The Letters and Diaries
of
John Henry Newman

The Letters and Diaries
of
John Henry Newman

Edited at the Birmingham Oratory
with notes and an introduction

by

Charles Stephen Dessain

of the same Oratory

Volume XVIII
New Beginnings in England
April 1857 to December 1858

NELSON

THOMAS NELSON AND SONS LTD
36 Park Street London W1
P.O. Box 2187 Accra
P.O. Box 336 Apapa Lagos
P.O. Box 25012 Nairobi
P.O. Box 21149 Dar es Salaam
77 Coffee Street San Fernando Trinidad

THOMAS NELSON (AUSTRALIA) LTD
597 Little Collins Street Melbourne C1

THOMAS NELSON AND SONS (SOUTH AFRICA) (PROPRIETARY) LTD
51 Commissioner Street Johannesburg

THOMAS NELSON AND SONS (CANADA) LTD
81 Curlew Drive Don Mills Ontario

THOMAS NELSON AND SONS
Copewood and Davis Streets Camden New Jersey 08103

———

First Published 1968
© The Birmingham Oratory 1968

17 135034 0

Nihil obstat
REGINALD BUTCHER, M.A.
Censor

Imprimatur:
✠ PATRICK CASEY, V.G.
Auxiliary Bishop of Westminster
20th December 1967

Printed in Great Britain by
Thomas Nelson (Printers) Ltd, London and Edinburgh

Preface

WITHOUT the gradual building up at the Birmingham Oratory of a very full collection of Cardinal Newman's correspondence (an account of which will be found in the Introduction to Volume XI), the present work could not have been undertaken. Its aim is to provide an exhaustive edition of Newman's letters; with explanatory notes, which are often summaries of or quotations from the other side of the correspondence. Some of these letters *to* Newman, when they appear to have particular importance, or to be necessary for following a controversy, are inserted in the text. Every one of the letters written *by* Newman is included there, in chronological sequence. Should there eventually be any of his letters, whose existence is known to the editor, but of which he has failed to obtain a copy, this will be noted in its place. On the other hand, no attempt has been made to include a list of letters written by Newman and now lost, nor the brief précis he occasionally made of his reply, on the back of a correspondent's letter, although these are utilised for the annotation.

In order that the text of each letter may be as accurate as possible, the original autograph, when it still exists, or at least a photographic copy of it, has been used by the editor as his source. (The very few cases in which he has been content with an authenticated copy will be noted as they occur.) Always the text of the autograph is reproduced, or, when the autograph has disappeared, that of the copy that appears most reliable. When only Newman's draft exists, that is printed. The source used in each case is to be found in the list of letters by correspondents.

Such alterations as are made in transcribing the letters aim, without sacrifice of accuracy, at enabling them to be read with ease. Newman writes simply and has none of those idiosyncrasies which sometimes need to be reproduced for the sake of the evidence of one kind or another which they provide.

The following are the only alterations made in transcription:

ADDRESS AND DATE are always printed on the same line, and at the head of the letter, even when Newman puts them at the end. When he omits or gives an incomplete date, the omission is supplied in square brackets, and justified in a note unless the reason for it is obvious. The addresses, to which letters were sent, are included in the list of letters by correspondents. The information derived from postmarks is matter for annotation.

THE CONCLUSION of the letter is made to run on, irrespective of Newman's separate lines, and all postscripts are placed at the end.

NEWMAN'S CORRECTIONS AND ADDITIONS are inserted in their intended place. His interlinear explanations are printed in the text in angle brackets ⟨⟩, after the word or phrase they explain. His erasures are given in footnotes when they appear to be of sufficient interest to warrant it. Square brackets being reserved for editorial additions; all Newman's brackets are printed as rounded ones (the kind most usual with him).

NEWMAN'S PARAGRAPHS AND PUNCTUATION are preserved, except that single quotation marks are printed throughout, and double ones for quotations within them. (Newman generally used the latter in both cases.) Further, a parenthesis or quotation that he began with the proper mark but failed to complete, or completed but did not begin, is supplied. All other punctuation marks supplied by the editor are enclosed in square brackets. Newman's dashes, which frequently do duty either for a full stop, a semicolon or a comma (especially when he is tired or writing hurriedly), are represented by a '—' with a space before and after. His spelling and use of capitals are left unchanged, but 'raised' letters are lowered in every case.

NEWMAN'S ABBREVIATIONS are retained in the case of proper names, and in the address and conclusion of each letter, since these are sometimes useful indications of his attitude at the time. In all other cases, abbreviations are printed out in full, where Newman employs them.

When he uses the initials of proper names, the full name is normally inserted in square brackets after the initials, at the first occurrence in each letter, and more often if it seems advisable in order to avoid confusion. No addition of the full name is made in the case of Newman's correspondent, whether his initials occur at the beginning of the letter or in the course of it.

When Newman uses only a Christian name, the surname is sometimes added in square brackets for the reader's convenience. The Christian names of members of the Oratory, since they are of frequent occurrence, are listed in the index of proper names and the reader is referred to surnames.

When transcription is made from a PRINTED SOURCE, typographical alterations clearly due to editor or printer are disregarded.

Sometimes Newman made HOLOGRAPH copies of his letters or of portions of them, when they were returned to him long after they had been written. In order that the reader may be able to see how much he copied and what changes he introduced, the copied passages are placed in quarter brackets ⌐ ⌐, and all additions of any importance included in the text in double square brackets, or, where this is impracticable, in the annotation.

Newman's letters are printed in CHRONOLOGICAL ORDER, with the name of his correspondent at the head (except that those of each day are arranged alphabetically), and, when more than one is written to the same person on the same day, numbered I, II. In the headings the name of the correspondent is given in its most convenient form, sometimes with Christian names in full, sometimes only with initials.

THE LIST OF LETTERS BY CORRESPONDENTS, at the end of each volume, shows whether the source used was an autograph, draft, printed source or copy, and in the last case, whether a holograph made by Newman later; and gives the present location of the source, as well as of any additional holograph copies or drafts. When a letter, or a considerable portion of it, has been printed in a standard work, references are given; but mistakes or omissions in these previous publications are noticed, if at all, in the annotation.

THE LETTERS WRITTEN TO NEWMAN, when inserted in the text, are printed in type smaller than that used for Newman's own letters, and headed by the name of the correspondent. These letters are not arranged in chronological order, but are placed either just before or just after the letter of Newman to which they are related. A list of them is given at the end of each volume in which they occur. These and the quotations from letters in the annotation are always, unless otherwise stated, printed from autographs at the Birmingham Oratory, and are transcribed in the same way as Newman's letters.

NEWMAN'S DIARIES COVER THE YEARS 1824 to 1879 (with a gap from July 1826 to March 1828). They are written in a series of mottled copy books, $12 \times 18\frac{1}{2}$ centimetres, printed for a year each, and entitled *The Private Diary: arranged, printed, and ruled, for receiving an account of every day's employment . . .*' with the exception of the four periods July 1847–May 1850, January 1854–January 1861, January 1861–March 1871, March 1871–October 1879, each of which is contained in a somewhat thicker copy book.

These diaries are printed complete for each day in which Newman has made an entry, except that the lists of people to whom he has written or from whom he has received letters are omitted, as not being of sufficient general interest. The original diaries are, of course, available for consultation. At the end of each diary book are various notes, lists of addresses, of people to be prayed for, accounts, etc. These, also, are omitted, except for occasional dated notes of events, which are inserted in their proper place. Of the rest of the notes, some are theological and will be reserved for a volume of Newman's theological papers, and others will perhaps have room found for them in any fuller edition of *Autobiographical Writings*.

Newman compiled with his own hand, on quarto sheets sewn together, a book of *Chronological Notes*, drawn largely from the diaries. Any new matter in these *Notes* is printed in italics with the appropriate diary entry. (It should be noted that the diary entries themselves were sometimes written up considerably later than the events they record.)

Each volume is preceded by a brief summary of the period of Newman's life that it covers. Summary, diaries and annotation give a roughly biographical form to the whole, and will, it is hoped, enable the ordinary reader to treat it as a continuous narrative.

THE BIOGRAPHIES OF PERSONS are collected in the index of proper names at the end of each volume, in order to simplify the annotation of the letters. Occasionally, when a person is mentioned only once or twice, and a note is required in any case, biographical details have been given in the notes, and a reference in the index. Volume XI, being the first of a new period in Newman's life, contains an account of every person mentioned, with the exception of a few for whom a notice seemed unnecessary, and of still fewer who have not yet been identified. The indexes of Volume XII and of subsequent volumes contain notices of persons who appear in them for the first time, and references back, in the case of those who have been noticed in an earlier volume. (The editor will be grateful for information as to persons not identified.)

These notices have been compiled from such various sources—books of reference, letters at the Oratory, information supplied by the families or religious communities of the persons concerned, and by librarians and archivists—that the giving of authorities would be a very complicated and lengthy process. Like others faced with the same problem, the editor has decided usually to omit them. References are given, however, to *The Dictionary of National Biography*, or *The Dictionary of American Biography*, in all cases where there is an article there, and failing them, to Boase's *Modern English Biography* or Gillow's *Bibliographical Dictionary of the English Catholics*. When all the volumes of letters have been issued, a final index volume will be compiled for the whole work.

Contents

Acknowledgements

FIRST of all thanks are due to the Knights of Columbus in America, whose generosity has made possible the publication of this volume.

Then, the editor wishes to renew his thanks to many of those mentioned in the acknowledgements of earlier volumes, who have continued to assist him. In addition he is grateful for the help given him by Fr J. Derek Holmes, and for information supplied by Fr Gaston Bergeron, O.F.M., Fr Patrick Brophy of Carlow, Padre Cistellini of the Florence Oratory, Fr R. C. Gorman, S.J., of Farm Street, the Revd V. H. H. Green, Chaplain of Lincoln College, Oxford, A. Nicholls, Sub-librarian of Birmingham University Library, Abbot Aelred Sillem of Quarr and Fr Dermot Walsh, O.P. He wishes to thank also Mr Douglas Woodruff who gave the permission of the family for the inclusion of Lord Acton's letters.

Among those who have provided further Newman letters or arranged for copies to be made available are Mrs E. B. Given, the British Records Association, Mr David Horn, Père M. Join-Lambert of l'Oratoire de France, the archivists of the English Rosminians, Mr Frank Strahan, archivist of Melbourne University, Mgr G. A. Tomlinson, the University of Iowa Libraries, Lincoln City Library, the Miriam Lutcher Stark Library of the University of Texas, Maison Charavay, Christie's, Dawson's of Pall Mall, the House of El Dieff, C. & I. K. Fletcher Ltd, Goodspeeds of Boston, Maggs Bros, and Sotheby & Co. For any omissions in these acknowledgements the editor begs indulgence, and will try to remedy them in a later volume.

Abbreviations in Volume XVIII

THE abbreviations used for Newman's works are those listed in Joseph Rickaby, S.J., *Index to the Works of John Henry Cardinal Newman*, London 1914, with a few additions.

References to works included by Newman in his uniform edition are always, unless otherwise stated, to that edition, which was begun in 1868 with *Parochial and Plain Sermons*, and concluded in 1881 with *Select Treatises of St Athanasius*. From 1886, until the stock was destroyed in the 1939-45 war, all the volumes were published by Longmans, Green and Co. They are distinguished from other, usually posthumous, publications by having their date of inclusion in the uniform edition in brackets after the title, in the list of abbreviations below. The unbracketed date is, in every case, the date of the edition (or impression) used for giving references. (Once volumes were included in the uniform edition the pagination usually remained unchanged, but there are exceptions and minor alterations.)

Add.	*Addresses to Cardinal Newman with His Replies etc. 1879-82*, ed. W. P. Neville, 1905.
Apo.	*Apologia pro Vita Sua*, (1873) 1905.
Ari.	*The Arians of the Fourth Century*, (1871) 1908.
Ath. I, II	*Select Treatises of St Athanasius*, two volumes, (1881) 1920.
A.W.	*John Henry Newman: Autobiographical Writings*, ed. Henry Tristram, 1956.
Call.	*Callista, a Tale of the Third Century*, (1876) 1923.
Campaign	*My Campaign in Ireland, Part I* (printed for private circulation only), 1896.
D.A.	*Discussions and Arguments on Various Subjects*, (1872) 1911.
Dev.	*An Essay on the Development of Christian Doctrine*, (1878) 1908.
Diff. I, II	*Certain Difficulties felt by Anglicans in Catholic Teaching*, two volumes, (1879, 1876) 1908.
Ess. I, II	*Essays Critical and Historical*, two volumes, (1871) 1919.
G.A.	*An Essay in aid of a Grammar of Assent*, (1870) 1913.
H.S. I, II, III	*Historical Sketches*, three volumes, (1872) 1908, 1912, 1909.
Idea	*The Idea of a University defined and illustrated*, (1873) 1902.
Jfc.	*Lectures on the Doctrine of Justification*, (1874) 1908.
K.C.	*Correspondence of John Henry Newman with John Keble and Others, 1839-45*, ed. at the Birmingham Oratory, 1917.
L.G.	*Loss and Gain: the Story of a Convert*, (1874) 1911.
M.D.	*Meditations and Devotions of the late Cardinal Newman*, 1893.
Mir.	*Two Essays on Biblical and on Ecclesiastical Miracles*, (1870) 1907.
Mix.	*Discourses addressed to Mixed Congregations*, (1871) 1909.
Moz. I, II	*Letters and Correspondence of John Henry Newman*, ed. Anne Mozley, two volumes, 1891.

O.S.   *Sermons preached on Various Occasions*, (1870) 1927.
P.S. I–VIII   *Parochial and Plain Sermons*, (1868) 1907–10.
Prepos.   *Present Position of Catholics*, (n.d. 1872) 1913.
S.D.   *Sermons bearing on Subjects of the Day*, (1869) 1902.
S.E.   *Stray Essays on Controversial Points*, (private) 1890.
S.U.   *Sermon Notes of John Henry Cardinal Newman, 1849–1879*, ed. Fathers of the Birmingham Oratory, 1913.
T.T.   *Tracts Theological and Ecclesiastical*, (1874) 1908.
U.S.   *Fifteen Sermons preached before the University of Oxford*, (1872) 1909.
V.M. I, II   *The Via Media*, (1877) 1908, 1911.
V.V.   *Verses on Various Occasions*, (1874) 1910.

*   *   *

Altholz   Josef L. Altholz, *The Liberal Catholic Movement in England*, London 1962.
Boase   Frederick Boase, *Modern English Biography*, six volumes, Truro 1892–1921.
Culler   A. Dwight Culler, *The Imperial Intellect, a Study of Newman's Educational Ideal*, New Haven 1955.
D A B   *Dictionary of American Biography*, London 1928–36.
D N B   *Dictionary of National Biography*, to 1900, London, reprinted in 1937–8 in twenty-two volumes, the last being a Supplement, *D N B*, Suppl.
D N B, 1901–11   *Dictionary of National Biography*, 1901–11, three volumes in one.
D R   *Dublin Review*.
D T C   *Dictionnaire de Théologie Catholique*, Paris 1903–50.
Gasquet   *Lord Acton and his Circle*, edited by Abbot Gasquet, London 1906.
Gillow   Joseph Gillow, *Bibliographical Dictionary of the English Catholics*, five volumes, London 1885 and later.
Harper   Gordon Huntington Harper, *Cardinal Newman and William Froude, F.R.S. A Correspondence*, Baltimore 1933.
Liddon's *Pusey* I–IV   H. P. Liddon, *Life of Edward Bouverie Pusey*, four volumes London 1893–7.
de Lisle   E. S. Purcell, *Life and Letters of Ambrose Phillipps de Lisle*, two volumes, London 1900.
MacDougall   Hugh A. MacDougall, *The Acton-Newman Relations*, New York 1962.
McGrath   Fergal McGrath, S.J., *Newman's University Idea and Reality*, London 1951.
Trevor I   Meriol Trevor, *Newman the Pillar of the Cloud*, London 1962.
Trevor II   Meriol Trevor, *Newman Light in Winter*, London 1962.
Ward I, II   Wilfrid Ward, *The Life of John Henry Cardinal Newman*, two volumes, London 1912.

Introductory Note

1 April 1857–31 December 1858

AT the beginning of April 1857 Newman notified to the Irish bishops individually his intention of resigning the Rectorship of the Catholic University in the following November. Six years would then have elapsed since his appointment, and three since the opening term. By the end of the year he would have crossed the Irish Channel fifty-four times in the service of the University. He was in his late fifties and the strain was telling. Furthermore, it was evident that his Oratory, forgotten in a provincial and industrial town, would hardly survive without his presence and guiding hand. Prolonged absence was 'simply incompatible with his duty to St Philip'. Then, although Newman was held in great esteem by all classes in Ireland, and had the confidence and affection of his staff of professors, he was kept at arm's length and at the same time hampered by Archbishop Cullen, with whom in practice the ultimate control of the University lay. Cullen had his own difficulties with other Irish bishops, but the correspondence shows with what gratuitous hindrances and frustrations he encumbered Newman. Also, it was becoming increasingly obvious that all hope of the University being English as well as Irish was at an end. Newman considered that his own countrymen had the first claim upon him, and even that he was neglecting his duty to them in a time of trial. 'It seems to me that a time of great reaction and great trial is before us,' he wrote to Ambrose St John on 7 May 1857, 'it seems that really I may be *wanted* in England . . . I have too little perhaps made myself felt.'

The immediate cause of these remarks was the growing breach between the more open-minded and critical Catholics and the Ultramontanes. The *Rambler* was about to pass into the hands of Sir John Acton and Richard Simpson. Its standard improved steadily, but its opinions and tone alienated Cardinal Wiseman who was still the patron of the *Dublin Review*, while its approval of Government aid and supervision for Catholic schools alarmed Bishop Ullathorne. Then the *Union* newspaper had just been launched on its career by the Anglican F. G. Lee, as the organ of the movement for corporate reunion. A. L. Phillipps was unrestrainedly enthusiastic in his support, from the Catholic side. Newman urged caution, and in July 1857 wrote Phillipps a series of letters remarkable not only for prudence and common sense, but also for breadth, and, as it would much later be called, the ecumenical spirit. In that same month the Association for the Promotion of the Unity of Christendom was founded.

An efficient school for the sons of educated Catholics, especially from the families of converts, was another crying English need. This emerges vividly

xiii

from the correspondence, and it led Newman to make plans for a school at the Oratory in Birmingham, which might also prepare boys for the Catholic University. Meanwhile, another work of great importance was laid on his shoulders. At the end of August 1857 Wiseman invited him, in the name of the English bishops, to make a new translation of the Bible into English. Experience had made him cautious about episcopal invitations to labour, but such a request could not be refused. He collected helpers, almost all of them either old Catholics or members of his own Oratory, bought books and made other preparations. When he asked how expenses were to be met, the answer was long delayed, and then a new complication arose. Archbishop Kenrick of Baltimore had almost completed a translation of the Bible, and in May 1858 the American bishops asked the English Hierarchy to agree to a joint translation. Newman was informed of this, but the English bishops neither replied to the American proposal, nor gave instructions to Newman. He had been asked to embark on a great undertaking, and the first serious difficulty was met by silence. Hopes had been raised, only to be dashed, and meanwhile, the work Newman had planned on the relations of faith and reason was inevitably interrupted and postponed.

Although he remained in England from the latter part of November 1857 until his farewell visit to Dublin at the end of October 1858, and had so much to occupy him in Birmingham, Newman was still devoting most of his energy to the Catholic University. He had hoped that a working compromise might have been reached, which would have enabled him to continue as Rector. He was prepared to spend two or three weeks each term in Dublin, which would have kept for the University the prestige of his name, so valued by many of the Irish bishops. It would also have sufficed to supervise and maintain the efficient organisation he had built up. The compromise depended for its success on there being a resident Vice-Rector whom Newman could trust. Until the summer of 1857 when he became Archbishop of Cashel, Patrick Leahy had been the (generally absent) Vice-Rector. Newman proposed that Leahy's successor should be one of the lay professors, familiar with the working of the University, and acceptable to his colleagues. The Irish Archbishops insisted that the Vice-Rector must be a priest, but they had the greatest difficulty in filling the post; nor did they consult Newman about it, although the matter concerned him so closely. The compromise plan fell through, and an effective Vice-Rector was not appointed until the end of November 1858, after Newman had finally resigned. Newman in fact, for the sake of the University, delayed his resignation for a year longer than he had intended, and from February 1858 declined to take his salary. During the time that the University was without a Vice-Rector, breaches of discipline had to be referred to Newman at Birmingham. The correspondence thus caused brings out vividly his conception of University discipline, which he thought should be a combination of firmness and humanity.

At the beginning of 1858 Newman succeeded in launching the *Atlantis*, 'a Register of Literature and Science conducted by Members of the Catholic University'. This learned periodical, published twice yearly, added considerably to the prestige of the University. To the first numbers Newman contributed his essays on the Benedictines. During the Summer of 1858 an attempt was made to obtain a Charter for the University. Newman drafted a memorial, signed by the Professors, which was presented to Disraeli, Chancellor of the Exchequer in Lord Derby's government. Newman himself tried to canvass Cabinet Ministers whom he had known as undergraduates at Oriel. This memorial or letter to Disraeli, of 19 July 1858, described the achievements of the University, including the establishment of successful evening classes for young men who were at work in Dublin during the day. The Catholic University was a pioneer in the sphere of University Extension Lectures, which were not begun in England until 1873.

In the Summer of 1857 Newman published *Sermons Preached on Various Occasions*, and at the end of 1858 delivered lectures at Dublin on 'Literature', 'Discipline of Mind', and 'Christianity and Medical Science', which now form part of *The Idea of a University*.

Except for his ten-day visit of farewell to Ireland, Newman spent the whole of 1858 at his Oratory in Birmingham, which was depleted by the long illnesses of two of its members. Newman was made anxious as to the future recruitment of the Oratory. In spite, or rather, because of this, he was on the look-out for new spheres of activity for his Community. The plan for a Catholic boarding school, after languishing for a time, was revived, and as a first step the temporary church of the Oratory was improved and renovated, for, as Newman remarked to Serjeant Bellasis on 13 April 1858, 'as far as I see, children and boys take in religion principally through the eye'. Newman also tried to improve the position of English Catholics by encouraging the *Rambler*, about the future of which he corresponded with Sir John Acton, during the second half of the year. In December Döllinger was denounced by the English Ultramontanes for his article in the *Rambler* on 'The Paternity of Jansenism'. The stage was set for the collision between that periodical and the English bishops, which was to lead in the Spring of 1859 to Newman's reluctant acceptance of the editorship, and his plea for the consultation of the laity.

Summary of Events covered by this volume

*   *   *

1857

3 April   Newman in Dublin sends out letters to the Irish Bishops, announcing his intention of resigning the Rectorship of the Catholic University on 14 November. He returns to Birmingham for Easter.

28 April	Newman in Dublin for the Summer Term. He goes back to Birmingham twice during it, for the Feast of St Philip, 26 May, and for that of Corpus Christi, 11 June.
3 May	*The Church of the Fathers* is republished in Dublin.
18 July	Newman returns to Birmingham. *Sermons Preached on Various Occasions* is published soon after.
6 Aug.	The Oratorians at Birmingham refuse the request of the Irish Archbishops to allow Newman to be absent from the Oratory as heretofore for long periods.
27 Aug.	Newman receives Cardinal Wiseman's letter asking him in the name of the English Bishops to undertake a new translation of the Bible into English.
29 Oct.	Newman goes to Dublin in time for the opening of the Autumn Term on 3 November.
19 Nov.	Newman returns to Birmingham, and, since neither a successor nor a Vice-Rector is yet appointed, continues in his office of Rector of the Catholic University.

1858

1 Jan.	Publication of the first number of the *Atlantis*, with Newman's article, 'The Mission of the Benedictine Order'.
20 Jan.	J. S. Flanagan gravely ill.
22 Feb.	Henry Bittleston gravely ill.
19 April	Plans are drawn up for the Oratory school, which opens a year later. Evening classes resumed in Dublin, with an attendance of a hundred.
28 July	The Memorial drawn up by Newman requesting a Charter for the Catholic University is given to Disraeli.
4 and 30 Sept.	Sir John Acton and Döllinger visit Newman at Birmingham.
26 Oct	Newman pays his last visit to Dublin, and delivers three lectures in the University.
4 Nov.	Newman leaves Dublin for Birmingham.
12 Nov.	Newman resigns the Rectorship of the Catholic University of Ireland.
7 Dec.	Newman replies to the Bishop of Charleston about the translation of Scripture, that he awaits instructions from the English Bishops.
20 Dec.	Novena at Birmingham about the proposed Oratory school.
30 Dec.	Acton visits Newman and tells him of the denunciation of Döllinger.

The Letters and Diaries
of
John Henry Newman

TO JAMES HOPE-SCOTT

[[Personal]]   ⌐6 Harcourt Street April 1. 1857

It is hard indeed, if others may ask you, and you not refuse them; and a shame that you should feel a difficulty in doing so. I assure you, your refusal is the greatest consolation to myself possible, for it makes me not afraid to ask.[1]

And I shall feel it a second consolation if you force Badeley to give instead of you, and for himself and you too — for he put a match to the smouldering fire of my project [[the Atlantis]], when I happened, in order to fill up my letter, to tell him some of my half-devised schemes. As he sent me to you, send me yourself to him[12]

TO MICHAEL BLAKE, BISHOP OF DROMORE; GEORGE BROWNE, BISHOP OF ELPHIN; JAMES BROWNE, BISHOP OF KILMORE; PATRICK FALLON, BISHOP OF KILMACDUAGH; THOMAS FEENY, BISHOP OF KILLALA; WILLIAM KEANE, BISHOP OF ROSS; FRANCIS KELLY, COADJUTOR BISHOP OF DERRY; PATRICK MCGETTIGAN, BISHOP OF RAPHOE; CHARLES MCNALLY, BISHOP OF CLOGHER; DANIEL VAUGHAN, BISHOP OF KILLALOE; AND JAMES WALSH, BISHOP OF KILDARE

[2 April 1857][3]

My dear Lord

⌐I am so sensible of the honor which the Bishops of Ireland have done me in intrusting me with the high office of Rector of their University, and so grateful to your Lordship personally for the kindness (and confidence)[4] you have shown me, that I feel a corresponding pain in being obliged to resign into their hands the charge which I have unworthily sustained. This I propose

[1] Badeley had forwarded to Hope-Scott a letter of Newman's about his plan for starting the *Atlantis*. Cf. letter of 22 April to Badeley. Hope-Scott wrote from Abbotsford to Newman on 30 March, 'I have no money at present to help you with. In fact I find even my resources, which are D.G. considerable, scant for all I have in hand. This off my mind I will read your letter again and see if I can assist in any other way.'

[2] Badeley had written to Newman on 21 March, 'I hope you will carry out your scheme of a "Literary and Scientific Journal"—and I think there will be no difficulty in getting your friends to secure the sum you want for the period you mention—I, for one, shall be very glad to contribute my share for this purpose—I shall send on your letter to Hope as I am sure he will be interested . . .'

[3] The source of this letter is Newman's draft. He later wrote in pencil on most of the drafts of his letters of resignation to the Irish bishops 'March 1857.'

[4] [[the bracketed words were inserted in writing to the Bishops of Elphin, Ross, Dromore, Clogher, Killaloe and Raphoe]]

3

to do in November next. Believe me to say sincerely, that I would not take the initiative in such a step, unless I felt I could no longer fulfil the arduous duties which the office involves.[1] To go into this subject, which is so personal to myself at any length would be impertinent;[1] ⌐it is enough to say that my Congregation at Birmingham has growing claims upon me, considering the few years which possibly may remain to me of active work, and that I shall have been taken from its service for six years when November comes; nor does my strength any longer suffice for such frequent journeys between Dublin and England, as my double duties render necessary. I shall always entertain a most grateful sense of the honor you have done me in making me your first Rector, and begging you to pardon my shortcomings in that responsible position,

I am &c.[1][2]

TO JOHN CANTWELL, BISHOP OF MEATH

[2 April 1857]

My dear Lord,

⌐You have shewn such interest in my proceedings in the anxious office which I hold, and have treated me so kindly, that I cannot address this letter to you without regret that I should be obliged to send it. It is to say that my strength will not allow me to continue much longer in the charge of duties which involve so frequent a passage to and fro between this place and Bm [[Birmingham]]. I am therefore obliged to place the Rectorship into the hands of the Bishops of Ireland, who have so condescendingly honored me with it; and to assign November next as the date of my actual resignation, when I shall have more than completed 6 years since it [[the University]] has occupied my time and thoughts[1]

Believe me to be, with much gratitude to your Lordship &c.

[1] This sentence was omitted in the letter as sent.
[2] The aged Michael Blake, who as a young man had refounded the Irish College in Rome, replied on 13 April, 'I can easily conceive the yearning anxiety with which your venerable Community in England count every day of your absence . . . and considering the excessive fatigue you have to undergo in making those frequent journeys between Dublin and Birmingham, which are involved in your duties in both places, so far from thinking it wonderful that your mind begins to feel uneasy and suggests to you the thought of discontinuing your exhausting and almost superhuman labours over the Catholic University . . . it appears to me wonderful how you have been able to acquit yourself so successfully of all your duties within the compass of six years. . . . Ireland can never repay you for the benefits you have conferred upon her. But she will always remember your invaluable services . . .'
George Browne replied on 10 April, 'I regret exceedingly that any circumstance should deprive us of your invaluable services. I still hope that the Archbishop of Dublin may devise some means of averting the separation. Your loss to the University will be irremediable.
Wherever you are you shall always have the best blessings and the most affectionate regards of
Your most sincere & ffual Servt Geo. J. Browne'
For the reply of William Keane see letter of 14 April to him. All the extant replies of the Irish bishops are quoted or summarised in the notes.

TO ARCHBISHOP CULLEN

Dublin April 2/57

My dear Lord,

⌐The time is now approaching for the resignation of the high office which the Bishops of Ireland have so condescendingly committed to me. I named the subject to your Grace just a year ago this month, and now I beg leave to name the day.[1]

I will name next St Laurence's day, November 14th; when the six years will be more than completed since I began to devote my thoughts and exertions to the service of the University, and when the term of absence from my Congregation will have arrived for which I have asked permission.

My most urgent reasons for this step are, the fatigue which I experience from my frequent passages between Dublin and Birmingham, the duty of the Rector to show himself in public more than my strength will allow, for the good of the University, and the need to [my Congregation] of my services, which have been [so long] intermitted.⌐[2]

I am, My dear Lord, Your Grace's faithful Servant in Xt

John H Newman of the Oratory[3]

His Grace The Archbp of Dublin

TO WILLIAM DELANY, BISHOP OF CORK; CORNELIUS DENVIR, BISHOP OF DOWN AND CONNOR; AND JOHN DERRY, BISHOP OF CLONFERT

[2 April 1857]

My dear Lord,

⌐The courtesy you have shown me whenever it has been my good fortune to meet your Lordship, makes it incumbent on me from a feeling of gratitude as well as of duty, to signify to you, as early as I can, and to the other Prelates of the Irish Church, my intention of placing in your hands my responsible office at the end of this year. I cannot bear the fatigue which it gives me at my time of life to make those frequent journeys between Dublin and Birmingham, without which I cannot fulfil my duties in both places. I propose to resign in November, when I shall have had the satisfaction of completing six years, since I was first called on to give myself to the service of the University.⌐[1]

I am &c J H N

[1] See letter of 14 April 1856 to St John.

[2] The last page of the autograph has been torn, and the words in square brackets are supplied from the draft. Newman later dated the draft in pencil, 'About March 1857', and, when copying, slightly altered the last sentence to read [[and the need of my Congregation for the services which I have so long intermitted.]]

[3] Cullen seems not to have replied. See letter of 18 April to H. Wilberforce.

5

TO JOSEPH DIXON, ARCHBISHOP OF ARMAGH

[2 April 1857]

My dear Lord

⌐Your Grace has ever treated me with such singular kindness, that I have great pain in communicating to you a resolution, which may look like ingratitude, but which the lapse of time imperatively imposes on me.

In truth I have no choice but to resign into the hands of the Bishops the high office in the Catholic University with which their Lordships have honored me. My strength, I lament to say, is not equal to the frequent journeys to and fro between Dublin and Birmingham which the Rectorship exacts of me; and, even were I quit of the fatigue, as I am not, there is a growing call on one who holds that office, to show himself personally in all parts of Ireland as the representative of the University, and to that duty neither my years nor my habits enable me to respond.

Were other reasons required besides the above, I should add that, having, when this session ends, devoted as much as six years to the University at a time of life when time is precious because it is scarce, I feel that, great as is that object, I have no right to subtract what remains to me from the service of my own Congregation, and from those special duties, which, when no existing engagements interfere, are the natural and fit termination of this state of probation.[1] Nor have I any reason to suppose, that my Congregation will dispense with my presence at Birmingham for a longer period than that which I originally contemplated and they granted to me.

I wish respectfully to name the next St Laurence's day, November 14, as the day of my resignation, and begging you to believe that I shall retain to the end of my life a most grateful recollection of your uniform kindness to me,

I am, &c¹ J H N²

[1] [[termination of life]]

[2] Dixon replied on 6 April, 'I am in receipt of your esteemed favour. I need not say that I deeply regret your determination to withdraw from the University. Indeed the perusal of your last annual report prepared me for this. I have more reasons for my regret than I could express within the limits of a note. I know that your determination cannot now be changed. Yet I shall find a satisfaction in unburthening my mind fully to you, on this matter, on some occasion, please God before your departure from Ireland.' See Newman's reply on 15 April.

At the end of 'The Rector's Report to the Archbishops and Bishops of Ireland 1855–6,' dated 31 Oct. 1856, Newman spoke of the internal consolidation of the University as reconciling him to the inevitable prospect of his own separation from it. *Campaign*, pp. 72–3.

TO PATRICK DURCAN, BISHOP OF ACHONRY; THOMAS FURLONG, BISHOP OF FERNS; LAWRENCE GILLOOLY, COADJUTOR BISHOP OF ELPHIN; JOHN KILDUFF, BISHOP OF ARDAGH; JOHN MCEVILY, BISHOP OF GALWAY; AND DANIEL MCGETTIGAN, COADJUTOR BISHOP OF RAPHOE

[2 April 1857]

My dear Lord

⌐I am sorry that my first letter to your Lordship should relate to the prospective termination of that intercourse which it has been my privilege to enjoy with the Bishops of Ireland. However, the lapse of time has brought me near the conclusion of that leave of absence, which my congregation gave me from my duties at Birmingham. Independently of this my strength will not allow [me] to undergo those frequent journeys to and fro, without which I cannot satisfy even that partial observance of my Rule, from which my Congregation cannot release me.

I therefore propose to place my resignation in the hands of the Bishops in November next.

I cannot withdraw from this great undertaking, without expressing my grateful sense of the confidence which has been shown me by the Bishops of Ireland in placing me at the head of it, and of the kindness with which, according to their opportunities, — so many of your Lordships have supported me in it⌐[1]

I am &c

TO JOHN LEAHY, COADJUTOR BISHOP OF DROMORE; DOMINIC O'BRIEN, BISHOP OF WATERFORD; JOHN RYAN, BISHOP OF LIMERICK; AND EDWARD WALSH, BISHOP OF OSSORY

Dublin April 2/57

My dear Lord,[2]

⌐I fear you will think it but a poor return to you for your unvariable kindness to me, if I write to announce my approaching resignation of the Rectorship of the University.

I have more reasons for this step than it is easy to enumerate on paper. My age is now considerable; my contemporaries are dying or failing around me; I cannot tell what time is left to me for any work; and I do not like the prospect of being taken away without having given my last years to my Congregation at Birmingham. These are some of the considerations which I trust will justify me in your Lordship's eyes for the step I am taking.

[1] For the reply of Thomas Furlong see letter of 14 April to him, and for that of Lawrence Gilhooly, see letter of 18 April to H. Wilberforce.

[2] This letter is printed from the autograph sent to John Leahy. The draft, reproduced in *Ward* I, p. 631, has slight differences.

I propose to resign in November next, when I shall have given more than six years to the work of the University, though for only half of them I have had any continuous residence in Dublin. This space of time is equal, in preciousness to myself, to twice the number of years to a younger man.

I shall ever entertain a grateful sense of the confidence with which you have honoured me, and the support you have given me, and, begging your Lordship's blessing, I am,[1]

My dear Lord, Your faithful & affte Servt in Xt

John H Newman of the Oratory[1]

The Rt Revd
the Coadjutor
  Bp of Dromore

TO JOHN MACHALE, ARCHBISHOP OF TUAM

Dublin, April 2, 1857.

My Lord Archbishop, ⌐I beg to acquaint your Grace that the term of years is now nearly completed which I proposed to myself to devote to the service of your University. It is my intention to resign the office of rector, with which you have honored me, next St. Lawrence's Day, November 14.[1]

I have the honor to be, my Lord, Your Grace's obedient servant,

John H. Newman, of the Oratory.[2]

His Grace the Archbishop of Tuam.

[1] Leahy replied on 8 April, 'I read with great sorrow the letter in which you announce your determination to resign the Rectorship of the Catholic University in the course of the present year. . . . No doubt your position is not only very laborious but also very irksome, still I know not another where you could so effectually promote the honour of God and the good of religion, and it is I believe a very general feeling that divine Providence seems to have prepared you in a particular manner for the situation. Your name is in itself a mainstay to the University and if you leave it I fear it will at once sink in public estimation. I trust then, and shall pray that you may be induced to change your determination . . .'

For the reply of Dominic O'Brien see Newman's letter of 14 April to him.

[2] The see of Cloyne was vacant at this time. So also was the Archbishopric of Cashel, but Patrick Leahy who was about to succeed to it, wrote on 4 April, 'You cannot, I always thought and think, be done without so soon.

Providence will, I trust, arrange things so that you may be induced to change your mind. Your separation from the University in its present infant state would be most injurious, if not fatal, to it's best interests.'

There is no trace of the letter of resignation to Newman's friend David Moriarty, Bishop of Kerry, but he wrote on 15 April, 'I can not yet believe that this is in the way of Providence, at least so soon. Even a year or two more would make much difference. I suppose Dr Leahy will be the next Archbishop of Cashel. He ought to know the wants of the University and your difficulties, and his position would enable him to give you that help and prop which you should have, but have not received from the Episcopal body.'

Memorandum[1]   On my Letters of Resignation.[2]

(N.B. It may seem strange that I have rested my retirement in so marked a way on the fatigue of journeying between Birmingham and Dublin. But it was a real great difficulty, and it went to the root of the question how I could continue Rector — leading as it did immediately to the quantum of residence to be required of me at Dublin, Dr Cullen really wishing me to be there throughout the year. Thus *he* settled the difficulty.

My health was far from strong at this time and I felt the journeys much. I was told something was the matter with my heart, and was not made easy on the subject till I consulted a medical authority in London at Christmas 1857–1858.

I cannot bear journeys now more than then — and I question whether I should not have been fairly knocked up then, as now, if I had continued them.)

FRIDAY 3 APRIL 1857   sent my Letters to the Bishops resigning Rectorship, dated yesterday   At night went to *Birmingham* England

TO JOHN STANISLAS FLANAGAN

April 4. 1857[3]

I should say, (as I thought to myself, when I read your letter at Dublin,)[4] if he has faith in us, let him stop — if he has not, by no means let him stop.

It is not consistent with the duties I owe to the Congregation, to let any one stop in it without faith in it.

I anticipate he will *not* be able to say that he has simple faith and confidence in the Congregation.

This being the case, I recommend his paying his father a visit for a month — and thus to be thrown on himself and his own thoughts. This will oblige him seriously to make up his mind consulting whom he pleases.

---

[1] Newman wrote this Memorandum in 1872, when copying his letters of resignation at the end of 'Memorandum about my connection with the Catholic University.'

[2] Wilfrid Ward described the letters of resignation as 'carefully graduated in cordiality of expression.' *Ward* I, pp. 630 and 375. Fergal McGrath, however, says of this remark that it 'is misleading, and would appear to impute to Newman a singular want of dignity and taste. With two exceptions, the letters are markedly cordial, and their different wording is naturally explained by the varying degrees of intimacy which existed between the writer and the recipients. The letter to Dr. Cullen is strictly formal, and that to Dr. MacHale almost curt, but it is difficult to see how, under the circumstances, they could have honestly been written otherwise.' *McGrath*, pp. 438–9.

[3] This letter has no name of a correspondent, but was evidently written for Flanagan, who had charge of the novices.

[4] Flanagan had written on 31 March his agreement with Newman's opinion, that the novice, Henry Ignatius Dudley Ryder, who was unsettled, ought to be allowed to leave the Oratory if he wished it, but ought not to be sent away. See letter of 29 March.

He shall return at the end of the month, if he wishes it and can say 'I have faith in the Congregation.' And then no one will be the wiser as to the difficulty he has had.

If he cannot say 'I have faith,' he will not return.[1]

PALM SUNDAY 5 APRIL 1857 took the function — and procession. preached

TO J. M. CAPES

The Oratory Birmingham April 6. 1857
My dear Capes

I am very sorry to have the question I asked you about our Bishop in a way answered in his letter in yesterday's Register. He there speaks of you as going out of your way, to be Erastian and Protestant. I have not yet referred back to your Article — but I very much grieve that such should be his impression.[2]

[1] Newman made a Memorandum on 6 April:
'It must ever be a very strong act to take a youth under age into the Community against his Father's will.
For myself, my ground all along for so acting in the case of H.R. has been, that the boy resolutely chose us—and I felt I had no right to deprive St Philip of a subject.
And to test his resolution, I wished him to separate from us, and then act. His response was, after being a year at Rome, to break up the engagements and prospects, into which I had let his Father introduce him, and come to us. The only condition I had put on him was, that he must come at the end of the year, or not at all.
Still he came, in spite of his Father. But still I said, when, in consequence of this, I agreed to admit him into the Congregation, that it was impossible that this state of things could go on—but that either his Father must be reconciled to us, or he would go.
We did all we could in determining among ourselves, that, certainly for the first year, he should not go home, to be unsettled.
Now, however, his Father writes to him—and for the first time he listens to what his Father says. For the first time he gives an evident token that, instead of having faith in us, he is criticizing us, and looking towards the London Oratory.
I cannot recognise the idea, that we may allow a Novice in the House who doubts of us: who, not only doubts of us now, but whom we find, viewing the past in the light of what we know, has been divided in mind about us, in spite of his acts, for this year and a half past.
Too long, poor fellow, he has halted between two opinions. It is for his own good, as well as for our peace and dignity, and the honor of St Philip that he should decide. He is unfair to himself and to us just now.
I propose then that he is sent home for a month, to consult whom he will, to decide finally, to return here, or to go to London, or to be a secular priest: but any how not to return, to plague us with his doubts.'
A further Memorandum on Ignatius Ryder, which throws light on Newman's ideas about vocation, will be included in the volume of his Oratorian papers.
[2] In his letter of 30 March Newman asked Capes, who was now again editing the *Rambler*, 'How do you stand with Dr Ullathorne?' On 31 March Ullathorne wrote a long letter on the question of Government aid for Catholic schools, published in the *Weekly Register* (4 April), p. 5, and in the *Tablet* (4 April), pp. 218–19. His letter began:
'Dear Sir—In reviewing my Notes on the Education Question, the *Weekly Register* has argued in favour of accepting Building Grants on the conditions of the Model Trust Deed, whilst the *Tablet* has maintained the same position without adducing argument. And the *Rambler* has boldly advocated the right of her Majesty's Inspectors to instruct the managers of our Poor Schools on the religious teaching of those schools through the medium of documents addressed to the secular government. These facts are so many proofs of what will

The Register says that the Bishop of Salford is the other way — and he it is who has headed your subscription list.[1] What does all this mean? What pains me is to find that you and our Bishop are quarrelling. I hoped you would have been together.[2]

I stop here till about April 22 — and fear I shall just miss you. I wish you could come here for a day or so before I return to Dublin. I am so curious and anxious to know how things stand.[3]

Ever Yours affectly John H Newman of the Oratory

J. M. Capes Esqr.

TO EDWARD HEALY THOMPSON

The Oratory Birmingham. April 6/57.

My dear Thompson

I am glad to see from the Register and Union that you, or at least your argumentative powers, are in so good case — and I shall be glad to know that I am right in believing it of your whole man, that is, your body, which was

ultimately result from making the lay element preponderate in the management of our schools. For, whilst the *Rambler* has adopted a purely Protestant and Erastian view of the duties of inspection, the two Catholic newspapers have failed to discern that the Committee of the Privy Council deliver into our hands a Model Trust Deed, accompanied with a Protestant and Erastian interpretation of its provisions.

It has been industriously stated that the Bishops have formally approved the Model Trust Deed, and that even the Holy See has sanctioned the government system. Both statements are incorrect. . . .'

Ullathorne complained that while Bishops had the right to exclude a book or a teacher from Catholic schools on religious grounds, it was left to a lay authority to decide in what 'religious grounds' consisted.

Ullathorne in his letter was referring to the review of his *Notes on the Education Question* in the *Rambler*, (March 1857), pp. 236–7 which pointed out that to insist on Government Inspectors instructing themselves only with secular teaching was to play into the hands of those who wished for a total separation of religious instruction from education. 'Why insist,' the *Rambler* asked, 'on the inspectors being Catholics, if their religion is to be entirely forgotten during the inspection?'

The *Weekly Register*, (18 April), p. 4, published Capes's letter of 6 April to Ullathorne, protesting that he had been misunderstood, and the latter's reply of 8 April: 'On examining the paragraph in the *Rambler* again, I perceive that I should have expressed myself more accurately if I had said—"The *Rambler* has boldly advocated the *expediency* of Her Majesty's Inspectors instructing the managers of our Poor Schools on the religious teaching . . ."'

[1] The *Weekly Register*, (4 April), p. 9, had a leading article which began: 'Among English Catholics the question of the moment is, whether we may lawfully and prudently accept aid from the Parliamentary Grant towards the building of Poor Schools. We are this week honoured by being made the instrument of publishing a letter of the Lord Bishop of Birmingham, giving reasons against the acceptance of the Grant. On the other hand, the Bishop of Salford and the Vicars Apostolic of Edinburgh and Glasgow have, almost at the same moment, expressed a strong opinion in favour of it. . . .'

Capes, who had been lecturing in Manchester, was in the middle of March presented with £70 by the Catholics there, the Bishop of Salford, William Turner, heading the list of subscribers. See letter of 30 March to Capes.

[2] The divergences between the *Rambler* and some of the English bishops, in which Newman was to be as involved exactly two years later, were already obvious. Cf. Joseph L. Altholz, *The Liberal Catholic Movement in England*, London 1962, pp. 36–44.

[3] See diary for 15 April.

the ailing portion of it. I have heard nothing definite about you for a long time.[1]

But what I write to you about especially is to congratulate you on fixing A. Phillipps on a spit, if he is made to see it. I wanted it to come out as the turning point of the controversy — viz that we did not pray for the conversion of the Church of England as such, any more than we pray for the Fishmongers Company as such, because we did not allow its religious existence.[2]

This is the sole difference between you and him — will he accept it? will he maintain that the Church of E has a religious existence? and if so, will he give you on paper *what* the notes are of its religious existence?

It has pained me exceedingly lately that the Rambler should have come into collision, not only with the Cardinal, but with our Bishop. Is not the Liverpool Catholic Institute Magazine the Cardinal's representative against the Rambler?[3]

Ever Yrs most sincerely John H Newman of the Oratory

E. H. Thompson Esqr.

TUESDAY 7 APRIL 1857   in retreat   [also Wednesday and Thursday]

THURSDAY 9 APRIL   The Bishop called   took the functions [also Friday and Saturday]

SATURDAY 11 APRIL   Fr Wm Neville returned to Oratory, after having been in Italy a year.

EASTER SUNDAY 12 APRIL   preached

[1] Frederick George Lee (at this time Minister of the Berkeley Chapel in London), having bought the *Church and State Gazette*, transformed it and founded in Dec. 1856 the *Union* newspaper, 'in the interests of Anglo-Catholicism and Union with Rome.' To the issues of 27 Feb. and 20 March 1857 A. L. Phillipps contributed letters, advocating the corporate reunion of the Church of England with that of Rome. Thompson controverted with him both in the *Weekly Register* and in the *Union*. One of Thompson's letters to the editor was published in part in the *Union*, (27 March 1857), p. 208 and in full in the *Weekly Register*, (4 April 1857), together with another letter on the subject, addressed to the editor of the *Weekly Register*.

[2] In his letter to the editor of the *Weekly Register*, (4 April 1857), p. 4, Thompson wrote of himself and those converted by the Catholic movement in the Church of England: 'We do not take the same view as Mr. Phillipps of the character and prospects of the National Church. We do not hope for its restoration to Catholic Unity, for the simple reason that we do not believe it has the sort of existence Mr. Phillipps attributes to it. For my own part I honestly declare that I do not hope and I do not even pray for the Anglican Church in its corporate capacity. I hope and pray for England, for all my countrymen; I hope and pray for the members of the Anglican Church, and especially for those who profess the principles which were the occasion of my own conversion, and who are sincerely seeking the Truth, or earnestly acting upon such truths as they already possess, careless of consequences. But for the Anglican Church as an ecclesiastical body, or as a body at all, I have no sort of feeling whatever. Nor ought this to shock or surprise Mr. Phillipps when he recollects what has been written by the very leader of the movement, by him to whom the children of the movement looked up as their master and teacher. It is curious to compare the language used by Mr. Phillipps in his letter to the *Union*, with that employed by Father Newman in his "Lectures on Anglican Difficulties." '

For Newman's view at this period about corporate reunion see letters of 1, 4, 9, 13 and 30 July 1857 to A. L. Phillipps.

[3] The *Liverpool Catholic Institute Magazine*, began in 1856 or 1857, in Liverpool, and then was published by Burns and Lambert in London. It came to an end in 1858.

TO WILLIAM HENRY ANDERDON

(sent)   Easter Day April 12/57

My dear Anderdon

I am much grieved to see from your letter that you think me hard on you in my interpretation of my words about the gas. Sooner than that, I freely consent to your putting in gas into the church at once. Thus you will save the £30, which I did not know you were losing.[1]

As to the Candelabra, I suppose you simply wish them away. If so, this Oratory will purchase them of me, and you have only to give Beardwood directions to send them here by luggage train.[2]

Thank you for what you tell me of your payments. Best Easter greetings, in which all our party here join

Ever Yrs affly J H N

P.S.   If there was a 5 years lease, you know the sense of the words would not be either yours or mine — but the Law's. We don't know, I am sorry to say, the two Priests whom Lord C. [Campden] mentions

TO EDWARD HEALY THOMPSON

The Oratory Birmingham. April 12. 1857.

My dear Thompson,

The best Easter Greetings to you and Mrs Thompson. I suppose Southwell Lodge is your home — I fancied you were at a friend's house.

Your letter to the Editor of the Union is a good one, and I hope will do him good, and I thank you for letting me see it.[3] As to the bearing of the controversy, however, on him and his friends, I have not much considered that. What I do feel is the great impropriety of a person like Mr Phillipps a

[1] Anderdon wrote on 9 April, 'I shrink from a 5 years' Lease . . . because I never feel certain of our not misconceiving each other upon some point or other of the arrangement. The words e.g. of your former letter from Birmingham seemed to me as plain as could be, that "in any arrangement" I might put in Gas . . . I thereupon went to an expense of some £30. If this has been so in one case, it might be in a multitude of others. Perhaps it will be safer for me to be your tenant for the year ending Feb. 18, 1858.'

[2] Anderdon asked if he might buy the Candelabra, and added, 'Pollen does not like them, and wishes them away.' Anderdon replied on 14 April, 'Thank you for your kind letter, received yesterday. I will not deny that I had all along felt it—what shall I say? hard, aut quid simile—but your kind permission now sets it all right.

You must let me have my own way about buying the Candelabra.' Anderdon added, 'We are in imminent danger of becoming *fashionable*—The aides-de-camp attend regularly from the Castle, and astonish our weak minds by their moustaches . . .'

[3] No letter from Thompson (who was living at Southwell Lodge, Taunton), was published in the *Union*, by the editor, F. G. Lee, later than that inserted incomplete on 27 March.

Catholic, coming forward and saying what in effect is not true, whatever the words mean in the letter. If we did not protest against him, we might fairly be called double dealing — willing to mislead the Anglican party into a belief of what is not.

As to acting upon the Editor of the Union, and trying to convert him individually, a number of questions then come in — which do not enter into the re Phillipps except that I wish he would ask himself whether he is taking the way to convert the Editor or not.

Can you tell me anything about Dr Hendren — if you see him, say every thing kind and respectful from me to him.

Ever Yrs most sincerely in Xt,   John H. Newman of the Oratory

TO THOMAS FURLONG, BISHOP OF FERNS

Oy Bm April 14/57

My dear Lord

I feel most deeply the kindness of your note,[1] and I trust I may take it as an assurance that, as years advance and my end is drawing on, I shall have the benefit of the good prayers of those who show now so kind a feeling towards me

I am &c J H N

TO WILLIAM KEANE, BISHOP OF ROSS

April 14/57

My dear Lord

I do not know how enough to thank your Lordship for your most kind letter.[2] It is a great consolation to me to find that what might appear like

---

[1] Furlong wrote on 7 April, 'It is with much pain and regret that I learnt from your kind communication that the Catholic University is to be deprived of your invaluable services. . . . A hope was fondly cherished that under your fostering care, it would be enabled to surmount the difficulties, which beset its infancy and would finally become a rich fountain of Catholic feeling and Catholic literature in a country where in certain classes they are much needed—But Providence it would seem deems us unworthy of such a blessing. Our unfortunate divisions entail upon us a well merited chastisement. . . . believe me you will be followed by the affection heartfelt regrets of the clergy of this Diocese and very specially of your faithful & attached Servt in J.C.

Thomas Furlong'

[2] Keane wrote on 7 April, that Newman's letter took him 'quite by surprise,' and he read it 'with feelings of more than regret.'

He added that the University was 'as yet only struggling for its existence—Struggling, no doubt, bravely and to a certain extent successfully, but still struggling so as to require the continual aid of the directing head and firm hand that have already achieved so much to give it a position. It is also to be feared that as the friends of the Institution will be dispirited, its enemies, numerous and powerful, will interpret your resignation in a way to suit their own purposes and to injure the work you have so nobly begun.

ingratitude though it is not has not forfeited for me your good opinion. What I feel is that a Rector should be 20 years younger than I am, and should be able to give his life to this one work. I have done substantially all I could do at my age in setting the University off, and I doubt not Providence will not be wanting to this one purpose, but, as he has begun its execution so he will continue and complete it

J H N

TO DOMINIC O'BRIEN, BISHOP OF WATERFORD

April 14/57

My dear Lord

If any thing could make me repent of the resolution to which I have come, it would be the receipt of so feeling and earnest an appeal as that which I have received from your Lordship.[1] But nothing can undo the fact that my strength is not what it has been — and I have a sure confidence that the same Providence which has carried on the University to this date, will not be wanting to His own work and carry it on His own wise and good way. He has no need of men, and can find them, when He wills to use them. This thought consoles me, under that anxiety with which the step I have taken is necessarily accompanied

J H N

WEDNESDAY 15 APRIL 1857   Capes came and slept at Oy [Oratory]

TO JOSEPH DIXON, ARCHBISHOP OF ARMAGH

April 15/57

My dear Lord

I write a line merely to acknowledge the receipt of your Grace's most kind letter[2] — and to assure you how grateful I am for your promise to

---

Of course health and the claims of previous duty involve considerations against which no one could venture to dispute. But if at the approach of November both the one and the other still leave you the liberty of reconsidering your determination to resign, I do sincerely hope that the Catholic University will not lose the services of one to whom the special choice of the Holy Father confided the officer of Ruler.

Be assured, My dear Doctor Newman, that at all times you have the fullest confidence and the best wishes of

your faithful & devoted Servt in C. Wm Keane'

[1] O'Brien implored Newman to defer his resignation, 'Consider the glory you give to God, the great good you confer on Catholic Society by directing the education of our Catholic Youth, the difficulty of finding a person qualified to fill the Office you hold with so much advantage to Religion, such service to education and so much credit to Yourself. If my words would have any weight with you, I would beseech you to ponder a little before you take a step so ruinous to an establishment so gloriously commenced, so steadily progressing, yet still in want of the guidance of so firm a hand.'

[2] See letter of 2 April to Dixon.

converse with me on the subject on which you write and how desirous I shall be in all respects to be as frank and open myself as you can wish.

I am &c J H N

TO JOHN LEAHY, COADJUTOR BISHOP OF DROMORE

The Oratory, Birmingham, April 15, 1857

My dear Lord,

I knew perfectly well how kind an answer I should get from you, but that neither diminished my pain in writing to you, nor diminishes my gratitude now for what you have written.[1]

Gladly would I do for the University anything which really was in my power, but I ought rather to return thanks that I have been allowed to do anything for it, than wonder that what I can do should find its natural limit.

I am greatly consoled by your assurance that you will not forget me in your good prayers, and begging your Lordship's blessing,

I am, my dear Lord, Your faithful and obedient servant in Xt

John H. Newman, of the Oratory.

The Right Rev. the Bishop Coadjutor of Dromore.

THURSDAY 16 APRIL 1857   Mrs Poncia ill
FRIDAY 17 APRIL   Lord Campden called — or next Friday

TO SIR JOHN SIMEON

The Oratory, Hagley Road Birmingham April 17/57

Private

My dear Sir John

I am going to take the liberty of writing to you on a subject, about which I have already been talking with John Pollen.[2]

I believe, (though I do not wish it known just now) that I certainly shall get away from Dublin at the end of this year, having set the University off, which is all I proposed to do. If, having done this, I could be instrumental also, in setting off another great Catholic desideratum, a public school, I should have cause of great thankfulness to Him who gives strength and opportunity for useful undertakings.

Of course the idea of a large school implies the existence of boys to fill it, and I suppose that in fact there are plenty, if their parents would send them.

[1] See letter of 2 April to Leahy.
[2] See the letter of 28 Jan. 1857 to Pollen.

However, it cannot be supposed that any great number would be got together at once. The school then would necessarily have a very modest beginning. And moreover, it would meet with great difficulties, as involving an opposition to existing Catholic schools, *if* it started with any great pretension.

It is this circumstance that leads me to think, that the Oratory could help in it. Ultimately a school must be in the country, but, while it is small and the members of it children, this neighbourhood, which is airy, high, and covered with trees and gardens, would not, I conceive, be inappropriate.

It would not be difficult to find a convenient house with a paddock close to us. And I should propose to start, if possible, with children about nine years old, under the care of some lady, Father Darnell, who is a Wykehamist, being the Paedagogue. In the course of four or five years, when the boys became old enough for a public school, some change in the plan might take place, and the Oratory would retire from the charge or not, according to circumstances.

However I am going too far, considering I know so little at present, whether others will think such a project possible. You will be more able than I am to decide both on the idea itself and on the mode of carrying it out. All I have to add is, that the Oratory would not like to be concerned in the financial part of it, or to receive any remuneration.[1]

Believe me, My dear Sir John, with much esteem Yours most sincerely

John H Newman of the Oratory

Sir John Simeon Bart.

[1] Sir John Simeon replied on 30 April, 'No one feels more keenly than myself the necessity of some better education for our children than I believe to be provided in any Catholic institution.

I have not yet seen a single old Catholic, Priest or Layman, whom with my old Oxford memories still alive, I can consider a well educated man. . . . It is to my mind axiomatic that, unless something can be done to improve the Education of our boys, it is impossible for the Catholic body in England to elevate themselves into intellectual equality with their fellow Citizens. . . .

The defects which strike me as pervading the present system of English Catholic Education are Want of Manliness, Want of Completeness, Want of definite purpose; and consequent want of influence on the future pursuits and character of the man.

I give, as far as I am able to judge, the fullest credit to that system for its many most important advantages, especially as regards the inculcation of purity, and the consequent production of a high moral standard. Still this is apparently purchased at the expense of many valuable qualities of manliness[,] energy, and readiness to face the world.

To my mind Eton, minus its wickedness, and plus the inculcation of the Catholic faith would be what I should best like to see . . .

There is no one in whom I could feel such entire confidence as yourself, were you to undertake this great work; and may I say why I feel this confidence in you, and why I could not offer it with equal sincerity to some others? It is because, with all that you have gained by becoming a Catholic, you never seem to me to have forgotten what you have left, and some of which you have perhaps, as I have myself, lost.

Now I am, and cannot help being, although a thorough Cosmopolite in many ways, emphatically English in all that relates to freedom, whether of individuals, of thought, of discussion, or of institutions. I fear that I carry this feeling too far on some points; but be that as it may, there is nothing that I look on with more jealousy and distrust in the present day than the disposition to denationalize the English Catholic, and to set up as a model for his imitation, some foreign type, which except as regards the accident of the Faith, I look

TO W. G. WARD

The Oratory, Birmingham April 17. 1857

My dear Ward,

I have just received Mrs Ward's letter, and write to you at once. Thank you for your kind inquiry after my health, which, thank God, is excellent, but at my time of life and after so long a spell of head work I never should have cause to be surprised, if I had some sudden visitation, — paralysis.

You have no need to inquire about your subscription to the University. I don't know to whom you can have made the promise to subscribe. If to me, I release you from it at once. But, even if I set about it, I could not tell you what it was, or how long unpaid. I have nothing to do with the accounts myself; and, though some few sums have been paid me, I have at once passed them on into the Bank. Nor do I know *who* can tell you — for I cannot make out that any accounts are kept at all. There is no secretary, no board, of finance — and I have in vain preached about its necessity.

How singular it is, that you should disapprove of my work at Dublin, and that I should think you in a false position at St Edmund's; — and that, while you are thinking of moving from St Edmund's to the isle of Wight, I should be returning from Dublin to Birmingham![1] My letters of resignation have gone to the Bishops, and have been accepted, as far as my answers hitherto go;[2] and I doubt not, as far as residence goes, my connection with the University is drawing to a close, (*though I don't wish this known*). — However,

upon as in every way inferior. It seems to me that the Convert element amongst us has much to answer for in this respect, and, in perfect candour I must say that, as a body, I confess to a little dread of the Oratorians in this particular. I should be sorry to see my boys encouraged to throw overboard their distinctive English character in favor of something which is by some people considered Catholic, simply because it is Antinational. I have not the pleasure of knowing Fr Darnell, and with little boys it is hard to say that such an influence as I deprecate could come in; but your letter contemplates a large and continuous plan, and I cannot help fancying that your idea to be entirely successful would require to be kept entirely clear of the tendency to which I have alluded. . . .

. . . . If I felt that yours was to be the presiding head, and the guiding hand, I should have no fear of intrusting my boys, when old enough, to such a school. . . .'

Newman commented that there was 'a vast deal of truth' in this letter. But it was 'a painful one,' because it attributed to the English Oratorians as a body attitudes which were repugnant to Newman and his Oratorians at Birmingham. See letter of 4 May to St John, and his comment in second note there.

[1] In 1858 W. G. Ward gave up his position as Professor of Dogmatic Theology at St Edmund's College, Ware, and went to live at Northwood, his family place near Cowes in the Isle of Wight. He objected to what he called (in an undated letter, probably written in 1855) 'the predominance of secular literature' in Newman's plan of University education. Newman thought that an untrained layman teaching dogmatics at a seminary was in a false position. Cf. a letter from Ward to Newman in Wilfrid Ward in *William George Ward and the Catholic Revival*, London 1893, pp. 448–9, and Newman's letter of 19 Jan. 1857 to Capes.

[2] The draft has, 'My letters of resignation have gone to the Bishops, and it has been accepted in all but one of the answers I have received.' See last note to letter of 18 April to Wilberforce.

you, I suppose, do not change in your views about St Edmund's, nor can I in mine about the University.[1]

Mrs Ward does not say anything about your health — and I take no news to be good news.

God bless you, My dear Ward, and believe me to be, Ever Yours affly in Xt

John H Newman of the Oratory

W G Ward Esqr

TO HENRY WILBERFORCE

The Oy Bm April 18/57

My dear H W

Thank you for your capital article against the Queen's Colleges. It is a line which ought to be pursued.[2]

By the bye, it somewhat pained me that you should alter dear Robert's word 'worship' into 'devotion — ' in your printed copy of it — for it *implies that he was without devotion* before that time — which would be most unfair to him. His meaning rather was the *cultus*. Besides, you make me misquote.[3]

Best wishes from us of this Holy Season

Ever Yrs affly J H N

[1] Ward replied on 22 April, 'I have been pondering with some interest, on your comparison between your own movements and mine. I think my difficulty in entering into your University views, and your disapproval of my position here, both arise in some degree from the same difference of view; the same indeed, which tended at one time to make me an Arnoldian, to which you, I think, were never the least drawn;—I mean this, that I never have been able to understand (even as a theory, apart from the question of agreement or disagreement) the opinions which I find so generally prevalent as to the essential distinction between ecclesiastical and secular education.

However, my humble divergence has probably troubled you little enough; whereas, I assure you, it has been a very real pain to me, the thought of your disapproval of my work here. You may remember you first mentioned it in a letter some three years ago.

In one respect your "position" in Dublin has been as "false" as you think mine here, though in a most different sense. For you have been called Rector and made responsible, while having very far from a real control over the course of events. The Cardinal [Wiseman] was speaking here the other day in extremely strong terms on the subject, and regretting deeply that you had not been made a bishop as was proposed.

However, I am extremely glad—not selfishly alone, but on public grounds—that we are now likely to get some more theology out of you. I suppose you will think of looking at your M S. on Faith again. . . .

I hear that among the poor of Dublin you are perfectly idolised, and also (of course) among your students. To them, what a calamity!' (Wilfrid Ward, *op. cit.* pp. 449–50, where the letter is printed in full.)

[2] The *Weekly Register*, (18 April 1857), p. 8 had a leading article, 'Financial Reform— The Godless Colleges,' which pointed out what an expensive failure the Queen's Colleges in Ireland had been. They cost £38,200 a year, and a capital sum of £308,000 had been spent on them, yet the number of students at the Catholic University was more than double those in the College at Galway, and exceeded those at Cork. Here was an opportunity for Gladstone to retrench.

[3] In his last letter to Newman, Robert Wilberforce spoke of usages which had seemed an impediment to his conversion but, after it, became an object of attraction. 'This is especially the case with the worship of Our Blessed Lady . . . whereas I have come to regard it as a reward to my faith, in being a Catholic.' Henry Wilberforce altered this. See letter of 8 March 1857 to the Editor of the *Weekly Register*.

P.S. ⌐I follow you in your Education views — but I agree with our Bishop that the State must be narrowly watched — and I fear the State *books*. As to Formby, he is making himself intolerable.[1]

I have written my prospective resignation to every Bishop in Ireland — The answers, as far as they have come, are *most kind* — only one (and he a Co-adjutor) threatens me with the Pope.[2] Dr Cullen writeth not — nor of course McHale⌐

MONDAY 20 APRIL 1857   R. Ward came and slept at Oy. [Oratory]

TO D. B. DUNNE

The Oratory, Birmingham April 20/57

My dear Dr Dunne,

I send you a letter from Mr Keane, and think, if you will be kind enough to do so, that you will talk with him to more effect than I could write.

I think you will agree with me that I have no 'understanding', nor you either, that he would 'be able to acquire some position in the University at the end of two years.' What I said and say, is that a person, like him, who comes and distinguishes himself in it, is the man to get on in it — will have both a claim, and will in fact get on. But the University cannot find places at will, and at a moment — and it is plain I cannot either predict nor create them.

My notion is that he would be a desirable person, first for a Tutorship — and so he would get on, as openings occur. His line seems to be the Oriental languages; this, as you know, is open. There is no chance, I suppose, of a Professorship being founded just now — and, if the time at length came — no one can prophecy [sic] there would not be other candidates — but no one would have the claim of Mr Keane, and the very fact of his being on the spot with testimonials, or writings attesting his proficiency, might hasten the appointment, as well as decide it in his favor.

I think you will bear me out that this corresponds to what I said to you when he talked of coming to us — I could have wished I had put it down on

---

[1] Henry Formby was violently opposing the acceptance of State aid for Catholic Schools.

[2] Laurence Gillooly, a Vincentian, and Coadjutor Bishop of Elphin, acknowledged, on 13 April, Newman's letter of resignation, 'The motives you alledge [sic] are strong ones and have been of course well considered—Yet I cannot help thinking and expressing to you my conviction that your retirement at the present time will imperil the very existence of the University; and that reasons even more cogent than those which first secured your services, now claim the continuance of them. I should feel anxious for the future, had I not a confident hope that the will of God will be somewhat differently manifested to you thro our Holy Father and the Bishops . . .'

paper then — but I think I was in Dublin, and every thing passed in conversation.

As to his stopping another year or not, why, *we* can only advise him on *our* side of the matter. I should say, yes — for the more I think of it, the more I think there is much to do, for his getting really good honors. But of course his Father must decide what *he* considers best, with this uncertainty of his academical future.

My memory is so bad, I don't recollect what prizes etc he has got — but don't they help him out a certain way? and may they not next year?[1]

Best Easter greetings to you and yours

Very sincerely Yours in Xt   John H Newman

TO EDWARD BADELEY

The Oratory Birmingham April 22. 1857

My dear Badeley

I meant to have written to you within the Easter Octave, when I might more fitly have sent you the best greetings of the sacred season, than I can do now, when Low Week is running on. I suppose you don't know much how things are going on external to the venerable precincts of the Law, else I would say how anxious I am about the Education and other questions now pending, and would ask for light.[2] However, what I am writing about is the matter on which you gave me a kind encouragement when I last wrote. I want to set going a Dublin University Scientific and Literary Journal; at first, to come out only twice a year. I expect the cost will be £100 a number. I want to find the money for three years, if I can, and then leave it to itself — but I must be content with two years, if I can't do more. Lord Dunraven has promised me £10 for three years — but this is all I have got. Hope Scott is quite over done, and can do nothing for me. Can you do any thing? If I get a few promises, I will print a sort of prospectus.[3]

I have sent in my letter of resignation — i.e. I have written to every one of the Irish Bishops saying I mean to resign next November. There is a report among the Dublin Whig Protestants, that the Queen's Colleges are simply to be given to the Protestants — and Maynooth and our University

---

[1] Augustus Henry Keane was at St Patrick's House. In Nov. 1856 he won a Classical Scholarship at the University and also prizes for Greek Criticism and English Essay. He was appointed a tutor at St Patrick's House in Nov. 1858, and later became a renowned Orientalist and Professor of Hindustani in University College, London.

[2] Badeley replied on 30 April that the Bishops and the Poor School Committee had met, 'when those who were opposed to the Government grants gave up their opposition.' The *Tablet*, (2 May 1857), p. 275, reported that a unanimous resolution had affirmed that grants could be safely accepted for the Catholic schools.

[3] See letter of 1 April to Hope Scott. Badeley promised £5 for two or three years towards what was to become the *Atlantis*. For the prospectus see second note to letter of 20 Oct. 1857 to Sullivan.

in some way to be consolidated. This is really wise in Government — if they mean it — but I do not know how to believe it.

Duffy is publishing my Lectures *with* the Achilli passage. I have distinctly stated to him that he must do it on his own risk — and that I cannot be answerable — but *does this exculpate me in the eye of the law?*[1]

Ever Yours affly John H Newman of the Oratory

E Badeley Esqr

TO MRS WILLIAM FROUDE

Oy Bm April 22/57

My dear Mrs Froude,

Best Easter greetings. I have not written to you, because I don't like to seem to be corresponding. I always think of you.

So many persons have been deeply interested for you, and are looking out, that it is impossible your secret can be kept. The other day a friend called who was passing through — and *entreated* me to tell him. It was impossible that he should not infer something, though I said nothing[2]

Ever Yrs affly J H N

TO ANDREW ELLIS

The Oratory, Birmingham April 26/57

Private

My dear Dr Ellis

Thank you for your letter just received, which puts me au courant with the Medical Bill Proceedings.

I wrote to Mr Monsell (between ourselves) immediately on your speaking to me several weeks ago, and got a very satisfactory answer. I know quite well he will do whatever he can, and make an effort to do much — what he *can* do, neither he nor I can tell.[3]

I am kept here by a cold — and I don't think any thing I can say now,

---

[1] Badeley replied that 'every fresh publication is a new offence,' and that if Newman were in any way concerned with the new edition of *The Present Position of Catholics in England*, or had the right to prevent it and did not, he would be in danger of prosecution. The passage denouncing Achilli was omitted from the edition of *Prepos.* published by Duffy, Dublin 1857.

[2] This friend was most probably Richard Ward (see diary), who was related to the Froudes. Mrs Froude had become a Catholic on 19 March.

[3] See letter of 31 March to Monsell. Ellis was anxious that the Medical Faculty of the University should be represented on the Board which it was thought the Bill would establish.

will make Mr M. more zealous than he is; else, I would attempt to go up to London. However, I will turn the matter in my mind

     Yours most sincerely John H Newman of the Oratory

A Ellis Esqr

P.S. Mr M. told me that he had *not* charge of the Bill

TUESDAY 28 APRIL 1857 set off to Ireland at night *to Dublin* Penny left Dublin for a fortnight

WEDNESDAY 29 APRIL about this time Br Charles put off habit.

TO ARCHBISHOP CULLEN

     6 Harcourt Street April 29. 1857

My dear Lord,

 I have to beg of your Grace the favor of your putting at my disposal the sum necessary for defraying the Quarter's Expenses of the University. It is made up as follows:—

	£
Fourth of £5000 for the Faculties of Medicine, Philosophy and Letters, and Science, the annual sum which I asked of the Bishops in my statement of June 1856[1]	1250
Fourth of £1200, the interest of the Trustee Fund, as by the same statement	300
	1550
In lieu of fees of the Students, not yet exacted, except in part	. . .
	£1550

As I have cheques of his Grace the Archbishop of Tuam to the amount of £1500, which I have acknowledge to him, but which I have never used, I send them for your Grace's counter signature, as nearly meeting the Quarter's expenses. But, should your Grace prefer new cheques, I will send them to you.[2]

 I am, My dear Lord, Your Grace's faithful Servant in Xt

     John H Newman of the Oratory.

His Grace The Archbp of Dublin

[1] Letter of 19 June 1856 to the Archbishops and Bishops of Ireland.
[2] Cullen returned the cheques signed, on 2 May, and added 'I hope I shall have the pleasure of paying you a visit on some day next week
 Believe me to be with great esteem Your devt Sert'

TO JOHN STANISLAS FLANAGAN

6 Harcourt Street April 29/57

My dear St

A calm good passage.

On second thoughts don't show to M. [Monsell][1] that you know the contents of the letter I showed you, till he speaks to you.

I have just been showing Smith O'Brien over the University. He seems to me an amiable, prosy, not very strong man; by amiable I mean, a person one should love.[2]

Renouf is going to be married (don't tell) He won't take pupils.[3] It is generally known that I have sent in my resignation. E. de Ligne and Fraser have said that they shall not stay, if I go. Do consider what a kettle of fish I am in — What am I to do about the house! The bills this spring are *frightful*

Ever Yrs affly J H N

P.S. Dr Renehan has had more than one serious stroke in Holy Week. I have had the whole account of his case from Dr Lee, and, I assure you it increases the seriousness with which I have already applied it to myself. It has been brought on 1. by anxiety about the Maynooth Commission. 2. by rapid rail road travelling.[4]

TO WILLIAM MONSELL

6 Harcourt Street Dublin April 29/57

My dear Monsell

I have just had a talk with Lynch on the subject which you have so kindly confided to me.[5]

Certainly, my own impression is, that you have come to just the conclusion which becomes you. It seems most strange that a man of your political standing and character should have had such an offer — nor could you do any thing but decline it.

For myself, I cannot conceive that things will rest there — or that no

[1] See next letter.
[2] William Smith O'Brien, who had been sentenced to transportation for life after his insurrection in 1848, received a conditional pardon in 1856, and returned to Ireland in July of that year.
[3] In the summer Renouf married Ludovica, eldest child of Christian Brentano. Döllinger had known her from infancy, and gave a party for her engagement.
[4] Laurence Renehan, President of Maynooth, died on 27 July 1857. Walter Lee had been Dean of Maynooth, and then in 1856 became Secretary to the Trustees of the College. The Royal Commission on the management and studies sat from 1853 to 1855.
[5] Henry Lynch was Monsell's private secretary. It would seem that when Parliament met in April after the General Election, Palmerston made some offer to Monsell, who was President of the Board of Health Feb.–Sept. 1857. 'Lord G.' is probably Earl Granville, who was Lord President of the Council.

other offer will be made. At the same time, I know well it is impossible to answer for the movements of such a man as the person offering.

Any how, I should be sorry that you had acted otherwise than you have done — and I can't think a man like Lord G. would have any other opinion.

Ever Yrs affly John H newman

The Rt Honble Wm Monsell M P

THURSDAY 30 APRIL 1857   Dr Lee of Maynooth and Robertson to dinner.

TO J. I. TAYLOR

[End of?] [[April? 1857]]

Private

My dear Dr Taylor

┌Thank you for your very kind letter. It is quite true, in answer to your question, that I cannot long remain here, but it is from no 'disgust' on my part, as you suppose, but from the prospect of old age and the many claims which are made at present on my time and strength. I came here only for a season. My Congregation at Bm [Birmingham] only spared me for a season. You recollect how eager I was to get to work — this was because I saw precious time going, which was irrevocable. When this Session ends, I shall have given *six years* to the University. At my time of life six years is as long as twelve years of a younger man. For six years shall I have given up my confessional and the other duties of an Oratorian. For six years all my other work, all my reading, has been suspended. The first three years were wasted indeed, as far as active proceedings here went, but they were not therefore the less lost to my congregation.

I have ever said that I could be here but for a time. In 1852, in my University Discourses, I said 'neither you nor I must ever be surprised, if the Hand of Him, with whom are the springs of life and death, weighs heavy on me.'[1] In the Catholic Gazette in 1854 I said I only 'aspired to the preliminary task of breaking the ground and clearing the foundations of the future.'[2] In my report to the Bishops in 1855 I spoke of 'the time being so limited, which at my age, and with my engagements elsewhere, I can hope to be allowed to employ' in their Lordships' service.'[3] It is near a year since I mentioned the term of my stay distinctly to Dr Cullen. I could not do more than all this. To have stated my intention of going publicly, would have tended to defeat the good of my being here at all.

[1] At the end of the last Discourse, *Idea*, p. 239.
[2] The reference must be to Newman's Inaugural Lecture in the Faculty of Philosophy and Letters, The *Catholic University Gazette*, (16 Nov. 1854), p. 200, 'Christianity and Letters,' *Idea*, p. 267.
[3] *Campaign*, p. 55. The 'Report for the Year 1854–1855' is dated 13 Oct. 1855.

The University wants a Rector 20 years younger than I am — one who can form *plans* for the future — who can give a life to its service; again, who has no other engagements, and can give his whole heart and strength to it. I have set it off. This is all I proposed to do. I cannot longer carry on both my Dublin work and my Birmingham work. I cannot bear the fatigue of going to and fro between England and Ireland. And the University has had out of me pretty nearly all it can squeeze.

I have never for a moment doubted of the success of the great undertaking which brought me here.

It has steadily advanced month after month ever since it began. Its establishment is only a matter of time; but time is just the article which I cannot promise myself. Meanwhile St Philip has a demand on what remains to me.[1]

J H N

TO D. B. DUNNE

6 Harcourt Street May 1/57

My dear Dr Dunne

I have not the wording of the Statute of January before me, but I conceive that any one who submitted himself to St Patrick's House's discipline for the portion of the day which may be called 'the business hours' beginning with Mass, is a resident. Am I not right?

If he was thus connected with St Patrick's House, he would no longer be an Extern, and would have the advantage of both Professorial and Tutorial instruction.[1]

Mr Flannery would pay the University at the rate of £10 a year for him, and would count him as one of his students for the grant of money made to his house.

What *he* paid to Mr Flannery would be a private arrangement between them.

I have tried to find Renouf, to see if he agrees with me — but he is out of the way. Please, read the above to Mr Butler, or some other Professor — to see if he agrees with me — and consider it yourself. If two opinions corroborate me, yours and his, I suppose I am right.

I have this morning received your most kind letter returned from Birmingham.[2] I feel myself quite unworthy of so much consideration and

---

[1] This perhaps refers to A. H. Keane.

[2] Dunne wrote on 24 April:

'I have heard that you have tendered your resignation, nay, that no circumstances could induce you to stay among us longer. I could not tell what sadness this piece of news has caused me. I had never realized the idea of your going away at all—and even ideally such an event seemed too distant to excite apprehension. Now when it seems imminent, it appears to involve too general, and too personal a misfortune to be permitted. I cannot but cherish the hope that God and the Blessed Virgin who have established this University and preserved attachment. All I can say is, that any thing I can do which does not come across clear duties which are upon me, I will gladly do — but I could not die in peace, if during my last years I had separated myself from my Congregation — nor can I hope St Philip will do any thing for me, if I only give him the dregs of my life.

Ever Yours affectly in Xt   John H Newman of the Oratory

MONDAY 4 MAY 1857   M. de Bamville and Wallis to dinner

TO AMBROSE ST JOHN

⌐6 Harcourt Street May 4. 1857¬

My dear A

In the Union which I sent to Bm [Birmingham] yesterday, is an account in the letter of a Correspondent, of one Gest's writing one of the Church of E.'s [England] articles, with his *meaning* when he wrote it. As it bears upon Number 90, I wish you would ask Robert [Tillotson] to be so good as to cut the letter out of the Paper, and keep it for me.[1]

2. ⌐I inclose a letter, which, please, *send me back at once*. It is a painful one — but I think there is a vast deal of truth in it. Don't tell any one that you have seen it.[2]

3 There was a meeting of the Deans of Faculties today; and⌐ as I have not been told even the fact of their meeting ⌐my suspicions,¬ otherwise alive from the sensation my leaving is making, ⌐are roused, that it is about *me*.¬

it to the present moment, will not now subject us to such a calamity:—for I am convinced it will immensely hinder the success of what, under all circumstances you must regard as emphatically your own work.

Among both Professors and Students, I am sure there will be only one feeling of intense sorrow: and this, apart from any other motive, from the deep feeling of veneration and regard which you have created in every heart. For myself, I feel as if I had been informed of my separation from my father.

But, I do hope, we shall be spared this great affliction: and that when you return to us you will see more than sufficient motive for continuing to develop your own commencements.'

[1] The *Union*, (1 May 1857), p. 291, published a letter containing a copy, from the original in the State Paper Office, of a letter of Edmund Geste, or Guest, Bishop of Rochester, to Cecil, dated 22 Dec. 1566. Geste, who was a defender of the Real Presence, wrote, 'I suppose you have heard how ye Bisshop of Glocestre Cheney found himself greived with ye plasynge of this adverbe *onely* in this article "The body of Xt is gyven, taken and eaten in the Supper after an heavenly and spiritual manner *onely*," because it did take away ye presence of Xt's body in ye Sacrament. . . .

I told him plainelye that this word *onelye* in the foresaied Article did not exclude ye presence of Xtis Body fro ye Sacrament, but only ye GROSSENESS AND SENSIBLENESS in ye receiving thereof. For I said unto him *tho he took Xtis Body in his hand . . . yet did he not for all that see it, feale it,* smelle it, nor taste it. And therefore I told him I wold speak against him herein, and ye rather bycause YE ARTICLE WAS MY OWN PENNYGNE. . . .'

[2] This was Sir John Simeon's letter of 30 April, quoted in note to Newman's of 17 April to him. St John replied on 5 May, 'Sir John Simeon's letter is indeed very interesting—I do not think it right to keep him in the impression that we and London are one. It is too bad— They get all the praise we all the blame of their misdeeds,' namely the 'anti-national' and 'Italianate' attitude at the London Oratory, complained of by Simeon.

I know Fr O Reilly has spoken to Dr Cullen on the subject of my going —
and ⌜Father O'R. came here today just after, (I suppose,) the meeting⌝ had
been held, — tho' *he* said nothing of the meeting. ⌜He spoke of my intention
of going, and said that many things might happen before November⌝ or
something of the kind. ⌜The form which my suspicions take is, that some
document signed by the Deans is to be sent to Dr C. for Rome. Of course all
this may be a mares nest — but you may be sure I shall keep a sharp look out
— and,⌝ if I get hold of any application to Rome whatever, I shall set you at
Bm on applying also

Ever Yrs affly J H N

P.S.   ⌜It is also possible that an address is to be presented to *me* from the
Professors, and that the Deans are concocting it.⌝ I think then *you should do
the following at once*, viz let the General Congregation pass a Decree, and send
it me, (so that I may present it with a previous date affixed to the Professors,
if they present any thing to me) to this effect, 'Whereas by Decree of such
and such a date' (if the date is not as early as 1851 or 1852 perhaps it had
better not be set down?) we gave permission to our Father Superior to be
absent from this House for the purpose etc and whereas the time has expired
etc and whereas we find that we cannot continue longer the great inconvenience etc. we hereby unanimously determine, in General Congregation
assembled, that his leave of absence shall end, and that by virtue of obedience
to St Philip, he must return etc etc

TO AMBROSE ST JOHN, I

6 Harcourt Street Dublin ⌜May 6. 1857

My dear Father Dean,

I have just received your letter containing Decree of General Congregation
withdrawing my leave of absence from Birmingham. I need scarcely say I
feel bound to obey it.[1]

---

[1] St John wrote:

'The Oratory, Birmingham. May. 5.

My dear Father Superior,

   Our Fathers have requested me to forward to you a Decree passed by them this day in
General Congregation:
It is as follows—"C. G. May 5. 1857.

   Whereas by Decree of May 6. 1852 we gave permission to our Father Superior to accept
the office of President of the Catholic University and whereas the time has long since expired
which we contemplated for his absence when we gave him that permission; and whereas we
find we cannot continue longer the great inconvenience arising from his protracted separation
from us, we hereby unanimously determine in General Congregation assembled, that his
leave of absence shall end, and that in virtue of obedience to St Philip he must return to us."

   Ever my dearest Father Superior Yours most affectionately in St Philip

Ambrose St John. Dean of the Oratory—in the absence of the Superior.
The Very Revd Fr J. H. Newman.'

However, I do not interpret it to mean, that I must return at this moment without any delay. I assure you, I will do so at once, if such is the wish of the Congregation; but it may only mean to fix a limit to my absence.

The words of the Decree are these: 'We hereby unanimously determine,[1] in General Congregation assembled, that his leave of absence shall end, and that in virtue of obedience to St Philip, he must return to us.' ⌐I wish to ask of you, as interpreting the intention of the Congregation, whether I am to return at once, or, if not, within what time.⌐[1]

I am, My dear Fr Dean,

Most affectly Yours in St Philip   John H Newman Praep.

The Revd Father Dean

TO AMBROSE ST JOHN, II

May 6/57

My dear A

The Decree will strengthen my hands uncommonly. I feel the matter is now really a matter of obedience, and I shall observe it as such. I can only act under the directions of the Congregation

Ever Yrs J H N

P.S.   I don't see that the Congregation *need* answer my question at once, *unless it wishes to do so* — I mean, if it had rather not.

P.S.   I thought the Cardinal's Letter the most tremendous set down possible. But Mr Langdale will resign, if any thing else stands good[2]

TO AMBROSE ST JOHN

6 Harcourt St May 7/57

My dear A [[Ambrose]][3]

I read the Rambler for May last night, and am pained, and almost frightened, at the first article.[4] It is the second or third successive stroke, each

---

[1] Newman copied the essential part of St John's reply:

'Oratory. May 7. 1857

My dear Father,
    We will write to you an official letter in answer to your question in due time. Meanwhile we all understand you will not come for good before November. . . .
                                Yours most affectly (signed) Ambrose St John

[2] See letter of 7 May to Ullathorne.

[3] This is the first of the letters Newman inserted in the collection he made 'In Re Rambler 1858–1862.'

[4] 'The Political Future', the *Rambler*, (May 1857), pp. 323–37, drew attention to the divisions among Catholics and claimed that they were lacking in political sense and prone to

louder than the one before. Capes is too good a fellow, for one to have any fears of *him* — but his articles both register, and will blow up and spread, bad feeling, very bad feeling. I look at them in connection with a letter I sent you a few days ago — and the more anxiously, because the two complaints are so entirely independent of each other.[1]

It seems to me that a time of great reaction and of great trial is before us. I earnestly trust I may be wrong. I will do my best to prove myself wrong. But it seems to me that really I may be *wanted* in England, and that there may be a providential reason, over and above the compulsion of the Fathers at Bm [Birmingham], for me to return. I have too little perhaps made myself felt — and, while some like Fr Faber are going ahead without fear, others are in consequence, even if not inclined of themselves already, backing and making confusion.

The Bishops are necessarily engaged in the great and momentous ecclesiastical routine. They are approving themselves good stewards in the sense in which St Carlo or St Francis were such — meanwhile, the party of the aristocracy and the party of talent are left to themselves without leaders and without guides.

It makes me wish I were to live twenty years in full possession of my mind — for breakers are ahead. Yet the battle is not given to the strong, and divine purposes are wrought out by the weak and unarmed — so that I am making myself of more importance than past history justifies. Still here I am, as yet alive and well — and I assure you my thoughts have turned among other things to the subject which Ward wishes me to pursue, more than they did.[2] Do pray for me that I may find out what use God wishes to put me to, and may pursue it with great obedience

Ever Yrs affly J H N

TO BISHOP ULLATHORNE

6 Harcourt Street Dublin May 7. 1857

Private

My dear Lord

It is with great anxiety and concern that I first read the Cardinal's Letter in the last Tablet, and then heard from Birmingham something you said about it to some of our party there. When I read the Letter, I saw that it involved a history to which it gave us no clue, and I was amazed at what seemed the

intemperate criticism. It decried the Independent Irish Party, spoke slightingly of Cardinal Wiseman, and remarked 'that the clergy and laity of Ireland happen to exercise their privilege of disagreeing in what is not of faith to a most wonderful extent.'

[1] This was Sir John Simeon's letter, quoted in note to that of 17 April to him. Cf. also letter of 19 Jan. 1857 to Capes.

[2] i.e. the subject of faith and certainty.

verbal references to your Lordship's Notes.[1] What Fr St John tells me deeply pains me.[2]

No one can hate differences of opinion on doctrinal or practical subjects more that I do — no one could hail more than myself the news you gave me, when I last saw you, that the differences on the Education Question were shortly to be arranged. I earnestly trust they will be so, still; but it is miserable, if deference is not to be paid to those who have a right to have, and a duty to express, their own view of the subject. For myself, I am not in a *position* to be able to form my own private opinion on this particular matter, but it does not require any thought or deliberation whatever, to be earnestly desirous that the difference should be settled, and settled without disrespect or slight towards any of the venerable Fathers of our English Episcopate.

I cannot help writing these few lines, first to express my true devotion to your Lordship, and deep concern at the trial, to which (it seems to me) your Episcopal Sollicitude has been subjected — and next, my anxiety about what is to follow. Every one sees his own side of Catholic affairs — perhaps no side is just now pleasant. Your Lordship, doubtless, as Bishop, has presented to you an aspect of the state of the Church, peculiar to yourself, and of peculiar anxiety. I have my side, and it too is full of forebodings for the future, which I pray God may be utterly mistaken — If, in addition to these existing prospects of evil or occasions of sorrow, there should appear to the world to be a discordance in the highest quarters, what may not be the consequence? Cannot the Holy See, in this matter, save us from such a danger?

Pray excuse me if I am too free — but, I may be wrong, but I fancy a time of trial is coming on us

I am, My dear Lord, with the greatest respect, Your Lordship's affectionate Servt in Xt

John H Newman of the Oratory

The Rt Revd The Bp of Birmingham

[1] A long letter from Wiseman to Charles Langdale, the Chairman of the Catholic Poor Schools Committee, was published in the *Tablet*, (2 May 1857), p. 281, and also in the *Weekly Register*. It made known that Catholics could safely accept the Government grant for their schools. Wiseman went into the recent history of the matter, and at least by implication criticised Ullathorne for the cautious attitude he had adopted in his pamphlet, *Notes on the Education Question*, London 1857. See also Newman's letters of Feb. 1857 to Ullathorne.

[2] St John wrote on 5 May, 'The Bishop has just been here. He has come to say that the Cardinal's letter in the Register purporting to come from the Bishops was written without his sanction unseen by all the Bishops and unapproved by the *majority*. He is going to write publicly about it as he thinks it will seriously compromise himself and others—Here's a go —Poor little Bishop he is excessively cordial, and *felt* evidently at home here.'

On 12 May Ullathorne issued a printed circular to his clergy, explaining that Wiseman's letter to Langdale was approved at an unofficial meeting of bishops. Ullathorne was not present, and had since received a distinct denial that any allusion to him or his writings was intended by Wiseman.

TO BISHOP ULLATHORNE

6 Harcourt Street Dublin May 10. 1857

My dear Lord,

I feel very grateful for your confidential and painfully interesting communication.[1] I hope your health will not suffer from these anxieties, and propose, for it is all I can do, to say a weekly Mass for your Lordship's intention in this matter for some time to come.

Begging your Lordship's blessing I am, My dear Lord, Your affte friend & servant in Xt

John H Newman of the Oratory

The Rt Revd The Bp of Birmingham.

MONDAY 11 MAY 1857   Dr Leahy's appointment to Archbishoprick [of Cashel] known about this time

TO D. B. DUNNE

6 Harcourt Street May 11. 1857

My dear Dr Dunne

I see no difficulty in your going to Maynooth, and most willingly give leave to A. Bethell to go with you. It will be a great advantage to him.

As to the application to London, I suppose I shall hear something about it from Dr Hayden.[2]

I cannot think what I have said in my last to deserve so very kind and and affectionate a notice from you. But I am very glad to have it, and hope it is a pledge that you will not forget me in your prayers

Yours, My dear Dr Dunne, Affectly in Xt

John H Newman of the Oratory

D Dunne Esqr

P.S.   I like the idea of Augustus defending some theses at the end of term.

TO THOMAS SCRATTON

May 11/57

My dear Scratton

In answer to Mr Hanley's question, I may observe, in addition to what you have so well said to him, that, if his son attaches himself to St Patrick's

---

[1] This is not to be found.
[2] This must refer to the Medical Bill. Cf. letter of 26 April to Ellis. Hayden was Dean of the Medical Faculty.

house in such sense as to be there during the business hours of the day, he will be considered as an Intern and have the *benefit of the Tutor's Lectures and instruction*.[1] As to the expense, that will be a matter of arrangement between him and Mr Flannery — but I don't suppose it would be a large sum.

You can explain this to him, and send him a copy of the Statute of January[2]

Yrs affly John H Newman

Thos Scratton Esqr

P.S. The inclosed bill has to be paid. If Anderdon uses the Organ, he should pay half of it.

TUESDAY 12 MAY 1857 Dr Leahy called, and then Dr Cullen

TO AMBROSE ST JOHN, I

⌐6 Harcourt Street May 12/57⌐

My dear A

⌐Dr Leahy has just called — he began the subject of the Rectorship — he was kind and appreciative and earnest as much as my warmest friends could desire — said that I could not understand the full confidence the Bishops had in me — that I was the man, he verily believed, intended by Providence, before I was a Catholic, for the work — that I should destroy it if I went, — that he would not, could not, believe I was to go etc etc.

I showed him the Congregation's Decree of May 5, which was a simple quietus to him, as it has been to every one to which [[whom]] I have shown it.

He said that he hoped I would persuade the Congregation to spare me, at least a year or two longer. I said I could not in conscience — that no words could do justice to the intensity with which I felt the evil of my absence — that we had all borne it very long; that no one could tell how long my life was to be — that I could not leave the world with a good conscience, if I had not given my last years to St Philip. On the other hand, that the setting up of a University was the work of years, the work of a life — that I could only be here at most a year or two more or less — that the Bishops should get a man 20 years younger etc etc.

Then he said, would not the Congregation yield if the Archbishop wrote to them in the name of the Archbishops? I said, I did not think it would be any use.

Then after a minute or two, it struck me this was imprudent to say —

---

[1] Mr Hanly complained that non-resident students received no tuition in the University, and that he had been unable to find private tutors among its staff. Joseph Hanly came to the University in Nov. 1855, when he was *proximus* for the Historical Essay Prize. (Cf. James Meenan, editor, *Centenary History of the Literary and Historical Society of University College Dublin 1855–1955*, Tralee, n.d. [1956], p. 10.)
[2] See diary for 15 Jan. 1857.

that if a correspondence once began, the Congregation might make terms, grant *some* absences etc. So I recalled my words — I said that I was wrong to go so far as to prejudge what the Congregation would do — that they would feel deeply the condescension of the Archbishop writing etc etc. I said this once or twice, but Dr Leahy did not respond. I suspect he had thrown out the notion to see what I should say, and did not like to commit himself further.

He still urged me to persuade the Congregation. I pointed to the letter and said that it was out of my hands etc etc. So he went. ⟨The notion of a partial residence, or of non-residence was not mentioned between us.⟩

Your Decree has done me incalculable service. Butler, when he first saw it, seemed to realize what before was to him in nubibus. And so of others. I expect Dr Leahy will recommend to Dr Cullen to write a letter to the Congregation — so be prepared what to say in anticipation. I recommend you without delay to get a view what your answer should be, and let me know it.[1]

Ever Yrs J H N

TO AMBROSE ST JOHN, II

⌜2½ oclock PM May 12/57⌝

My dear A

⌜The poor Archbishop [Cullen] is just gone — I say 'poor,' because he was evidently so nervous and distressed, as to melt me internally, though I was very stiff or very much moved, both at once perhaps, during the short interview.

First he begged me to stop, for everyone said I must — for three years more, so as to make six from the opening of the University.

I reminded him how I had urged him to begin sooner, for I had lost my first years in waiting. Also, that I told him a year ago what was to be.

Next he said Propaganda would give a dispensation, he was sure, of non-residence [[at Birmingham]].

I said I was sure that the whole Oratory would go off to Rome to present in person an expostulation, rather than let such dispensation pass sub silentio.

Then he said some arrangement perhaps might be made, by which I should be more time at Birmingham — and a Vice Rector who might reside always [[in Dublin]].

I said I was sure the Fathers, as I myself, would do every thing possible to serve an undertaking which they expected so much from.

Lastly he said that perhaps some of the Bishops, perhaps an Archbishop, might write to the Birmingham Congregation.

I said that I knew well how grateful the Bm Fathers would be for such condescension — for myself, I felt extreme gratitude to the Bishops, some of whom had sent me most touching letters in answer to my announcement.

All this took place with pauses of silence on my part and his — and when I spoke, I spoke with great momentum [[?]]. I say all this to bring the scene before you.

Then he rose, and I rang the bell — and there must have been something unusual in our faces, for when Frederic came in, he [[F.]] looked frightened.

He then said that he had spoken to some Bishops about my Church — delay had been unavoidable — but he thought they would buy it for the University — and they would settle it when they met in a few weeks.

I think your answer should be most courteous, warm, and grateful. Apologetic, on the ground of the *real* need of a Superior at Bm — expressive of your desire to do all you could — and saying that you answered without delay out of reverence and gratitude, but you wished to be allowed maturely to think over the proposition[1]

Ever Yrs affly J H N

TO THOMAS SCRATTON

6 Harcourt Street May 12/57

My dear Secretary

Will you write an official letter to *each* of these three Gentlemen, Mr Mc Dermott, Mr Cox, and Mr Hamy to the following effect respectively:—

that I have carefully considered the letters addressed by them to the Professors on the subject of their presenting themselves at an early date for their scholarship examination, and that, not content with my own judgment, I have submitted the question to the Council of the Faculty of Philosophy and Letters, and that I find my own view confirmed by that Faculty

Accordingly I think it right to abide by it — and that I send them the formal decision of the Council of the Faculty, as expressive of it.

To Mr Mac Dermott, then, you will say that 'he has shown no sufficient reason in his letters to the Dean of Faculty, why Rule 26 prescribing the conditions, under which Medical Burses are held, should be dispensed with in his favour:'

To Mr Cox you will say that 'he is referred to Rules 26 and 24.'

To Mr Hamy that 'he has not shown sufficient cause why Rule 26 should be dispersed with.' But I should not be altogether unwilling, from his particular circumstances, to give him for a while a dispensation from residence.[1]

I am, My dear Secretary, Affectly Yours John H Newman

The Secretary of the Cath. Univ.

---

[1] Among 'Rules and Regulations of the University', 24, 'Candidates for Examinations', and 26, 'Medical and Scientific Burses' insisted on residence during the first two sessions.

Hugh MacDermott was nominated to a burse by the Bishop of Achonry and Alfred Francis Hamy by the Bishop of Dromore.

P.S.   Will you draw Arnold a draft for £5 on account of Tutor's money due to the House at end of term?

I send the Reviews for Arnold, who will call for them[1]

WEDNESDAY 13 MAY 1857   new edition of Church of Fathers published just now.[2]

TO VISCOUNTESS CAMPDEN

6 Harcourt Street Dublin May 13. 1857.

My dear Lady Campden

I have just now received your letter, and will, as you wish, consider it strictly confidential.

I do not deny I have been for many weeks very anxious about the health of Mr Anderdon — or rather about his exertions and the effect they *may* have on him. Indeed, as my friends here know, I am continually speaking on the subject.

As to himself, my words are simply thrown away, and I can do nothing. I have urged him to do less, and to get assistance, till I have fairly teazed him, without producing any other result. I have been obliged to give over.

The accounts you have heard of his work are exaggerated, but there is no doubt he ought to do less, and is in the way to knock himself up.

Again I should say that in Lent, when the Monsells passed through Dublin, and I had been discoursing to Mr Monsell on the subject and on my anxiety about him, when he made his appearance, (for I hardly get to see him once a month, and he looks grave when I go to him or send for him,) Mr Monsell thought him looking very well — and I cannot deny he did.[3] I have not seen him since, except when he once rapidly passed me. I am afraid I must say, you underate my influence. He has got a great work before him, of great promise, and is making a great name here. He is doing a vast deal of good, he is opening a new field of missionary exertion here — and he thanks no one who interferes with him.

I should say too that he is certainly surrounded by a number of kind people who are as anxious about him, if that be possible, as you can be. You know that, wherever he is, he will be loved and valued — and their keen eyes

---

[1] Among Newman's letters to Scratton is an undated note, which is inserted here for completeness:

'My dear S I believe "John Conelly" is a gentleman, and you should have called him Esquire.

Ever Yrs J H N'

[2] This was the third edition of *The Church of the Fathers*, with a new 'Advertisement,' dated 'Lady Day, 1857,' and published by James Duffy, Dublin.

[3] See letter of 20 March 1857 to St John.

are sure to detect whenever he is unwell, and their homes are open to him at any moment.

He professes to be taking care of his health — there is one thing certainly I should like to do — that is, to limit his work to the University Church. Instead of this, he preaches about the place for various charities — he preaches next Sunday, for instance — but I neither can break engagements which he has made, nor hinder his making them. However, I will say, in corroboration of what I observed above, that one Sunday some weeks ago, a lady who lives near, observing him tired after his morning mass, obliged him to come to her house, forced on him a very substantial meal, and obliged him to put off a sermon he was to have preached for some charitable object in the middle of the day. So you see he is in more potent hands than mine.

On the whole, taking things as they are, taking into account his determined zeal, I think he has, in the deep veneration and affection of those who surround him, the best safeguard or alleviation of the difficulties of his position which is possible.

Believe me to be always, My dear Lady Campden, Yours most sincerely in Jesus and Mary

John H Newman of the Oratory

The Viscountess Campden

THURSDAY 14 MAY 1857   Lloyd called

TO RICHARD SIMPSON

6 Harcourt Street Dublin May 14. 1857

My dear Simpson

I thank you for the zeal you show for the University.[1] We are not in the most favorable position just now as regards Theology — but I hope we shall be so soon. I shall be at Birmingham, if all is well, on St Philip's day, the 26th. Could Mr Livius be our guest for that day? It is Tuesday week — I could then talk with him — I suppose I shall remain there several days — but the 26th or 27th would be safest

Very sincerely Yours in Xt   John H Newman of the Oratory

R. Simpson Esqr

[1] Simpson wrote to ask whether Thomas Livius, just become a Catholic, who had been at Oriel College, and an Anglican clergyman, could study theology at Dublin. See letter of 27 May to Simpson.

TO JOHN WYSE

[14? May 1857]

Dear Revd Sir

I assure you I have not been aware of any such differences between the Fathers of the Birmingham Oratory and yourself as you seem to consider to exist, and what you say is quite news to me and I think will be to the rest of our party.[1] I really believe none of us have unkind thoughts of you, — I never heard one expressed. As to your views on Church matters, to which you allude, I do not know what they are, and never was so rude as to think about [them]. However, I consider it very kind and considerate of you to have written as you have. For myself, I have never, I assure you, given the letter to which you so frankly refer a second thought, nor did I mentioned [sic] it to others, though by accident I believe two of the Fathers heard of it.[2] I beg you will not think more of it yourself. It is very kind and generous of you to feel it.

I am &c J H N

TO JOHN STANISLAS FLANAGAN

May 15/57

My dear S

Get the Father Secretary to put up a notice on the Board, to the effect that no one should leave on absence without writing up, not only his day of coming back, but where letters may be addressed to him. I meant to have done this before now. And I will take care to direct all Congregational letters to 'the Dean' so that they may be opened, if the Dean is not at home, by the Secretary.

Formby has given me a most magnificent opportunity of flooring him. He has asked me to take part in appealing to Rome against the Cardinal's Letter.[3] So I am *candidly* giving him my opinion of his letters to Marshall, and showing him, how, while I understand the Bishop, I utterly disagree

[1] John Wyse, the priest in charge of the former Oratorian church at Alcester Street, Birmingham, had recently made a retreat in Rome. As a result he wrote, on 11 May, his wish 'to remove any unpleasantness that may exist between the Fathers of the Oratory and myself ... There is doubtless a great deal that ought to be forgiven and forgotten on both sides ... Referring to myself personally, I have but one wish, namely to atone for the disrespectful letter I once in the heat of a moment wrote to you—as also for the many hard things I have said of you and your Fathers to persons of my acquaintance. You will not expect that I should change my opinions on Church matters ... I ... acknowledge myself guilty of frequently speaking ill of you and your Fathers to others [sic] priests and to a very few lay persons. For this I am really sorry ...' See also next letter.
[2] See last note to letter of 19 June 1855 to St John.
[3] i.e. Wiseman's letter to Charles Langdale in favour of accepting the Government grant for Catholic schools, to which Formby was violently opposed. See letter of 7 May to Ullathorne.

38

with him.[1] He is too imperturbable ever to be put out, but I shall write in the sweetest manner (not so very sweet, either). I must take care, for I am not sure the Bishop is not at the bottom of his letter, tho' he may not agree with him.

Will you, as Father Minister, seriously turn in your mind *what to do* with Frederic, John and James[2] in the Vacation — whether you will receive them into the House — if not what you advise me to do — whether they could be at Rednall etc.

Mr Wyse has written me a kind letter hoping that differences between the Oratory and him may now cease ('there had been faults on both sides'), and a new start be made. I have answered by thanking him and assuring him that I really believed there was not one of us who had had an unkind thought of him, and that I had never heard one expressed. That, with respect to his church views of which he spoke, I had never thought about them, and had not been so rude as to do so. I record all this, because I did not dare allude to the original and only quarrel I have with him, lest I should annoy him and put all out, that he turned St Philip out of a Chapel which St Philip founded. I never can go out of my way to assist him in that Chapel with that slight unatoned for. Aliquid desideravere oculi mei[3] in that Chapel — but that has never coloured my thoughts of him, much less my words. He seems to think we have been *acting* against *him*. I believe not.

Ever Yrs, J H Newman

TO MRS JOHN MOZLEY

6 Harcourt Street Dublin May 15. 1857

Mr dear Jemima

I write just in time to wish you many happy returns of your birthday. It rejoices me to hear you give so good an account of yourself.

I had heard nothing of Frank's accident before your letter. Pray give me some account of it. I always forget his direction, or I would write straight to him.[4]

I inclose a draft of £20 for Charles. As before, I give it while I can, — and suspect it will be my last. At least my last large sum, for, in consequence of my years, my stay here is very precarious. I should have resigned now, if it depended on myself.

Ever Yours affly John H Newman of the Oratory

P.S.   I am quite well, thank God.

---

[1] i.e. Formby. For his letters to T. W. Marshall see letter of 24 Feb. 1857 to Ullathorne.
[2] These were servants in Newman's house at Dublin.
[3] *Ecclesiastes*, 2:10.
[4] See letter of 31 Aug. to Mrs John Mozley.

SATURDAY 16 MAY 1857   Dr Russell of Maynooth and Robertson to dinner

TO MISS HOLMES

6 Harcourt Street Dublin May 16. 1857

My dear Miss Holmes,

I am glad to hear so good an account of you, inspite of the badness of the season at Boulogne. I always feared that the report of fever would frighten away visitors — but I suppose there is an average in these things, and if one season is bad, another is good. It is a great thing being so near England, while in France — and that makes Boulogne preferable to any other place. Thank you for the pains you are taking with my stole.

I go back to Birmingham for good in July. I shall either relinquish the Rectorship, or at least shall only come over occasionally after that, and that only for a time. We consider that the University is getting on very well, and that the neck of the difficulty, as regards it, is broken. I should not like to be away from Birmingham during my last years. At present, thank God, my health is perfectly good, and I am quite up to work — but at my age it is impossible to say how long I shall last — and I have warnings around me. Dear Robert Wilberforce's death, who was younger than I am, has been a great shock to us all — and the Papers say that Dr Pusey is seriously ill. I heard in February that it was a softening of the brain — and he is about my age.

I am glad you have been profited by Father Faber's books. I have heard others say the same thing. I see by the Advertisements that he has just published another.[1]

Callista is at last being translated into French. They began a year ago — I don't know the reason of the delay[2]

Yours affectly in Xt   John H Newman

SUNDAY 17 MAY 1857   Lloyd and Scratton to dinner.

[1] *The Creator and the Creature*, London 1857.
[2] *Callista*, translated by l'Abbé A. Goemaere, was published at Brussels in 1857. Other distinct French translations were published in 1859, 1867 and 1908.

TO JOHN STANISLAS FLANAGAN

6 Harcourt Street May 17/57

My dear Stanislas,

Tell me if any thing strikes you in the inclosed, or if there is any thing to add.[1]

The *Deans were* moving in my matter, as I thought. And their moving frightened Dr Leahy — who moved, that *they* might *not* move.

Dr Leahy made the Archbishop move. I do not think the Archbishop would have moved except from the strong feeling of Dr Leahy and of the Catholics in Dublin.

Every one tells me that my going is the only subject talked about in every society, and I think Dr Cullen has in this way been brought to what otherwise he would not come. Nothing shows me yet, that he has any thought for *me* — but that every one tells him that he is in a difficulty.

I think the effect of this will be to increase my power wonderfully — but feeling, as I do, my extreme incapacity, and knowing how vague and illogical the belief[2] of my capacity is, I assure you, I wish more than ever to get away, before I am found out — for I am an ass in a lion's skin.

Dr Leahy is very anxious the whole matter should be arranged *at once*

[1] The enclosure was as follows:

'May 16. 1857

Requests humbly presented to the Archbishops by the Rector, during the negociation for his continuance in his office.
1. The annual grant, to be made for University purposes by the Trustees, shall be (according to the Rector's letter of June 20. 1856) £5000 and the annual interest of the Trustee Fund £1200, together with the annual Students' Fees, which, till they reach £500, shall be made up to that sum by the Trustees. In all £6700.
2. Of these items, the £5000 shall be devoted to the three Faculties of Medicine, Philosophy and Letters, and Science, and to the University Administration. Out of the £1200, a sum not exceeding £1000 shall be devoted to the Faculty of Theology, to the Preachers, and the Altar Service in the University Church. The remainder shall provide for sundry and occasional expenses. The payment of the Bishops' Medical and Scientific Burses shall not come out of the above annual grant.
3. This grant shall be paid in quarterly payments on November 3 February 2 May 1 and July 22 respectively, being transferred by the Bankers from the Trustee Fund to the Cullen and Newman Fund on the presentation of the Rector's receipt.
4. The Rector is not to be answerable for the expenses of the Collegiate or other Houses, nor to include them in his statement of account.
5. The Rector's accounts shall be audited every November, and the balance sheet shall be appended to his annual Report.
6. A Secretary shall be appointed under the Trustees for the management of the annual collections throughout Ireland, and a statement of receipts and payments made to and by the University, shall be annually appended to the Rector's Report.
7. Once at least in every term a Board shall sit, consisting of the Archbishops, or their representatives or nominees, or others having their authority, before which the Rector may bring questions requiring settlement, applications for extraordinary grants of money etc.'
At the head of drafts of this paper Newman placed two other conditions, 'N.B. to have the Vice Rector named — and, if an untried person, to have him Pro Vice Rector for a year.
Arnold's appointment.' [See letter of 30 March 1857 to Cullen].
Newman included the substance of this paper in his second letter of 16 Oct. 1857 to Archbishop Leahy.
[2] Newman first wrote 'notion.'

41

before it gets into the Papers. He returns here in a day or two. I have found out that the Vice Rector need not be a Priest — and, though I shall not effect any thing by this, yet it will strengthen my power to interfere in the appointment.[1]

Sir R. Kane wrote off at once to Lord Carlisle in London that I was going. I have some fear they are concocting a government school measure just now — and that the report will do us harm.

Ever Yrs affly J H N

TO MOTHER MARGARET MARY HALLAHAN

Oratory, Birmingham May 18. 1857

My dear Revd Mother

We are beginning our own Novena, and I have taken care to enter your intention on our list. Do not forget us on St Philip's day, which *we* keep on its proper day, the 26th — but do as you find best for the convenience of your holy Community, whether the 26th or 27th.[2] Our dear Patron and Founder has been so good to us since we have been here, that I am sure he would have nothing else for any one else, were he not a Saint, as he is. The more we ask, the more he gives.

His Congregation has just been re-established in Spain, with St Vincent of Paul, and it really looks as if he was to do great things all over the Church.[3] Please to pray for us, that he would make us worthy of him.

Yours, My dear Revd Mother Very sincerely in Christ

John H Newman Congr. Orat.

TUESDAY 19 MAY 1857   Harry Bethell went to Scratton's at Kings town about now.

---

[1] Flanagan replied on 17 May, 'There is not a single Catholic layman of education in Ireland that would not tell you that the University is doomed the moment you leave it. . . . what riled me was to know this, and yet see that the Bishops did not act towards you, as they should towards the sole prop of the Institution. . . . You must not give in on any point . . .'

[2] In England at this time the feast of St Augustine of Canterbury was kept on 26 May, and St Philip the next day. The intention of Mother Margaret Hallahan and her nuns appears to have been the success of a school primer to facilitate 'the religious study of history,' which they hoped to publish.

[3] Article 29 of the Spanish Concordat of 1851 laid down that houses of the Congregations of St Vincent de Paul and of St Philip Neri were to be established where there was need of them. This became possible in 1856, when a liberal government was succeeded by one more favourable to the Church.

TO JOHN STANISLAS FLANAGAN

May 19/57

My dear S

I kept A's letter[1] open till the post went, in hopes of the Post coming in — but it has been very provoking lately.

Go at once to Campden without loss of a day — unless you have some reason I don't know.[2]

Robert will take care of the novices

Ever Yrs affly J H N

TO AMBROSE ST JOHN

⌈6 Harcourt Street May 19/57⌉

My dear Ambrose

⌈As to an Irish Car, I think it is the perfection of riding in fine weather, but I never will get on it in a hard shower.[3]

I believe that in the Union of last Friday, which will come to you today or tomorrow, you will find a small statistic account of German Universites. However, I wish Robert to find it, in order to improve his intellectual eyes. Will you tell him to cut it out for me? I am not sure it is there — but if it is not, it will be a still greater improvement to him to find it there, and will really do him credit.[14]

I expect to set off for Birmingham next Sunday night. How long I stop is to me a puzzle — If I am to be at Bm on the Sunday in Octave of C C [Corpus Christi] I must come back here in the interval. If I give up that Sunday, I don't see the banners and bows[5]

Ever Yrs affly J H N

TO ROBERT WHITTY

6 Harcourt St Dublin May 19. 1857

My dear Fr Whitty

I thank you for your kind letter from Rome, and I congratulate you with all my heart on your entrance into the great Society, of which I feel sure you

---

[1] i.e. the one of this day to St John.

[2] Flanagan had already refused the pressing invitation of Viscount Campden and his wife to visit them.

[3] St John asked on 16 May, 'Would you object to go to Rednal in an Irish car?'

[4] The *Union*, (15 May 1857), p. 322, quoted from the *Allgemeine Zeitung* of 4 May, a detailed account of the German universities, other than those in Austria.

[5] The confraternities and schools at the Oratory had provided themselves with banners, which would be used for the first time in the Corpus Christi procession.

will prove worthy.[1] I am glad too that you are not making your novitiate at Rome; for Verona, though cold in winter, will, I think, suit you better. Thank you for your kind words about myself, you must not forget me at holy times and places.[2]

I sent in notice of my resignation in November to the Bishops six or seven weeks ago. Those who answered me wrote most touching letters, for which I feel deeply grateful. My Congregation has formally recalled me, and the Archbishops are to correspond on the subject with the Fathers. What the latter will determine on, I really do not know. I don't think they have made up their minds themselves yet — but I suppose it will be to allow me to be here for a month or two in the year for a year or two more — and, if the Archbishops do not think this enough, I do not know what can be done, as far as I am concerned. I doubt whether Cardinal Barnabò will interfere.[3]

Thank you for the interesting papers you inclose in your letter.[4] It does not seem to me strange that nothing immediate has followed the definition of the Immaculate Conception — rather, if would have been unlike the course of ecclesiastical history hitherto, if it had. Meanwhile, surely there is a growing rise in the prospects of the Church every where. How dismally disappointed the Fathers of Nicaea must have been at the immediate consequences of the Great Council!

Ever Yours affly in Xt   John H Newman

WEDNESDAY 20 MAY 1857   meeting of Council

[1] Whitty, who was about to become a Jesuit, wrote to Newman from the Gesù in Rome on 11 April, 'I leave Rome on Wednesday next (Easter Week) with Dr Manning for Loretto and thence on by myself to Verona where I am to pass my Noviceship.' He also said, 'You will I think rejoice with me that the Holy Father has been pleased to make Dr Manning Provost of the Chapter of Westminster—vacant by my own resignation. The Holy See has done this with full knowledge—tho' of course it involves likewise our own Cardinal's most willing consent and a zeal for the general good on the part of Mgr Talbot.'

[2] Whitty had written, 'I hope you will sometimes remember one who has not lost one particle of his veneration and affection for you.'

[3] Whitty said in his letter, 'I have no news to give you from Rome. The influence of Dr Cullen is very great on all Irish matters and he takes care to preserve it by having the first word on every point and by committing the Authorities here beforehand themselves to any important measures of his own. So at least I am told. I have remarked myself a very distinct impression—almost an exaggerated one—of the antipathy between the English and Irish races and a decided resolve to listen to nothing from Englishmen about Ireland. Should you persist in the resolution you told me of in Dublin last November I trust you will be called to Rome to give a detailed account of your work in Ireland.'

[4] Whitty sent Newman a copy of some prophecy about the spread of the Church in China, and said that he and Manning had remarked that 'we had seen no outpourings of mercy such as we might expect,' as a consequence of the definition of the Immaculate Conception, 'which unquestionably was the great event of this century.'

TO HENRY WILBERFORCE

TO HENRY WILBERFORCE

6 Harcourt Street Dublin ⌐May 20/57⌐

My dear Henry

As we have just bought a large Munich Medical Library, which is shipped for this place, we now have need of your bookcases, if you are willing to sell them.[1] Will you make up your mind? or name your price? Then the Medical Professors will determine whether to accept it or not. If you or they decline, you shall have the bookcases at once — for it is not right you should be kept out of them — and I am very sorry that it should have been the case so long. — I am here till Sunday night, then at Birmingham.

⌐I sent round my letters to the Bishops,⌐ announcing my intended resignation in November, ⌐at the beginning of April. And my Congregation has formally recalled me.⌐ Of course I would be in two places at once if I could be — but life is very uncertain, and, whether here or not, any how I must be at Bm [Birmingham]. ⌐I suppose it will result in a compromise, by which I shall be two months in the year here [[Dublin]] for two or three years to come. A non-resident Rector will be a bitter pill⌐ for the Irish clergy — ⌐but at the moment it seems they will be forced to it, and in all things I am likely to carry things with a high hand. What a great thing it is to be independent or detached — good people here don't seem to have comprehended that nothing brought me here, nothing keeps me here, but the simple wish to do some service to Catholic Education. Even the Nation, in puffing me, talks of an honourable or natural ambition. Nor is the irksomeness of being here compensated by having every thing my own way — for the more autocratical I am, the more may fairly be expected of me — which is not pleasant.

I have a number of very good and kind friends, and the answers of such Bishops as have written to me are most touching — but⌐ I never should be surprised at the country discharging me suddenly, almost without notice, when they thought they could do so.

Ever Yrs affly J H N

ASCENSION THURSDAY 21 MAY 1857   Cincinnati lady called about now
SATURDAY 23 MAY   meeting of Council

TO MICHAEL FLANNERY

May 23. 1857

My dear Mr Flannery

It has been matter of great concern to me to have it brought home to me from time to time, that you feel you cannot enter with interest or heartiness into the regimen which I have laid down for the Collegiate Houses.

---

[1] For the medical library see letter of 10 Jan. 1857 to Pollen, and for the bookcases letters of 20 Jan. and 8 March 1857 to Wilberforce.

This feeling has shown itself at this moment in your little desire or care to have a second Tutor, for your increased numbers; but this instance is merely the occasion of my writing, for it does not stand by itself, but, as you must know well, is only the expression of a state of opinion and judgment in the subject of your house, which is habitual to you.

You have been uniformly desirous of classes in your House and of compulsory lectures, and you have wished, instead of Tutors, to have subdeans, or, what answers to them, Tutors with collegiate authority; and you are deliberately of opinion that your House will not be in a good condition, till those or similar measures are carried out.

It seems to me unfair on any one who is in a responsible situation, as you are, unnecessarily to be subjected to control in things on which he has a definite and permanent opinion. This is the reason why I have now come to the resolution, that, after this term, you shall do just as you will with your House. After this term I will not interfere, but you shall in all things has [sic] as much freedom as Dr Quinn, within the limits, that is, of the Rules and Regulations.

I am &c J H N

TO PATRICK LEAHY, ARCHBISHOP ELECT OF CASHEL

[23 May?] [[June 1857]][1]

My dear Dr Leahy

⌐The question of Vice Rector makes me very anxious — for any how the finding a successor to yourself will be the cardinal difficulty of our prospective arrangements, and what you say seems to me to add materially to its urgency.[2]

It is surely most desirable not to bring a Vice Rector into the existing body of Professors, but to take a Professor already familiarized with our way of going on. And if at length an arrangement were made which contemplated my continuance here with less of residence, still more important would it be⌐ to the wellbeing of the University, ⌐that the Vice Rector and Professorial Staff

---

[1] This letter was later dated thus by Newman. On Leahy's letter to which it is a reply, Newman wrote in pencil 'June? 1857.' Leahy's letter is dated 'Thursday Morning,' and the contents show this must be 21 May.

[2] [[magnitude]] Newman had sent his congratulations to Leahy on his nomination as Archbishop of Cashel, and raised the question of his successor as Vice-Rector of the University. Leahy replied in his letter of 21 May,

'Your note gives me the liberty to offer an opinion as to the substitute for the Vice-Rector. However you manage, do not name one of the Lay-Professors. Though not stated in terms in the Decrees of the Synod of 1854 that the Vice-Rector as well as the Rector should be a priest, it was certainly in the intention of the Bishops. And it would scarcely be seemly or fit that in a Catholic University a Lay-Gentleman should exercise authority over Priests. Such at any rate would be the notion of many—most persons.

Assuming that the Vice-Rector must be a priest, his substitute should be a priest.

For Mr Butler I have the highest respect. To appoint him, however, substitute for the Vice Rector would, to say the least of it, be considered a strange proceeding.'

should be of one mind. The existing Professors have been tried, a stranger will be an experiment.

If we look towards the existing clerical Professors, there are but two. *Fr O'Reilly would suit admirably*, if he could be persuaded to act. Every one would be content with him, but hitherto I find him more than reluctant. He will not do anything as Pro Vice Rector. Dr Forde is a man of talent, of decision, and of presence — but I am grieved to have to believe that even a stranger would be more popular than he.

Let me add that it seems dangerous to interpret the meaning of an assembly of bishops on a subject not proposed to them. Discussion might have changed their primâ facie opinion. The documents of the Synodal meeting as they stand are strong in favour of the more liberal view of the qualifications of Vice Rector. The Fathers [[Bishops]] have actually inserted in the case of the Rector, 'sacerdotii dignitate insignitum', which I believe is not found in the Louvain Statutes, but they have left the qualifications of Vice Rector as they stand at Louvain, where the clerical state is not required, nor in matter of fact, demanded [[called for]].[1] Further they actually have altered in another way that very Louvain Statute concerning Vice Rector, for they have taken away the Rector's participation in the appointment, omitting the words 'post expositam Rectoris Magnifici sententiam', of Louvain; and this shows that the statute about Vice Rector actually was discussed.[1] Moreover, I think it clear that the Holy See has confirmed no statute except what has actually been before it. For these reasons, fully granting that a clerical appointment is the more obvious, ⌐I should much regret if the door is closed in limine to any other [[but ecclesiastics]]⌐[1] Excuse this freedom &c[2]

SUNDAY 24 MAY 1857   Colonel Vaughan to dinner[3] — after dinner went off by boat

---

[1] The Belgian Bishops, when refounding the University of Louvain in 1834, decreed: 'Nobis pariter, post expetitam Rectoris Magnifici sententiam, reservamus nominationem et revocationem Vice-Rectoris, qui adinstar coadjutoris consilio et auxilio praesto sit eidem Rectori, quique eo absente, aegrotante vel moriente, ipsius vices provisoriè suppleat, ne Academia aliquod detrimentum patiatur.' *Oratio . . . P.F.X. de Ram . . . Quum Archi-episcopus Mechliniensis . . . Universitatem Catholicam inauguraret. Accedant Monumenta ad ejusdem Universitatis constitutionem spectantia*, Louvain 1834, V, p. 62.

The decree of the Irish Bishops on 18 May 1854 ran: 'Nominandum etiam decernimus Vice-Rectorem, qui consilio et auxilio praesto sit rectori, quique, eo absente, aegrotante, aut moriente, ipsius vices provisoriè suppleat, ne quid detrimenti res academica capiat. Vice-Rectoris nominationem et revocationem nobis reservamus.' *Campaign*, p. 89.

[2] Leahy replied on 24 May, 'You had as well not put any one in nomination just now for the Vice-Rectorship, as I do not mean to resign the Vice-Rectorship till the meeting of the Archbishops, which will be towards the end of June or the beginning of July.

As to a Pro-Vice-Rector, I am still of opinion that he, as the Vice-Rector, should be a priest. And I still think it was the intention of the Bishops that the Vice-Rector should be a priest. . . .'

[3] John Francis Vaughan (1808–80), of Courtfield, Herefordshire, father of Cardinal Vaughan.

TO BARTHOLOMEW WOODLOCK

(Copy)   6 Harcourt Street May 24. 1857

My dear Dr Woodlock

The Council has had two meetings on your proposal. This shows we have felt its importance and desirableness — however, we have decided against it. The votes were all one way.

I think we have been called upon by the Archbishop to decide suddenly on a great question. We could not take your proposal, acceptable as it was, as an isolated case and we could not form a system for the theological schools in a week or two. You wanted an answer at once. Your latest day for the Act was not much more than a month from this time.

I do not know that we should have felt the difficulty so great, if your candidate had asked to make an Act for his Baccalaureate, not his Doctorate.[1]

I am, My dear Dr Woodlock, Sincerely Yours in Xt

John H Newman of the Oratory

The Very Revd Mgr Woodlock.

MONDAY 25 MAY 1857   to Bm [Birmingham] found Wingfield here

TUESDAY 26 MAY   St Philip's day. I sang High Mass. Dr Weedall preached in evening

WEDNESDAY 27 MAY   Mr J. O'Reilly, surgeon, came suddenly — took him into the house

TO RICHARD SIMPSON

The Oratory Birmingham May 27/57

My dear Simpson,

Thank you for your zeal about the University, — but it was a shame in Richard Ward to tell what I said to him confidentially, and which was not true except at the moment.[2] The theological Professors are sanguine about starting next October — whereas R Ward wished a decision last *February*, I think

Very sincerely Yours John H Newman

R Simpson Esqr

[1] Woodlock, who was President of All Hallows Missionary College, evidently asked that measures should be taken for conferring a Doctorate in Theology.

[2] Simpson wrote on 25 May, that before he received Newman's letter of 14 May about Livius taking the theological course at Dublin, he met Richard Ward, who had thought of doing the same. The latter told Simpson that Newman had 'rather discouraged his idea . . . for that there were only two others in it.' As a result Livius altered his plans.

TO HENRY WILBERFORCE

The Oratory Bm ⌜May 27/57⌝

My dear Henry

⌜The Cardinal [[Wiseman]] has a thousand good points, but you must never *trust* him. My first severe lesson on the point was the Achilli affair, but I have had other serious ones since.⌝[1]

As to Mr MacW. [MacWalter] he is a clever man, if he is the person of whom the Times took a leading article, and gave him money for it. I had heard he was to have the *Dublin*. I think it very likely that he considers you not equal to conduct a paper, and tells the Cardinal so. I am glad you are getting out of Richardson's hands.[2]

Ever Yours affly John H Newman of the Oratory

H W Wilberforce Esqr

THURSDAY 28 MAY 1857   cold, windy, ungenial weather.

TO PATRICK MAXWELL

Oratory Bm May 28/57

My dear Sir,

Mr Scratton has forwarded your letter of the 26th to this place. I thank you for the information which it contains.[3]

I beg you to return answer to Mr Hone that circumstances have materially changed since last year when I brought the matter before the Board of the Blue Coat School, and that I am sorry I have not the power, which I had then, of answering their proposal at once; but that I will lose no time in bringing the subject before the Trustees of the Catholic University, to whom it belongs

I am &c H N

[1] Cf. letter of 26 Nov. 1851 to W. G. Ward.

[2] Wilberforce, editor of the *Weekly Register*, must have written his complaints to Newman, already recounting what he repeated in a letter of 17 Jan. 1859 as follows, 'I should have no fear of the Tablet, but for the Cardinal. I do not like to say a word against him; and we know what he is. But giving him full credit for his *intentions* his conduct to me has in fact been *perfidious*. He *entirely* got me to buy the paper [The *Weekly Register*], (which has cost me £1,600) by his solicitation and by promises of giving me *assistance, secret intelligence* etc which would compel the Times to quote me etc.

He might really have done this . . .

However he was quite friendly with me, till that unhappy Mr MacWalter got about him; about 2½ years ago. He made a plan to push me out and get into my place and as the means set the Cardinal against me, by *what* lies I do not know. But such a man would, of course, scruple at nothing.

I have been told by a Bishop, that since that time the Cardinal's tone *quite changed* as to me; and it is now said in London that he is my enemy. He is barely civil to me.'

[3] Patrick Maxwell wrote that the Board of the Blue Coat School, who were the ground landlords of 87 Stephen's Green offered to renew the lease for forty-one years. This was the site of the University Church and eventually the lease was renewed indefinitely.

TO THOMAS SCRATTON

Oy Bm May 28/57

My dear Scratton,

Will you send the inclosed letter to Mr Maxwell — and write the copy I send from yourself, for him to take to the Archbishop. I hope you had my letter on Sunday about Mr Hughes.

As to the query of Mr Gabb, will you write to say that we would gladly do any thing to serve him, but that 'we could not educate a young man in order to his taking a degree at the London University.'

Ever Yrs John H Newman

Thos Scratton Esqr

FRIDAY 29 MAY 1857   The Bishop called
WHIT MONDAY 1 JUNE   Dr Forbes called and dined (from New York)

TO EDWARD FRANCIS COLLINS

The Oratory, Birmingham June 1. 1857

My dear Sir,

I shall be flattered by hearing from you on any subject which you have at heart.

One thing, however, you will allow me to add that I am neither a good canonist on difficult questions, nor on the other hand have I any great time for correspondence. It may seem ungracious to say so, but I fear to promise more than I can perform —[1]

Most truly Yours in Xt   John H Newman

E.F. Collins Esqr

P.S.   Pray accept my best thanks for your little book.

TO JAMES STEWART

The Oratory Birmingham June 1. 1857

My dear Stewart,

Thank you for your letter of this morning.[2] You are quite at liberty to put into the Freeman and Tablet a notice to the following effect:— 'We hear

---

[1] Edward Francis Collins (1807–72), was a devout Catholic journalist at Hull. He published anonymously in 1859 a little book on the Rosary. In 1868 he was for a short period sub-editor of the *Tablet* under Herbert Vaughan.

[2] Stewart wrote on 30 May, 'You asked me to let you know when any thing appeared in the Newspapers about your resignation. I have just heard of . . . a very damaging notice in

on authority which we entirely trust, that, so far from the broad statements of the Times about Dr Newman's retirement from the Catholic University being true, he has neither sent in his resignation, nor has he any intention of leaving Dublin.'[1]

Alter it in your own way. By the bye, if it goes into the Freeman before Saturday, the Tablet will not thank you for sending it to it (the Tablet) also — The two Papers are not on the best terms just now.[2]

I would have put in something *myself* three weeks ago, — but I am sorry to say (entre nous) there is some shilly shallying just now in high quarters, and I am not so sanguine as I was a little while ago.[3]

Ever Yours affly John H Newman

P.S.   I propose to return in a day or two.

TUESDAY 2 JUNE 1857   Mr J. O'Reilly went to Drogheda with Scully   went in afternoon to Rednall and back   Wilkinson and Mr Kirwan Brown dined and slept[4]
THURSDAY 4 JUNE   went at night to Dublin

the Times . . . to the effect that you were about to leave, and the whole institution immediately broken up. We are all so anxious that a contradiction shall appear . . .' *The Times*, (25 May), p. 7 had a paragraph: 'For several days past reports have been current to the effect that there is a screw loose in the machinery of the Catholic University, and that unless prompt aid be administered the notable scheme devised by Dr. Cullen for closing the gates of the Godless Colleges will only be remembered among the things that were. No one will deny that thus far the project has disappointed the expectations of its promoters, and the rumour now is that the learned rector himself (Dr. Newman), having no taste for sinecures, is about to be transferred to England, where a more suitable appointment has been provided for him. . . .'
   [1] Newman had announced to the Irish Bishops his intention of resigning on 14 Nov. 1857. In fact he postponed his resignation until 12 Nov. 1858. As his letters, for instance that of 20 May 1857 to Wilberforce, show, he expected that an effective Vice Rector would be appointed, and that he would continue to reside in Dublin for two months of each year.
   [2] A disavowal was sent to the *Freeman's Journal*, but no such notice as Newman suggested appeared, in the *Tablet*. However, the *Tablet*, (13 June 1857), p 376, devoted its first leading article to the matter: 'How far a man can be said to "resign" an office taken for a limited period, when that period is completed, we do not exactly know. We are led to the remark by the ingenious conclusions which so many of our contemporaries have drawn from the fact that the period for which Dr Newman consented to undertake the laborious and anxious post of head of the University, which he has founded and built up, is now about to terminate. . . .
   . . . there is sure to be a strong and very general wish that Dr. Newman should not materially alter the nature of his connexion with the University, even if he should prefer to fill some other than his present post, and one which did not require more than occasional residence. It is quite obvious that Dr. Newman, by short but regular residences, at intervals, with the aid of correspondence, could be all, and more to the University than anyone is now entitled to require him to be. . . .
   Some such course the Bishops will probably desire to see pursued, and if so, efforts will probably be made to induce Dr. Newman to continue in his present post with stated periods of residence in the University, as we believe was the custom of the late Vice-Rector, the most Rev. Dr. Leahy. . . .'
   The *Weekly Register*, (20 June 1857), p. 8, had a similar statement.
   [3] See letters of 12 May to St John and 23 May to Leahy.
   [4] Thomas William Wilkinson, a curate at St Saviour's, Leeds, who became a Catholic in 1847, was a priest in the Hexham diocese, of which he was made Bishop in 1889. Edward George Kirwan Browne, curate at Bawdsey, Suffolk, became a Catholic in 1845.

TO HENRY WILBERFORCE

June 4/57

My dear H W

Sophy Ryder tells me that you are going to put an advertisement in your Paper about her needs at Brislington.

Will it not be good if you told your printer (if it could be done) before breaking up the type to print, (say) 100 copies of it, which her friends might distribute[1]

Ever Yrs affly J H N

P.S. I meant to have written to you in answer to yours, but have no paper and no time. I had nothing more to tell on the subject you wrote to me. I am much concerned to think you contemplate giving £900 — You spoke to me in November of £200.[2]

TO JAMES HOPE-SCOTT

⌐6 Harcourt Street⌐ Dublin ⌐June 5. 1857⌐

My dear Hope Scott

⌐I have only just got your most joyful letter of the 2nd and with you I return thanks to the Author of all good that you have been able to write it.[3] I congratulate you with all my heart. I had made a special memento in Mass for your intention — but I shall not cease to give my unworthy prayers that He who has not forgotten you will continue His blessings.⌐

I am going to and fro just now — and perhaps may be in London the week after next. But it is in vain to expect to see you, as I should not sleep there — but Badeley will tell me something about you. I have a vast deal to talk about but have doubts how far I could bring it out all of a sudden. You may take interest in seeing my project, I spoke of, more in shape — so I send it you.[4] I wish you were enjoying otium cum dignitate and could *write me an article*

Ever Yours affly in Xt   John H Newman of the Oratory

J R Hope Scott Esqr

[1] No such advertisement seems to have been published in the *Weekly Register*. The Good Shepherd nuns at Bristol, among whom was Sophie Ryder, had opened a reformatory for girls.
[2] This seems to refer to Wilberforce's purchase of the *Weekly Register* from Thomas Richardson.
[3] This letter announced the birth on 2 June of a son and heir to Hope-Scott, Walter Michael, who died a year later.
[4] This was a copy of an advertisement for what was to be called the *Atlantis*. The advertisement was also published in the *Weekly Register*, (13 June 1857), p. 3.

P.S. I direct to London since you seem returning — yet without knowing your direction.

⌐My best congratulations to your wife, of course.¬

SUNDAY 7 JUNE 1857   dined at Sergt O'Brien to meet Mr More O'Ferrall

TO F. S. BOWLES

June 8/75

My dear Fr Frederic

Your letter is just come.[1]

1. Pange Lingua.

2. Lauda Sion. The choir may do what they please in the Lauda Sion. Nothing will be better than their taking alternate verses. Only the guild must be *answerable* for the whole. If you give out say 'the guild shall take one verse, the choir *another*' there will be a hitch to a certainty — especially when the guild is in the open air, and the choir still in the corridor. (Besides the choir will want to take breath perhaps after the Pange Lingua)

3. Tantum ergo — Webb's if you like, and Benediction music as you like.

4. Roman Litany. I am any thing but averse to harmony here. I like it better *with*. But in answer to your captious objection 'We don't know *what* the harmony *is*' — I answered 'Well then, do it *without* harmony.'[2]

TUESDAY 9 JUNE 1857   meeting of Council — came off at night to Birmingham

TO HENRY WILBERFORCE

Dublin June 9/57

My dear H

I have received the inclosed this morning — who is Mr Monro?[3] He tells me to send my answer to you — will you send it on? and send back his letter

---

[1] Bowles asked about the music for the Procession on Corpus Christi.

[2] Newman left his letter unfinished.

[3] Philip Munro (1825–1901), at Magdalen Hall, Oxford, and then curate at Ware, Hertfordshire, became a Catholic in 1852, and later a priest in the diocese of Southwark. He wrote on 2 June from Naples 'on behalf of a Neapolitan friend here who is desirous of founding a certain number of exhibitions at some College in England. His object is to provide a thoroughly sound and complete education there for a certain number of Neapolitan youths, as he feels that there is a great shortcoming in this respect at Naples.' Munro recommended the Catholic University and asked what course his friend, who hoped to found five or six exhibitions, should pursue.

Newman made a note on Munro's letter, 'answered June 9/57 recommending his friend to hire a house in Dublin (say for 3 years) and stock it with inmates, they paying the *board*. J H N.'

to me, which I send you to identify him. I go to Bm [Birmingham] this evening[1]

Ever Yrs affly J H N

THURSDAY 11 JUNE 1857 Corpus Chr. [Christi] sang high Mass — no Procession. went to Rednall and back.
FRIDAY 12 JUNE cold. n w wind — still fires in the evening.

TO MICHAEL BLOUNT

(sent in substance) June 13/57

Dear Sir

I thank you very much for your notice of the liberality of Mr Canning towards the University. As yet I do not see that we can claim it — I have built a Church for the University and provide a weekly Mass there for benefactors — but the Trustees have not yet recognised it, and till they buy it of me and pass some resolution of their own on the subject of the Mass, they cannot comply with your condition.[2]

When this will be, I cannot tell — meanwhile I will suggest the great desirableness of making a separate Fund for the purposes of *England* at the University in Dublin. We have the rudiments of four Colleges there already. When there is a seminary, there will be a fifth. I should recommend an English College, the funds being in the hands of English Trustees. But this is for consideration. I could give many reasons in favour of the plan.

J H N

[1] Munro replied on 23 July that his Neapolitan friend was Commendatore Caprioli, a priest aged 75, who had been private secretary to Francis I and after that to Ferdinand II, until 1848. 'He then fell into disgrace, I imagine from his holding "liberal" principles. He sees, he says, the great defect in the general education of the youth of this country . . .' Caprioli did not take to the idea of leasing a house in Dublin, but preferred to found a number of exhibitions at once.
Newman made a note of his answer on 30 July, 'wrote that his friend had better not commit himself to any *plan*—but leave his money, *with fullest instructions*, in the hands of the Naples Oratory, or the Birmingham, in trust for the University of Ireland.' Cf. letter of 30 July 1857 to Stanton. See also letter of 18 April 1859 to Flanagan.
[2] Michael Blount was acting for his cousin, Edward Canning, who had left considerable sums for charity, and in particular £100 for the Catholic University. But to all his donations the condition was to be attached 'That his soul should thereby receive the benefit of perpetual Masses.' Eventually £100 was devoted to the University church, and Canning's name included in a list of benefactors for whom a weekly mass was to be said in perpetuity.

The Oratory Birmingham June 13. 1857

My dear Scratton

Mr Butler thinks I had better answer him through you.

You must write, please, to Waterford to say that the University has not received into affiliation the *ecclesiastical* department of any college or seminary, but only the lay portions, and grammar schools — and that the Bishop's request for the affiliation of the Waterford College was understood to apply only to the lay department.[1]

Will you tell Mr Butler, too, that I agree with him that it will be best for him and Stewart to go to Armagh on Tuesday next. If so, the Armagh people should be written to *at once*.

Ever Yours affly John H Newman

T. Scratton Esqr

Oy Bm June 13. 1857

My dear Mr Sullivan

I am sorry to say that I *am* committed to Fowler for the Scientific Register; this, however, does not at all bind the Professors, who are much more concerned in the undertaking than I am, nor need it. Let them choose another printer, provided they have a clear plan before them.[2]

But I have great misgivings about Brown and Nolan doing our work well amid their stationery. I had experience of this sort of thing in the beginning of the Tracts for the Times. They were printed in Oxford, but we lodged them at a Stationer's in Regent Street. The plan did not answer at all, and at the end of the year we took them to Rivington's, where they are still.

If B. and N. have the *printing* of our work, they should do more for it; but for so problem[at]ical a benefit (to us), which puts them to no trouble at

---

[1] It is clear from a telegram Newman sent next day to D. B. Dunne, that the University was asked to provide examiners for St John's College, Waterford. They were to examine church students as well as lay students, and Edward Butler, the Professor of Mathematical Science, suggested that to circumvent the difficulty as to affiliation, he and Dunne should be invited as guests. Butler thought they ought to attend, even as spectators. Newman telegraphed, 'I agree with Mr Butler.'

[2] Sullivan wrote on 11 June that it was felt to be important that the *Atlantis* should be connected with Dublin, even though it 'must be published by a first class publisher in London.' It was suggested that Longman should take the Catholic printers and stationers, Browne and Nolan, for agent in Dublin, but these last would only agree to this if they were also the printers of the periodical.

Eventually the *Atlantis* was printed in Dublin by John F. Fowler, and published by Longman, Brown, Green, Longmans and Roberts.

all and which is repaid by the percentage, I do not think they have a right to bargain for the *printing*.

Further, they have to be taught their trade as University Printers. Did they ever print Latin? I know what work it was to teach Fowler; he can do it now. Can they print French, Greek, or Hebrew? Their mistakes in proof would be a heavy addition to the expense. Again, can they set up a title page? Here again Fowler gave me a great deal of trouble. I don't say he is perfect now — far from it — but I think we should have to begin over again with a new printer.

On the other hand, what you say about Longmans' suspends my going to them. You and Mr Hennessy are the only two who have not felt reluctant to enter into relations with them. I should not have thought of doing so, unless you had suggested it. I think it prudent then to wait first for the opinions of the Professors of the two faculties of Science and of Philosophy. There is no need we should hurry things. Nor am I clear that, did we propose it to Longmans', they would not bargain for *their own Dublin* agent.

I am &c J H N

TO HENRY WILBERFORCE

Oy Bm June 13. [1857]

My dear H W

I propose to come to London for some hours on Thursday ⟨June 16.⟩ — and will call on you, with the chance of seeing you, at 3 Brydge's Street about noon

Ever Yrs affly J H N

I could not read your last.

SUNDAY 14 JUNE 1857   sang high Mass and had procession of Blessed Sacrament

TO THOMAS HAYDEN

The Oratory, Birmingham June 15/57

My dear Dr Hayden,

I shall be glad to do all in my power to forward the scheme of a medical lodging house — and am glad you have reminded me of it.[1] A year ago, I would, on my own responsibility, have engaged in it — but Dr Cullen is, I

---

[1] Hayden wrote on 13 June that the new Medical School at Stephen's Green Hospital was about to open a house of residence for students, and that if the similar long proposed house in connection with the Faculty of Medicine at the Catholic University were not soon established, the consequences would be harmful for the latter body.

think, rather anxious lest more money should be spent than is included in the ordinary estimate for the year. I dare say, he would be ready to give more, but perhaps he does not know how much there is to give, and he has in fact appeared to wish to curtail even the sum which I actually set down for ordinary expenses.

Under these circumstances, I should advise a statement *from the Faculty* of the desirableness of a medical House, of the fear of our being rivalled in the place by other bodies, and of the anticipated cost of it — It might be addressed either to the Archbishop or to me. In either case I would present it to him. Perhaps it would be better to address it to the Trustees, than to Dr Cullen only. I hope to be back again directly

Yours most sincerely John H Newman

Thos Hayden Esqr Md

TUESDAY 16 JUNE 1857 went to London and back — ἄπρακτος — doing nothing.
WEDNESDAY 17 June went over to Rednall to see Fr Ambrose and back

TO PATRICK LEAHY, ARCHBISHOP ELECT OF CASHEL

The Oratory, Birmingham June 17. 1857

My dear Lord,

I feel exceedingly the kindness of the wish expressed in your letter, which came to me last evening, and I shall keep it as a record.[1]

And I am as eager that you should not think me ungrateful in asking you to let me answer it in the negative. I really am obliged to do so; — not only have I not the gift of preaching, but I have not power just now to turn my mind to any duty which will require so much thought and effort to discharge it suitably. I am oppressed with cares and anxieties both here and in Dublin, and have too much on my hands even to fulfil the responsibilities of each day as it comes.

I trust to your goodness to accept this honest excuse, and to believe me, My dear Lord, Your Grace's sincere friend & Servt

John H Newman of the Oratory

The Most Revd Dr Leahy

[1] Leahy asked Newman to preach at his consecration on 29 June at Thurles. See also letter of 20 June to Leahy.

TO JAMES STEWART

The Oratory, Bm June 17/57

My dear Stewart

I am sincerely sorry to hear of your illness — but really every one is ill almost, with this praeternatural wind. Here I am just now very anxious about Fr St John who is troubled with Asthma, and has had to leave his duties, just at the moment when they are unusually urgent. I attribute it to the keen wind. I am on the point of crossing, and shall not be much outstripped by this letter. I am very sorry to be absent — but it is very difficult to be in two places at once.

Ever Yours John H Newman of the Oratory

J. Stewart Esqr.

THURSDAY 18 JUNE 1857   in evening, came off to [Dublin]

TO RICHARD STANTON

The Oratory, Birmingham June 18. 1857

My dear Fr Richard,

I have pleasure in sending you by rail the volumes of St Athanasius — Pusey sent me several copies a few years back. I have the Suffragan Bishops, thank you, and have no need, that I know of, for a second copy. Yet should you have no prospective use of it, I should like you to leave it me in your will, for duplicates sometimes are very acceptable.[1]

I am resolutely fixed to return here — though I will do as much to seem in two places at once as it is possible for one who has not the gift of bilocation. I don't object, for a year or two, to be a non-resident Rector, with a real acting Vice-Rector — but it will be a very large pill for the Irish clergy to swallow — and I doubt the capacity of their throat.

What strange weather is this for the time of year!

Ever Yours affecty John H Newman

The Revd Fr Stanton

P.S.   Since writing this, I see you want the Latin. I read wrongly. I send it by post, and not the volumes.

[1] Stanton wrote on 11 June, 'I believe I am writing principally from an earnest desire to hear something of you, or at least to see your handwriting again.
I wish however at the same time to beg a copy, if you have one to spare, of the Latin version of your dissertations on St Athanasius . . .' *T.T.* pp. 1–91. Stanton offered Newman *The Restoration of Suffragan Bishops, V.M.* II, pp. 49–92.
Stanton's previous letter to Newman was on 3 Oct. 1856. See letter of 5 Oct. 1856 to him.

FRIDAY 19 JUNE 1857 Dublin. called on Mrs O'Brien

TO LAURENCE FORDE

June 20/57

My dear Dr Forde

I am much obliged to you for showing me Mr Duffy's title page, and I agree with you that it gives rise to questions which require consideration. One is whether Duffy does not by means of it (unintentionally) make himself University publisher. If you do not object I should like to show it to the Council, which will meet in little more than a week.[1]

I am &c J H N

TO PATRICK LEAHY, ARCHBISHOP ELECT OF CASHEL

6 Harcourt Street June 20. 1857

My dear Lord,

I know how ungracious it must seem to you, for me to repeat what I wrote to you the other day; but it is from no indolence or mere diffidence that I do so. At my age there are things which I cannot do, as I cannot run or climb; I can exercise no act of volition on my mind sufficient to compel it to do at a moment what you ask me to do. And, if I could not do it, though my mind were unembarrassed, much less can I, when I am really burdened with care and anxiety.

Additional motives for preaching, such as you suggest, are not wanted; I should not want any other besides that of wishing to show gratitude to your most friendly wish.[2]

As regards the interests of the University, I know quite well, the Rector ought to go about, and show himself, and make himself heard, more than I do. Conviction of this is one of my reasons for wishing to resign.

Gladly will I come, as you so kindly ask me, to listen to the better instruction which will issue from the lips of whomsoever you assign, instead of me, to take upon himself the honorable and important duty, which I am obliged to decline.[3]

I am, My dear Lord, Your Grace's faithful and affte servt in Xt

John H Newman of the Oratory

The Most Revd Dr Leahy

[1] On the frontispiece of a book by Forde, Duffy proposed to employ a woodcut used as the device of the University Committee. Rather than delay his book, Forde decided to omit the woodcut.

[2] Leahy wrote on 20 June importuning Newman to preach at his consecration, and added, 'your presence with your Sermon would render great service to the University in a Province from which it has much to expect . . .'

[3] See letter of 28 June to Leahy.

SUNDAY 21 JUNE 1857   Scott to dinner

MONDAY 22 JUNE   Senate for confirm Examiner [sic]

TO RICHARD STANTON

6 Harcourt Street Dublin June 22/57

My dear Fr Richard

Fr O'Reilly S.J. expressed himself today as desirous I should make inquiry on a subject, which leads me to write to you. He says that the Fr Provincial in Upper Gardiner Street has sent a letter to your Fr Ball, and never got an answer. Having done as much as this, I have done all I promised Fr O'Reilly that I would do[1]

I thank you for your letter   Ever affly Yours

John H Newman of the Oratory

The Revd Fr Stanton

TUESDAY 23 JUNE 1857   Examinations for License — Louis [de Vaulchier], Reginald [Barnewall] H Bethell

TO MANUEL JOHNSON

6 Harcourt Street Dublin June 23. 1857

My dear Johnson,

I hear you are coming to Dublin in August for the meeting of the British Association. I regret I shall not be here — but my house will, and empty, and able to receive any number of savants. My house keeper, though not one herself, will provide those necessaries which not even the most intellectual can do without, and any number of beds.

Do take possession of it, if you come, and have no more hospitable quarters to go to — and let me offer it to any one else, who comes from Oxford.

And if you come, I hope you will be able to take Birmingham in your way, where you will find me, if all is well[2]

Ever Yours affly John H Newman of the Oratory

M. Johnson Esqr

[1] Antony Ball was a young Irish priest at the London Oratory, from which he was expelled in 1862.

[2] Johnson replied on 30 June that he would not be in Dublin, but would tell others at Oxford. He then gave his own news: 'We have just returned from a most agreeable visit to H. Bowden—I never saw him or his folk more flourishing. . . . The Grosvr Place people [Mrs J. W. Bowden] are also very well. . . . I have to thank you for a prospectus of your forthcoming Review. . . . My wife and five children are all I am thankful to say very flourishing —It seems funny that a generation of one's own folk should have grown up as much as they have without having seen *you*. . . .

James Mozley and his wife are with us at present on their way to Derby.

I hope some day we shall meet for it is long since we have. If any thing should take me to Birmingham I shall not forget Edgbaston. . . .'

TO DANIEL VAUGHAN, BISHOP OF KILLALOE

June 23/57

My dear Lord

I thank you very much for your most kind letter.[1] Most fully will I do my part in coming into any arrangement which is possible for my still taking part in University affairs — but at present the state of things is exactly where it was on my writing my letter to your Lordship and the other Bishops on April 2.

Repeating my acknowledgments for your most kind interest in me, and asking your blessing

I am &c J H N

WEDNESDAY 24 JUNE 1857 These days very hot
THURSDAY 25 JUNE called on Lord Lieutenant, (Lord Carlisle) and went to All-hallows for disputation Reginald went. Louis went for good

TO H. E. MANNING

6 Harcourt Street Dublin June 25/57

My dear Manning

Your most kind letter has just come. I need not say how gladly I would be with you, if I could — but already people think I have been away from Dublin too long, and I wish, since I am leaving, not to put them out.[2] I am returned from England now about a week, having been away not much short of a month together. I shall not fail to say Mass for you on the 2nd, which is a Feast for which I have a special devotion. I have now before me, passing through the Press, my Oscott Sermon which is really written for the Visitation, tho' preached some days later; and your letter flanks it.[3]

I hope some time I shall hear from you some particulars of your Rule, which interests me very much. When Fr St John and I were in Milan in 1846, we inquired a good deal about it, but could learn nothing.[4]

I am going to call on the Lord Lieutenant this morning. He wished to see me out of civility. I don't expect I shall learn much of our University prospects

[1] The Bishop wrote on 20 June his pleasure because he has been told that Newman was not to leave the University. 'A greater loss the University could not sustain than your leaving it just now.'
[2] The church of Manning's Oblates of St Charles, St Mary of the Angels, Bayswater, was to be opened on 2 July.
[3] Newman's Oscott Sermon, 'The Second Spring,' was preached on 13 July 1852, and Manning was present. Newman included it *Sermons preached on Various Occasions*, and his letter dedicating the volume to Manning, is dated 'In Fest. Visit. B.V.M. [2 July] 1857.'
[4] i.e. the Rule of the Oblates of St Charles, which Manning was introducing into England.

from him, both because it *is* a mere call of civility, and secondly because he has no[t] any great influence. Lord Clarendon is the real man.[1]

Remember me to all of your Community whom I know — and congratulate them all, and believe me to be Ever Yours most affectionately

John H Newman of the Oratory

The Very Revd Dr Manning

TO AMBROSE ST JOHN

⌜6 Harcourt Street June 25/57⌝

My dear Ambrose,

⌜Manning opens his Church on the 2nd July. I think it would be a good thing, if you and some one else⌝ (whom does he know best?) ⌜went to represent me. But I don't urge it. He writes, wishing me and the Fathers to come.⌝ As to the expense, I could afford one, not two — I would pay for one return ticket for ⌜e.g. Edward or Nicholas,⌝ and then it struck me that you *talked* of going to London yourself. But if you are *not* going, then I will pay your return ticket, and only you will go.

⌜Mind, I am putting nothing upon you — but I think it would please him.

I wish to do *nothing* of course to risk your recovery —⌝ so by no means think of going, if you think it will hurt you.[2] By the bye, ⌜*you* must not return the same day —⌝ but might sleep, I suppose, at your sister's, or at Zulueta's.

Harry B. Louis and Reginald are leaving. We have not yet heard from the Princess and Countess.[3] ⌜I am now starting to call on the Lord Lieutenant [[Lord Carlisle]]. Next Monday I groan to say, I have to go down to Thurles for Dr Leahy's Consecration. It is just the sort of thing that knocks me up, and *no one will believe it*. I thought some *business* would be done there, the three Archbishops being together —- but Fr O'Reilly says no; and no one has said yes.⌝

Ever Yrs affly J H N

TO F. S. BOWLES

June 26/57

My dear Fr Frederic,

I agree with you that it is best to stave off arrangements till I come. I don't like the thoughts of giving up the choir — *Could* Sister Mary Philip

---

[1] The Earl of Clarendon, Foreign Secretary, had been Lord Lieutenant of Ireland from 1847 to 1851, and was a supporter of the Queen's Colleges.

[2] St John was recovering from asthma.

[3] Henry Bethell, Louis de Vaulchier and Sir Reginald Barnewall left Newman's House and the University at the end of the term, but Princes Edward and Charles de Ligne and Count Stephen Zamoyski remained on.

do the evening services? I thought Mr Jones was, not to play, but find a player.[1]

Ever Yrs affly J.H.N.

The inclosed are from Lawrence's Hymn Book.

TO CATHERINE ANNE BATHURST

6 Harcourt Street June 27. 1857

My dear Child

What you tell me is most shocking — but I think the child is too young to gain any moral harm. Perhaps it may have the reverse effect.

Punishment, I suppose, is inflicted as a preventive — three months hard labour is a tremendous penance, as it is inflicted. When we go to the question of what culprits *deserve*, we are lost. For some crimes, no punishment seems quite enough.

You need have no scruple — your *contrition* in your own room will be quite enough — without going to the Confessional.

I cannot promise myself a fixed day for my Mass, nor hour

Ever Yrs affly JHN

TO THOMAS HAYDEN

(Substance)   ⌈June 27⌉ [[1857]]

My dear Dr Hayden

⌈If there is [[was]] any thing which would decide me on not going to Thurles,⌉ independent of my physical feebleness, ⌈it is the news you report.[2] I could present papers such as those you have given me — but as to a discussion about the University, I should simply be in a false position, because the Archbishops have not yet at the end of three months communicated with my Oratory.

E.g. Suppose the subject of a Vice-Rector was mooted, if I heard any name mentioned and gave an opinion on it, I should be compromising my

---

[1] Mr Jones was the organist, and Sister Mary Philip was Catherine Anne Bathurst, who had come to Edgbaston at the end of March 1857, to take charge of the orphanage for boys.

[2] Hayden wrote,

'30 Harcourt St June 27. 2 P.M.

Very Rev. dear Sir

I may take the liberty of mentioning that I heard from a Professor who had the information directly from Dr Leahy, that the University *is* to be under discussion by the Archbishops at the forthcoming meeting and that Dr Leahy is "determined it shall be."

Very truly &c, Your's

T. Hayden'

The Archbishops would be assembled for Leahy's consecration at Thurles. In fact they did not discuss the University. See letter of 5 July to Mills.

Congregation, and implying without its consent that I intended to stay as Rector. If on the other hand, I said nothing, I should appear to their Graces to have assented by my silence.

If, however, I gave them the reason for wishing to give no opinion at all, I should seem to be complaining of them, which would have a most ungracious appearance. And, to get out of an embarassing position, I might be led to do something or other which I might be sorry for afterwards.

I am still of opinion, that nothing will be done or even attempted. Any how the first step is to write to Birmingham[1]

I am &c J H N

SUNDAY 28 JUNE 1857   Wallis to dinner

TO PATRICK LEAHY, ARCHBISHOP ELECT OF CASHEL

June 28/57

The Report in Dublin is, that the Bishops mean to determine something at Thurles tomorrow about the Rectorship, that is, I suppose, about writing to the Oratory. If so, sorry as I am to be away from your Consecration, there might after all have been an awkwardness in my presence.[1]

MONDAY 29 JUNE 1857   Dr Leahy's consecration — Ornsby, Robertson, Hayden, Sullivan, Hennessy went.[2]

TO HENRY BITTLESTON

6 Harcourt Street June 29. 1857

My dear Henry[3]

I have not been able to read over what I have written.[4]

If I have not corrected yours, but written my own, it is because you have sent me little bits of paper like Sibyl's leaves, and those written partly in ink, partly in unintelligible pencil.

The fault of yours is the *want of logical sequence* — and that in two ways.

---

[1] Newman, who excused himself on grounds of health from attending the consecration at Thurles, added a note at the foot of this draft, '(N B. Not a word had been said to me by any Bishop about the *chance* of a consultation about the University at Thurles—and as to the office of Vice Rector Dr Leahy had said I had better say nothing at all about candidates etc.)'

[2] Newman added in pencil later 'to it?' According to the *Tablet*, (4 July 1857), p. 421, the Professors attended in 'University costume,' to represent the University at the consecration of its Vice-Rector as Archbishop of Cashel.

[3] Bittleston had sent the draft of an article 'Sacrament' for the theological and ecclesiastical dictionary Newman hoped that the Birmingham Oratory might produce. He had placed a notice in the Congregation Room: 'April 27. 1857.

Fathers who wish to take part with the Fr Superior in the Theological Dictionary, are requested to place their initials against the Articles they undertake and to place them, when written, in rough copy, in the hands of Fr Secretary.'

The method Newman laid down for this Dictionary and the sample articles he drew up will be included in the volumes of his Theological Papers.

[4] i.e. Newman's own sketch, which he enclosed, of the article 'Sacrament.'

1. things put out of place. 2. three or four ideas stuffed into the same sentence, as into a carpet bag.

I know it is very difficult to be logical. A matter of degree always — in part a matter of opinion. I don't set up mine as a model — but I think it better than yours. You may write one better than mine.

Excuse me if I say that I think having to do these little essays will improve you very much generally — by obliging you to observe order. I hear criticisms on your Sermons, which are what *I* should make on your bits of paper.

I hope you won't think all this very savage.[1]

Postscript

1. Sacrament, (Lat. Sacramentum etc) is the received name for the seven special sacred rites of the Catholic Church; viz Baptism, etc (enumerate them)

2. In the original sense of the word Sacramentum, it signified the military oath etc etc (don't put in about μνέω, μνστης etc which belongs to the title Mystery.) or any oath — and hence the oath or vow on being initiated into the Sacred Rites of Religion — and hence those secret and sacred Rites themselves.

3. Sacraments are distinguished from all other rites, as being both signs and means of grace, instituted by our Lord Himself, whether immediately or through His Apostles. By their being *means* of grace, is meant that they are instruments, through or together with which supernatural grace is given to the recipient; and by their being *signs*, that the visible rite is symbolical (or analogous) of the particular kind or virtue of the grace given.

4 The grace given in a sacrament is two fold — first habitual grace, by which the soul is sanctified and united with God and lives, and secondly the grace just alluded to or the sacramental grace ⟨grace of the sacrament⟩, which is that which is denoted under the outward sign.

5. This sacramental grace implies a certain analogy between the requirements of body and soul. Thus Baptism gives life, Confirmation etc.

6. It has already been implied that a sacrament consists of two parts, a sign and a thing signified. Hence St Augustine defines it. . . . . and the Council of Trent . . .

7 The outward sign may be considered more distinctly under the division into matter and Form; the matter being the ordinary element or natural

---

[1] The rest of the covering letter is missing. Bittleston replied gratefully on 7 July, and spoke of wincing 'under the revelation of my own folly in attempting what I could not do.'

substance (as water in Baptism) which is used for a religious or supernatural purpose, and the form being the ministerial words which appropriate it to that religious purpose, and thereby separate it from other matter of the same kind, as water used for washing the face etc. Hence St Augustine says, 'Accedit verbum ad elementum etc.'

8. Hence the matter and form are all that are intrinsically required for the constitution or *confection* [of] a Sacrament, it produces its effect, that is, it confers grace ex opere operato, i.e. by its own vis ⟨without depending⟩ on the recipient.

9 This must be qualified so far as this 1. that more or less grace is given, or more effectually given according to the disposition of the recipient. 2 that he can suspend its effect altogether, e.g. 3. that he may make it invalid, by the absence of a negative ⟨?⟩ ⟨passive⟩ intention.

10. Hence, the distinction between the Sacramentum and the *Res* Sacramenti — Explain

11. This introduces us to the question of the *Minister* of Sacrament and his intention, which is another extrinsic condition of the validity of a Sacrament. Explain *who* are the ministers.

12 As to intention merely refer to the word 'Intention.'

13. Another effect of Sacrament, is Character — impossibility of repeating three

14 Sacraments of dead and living

15 Jewish Sacraments.

16. Greek, Armenian, Nestorian Sacraments.

17 Lutheran, Calvinistic.

TO MICHAEL BLOUNT

(substance)   June 29/57

My dear Mr Blount

I am quite willing to act upon the proposal you have selected from those I suggested.[1]

Will you put down on paper the kind of acknowledgment or receipt you wish me to give you. It would state the fact that you had put into my hands Mr Canning's hundred Pounds for a University purpose such as I should select, the interest being used for masses for his soul till the money is applied as intended — but it is not to be so applied till there is a guarantee that there shall be a (weekly?) mass for Benefactors such as to include Mr Canning. If you would send me a draft of it, I would make any remark on it which struck me.

[1] Cf. letter of 13 June to Blount. In a letter of 20 June Newman made the proposal now outlined further. His other proposal was that the capital from Mr Canning's legacy should be preserved with the interest accruing, until it could be spent on the University. See also letter of 8 July to Gilbert Blount.

You can invest it in my name when you please, but in that case I suppose I should not be answerable for the security of the investment. If I vested it, I should be answerable.

I am &c J H N

TO JOHN STANISLAS FLANAGAN

Dublin June 29/57

My dear S

As to I's [Ignatius Ryder] going to St Leonard's, what is he to do there? for how long? etc etc. And then, why to St Leonard's, which is so far off? The Lancashire coast is much nearer, or the Bristol Channel — but I think it a difficulty his going at all. It is a question whether he would not be better at Edgbaston than at Rednall — but then I suppose you will say, he must naturally *do* more at Edgbaston.

I am exceedingly concerned at William[1] going without having been to confession. Perhaps he would rather go to a stranger at Sheffield, than to a Confessor he has been to before.

Have you thought about what is to be done about the waiting? I really don't think it would be bad to put several good school boys in cassocks. It is sad that we are so broken up by Ambrose and the novices being away, not to mention myself.

The report is that Mr Flannery is to be made Vice Rector. I thought it fair to tell Dr Leahy, that, since I had no opportunity of giving an opinion on the object of their choice (whoever it should be) before appointment, I should claim a right to criticize after. It is wonderful, if they do it without consulting me. I told him how much it concerned me, if I were to be non-resident. I also have given him a hint about writing to the Oratory — for in truth I am inclined to think they will put the thought aside — though they may be writing, or debating about writing, this very day. One Bishop went away from Dr Cullen saying that it was all settled, and I was going to remain — another wrote to me to express his pleasure that I was to remain. I am obliged to answer that *nothing* is settled, but things are just where they were three months ago.[2]

Perhaps H Bethell and his Father may be coming to the Oratory in their way from Manchester to Bristol. H. leaves for Manchester tomorrow. He passed a good examination. Louis [de Vaulchier] behaved very well in parting, and spoke feelingly. He certainly has done us much good, and Renouf much credit.[3] Reginald [Barnewall] is determined to go up again. I am glad

---

[1] '(Kenna?)' has been added here later. Flanagan wrote on 28 June that William McKenna, the former laybrother, had returned to his mother at Sheffield. 'I regret to say that he left the house without going to his duties.'

[2] See letter of 23 June to Daniel Vaughan.

[3] Renouf had been de Vaulchier's tutor for ten years.

to recollect that I wanted him to stop another year. His failure will do good. He too is to go (with his mother) to Manchester, and is to get to the Oy [Oratory] about the time I get there.

Ever Yrs affly J H N

P.S. The elder Blunt is leaving Oscott, and talks of being a soldier! He is going to pay the Bethells a visit. I wish I could make a move towards him — I don't know how.[1]

P.S. Three of your packets have been overweight. I inclose a letter from Crawley. Keep it to yourself[2]

J H N

TO AMBROSE ST JOHN

⌐Dublin June 29. 1857

My dearest Ambrose

I wish you many many happy returns of this day, but I never will forgive you for not telling me of it in time for me to say Mass for you. I am saying Mass for you once a week, and might as well have said it this morning as not.

As to the anonymous £50, *how* will it be administered?[3] First, it will be sent to Nicholas as Treasurer? then, ⌐are you to *charge* for dinner etc at Rednall, the Fathers paying out of the £50?⌐ Further, should there not be some little charge for sleeping, which would give *you* an excuse for paying, and save you from seeming to *monopolize* the house?

⌐I exceedingly rejoice at your improvement in health — but am not at all satisfied you may not have a relapse any day.⌐ E.g. should the weather change and the barometer fall suddenly. ⌐Do be on your guard.

As to H W's [[Henry Wilberforce]], I should like you of all things to go there.[4] I have a mixture of pity and disappointment about him I cannot describe.⌐ See how they all are there, for his wife has not been well. ⌐As to the [[Brompton]] Oratory there, be as kind to every one as you choose — but don't take a meal there. (H W's being so near is a sufficient excuse) and of course don't talk about us or our doings. Don't talk about Rednall.⌐

I don't know what you allude to as to this house. Reginald [Barnewall] and Louis [de Vaulchier] are gone, Harry B. [Bethell] goes today — *their time being up.*[5] ⌐As to the other leach,⌐[6] of foreigners, they are all in a precious

---

[1] This was Francis Scawen Blunt (1839–72), elder brother of Wilfrid Scawen Blunt.

[2] George Crawley wished to join the Birmingham Oratory.

[3] St John, who had come into a share of his family inheritance, offered £50 for the board of Oratorians who went to their house at Rednal.

[4] St John proposed to stay with Wilberforce at 77 Onslow Square, near the Oratory at Brompton, when he went to London for the opening of Manning's church on 2 July.

[5] St John thought they were leaving on account of a breach of discipline.

[6] 'Dish of . . . coagulating material.' *O.E.D.*

stew, and trying to make up. Z. [Zamoyski] *must* go — as to the two Princes, ⌜I would keep them, if I dare — but I know well that mischief has got into the House, though I am very much in the dark. My fear is — I can't in honesty and charity take fellows, like young Errington, from Ushaw, if lax youths are my inmates.⌝[1]

I hope you don't mean to miss Pollen — rather, put him off. Recollect he comes at your strong wish, and with out any wish of mine. As to the colour of the House, let Pollen decide.[1]

⌜I congratulate you on your money.⌝ We must thank God. ⌜Don't squandor it like a sailor, which you are disposed to do.⌝

You had better write the Preface to the Raccolta,[2] and then I will cut it up. How does the printing go on?

Ever Yrs affly J H N

TUESDAY 30 JUNE 1857   change in weather — glass falling 10 degrees   Harry Bethell went.

TO THE DUKE OF NORFOLK

6 Harcourt Street June 30/57

My dear Duke of Norfolk,

I have received from you with very great gratitude the gift of your volume.[3] It is most pleasant to know I am remembered by you. For myself I never shall forget the great kindness and sympathy you showed me in the Achilli matter — and unworthy as they are, you and yours are continually in my prayers.

It is a source of great gratification to me to hear with what hope and interest English Catholics are looking to you as their head, and I doubt not at all that you will have all the graces given you necessary for that position

Say everything kind from me to the Duchess, and believe me   &c

J H N

[1] St John was staying for his health at Rednal, where the outside of the house was being painted.
[2] *The Raccolta, or Collection of Indulgenced Prayers*, which St John was translating.
[3] *The Lives of Philip Howard, Earl of Arundel, and of Anne Dacres, his wife*, edited from the original MSS. by the Duke of Norfolk E.M., London 1857.

TO A. LISLE PHILLIPPS

6 Harcourt Street Dublin July 1. 1857

My dear Mr Phillipps

I thank you very much for your new pamphlet, and should have acknowledged it before this, except that I wished to read it first.[1] The subject is of all others the most interesting to an English Catholic, and you have treated it with that gentleness and affectionateness, which it not only requires, but which it gains from you on all occasions. I thank you especially for the very kind mention you make of me.[2]

You know enough of my feelings on the whole subject, to know that there are some things in it, in which I am afraid to follow you — but I earnestly pray that those consequences will in no respect happen in fact, which seem to me so legitimate and likely. I mean, as you will anticipate, that the tendency of a portion of your pamphlet is, far indeed from your intention, to persuade individual Anglicans to wait out of communion with the Catholic Church, till they can come over with others in a body. There is such an extreme difficulty in rousing the mind to the real *necessity* of leaving the position into which men have grown up, their professions perhaps, their neighbourhood, or their family, or their work, that they will easily avail themselves of any the slightest excuse — and even a hint from a person so deeply respected as yourself, so beloved, yourself too a convert, is more than sufficient to turn the scale, when the mind is in suspense. And then suppose, if these very dear and precious souls, say Dr Pusey, are taken away in this state, when grace has been offered them, and they have not followed it up.

I perfectly agree with you in thinking that the movement of 1833 is not over in this country, whatever be the state of Oxford itself; also, I think it is for the interest of Catholicism that individuals should not join us, but should remain to leaven the mass, — I mean that they will do more for us by remaining where they are than by coming over, but then they have individual souls, and with what heart can I do anything to induce them to preach to others, if they themselves thereby become castaways?

You will see that I am alluding especially to the passage on pp. 31 32, in which you say, the Church 'calls her separated children individually, but etc'[3] — the effect of which passage I really think is to imply that, since there

[1] *On the future Unity of Christendom*, London (Charles Dolman . . . and . . . 'The Union' office) 1857. For the reunion movement see letter of 6 April 1857 to Thompson; also Cuthbert Butler, *The Life and Times of Bishop Ullathorne*, London 1926, I, pp. 334–44; W. Ward, *The Life and Times of Cardinal Wiseman*, 2nd edition, London 1897, II, pp. 477–90; and H. R. T. Brandreth, *Dr Lee of Lambeth*, London 1951, pp. 76–83.
[2] When quoting from *On Romanism and Popular Protestantism* that belief in the Thirty-nine Articles was necessary for salvation only in so far as they embodied Articles of the Creed, Phillipps described Newman as 'one of the most eminent and powerful writers that the Church of England ever produced' *On the future Unity of Christendom*, p. 9.
[3] In this passage, basing himself on the Council of Florence, Phillipps maintained that the conduct of the Church 'consists in a conciliatory dealing with the separated *bodies* of Christians in their *corporate capacity*. No one who maintains this is, of course, blind to

is a prospect now of the nation, or the Church Establishment, of England becoming reclaimed, therefore individuals, say Dr Pusey, are not called upon by the Catholic Church to come over to her at once.

I should not be honest, or satisfy my own conscience, if I did not say as much as this, when you have seemed to ask my opinion, by being so good as to send me what you have written — but do not suppose me to be blind to the most happy effect, which a composition, written in so Christian a spirit, that is, with such tenderness and consideration for those whom it principally addresses, must have, in opening their minds to give a patient hearing to the all important subject to which they are invited.

Believe me, My dear Mr Phillipps (with the full certainty you will pardon my frankness) Most sincerely Yours in Xt

John H Newman of the Oratory.

A. L Phillipps Esqr.

P.S.   Has it ever drawn your attention that the English nation would have come back, or probably so, except for the Scotch? It is the Scotch Protestant party now, which is the life of the opposition to us in Parliament and Exeter Hall. So it seems to me. James ii, I suppose, is the other human cause.

You must not suppose I am one of those who wish the Church Establishment of England overthrown, though I cannot regard it, *as a Catholic*, in any 'corporate capacity.' I quite agree with you that we may contemplate the English *Nation* as a body. The words are 'teach all nations', not 'teach all Churches.'

TO CARLO ROSSI

Patri Rossi Praep. Orat. Rom. &c   July 1 [1857]

Litteras Tuas, Pater Reverendissime, hodie recepimus, in quibus, pro tuâ humanitate, exilitatem meam et universam Congregationem meam certiores fecisti, te per suffragia Patrum Romanae S. Philippi Neri Congregationis in

another important fact, viz., that the Church does not limit her dealings with her separated brethren to this course: it is quite certain that she calls upon them, singly and individually, to return to unity; and when any of them hear her voice, she rejoices over the return of the wandering child: but this for the most part, is her course of action, when the rebellion against her authority is at its height, when a corporate reunion appears hopeless, and when the heads of the separated communions obstinately refuse to listen to any overtures for peace. The moment, however, that a favourable opportunity occurs; the moment the separated portions of the Church manifest a desire for peace, for the restoration of unity, then at once the Church comes forth, with all the tenderness of a loving mother, to effect a reconciliation with her separated children . . .

It is obvious, then, that if some Catholics are averse to the idea of a corporate reunion of the separated communions of Christendom, there is no such difficulty on the side of the Church as such; it is a mere caprice or prejudice of individual Catholics, and repugnant to the established policy and traditional practice of the Catholic Church herself.'

ipsam sedem et dignitatem Beatissimi et Amantissimi Fundatoris nostri evectum esse.[1]

Quasì sine ullâ morâ et sincerissimo cordis affectu haec qualiacumque Paternitati Tuae scribo, Tu qui tot nominibus Pater à me et à nostris jure dicendus es, quò tibi maturissime possim exprimere, quantum ex illâ litterarum tuarum lectione tum ego tum Patres Congregationis nostrae Birminghamiensis, praesertim Patres Ambrosius StJohn, et Fredericus Bowles, gaudium perceperimus.

Item, Pater benevolentissime, pro certo habeas velim, nos neque oblivisci Tui, neque supplicationes nostras omissuras, indignissimas licèt, quas pro Te, muneri amplissimo fungenti, à nobis postulasti

Valeas, et vigeas semper in prosperis in plenitudine charitatis illius principalis [?] quam S Philippus suis largiri solet

Carolo Rossi Praep.

THURSDAY 2 JULY 1857 (Manning's Church opening. Ambrose and Nicholas there)
Mr Doane to dinner

TO JOSEPH DIXON, ARCHBISHOP OF ARMAGH

Private   Copy

⌐July 2/57⌐

My dear Lord

I am taking a step which requires an apology and I hope you will not think it impertinent in me either towards your Grace or the Prelate of whom I am going to speak. But I cannot help giving utterance to the feeling of many months, that ⌐Dr Moriarty is *the* man for Rector of the University, and I shall be more easy in time to come to have said it, though nothing comes of it,⌐ than to have kept silence thro' delicacy

⌐You may well think me intrusive, you may well think me audacious in thus writing to you — but⌐ I have the University so much at heart, that ⌐I will risk seeming so.

Really, I do think the University has had out of me all that it can have — I have not energy in me to go on; I am quite wearied out, and want rest. If I retire now, I shall seem to have done, something — if I do not, I shall by my incapacity in time to come, undo what little credit (and it is little enough) I deserve for the past[2]

Dr Moriarty would kindle an enthusiasm for the University all thro'

---

[1] Rossi, who had been the teacher of the first English Oratorians at Santa Croce in 1847, wrote on 23 June to announce that he had been elected Superior of the Roman Oratory.

[2] [[undo what little (and it is little enough) I have done]]

Ireland — He would, more than any one, bring all parties round to it. He would be popular with clergy, with what once was the young Ireland party, with our Whig friends in Dublin, and with the English Professors. He has a great zeal for the University himself, and he knows, not only Ireland, but France and Italy. And as having so much to do with All hallows, he would come with a great prestige. Then he is an eloquent preacher, and speaker, and he would be able to show himself, and make the University felt in Dublin and Ireland.

It is, I know, a very cool thing in me, to contemplate a diocesan Bishop* descending to the Rectorship — but the University is a great object, and requires some great assistance at starting.[1]

I am too old to be Rector, but any help I could give him, without leaving my present responsibilities, I would gladly offer. Begging your Grace's blessing &c

J H N

The Most Revd The Primate

[[*(Did I mean maliciously to suggest that it was a cool thing in the Irish Bishops to ignore the Fathers of the Oratory, and make me give up the duties that lay upon me towards them?)]]

TO AMBROSE ST JOHN

Dublin. July 2/57

My dear A

I fear there will be some contretemps between you and Pollen. He told me he was coming to you on the *3rd*. Says I, 'Why Fr St John will be in London till the 5th, and I know he wished to stop even over the 5th.' Says he 'Well, there's no *need* of my going at all —' Says I, 'that's what I tell him.' Says he, 'I won't go.' Says I, 'Why should you?' Says he, 'I'll write and tell him so.' Says I, 'But you don't know how to direct to him?' Says he 'Where does he put up in London?' Says I 'at H W's.' [Wilberforce]

So I suppose he has written to you. And the chance is you have said something to him in the letter I have taken to him today. And therefore the upshot will be, that he will not go to Birmingham on the strength of his letter to you — and you will go back to Birmingham on the strength of your letter to him.

⌜Mr Doane called here today and dined. You know how he plagued me almost, by his dependence on me last year. Now he has cut Birmingham⌝ and almost me. He was not coming here,[1] nor did he come to see me — but he had some time on his hands when he got to Liverpool for he is going to Killarney. ⌜He has been to the London Oratory⌝ and talked to. ⌜Asked me, if H.R. [Harry Ryder] was with us?⌝ for his father had sent him to Rome that

[1] [[He was not here on purpose, but had some time on his hands.]] Newman rearranged a number of the sentences in this letter, when copying later.

73

he might not join us hastily — ⌐Asked how many novices we had — asked if we were not [[too far]] in the country[1] — asked if we had a parish, as the Oratory has at Brompton. Whether Father Neville had come back, how we could have the face to steal Fr Tillotson? etc etc. Now, my dear A, *Whence* did he get all this? He was quite surprised to find that I was leaving Dublin.⌐ I suspect all this is the gossip of the Collegio Pio derived from London, and strenghtened by Brompton. ⌐Certainly it does us most extremely harm —⌐ Something like eight persons joined Manning from the Collegio Pio. It is odd ⌐none have ever *thought* of us.⌐ Coleridge is, they say, to be a Jesuit, as well as Wynne. As to the Collegio Pio, it is quite true, I have subscribed nothing to it; so I deserve nothing.[2]

I should say that ⌐certainly Doane knew there was a separation between the two Oys [Oratories]⌐ from his never speaking to me of Fr Faber etc. ⌐He had been three months during the winter next door to Mrs Bowden at Bonchurch, and had seen a good deal of John Bowden. I should never be surprised to find that at Rome or elsewhere the report was we were breaking up. I here, others ill, Fr William leaving (as Miss Giberne asked⌐ with an allusion to Penny) Penny and Fr Dalgairns gone — kidnapping Fr Robert, kidnapping H Ryder, desperately.

I have told Nicholas that some one has promised me £50 for Rednall board — but, ⌐as to your property, one thing occurs to say, in consequence of what you observe about it. It is my earnest wish and hope, and belief, that you, who are so much younger than I, will survive me — and so, when I get older and cannot make money by my books, will [[out of your fulness help]] sustain me, (for you know I have not above £48 a year) — but, in case I should live longer, I should perhaps be in difficulty. I wish you would in your will (at some time) give me a life interest in enough of the money you leave to the Congregation to make up to £80⌐ (— e.g. does not the Congregation owe you £500 and more? something of that sort —) [[i.e. £32,]] or there about. But this I only suggest.[1][3]

Ever Yrs affly J H N

July 3/57

[1] This was an implied criticism, for Oratorians are meant to be in towns. Edgbaston was a rapidly growing suburb.

[2] The Collegio Pio was founded in Rome, in 1852, for converts and late vocations. Newman now sent £5 for the College to the English agent, Mgr Ferdinand English, whom he had known in Rome in 1846–7. English replied on 9 July, 'Your revered hand brings back to remembrance the happiest, sunniest part of my life,—when together in beautiful Italy. And nothing will give me greater pleasure than to visit you,—though in smoky Birmingham.'

[3] St John replied on 5 July, 'I begin with the last page of your letter because it is most pleasing to me. It is the kindest thing you ever said to me . . . What I propose now is if you will let me to give into your hands when the bulk of the property sells £1000 for *yourself* to meet what you mention.'

FRIDAY 3 JULY 1857 Crofton to dinner

TO J. R. BLOXAM

6 Harcourt Street Dublin July 3. 1857

My dear Bloxam

I thank you very much for your kind offer to subscribe to our Periodical.[1] Should we want a subscription list, I will gladly avail myself of your liberality, but Ireland ought to do it of itself.

For myself, I shall not remain here longer except nominally, that is, except so far as to connect myself in name with the new University, as far as ever I can — Hence, I *begin* with being Editor of the Journal — but I have quite enough to do at Edgbaston, without going from home — nor is there a necessity now, for we are going on here with great promise.

I have not seen either Dr Oliver's work nor J B Morris — and cannot guess how Dr O. has managed to introduce Morris.[2]

I am deeply grieved to hear the accounts of Marriott, which come to me. I heard too a very bad account of Pusey in February, but no news is good news, and many months have elapsed since

Ever Yours affly John H Newman of the Oratory

The Revd Dr Bloxam

TO JOHN STANISLAS FLANAGAN

Dublin. July 4/57

My dear S

Mr Doane, who dined here the day before yesterday, in his way to Killarney and Cork, supplies to me the most striking instance, I have met with, of the way, as I think, we are whispered against. It has grown on me ever since he went. His manner was as altered as possible from the time I saw him at Paris and Rome.[3] At first I thought he had merely grown graver and older — and I said to myself, see what the effect of Rome and sacred orders is — for he was far too much of a boy at St Sulpice — but I do now really think that it was caused by a feeling of suspicion or unpleasant association in which he now views me. He was three months next door Mrs Bowden in the Isle of Wight in the winter, and saw a good deal of John Bowden; but he dribbled all this out in a grave way; and it is certain, if he saw much of J.B. and walked with him, he must have heard their version of

---

[1] i.e. the *Atlantis*, the first number of which appeared in Jan. 1858.

[2] Bloxam must have mentioned the work of the antiquary Canon George Oliver, *Collections illustrating the History of the Catholic Religion in the counties of Cornwall, Devon, Dorset, Somerset, Wilts, and Gloucester*, London 1857, in which there is an account of John Brande Morris, pp. 357–9.

[3] In the winter of 1855–6.

every thing. When he was in London he went down to Brompton — and it was quite plain from the way he mentioned it, that he knew there was a distance between us and them — If it were not for all this, I should have thought that what he said or asked about us was from the gossip of the Collegio Pio — but I suspect this had not much to do with it, though it might have something. He asked whether our Oratory at Bm [Birmingham] was not in the *country*. He asked whether, as the Brompton Oratory, *we* took a parish, implying, as I thought, that we did not. He asked how many novices we had, in a mysterious way? He rather pressed me on the point *where* HR. [Harry Ryder] was at this moment. Was he at Bm? *where* was Rednall? 'His Father' (he said) 'had sent him to Rome wishing him not to join us without a trial.' He said we had kidnapped Fr Tillotson, at which the Americans were highly indignant.[1] I was tempted both to say nothing at all in answer, and to say a great deal. I said that we had established our Mission at *another* part of Bm before we came where we were — at which his eyes opened with surprise — and that our present Church was so full that we had thought of enlargeing it. I asked him to take a room in this house — but he would not.

I think, as time goes on, we may expect any quantity of contempt from the influences which are at work against us — and that our line is to make ourselves in every way *strong in Birmingham* — and depend upon it, we shall have numbers [?] elsewhere falling back upon us — And what I said, as against *Protestants*, in my last Corn Exchange Lecture, I say now of our position in the *Church* — What people *say* against us, is worth nothing — we only have to care when saying becomes doing — but, while we have *local* opinion, we may defy public, and while we are strong at home, we may defy the world.[2]

I still think that the tone of Mrs Ward's first letter, some months ago, was caused by a sort of fear *where* to find me.[3] And did I tell you that Mrs Bowden (who used every February 21 to send me a letter every year on my birthday) has now ceased — and I have not heard from her but once, I think, since last November year.[4]

Ever Yrs affly J H N

The Post, which I was waiting for, has not come in.
Will you direct and forward the inclosed?

[1] Tillotson wrote from Birmingham to Newman on 6 July, 'As to what he said to you about me of course my dear Father you did *entrap* me, but it was in St Philip's spirit, and you saved me from Hell, and I owe you myself and my all, for it, little or nothing as it is. Besides all that, the little spiritual life even of *sentiment*, which I had before I ever saw you, it was you who formed it in me by your "Parochial Sermons." I am yours therefore by this double tie, to say nothing of the greater one of *privilege*, which I grant I have never sufficiently valued, but which in reality is priceless. I never will *leave* you my dear Father, and such an invidious report shall by God's grace make me redouble my exertions for you, and your House, my happy Home. As to the United States I ignore it, and I desire never to set foot on it again, except you *wish* it.' But see letter of 7 Nov. 1859 to Tillotson.
[2] *Pre. Pos.*, pp. 382–8.
[3] Cf. letter of 17 April to W. G. Ward.
[4] Cf. letter of 14 Nov. 1856 to St John.

TO ROBERT D. LYONS

⌜July 4⌝ [[1857]]

⌜My dear Dr Lyons,⌝

I cannot give you an opinion myself on the matter about which you write, because I know too little the feelings of Dublin people about it. ⌜For myself, I have always advocated an approximation [[approach]] to the Queen's *University* (as distinct from the Queen's Colleges) but the two are so closely associated together in the minds of the people of Ireland, that I have not got one single person to second me.[1]

This being the case, I dare not go by my own judgment on your question — but I will try to find what *would be thought of it* as quickly as I can

Yours &c J H N⌝

TO A. LISLE PHILLIPPS

6 Harcourt Street, Dublin July 4. 1857.

My dear Mr Phillipps,

I thank you very much for your most confidential letter, and the very interesting information it contains.[2] It cannot but bring the smaller and weaker party to the stronger, for any number of Anglicans to meet in

[1] Lyons wrote on 3 July asking whether he could accept an appointment 'of considerable distinction and with an emolument of £100 p. annum,' as Examiner in Theory and Practice of Medicine to the Queen's University. The Queen's Colleges were constituent parts of the Queen's University, which was established in 1850.

[2] Phillipps replied the next day to Newman's letter of 1 July:

'. . . I will communicate to your discretion what hitherto I have kept secret from all but the Cardinal of Westminster and three other Bishops; you are aware how vexed a question it has been of late years in the English Catholic Body whether it was or not a tenable proposition, that there *could* be a Corporate Reunion between the National Church of England and the Catholic Church . . .

Now it having been officially intimated to me . . . that there was now a powerful Party in the Established Church *ready to take definite steps towards* the realization of such a measure, I was induced in the early part of the year to write the Letters which appeared in *The Union*, and when subsequently those Letters occasioned a strong out burst of remonstrance in some of the Organs of the Catholic Body, I felt we could take no further step, until we had ascertained from the Voice of Authority how far we could with safety proceed on our course. At first I applied to Authority at home, but unable to get a sufficiently definite decision, tho' the answer was far from unfavourable, and being moreover sorely perplexed by many harsh letters from several quarters chiefly of Converts from this very movement . . .' Phillipps felt inspired to lay the whole matter before the Pope himself.

With the approval of leading members of the Anglo-Catholic party, Phillipps wrote to Barnabò, the Cardinal Prefect of Propaganda, and on 20 June received an encouraging reply. The Cardinal 'assures me of his entire and cordial approbation of the Project [for corporate reunion] I had laid *before him*, [and] promises to lay it before the Pope *immediately* on his return to Rome . . .' Phillipps communicated this reply to Wiseman and three other bishops.

'. . . I next communicated this wonderful intelligence to the heads of the Anglo-Catholic Committee in London, where it was received with the greatest enthusiasm, and on Saturday of this very week I am to meet them in London in order that we may make a second communication to the Holy See.'

See also *de Lisle* I, pp. 375–80.

conference Catholics like yourself and those whom you will represent. I trust it will issue in many conversions.

The four resolutions or steps which you name will be very important ones.[1]

I am still somewhat uneasy lest persons, who ought to be Catholics, should allow themselves to *bargain* and make *terms*. Should not they have some [presumption?][2] from the Holy See — or in some formal way surrender themselves?

I will soon begin by giving you a Mass once a week for your intention — and hope you will give me any information of any steps that shall have taken place. I shall keep your secret very faithfully.

> Very sincerely Yours in Xt   John H Newman of the Oratory

A. L. Phillipps Esqr.

SUNDAY 5 JULY 1857   no University Sermon by accident

TO ROBERT D. LYONS

Dublin July 5/57

My dear Dr Lyons

I have taken what seemed to me good advice on your question, without of course giving any hint who asked it or whom it concerned. And I am sorry to say the answer was decidedly contrary to your wishes. It is as plain as possible that the Queen's University excites the greatest irritation in the minds of numbers — I am sorry it should; but there is no doubt of the fact.[3]

[1] Phillipps wrote that he and those with whom he was acting had already arranged as follows: '(1) a magnificent Chalice of Australian Gold set with precious jewels and a Paten of like nature is to be conveyed to the Cardinal Prefect in gratitude, and in token of the coming restoration of Communion. [Barnabò declined the chalice.]
(2) an association will be enrolled on Saturday next for the Promotion of Unity
(3) The Imprimatur of some of our Bishops on the Catholic side, and of the Bishops of Salisbury, Oxford and Brechin on the Anglican side will be prefixed to a Prayer for Unity to be used by the members of the Association.
(4) a Body of Preachers (Anglican) is to be enrolled to preach the Reunion all over the Kingdom, wherever it *can* be done—'
[2] The copyist, H. L. Bellasis, left a space here, the word being illegible. In *de Lisle*, I, p. 369 it is printed as 'presumption.'
[3] In connection with this letter Newman copied out the following, in the correspondence at the end of 'Memorandum about my connection with the Catholic University,'
'From Mr Hennessy to Dr Newman
Oct 10
I am glad to see the favorable impression which the University is making (at Cork) a circumstance which will be the more enhanced, the more the University avoids official contact with the Queen's University.
(signed) H. Hennessy
In November 1856 when Sir R. Kane wrote a letter to the Cork Examiner, stating that, in the Senate of the Queen's University, in consequence, as he seemed to imply, of some overture on the part of the Catholic University, "the subjects under consideration have been *the relations, which are to exist*, between the Queen's University and the so called Catholic University" the Dean of our Faculty of Medicine at once wrote to the Examiner denying the fact altogether.'
See letter of 10 Nov. 1856 to Hayden.

Under these circumstances I do not see that any thing is left to me, but to say that I think a connexion with the Queen's University is impossible in any of our Professors

Very sincerely Yours John H Newman of the Oratory

R D Lyons Esqr M D &c &c.

TO AUSTIN MILLS

6 Harcourt Street Dublin July 5/57

My dear A

I am glad to hear the success of Loss and Gain, tho' I can't understand it. I suppose Lewis saw to the correctness of the translation.[1]

As to the Anglican Church, I should at first sight recommend M. Ségondy the following works — Lingard. Short's History of the Church of E. Neale's Puritans. Butler's English Catholics. Challoner's Missionary Priests — Flanagan's History. *But wait till I come* — I wish I could afford to give them to him.[2]

I am very sorry the wood is not put up in the Library — Do send to Haywood — for this very bright weather will do the books additional harm.[3]

Tho' Ambrose has returned, you don't say anything about the Bayswater matter — and the paper gives nothing but the Cardinal's sermon. Billing will wait *till the proof goes back* — did I not give it you? What to *look at* is the year and the number of the Volume in *each*. Depend on it, the *bookbinder* will be able to do nothing.[4]

Dr Leahy wishes to keep me here after the term ends, on the wild goose chase of the Archbishops meeting in Dublin about the University. *People were confident* they would confer at Thurles, and were eager for me to go there *on that account*. Of course they never dreamed of it.

Ever Yrs affly J H N

[1] Mills reported that he had heard from the Abbé Segondy, whose translation of *Loss and Gain, Perte et Gain*, Tournai 1856, had been a great success. A second edition was called for, and this appeared in 1859. David Lewis, who was living at Brussels helped Segondy with his work. Cf. F. Segondy, *Essai sur l'Eglise Anglicane*, Paris 1878, p. 555.

[2] Segondy wanted to write a book about the Church of England and also the Nonconformists, which became *Essai sur l'Eglise Anglicane*, and asked for a reading list. John Lingard, *A History of England from the first Invasion by the Romans to the Accession of William and Mary*, eight volumes, London 1819–30; Thomas Vowler Short, *Sketch of the History of the Church of England*, Oxford 1832; Daniel Neal, *History of the Puritans*, five volumes, London 1732–8; Charles Butler, *Historical Memoirs respecting the English, Irish, and Scottish Catholics since the Reformation*, four volumes, London 1819–21; Richard Challoner, *Memoirs of Missionary Priests and other Catholics . . .*, two volumes, 1741 and 1742; Thomas Flanagan, *A History of the Church in England from the earliest period to the Re-establishment of the Hierarchy in* 1850, two volumes, London 1857.

[3] The roof of a large skylight in the library at the Oratory was to be blocked by planks.

[4] New title pages and prefaces were being printed for the set of *Bibliotheca Patrum* in the library.

TO D. B. DUNNE

July 6/57

My dear Dr Dunne

Augustus [Bethell] seems so cast down at the idea of his labours having no issue, that I am led to ask you whether you could persuade your brother to be so kind as to take your place in the whole conduct of the Disputation, including rehearsals.[1]

I don't know whether this is possible — but I shall send Augustus to talk to you, or rather to be talked to, on the subject — if, as I hope, you are sufficiently well to see him

Ever Yours affly John H Newman of the Oratory

D Dunne Esqr D D &c &c

TO W. G. WARD

6 Harcourt St Dublin July 6. 1857

My dear Ward,

I have read your lectures with great interest, but am not sure that I have mastered the whole argument.[2] In the case of your essay three years ago, I had nothing to say — because I thought the customary teaching was so much the other way that there must be a mistake in the argument somewhere, though I did not see where.[3] I hope that your present argument is not bound up with *it* — I do not see that it is.

All my feelings and habitual convictions go with your present — and no one, I am sure, will be able to read it without gaining personal good from it, and thanking you for the deeply serious, real and practical tone with which you handle scientific questions — But I want you to explain to me this:—[4]

You say, if act Z, which is compatible simultaneously with an act of mortal sin, be all that a man has to produce when he is dying, he does not really renounce sin, since he has, not a nolitio, only a nolleitas.

[1] Bethell was to have taken part in a scholastic disputation. Dunne's younger brother, born in 1830, later became Archbishop of Brisbane.
[2] *Five Lectures on Attrition, Contrition, and Sovereign Love; with a practical application of the Doctrine:* delivered in St. Edmund's Seminary by William George Ward, D.Ph. Dogmatical Lecturer in that Seminary. Privately printed. The preface is dated Ascension Day 1857. Cf. letter of 13 Feb. 1858.
[3] *De Obduratorum Peccatis Mortalibus*, p. 79, privately printed, in the form of a letter addressed to Manning, and dated from London, 18 Jan. 1854. Ward argued against the common thesis that for a sin to be grave, there must be explicit realisation of its wickedness.
[4] Ward was arguing for the difficulty of a deathbed repentance on the part of a hardened sinner. Nolleitas means 'I could will to avoid mortal sin, and obey God,' Nolitio 'I do will such avoidance.' Act Z is 'I am unwilling to do wrong because of my Creator's claim on my obedience,' but it is made simultaneously with act Y, 'I do what is wrong for the sake of the pleasure it affords.' Act Z is called a 'Velleitas' or 'Nolleitas', act Y a 'Volitio' or 'Nolitio.'

On the other hand you will allow that a man may have a nolitio one moment, and that the next an overpowering temptation may drive it out, and it may become only a nolleitas. I suppose you must — else, once a nolitio, always a nolitio.

Why then may not the cases mentioned by Recupitus p.54, be cases of a nolitio becoming a nolleitas or less, i.e. of a nolitio *going*?[1]

If so, you cannot argue from any case, any number of cases, in which the *will seems weak* at the last, that dying men have commonly only nolleitas — for the phenomenon of weakness and lapse is equally solvible [sic] by the hypothesis of a nolitio not lasting, as a nolleitas being from first to last. Therefore, giving up the *phenomena of deathbeds*, you must fall back on your general antecedent abstract principle, 'qualis vita, finis ita.'

This principle is argued out *merely from antecedent probabilities*. On the other hand, why may I not allege the *circumstances* of the fact of a man knowing that he is dying, as likely to *throw him* into a state of mind he never had before? 'Qualis vita, finis ita.' i.e. it is true of vita and finis under the *same circumstances*; I mean in the case of a person not *knowing* he was dying. But take a man with clear firm faith, an absolute belief that hell is opening upon him, and a vision, not simply of a priest with a stole and the last sacraments, but of a judgment seat, why should not his nolleitas, habitual up to that moment, be suddenly raised and transformed into a nolitio? Which is not proved not to be a nolitio, because, being a great strain to his mind, it can only last a short time — And if the priest finds him thus rightly disposed, why may not the grace of absolution and the other Sacraments leave him in that abiding state of grace that death may find him justified?

Excuse my imperfect wording of my meaning, as well as whatever there is of confusion in my meaning itself.

Another, though less important difficulty, occurs to me as regards your view of the donum perseverantiae. I had been accustomed to view it in a way more compatible with that doctrine of deathbed repentance which you oppose. You know *I* do not feel the intellectual and moral difficulty of predestination which you do — and it would not strike my imagination, or be a trial to my faith, to find good men falling away (awful as it is) and bad men pardoned, on their deathbed. Now what is commonly said about the donum perseverantiae has led me to say to myself 'After all you do, you are simply in the hands of God; after all, you are thrown upon simple prayer, not on merit — God has not *promised* to save you, *whatever* fair show you may have —' You, however, from your absolute taking of 'Qualis vita, finis ita,' as a principle, are led to hold that the donum perseverantiae may, (practically,) be reduced to law, and become the manageable result of certain assignable antecedents. You say: 'We shall next year study the CONDITIONS on which we may SECURE the "magnum perseverantiae donum"' — the principal of course being prayer.

---

[1] These were cases of people subjected to strong temptation just before death, and apparently succumbing.

We shall see that it is both EASY to comply with these conditions, and also EASY to have a MOST WELL FOUNDED AND CONSOLING CONFIDENCE that we *do* comply with them.' p.69.

This is delightful doctrine — but is it not rather startling? Must we not all humble ourselves under the mighty hand of God, more than this leads us to do? Must we not all recollect that we were lost every one of us, when God finds us, and that He may do what He will with us?

Ever yrs affectly John H Newman

TO CHARLES BIANCONI

[[Copy]] ⌐*Private*

Dublin July 8. 1857

My dear Mr Bianconi

I forgot to give you our Prospectus just now — and therefore I send it you by post.

While I am writing, I will put on paper what I said to you just now, as the matter, which you introduced, was of a serious and delicate nature.

I hold it to be absolutely necessary for the welfare of the University, that there should be a committee of Finance, to register and apply the collections, under the Bishops; with which committee, and not with their Lordships, the Rector should transact business.

On the other hand, as to any ecclesiastical questions about an Apostolic Legate, the power of the Archbishop etc — it would ill become me, a foreigner and a guest of the country, who have been most kindly and honorably received by all parties, to interfere.[1]

I am My dear Mr Bianconi

Sincerely Yours John H Newman

Charles Bianconi Esqr[1]

TO GILBERT BLOUNT

[8 July 1857]

My dear Sir,

I thank you for the Bank receipt of £100 placed to my deposit account in the London Joint Stock Bank, as a donation from the late Mr Canning through your Father to the Catholic University of Ireland; and I return the counterfoil filled in, as you wish.[2]

---

[1] Newman made a note of his reply on 18 July to a letter, perhaps from Bianconi, 'answered that I was very sorry that there was no "committee of management," of which he spoke; that I had long desired it. I hoped it would soon be appointed, but that there was no one to lay his case before J H N'

Cullen was appointed perpetual Apostolic Delegate for Ireland in March 1852.

[2] See letters of 13 and 29 June to Michael Blount. Gilbert was his son.

I inclose a receipt, hoping I have used the right stamp, I send a copy of the receipt to our Father Treasurer at the Oratory, Birmingham, who will place it among the papers of the Congregation.[1]

May I ask for the late Mr Canning's Christian name and place of residence?[2]

I am &c J H N

Gilbert Blount Esqr

TO ARCHBISHOP CULLEN

Catholic University, Dublin.   Office of the Secretary
87 Stephen's Green, South,   July 8 1857

My dear Lord,

In anticipation of the end of the Session and the dispersion of the Professors of the University I beg to ask the kindness of your signing the inclosed Draft for £1600 for the Salaries etc. due for the quarter ending on August 1 next.

The sum of £1600 is made up as follows

¼ of £5000 for the Faculties of Philosophy Medicine and Science	1250
¼ of £200 [sic] interest of University Fund	300
Sum paid short of £1550 in the foregoing Quarter viz. 1500 instead of 1550	50
	£1600

I beg to present to your Grace and to the other Archbishops — for the Professorship of Architecture J. J. Mac Carthy, for the Professorship of English Literature T. Arnold Esq.

---

[1] Newman's letter of 8 July to the Father Treasurer, Nicholas Darnell, repeats what is here said. Newman sent a similar letter to the Father Sacristan, William Neville,

'July 8. 1857

Dear Fr Sacristan

I wish you to be so good as to provide Masses to the amount of £5 a year till further notice for the soul of   Canning Esqr of   for the payment of which I will be responsible.

The interest (£5) on the principal begins from this day—but it will not be actually paid, I suppose, for half a year

Yrs affly J H Newman praep.

The Revd Fr Sacristan

[2] Gilbert Blount replied on 9 July, 'Mr Canning's christian names were Edward Joseph, and his last place of residence 15 Cunningham Place St John's Wood Lon. He was the last in the male line of the Cannings of Foxcote in Warwickshire, but did not possess the place or property.'

Neither of these appointments involve any additional expense to the University.

I am, My dear Lord, Your Grace's faithful Servt in Xt

John H Newman of the Oratory

July 10[1]

TO MRS HOPE-SCOTT

6 Harcourt Street Dublin July 8. 1857

My dear Mrs Hope Scott

It is very kind your writing to me. I have congratulated with you and Jim with all my heart, since I heard the good news. It struck me, as well as your Protestant friends, that Sir Walter Michael was to turn out a conjuror.[2] I missed your husband in London lately to my great regret. It is wonderful what work he does — but I wish it tried him less.

The Henry Kerrs, I believe, are in London, so it is no use asking after them.

I *won't* forget Mary Monica, in spite of Walter, and send her as well as him my best love.[3]

I am, My dear Mrs Hope Scott Affectionately Yours in Xt

John H Newman of the Oratory

Mrs Hope Scott

TO AMBROSE ST JOHN

⌜July 8/57⌝

My dear A

⌜The inclosed letter, just come, has disconcerted me a great deal.[4] It is aimed *at you*. I don't like to disoblige the Campdens, if possible.

This struck me, whether it could be made to square with your plans to be there ten days — I mean to prepare the children for confirmation and to be present at the ceremony.⌝

Of course the confirmation is a mere *excuse* for getting out of us the whole two months — but still if we did as much as I said, we should be taking her at her word.

---

[1] This date and the conclusion of the letter are in Newman's hand, the rest being written by Scratton. Cullen returned the cheque signed, on 12 July, and said that the appointments could be arranged when the Archbishops met in Dublin on 21 July.

[2] Mrs Hope-Scott, granddaughter of Sir Walter Scott, wrote on 5 July to thank Newman for his congratulations of 5 June on the birth of her son, Walter Michael. She said, 'our Protestant friends conclude he is named after *the* Michael Scott,' the magician in *The Lay of the Last Minstrel*, canto II.

[3] Mary Monica, Mrs Hope-Scott's daughter, was born in 1852.

[4] A letter from Viscountess Campden, asking for Oratorians to stay at Campden House, Gloucestershire.

ˈAnother question is whether *Nicholas* would like to go for ten days or more — the two or three months is IMPOSSIBLE — [1] but I should like us to do something. Will you see what N. says — and let me know about yourself too. I can't read her rigmarole, and it cost (not me) four pence

Ever Yrs J H N

THURSDAY 9 JULY 1857   Stewart and his son to dinner

TO JOHN STANISLAS FLANAGAN

Dublin July 9/57

My dear S

Yesterday A. Bethell rehearsed a latin philosophic dispute — and though he did very fairly, did not do well enough for an exhibition. He talks of coming some time in the Vacation to Birmingham. I wish we could promise him practice in this line. Don't *you* dispute? did not Harry ecleped Ignatius learn it at Rome?

It struck me Ignace would like it — it might give him some spirit — and it would be a great thing both for I. and A. to practise speaking Latin.

Would it be possible to persuade H R's [Harry Ryder] friend up at Oscott — Dr M. [Meynell] who has lately come from Rome, to give us a few lessons.[1] The worst is that Augustus knows *his* part pretty well. It is the Moderator who has to learn.

Don't you think we might screw some philosophy in this way out of Henry, Austin, etc.

I want to have some talk with you about H.R. when I come back. I suppose you are letting him go on as usual now. If, by the time I come, he is just as impatient under the daily rule as before, what I have to say will come to be considered — I was talking to a person the other day, who had tried his vocation in a regular house. He is a religious good person, but broke down under the multitude of *little duties* one succeeding another, and each of which he aimed at doing perfectly. His health suffered, and I think he said he had not recovered yet. He is a very clever man, and not soft. Then, it struck me, whether we must not avoid, if possible, any thing of the kind.

Now what are a novice's duties between 10 AM and 5 PM? his duties, as such, are only a visit to the Blessed Sacrament and a quarter or half an hour's spiritual reading — is it not so? Now the *effect* is a great deal more, and perhaps affects the imagination, if you parcel out the time for him, and say from 10 to 11 Lecture, and 11 to 1 study 1 to 1½ visit and examen, 1½ to

---

[1] Charles Meynell (1828–82), was at the English College, Rome, from 1849 until 1856, when he came to Oscott as Professor of Philosophy. Newman consulted him during the writing of *A Grammar of Assent*.

$3\frac{1}{2}$ exercise, $3\frac{1}{2}$ to 4 spiritual reading — 4 to 5 time to himself — On the other hand, if you could say, Do what you will from 10 to 5, so that you make your visit and your reading, he would *do* precisely the same [as] in the other case, and would *seem* to be bound a great deal less — The utmost he could do, would be to throw off his visit and reading till towards 5 o'clock, and be lazy about exercise — so as to have a long swing of reading — Well, this would be an evil to meet, when it got excessive — But we will talk together. Any news of Victor?

Ever Yours affly John H Newman

P.S. Since writing the above your letter has come.

1. I know perfectly how painful H R is to you, without my needing to be told. Yet how can we help it?[1] His staying may be of use to A. Bethell. If you ask me, *I think you do too much with him.* You are looking to do too much with Crawley. I shall, not only *ease* your conscience, but *put it* on your conscience, i.e. your obedience, to *do less*. Give HR. *his head*, and see what comes of it.

2. I shall be ready for H Lynch after your hints.[2]

3. Victor had better remain.[3]

4. Doane was very affectionate to me personally, and said all that is contained in his letter to Robert. *I* recommended him to write to Robert for my portrait. I think the sight of me revived his prior feelings — still I think he at first viewed me differently.[4]

5 *See that my twopenny letter to Ambrose of this morning goes to him at once.* It is from Lady Campden.

6. I shall be back Monday or Tuesday week, July 20 or 21. I can't help thinking that, now that it comes to the point, the Archbishops don't like to write to the Oratory. Of course, if they like to write to me, or to tell someone else *from* them to write to me, in order that you may hear in that round about way, well and good. One is not stickling for forms — but some how or other the Oratory must be consulted. It cannot be denied they have great difficulties. They cannot choose Rector or Vice Rector without Dr McHale, and he won't act — so they either have to put off or to come to an open rupture with him. Then again I hear that, because no one knows the state of accounts, we are overdrawing frightfully at the Bank — and that we have been charged £200

---

[1] Flanagan wrote, on 8 July, of Ignatius Ryder, '. . . he *is* a wonderful trial to me. . . . I hope I do not show it, and that I am unvaryingly kind to him, and receive him with a cheerful countenance if he comes to my room a dozen times a day.' Flanagan was anxious, too, as to how he would cope with George Crawley, a convert and a priest, who wished to come to the Oratory as a novice.

[2] In his letter Flanagan gave advice concerning the request Newman dealt with in his letter of 10 July to Lynch.

[3] Flanagan's second novice, Victor Duke, was unwell and staying with his family at St Leonards. He returned on 14 July.

[4] In reply to Newman's letter of 4 July Flanagan said, 'I have no doubt whatever that your surmises about Doane are true. . . . I enclose a letter from Doane to Robert [Tillotson], which would seem to show that he (D) retains his feelings towards you personally.'

or £300 interest. I have again urged Dr Moriarty on Dr Dixon; and I really think he would do what no one else can do.[1] I never should be surprised at Propaganda being advised to put *every thing* into my hands, making be [me] absolute manager of the whole.

I sent back one of Ward's pamphlets yesterday to Bm. [Birmingham] I have written to Ward making two objections. His view is serious, important, and well argued — but I want some things explained.[2]

TO MISS HOLMES

6 Harcourt Street Dublin July 9. 1857

My dear Miss Holmes

I was thinking about writing to you this morning, when your letter came.[3] It always concerns me to find you in the sort of troubles which you mention in it. Every thing you have told me from time to time makes me agree with you in thinking that you have a good director, and that you have made an advance under him, though it is quite as certain that every now and then he distresses you and you distress him. He is, and what is more, you know him to be, a holy and a clever man. What will you get more any where than this? You pay the price of it in the occasional penances which I have alluded to — but we *must* suffer here, and it is very rare to find a man who has so many qualifications as your good priest. Some, whom you at first sight would prefer, have not the qualification of learning, and could not direct you, if you wished. Every good working priest must be 'narrow minded — ' as every lawyer, physician, or chemist, is narrowminded. To know your own business *well*, is, in this world, to know *nothing else*. This is the *rule*, depend on it — tho' we may *try* to make it otherwise. Those who are more philosophical, are unpractical — they talk, give unmeaning advice, get tired, get impatient, and throw up the matter. Your director may seem to you from time to time unjust, but he is patient, patient on the whole. He may seem to you harsh or stern, but he listens, desires, aims, labours to do you good. I know able men who are warm, pleasant, sanguine, full of promises, but *do-nothings* — every thing which looks so bright, suddenly vanishes in smoke.

For myself, my dear Miss Holmes, I have not the knowledge, the presence of mind, or the patience, for a director — and the only feeling I have on reading how you speak of me, is a feeling of satisfaction that, with such ideas, you are *praying* for me. For I am very weak and bad — and, though I am (thank God) very well, I am getting *old*. It is very affectionate in you being so distressed to think of it — but, if it makes you pray more earnestly for me, I shall gain by your pain.

God bless you, my dear Child, and believe me ever, Yours affectly in Xt

John H Newman of the Oratory

Miss Holmes

[1] Letter of 2 July.   [2] Letter of 6 July.   [3] Miss Holmes was still at Boulogne.

TO A. LISLE PHILLIPPS

6 Harcourt Street Dublin. July 9. 1857

My dear Mr Phillipps

I have read your letter, just received, with the greatest interest.[1] As also the Form of Devotion which I return.[2] Especially I am delighted to see the devotion expressed in it to our Lady — because it seems an encouragement to believe, not only that she *will* have, but that she *has* had, a part in the work.

The only thing that pains and disappoints me is that you say not a word of Pusey as having anything to do with the work — or of Isaac Williams — or of dear Keble. Is it possible that the first generation has had its vintage, and that the second gathering of grapes belongs altogether to a second? Oxford certainly seems almost without hope just now.[3]

Pray do not fail to let me know more. When it is prudent, I would get a Mass once a week from our Oratory at Edgbaston

Excuse haste & believe me Most sincerely Yours in Xt

John H Newman of the Oratory

A. L. Phillipps Esqr.

TO EDWARD CASWALL

July 10/57

My dear Edward

Now that the High and 12 o'clock Masses may be said by one Priest, would it not be possible to have the *School mass* in the Oratory, which was only omitted for want of Priests enough. I mean a mass which *all the children* Sunday and week day, boys and girls, might attend

Ever Yrs J H N

P.S.   I declare I think they will not continue me as Rector. Of course I

[1] Phillipps on 7 July thanked Newman for his letter of 4 July, and accepted the statements in it about individual conversions. Phillipps maintained, nonetheless, that the letter he had received from Barnabò allowed a Catholic to encourage the desire for corporate reunion among Anglicans. Phillipps went on to recount the evidence he had found in London of the spread of Catholic ideas and practices in the Church of England. He described the meeting he had attended, 'It was a large gathering, of course strictly private, all the Clergy present belonged to the Metropolis, and all wore the Roman collar: there were also some distinguished laymen: the plan of action I have already said I cannot divulge, but I was by no means prepared, tho' I had expected a great deal, to find the whole body so thoroughly Catholic in their belief . . .'

[2] This was being circulated among the Anglicans with whom Phillipps was in contact.

[3] Newman's impressions were correct. See H. R. T. Brandreth, *Dr. Lee of Lambeth*, pp. 86–9, 'The older generation was mainly alarmed by the *Union Newspaper*.' On 23 July Phillipps wrote to Newman that he had met a friend of Isaac Williams's, who reported that the latter 'did not approve of the Romanizing tendencies of "the Union," or of the movement of TOTAL surrender.'

88

must have a voice in the appointment of Vice Rector, if he is to represent me in my absence. Thus I am asking *two* things. 1. non-residence. 2 appointment of Vice Rector. To ask one of these is trial enough of their forebearence — but to ask both! Rome may do it, but they won't. *Will you let Fr Ambrose have the inclosed.*

TO HENRY J. LYNCH

6, Harcourt St Dublin July 10th 1857

My dear Mr Lynch

I assure you I fully feel the force of the considerations you urge on me in your letter just received and gladly would I show practically my sense of the peculiar deference and respect with which any communication from you on the subject of Rathtarman ought to be received.[1]

On the other hand you must be so kind as to recollect that it is now ecclesiastical property.

It is in the eye of the Church simply the Pope's property, and no one else's. — I believe he has the abstract power without assigning a word of reason of taking it from us to-morrow, and giving it to the Redemptorists, Jesuits, Vincentians or any other body. — So much in matter of fact. — Moreover, in a strictly Catholic Country we should not have the *power* of selling it; as it is whatever power we exercise over it is only from custom.

Nor does the circumstance that this stringent law is suspended in these Countries exempt us from its moral obligation. — We are Trustees of property which the Church would if she could subject to it. — And at any rate I suppose the Pope might appoint a Visitor at any time to report how we managed the property accidentally left in our hands and deal with us accordingly.[2]

I say all this to show that we cannot simply direct our conduct to personal feelings towards yourself, but as being the holders or tenants of property which belongs to a higher power. — I am not prepared to say that a restoration of property to a family to whom it had belonged would not be a legitimate proceeding on our part provided the Church did not suffer by it but in order

[1] This refers to the Rathtarman estate in County Sligo, which the Oratorians had purchased from Henry Lynch in 1852. It originally belonged to the Flanagan family, into which Lynch's father had married. Lynch now wanted to buy it back, so that it might return to the family and give him political influence, but he had no money, and could only repurchase the property by heavily mortgaging it. As Stanislas Flanagan pointed out to Newman in his letter of 8 July, this meant that it would eventually fall into the hands of the mortgagee, and be lost to the family entirely. In 1861 it was sold to Stanislas's cousin, Stephen Woulfe Flanagan, and Henry Lynch's consequent recriminations were to cause embarrassment to the Oratorians in 1866–7.

[2] These remarks of Newman, writing to a friend, were incautious. In view of them, it was later suggested that the sale of Rathtarman to the Oratorians could be set aside under the Mortmain Act. See letter of 23 Oct. 1867 to W. Williams.

to be thus legitimate and justifiable it must be a *bona fide* restoration with a certainty of its being final. —

I am led to say this by a startling hint you threw out 'that the purchase money might be left as a mortgage on the property on interest'. — I know very little of business matters, but the notion of *our still* having power over the property seems simply inconsistent with such an honorable surrender of it to you as the respresentative of former proprietors as would be satisfactory to our feelings. — We should not be respectful towards yourself in parting with it to you on such terms and the very circumstance you suggest them seems to imply a great difference between our respective views on the subject. —

Excuse me if I am writing under a confusion of ideas as well as in great frankness but I cannot help looking at you not only in your own person but as a representative of the family [there would be] no respect if I pretended to give up to them with one hand what with the other I was forcing them to mortgage.

I am sure you will give me credit for every friendly and cordial feeling in thus stating to you honestly what has struck me on the perusal of your letter.

I am, my dear Mr Lynch most sincerely Yours

John H Newman of the Oratory

SATURDAY 11 JULY 1857   Robertson to dinner

SUNDAY 12 JULY   Renouf went for good   very hot again

MONDAY 13 JULY   Ornsby and Scott to dinner   Fr Guerritore of the Naples Oratory came down to Birmingham.

TO MISS M. R. GIBERNE

6 Harcourt Street Dublin July 13. 1857

My dear Miss Giberne

I have just got your letter, and learn you are in England, which I did not know nor hear of. You wrote to me from Rome to say that you thought of coming; but for that very reason I could not answer your letter. I shall be at Edgbaston at the Assumption and shall be rejoiced to see you.

You don't say how your leg is — or how you are in health. Where were you our very hot week?

I have not seen Grace since she was 3 or 4 years old.[1]

Ever Yours affly in Xt   John H Newman of the Oratory

Miss Giberne

[1] Newman did not see Grace Mozley, the daughter of his sister Harriett until July 1890, when she came to visit him a few days before he died. *Trevor*, II, pp. 643-4.

6, Harcourt Street, Dublin July 13th 1857

My dear Mr Lynch

Thank you for your explanation on the subject of the mortgage.

I think we certainly should have a great difficulty in negotiating a sale of Rathtarman to you unless we had the certainty it would become bona fide yours without any incumbrance. — We should not gain our object else. — You will kindly understand my reason for saying so from my former letter[1]

I am, my dear Mr Lynch, Sincerely yours, John H Newman

TO A. LISLE PHILLIPPS

6 Harcourt Street Dublin. July 13. 1857.

My dear Mr Phillipps,

I am extremely obliged to you for your information — and shall destroy your letter, as you wish me, when I have read it once or twice again.[2]

On second thoughts, perhaps the time is not come for the Oratory Mass. I should be led, without knowing it, to let out something — but I think I can get you one certainly, whenever things are a little more known.

I am very anxious, lest the people at Rome should throw back and disappoint your friends. I know the tone of Propaganda is, on principle, very different to priests and laymen, to laymen and Protestants — but still, they know so little of the English character, and have so little tact, (as much as I should have in dealing with the Sepoys,) that they may give great offence, as soon as ever they emerge out of the vague terms of courtesy and kindness which Christian charity will elicit from them at the outset. I doubt not, Fr Pagani, as knowing England, will have his eyes about him here.[3]

Then again, there is one thing which, I suppose, the Church by her principles cannot concede — Every Anglican clergyman who comes over (even if the marriage of priests was allowed) would have to *go through* the form of Ordination — merely because the Church goes by what is *safest* in the Sacraments. However, that the movement will end in the coming over of many individuals, who set about it with larger ideas, I trust there is no reason

---

[1] Lynch renewed his request in May 1859.

[2] This letter evidently contained further information about plans for corporate reunion.

[3] John Baptist Pagani, the Rosminian, who came to England in 1838, had become the General of his Order at Rome in 1855. In the summer of 1857 he was in England and heard of Phillipps's projects for corporate reunion. The latter wrote to Newman on 23 July, 'when I told him that we wanted an agent in Rome . . . through whom the Anglican Bishops might communicate with the Holy See . . .' he 'most generously and enthusiastically offered his services for the blessed work.'

at all to doubt. And even one soul is worth 'Sweeping the house' for — I conjecture.[1]

    Most sincerely Yrs in Xt John H Newman of the Oratory

A.L. Phillipps Esqr

TO AMBROSE ST JOHN

            ⌜6 Harcourt Street July 14/57⌝

My dear Ambrose

 ⌜I hear a good account of you. I hope truly. I long to see you, and am getting somewhat melancholy, which is very ungrateful.

 In truth, I get fidgetted from the notion that people are at work against us, if not voluntarily and intentionally, at least in their own feelings.[2] Did Henry Wilberforce ask you to go with him to Boffin Island? he goes in a few days with all his family. It would have been just the thing for you; but he takes Fr Ballard as his chaplain. Arthur will be with them.[3] Fr B. passed through today, but did not say a word of his intention of joining the Wilberforces.[4] On the other hand Mrs W. writes to Scratton to take Arthur in for a night, and does not say a word to me, though I shall have an empty house, and she says she wants room for the rest of them. I think HW took a disgust to Bm [[Birmingham]]. You recollect how Fr Faber wished *me* to go to London, and leave all of you in Bm[[!]]⌝ and *prophesied* I *should* go to London.[5] I think he has said to others, as to the Bowdens, and Ws [Wilberforces], that nothing can be done at Bm — that I am thrown away etc. ⌜Then again H.W took a disgust to (many of) the Bm Fathers — he spoke against Penny and Fr Frederic — he spoke against Austin — Fr Stanislas he liked. Then again I think that it is given out in whispers that I, that we, 'cannot manage young men,' and therefore never shall have novices.⌝

 I am *made* suspicious — another thing is this. A. Bethell said, on my proposing it some time ago, that he should like very much to come some part of this vacation to Edgbaston. His brother, Harry, took it for granted. It was settled that it was to be October. I had occasion to write to his Mother (a fortnight back) and said that A. had told me his wish for the Oratory — said I hoped it would be God's will — that I should look on him as filling up the

---

[1] *St Luke*, 15: 8.

[2] [[In truth I have the notion that people, if not intentionally, yet in their own feelings, are at work against us.]]

[3] Arthur, Henry Wilberforce's eldest son, was studying for the priesthood at Ushaw. Fr Ballard was an Oratorian from London, but apparently stayed for only a few days with the Wilberforces. An invitation to St John, to accompany them, was on its way when Newman wrote. St John, who had recovered his health at Rednal declined. See letter of 30 July to Wilberforce.

[4] [[Fr Ballard passed through this place today—he would not dine with me, and said not a word of his joining the Wilberforces.]]

[5] Cf. the correspondence at the end of March 1849.

place of Fr Joseph — and hoped I might ask her to pray that it may be brought about. My letter for other reasons required an answer — but she has never answered me. Now he comes to me tonight to take leave, and says that 'his plans are quite uncertain for the Vacation,' on my speaking of his coming to us in October. This may be all accident, I know, but it depresses me.

Ever Yrs affly John H Newman

ᴦP.S.   July 15/57 As to what I wrote about above, one special cause why it distresses me is that I put it down to my own sins, as being a bad Superior of the Oratory — however, it is intended as guidance as well as penance, and I make the following remarks as to the course which it suggests to us.

I almost give up, or am willing to give up in thought, any connection we may have had rising out of our antecedents, which ought to bring novices to Birmingham.[1] Practically it is likely to prove worthless. ᴦAll the world goes to London — to know people up and down the world, is to know people in London.[1] That is Fr Faber's position — and he is, as they say, master of the situation. I knew it, when I let him go there — I refused it myself, because it is not my line [[to be in London]]. I never have liked publicity, and could not do justice to it.[2] I should have been in a most false position. Providence did not mean it [[for me]] — but it follows that my whole Oxford connexion, and whatever comes through it, and again all the interest I might have excited by my former works [[and history]], goes to London, not to Bm, and so to [[the Brompton House and]] Fr Faber. All he has not himself, and wished to have, is [[the prestige of]] my *name*. As long as he can make his Oratory looked on as mine, he has all from me he wishes [[to have]]. He inculcates this [[by what he says to others]]. C. Bowden wrote to me in the autumn that 'his wish to join the London Oratory was a wish *to be near me* — ' This is what is inculcated — [3] When they pressed me to go to London seven years ago, Fr Antony said in his [[off hand]] way in answer to my objections 'O, what we think you would do, is to sit in a library with books before you, and then we should [[be able to]] say 'Father Newman' to people who came in, and should bring people to see you.'[4] [[For this reason]] I never should be surprised [[even now,]] if they put up my portrait in a conspicuous place [[in their house]] at Brompton — the guest room — and thus would have a double advantage, would show gratitude and forbearance, and would use my name.[5] All this, you see, shows that I must not allow myself *of my own act*, to be

---

[1] [[to know people up and down the country is to know a metropolitan circle.]]
[2] [[to a situation which involved and called for it.]]
[3] [[This is what had been set before him as his inducement.]] See letter of 17 Oct. 1856 to Charles Bowden.
[4] Cf. Hutchison's letter to Newman at the end of March 1849: 'Is it however quite certain that you would have the quiet and freedom from being bored which you would require for the "literary line" in the helter-skelter racketty house at Birmingham[?]. It was only last night that F. Wilfrid was saying that you ought to be in London in a room with books up to the ceiling all round, where you could be reading and where people could come and see you.'
[5] [[and of availing themselves of my name.]]

mixed up in people's minds with them. This, however, is a digression — what I mean is, that we must dismiss the prospect of novices arising out of the connections of the past. Mrs Bethell, when she sent her sons here, said 'she hoped her dream of years had been fulfilled, to bring them near me.' It will be strange, but it must not surprise us, if this, as other dreams, flits away and has no accomplishment.

There is another reason. To the rising generation itself, to the sons of those who knew or read me 15 or 20 years ago, I am a character of history — they know nothing of me;[1] they have heard my name, and nothing more — they have no associations with it. Some time ago Miss Bathurst expostulated with some one [[some youth]] who was going as a novice to the London Oratory 'how is is possible,' she asked, 'you don't go to Bm?' I should think he was more astonished than she, at her question.[2] I made influence at Oxford by my Parochial Sermons — they are not only Protestant but simply unknown, unheard of by the young generation. Fr Faber's books are to it, just what those sermons were to the foregoing, and do the same work of creating influence.[3]

Here then are *two natural* reasons in the *course of things*, they show it is exceedingly improbable that *I* shall do any thing for the Bm Oratory in bringing novices, (1. my own connexion in the country, or the old generation, congregating in *London*, and 2. the young generation running after Fr *Faber*'s writings) — They arise from the natural course of things — not to be lamented — not to discourage us — not any punishment for any thing we have done or not done. And to this must be added the unpopularity of Bm as a site, far worse than Manchester or Liverpool.[4]

What *does* annoy me, over and above the apprehension that I am out of favor with St Philip, is the spirit of scheming, encroachment, unfairness, and contempt which some of our London friends have shown and show.[5]

But now, what is the lesson — why, I cannot help looking *there*, most unlikely and umpromising as it seems, whither I have been drawn, as you know, from a very different motive — to the wealthy Protestants about us. It is plain, the Oratory should in the main be supplied from its own neighbourhood.[16] The Pope has sent us to the lautiores, opulentiores etc

[1] [[or read what I wrote fifteen or twenty years ago. I am a mere page of history. I do not live to them; they know nothing of me]]

[2] [[I think he was more astonished at her question than she at his act.]]

[3] [[It was at Oxford, and by my Parochial Sermons that I had influence; all that is past: Fr Faber takes my place, and is gaining influence by his Catholic books.]]

[4] [[Here then are two natural causes in the course of things which serve to show that *I* shall do nothing for my Oratory in bringing novices to it; the old generation congregates in London not in Birmingham—and the new generation gravitates to Fr Faber. They are not to be lamented—nor must they discourage us. We must take facts as they are. I ought to have added the unpopularity of Birmingham socially, compared with Manchester or Liverpool.]]

[5] [[which some of our good friends have evidenced and evidence.]]

[6] [[I do think we are bound to make an attempt on the Protestants around us. I wish I knew how to do it. An Oratory should be in the main supplied from its own neighbourhood.]] Newman proceeds to quote words from the Brief of Pius IX in 1847, empowering him to set up the English Oratory.

These are *ours*. 'Opulentiores.' I do think we are bound to make an attack on them.

I wish I knew how to do it — ⌐you know from the time we came up to Edgbaston, I have wished to attack them. Last year, I talked, in anticipation of my coming back of having a lecture every Sunday at 4 in the Oratory. I wonder what the effect would be of this persevered in for years. The immediate difficulty is, that you are all so hard up, and require relief from me rather than an addition, on my part, to the work of the Oratory. The intention I have given to the Mass you say for me, is 'my coming back — ' to Fr Nicholas's 'our making an impression on the rich people about us — '⌐ You see I have been looking one way some time.

⌐On the other hand, my mind does require rest.⌐

Ever Yrs affly J H N

WEDNESDAY 15 JULY 1857 Terminal examinations began. Archbishop gave away medical prizes. Augustus Bethell, and Charles de la Pasture went. Council held.

TO HENRY WILBERFORCE

6 Harcourt St ⌐July 15/57⌐

My dear H,

⌐My house will be empty in a day or two, except by the Servants.⌐ I shall go, if all is well, on next Saturday night.

⌐Come with bag and baggage and take possession — upstairs and downstairs — and do the same going back.

At the end of August the British Association takes possession of it. In September Renouf and his Bride⌐

Ever Yrs affly J H N

THURSDAY 16 JULY 1857 Examinations 2 de Lignes, Zamoyski, Frazer, White went. Scott went.

TO JOHN STANISLAS FLANAGAN

Dublin July 16. 1857

My dear S

I have just received your memorandum, which I return.[1]

You all know how false such charges are. I only hope that it will lead you all, as feeling it, to give me some hearty prayers.

[1] In a letter of 15 July Flanagan said 'I write now simply to enclose you a memorandum of a conversation which took place yesterday between Fr Enrico Guerratore of the Naples

My own indolence, as well as my feeling of what St Philip would have done in his own case, leads me to wish, or rather to resolve, to do nothing.

But I do not know that we have a right, as a matter of truth and falsehood, to hear a thing said which we know to be false and not protest against it at once. But this concerns you, not me.

If you ask me what I think you should do, it would be this — for the Fathers to meet at once, and to address a joint letter to the Secretary of the London House, quoting the Naples Father's words, and asking the *fact* whether the London House said what he reports, and has written to foreign Oratories to say it.[1] This cannot be done at a *formal* meeting, I being away, and therefore must not be written by the Secretary, but I suppose by Ambrose in the name of the Fathers assembled.

On the answer coming from the Secretary of the London House, it will either be yes, no, or (which is more likely) with distinctions. However, you will be able to deny what they say, whatever it is, if it is any thing (broadly to the one fact about unsurping *power* etc). And so I should think you ought to meet again, and answer it in a few words.

There I should leave the matter, not going into the controversy. It would be a matter of consideration, whether the correspondence should not then be sent round to the principal foreign Oratories.

My only fear is that their answer should be a very long one; taking up many little bits, and misrepresenting them — which would require a separate answer. *But I think you should keep yourself to the the great one point whether I wished to interfer with their independence.* And if they were *long*, you would not send round the correspondence but merely *one* letter of your own to the Foreign Oratories, if you wrote at all.

This is what strikes me. The sooner we can get it off our hands the better

Ever Yrs affly J H N

P.S.   On second thoughts, tho' it is not a thing you need determine at once. I think you *need not* send round to foreign Oratories at all — and that it will be enough to protest at home.[2]

FRIDAY 17 JULY 1857   Examinations

Oratory and Fr Ambrose. Fr A. came to my room a few moments after leaving Fr G. and I wrote down the notes which I now send—It is most amazing how the Londoners could have been guilty of such misrepresentation, not to give a worse name to it.'
[1] This refers to the circular letter sent by the London Oratorians to the Italian Oratories on 28 Dec. 1855. See note to diary for that day.
[2] The Birmingham Oratorians decided to wait until Newman's return, when he would see Fr. Guerritore himself.

TO PATRICK LEAHY, ARCHBISHOP OF CASHEL

July 17 [1857]

My dear Lord

I beg to present to your Grace and the other Archbishops, according to the provisions of the Synodal meeting of 1854, and the directions of Propaganda, J.J. MacCarthy Esqr the celebrated Architect for the Professorship of Architecture in the University, and Thomas Arnold Esqr, late of University College, Oxford, for that of English Literature.

Their appointments involve no increased expense to the University.

I am obliged to go to Birmingham at once to meet Fr Guerratore, of the Naples Oratory, on important matters. He had intended leaving England before this and stays over Sunday in order to see me.[1]

I am &c J H N

SATURDAY 18 JULY 1857 Examinations for Scholarship and Inceptorship. I went in evening to Bm [Birmingham] Penny went in morning.

TO ARCHBISHOP CULLEN

6 Harcourt Street July 18. 1857

My dear Lord,

Father Guerratore, of the Naples Oratory, is waiting for me at Birmingham. He was to have left before this; but has been prevailed on to stop over tomorrow, having been there nearly a week already, in order to see me on important matters.

This obliges me to leave Dublin without delay.[2]

I am, My dear Lord, Your Grace's faithful Servt in Xt

John H Newman of the Oratory

His Grace The Archbp of Dublin

[1] Cullen had written on 12 July, 'I expect that the Archbishop of Cashel and the other archbishops will be in town before the 21st of this month, when we can arrange with you about the appointment of the new professors.' The Archbishops confirmed the two appointments at a meeting on 21 Oct. 1857.

[2] This letter crossed one of the same day from Cullen, 'Will you do me the favour of dining with me on Tuesday next, at a quarter to 6 o'clock . . .'

TO JOSEPH DIXON, ARCHBISHOP OF ARMAGH

6 Harcourt Street Dublin ⌐July 18. 1857⌐

My dear Lord,

I acknowledge with many thanks the receipt of your signature to the cheque — and your consent to Mr McCarthy's appointment.

⌐I am obliged to go to Birmingham to-night⌐, in order to catch Fr Guerratore, of the Naples Oratory, who is stopping over tomorrow in order to see me on important matters. I did not hear of the Archbishops wishing for me here, till after he arrived at Bm. ⌐However, I do not think my remaining in Dublin would have been desirable⌐ — though I had not had this engagement — ⌐for at present my hands are tied. My Congregation has called me to Birmingham for good — and, this being the case, I could not have had any conversation with their Graces on the future of the University, had they honored me with proposing it, without compromising my duties to the Oratory.

Dr Leahy proposed six weeks or two months ago to write to the Oratory on the subject. That certainly would have set me free to speak — but I dare say very good reasons have occurred for not doing so.⌐

J H N

TO EDMUND O'REILLY, S.J.

July 18/57

My dear Fr O'Reilly

I inclose the list of University Preachers, which the Archbishop sanctioned in 1856.

I have thought best at once to put in to your and Dr Forde's hands, as representing the Faculty of Theology, the appointment of Preachers for the ensuing Session. The first sermon will be upon Sunday November 8.

I shall be sure to approve of any arrangements which you make. I suppose the Preachers will be glad to have as early a notice as possible

Yrs most sincerely J H N

SUNDAY 19 JULY 1857   arrived in Bm [Birmingham] for Mass.   Ambrose came in from Rednall   had talk with Fr Guerritore.

MONDAY 20 JULY   Fr Guerritore went.   Harry [Bethell] came

TUESDAY 21 JULY   Harry went.   I went over to Rednall with Ambrose, and then back.

WEDNESDAY 22 JULY   2nd box of books having come, began to put room to rights.

THURSDAY 23 JULY   went into retreat — letters came to Oratory from the Irish Archbishops about my continuing Rector.

SATURDAY 25 JULY   W H Scott came

SUNDAY 26 JULY   Stokes in Bm; called.

TO WILLIAM DODSWORTH

The Oratory, Birmingham July 26. 1857.

My dear Dodsworth,

I thank you very much for your £5 for the University. The accounts have been very badly kept — and I will insist, as a condition of my still having to do with it, on a better, or rather, *some*, management.[1] There should be an English Receiver. I am rather desirous of collecting for some definite English purpose. What I aim at is the establishment of an English Collegiate House — and I wish you would let your £5 go towards it. *My* house is at present the English House — and I have Oxford men! don't be jealous, because it is not Cambridge as Dean and Tutor — but I want to put this on a permanent footing. What I should like to do would be to take a good house on lease, and stock it with Dean and Tutor. Then whether it was full or not would not much matter — for the pension of each inmate would be sufficient for his cost.

At present, as is the case in all establishments of the kind, the difficulty is the setting off. Had it not been for my income as Rector, I should have been seriously in debt in my Housekeeping, tho' I take £100 a year, from the house never having been quite full, and at times or rather at first, half empty. But, could I once establish a House as I propose, every thing must go well. It would be an independent body, whoever was Rector — tho' he has jurisdiction to a certain extent over all the Houses. It would have good tuition provided at home — and its students would have the run of the University Lectures. I venture to say that no where else are they likely to have better. Our Professors in Letters are at once able and zealous; and our Medical and Science Schools are likely to be the first in Dublin.

You kindly speak of your confidence in me with reference to the University, but, if you knew the Staff of Professors and the Statutes you would understand that all that is wanted for its success (under heaven) is time and to be let alone — and, as it is, it would be a very difficult task for anyone external to it, who attempted *not* to let it alone. Moreover the Holy See is most eager for its success and stimulates the Bishops in every way.

Ever since you have been in England, I have tried to find your whereabouts — and, when in London the other day for a few hours, a rare event, I meditated a call, but drew back, thinking, (what turned out to be the case) that you would not be at home, but at the Oath Meeting.[2]

---

[1] When sending his donation on 24 July Dodsworth wrote, 'It being a Procurator's rather than a Rector's business, I would not have troubled you with it, but that after some search and enquiry in London, I could not find any one authorised to receive it.'

[2] Newman was in London on 16 June, the day on which a meeting was held at the Stafford Club, to protest against the Oaths Bill. This proposed a new oath of allegiance, which while omitting what was repugnant to Jews and other classes of British subjects, retained phrases obnoxious to Catholics. The Bill was thrown out in July, on its second reading in the House of Lords.

So Wilberforce has sent you my criticism, which I thought was made on *him*, when I sent it.[1] There is a vast deal of movement among the Anglicans just now — they cling to points which never can be granted, but to tell them so, will either throw them back, or, if they become Catholics, indispose them towards their faithful monitors. This was the reason for what I said to H.W.

I should rejoice to see you, and wish any thing brought you this way — we have oceans of room, if you want a bed suddenly.

Ever Yrs affly in Xt   John H. Newman of the Oratory

W. Dodsworth Esqr

MONDAY 27 JULY 1857   Frederic Godwin went to Dublin about now —

TO D. D. LISSONI

The Oratory Birmingham July 27. 1857

Sir,

I was not neglectful of your first letter, and now beg to acknowledge both it and your second.

I have to thank you also for a copy of my 'Loss and Gain' translated — which I looked into with much interest.[2]

I did not write to you as wishing to send you an opinion worth having on the manner in which the Tale is translated. It is *a very difficult* book to translate.

I am much flattered by your wishing to translate other works of mine. I will gladly give any authorisation which you require, if it comes to me through the good Fathers of Charity, the disciples of Father Rosmini.

Do you know Father Caccia, who is a Milanese, and lives in England? I will attend to any thing which comes through him.[3]

I am, Sir Your obedient Servant

John H Newman of the Oratory

Al Signor Il Signor D.D. Lissoni

[1] Newman had evidently written to Henry Wilberforce criticising his hostile attitude in the *Weekly Register* to the *Union* periodical, with its hopes of corporate reunion. Dodsworth wrote to Newman on 24 July, 'You think it impolite to attack the *Union*. I also have doubts, but some of my old friends are inclined to shelter themselves under their sham, and one is apt to think more of old friends than of the *public at large*. It is certainly a curious phenomenon in the Establishment that such a thing can find support there, and makes one hopeful that there are yet many to come.'

[2] This was a copy of the second edition of *Perdita e Guadagno ovvero Storia di un Convertito*, Milan 1857. In the first edition *L. G.* was described as translated by A. S., so that Lissoni was presumably the publisher. The first edition was published by the Stabilimento Volpati, and the second by its successor, Natale Battezzati.

[3] Charles Caccia (1807–82), ordained priest in 1830, parish priest of San Satiro at Milan from 1841, joined the Rosminians in 1850, and knew Rosmini intimately. He came to England in 1851, and from 1857 until 1865 was at Market Weighton. In 1872 he became General of the Rosminians.

TO THOMAS FLANAGAN

The Oratory, Birmingham, July 28, 1857.

My dear Mr. Flanagan,[1]

My copies of your new History came to me last evening, and I doubt not I shall derive much instruction and pleasure from its perusal.[2] However, I cannot help writing at once to thank you for what, on cutting open some of its pages, I find you say of myself. While the narrative preserves the sustained tone proper to history, and is written with due dignity and gravity, it is impossible not to discern in it a feeling of personal kindness towards me — and I hope I may take it as a pledge that you do not forget me and all of us here in your good prayers, (as I assure you I wish to remember you) that we may do our own work, which God has given us, in our day and in our place.

I had already promised a copy of your volumes to a French Priest, who is going to write some account of religion in England, and they shall go to him at once.[3]

As I am writing, I am tempted to add, what I assure you is in no sense the *cause* of my writing, that there is just one point in your chapter which requires a remark. It is a very minute one, and relates to just one half sentence.[4] I think it was Mr. Oakeley's view, that he might 'profess all Roman doctrine' in the Church of England, or at least 'hold it' — and consequently that the 39 Articles allowed of it. I never took this view. I knew that they bound me in various ways to oppose the Roman doctrines, and my conscience *approved* of this opposition — I mean, I thought ill of various tenets and principles of the Roman Church. Accordingly in 1841, after Number 90, in a letter which the Bishop of Oxford required of me, I wrote with great violence against the doctrines received at Rome and in her communion; with violence, but if I may so say, not violently — I mean, I spoke what I internally felt, and what I was called by my Bishop to say, but what (from my love of the Roman Church) I would not have said *then*, (though I had said worse things in years past,) unless it had been extorted from me by what I held to be then competent authority, — and I called it in that letter a 'confession,' as if I could not help saying it before such a tribunal. I recollect saying to Dr. Manning at the time, '*I* can't help it — the Bishop asks me — *I* don't wish to speak against

---

[1] This letter was first published by William Neville at the beginning of the first popular edition of *Apo.*, London 1904. From then onwards it began to be inserted at the end of the uniform edition of *Apo.*

[2] Thomas Flanagan, *A History of the Church in England from the earliest period, to the Re-establishment of the Hierarchy in 1850*, two volumes, London 1857.

[3] See letter of 5 July to Mills.

[4] In his second volume, pp. 453–60 Flanagan described the Oxford Movement and the conversions. On p. 458 he wrote of *Tract XC*, 'This tract maintained that the Thirty-nine Articles were susceptible of a Catholic interpretation, and could be subscribed to by a person holding all the dogmas of the Council of Trent.'

the Church of Rome — but it is a fact I think this and that of her, and I *must* tell out my opinions on the subject.'

Number 90 then was not a resolution of the 39 Articles into the Council of Trent, but an experimental inquiry *how far* they would approximate to it, under the notion that the Church of Rome would have in her turn to approximate to Protestants. The Tract had no wish to force a sense upon the 39 Articles, which they would not admit, but it considered them[1] *'patient of a Catholic interpretation,'* and that on two grounds — (1) historically, because in fact they were drawn up so as to admit the assent of (professed) Catholics, of which Gesti's letter, which has just come to light, is a remarkable confirmation;[2] next, logically, that is, on the assumption that the Anglican Church was a branch of the Catholic — for, if so, its formularies *must* necessarily admit of an interpretation consistent with the *Quod semper, quod ubique, quod ab omnibus,* of the Catholic Church, with which also, in spite of its *practical* and *popular* errors, as I called them, the Roman teaching was allowed by me to be consistent.

I never to this day have felt necessary to be dissatisfied with the drift or the substance of Number 90, though in detail there are strained interpretations.

When at length I found my objections to the Roman Creed disappearing, and that, where my heart had been, there my best and truest reason might and ought to rest also, I publicly retracted all that I had said against it up to 1841, and at once took steps for resigning my living of St. Mary's. This was in 1843.

That I let two more years pass before I submitted myself to the Church arose from my friends saying to me, and my saying to myself, 'Your new views may be a delusion — and, if you act on them without a fair trial of their enduring, you may find out they are so, when it is too late.'

Excuse this long account. See what it is to begin speaking about myself. I did not intend to write more than a sentence when I began.[3]

I am, My dear Mr. Flanagan, Yours most sincerely in Xt,

John H. Newman, Of the Oratory.

The Very Rev. Canon Flanagan.

WEDNESDAY 29 JULY 1857 consulted Dr Evans about my knee and generally

TO JAMES HOPE-SCOTT

⌐The Oratory⌐ Hagley Road Birmingham ⌐July 29. 1857⌐

My dear Hope Scott

⌐The books you lent me in 1852, for University purposes, are done up in

---

[1] Newman omitted at this point 'in Sancta Clara's words,' which were in his draft. Cf. J. B. Dockery, *Christopher Davenport*, London 1960, p. 92.

[2] See letter of 4 May 1857 to St John.

[3] Flanagan replied on 1 Aug., 'My view of Number 90, is indeed not mine: it is one of those rare instances in which I have looked through other people's spectacles . . .'

the selfsame box in which they came, nailed up and corded, waiting for a direction.[1] I don't know your number in Parliament Street, and wait to be informed till I despatch them.

I hope you are not breaking down with work and the heat, and that you have good news from home, if Mrs Hope Scott is still in the North — at home, if she is with you in London.

⌐I trust I am here for good, though the Congregation has to answer a letter from three Archbishops asking for my continued residence at Dublin. I can't reside — but if I can do good without residence, I will. I am getting old, though, thank God, I am very well⌐[1]

Ever Yours affectly John H Newman of the Oratory

JR Hope Scott Esqr

List of books.

⌐Mendez de Jure Academico fol	Collectio Legum etc Romae.
Monumenta Univ. Pragensis. oct. 3 volumes.	Conringius
Raccolta etc. quarto	Gymnasium Romanum
Priviligia Acad. Louvan. small quarto	5 MS books.

The Acts of Parliament in favour of the Universities of London and Durham are locked up at Dublin, and shall go to you, when I return.[1]

TO A. LISLE PHILLIPPS

The Oratory, Birmingham July 30. 1857.

My dear Mr Phillipps

Your most interesting letter has just reached me, having been forwarded from Dublin.[2] I thank you for your great kindness to me, and hope you will give me a good prayer, that, as I get older, I may get nearer heaven.

As to my view of 'the Re-union of the English Church' to Rome, I say

---

[1] Hope-Scott replied on 1 Aug., 'I am *very* glad to hear that the 3 Arch Bishops are sensible of your value, and I hope you will not resist them too sternly.'

[2] In his letter of 23 July Phillipps described the encouragement he had received from the Rosminians, and how Gentili had foretold to him 'that the English Church *would be restored to Unity.*' On the other hand, 'The English Catholic Body, as a Body, sneers at the work, will not believe it's possibility, and looks at those engaged in it as fools and madmen: of course there are exceptions, we have one English Catholic Bishop with us and a few Priests: but how different is the way in which the Holy See has taken it up! The answer from thence has been one of enthusiastic encouragement . . . Alas! at this moment influential Persons in the English Catholic Body are doing their utmost to poison the feeling at Rome against us . . .' Phillipps also emphasised how strong in his opinion was the Anglican party working for corporate reunion.

this — that it is my duty not to set up my own view, but to follow the leadings of God's Providence, and if He shows me that I have been mistaken, or leads me to suspect it, not to be stubborn.

This even if I had ever so much to say in the way of proof against Anglican Orders but I will go further. I never have been able to prove them not valid by any clear logical process, and I was surprised, when I got to Rome in 1846, to find various persons there in the belief that they were valid, and none, I think, clear that they were not.[1]

But there are many strong *indirect* proofs against their validity, and many reasons for *wishing* them invalid. I will only mention one of the latter description. I mean, the ineffable sacrileges offered to our Lord in the Blessed Sacrament, if the Anglican Clergy are priests. You know this, as well as I can tell you — but it seems to me impossible that God should allow this almost universal sacrilege for three hundred years — and therefore that the fact of the contempt of the elements in the Sacrament in the Anglican Church is a proof that it is not possessed of the virtue of a real consecration. Only within the last fortnight, one of our Fathers happens to go into a Church 20 or 30 miles from this place, when waiting for a train, and finds the consecrated (so called) particles thrown out of the vestry window for the birds. I recollect how shocked Hurrell Froude was, at the Anglican Chapel at Rome, at seeing the consecrated wine put back into the bottle. This surely is a very common practice; yet it follows from it, since wine keeps for years and years, that Christ may be confined sacrilegiously an indefinite time (considering how infrequent the administration is in some places) in a vestry closet, or drunk at a vestry merry meeting.

To this you may say, and there is comfort in the thought, that there may be some defect in the *matter*, enough to invalidate the consecration. Perhaps the bread is adulterated with alum, rye etc in such quantity as to destroy its qualifications for the sacred purpose — perhaps the tent wine,[2] which is commonly used is half treacle and half brandy (you saw perhaps lately, that in one place the communicants were half poisoned with catsup, ketshup) — but I really think it is a duty on the Anglican Clergy, who wish their Orders acknowledged, to meet this great difficulty. Can they wonder, is it any insult to their body, that Catholics should scoff at the notion of their Orders, when *love for their common Saviour* ought to make themselves as well as Catholic desirous that those Orders should not be valid? *They* are zealous for *themselves*; why may not we be zealous for *Christ*?

I think, when Alexander Knox maintained the doctrine of the Real Presence in the Sacrament, we of Oxford at that day *argued thence* the doctrine

---

[1] Phillipps wrote on 23 July that he had been sent 'a French treatise entitled "La vraie manière de Réunir l'Eglise Anglicane a l'eglise Catholique—" This Book was published in 1727 and expresses the author's conviction of the validity of the Anglican Orders . . .' This was presumably François Vivant, Vicar General of Paris, *La vrai manière de contribuer à la réunion de l'Eglise anglicane à l'Eglise catholique*, Paris 1728.

[2] 'A Spanish wine of a deep red colour and of low alcoholic content.' *O.E.D.*

of a Priesthood.[1] For it was impossible (we said) that God should leave so great a gift at random on the face of the world — if there was a Present Christ, there must be a Guardian and Keeper of the Presence — if there was a sacrifice there must be a Priest. Thus the Apostolical Succession is cogently implied in the doctrine of the Presence of Christ in the Holy Eucharist.

Now I continue this argument — and say that in like manner the Presence of Christ implies, of congruity, a *rite* in which He should be present. A minute ceremonial, a rubric, is involved in the idea of the Supernatural Gift. And the absence of a rubric, guarding the Gift, is the strongest of presumptions that the gift is not there. The Greeks *could* not scatter the consecrated particles to the winds of heaven, they *could* not pour back the Blood of Christ upon the natural wine and use it for common purposes. As Solomon discovered the true mother by the instinct of love, so the absence of this instinct in the Ruling, directing, Service — compiling, rubric-making Church of England is the best of practical proofs that that Church has no claim to be supposed to conceive in her bosom, to present to her people in her arms, the Invisible Incarnate Son of God.[2]

However, I have run out at great length, and begging you to pardon me and give you my good prayers, I am My dear Mr Phillipps.

Affectly Yrs in Xt,

John H Newman, of the Oratory.

P.S.   We are praying here for your dear son. How anxious you must be![3]

If England is converted to Christ, it will be as much due (under God) to you as to any one.[4]

[1] Alexander Knox (1757–1831), Anglican divine and friend of John Wesley, anticipated much of the teaching of the Tractarians.
[2] Phillipps replied on 12 Aug., 'I owe you more thanks that I can well express for your truly beautiful letter . . . I hope to call on you at the Oratory at Edgbaston . . . it will be delightful for me to thank you in person for the kind sympathy you have shown me in the attempt I am making . . . *to lay the foundation* of what may lead ultimately to a reconciliation . . .' Phillipps recognised that the obstacles were immense, and complained of 'the bitter and ungenerous way in which I have been attacked in the Rambler, the special organ of the Recent Converts.' He added, 'I read with the deepest interest the remarks in your last letter on the Anglican orders,' and said he agreed with Newman's view 'that facts and reasoning are rather in their favour than against them.' He admitted the force of the argument from the habitual profanations even of the Clergy, but thought it was offset by the profanations of which Catholic apostates were guilty.
Phillipps concluded, 'The Authorities at Rome *are as anxious as I am* for a Reunion of Churches, for they know there is no other chance of getting England as a nation, and I am certain they will not easily cast aside an opportunity of recovering so great a country to Catholic Unity . . .'
[3] Phillipps's second son Everard (1835–57), was an officer in the 60th Rifles at Delhi. The Indian Mutiny began in April. Everard Phillipps was killed at Delhi on 17 Sept., three days after he had earned the Victoria Cross.
[4] Phillipps heard, soon after this, that an attempt was being made, seemingly by Manning and W. G. Ward, to have his pamphlet *On the future Unity of Christendom* put on the Index. De Lisle, I, p. 380.
However, about this time Barnabò received from Wiseman a long 'Report on the Party called the "Union" Party in the Anglican Body.' It ended: 'In submitting this report . . . the

TO RICHARD STANTON[1]

The Oratory Birmingham July 30. 1857

My dear Father

By this post I send a copy of our Statutes and Calendar for Father Guerritore, if he would kindly take it for me to Naples, and deliver it to 'Mr Munro, Palazzo Gallo, Riviera di Chiaia.' I direct it to you, and ask the kindness of your giving it to him with *the above direction*.[2]

Should he be gone, will you accept it yourself — or give it away.

Yours affly John H Newman

TO HENRY WILBERFORCE

The Oy Bm ⌐July 30/57⌐

My dear H W

I am sorry at your disappointment; ⌐as to Harcourt Street, I offered it to Johnson Observer, and other Oxford men, and a French Abbé, at the meeting of the British Association in August⌐ (I don't know the date) and to Mr and Mrs Renouf in September — else ⌐you have nothing to do but to keep Mrs Grady well informed about your movements.

As to Ambrose,⌐ I think he wishes to go to you — but I think I shall persuade even *you*, that he must not. He has been away from the Oratory for two months — ⌐he is sure to be away in October, *which is his bad time*.⌐ His absence overworks us seriously. Stanislas will knock up next, if we don't look sharp; I am sending him to London for three days, thinking so short a

undersigned Cardinal believes that he has exhausted the subject of which it treats. He does not think that there is room for any action on the part of the Holy See; on the contrary, he fears only the imprudence of those who represent his Holiness as favourable to the plea of disregarding the conversion of individuals, in the hope of an approaching national conversion; and he takes the liberty of adding that, if there should ever be the faintest movement towards so desirable an end, the Bishops, who watch with the utmost solicitude over the religious interest of England, would hasten to announce it to the Supreme Pastor, and would not leave this part of their duty to a layman.' W. Ward. *The Life and Times of Cardinal Wiseman*, II, p. 488.

Barnabò wrote cautiously to Phillipps on 17 Aug. but the latter successfully defended his pamphlet in a letter of 31 Aug. *De Lisle*, I, pp. 381–4. On 8 Sept. 1857 the 'Association for the Promotion of the Unity of Christendom' was founded at a meeting in London. Its formation was proposed by Phillipps and carried by acclamation. Neither Barnabò nor Wiseman objected to Catholics becoming members. The latter frequently corresponded with Phillipps and was on friendly terms with Anglican members of the Association. The decree of Sept. 1864 forbidding Catholics to belong to the A.P.U.C. 'came as a crushing blow, and above all to de Lisle [Phillipps], to whom it was the breaking of the master-idea of his life.' Cuthbert Butler, *The Life and Times of Bishop Ullathorne*, I, p. 347.

[1] This letter was evidently addressed to an Oratorian in London, and since the autograph is at Birmingham, almost certainly to Stanton.

[2] Philip Munro wanted documents about the Catholic University for his friend at Naples. See letter of 9 June 1857 to Wilberforce.

recreation better than none. He is getting downcast, which is unlike him. ⌐I assure you, you can't conceive how we are worked.

Moreover, just now, he (A.) is quite well.⌐ He is quite well at Rednall. Let well alone.

Moreover, ⌐he is getting into a way of hearing his penitents *in the morning*⌐ several times a week, ⌐which does not hurt him at all. For years have I been at the Fathers, telling them I was sure that at least half of their penitents could come in the morning, if they chose. They are *forced* to do so now, for Ambrose *can't* hear them of an evening — ⌐ and I don't like to destroy so promising a beginning, and one which *at the moment* (if it is nothing more) is a great relief to Stanislas

Ever Yrs affly J H N

Corollary. Therefore, please, you must engage your other Priest.

I well recollect July 29/33[1]

FRIDAY 31 JULY 1857   went over to Rednall with Scott, returning

TO THOMAS HAYDEN

The Oratory, Birmingham. July 31, 1857.

My dear Dr. Hayden,

It disappointed and annoyed me very much that nothing was settled about the Misericordia Hospital before I came away. I was in communication with the Revd. Mother till the last — I then wrote her an objurgatory letter. But it's not her fault. She answered promising to do what she could.[2]

There was the report you mention that the Jervis Street staff were to be appointed to the Misericordia. But I did not think it would be so, though Dr. Ellis knows far better than I — and if he says so, *go by him*. There was also the report, I think well founded, that there was to be an entrance fee for all other practitioners at the Misericordia — but not an extravagant one — not more than the sum you mention. But I grieve to think that nothing is settled.

I shall be very glad to see your Report, and am, My dear Dr. Hayden, Sincerely yours,

John H. Newman, of the Oratory.

T. Hayden Esq. M.D.

---

[1] This was the day on which Henry Wilberforce's father, William Wilberforce, the Emancipator, died.

[2] Hayden was considering taking an appointment at Jervis Street Hospital, where he would have to pay his predecessor £200 for making the vacancy. There was a proposal to transfer the medical staff of Jervis Street to the New Mater Misericordiae Hospital, and to reserve six vacancies there for professors of the Catholic University. Hayden wished to know how matters stood, before deciding his course of action.

TO PATRICK LEAHY, ARCHBISHOP OF CASHEL

The Oratory Birmingham ⌈July 31. 1857⌉

My dear Lord

⌈I thank your Grace and the two other Archbishops for your most condescending letter to our Congregation, the answer to which is in course of preparation. Also for your kind and liberal offer to purchase the Church of me, which I gladly accept.[1]

It has cost rather more than £5600, and I propose to your and their better judgment some such arrangement between us in round numbers as the following:—

— that of this whole sum (£5600) as much as £2400 (£2360) should be paid me at once, which would get me out of debt; — and that, in lieu of the remainder, I and my heirs should receive of the Trustees £120 a year, to remain as a first mortgage on the fabric (or first charge on the congregational collections) and to cease absolutely if ever the fabric ceased to be a Church, and to be applied by me and my heirs, while I and they receive it, to some University purpose or purposes to be approved of by the Coetus Episcoporum or the Archbishops.⌉

I am quite at a loss to conjecture how I can continue my duties at Dublin. The other day I had occasion to go to an eminent physician of this place about my knee — he was led on to examine my chest, without my desiring it, or having any suspicion how the examination would end. He said that my heart was not right, and bade me keep as quiet as possible — in a word to *rest*. I do not know how to have any doubt, that my continuing in Dublin will shorten my life.

If these initial and formidable difficulties are got over, I shall take the liberty of putting on paper for you some points which I am very anxious to secure.

I am, My dear Lord, Your Grace's affte Servt in Xt

John H Newman of the Oratory

His Grace the Archbp of Cashel.

[1] Leahy wrote on 20 July a letter (which Mills acknowledged at once for Newman, who was in retreat), 'The Archbishops propose to you to take the University Church off your hands, reimbursing you for all losses and releasing you from all liabilities on account of it.'

In a postscript he added, 'A letter goes by this post to the Fathers of the Oratory, laying before them the earnest wishes of the Archbishops that you should continue to fill the office of Rector of the University.

There will be another meeting of the Archbishops on Friday, the 21st August, by which time the reply of the Father's is expected.

The Revd Mr Flannery has been appointed Clerical Secretary, whose duty will be to organise the Parochial Collections for the University through Ireland and to attend to the correspondence connected with them.

Other appointments will be made on the 21st August.'

For the letter from the Archbishops see 6 Aug.

Postscript

1. The Church has cost from first to last rather more than £5600 — of which perhaps £540 have been donations.

2. The basis of the arrangement for purchase, proposed above, is as follows:—

Whole cost (say)		5600
deduct — donations — (say)	540	
proposed donation from myself	100	640
		£4960

Of this £4960	
to be paid at once	2360
to be left on interest at 5 per cent	2600
viz £130 — say £120	
	£4960

3. The Church is built on ground, of which I have a lease of 17 years to run, with the option of a renewal of the whole premises, on which the Church and Number 87 stand for 40 years from this date, on an increased rent of (say) £70 instead of (say) £58 — with the liabilities of repairs in the House Number 87. These repairs will amount to £200 at once; and, as the House is old, it might require rebuilding before the lease of 40 years expires.

4. The Collections at High Mass, for the first Halfsession, since the Church was opened, were above £10 each Mass, or at the rate of £400 the Session of 40 weeks; for the second half session, above £5, or at the rate of above £200 the Session. The Collections during the whole Sunday have been as high as £25.

5. I have given the use of the Church and the whole collections to Mr Anderdon, on a rent, till next February.[1]

[1] At the end of the draft of this letter Newman wrote: '(N B If they give £2360 with a rent of £120 and gain from the congregational collections £600 a session, say a year, then they will get above 20 per cent for their money, deducting the £120 rent—and, *not* deducting it, which is fair, since I give it back to the University above £25 per cent. However, expenses of Preachers, celebrants etc must be deducted, and the question is, whether £600 will cover these.)

celebrants	80	collections in the Long
choir	200	Vacation (12 weeks) may
preachers	120	be set against coal, light-
Anderdon	200	ing, servants, insurance.'
	600	

TO ANDREW ELLIS

The Oratory Birmingham August 1. 1857

My dear Dr Ellis,

Thank you very much for your zeal. I think you have done a great deal.[1]

You must not use my name with the Archbishop — he has so often, and, not the least, in the case of the Hospitals project thwarted me by his silence and simple inaction, that I cannot understand his feelings to me — or whether it will make matters easier or not, to introduce my name. About the Stephen's Green Hospital he never saw, (and so I suppose did not *wish* to see) a letter I had *told* him I had lodged for him with a friend of his, whom he had named as his representative — and at the end of 10 months, when I sent for it, it came back to me without remark.[2]

Of course I should be very glad if you saw him, because doubtless you would do good; but you must not go from *me*. I can point to two instances, when, to all appearance, his fancying persons came from me made his manner to them change for the worse.

This I say in confidence — I doubt not you will soon bring the whole matter to a happy issue yourself.

Yours I am, My dear Dr Ellis, Most sincerely

John H Newman of the Oratory

A Ellis Esqr &c &c.

SUNDAY 2 AUGUST 1857   Nicholas went away for a month
WEDNESDAY 5 August   Stanislas went to London. The Chapel at Rednal began.

TO JAMES HOPE-SCOTT

⌐The Oratory¬ Birmingham ⌐August 5/57¬

My dear Hope Scott

⌐I have forgotten to use your direction till this morning, when I have just directed the box and sent it off.[3] I hope it will arrive without injury to the books. I have packed it myself — this you would say is not the best precaution — but it ought to be, for I have had much experience, and have lately packed

---

[1] Ellis was negotiating with the Sisters of Mercy about the introduction of professors of the Catholic University into their hospitals. No final agreement could be reached without the consent of Archbishop Cullen. The negotiations about the Mater Misercordiae Hospital came to an end in the course of a few days because the professors were unwilling to accept the proposed conditions.

[2] Letter of 29 July 1856 to T. MacNamara, concerning St Vincent's Hospital, Stephen's Green.

[3] The books mentioned in the letter of 29 July were sent to Hope-Scott in London, at 44 Parliament Street.

two large boxes in Dublin for this place, and I am as tender of books as if they were little helpless children.

As to Dublin the three Archbishops write to ask to have me *as hitherto* — and do not hint at non-residence — this is simply impossible. No one can tell how long or short my life will be; — that being longer in Dublin will shorten it, I do not doubt. I am told I have a tendency to disorder of the heart — and am advised not to walk fast, or up hill, and in all respects to rest. You know perfectly well that anxiety is the worst of unrests. It is of extreme importance to a young community such as ours in Birmingham, that I should live as long as I can. If I could concentrate in a moment all I am to do in such length of time as God gives me, I should not secure that quality which the length itself gives. Things must go slowly to go well.

Our Fathers are writing in answer to the Archbishops, that it is now six years since I gave up my confessional here, my weekly lecture, and my various internal duties; that the Congregation has been established little more than eight years, so that I have given to Dublin two thirds of the whole time, and the University has had the use of me far more than the Oratory; — that the absence of a head, (Bishops must know as well as any one,) is almost ruin to a body of labourers — especially in a body which has not vows, and a new body; that at my age one year goes for as much as four or five years of a younger man; and that the anxiety which the University involves, may be taking from them the chance of the future, while it deprives them of the present; that we have lost two Fathers by death, that two Fathers in the last two years have been knocked up, one of them was a year invalided, and the other out of residence still; that over work in consequence is knocking up others; and that one has left us, as we believe, because *I* am not here.[1]

We do not oppose the continuance of my Rectorship, but my residence in Dublin. And I tell you fairly we shall fairly be wrecked here, if I am away longer. No novices will come, while I am away[1]

Ever Yours affly John H Newman of the Oratory

JR Hope Esqr

TO JOHN HUNGERFORD POLLEN

The Oy. Bm. August 5/57

My dear Pollen,

I had been just thinking of your Lectures this morning, and lo the post brings them. I thank you for them — they will be very serviceable — and I

[1] John Cooke and Joseph Gordon had died; Darnell and St John had been ill, and the latter was still away; Dalgairns had left.

shall despatch them at once to the Press. I wish I had my article done. I have so much to do here, that one article must go a good way[1]

The three Archbishops have written to our Fathers asking me to continue residence as *heretofore*. This is simply impossible, and we are obliged to say so: — but we would do everything we can, and we tell them so.

Why won't Renouf take your house? I fear it is the expense. He is evidently timid on launching. He was to be married on the 25th.

I thought Coffin looked sadly overworked when I saw him for half an hour two years ago in Dublin. He used to be fat, but he was quite thin.

As to the Unionists, certainly one has cause to doubt them, but I can't help hoping they will end in falling over the brink, or at least, if they keep their balance, be the occasion of their friends doing the like. There is a great movement just now, and after having delivered one's testimony or protest, I don't see the good of continuing to rail at them. I wonder at this going to Coffin, as generally speaking, they keep clear of converts.[2]

Pray say every thing kind from me to him and McMullen. I have not seen *him* for years.

Ambrose seems bent on having you down here. The church begins this very day, ad Nives.[3]

Ever Yrs affly John H. Newman

FROM THE ARCHBISHOPS OF IRELAND TO THE FATHERS OF THE ORATORY

Dublin, 20th July, 1857.[4]

Reverend Fathers,

Sensible of the great services which Dr Newman has rendered to the cause of Catholic Education and of Catholicity, not only by the prestige of his distinguished name, but also by the able and zealous manner in which he has discharged the duties of Rector of our Catholic University, we are as anxious now to perpetuate those services to our rising University as we were at first to secure them. And in expressing this our earnest desire, we but give expression to the wishes of the Bishops, Clergy, and People, of Ireland.

We are also very sensible, Reverend Fathers, of the sacrifice your Congregation has been making now for some years by consenting to his absence for the sake of our University; and we are not at all surprised to learn how anxious you are that your Father Superior should be released from his duties here and given back to his Oratory. Yet, we are not without a hope, and a strong hope, that the same disinterested regard for the welfare of our Catholic University which first induced you to consent for a time to be separated from him will reconcile you to the sacrifice, great as it is, for

[1] Newman was collecting articles for the *Atlantis*. The first number, that of Jan. 1858, included his 'The Mission of the Benedictine Order,' and Pollen's 'Structural Characteristics of the Basilicas.'

[2] R. A. Coffin, now Superior of the Redemptorists at Clapham was evidently in touch with the supporters of the *Union*, perhaps owing to his friendship with A. Lisle Phillipps, in whose family he had been tutor for a year after his conversion.

[3] Work on the chapel at Rednal designed by Pollen was begun on this day, the feast of the Blessed Virgin ad Nives.

[4] This letter, in Leahy's hand, was acknowledged by Mills, the Secretary, when it reached Birmingham on 23 July.

some time longer; for, in it's present infant state, the connection of Dr Newman with the University is undeniably a very great gain, as his separation from it would be a loss the magnitude of which it would not be easy to estimate.

We hope, therefore, Reverend Fathers, that you will forgo for a time the happiness of having your Father Superior at home in the midst of his Congregation, leaving him to pursue the high vocation, to which not only does he appear to have been specially called the day he was named Rector of the Catholic University, but for which, as it seems to us, Providence had been preparing him long years before he became a child of the Catholic Church. We have the honor to remain, Reverend Fathers, Your faithful Servants in Christ,

> ✝ Paul Cullen Archbishop
> ✝ Joseph Dixon abp.
> ✝ Patrick Leahy, Archbp

To The Reverend The Fathers of the Oratory, Birmingham.

TO THE ARCHBISHOPS OF DUBLIN, ARMAGH, AND CASHEL

The Oratory Birmingham August 6. 1857.[1]

My Lords,

We have anxiously considered, as we were bound, the important letter, with which your Graces have honoured us, on the subject of our Father Superior's continued residence in Dublin, — a letter which claims our most serious and respectful attention, not only as coming from revered and beloved Prelates, personally known to ourselves, but moreover as expressing, for so we understand its words, the undivided sentiment of all the Archbishops and Bishops of Ireland. ⌐Considering the language in which it speaks of our Father Superior, it is impossible¬ to overrate the honour thereby conferred on him, and indirectly on ourselves, who have lent him to the University; and impossible ⌐in consequence to refuse anything whatever to its writers, which is not inconsistent, we will not say with the convenience, but with the welfare, nay the safety, of our Congregation.

But such, we avow it with deep concern, is your Graces' request. You are anxious, in the words you have used, 'to perpetuate the services of our Father Superior to your University,' and therefore ask us 'to consent to be separated from him for some time longer.' We conceive we do not mistake in interpreting these words to mean, that your Graces wish to gain our consent to his residence in Dublin, as during the last three years, for an indefinite time to come. Now we are sanguine that we shall be able, by a statement of some of the circumstances of the case, even to carry your Graces with us in the conclusion to which we have come, that such a further leave of absence from the Oratory to be granted our Father Superior is simply incompatible with

---

[1] Not only does internal evidence show that Newman wrote this letter, but his own draft of it exists, and was copied exactly. In the letter as sent, the last ten words, directing it to the three Archbishops, are in Newman's hand.

The letter was sent off on 11 Aug. See letter of that day to Leahy.

our duty to St Philip, and that we cannot with a clear conscience make ourselves parties to it.[1]

My Lords, none know so well as Bishops the need of a Head for the superintendence of a body of labourers; and assuredly that need is not lessened by the circumstance of its consisting of persons brought together into one House, and subjected to a common rule of life; — when too, in addition, they are held together, as is the case in the Oratory, not by any irrevocable vow, but mainly by the personal influence of the individual into whose hands they have freely committed themselves; — and further still when their body is of very recent formation and is struggling with the various special difficulties which beset every new undertaking. If the University, as you remind us, is a new work, so is the Oratory also; it has existed little more than eight years, and out of these eight years we have given your Graces our Father Superior for six. His Grace, the present Archbishop of Cashel, honored our Oratory with a visit on the subject of the University in September 1851; our Father Superior went to Thurles at the end of the same month; and from that time his thoughts have been devoted to the great object you have at heart. In consequence he has been all but lost to his community; it is near six years since he gave up his Confessional, and stopped his weekly instructions in the Church, as well as his theological lectures to ourselves, not to say his own private studies. He turned aside out of his appointed duties, and that under cover of the bare permission, which our Rule gives in extreme cases, to devote himself to your University, from simple zeal for so great an object: — He has been rewarded by your Graces' praise; we rejoice and return thanks to God that we have been able to permit him to gain it; but such is the fact, that since he has been our Superior, your University has had the use of him far more than ourselves; it has had two thirds of his whole time

Nor can we forget that our Father Superior is no longer in the prime of life so as to admit of our counting on his future years as a compensation for the past. Rather, My Lords, you must allow us to add it, the very occupations to which you call him tend to shorten the term of years, on which he might otherwise reckon. He has been especially warned by his medical adviser against anxiety, which comes upon him with double force, both from the direct responsibilities of his work in Dublin, and from the fact of his being unable to fulfil his prior and more sacred responsibilities in Birmingham. Thus, for what we can tell, you may not only be taking from us the present, but forfeiting for us the future. —

Grave as these considerations are they weigh still more heavily on our minds, when we turn to reflect upon the difficulties of other kinds which press upon our Congregation. We have lost two Fathers in Birmingham by death; one of them, from his varied talents, an irremediable loss, has been taken away since we allowed our Father Superior to go to Dublin. We have lately had the labours of two others interrupted by serious illness; one of them was disabled for the greater part of a year, the other is still obliged to absent himself from the Congregation. The work of many is thus thrown on a few; they in turn give way under the unfair accumulation of duties. Another great evil connected with our Father's absence is the unsettlement and general despondency arising from the want of a resident Superior, and it is to this that we attribute the loss of another of our body, of considerable reputation, whose departure was not to have been expected, had our Father Superior been with us.[1] There are other points of importance, too minute, or too private to insist upon. Some will suggest themselves to your minds; — your Graces are kind enough to make much of Father Newman's name; what is a gain to Dublin must be a proportional loss to Birmingham.

Have we not said enough, My Lords, to make you feel for us some of that sympathy, which we have felt for you, in lending to the University one so intimately bound up with us and with our history? May we not feel assured that you will be as generous towards us, as we have wished to be towards your great undertaking? Will you not come to the conclusion, that the loan, which it has been our privilege to offer, is our claim on you for its restoration at this date, not your plea for its renewal?

We entreat you to pardon our freedom: everything we *can* do, we will gladly offer; but we can consent to a non-resident Superior, even less than you perhaps can contemplate a non-resident Rector.

Humbly begging your blessing, My Lords, we beg to subscribe ourselves, Your Graces' faithful Servts in Xt

Ambrose St John. Henry Bittleston.
Frederick, S. Bowles. Edward Caswall
Henry Austin Mills. William Neville
Nicholas Darnell. Robert B Tillotson
John S. Flanagan

To their Graces The Archbishops of Dublin, Armagh and Cashel.

SATURDAY 8 AUGUST 1857 Stanislas returned

TO PATRICK LEAHY, ARCHBISHOP OF CASHEL

Aug 8/57

My dear Lord

I hope you will excuse our delay in sending you our answer. As we are not all at home, it is travelling for signature. I hope to send it tomorrow.

We ask you to be so kind as to tell us whether we ought, in courtesy, to

[1] See second note to letter of 5 Aug. to Hope-Scott.

send the Archbishop of Tuam a copy of our letter to the three Arch-bishops.[1]

ᒥIt has concerned me much to find that you have felt it right in your most kind and condescending letter to us, to ask for my services in Dublin as in the last three years, instead of proposing, as I was sanguine in expecting, some middle plan. It is quite impossible our Fathers should return any but one answer to a proposition, which is almost destructive of our Congregation.ᒧ How can I in conscience let the time, labour and money spent upon it to be thrown away. I went to Rome eleven years ago — I remained there a year — I came home, and had a great deal of work and anxiety — and friends have given us very large sums to establish ourselves here. Our house itself has cost £10,000. I am betraying this, I am stultifying myself, if I let the Oratory come to nought.

ᒥHad some measure of compromise been proposed, I should have sent you some points of detail about the University, which affect me personally, and which I had hoped to be allowed to secure.[2] This, alas, is unnecessary now.ᒧ[3]

TO WILLIAM MONSELL

The Oratory Bm August 8/57

My dear Monsell,

Mr Sullivan, our Professor of Chemistry, sends me the inclosed. I have told him you were not likely to help him, but I send it to you for the chance[4]

Ever Yrs affly John H Newman of the Oratory

P.S.   I am glad there is a chance of my seeing you so soon.

[1] Leahy replied in his letter of 13 Aug., 'It might be well to send a *copy* of the reply of the Fathers to each of the Archbishops. Or, if you send the reply to Dr Cullen for all, nobody, as I think, will charge you with a want of courtesy.' In the meantime the letter was sent to Leahy. See letter of 11 Aug. to him.
[2] [[vid. below—letter of October 16.]]
[3] To Newman's remarks about a 'middle plan' Leahy replied on 13 Aug., 'The exact terms of our Letter I cannot call to mind. My impression, however, is—that we simply asked the Fathers to consent to your continuing to fill the office of Rector of the University without saying whether you would be expected to devote as much time to it as heretofore, or what time, or upon what conditions. . . . But, whether, or how that absence [from the Oratory] might be regulated, whether it might be long or short, we abstained from saying, because—
We did not consider the question at all. That you looked forward to the adoption of a "middle plan," or that the Fathers of the Oratory expected it, we really did not know. . . .'
Newman commented, when copying this letter in 1872:
' [[(That is, the main point had been slurred over—perhaps because Dr Cullen did not agree on the point with the other two Archbishops. He had always spoken as if I must reside the whole year, and in the letter of the three Archbishops (consequent upon this correspond-ence between Dr Leahy and me) viz of August 25, they are only willing to "try the 'middle plan' for *one* Session.")]]'
[4] See letter of 9 Aug. to Sullivan.

SUNDAY 9 AUGUST 1857   began Mass for Pia Unio at ¼ past nine *they present*[1]

TO ROBERT ORNSBY

The Oratory Birmingham ⌐August 9. 1857⌐

My dear Ornsby

Excuse the delay of a day or two. I have been in search of an article for our new Journal in our Library here, but have not yet found it. I want to find it like Minerva, finished and ready to hand.

I am very much interested in Mrs Buckle's work. We want such books so badly. The money is the great difficulty. I wish I could be editor of an historical series. Tell her that, if she wishes me to give my opinion upon it, I will gladly read a portion, if she will allow me.[2]

⌐The Archbishops have asked for my services in Dublin *as hitherto*. This is simply impossible — and we can only return a negative. They meet on the 21st. I can't conceive why they did not come to some middle plan.⌐

Ever Yrs affly J H N

R Ornsby Esqr

TO WILLIAM KIRBY SULLIVAN

The Oratory Birmingham August 9. 1857

My dear Mr Sullivan,

I am sending your representation to Mr Monsell by this post — but I fear he won't be able to do any thing, as he is not on good terms with government — and in consequence of the Divorce Bill, will soon, they say, have nothing to do with them.[3]

At first sight I do not see the appropriateness of sending the Science Scheme to the Clergy — to send it to schools, learned societies etc is quite intelligible.[4] I would have the Scientific Journal Prospectus with the Scheme Scheme [sic] appended sent to the *latter*, if I had a list. This would involve

---

[1] The Pia Unio was a kind of 'secular institute,' for which Newman obtained privileges, when he was in Rome in Jan. 1856. It consisted of women who devoted themselves to good works, without the obligation of vows. It was responsible for the guild of young women, which at this time had 150 members.

[2] Cf. letter of 14 Feb. 1858 to Mrs Buckle. Her works seems not to have been published. There is no book of hers in the British Museum catalogue of printed books.

[3] Sullivan was concerned about his position at the Museum of Science and Industry. See letters of 3, 6 and 25 Oct. 1856. Monsell, who was President of the Board of Health, resigned in Sept., but not before he had put Sullivan's case to Earl Granville, who was Lord President of the Council. See letter of 28 Aug., to Sullivan.

The Divorce and Matrimonial Causes Bill, against which Sir George Bowyer presented a large number of Catholic petitions on 24 July, passed the House of Commons on 21 Aug.

[4] Sullivan wanted to send a copy of the Scheme of the Faculty of Science to every parish priest in Ireland.

sending it a great many places all thro' Ireland — but the majority of parish priests would feel it to be out of their way, and simply put it aside. To send the whole calendar[1] to all the priests would be a better thing, for it would carry its own meaning with it — but this would be double the expense.

Mr Penny is vanished. I wished him to go thro' this place, but he rushed up to his Mother — who is at some watering place — I will send him a note on the chance of its finding him.

I want to know which you would like — viz: the Literary part of the Journal (in which your *present* article will come,) is now setting up in the breadth of page of the Edinburgh and other Reviews — This is the most natural course; — but it has struck me to ask whether it would not be better rather to *curtail* the breadth, so as to admit of marginal notices down the page — as it is in the case of Reports, etc. The reason I say this is, that, the *possibility* of putting running headings to the paragraphs will be the *test* whether the Article has really good *mattér*, or is mere verbiage. Here then would at once be a mode for an Editor's ascertaining whether an Article (Literary) ought to be taken or not. (But it might look odd — will *you* decide?)[2]

I am, My dear Mr Sullivan,

Very sincerely Yours John H Newman of the Oratory
W K Sullivan Esqr

P.S.   I am sorry to say that the Archbishops have asked me of the Oratory for full residence as hitherto — which makes it quite impossible for us to grant it.

MONDAY 10 AUGUST 1857   called on the Bishop with Scott — but I did not see him
TUESDAY 11 AUGUST   Ambrose went to London. Sent off Congregation Letter to the Archbishops   went over to Oscott with Scott to meet the Cardinal at dinner

TO PATRICK LEAHY, ARCHBISHOP OF CASHEL

The Oratory Birmingham August 11. 1857
My dear Lord

I beg to transmit to your Grace the answer which our Fathers have written to the letter addressed to them on the subject of my continued residence at Dublin by the Three Archbishops; and ask the favour of your putting it into the hands of the Archbishops of Dublin and Armagh, after reading it yourself

I am, My dear Lord, Your affte Servt in Xt

John H Newman of the Oratory
His Grace The Archbp of Cashel

[1] Of the Catholic University.
[2] The *Atlantis* appeared with the marginal headings Newman here describes.

118

WEDNESDAY 12 AUGUST 1857   put blister on my knee.   Northcote called.
THURSDAY 13 AUGUST   Bishop called (Miss Giberne came)
FRIDAY 14 AUGUST   Mr A. L. Phillipps called.   Ambrose returned

TO MISS M. R. GIBERNE

Augst 14/57

My dear Miss Giberne

I am very sorry to hear you are suffering in so many ways, and not up. My own ailment is very slight, and I trust will be over by tomorrow. The thunder very likely has affected you, added to the travelling.[1]

I said Mass for you this morning.

Wishing you by anticipation a happy feast

I am Yours affectionately in Xt   John H Newman of the Oratory
Miss Giberne

SUNDAY 16 AUGUST 1857   Ambrose much better
MONDAY 17 AUGUST   Stanislas went with Harry to Rednal for the week.   began lecture to Pia Unio, once a fortnight   Frederic [Godwin] came from Dublin

TO THE ARCHBISHOPS OF DUBLIN AND ARMAGH

Aug 17/57

My dear Lord

I beg to inform you that I have sent the answer of our Congregation to the letter of the three Archbishops to his Grace the Archbishop of Cashel, who has kindly informed us that he will bring it before your Graces at Dublin on the 21, instant

TO PATRICK LEAHY, ARCHBISHOP OF CASHEL

Aug 17. 1857

(Rough copy)

My dear Lord

Your two letters of the 13th came to me yesterday and today. I am very much obliged to you for them.[2]

---

[1] Miss Giberne was staying in Birmingham.
[2] The first of these letters acknowledged the receipt of the reply of the Fathers at the Oratory and said that it would be laid before the other Archbishops on 21 Aug. The second is quoted in the letter of 8 Aug. to Leahy.

In consequence of them I think you will like me to observe as follows: —
⌐Neither the Archbishops' letter nor our Congregation's, touched upon the question of my remaining *Rector*, but about my *residing as hitherto*.

Their Graces' letter said 'We hope that you will forego for a time the happiness of having your Father Superior *at home in the midst of his Congregation, leaving* him to pursue the high *vocation* — for which, as it seems to us, Providence had been preparing him etc.' Kinder words could not be used, but they implied to our Fathers here *absence* from this Oratory.

On the other hand they felt that it would be disrespectful to do any thing else than answer your direct [[distinct]] proposition, so they wrote: 'We have anxiously considered the important letter, with which your Graces have honored us on the subject of our Father Superior's *continued residence* in Dublin.' And again 'You ask us', and they quote the Archbishops' words, 'to consent to be *separated* from him for some time longer.' And they add 'we conceive we do not mistake in interpreting[1] these words to mean that your Graces wish to gain our consent to his *residence in Dublin*, as during the last three years for an indefinite time to come.'

⌐When I spoke of a 'middle plan,' I meant some plan such as I had fancied first your Grace and then Dr Cullen suggested to me; viz a plan which involved residence for no more than a limited number of weeks in the year. If you wish to know what I consider to be such a residence I should say residence for some time in each term, say nine weeks in the course of the Session. Such a plan I think our Fathers would find possible for two Sessions — ⌐ viz 1857–58 and 58 – 59 But if I must give my opinion ⌐its feasibility in matter of fact would depend nearly entirely upon the selection made by your Graces of the Vice Rector, which, if the Rector is not to be in continual residence, is the cardinal point of the whole arrangement⌐

I am &c J H N

TUESDAY 18 AUGUST 1857   Pollen came in evening

WEDNESDAY 19 AUGUST   Austin went to Campden for 10 days   went over with Pollen to Rednall who went to town in evening

MONDAY 24 AUGUST   Ambrose went to Abergele   Mr Bridges came   Mr Edwards dined

WEDNESDAY 26 AUGUST   Dear Victor went away[1]   Mr Bridges went.   Frederic went to Capes.   answer of Archbishops came to our letter

FROM PATRICK LEAHY, ARCHBISHOP OF CASHEL

Tipperary, 25 Augt '57.

My dear Dr Newman,

The Meeting of the Archbishops was held in Dublin on last Friday, the 21st. Inst. There were present the Archbishops of Dublin, Armagh, and Cashel.

[1] On 20 Sept. Victor Duke wrote that he had decided to give up being a novice at the Oratory.

The Letter of the Fathers of your Oratory was laid before the Archbishops, as were your Letters,—that, in which you accept their proposal to take the University Church off their hands, and the other suggesting a 'middle plan',[1] the adoption of which would, it is hoped, sufficiently provide for the preservation of your own health and the necessities of your Oratory, and would at the same time continue to the University your valuable services as Rector.

The Archbishops have commissioned me to say how much pleased they are with the terms on which you offer to surrender the Church into their hands, and that, [as] soon as the necessary papers are drawn up, they will advance the sum you require now.

They have also desired me to say to yourself and to request you will have the goodness to make known to the Fathers of the Oratory, that, unwilling as they are to imperil your health or the good of your Community, yet, anxious to retain your services for the University as far as may consist with the paramount claims of both, they will gladly try for One Session the 'middle plan' suggested in your Letter to me, releasing you from permanent residence in the University and from residence for any longer time than you have indicated. 'If,' say their Graces, 'the experiment shall be found to have worked well, it can be tried for another Session.'

Of course, your own and the Fathers' consent is supposed, and is hereby asked.

It was late on Friday night when I arrived here from Dublin. It was impossible for me to write to you an hour sooner.

I remain, My Dear Dr Newman, Sincerely and affectionately Yours,

⊹Patrick Leahy Archbishop &c

The Very Revd Dr Newman, The Oratory, Birmingham.

TO PATRICK LEAHY, ARCHBISHOP OF CASHEL

Augst 26/57

My dear Lord

Thank you very much for your letter of this morning, and the kind proposal of the Archbishops. ⌐I will bring it before our Fathers as soon as possible — meanwhile I write to say that I anticipate no difficulty on their part to it.

For myself, I wish to urge upon your Graces that the success of the attempt depends on the person to be selected for the Vice Rector. It must be one in whom both the Professors and the Rector can place confidence, else I shall despair of being able to make the arrangement work[12]

The Archbishop of Armagh has most considerately given his assent to the provisional appointment of Mr McCarthy and Mr Arnold till the next meeting of the Bishops upon my writing to him. The Archbishop of Dublin said it would be determined at your late meeting. I suppose I may take it for granted that your Graces have given your assent to both appointments — and therefore, unless I hear from you to the contrary, I shall write to these Gentlemen to say so[3]

I am &c J H N

---

[1] i.e. Newman's letters of 31 July and 17 Aug. to Leahy.

[2] On this subject Leahy wrote, on 25 Aug., a second letter which had not yet reached Newman. See letter of 12 Sept to Leahy.

[3] Leahy replied on 28 Aug. 'The Archbishops considered your recommendation of

THURSDAY 27 AUGUST 1857   Cardinal Wiseman's letter came about version of Scripture
Miss Giberne went   Ambrose returned

FROM CARDINAL WISEMAN

London, Aug. 26. 1857

My dear Dr Newman

I beg to call your attention to the ninth Decree of the 2d Provincial Synod of Westminster, of which you, no doubt, have now a copy (P. 30) 'De Versione canonicarum Scripturarum.' [1]

You will easily understand, how it would have been inconvenient, not to say unfair, to have inserted the names of any persons in a Decree subject to approbation or disapproval, in substance and in details by a higher authority. And therefore no persons were named in the decree itself.

But the Bishops in reality had agreed, at the time they drew up the decree, that to you was to be committed the grave and most important work proposed in it, and that you had to select and name the persons whom you would wish to have for assistants in the undertaking. It was understood that most naturally they would be members of the Congregation of the Oratory.

But further, it is right for me to state, that in the letter, explanatory of the Decrees, which I forwarded to the Sacred Congregation of P. F. [Propaganda Fide] with the Acts of the Synod, I explained who were the 'viri docti' contemplated in this decree, that is, yourself and your Colleagues. So that the approbation of this Decree has been granted by the Holy See, with the cognizance and approbation of this circumstance.

The approbation of our Synod did not reach me till after Easter; and then I had to give up the only authentic copy in my hands, the Duplicate, for the press, at Paris. The printed copies have only just returned, and since they came I have been absent from home. Hence, not feeling that I could act officially till you had the approved Decree before you, I have not communicated with you on its intended application.

I now, therefore, on behalf of myself, and my episcopal Brethren request you to accept this expression of the confidence reposed in you by the English Episcopate, and to undertake the long contemplated and desired work of giving to English Catholics, and probably to many more who speak the English language, an accurate, idiomatic, and well-annotated translation of the Bible.[2]

I trust that you will accede to this request, and pray earnestly that the Holy Spirit may assist by His lights and grace, yourself and all who may be associated with you in this noble, and most religious work.

I am ever My dear Dr Newman Your affecte Servt in Xt

N. Card. Wiseman

The Very Rev. J. H. Newman DD. Superior of the Birmm Oratory Rector of the Irish Univty

Mr Arnold and Mr McCarthy. There was no difficulty or hesitation about either appointment, but they thought it as well not to make an appointment till we met in October, especially as this is Vacation and no inconvenience can arise. . . .'

[1] For this see note to letter of 14 Sept. to Wiseman.

[2] The second Provincial Synod of Westminster was held at Oscott in July 1855. As to the long delay in notifying Newman, see the Memorandum of Nov. 1857, at the end of that month.

The Oratory Birmingham August 27. 1857

My dear Lord,

I beg to acknowledge the receipt of Your Eminence's letter of this morning, containing the announcement of the singular honor which the Synod of Westminster has done me in proposing to intrust me with the revision of the English translation of the Bible.

As the Decrees of the Synod have not yet reached me, and the undertaking is so arduous, especially at my time of life and with my existing engagements, I hope I shall not be considered disrespectful or ungrateful to the Bishops, if I ask to suspend my answer till I have seen the words of the Decree.[1]

I am, My dear Lord, Your Eminence's faithful and affte Servt in Xt

John H Newman of the Oratory

His Eminence The Cardinal Wiseman

FRIDAY 28 AUGUST 1857   went over to Rednall and back

The Oratory Birmingham Aug 28. 1857

My dear Pollen,

(Private)   The Archbishops' plan is —

1. that I should be in Dublin 3 weeks a term for *one* Session as a trial.
2. Dr Ford Vice Rector. Nothing yet is definitely settled. Dr Cullen is said to have gone to Rome.

Will you learn for me, as soon as you can conveniently, what Manning's formal title is? — e.g. in dedicating a book to him. Is he Dr Manning or Father Manning.[2]

Ever Yrs affly J. H. N.

P.S.   I am just going over to see the Chapel.[3] It is as high as the top of the windows I believe

---

[1] Newman answered on 14 Sept.

[2] Newman was dedicating *Sermons preached on Various Occasions* to Manning. He addressed him as 'My Dear Dr. Manning.'

[3] i.e. the chapel at Rednal.

TO WILLIAM KIRBY SULLIVAN

The Oratory Birmingham August 28. 1857

My dear Mr Sullivan

I have done all I can in reference to the matter, about which you wrote to me. Lord Granville is in full possession of all the circumstances — though I don't wish you to mention this. Of course he cannot express any definite opinion on the existing arrangement until the year, for which it was settled that it should be tried, expires.[1]

As to the Science Faculty Paper, I think the best way will be to append it to the Scientific Journal — the first number of which, I trust, will not be long delayed. Have you thought of a name?[2]

Yours most sincerely John H Newman of the Oratory

W K Sullivan Esqr &c &c.

TO MRS JOHN MOZLEY

The Oratory Birmingham August 31. 1857

My dear Jemima

Will you kindly tell me Frank's direction? He always expresses it in initials, which I fear the Post Office would not recognise.[3]

I should not wonder, from what she says, that Miss Giberne will be paying you a call. If she should ask for any thing early of mine, handwriting, letters to me, letters from me, pictures etc, pray do not give her any thing. I can't help having the suspicion that she means, if she lives longer than I, to write some account of me — which I should not know indeed then, but the prospect of which I cannot endure.

I hope you are well and am My dear Jemima Ever affectly Yours

John H Newman

Mrs J Mozley

FRIDAY 4 SEPTEMBER 1857   pretty well finished article on Benedictines
SATURDAY 5 SEPTEMBER   Bishop called   Fr O Reilly came
SUNDAY 6 SEPTEMBER   Fr O Reilly went in evening

[1] See letter of 9 Aug. to Sullivan.
[2] See letter of 9 Oct. to Sullivan.
[3] Francis Newman's address was 7 Park Village East, London, NW, which he abbreviated 7 PVE, NW. He was writing to Newman at this period about Latin grammars, and about politics. On 13 Oct. he explained why, although he was a supporter of Kossuth's rebellion in Hungary, he did not support the Sepoys in the Indian Mutiny.

TO ROBERT ORNSBY

The Oratory Birmingham ⌈Sept 6/57⌉

My dear Ornsby

I really must not let a post go, or you will think me the rudest person in the world. Fr St John used my name yesterday, to send you a telegraphic message yesterday — for we wanted to anticipate the Birmingham post to Wilberforce, and did not recollect who else would be in Dublin but you — Then as for me, I have been over worked with my article for the Journal, which would not come to an end — [1] and then again ⌈I hoped,⌉ if I waited writing to you, ⌈to have something to tell you about my Rectorship.

But I have nothing. The point unsettled is the Vice Rectorship, and every thing depends on this — [1] but I don't wish this said.

Thank you for your extract from the Paper.[2] Thank you also for the insurance receipt, tho', how you came by it, I can't conjecture — through Copeland, if I must hazard.

I like the idea of your pursuing Greek and Roman Education — and hope you will make progress in it.

Fr O'Reilly is here today in his way to Scotland.

⌈The Archbishops are to meet in October — nothing will be settled about the Vice Rectorship till then. Of course the choice might be such, as to make any arrangement in which I was included impossible. But I trust the selection will be a good one.⌉

Ever Yours affly John H Newman of the Oratory

R Ornsby Esqr

MONDAY 7 SEPTEMBER 1857 Robert went to London   Edward went   Sir Arnold Knight called[3]   Frederic Godwin went home.

TUESDAY 8 SEPTEMBER   Austin and Scott went to opening of new Church at Stoke Robert returned

TO THOMAS HAYDEN

The Oratory, Birmingham. Septr. 8/57

My dear Dr Hayden,

I suppose my letter has crossed yours of this morning. I wrote, I think, on Sunday, to say that Mr O'Reilly had nothing whatever to do with us so you must not let him have the room, or come into the building.

Very sincerely yrs, John H. Newman

Thos Hayden Esq.

[1] 'The Mission of St Benedict,' for the *Atlantis.*
[2] This was a paragraph from *Saunders' News-letter.*
[3] Sir Arnold Knight (1789–1871), at Oscott College, M.D. Edinburgh University, 1811, a doctor at Sheffield, was knighted in 1841. He died at Little Malvern.

WEDNESDAY 9 SEPTEMBER 1857   much rain these weeks.

TO WILLIAM KIRBY SULLIVAN

The Oratory Birmingham Septr 9. 1857

My dear Mr Sullivan,

Thank you for the very satisfactory account you give me of the way in which the University acquitted itself at the Meeting. I doubt not, it is a great step for us, and a very good introduction to our Register.[1]

1. If you refer to the Prospectus, marked *private*, I there contemplate in each number 104 Literary pages, 48 scientific — and Reviews etc 56 — making in all 208 or 13 sheets. This arrangement was made after the pattern of the Genevan periodical — [2] You think it perhaps too much — or do I misunderstand you as thinking 58 Literary and 48 scientific enough, or nearly so? Of course we must carefully consider what we *can* do.

2. Your ethnological paper should come in the first number. People will take the first number as a specimen, not only of execution, but of our *idea* what the Register should be, in point of subjects etc. Now I dread their looking out for light reading and not finding it, and being disappointed. If we have too much of what *might* be light, as far as *material* goes, *done* heavily, they will think that we have aimed at something which we have not fulfilled — if it is light material done *lightly*, it may please at the instant, but will give a very false idea of what our publication is to be. Therefore, the first number ought either to have a good deal of science in it, or to have the literary part done scientifically. Now your article on ethnology is such as we want to give a character to the work — for it *must* be a solid scientific article, though in the literary part of the Register. I am afraid of my own, which is historical, whether it be heavy *or* light, for the reasons above given — i.e. because its subject is a light and interesting one. I don't know what people would say to Mr Pollen's — it is *good* and *heavy*, — but *before* the standard was set, people would think it ought to be, and was meant to be, light. I think we had better accumulate articles, and then take our choice out of them.[3]

3. I quite agree with you, that the Reviews should not be off hand or currente calamo, but digests.

Altogether so much depends on the start, that we must not be hasty

Very sincerely Yours John H Newman

P.S.   *Will you tell me whether we should use 'we' or 'I'?*

---

[1] This perhaps refers to the Meeting of the British Association, in Dublin.

[2] Each number of the *Bibliothèque Universelle de Genève* was divided into literary articles, six sheets, scientific, three and a half sheets, and literary and scientific notices, two sheets each.

[3] The first and third articles in the literary part of the *Atlantis*, (Jan. 1858), were Newman's on the Benedictines and Pollen's on the Basilicas. The second article was Sullivan's 'On the

TO HENRY WILBERFORCE

The Oratory Birmingham ⌐Sept 10/57¬

My dear H W

⌐Will you put into the Register a paragraph to the effect that acting under the decrees of the last synod of Westminster, which have lately been returned from Rome, the Cardinal has committed to Dr Newman the preparation of a corrected Version in English of Holy Scripture.¬[11]

I am sorry you were troubled by Ambrose's letter — He went rather too far, or rather too fast. When I heard that he had written to you to *come*, I made him countermand you. Mr Bohn is a very extraordinary man — if every thing is smooth-sailing, it would be a wonderful catch — but he is too plausible to be trusted. He began by saying that he had been nearly put into confinement as a lunatic, an honest, but not an assuring avowal.

Ever Yours affly J H N

⌐P.S. Sept 11. We have got at the bottom of Mr Bohn — He is a clever man with a patent, which I dare say will answer — *but he has no money*, and wants a monied partner.¬[12]

FRIDAY 11 SEPTEMBER 1857 went to London and back. to dentist, Burns, Longmans, Stewart.

SATURDAY 12 SEPTEMBER Mr Robertson (of Clapham) called James Delany went home

influence which the Physical Geography, the Animal and Vegetable Productions, etc., of different regions exert upon the Languages, Mythology, and early Literature of Mankind, with reference to its employment of Ethnological Hypotheses.'

[1] The first leading article in the *Weekly Register*, (26 Sept. 1857), p. 8, was headed, 'Revision of the English Translation of Holy Scripture,' and began: 'We are authorised to state that, in accordance with the decrees of the last Synod of Westminster, which have lately been returned from Rome with the approbation of the Holy See, the Cardinal Archbishop of Westminster has entrusted the preparation of a corrected version in English of Holy Scripture to the care of Dr. Newman.

Never has it been our duty to make an announcement which has given us more heartfelt satisfaction; and we doubt not, it will be shared by all classes of our readers. . . .'

[2] It would seem that St John thought he had found someone to assist Wilberforce with the *Weekly Register*, namely James Stuart Burges Bohn (1803–80), a London bookseller, not to be confused with Henry George Bohn. James Bohn was twice unsuccessful as a bookseller, and after 1847 went in for journalism, contributing to the *Family Herald*, and acting as assistant editor of the *Reader*. In 1857 he worked on a catalogue of theological books for David Nutt, which ran to 704 pages.

TO PATRICK LEAHY, ARCHBISHOP OF CASHEL

Sept 12/57

(sent in *substance*)

My dear Lord

I write a line in answer to yours of August 28 — lest you should be in suspence — merely to thank you for it — [1] and to say that before the Archbishops' meeting in October, of which you inform me in it, I will answer your former letter from Templemore about the Vice Rector.[2] Then I will lay before their Graces what I have to suggest on the two proposals which they have been so kind as to mention to me[3]

I am &c J H N

SUNDAY 13 SEPTEMBER 1857   sung High Mass in want of Priests
MONDAY 14 SEPTEMBER   Miss Giberne returned   Bishop of Strasburg called[4]

TO CARDINAL WISEMAN

The Oratory, Birmingham September 14. 1857

(Copy)

My dear Lord

I have received the copy of the Decrees of the Second Provincial Synod of Westminster, which your Eminence has had the kindness to send me — and, having read the particular Decree to which you have called my attention, in your letter ot the 26th of last month, I now proceed to reply to the communication with which you have honored me in the name both of your Eminence and of the Bishops of England.[5]

[1] For this letter see letter of 26 Aug. to Leahy.
[2] After his letter of 25 Aug. from Tipperary, which Newman answered next day, Leahy wrote a second letter, from Templemore, as follows, 'In my Letter today from Tipperary I forgot an important part of my commission.
The Archbishops have desired me to ask you whether you have any objection to Dr Forde, as Vice-Rector—that is in the event of all parties assenting to the "middle plan", suggested in your Letter to me.
Should you have an objection to Dr. Forde, then their Lordships ask you to place before them the names of two or three Irish Priests, residing in Ireland, from amongst whom they may choose a Vice-Rector.'
[3] See Newman's letters of 16 Oct. to Leahy.
[4] Andreas Räss (1794–1887), became Bishop of Strasburg in 1842 and devoted himself to the formation of his clergy. He was a supporter of foreign missions and of the definition of papal infallibility. The chief of his publications was *Die Convertiten seit der Reformation*, thirteen volumes, 1866–80, an account of the converts from Protestantism to Catholicism, during the period 1540–1800.
[5] The ninth decree of the second Provincial Synod of Westminster, 'De versione canonicarum Scripturarum,' ran as follows:
'Ut versio accurata sacrae Scripturae ex Vulgata Latina quam primum habeatur, Patres censuerunt committendam esse viris doctis ab eminentissimo archiepiscopo eligendis ejus

A greater honor, I feel, could not possibly have been done me than that which your Eminence in that communication has conferred, in selecting me for the office of preparing an annotated English version of the Bible; and I beg your Eminence and through you the Episcopal Body, to receive the heartfelt and most humble acknowledgments, which so high and singular a mark of approbation and confidence demands at my hands.

If I accept the work put upon me without hesitation or reluctance, it is not as if I did not feel its arduousness to be as great as its honor, but because nothing seems left to me but to obey the expression of a wish which comes to me from your Eminence with the concurrence of a Provincial Council.

As soon as ever I am free from some great engagements which at the moment are pressing, I will without delay address myself to the work.

Meanwhile, I should very much wish to know, whether any general directions will be given me for its execution, beyond those which its object involves; and also, whether your Eminence wishes me to meet the initial and incidental expenses, which are involved in its preparation, and which I foresee will be considerable, by means of the copyright, or whether any other mode of covering them has suggested itself to your mind.

Kissing the sacred purple, and begging your Eminence's blessing, I am, My dear Lord, Your affte Servt in Xt

John H Newman of the Oratory

His Eminence The Cardl Wiseman

London, Oct 6. 1857

My Dear Dr Newman

I have communicated to all the Bishops, your kind acceptance of the important undertaking of revising our English version of the Vulgate.

Your observation and enquiry about the preliminary expenses, and the manner of meeting them, are matter for very serious consideration.

I do not think copyright could be conceded of a work so eminently belonging to the whole body of Catholics speaking English.

But before a plan can be formed for mature deliberation, I think it would be very expedient, or even necessary to have some approximating calculation of what the expense would be of translating, transcribing etc before the work goes into the publishers' hands, remunerating of course fairly all employed. If you could confidentially furnish me with such an estimate, leaving a wide margin, I could see how the plan I have thought of would answer, without dealing about it with others. If I find that the two could not be made to fit one another something else must be devised.

I need not say that all the answers which I have received from the Bishops have expressed great satisfaction at your having acceded to their wishes

I am ever My dear Dr Newman Your affecte Sert in Xt

N. Card. Wiseman[1]

The Very Revd Dr Newman

confectionem, servatis tamen regulis Indicis quoad operis revisionem, notas apponendas ex SS. Patribus et piis scriptoribus desumptas et permissionem et approbationem lectionis ejusdem.' *Acta et Decreta secundi Concilii Provincialis Westmonasteriensis*, Paris 1857, p. 30.

[1] For Newman's reply see letter of 7 Nov. to Wiseman.

TUESDAY 15 SEPTEMBER 1857 went to Rednall and back
WEDNESDAY 16 SEPTEMBER two Fathers of the London Ory [Oratory] called

TO D. B. DUNNE

The Oratory, Birmingham Septr 16. 1857

My dear Dr Dunne,

I must have seemed very rude to you in keeping silence after your kind letter, when you sent me too the Cork Calendar besides, but I hoped soon to have sent you some news in return for yours, and then, when time went on and the news was not forthcoming, there seemed no reason for writing one week rather than the next, particularly as I happened to be very busy.[1]

I wish I had any thing to tell you for certain now — but the meeting in July was adjourned till August, and now it is to be reviewed in October — and I really do not know how matters will go. They say that Dr Cullen is gone to Rome — I never should be surprised, if it were considered the simplest arrangement to have a new Rector at once.

Meanwhile, I hope we are getting on satisfactorily with the Scientific Register, though I don't think it will be prudent to publish till we have two numbers in type — and we have as yet several departments without specimens provided — and I suppose the first numbers should, if possible, be samples of what we intend to do.

Your information about the Irish College at Paris singularly corresponded to the account given by the writer of the Times Letter — where does he get his information? The most singular characteristic of those letters is, that they are so carefully doctored, that you cannot say on which side the writer is — as if in order that the source should not be discovered.[2]

I hope you and Mrs Dunne have been enjoying this fine summer, and that you are quite recruited after the labours of the Session.

Yours, My dear Dr Dunne, affectionately John H Newman

[1] On 25 July Dunne wrote to Newman all the news he could glean concerning the Archbishops' meetings about the Rectorship.

[2] Dunne wrote on 25 July, 'In the Irish College of Paris the government was shared between the President and his Council. This Council consists of the Vice President and Professors. Some of the Council have been in a state of direct antagonism with the President for a long time. Amongst them (I believe) was a nephew of Dr. MacHale. The three Archbishops, on Tuesday last, suspended the Council—thus committing the whole government to the President only. Dr. Miley, the President, is not much liked by Dr. MacHale;—at least, so rumour says.

This act, which is at least not one of censure on the President, may render Dr. MacHale still more hostile towards us.'

The Times of 20 Aug., p. 10, had similar information in a private letter from Rome quoted by its Paris correspondent. This letter stated 'that Cardinal Barnabò and Dr Cullen . . . persevere in their determination to remodel or reform the Catholic Church in Ireland,' in spite of the opposition of MacHale. A beginning had been made with the Irish College in Paris. The letter then gave a fairly accurate account of Newman's position at the Catholic University, and added, 'It is much to be deplored that all the Irish prelates and priests do not appear to afford this eminent man the moral support and sympathy to which he is so well entitled . . .'

TUESDAY 22 SEPTEMBER 1857   party went over to St Wilfrid's for Mass.[1]

THURSDAY 24 SEPTEMBER   Mrs Froude came from Bristol for some hours. (Dr Ogle died this day)

MONDAY 28 SEPTEMBER   called on the Bishop taking my article on Benedictines. Farfan came

TO MANUEL JOHNSON

The Oratory, Birmingham Septr 28. 1857

My dear Johnson,

Thank you for your letter, most sad as it is.[2] And thank all the dear children, whom I only recollect as little ones, for their thought of me. I knew their Father, and their Mother too, before they were born — and I know how much they must feel the loss they have sustained. It is more than the immediate loss, great as that is — for it is the snapping of a tie, which for so many years has bound so many in one. I recollect their Mother, more than some of them do; and I know how overwhelming was their Father's grief, when he lost her.[3] I know, as to both Father and Mother, how great were the claims of both of them on the affection and abiding remembrance of their children. You say nothing of Miss Homfray — where is she? — I have the greatest regard for her — and I wish you to say everything kind from me to her, as to all of them, particularly your dear wife. It seems but the other day when they were all little bits of things upon the floor — but I was young then also.

Thus I am carried back to a still earlier time, when John Bowden and I lived so much with their Father. That is near forty years ago. One by one, like the sparks upon burnt paper, my earlier recollections are going out. Henry Bowden and you are some of the earliest now which remain.

My dear Manuel, it is sad, that with my face deliberately turned, as it is, to the future, I should have such pain in looking back at the past, which cannot return. But the longer I live, the more vivid and the more tender are my recollections of my youth — and the longer I live, the fewer people are there on earth, who bear part in them, and who could sympathise in them, were they near me.

I never forget you all. My godson Octavius[4] is still continually in my prayers

Ever Yours most affectionately John H Newman

M. Johnson Esqr

[1] The anniversary mass for Mrs Caswall, who was buried at St Wilfrid's on 22 Sept. 1849.
[2] Johnson wrote on 26 Sept. from Shoreham, to announce the death of his father-in-law, James Adey Ogle, who died there on 23 Sept. Ogle had been Newman's private tutor, and close friend. Cf. *Apo.* p. 236.
[3] Ogle's wife, Sarah Homfray died in 1835. Miss Homfray was her sister.
[4] Johnson's brother-in-law, Octavius Ogle, Fellow of Lincoln College. See letter of 20 Oct. to him.

TUESDAY 29 SEPTEMBER 1857 Edward's speech and music[1] Farfan went. (Dr Forbes of America called and went with Robert to Rednall) (Fr Crowther came.)

FROM WILLIAM DODSWORTH

Tunbridge Wells 27 Sep 1857.

My dear Newman,

Along with many others I rejoice that the work of revising the Translation of the Bible is committed to you. Probably you will be inundated with suggestions. With less experience of your kindness I should not venture to send mine, but that will induce you, without apology on my part, to take them for what they are worth— and do not trouble yourself to reply.

I would suggest then the bold course, for such it certainly would be, of taking the English 'authorised Version' as the foundation of your Revise. The objections of course are great and obvious, but yet I think the advantages outweigh them. Many Catholics of the old school would be outrageous, and I suppose a terrible storm would be raised in Ireland. But in England that 'old school' is not powerful, and in Ireland might it not be possible to win over some of the Bishops? Then I suppose the Revise will only be recommended and not enforced so that time would be allowed for it gradually to supplant the Douay.

But how great would be the advantages.

1. A more beautiful translation than can be hoped for in any other method.
2. A better translation than the Protestants themselves possess, because corrected —it would be at once adopted by High-Church Anglicans.
3. It would remove a great hindrance to English conversions.
4. It would expose protestant methods of perverting truth.
5. It would save you an immensity of labour.

Besides is it not really the *common sense* view of the matter? If you had to revise a Bible for China, and there already existed one of surpassing beauty, and the idol of the greater number of the inhabitants, and only disfigured by a few gross errors —would not your course be obvious? Doubtless a song of triumph would be raised by Protestants. Well, let them have their triumph so far as it is a just one. Why should we grudge it? At the same time it would tend to convince the more candid amongst them that uninfluenced by prejudice we only seek truth, and independent of all circumstances wish to place it in the most attractive form.

It seems to me a great opportunity, and worthy of a great struggle as no doubt it would be.

Then if Irish prejudice *were* surmounted how much it might tend to remove that hatred of Saxons which we have too justly incurred.

Excuse all this, and do not give yourself the trouble to reply.

Ever yours very affecty W. Dodsworth.

[1] This was Caswall's report to people around the Oratory of the year's work. He spoke of the various guilds and schools, of the service of the Birmingham Workhouse, the Prison and the Asylum, about the attempt to start a Catholic hospital, and about the work at Smethwick, where a large population was congregating round the new foundries.

Caswall went on to speak of the translation of the Scriptures, entrusted to Newman, the members of the Oratory being associated with him in the work. He then asked his hearers to pray 'that the time of our Father's sojourn in Ireland may be shortened,' and that the Oratory might at once enjoy his presence. Newman wrote in pencil on the MS. at this point, 'I think you may say something stronger than this. I really have come back, except for 9 weeks—and that the Irish Bishops have only asked for one year.' In consequence Caswall added a couple of sentences to his speech.

TO WILLIAM DODSWORTH

The Oratory, Birmingham Septr. 29. 1857.

My dear Dodsworth,

I am glad of anything which gives me an opportunity of seeing your writing and I wish I had means of talking with you on the important subject of your letter.

I quite agree with you in the abstract, and think your arguments most weighty — but I much fear, when the matter is closely looked into, that what you suggest is impossible. For instance, take the Psalms — there perhaps the poverty of our version, and the beauty of the Protestant are best contrasted. Here first, *account* for the difference between the versions in Prayer Book and Bible. Is not the Bible version, (made *after* the Prayer Book version) said to be more correct, but the harsher? what does this mean, but that when the Psalms were to be adapted for *recital*, it was found necessary to doctor them? And this is not a solitary instance of that process in the Anglican Service books — what can be more harmonious and majestic than the language of the Collects? but I think Isaac Williams shows that they have been altered in translation, and I should say, for the sake of the rhythm. Take the Collect for last Sunday — see how the Reformers have diluted the original — yet how musical they have made it, 'diabolica vitare contagia' — 'to withstand the temptations of the world, the flēsh ănd thĕ devil.' I know, that for myself, I am apt to go into the other extreme, for, much as I like good music, I have sometimes too ruthlessly despised it in order to bring out strongly the very sense which had to be brought out — and have on that account been censured. However, the rule holds good, that we must not sacrifice sense to sound; — and, especially, in an inspired text.

But, if this would create a difficulty even in having to revise an Anglican version, much greater is it, when we have to translate from the Vulgate. Considering how much the Vulgate differs from the received Hebrew text, in the instance of the Psalms, how can I possibly *use* the Protestant version in my translation? E.g. mons coagulatus, mons pinguis — ut quid suspicamini montes coagulatos? — 'Even an high hill, as the hill of Bashan. Why hop ye so, ye high hills?'[1]

Again, in this very instance, what makes 'hop ye so?' tolerable to a Protestant but custom? would a Catholic, who never heard it before, endure it? — so that even in point of English, let alone the sense, there would be a difficulty.

I consider then it is indisputable, that 'the bold course of taking the English Authorized version as the *foundation* of our Revise,' to use your words, is impossible.

[1] *Psalm* 67 : 16.

When you come to the question of *availing* oneself of the Authorized Version, that is another question altogether — Challoner has done *this*; and certainly there is no reason I might not do it; but to do so does not answer the objects or secure the advantages, which you suggest.

Another enormous difficulty, if I were to continue my objections, would be found in the theological impress which has been put upon portions of the sacred text. 'Justice' is a theological term — and to say 'righteousness' would bring in great confusion. — 'Penitence' for 'penance', even if critical, which I doubt, would be untheological. — What are we to do with 'What is to me and to thee, Woman?' Dr Kenrick says 'What hast thou to do with Me?'[1] I would willingly accept it — but I fear the devotion of Catholics would (most irrationally) be offended.

And you must recollect altogether, that my labour has to be subjected, when completed, to English censors — and to Roman. I might find it rejected in toto; — or irreparably damaged, or utterly destroyed, by emendations.

Should you have any thing to say, on reading the above, pray give me the benefit of it — I assure you, there is no work I should less have liked committed to me. I had cut out my own work for myself — for which I consider myself adapted — [2] and here comes an undertaking, which I cannot decline, to occupy the few years of mental vigour which may remain to me.[3]

I am, My dear Dodsworth Most sincerely Yours in Xt

John H Newman of the Oratory.

WEDNESDAY 30 SEPTEMBER 1857   Austin and Henry went for holy day

TO H. E. MANNING

The Oratory, Birmingham Septr 30. 1857

My dear Manning

You will have my little volume in a few days.[4] I suppose I can scarcely hope you will not be disappointed with it. I should not have ventured to offer you so second rate a thing, had I not happened to be concluding it, on the 2nd of July. You will see several which you [have] seen before, out of the whole number of Sermons. Altogether, it is not worthy of its Dedication

Ever Yours affly John H Newman

The Very Revd Dr Manning

[1] i.e. Archbishop Kenrick's translation.
[2] See the end of Newman's letter of 27 Feb. 1857 to Ullathorne and last note there; also the first paragraph of W. G. Ward's letter to Newman of 29 Sept. in *Ward*, I, p. 420.
[3] See also letter of 7 Oct. to Dodsworth.
[4] *Sermons preached on Various Occasions*, dedicated to Manning.

TO ROBERT ORNSBY

The Oratory, Birmingham Septr 30. 1857

My dear Ornsby,

I have just received your kind present of the Life of St Francis;[1] and I have thanked you already in the best manner, by taking it up, and reading various parts of it. And now I must thank you again, not for giving it, but for writing it — for it is a very beautiful book, and leads one to regret that your duties should oblige you to do any thing else but write Saints' Lives, and should take you away from St Francis to Cicero and Seneca. But our Professors and Undergraduates will be of a different mind.

Ever Yours affectly in Xt   John H Newman of the Oratory

R Ornsby Esqr

TO JAMES STEWART

The Oratory, Birmingham Septr 30. 1857

My dear Stewart

I was very glad to see your handwriting, and to hear of your removal into the neighbourhood of the University, as, after Drumcondra, Great Charles Street certainly is — and, considering all negociations between great parties end in compromises, you certainly seem to have claims on the University, since you have met it half way, that it should go the other half, and settle down in Rutland Square. And the circumstance you have such a consensus in favor of your locality, as Ornsby, Butler, and Robertson, the Archiepiscopal Palace, and the Jesuit and Dominican Houses give you, puts Number 86 clearly in the wrong, if it does not cross over Carlisle Bridge before term commences. But as to yourself, I have always thought the walk in all weathers from Drumcondra to Stephen's Green too much even for an active man like you — so I am very glad you have moved.

You are always so very kind in wishing me to stay in Dublin, that I feel a bad conscience, as if it were ingratitude in me, to be so resolute in going. But really I do not know what *can* keep me. As the negociation is not concluded, I do not like to talk about it; but, as far as I am concerned, nothing shall I not think it my duty to do, in order to avoid further absence from my Congregation here. I will tell you in confidence (what it so happens I have told to no one) that all that the Archbishops now ask is a year more. And, even if Dr Cullen wished to ask the interference of Propaganda, (which I much doubt) I think he would not ask any more than my *full* residence during that one year, which my Congregation has not granted. But, if you ask me, I think

---

[1] Robert Ornsby, *The Life of St. Francis of Sales*, London 1856.

Dr C wishes me to go, and his only puzzle is to find a successor whom he would like. But he is so close a man, it is impossible to know.

Say everything kind from me to Mrs Stewart, and to Butler, Ornsby, and other friends. Yours, my dear Stewart Most Sincerely in Xt

John H Newman of the Oratory.

James Stewart Esq.

THURSDAY I OCTOBER 1857 Fr Crowther went
SATURDAY 3 OCTOBER   Robert went over with Northcote to Stoke
SUNDAY 4 OCTOBER   I duplicated   Robert returned
MONDAY 5 OCTOBER   Robert returned [sic]   Tooth ache *for some days.*
TUESDAY 6 OCTOBER   could not say Mass

TO H. E. MANNING

The Oratory, Birmingham Octr 6. 1857

My dear Manning

An unhappy tooth will bring me to a London Dentist — *perhaps* on Tuesday next. If you are at Bayswater then, I would call on you and save you the trouble of coming down here. Let me know your movements and engagements. Unluckily, with the risk of tooth ache, I should be obliged to see what the day was like, before I set out and might disappoint you

Ever Yrs affly John H Newman

The Very Revd Dr Manning

TUESDAY 7 OCTOBER 1857   communicated without saying Mass

TO WILLIAM DODSWORTH

The Oratory, Birmm Oct 7. 1857.

My dear Dodsworth,

Of course I do not mean to put aside your suggestions for good and all, which would be a poor use of what is very valuable — but I do not see how they can practically be acted on, at present.[1]

E.g. I translate from the Vulgate Mic. V.6. literally. I am *obliged* to be literal. 'Now shalt thou be laid waste, O daughter of a robber; they have laid siege against us, they shall smite with a rod the cheek of the Judge of Israel.'

Now the Douay. 'Now shalt thou be laid waste O daughter of the robber; they have laid siege against us, with a rod shall they strike the cheek of the Judge of Israel.'

[1] Dodsworth's reply to Newman's letter of 29 Sept. is not to be found.

Now the Protestant: 'Now gather thyself in troops, O daughter of troops; he hath laid siege against us; they shall smite the Judge of Israel with a rod upon the cheek.'

First: Is the Protestant version better English than the Douay? Secondly — *Can I*, consistent with the Vulgate, make my translation nearer the Protestant than the Douay?

Zeph iii. 1   I am taking these instances at random, or nearly so —

Literal.   'Woe to the city that provoketh and hath been redeemed, the dove. She hath not heard the voice, nor accepted discipline; she hath not trusted in the Lord nor approached unto her God.'

Douay.   'Woe to the provoking and redeemed city, the dove; she hath not hearkened [sic] to the voice, neither hath she received discipline; she hath not trusted in the Lord, she drew not near to her God.'

Protestant.   'Woe to her that is filthy and polluted, to the oppressing city. She obeyed not the voice, she received not correction. She trusted not in the Lord, she drew not near to her God.'

1. How can I so translate, as to be able to say that the Protestant Version is my *basis*? 2. Is not the Douay better than mine? is it not so on a par with the Protestant in English, that you could not say which was which?

Jer. xlvi. 21–22.   'Her hirelings also that lived in the midst of her, like fatted calves are turned back, and are fled away together, and they could not stand for the day of their slaughter is come upon them, the time of their visitation. Her voice shall sound like brass — for they shall hasten with an army, and with axes they shall come against her, as hewers of wood.'

(Protestant) 'Also her hired men are in the midst of her like fatted bullocks; for they also are turned back and are fled away together; they did not stand because the day of their calamity was come upon them, and the time of their visitation. The voice thereof shall go like a serpent; for they shall march with an army, and come against her with axes, as hewers of wood.'

I don't think you would know the one from the other, except for the word 'Also' coming first in the sentence, and 'because' for 'for', and 'thereof' for 'her'. But to preserve such archaisms is not to translate on *the basis*.

Then in the New Testament, I doubt whether some phrases which we are attached to are not from custom only good, though it is difficult to know what to put instead, when every translation must [appear] strange. Such as 'Men *and* brethren' — 'he answered and said' etc.

On the whole the more I think about it, the more I come to the conclusion, that, as far as *English* goes, I only have to *correct*. It is another thing if I must illustrate the text of the Vulgate by the Hebrew and Greek originals. I shall rejoice to see your Article — and shall be most grateful for your notes — but I am at present limited to Fathers of the Oratory as writers by the Cardinal's Letter.

Ever yours affly J.H. Newman

The Oratory, Birmingham Octr 7. 1857

My dear Sir,

I take the liberty of writing to you on the subject of a lady, with whom members of your family were, I believe, at one time intimate, and had opportunities of knowing and valuing more than I can have had. Yet, as I have heard of her several times lately, and you probably have not, I seem to have a reason for introducing her name to you — I mean Miss Holmes.

She is at Boulogne, and I fear in some pecuniary embarassment — to what extent I do not know — I suppose not much. The anxiety seems to have affected her health — a fresh letter has just come to me from her — and she speaks of having been confined to her room for a month, but now getting about. Her friends on the spot are afraid of her chest — else, she says, 'If I can only get strong enough to take a situation at a high salary in England, with my experience of the last ten years, I can manage to pay off every thing in a year.'

No one regrets more than I can, to find her so often change her plans. I have never attempted to offer her any advice on the subject, when she has happened to write to me, as knowing literally nothing, and having no means of judging, about the circumstances which influenced her — but I have been grieved to see that, as years go on, she is as uncertain about the future, and as destitute of means of meeting it, as ever.

I am writing to you, as I have written to a friend elsewhere who knows her, from the interest I take in her, and my own utter incapacity to give advice — and, while I have reason to believe that you take interest in her also, I am quite sure that you are far more able than I to make suggestions which may be of service to her in her present difficulties.

She has no notion whatever that I am writing to any one about her.[1]

I am, My dear Sir, with much respect, Sincerely Yours in Xt

John H Newman of the Oratory

Wm Leigh Esqr

The Oratory Birmingham Octr 7. 1857

My dear Dr Todd

I have received your circular about the choice of Books for Schools etc. It is a subject in which I take great interest, and shall be very glad in aiding according to my ability.

[1] See letter of 10 Oct. to Leigh.

Two points, however, strike me to mention.

First, I know nothing about Schools of Primary Education, and could be no judge as to what books are wanted, and what suitable. The difficulty which *I* feel great anxiety about is in the education of the upper class — We want Histories of Greece and Rome — General History — Lives of Great Men — Histories of Literature — of periods of the Church — of national or local Churches — of revolutions etc etc. e.g. Italian literature, the Normans, the Moors in Spain, the Inquisition, Roman Empire, French Protestantism, Cromwell, Origen, Revolution of 1688 etc etc. Again, Books of Evidences of Christianity — Introductions or Analyses of Scripture — Account of the Greek Church — Account of German Philosophy etc etc

Of course I might go on indefinitely — I mention these, not as hoping ever to see them all done, but to show how much there is to do. And that, not in the way of *instructive or entertaining Literature*; (in which line Burns is doing so much,) but in providing books *which are to be got up*. It is plain that I am aiming at *University Manuals*; but they would also be in request for the upper classes in Colleges, or ought to be.

Fr Darnell of this Oratory is translating Dollinger's new and important work on Heathenism and Judaism when our Lord came.[1] *This* is the kind of book I am desiderating.

I fear you will think I am travelling in a different direction from your own — but I think it best to say what I myself feel, and to ask for your thoughts upon it. It would be travelling to another subject altogether, if I went on to speak of the ways and means by which such books should be secured; yet I will touch on the subject, merely that you may more fully understand what I am interested in principally. There have been several attempts on the part of Dolman, which have failed, to get up subscriptions for 'Libraries — ' but certainly it is what ought to be done. Some authors would require payment, but others would not — and would be satisfied with getting their books printed free of expense. I think some good books would be written by nuns. Such works would ultimately pay at least their expenses, so that, if one could get subscriptions enough for (say) three years, the then incomings from the volumes printed in those three years would suffer one to continue on the series with out further subscription. A thousand pounds raised for this purpose would suffice. I wish I had it for the object.

And now, to return to my subject. You see that, though I will gladly take part in any plan for books of primary instruction, my heart is not with them, nor my power of being useful.

My second remark is more immediately important; — in what relation does your plan stand to the Bishops? Your Circular says, 'In the *absence* of any authoritative body — ' but surely there is a medium, between a formally appointed Committee and a self constituted set of revisors. If you are

---

[1] Döllinger's *Heidentum und Judentum* was published in 1857; Darnell's translation, *The Gentile and the Jew*, two volumes, London 1862. See letter of 25 Nov. to Acton.

contemplating parochial schools, it seems simply necessary in some way or other to speak with episcopal sanction[1]

Ever Yours most sincerely John H Newman of the Oratory
The Revd Dr Todd

THURSDAY 8 OCTOBER 1857   said mass upstairs   A. Bethell came   had leeches on my gum at night

FRIDAY 9 OCTOBER   said mass upstairs

TO WILLIAM MONSELL

The Oy Bm Octr 9. 1857

Private
My dear Monsell,

I have not written to you about the University, because there is nothing to say. The Archbishops are not to meet till the end of the month; — when, I *suppose*, Dr Cullen will have returned from Rome. They have suggested a person for Vice Rector who would be simply inadmissible.[2] I should be a traitor to the University if I concurred in such a choice. But they have asked me also to mention any names of *priests, Irishmen,* and who *live in Ireland —* and I have taken the advice of Dr Moriarty and Dr Russell on the subject.

This is how things stand, except that they have taken me only for *one* year more, with a few weeks residence in each term.

Pray say every thing kind and respectful from me to Mrs Monsell in prettier French than I can command

Ever Yrs affly John H Newman of the Oratory
The Rt Honble W Monsell M P

TO WILLIAM KIRBY SULLIVAN

Oy Bm Octr 9/57

Private
My dear Mr Sullivan

Dr Russell will give us his Paper.[3] I asked him in confidence about the name of the Register. He says 'I should decidedly object to Erigena as your

---

[1] Todd was the priest at Chiselhurst, Kent.

[2] i.e. Laurence Forde. See note to letter of 12 Sept. to Leahy.

[3] This was a paper Russell had read at the meeting of the British Association in Dublin, in Aug., 'On the Inhabitants and Dialect of the Barony of Forth, in the County of Wexford,' published in the *Atlantis*, (Jan. 1858), pp. 235–44.

title. Recollect that his errors were not merely in theology but in philosophy too — and those precisely which fall in best with the modern heterodox schools.' So *that* is settled — He adds 'Columba would be infinitely better — ' 'Of all the others Atlantis pleases me best — and yet it does not satisfy me.'[1]

Of course you will not repeat the above. I think we must take Atlantis — We ought to decide by the 25th of this month.

Yours most sincerely John H Newman of the Oratory

W K Sullivan Esqr

P.S.   I personally should like Columba from the sound — but I suppose it would surprise people. Some one has suggested Catholicon. What is to be thought of *Ierne — Eblana — [2] Hagionesus* ('Isle of Saints' being a received title) — *Ogygia*, a name of Ireland, I see? I mention these, because, titles which will not answer, often suggest others which will.

SATURDAY 10 OCTOBER 1857   said mass upstairs   had the tooth out   Mr Sukely, Robert's friend, came.

TO MISS HOLMES

Oy Bm Oct 10/57

My dear Miss Holmes

The Hope Scotts write very anxiously and kindly about you.

I wish you could make out *what your debts are.*

Ever Yrs affly J H N

If you stay the winter, you will make your debts greater. Surely it is well to leave at once.

TO WILLIAM LEIGH

The Oratory Birmingham Octr 10. 1857

My dear Mr Leigh,

I am very much pleased to receive so kind a letter from you. And I also thank you and Mrs Leigh very much, for showing me so promptly that I judged rightly in believing that you took a warm interest in Miss Holmes.[3]

---

[1] Sullivan wrote on 11 Sept., 'I suppose Mr Hennessy mentioned to you the name "*Atlantis.*" I think some name of this kind would be very good. It would be intelligible, historical, geographical and poetical.' On 5 Oct. Sullivan was writing that he preferred 'Erigena.' 'The derivation as you say is good, the man himself represents the best period of Irish History—therefore the period which would call up the pleasantest memories.'

[2] This was the name of Dublin on Ptolemy's map.

[3] William Leigh, who lived at Woodchester Park, Stroud, was well known for his generosity. On 21 Oct. he wrote to thank Newman for the gift of a copy of *O.S.*

I have sent on Mrs Leigh's letter. Pray convey to her my best respect — I do not forget that I once had the pleasure of being introduced to her

Yours, My dear Mr Leigh, Most sincerely in Xt

John H Newman of the Oratory

Wm Leigh Esq

TO WILLIAM KIRBY SULLIVAN

The Oratory, Birmingham Octr 10. 1857

My dear Mr Sullivan

I think your distribution of subjects very valuable, and shall keep it as a guide for the future — It may require some modification or expansion, as time goes on; but that will not interfere with its principle.[1]

I am still somewhat anxious whence the 30 pages of Notices and Reviews are to come, unless you mean that the Scientific will take up that — Perhaps you do.

I wrote at once to Mr Arnold, but I have some fear that the University Porter may have neglected to forward my letter — as Mr A. did not reply to a former letter of mine.[2] If you are passing the house any day, perhaps you will be so good as to inquire — though I don't think we shall want him this number.

I talked myself of reviewing the Plurality of Worlds controversy — this I shall not have time to do — but there is just a chance of my thoughts falling into the the shape of a semi-metaphysical paper, which might come under 'literature' in Number 2 or 3, but the ground is so delicate, that, when I got into it, I might find it safer to retrace my steps, than risk sticking in the mud or sinking.

As to Mr Scott, I am very anxious about his *conclusion* — he has tried it in different ways, I mean, to avoid giving offence, or saying what he should not say. He makes our Lord's life much longer than is usual — this is not any thing to be anxious about but then, he cannot help going on to consider the passage in St Luke which makes our Lord 30 at the beginning of his ministry. A chronological error does not seem to me a difficulty in an inspired writer — but many may think it is — and what *does* require exploration is, how a writer who ought to know (inspired or not) *came* to make it. I have some fear that I must take advice — and this may delay the article beyond next number. I cannot tell how long it would be — perhaps 25 pages. But, if

[1] In his letter of 8 Oct. Sullivan proposed to separate the various topics that would be dealt with in the *Atlantis* into two broad divisions, Literature and Science.

[2] Arnold apologised on 9 Oct. for not answering Newman's invitation to contribute to the *Atlantis*. He wrote '. . . if you think a short critique upon Chaucer would be worth insertion, I could soon send it you. Or a paper upon the Paradise Lost, something in the style of those in the Spectator.'

we have scientific notices to the amount of 30, above the 180 pages, we shall not want it. I don't think there is a chance of his conclusions being anticipated.[1]

Yours very sincerely John H Newman of the Oratory

W K Sullivan Esqr

P.S. I think it would be best to divide each beforehand with the words 'Literature' 'Science' and 'Notices' etc respectively — as in the Genevan publication

SUNDAY 11 OCTOBER 1857 Exposition of Blessed Sacrament for the war in India *on the Indian Mutiny*.[2] Mr Sukely spent the day here.

MONDAY 12 OCTOBER Nicholas went to his Father

TUESDAY 13 OCTOBER Ambrose Stanislas and William went for the day to the Manchester Exhibition[3]

TO PATRICK LEAHY, ARCHBISHOP OF CASHEL, I

The Oratory, Birmingham Octr 16/57

My dear Lord

I inclose my letter for presentation to the Archbishops at the meeting which you informed me would take place about this time.

The letter from Mr Tyrrell, which accompanies it, illustrates what I mean in my inclosed answer to the Archbishops by the necessity of their meeting, either themselves, or by their representatives, at stated times, for University business. I have been trying to set up a Medical lodging house now for three years. I mentioned it in my first Report. I sent you a representation of the Faculty of Medicine on the subject last June.[4] The Dean of the Faculty has, I believe, applied to you since, and *nothing is done*. Meanwhile the Protestants have taken our hint, and set up such a house in connexion with their own institutions.

As to Dr Cullen, I cannot get him to give to me any answer at all. He neither acts himself, nor will let me act. It is as long ago as last March, that I asked His Grace to let me put Mr Arnold in the Professorship of English Literature — he declined, (Dr Dixon assenting,) alleging the expense. There

---

[1] Scott's article 'On the dates of the Nativity and Crucifixion' was not published in the *Atlantis* until Jan. 1859. See letters of 25 May 1858.

[2] The Indian Mutiny which began in April 1857, was not suppressed until the spring of 1858.

[3] This was the Art Treasures Exhibition at Old Trafford, opened by the Prince Consort on 5 May, which attracted 335,115 visitors from the Queen downwards, until it closed on 17 Oct.

[4] See letter of 15 June to Hayden. Tyrrell asked for a loan in order to start a lodging house for medical students.

was *no* expense, as I told him, for Mr Arnold would take the place of Mr McCarthy — still he would not give me leave. Thus business is at a stand still.[1] So it has been about the appointments at the Hospitals.[2] If he said, as in the case of Mr Arnold, 'No', it would be a gain; but he keeps a dead silence, and gives a reason which I fear I cannot accept as his real one.

Now I do hope, my dear Lord, you will sanction me in promising Mr Tyrrell this advance of £150, *on condition* he is backed up, as I believe he will be, by the Medical Faculty

I am, My dear Lord, Your affte Servt in Xt

John H Newman of the Oratory

The Most Revd The Archbp of Cashel

TO PATRICK LEAHY, ARCHBISHOP OF CASHEL, II

The Oratory, Birmingham ⌜October 16. 1857⌝

My dear Lord,

⌜Since the time is now approaching, as I gather from your Grace's letter of August 28, for the October meeting of the Archbishops, I request your kindness to lay before them the following answer to the message which they were so good as to send me after their meeting in August.

First of all, I have to offer them the respectful thanks of our Fathers here, for the considerate kindness with which their Graces have listened to their representations on the subject of my continuance at Dublin. They beg me to say that they willingly accede to the proposal contained in your letter of August 25.[3]

For myself, on whom it next falls to express my feelings on the proposal of the Archbishops, first I have to thank your Grace⌝ for the ready assurance of your letter of August 28, that there was no difficulty on the part of any of them in receiving my recommendation of Mr Mc Carthy and Mr Arnold to ad interim Professorships till the next Synodal meeting of the Bishops.[4]

And I beg to convey by you to the Archbishops my humble thanks for the kind mode in which they have received and accepted my terms for the purchase of the University Church.

And, in the second place, ⌜as to the proposal, founded on my suggestion, and agreed to by our Fathers, that I should continue, as a trial, in the office of Rector for a year, with the residence of only a few weeks in each term, I did not conceal from you that the practicability of the plan depended on the choice which the Archbishops should make of a person to succeed your Grace

[1] See second letter of 21 March to Cullen.
[2] See letter of 1 Aug. to Ellis.
[3] This letter is placed before Newman's of 26 Aug. to Leahy.
[4] See second note to letter of 26 Aug. to Leahy.

in the office of Vice-Rector, since he would virtually be in great measure the acting Rector of the University. Your second letter of August 25, dated Templemore, informed me that the Archbishops condescended to place before me two propositions, and allowed me to choose between them.[1] Of these, I accept the latter, which was to the effect that I should 'place before their Graces two or three Irish Priests, residing in Ireland, from amongst whom they might choose a Vice Rector.'[1]

Proceeding, then, to avail myself of this permission, I am led to think that they would like me to mention as many names as I can, though, in setting down the names of those persons whom I select with most confidence, I have this difficulty, that I know them to be fitted for a higher office than that which has at present to be filled up; and I hope that their Graces will excuse in such instances the seeming unreasonableness of my choice, on the ground that I am not without the expectation that they may perhaps intend the person, now selected as Vice Rector, eventually to succeed to the Rector's Chair. What makes me the rather anticipate some such purpose on the part of their Graces, is the circumstance, that, though the Synodal Decrees do not require the Vice Rector to be a Priest, and though there are many reasons which make it, as I think, unadvisable, they exclude laymen from the number of those whom I am to name, and out of whom the choice is to be made.[2]

ⁱI beg then to submit to their Graces the names ofⁱ Dr Russell of Maynooth, Dr Kelly of Maynooth, Dr Kieran of Dundalk, Fr Murphy S.J. of Belvidere House, and, (if the state of his health would allow it, which is very problematical,) Dr James Quinn of Harcourt Street.[3]

[1] See Newman's letter 12 Sept. to Leahy.
[2] On 17 Sept. Newman made a 'Memorandum for the answer to be made in October to Dr Leahy's letter of last month dated Templemore.' After noting that he would accept the second of the Archbishop's alternatives, Newman added, 'What I should have liked best, would have been to have suggested persons already professors or officials of the University, but this I am debarred from doing, since their Graces have expressed a wish that I should contemplate none but priests, and far the greater part of the governing body are laymen. Looking then outside the University I would name the following:—Revd Dr Russell Maynooth, Revd Dr Kelly Maynooth Very Rev Fr Murphy S J Revd Father M. O'Ferrall S J.' Cf. letter of 23 May 1857 to Leahy.
[3] Newman made a note of a letter of 7 Oct. he received from Quinn, who said, 'Your little note gave me far more pleasure than you could have foreseen. It implies, though it does not say, that you are to continue to preside over the University. I have never seriously doubted that it should be so. I hope you may be spared over it long enough to see it flourishing. . . .'
Newman also copied part of a letter of 12 Oct. from Dr Russell, 'I have had a general conversation with Dr K. [Matthew Kelly], the result of which is pretty much what I anticipated, that he should much prefer that the matter, if possible, should not be mooted till after our Board (20th inst.)—that, if it came before him, he would be prepared to do whatever the two Primates and his own Bishop, Dr Walsh, thought best.
As to naming any other person, whom I think fitted for the office . . . the only priest whom I would suggest to you is Dr Kieran of Dundalk.'
Kelly, who had been Professor of Belles-Lettres and French at Maynooth since 1841, was on 20 Oct. promoted to the Chair of Ecclesiastical History. In Sept. 1858 he was at length appointed Vice-Rector of the Catholic University, but died in the following month. Dr Kieran was Parish Priest of Dundalk and Vicar General to Archbishop Dixon whom he succeeded in the See of Armagh. Francis Murphy was Rector of the Jesuit College, Belvidere House, Dublin.

It was with great satisfaction that I learned from your Grace's letter of July 20, that the Very Revd Mr Flannery was appointed by the Archbishops as Clerical Secretary, in order to organise the Parochial Collections, and to attend to the correspondence connected with them.[1] I am sure the best results will follow from that appointment, and ⌐I am encouraged by it to submit a suggestion to the Archbishops on the subject of one or two collateral arrangements, which seem to me necessary for the due administration of the University money.

Your Graces will recollect, that I made a request to the Synodal meeting of June 1856, that the Bishops would allow the yearly expenses of the Personel of the University to stand as follows: — *£5000* from yearly collections, *£1200* being Interest of the Fund, and *£600* from fees of students, (that is, supposing 60 students at £10 each,) — in all *£6800*; — ⌐ of this sum, the £5000 paying for the three Faculties of Medicine, Philosophy and Letters, and Science, the £1200 being devoted to the Faculty of Theology, the Preacher, and the High Mass, and the £600 paying other expenses, as (for instance,) the present advances of the separate Collegiate Houses: —

⌐I now beg of their Graces,

1. that, till the fees actually reach £600 a year, (for the Rule for enforcing them began only a year ago, and did not bind those students who were already entered,) they would be pleased to make up the deficiency of that sum,⌐ for the purposes of the University.

⌐2 that the £6200 (£5000 + £1200) together with the compensation of this deficiency, be transferred by the Bankers from the Trustee Fund to the Cullen and Newman Fund in quarterly payments, on November 3, February 2, May 1, and July 22, on the presentation of the Rector's receipt.

3. that the Rector be not answerable for the payments of the Bishops' Medical and Scientific Burses, or for the expenses of the Collegiate or other Houses, nor include them in his statement of account.

4. that his account be audited every November, and the balance sheet appended to his annual Report.

5. that a step be taken, which is of such importance to the interests of the University that without it I do not see how we can go on any longer, viz that the Archbishops, or persons they appoint to represent them, sit once in every Term in Dublin, to receive questions or applications, whether from the Rector himself, or from the Deans of Faculties.[2]

Nothing further occurs to me to say to your Grace, except this: — viz that, should no Vice Rector be appointed by the beginning of Term, I think your Grace will consider it right and necessary that I should myself appoint a Pro-Vice-Rector, for the emergency, according to the words of the Decree,

---

[1] See first note to letter of 31 July to Leahy.
[2] Cf. the paper Newman sent to Flanagan on 17 May 1857.

'nominationem Secretarii, aliorumque omnium Academiae officialium pertinere ad Rectorem decernimus.'[11]

I am, My dear Lord, with great respect, Your Grace's faithful and affecte Servant in Christ

John H Newman of the Oratory

To His Grace, The Most Revd The Archbishop of Cashel

SATURDAY 17 OCTOBER 1857   Charles de la Pasture came

TO RALPH PLATT

The Oratory, Birmingham October 17. 1857

My dear Mr Platt,

I do not forget I had the great pleasure of making your acquaintance at the Provincial Synod some years ago — and I avail myself of that introduction to ask you a favor.[2] The Cardinal, acting in concurrence with the Bishops, has put on me the most honorable, but most arduous duty of revising our version of the Scriptures. Now is it not possible that you have turned your mind to the subject? and if so, are there no suggestions which you can make me on the mode of fulfilling so great a work? I shall be very thankful for any. Also, will you allow me, when the work is more advanced, to send you either specimens or portions of it for your inspection?[3]

Excuse the liberty I take and believe me to be, My dear Mr Platt,

Sincerely Yours in Xt   John H Newman of the Oratory

The Very Rev R Platt V G &c &c.

[1] On 18 Oct. Leahy acknowledged Newman's letter, and added, 'On Tuesday next the Archbishops meet, when I will present your Letter and as far as possible second your wishes.
I will remind the Archbishops of the pending appointments of Mr Arnold and Mr McCarthy.' Newman noted in 1872, [[(He had already said to me in his letter of 28 Aug. that 'there was no difficulty or hesitation in either appointment, but the Archbishops thought it as well to (wait) till they met in October')]]
For the Archbishops' reply see letter of 30 Oct. to Leahy.
[2] Ralph Platt, Vicar General of the Diocese of Hexham, was learned in the Classics and Hebrew.
[3] Newman made a note on 16 Oct. that he was sending a letter of this type not only to Platt, Tate and Walker, whose letters follow, but also to Charles Newsham President of Ushaw, Manning, Husenbeth, Mark Tierney the historian, Canon James Waterworth, John Maguire Wiseman's Vicar General, Daniel Rock the antiquary, Canon Joseph Render at York, William Weathers President of St Edmund's, George Morgan at Oscott, John Williams Canon of Clifton, and John Dalton translator of the works of St Theresa.
Four others were asked 'not to revise, but to *suggest now.*' These were Dr Oliver, Bishop Hendren, Canon Thomas Flanagan, and Rudolph Bagnall Vice-President of Oscott.
The only convert in these two lists was Manning. In Sept. Newman sounded W. G. Ward as to how far he could help, (*Ward*, I, p. 421), and Ward's brother-in-law, William Wingfield, at about the same time offered his services, which were accepted.

TO ROBERT TATE

The Oratory, Birmingham October 17. 1857

My dear Dr Tate,

Our Cardinal, acting under the Decree of the 2nd Provincial Synod of Westminster, and with the concurrence of the Bishops, has done me the very great honor of committing to me the office of revising the English translation of the Bible. I am sure that it is a subject which before now has engaged your attention — and it is not wonderful that, in an undertaking which is as arduous and responsible as it is honorable, I should look about for all the advice and help which I can get. Will you then give me the benefit of any suggestions you have to make? and may I be allowed, when things are more advanced, to send you either specimens or portions of the revision for your inspection and criticism?[1]

I am, My dear Dr Tate, with great satisfaction at having a reason for writing to you,

Very sincerely Yours in Xt,   John H Newman of the Oratory

The Very Rev Dr Tate.

TO J. WALKER, OF SCARBOROUGH

The Oratory, Birmingham, ⌐October 17. 1857⌐

My dear Mr Walker,

⌐The Cardinal, acting under decree of the 2nd Provincial Synod of Westminister, and with the concurrence of our Bishops, has done me the great honor of committing to me the charge of revising our version of Holy Scripture. In undertaking a duty so responsible as well as honorable, I naturally look to such persons as yourself, for advice and aid in my attempts to fulfil it.⌐ Will you then let me ask you for any suggestions which strike you on the subject? Also, will you allow me, when I have made some progress in

---

[1] Tate suggested, in his reply on 24 Oct., that chapters should be divided by paragraphs and not by verses. Maguire, on 21 Oct., said the same, and he was highly critical of the 'servility' and unintelligibility of the Douay Version. Dr Rock wrote on 7 Nov., 'As far as mere language is to be considered the so-called English Protestant authorized version is a fine specimen of idiomatic racy English: the Catholic one is not. I strongly dislike Latin words with nothing but an English ending about them. . . .' Similarly Tierney, on 21 Oct., who wanted more than a mere revision, and said 'the superiority of the latter [Protestant Version] has often been a serious disadvantage . . .'

Husenbeth, on the other hand, wrote on 21 Oct., of 'a general feeling that the work of revision should be done with extreme caution and alterations introduced *very sparingly.* There is a serious apprehension lest an endeavour should be made to assimilate our version to that of the establishment.'

the work, to send to you specimens, or, it may be, portions of the translation, for the benefit of your inspection and criticism.[1]

I am very glad of this opportunity of writing to you — and am,

My dear Mr Walker, Most sincerely Yours in Xt

John H Newman of the Oratory

The Very Revd Canon Walker

MONDAY 19 OCTOBER 1857 went over to Rednall and back with Ambrose. Nicholas returned

TUESDAY 20 OCTOBER Ambrose went to London

TO OCTAVIUS OGLE

Oct 20/57

Thank you, my dear Octavius, for your very affectionate letter.[2] It gives me very great pleasure to have it; for it assures me, what I sometimes scarcely venture to hope, that there are persons, whom I never see or hear of, who yet have kind thoughts of me. I find that that love, which I have always felt for you, though I have seen you so little ever, and not at all for so long a time, is not a mere gratuitous feeling on my part, without encouragement or return, but is felt by you for me. And this will serve to keep up the thought of you in my mind to the end of my life, were it ever likely to fail, which I don't think it is.

Your letter is indeed a great comfort and reward to me. God bless you.

Ever Yrs affly J H N

[1] There is a letter of 6 April 1858 from Walker containing his suggestions as to details. On 23 Oct., Charles Newsham answered from Ushaw: 'I was really overjoyed, first from my affection for you, for a more distinguished honour could not be conferred upon you; but still more because I felt that now at last this most important work—*the most important of all*, as far as I can see, for the benefit of religion in this country—was about to be performed, *and performed well*. For more than 30 years I have been most anxious to see this essential work executed; for I have always felt that our very defective version was a real obstacle to much good; and I firmly believe that a person better qualified than yourself for the task does not exist in the world. I am convinced God has raised you up for *this* great work. The presidency of the Irish University, important as it is, dwindles, in my opinion, into insignificance when compared with the importance of furnishing a really good version of the Bible . . . for the sake of so many thousands spread over the world.'

[2] Ogle wrote from Lincoln College on 19 Oct., 'Your mention of my name in a letter to Johnson [28 Sept.] makes me bold to write you a few lines of thanks. It has often been in my mind to thank you for your remembrance of me, which I have from time to time heard of through the Mozleys. For I was brought up to esteem and regard you above all others save those of my own family, and my judgement, such as it is, has long since endorsed the feeling which was taught me. Believe me that it gives me much comfort and some courage to know that your prayers are with me to strengthen and intercede for me. You have never been absent from my thoughts and best wishes, and henceforth I trust will never be absent from my prayers. I dare say I shall never see you in life, nor, if I did, could I venture, for fear of exaggeration, to tell you, what influence my connexion with you has had over me, but I am sure that it has been a real influence, and for good.'

Ogle and Newman met when the latter visited Oxford as an old man.

The Oratory Birmingham Octr 20. 1857

My dear Mr Sullivan

I inclose *for your private reading* a letter which came last night from Mr Penny, with its inclosure. It is discouraging — what are we to do? I am not sure that Airey has done him justice — I know (between ourselves) that Airey sometime ago spoke contemptuously of us.[1]

I am glad you like the Prospectus.[2] The Longmans advised it to be *before* the publication of the Register. I could send it them to do what they choose with it — meanwhile it might be sent to various papers, and form an Advertisement in some. But I leave all this to your better judgment.

[1] This was evidently a criticism by George Airey, the Astronomer Royal, of the article Penny was contributing to the first number of the *Atlantis*, (Jan. 1858), pp. 145–70, 'On the Influence of the Great Inequalities of Jupiter, Saturn, etc., upon the Motions of the other Heavenly Bodies.' See Newman's postscript. The passage in the article referring to Encke's comet was omitted, and a note added which described Leverrier's work.

[2]

THE ATLANTIS

A HALF-YEARLY REGISTER OF LITERATURE AND SCIENCE

Conducted by Members of the Catholic University of Dublin

The object of the work, which these lines are intended to introduce to the public, is to serve principally as the repository and memorial of such investigations in Literature and Science, as are made by the members of the new Catholic University of Ireland. It is natural that men, whose occupations are of an intellectual nature, should be led to record the speculations or the conclusions in which their labours have issued; and that, having taken this step, they should consider it even as a duty which they owe to society, to communicate to others what they have thought it worth while to record. A periodical publication is the obvious mode of fulfilling that duty.

The prospects of their work are to be determined by its object and character. They cannot hope to interest the general reader; but from this very circumstance they are happily precluded from the chance of competition with those various ably-conducted periodicals which already possess the popular favour. They do not aspire to include Theology, as such, among the subjects to which their pages are to be devoted; but here again they have the compensation, that they will not be running the risk, in anything they publish, of provoking that most serious of all rivalries, which is founded on a principle of duty. Thus they hope to take their place among such writers as are absolutely unable to stand in each other's way, because they are all employed upon a field where there is room for all, and supply a market which cannot be overstocked, in which no one's loss is another's gain, but the success of each is the benefit of all.

Accordingly, instead of fearing rivals in those who are engaged in similar pursuits, the Conductors of the *Atlantis* are secure of friends. In undertakings such as theirs, success, from the nature of the case, is another name for merit; and failure can only arise from causes traceable to themselves. If they are sanguine that they shall be able to answer to the profession which they make in the very fact of their commencing, it is because they trust they have the elementary qualifications of zeal, industry, and determination.

The work will be published half-yearly, on the first of January and the first of July. Each number will be divided into three portions, devoted respectively to Literature, Science, and Notices, Literary or Scientific, the number of pages in each portion varying with the number.

The first number will appear on January 1, 1858.

The publishers are Messrs. Longman and Co., Paternoster Row.
Catholic University House, Dublin,
November 3, 1857.

An earlier Prospectus, dated 6 May 1857, was printed at the end of *The Calendar of the Irish Catholic University for the Session of 1856–57*, Dublin 1857.

I fully see the importance of making the Register our advertiser.[1] Already I have told Fowler to strike off some copies of your Science Scheme for it. What kind of 'General University Prospectus' would you think suitable? There *is* an abstract of the *Rules*, but perhaps that is too minute.

The reason I looked out for a motto for the Atlantis from Bacon was as if to *explain* the name — which I think will perplex people — It was for this reason that I looked out in Plato etc. But I have no other reason at all, and the specimens I sent had nothing in themselves to recommend them.

As to the number of copies, it should of course be such as we could dispose of, whether in the way of presents or sale — If you think we could get 500 + 100 copies off our hands in one way or the other, very good.

Very sincerely Yours John H Newman of the Oratory

P.S. I am sorry I should have missed any of your questions — through carelessness

As to the part of Mr Penny's article about Encke's comet, if it would not hold, it might be omitted and he might supply the gap at the end of the Article, by some account of what Leverrier really has done.

TO EDWARD BELLASIS

The Oratory. Birmingham Octr 21. 1857

My dear Bellasis,

Thank you for your kind letter of this morning. The truth is, I have been so much out of England for the last year or two, that I have a feeling lest my friends should think me dead. And then again, a feeling lest they should think that, though I came to London, I never cared to find them out. Now I *never* am in London, except literally for an hour or two, but they can't know that. And then, I recollect how kind you and Mrs Bellasis have been to me, and I especially bear in mind your kindness at the time of that Achilli matter, and while Cockburne was pitching in to old Campbell;[2] and I seem to my self, or at least seem to myself likely to seem to you, ungrateful. And now, I suspect I have been persecuting you with a second volume, a small set of Sermons which I have just published, but I meant to ask Mrs Bellasis to be so good as to accept them — but looking at my list, I fear it will go to you by mistake — so will you gain her consent to take it, if it comes to you?

I should like nothing better than to fall in with you — but that seems impossible. I missed you to my great disappointment this time three years at Alton, when the poor young Earl was there[3]

Ever Yours most sincerely John H Newman of the Oratory

---

[1] i.e. the *Atlantis* was to be used for advertising the activities of the Catholic University. Several pages at the end of the first two numbers were used for this purpose.
[2] See letter of 22 Nov. 1852 to John Joseph Gordon.
[3] See diary for 29 July 1854.

TO THOMAS SCRATTON

The Oratory Birmingham Octr 21/57

My dear Scratton

Fathers and Mothers have a voice in such arrangements as my letter implied. The young Princes are coming back to me. Had I had even an idea that you considered that any engagement had been made with you, I would have written to you.[1] What I wished was that you should take Zamoyski — which you recollect, when I mentioned to you, you did not relish. They are all three coming back to Harcourt Street — You need not do any thing about their money.

So Dr Russell is President of Maynooth; and Dr Kelly takes his place.[2] I suppose I shall hear tomorrow who is the Vice-Rector.

Renouf seems to have vanished. He *was* married, I heard from Germany — but I have had no 'cards.'[3]

I am much perplexed about Dr Hayden's expenses. I have promised him *certain things*; e.g. for a suit of clothes for the Porter ⟨Purcell⟩ — Let him send in such definite bills, and I will sign a cheque for them — but for indefinite expenses the Medical School must go to the Archbishops.

Ever Yrs affly J H N

Thos Scratton Esqr

SATURDAY 24 OCTOBER 1857   Ambrose returned
TUESDAY 27 OCTOBER   Mr Bethell called.

TO EDWARD BELLASIS

The Oratory Birmingham October 28/57

Private

My dear Bellasis,

It is one evil of my late absence from England that others have spoken for me, and have represented the Oratory. It is an institution which admits of very great varieties of character and work, as is seen by the Oratorians abroad, and, while we at Birmingham wish to see all other similar bodies 'abound in their own sense,' and follow out there own opportunities, we claim to do the

[1] Scratton understood that the Princes de Ligne were not returning to the University, but made a private arrangement to take them in as lodgers if they changed their mind.
[2] See fifth note to second letter of 16 Oct. to Leahy.
[3] Renouf was married in Aug. 1857.

same ourselves, and to be the spokesmen for ourselves. Certainly, as regards education, so far from not wishing to take it up, we have made three several attempts in vain, to engage in it.[1]

Our wish was to set up a public school, such as Eton and Winchester, for Catholic boys. When it *was once set up*, it could no longer indeed be in our hands — nay Edgbaston would not be enough in the country for it — but we thought that we could begin it, and that we should have opportunities which others had not. The normal age of coming ought to be 13 or 14 — but we thought that it would be better to begin with children of 8 or 9, who should *grow into* public school boys in the course of 5 or 6 years, by which time the plan would be formed, and we could gradually relinquish the task. In this way too we should not be interfering with the existing interests of other schools. (And for this reason I should be obliged to you not to talk of our scheme; for *in the first place* I should wish to mention it, if it came to any thing, to Dr Weedall, the Bishop, and others first.) We had some correspondence with Oscott years ago, on another educational scheme, and one of their conditions was that our terms should be higher than theirs — [2] and from the fewness of the number with which we should commence, as well as for other reasons this would be necessary.

About a year ago I talked over the matter with John Pollen, and in consequence wrote a long letter to Sir John Simeon on the subject — but his answer was so little encouraging, that we have dropped the subject, and turned to other things.[3]

Any plan such as I have been speaking of, would require a considerable outlay to commence it — and we have not any thing to give towards it. We will try to carry out any thing which others originate, but this is all we can promise, should our aid be desirable. Mrs Wootten was kind enough to say she would make herself Dame, if she were wanted, and take the boys under her charge — Fr Darnell would take the charge of their schooling. There are plenty of nice houses with gardens about us.

And now I have troubled you with pretty much all I have to say on the subject — It would be a great pleasure to us to find ourselves able to be of any service to yourself and other friends, in so very anxious and important a matter.

Pray thank Mrs Bellasis for me for her most kind letter which has just

[1] Bellasis wrote on 26 Oct. that he was anxious as to how to provide for the education of his eldest son, Richard, nearly 8 years old. He wanted a preparatory school, where he would have discipline as well as instruction, 'in a thoroughly Catholic atmosphere.' Bellasis continued, 'I asked some time ago, one of the Fathers of the London Oratory, whether it was at all likely that a school might ever form part of the plan of your Congregation, but I got so decided a negative that I turned my thoughts elsewhere. Yesterday I met Pollen, and he mentioned to me that you had thoughts of a school, though he had no authority for speaking of it, and advised me to write to you.' Cf. letter of 28 Jan. 1857 to Pollen. Attempts were twice made to start a school at St Wilfrid's, in 1849 and 1850, and again when the Oratory had moved to Edgbaston.
[2] See letter of 26 Dec. 1849 to Ullathorne.
[3] See letter of 17 April 1857 to Sir John Simeon.

arrived — and assure her with what pleasure I should see the goodly row of young Papists, whom she promises to show me at Northwood House[1]

Ever Yours most sincerely John H Newman of the Oratory

Edwd Bellasis Esqr

P.S. I am very sorry to hear from Mrs Bellasis that you have been so over-worked

TO MRS WILLIAM FROUDE

The Oratory, Bm Oct 28/57

My dear Mrs Froude

It is a great comfort to receive and read your letters, and all that you tell me about yourself, and your children.

I did not know dear Isy's direction, and answered through Sister Dominica.[2] At the same time I think it best not to correspond with her without her father's knowing — and you must not be disappointed, if, for a like reason, I think it best not to write to Hurrell. God will hear your prayers, and bring about your wish in some way known to Himself. What you said about him has interested me extremely.

I am going to Ireland in a day or two, and shall be there for about three weeks.

Ever Yours affly in Xt   John H Newman of the Oratory

Mrs Froude

TO LADY GEORGIANA FULLERTON

The Oratory, Birmingham. October 28, 1857.

My dear Lady Georgiana,

I ventured to send you that small book,[3] not as thinking that there was any thing in it which would be of special interest to you, but in order to bring me to your mind, for I am getting very old now, and need the prayers of all who will be so kind as to think of me. And therefore I cannot help taking pleasure in the good opinion of others, as in yours, though I know in my conscience I am so unworthy of it, because it serves to give me a hope that they will remember me in sacred times and places. Pray do not forget to do

---

[1] The Bellasis family lived at Northwood House, St John's Wood, London.
  Bellasis replied on 4 Nov. that he would discuss with others the possibility of providing the support Newman asked for, without mentioning his name. Bellasis was convinced that many Catholics were in the same difficulty as himself. See letter of 2 Feb. 1858 to him.
[2] i.e. Mary Anne Bowden at Westbury. Isy, born in 1840, and Richard Hurrell, born in 1842 were Mrs Froude's two elder children.
[3] Evidently *Sermons preached on Various Occasions.*

that, my dear Lady Georgiana, and be sure that I try to do the like charitable office for you and Mr Fullerton.

Ever yours most sincerely, &c.

TO THOMAS SCRATTON

Oct 28/57

My dear S.

As the drafts are not due till the 3rd, before which day I shall be in Dublin, I suppose all will be straight. I think you told me Dr Leahy had got us the money.

Ever Yrs J H N

P.S. You must insert, please, Mr Mc Carthy's (the *Architect's*) Christian names. You will see a review I suppose of the paper.

TO LADY CHARLES THYNNE

The Oratory, Birmingham. Oct. 28th. 1857.

My dear Lady Charles,

I am very grateful to you for having received so kindly the little volume I ventured to send you. Please do not forget to think of me sometimes in your prayers, as I do not, according to my ability, forget you and yours.

Give my kindest regards to Lord Charles, and believe me to be, My dear Lady Charles, Yours sincerely in Christ

John H. Newman of the Oratory.

The Lady Charles Thynne.

P.S. I am glad to hear so good an account of Frederic [Thynne].

THURSDAY 29 OCTOBFR 1857 at night went to Dublin

TO W. J. O'NEILL DAUNT

6 Harcourt Street Dublin Octr 30. 1857

My dear Sir,

I have just now arrived at Dublin, and hasten to acknowledge your kind letter, which I find on my table.

I thank you very much for your subscription to the University Fund —

and for the half note which you inclose. Will you kindly send the other half to the Very Revd Mr Flannery, 86 Stephen's Green, whom the Archbishops have made the sole recipient of subscriptions? I will send to him the half note which I have.

I am, My dear Sir, Most truly Yours

John H Newman of the Oratory

W J O'N. Daunt Esqr

TO DANIEL JONES, S.J.

6 Harcourt Street Dublin Octr 30. 1857

Dear Father Jones,

On arriving at this place an hour or two ago, I found your letter, and hasten to answer it. At the risk of saying what you know already, I will observe that Mr Ward has printed two pamphlets — one on the Voluntarium, in Latin, two or three years ago — and another in English lately on an opinion contained in Fr Faber's last work.[1] As to any answer from Fr Faber or any of his friends, to which you allude, I have not heard of any.[2] For myself, I have not read any one of Fr Faber's books — I have heard parts read, and thought there was a great deal very eloquent and poetical in them — as there was in one chapter of the Volume on the Holy Eucharist, which I read myself.

Your Reverence knows enough about the constitution and history of the Oratory of St Philip to know, that one House knows nothing whatever of what another House does — and this applies most fully to the two Houses which are at present in England. I am not unwilling to say this, as on various occasions we have found our own House judged of by words or acts of the Fathers of the London Oratory.

I am, My dear Father Jones, Sincerely Yours in Xt

John H Newman of the Oratory

The Revd Fr Jones S J

P.S. I am very glad to find that I am soon to have the pleasure of seeing you.

[1] See letter of 6 July 1857 to W. G. Ward. In the preface to *Five Lectures on Attrition* . . . Ward explained that he dissented widely from Faber's opinion in *The Creator and the Creature* on the subject. Jones, who was about to lecture in Dublin on this department of moral theology, had heard that some of the London Oratorians had replied to Ward's book, and he wanted to study the controversy. In fact there had been no reply.

[2] Jones wrote on 23 Oct., 'It occurred to me that perhaps your Reverence would not have any objection to give me a letter of introduction to some Father of the Oratory in London on receiving which I could write to him or what would be still better, (as time passes) that you would kindly give me any printed essay or book which may have been written on the subject by the Oratorians.'

Cf. Newman's letter of 21 Nov. 1856 to Alexander Grant.

Dublin ⌐Oct 30/57⌐

My dear Lord,

I thank you very much for having gained for me the assent of the Arch-bishops to the proposition of the Medical Faculty on the subject of setting up a Lodging House, and for the efficacious support with which they have accompanied their assent. I conveyed my message to Mr Tyrrell at once.[1]

Also I thank you for gaining their assent to the provisional nomination of Mr Mc Carthy and Mr Arnold to the chairs to which I recommended them.

And I am much pleased to find that the Archbishops so far have complied with my request that they should meet at stated times to receive applications from the University Authorities, that they propose to meet at a certain time to come to consider the University Expenditure.

I wrote at once to Fr O'Reilly to convey your message on the subject of the theological Lectures to be given this term by himself and Dr Forde.

⌐As to the payment of Dr Forde's Salary, I have never arranged to give him any definite salary, as your Grace seems to consider, but I have intimated to him from the first that I will give him any such sum which the Archbishop of Dublin (that is, the Archbishops) will name — but that I did not feel myself equal to naming the sum myself.⌐ Perhaps you will kindly give me the authority of the Archbishops for some definite salary, which then shall be paid him at once.

I am much obliged to you for informing me that the Salary of Vice Rector and Professor of Holy Scripture is available for that purpose from May 1st last[2]

---

[1] Newman copied out part of Leahy's letter of 24 Oct., 'The Archbishops met in Dublin —Dr McHale was not present.

1. The Lodging House for Medical Students, with Dr Tyrrell for the Head, was approved of. . . .

2 The Archbishops also approve of setting up the School of Theology . . .

3 The Archbishops also approved of Mr Arnold and Mr Mc Carthy as Professors respec-tively of English Literature and Architecture

4. The appointment of a Vice Rector is, under present circumstances of so much im-portance, that the Archbishops have thought it better to take time in considering it, and have therefore *deferred it until after Christmas*, leaving it to you in the meanwhile to name a Pro-Vice-Rector. They desired me to request you will name none but a Priest,—I should rather say, to suggest, because that is what they did say.

5. Your proposed expenditure of £6800 per annum, the ways and means of making out that sum, and the allotment of it, and the manner of applying it, these considerations *they wished to defer to another time*, as they require more leisure to deliberate on them than they really had.'

When copying in 1872 Newman noted: [[(It will be observed that a dead silence is kept about my cardinal demands, as stated in my letter to Dr Leahy ⟨Oct 16. 1857⟩, of a Vice Rector *who would really represent me*—and especially a Finance audit yearly and a terminal Episcopal Dublin meeting.)]]

[2] Leahy wrote again on 27 Oct.: 'Your cheque was duly signed by two Trustees. Shall it be forwarded you by Letter before your coming to Ireland, or shall it remain here until you come, and in whose hands?

Although Dr Forde, since his appointment to the Chair of Canon Law, had the opportunity

I thank you also for obtaining the signatures of the Trustees to the cheque. In answer to your question about the mode of disposing of it might I ask you to be so good as to pay it into the 'Cullen and Newman Account Hibernian Bank —'

ᒥAs to the Pro Vice Rector, I have asked Fr O'Reilly to undertake the office up to February 2 — If he declines, which I trust he will not, I am sorry to say that there is no one whatever to whom I am in a position to offer it — the interval being too short to offer it to any priest out of the place — and there being no one else here to whom *I* can satisfactorily offer it.¹

Thank you for your inquiry about my health, of which I am pleased to say I can give a very good account

I am &c J H N

TO JOHN STANISLAS FLANAGAN

6 Harcourt Street Oct 31/57

My dear Stanislas

I am glad of your talk with Augustus — and I cannot be sorry that I told his Mother at once, what he had said to me. No one can say we have done any thing underhand.¹

It seems St Philip's will that we should depend on our *neighbourhood* — every other hope seems to break under us. But the enormous difficulty is to find there, not merely vocations, not merely the class in society, but the education, both secular and theological, for our purpose. A's hint about our

of doing but little, he had because of his nomination to that Chair relinquished every other employment and was wholly at the service of the University. The fault was none of his that he did not do more than he did.' Newman commented, when copying in 1872, [[(he had not given even one lecture, or formed even one class. He had simply done nothing. It was occurences like these which made me wish to put the theological school into the Bishops' hands.)]] 'The Archbishops therefore were of opinion that he was entitled to a Salary since his nomination—such Salary as you may have arranged to give him.' Newman again commented, [[(N.B. There were three Theological Professors with salaries, but doing nothing. This was not my doing—and in consequence of it it was that I begged the Bishops to take the Theological Faculty into their own hands. Fr O'Reilly would not draw his salary. The other two did.)]]

'Might not the Salary of the Vice-Rector and Professor of Scripture for the last Half Year—since the 1st of May—be usefully applied in paying at least some portion of Dr Forde's Salary?

Let me hope the quiet of your Oratory, of course so welcome to you, has had a beneficial effect upon your health.

Dear Dr Newman, Very sincerely Yours, P. Leahy.'

Leahy himself had been Professor of Sacred Scripture until his appointment as Archbishop of Cashel earlier in the year. On Forde see letter of 8 Feb. 1858 to Scratton.

¹ Flanagan wrote on 30 Oct. that Augustus Bethell, who was staying at the Birmingham Oratory did not at all appear to have a vocation to it. He had evidently informed Newman some time earlier that he thought of joining the Oratory, and Newman mentioned it at once to his mother. His parents had advised him against it on the ground that 'England wants missionary priests so badly, that she cannot afford to have several living together in one place.' Another objection, wrote Flanagan, was that 'we labour under a disadvantage with respect to the study of theology.'

Cf. letter of 6 Nov. to Bellasis.

want of theology is true; — i.e. I mean as to appearances, for the only way in which an Oratory can have the *credit* of the theology which it may really have within it, is first by having a *school* of students, or secondly by having *writers*; — and neither comes within the scope of the Oratory. Were we a little nearer to Oscott our difficulty would be removed. We *did* consider it, when we took Rednall instead of a site near Sutton Coldfield; — but there certainly were good reasons for keeping our Novices in a Villagiatura out of sight, and near a theological School. This, however, would have broken up our Congregation. Well, we must leave this matter to St Philip.

The other objection about the want of secular Priests for the Mission will avail, till we do *things which secular Priests cannot do.* This is a reason for doing the New Version ourselves, if we possibly can. It is a reason for a boy's school. At present, while I am alive, no direct complaint is made against us — but, when I go, the objection against us will increase. The Oratory is an isolated body, and a local one. If the Jesuits or Redemptorists do not get on well in one country, they can betake themselves to another. But we must found a claim of merit, and exhibit a visible, tangible, serviceableness, in that red brick house which stands upon a triangular island close to the Plough and Harrow. We have yet to find our place, *as an Oratory*, in the English Church. Your letter has just come. What has made J's father change? James may come on Monday[1]

Ever Yrs affly J H N

TO LAURENCE FORDE

6. Harcourt Street Novr 1/57 *Sunday*

Dear Dr Forde

Your letter of the 30th has arrived here this morning.[2] In answer to it, I have to inform you that the Archbishop of Cashel has written to me to say that 'the Archbishops are of opinion that you are entitled to a salary since your nomination, such salary as I may have arranged to give you.'

I have answered His Grace thus: 'I have never arranged to give Dr Forde any definite salary, but I have intimated to him from the first that I will give him any sum which the Archbishop of Dublin (that is, the Archbishops) will name — but that I did not feel myself equal to naming the sum myself. Perhaps you will kindly give me the authority of the Archbishops for some definite salary, which shall be paid to him at once.'

I expect his Grace's next letter to me soon — meanwhile will you do me the favor of mentioning the date when I offered to name you for the Professor-

[1] James Delany, a servant of Newman's in Dublin.
[2] Forde, having heard from Leahy that an arrangement was being made about his salary, wrote on 30 Oct. to ask for its payment.

ship to the Synodal Meeting? I think it was in March or April 1856.[1] As you are desirous of an immediate advance, I will direct the Secretary tomorrow to prefer a cheque in your favor for a second £100 on account.[2]

I am glad to hear that the Archbishops propose your commencing Lecturing at once.[3]

Thank you for your inquiries after my health, of which I have no cause at all to complain

I am &c J H N

TO PATRICK LEAHY, ARCHBISHOP OF CASHEL

6 Harcourt Street Dublin ⌐November 1. 1857⌐

My dear Lord,

⌐I am very sorry to tell you that Fr O'Reilly declines the office of Pro-vice-Rector.⌐ He says, 'On the one hand, I cannot undertake the disciplinary part of the office; and on the other, what sort of an officer will a pro-vice-Rector be, who does not undertake discipline?'[4]

⌐What then am I to do? when I leave Dublin, in the course of a few weeks, the University will have no one at all to preside in it. The Archbishops have virtually given me the choice of *only four* persons [[(as Pro-Vice-Rector.)]] — Dr O'Reilly, Dr Forde, Mr Flannery, and Dr Quinn. Dr O'Reilly declines, Dr Quinn is away. Dr Forde and Mr Flannery, with great qualifications in their own lines, could not represent the Rector.

I feel it a duty to give you the earliest notice of a great inconvenience, which is impending over the University.⌐[5]

Excuse this trouble, and believe me to be Your Grace's affte friend & servt in Xt

John H Newman of the Oratory[6]

The Most Revd The Archbp of Cashel

[1] The Synod was that of June 1856. Forde replied on 2 Nov. he had been offered the Professorship two or three months earlier, but considered he had no claim on University funds until after the Synod had approved his appointment.
[2] Newman had given Forde £100 on 17 Nov. 1856.
[3] Forde wrote, 'I am well pleased with the prospect of having something to do in my department next Session, and trust to make my course of interest enough to attract others, besides the comparatively small number who will follow it regularly—'
[4] Letter of 30 Oct.
[5] When copying out this letter in 1872, Newman added a note: [[(I wanted a *Lay* Vice Rector or Pro vice Rector because else, since I wished to choose out of the existing academical body, I had so small a choice. To insist on a priest, as the Archbishops did, was to drive me into a corner. Not that they now put the choice of a Vice Rector into my hands — only of a temporary Pro-vice-Rector.)]]
[6] Leahy replied on 2 Nov., 'The inconvenience impending over the University for want of a Pro-Vice-Rector is most serious.
It shall without delay be made known to those whom it concerns.'

TO HENRY WILBERFORCE

6 Harcourt Street Dublin ⌐Novr 2/57⌐

My dear H W

Your letter has just come — it is very wonderful. I trust it is a good conversion, and the effect of his mother's prayers. He may retain the gift of faith, even though he still acted waywardly. What a great trial he must be to her! an only son. What you say about his wife grieves me. It is news.[1]

⌐Every one remarks how the Register is improved. Some of your last articles have been especially clever. Our Bishop (Dr Ullathorne) was praising you. I told him I should let you know.⌐

I was very glad that you found it convenient to come here a second time. Have I written to you since? ⌐We have no Vice Rector appointed. The Archbishops let me appoint a *Pro* Vice Rector — *but* wish him to be a *priest*. This limits my choice to four persons. Fr O'Reilly, Dr Forde, Mr Flannery, and Dr Quinn. Dr Quinn is away, Father O'Reilly won't. Dr F. and Mr F. *I* won't. So we stand. *I* want a lay Professor to be Pro Vice Rector. Meanwhile, I have not yet engaged to stop after November 14.[1]

Ever Yrs affly John H Newman

TUESDAY 3 NOVEMBER 1857 the youths came. Term began. Dr Hayden's Lecture in Medical School Monsell in Dublin. called on the Prince de Ligne and he on me[2] Scott came into my House in place of Renouf.

WEDNESDAY 4 NOVEMBER The Prince de Ligne called.

TO MISS HOLMES

6 Harcourt Street Dublin Novr 4. 1587

My dear Miss Holmes,

I must adopt your fashion, and take two half sheets since I have nothing else, to thank you for the most splendid stole, which you have sent me, and

---

[1] This refers to William Wilberforce (1821–1900), only surviving son of William, eldest brother of Henry Wilberforce. In 1849 William Wilberforce junior married Rosa Elizabeth, daughter of William Jones, of Pentir Hall, Bangor. She died in 1878. On 22 Oct. 1856 Henry Wilberforce wrote to Newman about his eldest brother's wife, Mary, née Owen, who became a Catholic in 1852, 'Poor Mary is very deeply tried . . . You know her son has gone off 4 years ago to Australia and they have heard nothing of him for 8 or 9 months. She employs herself chiefly, I think, in prayer for him and her husband, and has a great confidence that his soul will be saved. His wife and 2 small children live with Wm.' [i.e. with William, Mary Wilberforce's husband]. Cf. letter of 25 Oct. 1856 to Henry Wilberforce.
[2] This was Eugène, ninth Prince de Ligne (1804–80), whose two sons by his third wife were in Newman's House at the University. Peel called him 'le plus grand financier de l'Europe.' He represented Leopold I of Belgium at the coronation of Queen Victoria and at that of Czar Alexander II. The Prince de Ligne was Belgian Ambassador in Paris 1842–8, and President of the Belgian Senate 1852–78.

which is one of the finest I have seen. The colours seem to me most beautifully blended, if I may talk of what I do not know — and St Laurence and St Cecilia were the two Saints, to whom I had a devotion (if you can use the word) when I was a Protestant boy at School.

I am much relieved to find that you are so much better, and so hopeful about your accounts. I had a very kind letter from the HopeScotts about you — but, from what I know of their plans, I don't think they are likely themselves to want a governess.

It was certainly most astonishing that the Curé should object to our Lady being incensed — and, if your banner was as good as the stole, it must have been a great mortification to have to unpick it.

I have got a most onerous, though most honorable, task on me now — viz to revise our Version of Holy Scripture. And I suppose I shall set to, as soon as I get back to Birmingham, which will be in about a fortnight.

Hoping you are getting quite strong, I am, My dear Miss Holmes,
Yours affly in Xt

John H Newman of the Oratory

Miss Holmes.

TO MANUEL JOHNSON

6 Harcourt Street, Dublin Novr 4. 1857

My dear Johnson

Professor Hennessy wants to read a book very hard to get, except to subscribers — Professor Forbes's Introduction to the 9th Edition of the Encyclopedia Britannica. Can you suggest to him any means of seeing it? I shall not be surprised, if you can't.[1]

Yours affly John H Newman

M. Johnson Esqr

THURSDAY 5 NOVEMBER 1857   The Pr de L. [Ligne] went.

TO CATHERINE ANNE BATHURST

6 Harcourt Street Dublin Nov 5/57

My dear Child

Certainly the letter which you send and I return (it has just come, though yours is dated the 3rd) is a very distressing one. I don't think what you say

---

[1] James David Forbes (1809–68), who described the polarisation of heat, was Professor of Natural Philosophy at the University of Edinburgh 1833–60, and after that Principal of St Andrews University. He wrote one of the prefaces to the *eighth* edition of Encyclopædia Britannica, which began to appear in 1853, *Dissertation Sixth: Exhibiting a General View of the Progress of Mathematical and Physical Science, principally from* 1775 to 1850.

about sweetness can have done any harm. She is wrong, if she thinks the bulk
of converts are *not* quite free from doubt. According to my experience, doubt
is quite the *extreme* exception. But at the same time sympathy, such as you
can show, will be an immense gain to her. Your letter is a very good one.
I don't see how she can mistake it — but sick persons are so unaccountable,
that never you mind if she does; though, *if* she does, the very doing so will be
a relief to her, and will lead to a fresh answer from you — which will do her
fresh good. My dear Child, who knows that it is not for this that your dear
Lord has let you be tried, that you may work to bring forward others?
⟨2 Cor i. 4.⟩[1] I will not forget her indeed, and, if I am able, to say a Mass
for her

Ever Yrs most affly J H N

TO AMBROSE ST JOHN

⌜Dublin Nov 5/57⌝

Charissime

⌜Thanks for your book [[Raccolta]] just come.[2] It looks very nice — and is
not too large.⌝ Not near so fat as follows from 'Who drives fat oxen etc'[3] —
⌜There is a wonderful deal of work in it, at first sight — and I wonder you
have ever got through. Well, it is a work *done*, which is a good thing
ἠνύστας καὶ τετέλεστας etc etc.[4]

Ever Yrs most affly⌝ J H N

TO THOMAS WILLIAM ALLIES

6 Harcourt St Dublin Nov. 6./57

My dear Allies,

Your letter has just reached me, and I thank you very much for the kind
thoughtfulness which has dictated it. How hampered I am! I am obliged to
act and cannot wait, and then after committing myself, I cannot do the very
thing which I wish. But I suppose this is the case with every one.[5]

---

[1] 'Blessed be the God . . . of all comfort, who comforts us in all our affliction, so that we
may be able to comfort those who are in any affliction, with the comfort with which we
ourselves are comforted by God.'
[2] *The Raccolta: or, Collection of Indulgenced Prayers*, London 1857.
[3] 'Who drives fat oxen should himself be fat.' Boswell's *Life of Johnson*, (L. F. Powell's
revision of G. B. Hill's ed.), iv, p. 313.
[4] ' Ηνυστας και τετέλεστας ὅσον ἐις την ἡμετέραν δυναμιν,' Lancelot Andrewes, *Preces Privatae*,
Oxford 1675, p. 220. 'It is finished and done so far as in our power . . .,' Newman's edition,
Oxford 1842, p. 146.
[5] Allies wrote on 4 Nov., 'Some one, I think, John Pollen, told me lately that you wanted
a Tutor or Dean at Dublin. If that be so, I think I can recommend one whom I take to be
among the ablest of unemployed Catholics—T. A. Pope, formerly Incumbent of a Church

163

As to the suggestion you make, what occurs to me, over and above these general difficulties, is this. If Mr Pope is a married man, he wants a good salary. Again what age is he? for our Tutors are young men, or are meant to be, answering to private Tutors at Oxford.

What we profess to give is £10 a head for each pupil (say £100) and board and lodging. The work is not much, or not a great deal; and is more of influence than of instruction. But at the same time influence is gained *through* the reputation of scholarship etc, and the very duty which comes on a Tutor is to do that which the pupil cannot do for himself, e.g. to explain difficulties in the works read in lecture, and to give aid in the higher classics, or to cram for examinations. At present Scott of B. [B.N.C., Brasenose College] is my Tutor here, and a capital one he is, but I don't know how long he will remain, and I sometimes doubt if he would have come at all at the beginning of term, unless he had found out that I had no one else. Now I am not in immediate want here, though I may be any day.

Then at the other house, where a Tutor is much wanted, Mr Flannery, who is at its head, has determined to do without Tutors.

I do not like the thought of losing a person such as Mr Pope, yet am much puzzled what to do. Could you answer the two questions I have suggested above. 1. his classical attainments and 2. the salary he would contemplate?

I tried to see you in London in the early summer, but you were away.

Ever yours affecly J.H Newman

P.S. I shall be in Birmingham in about a fortnight. Will you consider whether it is worth while for him to take the trouble, if he would, of paying me a visit then?

TO EDWARD BELLASIS

not sent

to be read at your leisure 6 Harcourt Street Dublin Nov 6. 1857
Private

My dear Bellasis

I am sorry to give you the trouble of reading another letter from me, but this will require no answer.

I think you quite understand our position — but I will add a word or two.

Of course I am looking out for the future. I cannot last for ever. While I

at Newington, who has been followed into the Church by more of his parishioners than any person I have heard of. . . . He was originally a Dissenter but went to Cambridge . . . He is a widower, with one son and daughter. The latter is just going to a French convent for some time; and the boy is at School at Yvetot, where two of mine are. . . .'

Thomas Alder Pope did not go to Dublin, but ten years later he joined the Birmingham Oratory.

live, I shall in a way defend my Oratory — but, when I am gone, people may begin to say 'What is the use of bringing together a number of priests into one House, when they are so wanted through the country?' and while the Bishops will naturally have an interest against us, we shall not have that defence which an extended order has, such as the Redemptorists, with its Fr General at Rome. Moreover, as our Property belongs to the Church, the Pope for the time being might at any moment turn us out and put others in, Jesuits, Redemptorists, or Vincentians, if *they* could turn the property to better account than we did.

It is then essential to the future existence of an Oratory that it should have a work and place of its own in the English Catholic Body. In a great town like London, it has an evident use, and there is no fear, if it is faithful to itself, of its ever finding work in its day to justify its existence — but I have ever said, and got it down in writing these 8 years, that till the Birmingham Oratory is something more than a flourishing mission, it has *not its place*. We were placed there by the Cardinal, we did not place ourselves — but we must *make* a place for ourselves, by taking root. We are in the midst of a very wealthy neighbourhood — could we convert any portion of them, we have our place at once; but at present there seems no hope of that. We began a hospital after several years preparation, and the two ladies who began it, one took a fever, the other a pleurisy, during the first week, and both died. This scheme failed, at least for the present — for money went away with one of them.[1] We have in mind to set up an apprenticeship for reformed boys — like the Somaschi of Milan; — [2] I mention this, as the other instances, to illustrate what I mean. One of our greatest difficulties is our want of money — for our Birmingham wealthy people are so scarce, that our Offertory and seat rents have never done so much, on the average, as pay the expenses of the Sacristy, and we have as missionaries to provide money for the poor and other objects from our own means, when we have not money enough for ourselves. A third class of plans has been connected with teaching. Whether it comes in the shape of middle school, or public school for the gentry, or (University) College, we would undertake any, which promised to give us something more than parochial work.

I know perfectly well that the parochial work which we have actually done and are doing is *very* important, and, as it never will be adequately known till the day of account, it is the most meritorious of works — but, as things are, unless we have a certain portion of visible utility more than the average, I fear we stand a chance in time to come of being swept away.

St Philip tells us to love to be despised — and the only difficulty I see in it is that there is a certain point of contempt, which leads from being ignored

[1] See diary for 22 Dec. 1856 and 3 March 1857.
[2] The Somaschi are an order of Clerks regular founded by St Jerome Aemilian in 1532. Newman visited one of their homes for boys in Oct. 1846. See letter of 14 Oct. 1846 to Walker, Volume XI, p. 261.

to being annihilated. We have ever neglected puffing ourselves at Rome — and the consequence is that we have no friend at court there. The Holy Father himself is a true friend to me and to us, but he is our only friend, and is surrounded by ten thousand influences. Nor should I care about being in the position of Cordelia in the play, were it not that practical consequences are involved in it, as in her case.[1]

And now I have written to you far more fully than I had intended when I began and have been obliged to write 'Private' as a second thought at the beginning of my letter. But it will enable you to understand our feeling. A body *lasts*; and therefore must have a *work*. The Oratory is a most versatile, elastic, institution, and can take any sort of work. Once that we have got a real work, I don't care, tho' the world did not know it — for it would turn up, and be known, as soon as any thing occurred to cause us to be looked at and into.

Another anxiety has been, though that is nihil ad rem here, that we have lost members. Father Gordon's death was a blow which we shall be long in recovering. It has told in various ways.

Excuse this very free letter. As to the immediate matter, *why not make Pollen do every thing*? if you wish to do any thing. He has at the moment time his own

Yours sincerely in Xt   John H Newman of the Oratory

Mr Serjeant Bellasis

TO F. S. BOWLES

6 Harcourt Street Dublin Novr 6. 1857

My dear Fr Frederic

I am sorry you have gone so far as to write to Fr Spencer without my knowing your intention — as it is an *extra*ordinary step to make a retreat out of the Congregation.[2]

You may be quite sure I will not be slow to do any thing, which is really St Philip's will, towards you as towards others — but I do not see I can give you an answer without a great deal more thought. It will be better, I think, to wait till my return to Birmingham, which is not very distant.[3]

Ever Yours affly John H Newman of the Oratory

[1] Cf. the opening scene of *King Lear*.

[2] Bowles wrote to Fr Ignatius Spencer, the Passionist, suggesting he might make a retreat under him, if Newman approved.

[3] Newman sent Bowles's letter to St John who commented on 7 Nov. that he was glad of it, because it showed Bowles was 'coming to a crisis in his own mind,' and things ought not to continue as they had done. 'I think he has not said Mass except on Sundays since you left. And besides this he seems to live when you are away almost out of Community life altogether.'

Saturday Nov 7/57

My dear Fr Frederic

I think the improvement will be great and had better be done.[1]

Affirmativè also, of the boys school in the Music Room ad interim

Ever Yrs affly J H N

TO CARDINAL WISEMAN

(rough copy)

6 Harcourt Street Novr 7 1857

My dear Lord Cardinal,

My silence, since the receipt of your Eminence's last letter,[2] wishing me to estimate the probable expense of the projected Translation of Holy Scripture, has arisen partly from my anxiety to obtain the necessary information, and partly from my dissatisfaction with any answer I could make, even when I had got it.

What I propose to do, is as follows: — to engage three of our Fathers in the work: — Fr St John, who has in past times made Hebrew his study, and in some measure Syriac, — Fr Darnell, who, beside his classical attainments, has been giving himself to German, — and Fr Caswall, whose taste in translations sacred and ecclesiastical is well known. And I thought of employing as assistant translators, Mr Wingfield, Mr Ward's brother in law, who has already employed himself in collating the Hebrew and Greek texts of the Old Testament, and Mr Scott, late Fellow of Brasenose, Oxford, who is not only a good scholar, but has made the sacred text his particular study. I am fitting up a room in our Oratory as a Scriptorium, and propose working there with the friends whom I have named.

I intend, however, first of all, to print some preliminary queries and remarks, and to send them round to the most competent judges in the English Catholic body.

According as the translation is ready, I should print it in four portions, of which the N.T. [New Testament] would be the first; submitting each portion in succession to the Revisors whom your Eminence may appoint, receiving it back, making the corrections, and either striking off editions or taking off the stereotype plates; as the case may be, and then going on to another portion, till all four were through the press. Thus the quantity of type required will

---

[1] Bowles asked for leave to remove a wall in the boys' schoolroom to make it more serviceable for his musical party.
[2] That of 6 Oct.

be a fourth of the whole type of the Bible, or, as the required number of letter types may run unequally in different letters of the alphabet, say a third.

As to the size of type and the general getting up of the Edition, it may be either a Library book, with a large type and on good paper, to be sold at a high price as a Princeps Editio, or it may be a popular stereotyped low-priced edition of (say) 10.000 or 20.000 copies.

What then I have to calculate, is the *additional* expense of the translation, over and above that of merely bringing out an Edition of Holy Scripture, which of course can be made to pay itself by the sale of the copies printed.

The additional expenses are 1 the preliminary matter or prolegomena. 2. the books. 3 the desks, racks, tables the fittings of the work room. 4. the translators and transcribers. 5. the cost of type kept standing during the revision. 6. the press men for copies for Revisors, and the extra composition after correction. 7 sundries, (e.g. parcels) etc.

I attempt to calculate them thus: —

		£ s.d
1.	Prolegomena	100.0.0
2.	Books, (I have already laid out towards £40, in editions of the Bible etc)	200.0.0
3	Desks and other fittings up	50.0.0
4	Transcribers 0.0.0. Translators (Mr Wingfield £100 for two years)	200.0.0
5	Purchase of type kept standing of one third of the Bible (cost of type of *whole* Bible £1000 — sale of type after 3 years £250, resulting expenses £750 Therefore, for one third of the Bible $= \dfrac{750}{3}$ or	250.0.0
6	Press men 0.0.0. compositors for whole Bible are £220 — say half as much again for corrections	100.0.0
7.	Sundries	50.0.0
	Total	£950.0.0

⟨N.B. I shall add £50 for Scott — and to make the whole £1000.⟩

Of this £950, a good part would be ultimately recovered by the profits of the sale of 20.000 stereotyped copies.

The loan of the type, (the purchase and sale of which entered into the above calculation,) for the purpose of the selling edition should be deducted from the £950, and thrown on the edition. I do not know what charge printers make in printing a book for a customer, for the use of their type, but whatever it is, it should be put against the £250 for type which forms part of the £1000.

I have not thought of renting type (instead of purchasing it) because it is impossible to find enough available at any printer's, at least in Birmingham, where the printing must be.

I have not thought it necessary to take any account of the expense of notes, headings etc., because the calculations which I have used have been made from the copies of the Douay.

The large type (Bourgeois) which I inclose would be not only handsomer, but easier to read for the Revisors. As I have mentioned the Revisors, is it asking your Eminence too much, to express a wish, at the commencement of my anxious work, that you would inform me, who the Revisors are to be.[1]

I am &c J H N

His Eminence Cardinal Wiseman

TO JOHN HUNGERFORD POLLEN

Nov 8/57

My dear Pollen,

I sincerely condole with you and your wife — and feel how sad it must make you for a while. But the grief will go and the joy will last and increase — for you have, for all your lives, one who will ever bear you in especial mind before the Throne of God. You have a second Guardian Angel.

Thank you for the thought of Oxenham.[2] I am much hampered here — I wrote to Manning about him *at once* — but he ought to see how things go on, and learn [about] us, before he rushes in medias res. Yet how is he to do it? — Where am I to put him? However, I shall be too happy to have him anyhow, if we do not disgust [?] him.

Ever Yrs affly J H N

P.S.   I suppose Scott's place would be open for him, whenever he wished, but don't say this. S. is fairly well now but not strong.

MONDAY 9 NOVEMBER 1857   Meeting of Council

TO WILLIAM NEVILLE

Nov 10/57

My dear Wm

Thanks for the pains you have been at. I shall not decide one way or another about Okely at once — [3] I wrote about Oxenham directly — but have not heard yet. Thanks too for your pains about my room.

Ever Yrs affly J H N

[1] Wiseman replied in a letter of 13 Feb. 1858, placed before Newman's of 14 Feb.
[2] Henry Nutcombe Oxenham was received into the Church by Manning on 31 Oct., and Pollen suggested he might find employment in the University.
[3] Neville had suggested William Sebastian Okely, of Trinity College, Cambridge, who had just become a Catholic, as tutor at Newman's House in Dublin, in place of W. H. Scott.

WEDNESDAY 11 NOVEMBER 1857   Ornsby's Inaugural Lecture of the Session.   Archbishop there

TO THOMAS W. B. WOOD

Nov 11/57

Sir[1]

In answer to your letter of this morning in which you say that your parcel has reached me and that I am in full possession of all the information you could give me on the subject of my questions about it, I beg to inform you that I am not in possession of it, and have no idea whatever what it contains. I therefore beg to repeat my questions.

I am &c J H N

TO T. W. ALLIES

6 Harcourt St. Dublin Nov. 12. 1857

My dear Allies,

Thank you for sending me Mr Pope's letter. I have answered him, as inclosed, and beg you to be kind enough to direct and forward it.

Do you know anything of the circumstances of the House or Hall attached to the University Lecture Rooms? I think it is probable we shall lose the Dean, Mr Flannery. If so, this would be a great opening for me, and I could avail myself of Mr Pope at once. But alas, I cannot hasten matters. I have written to beg him, if not inconvenient to him, to spend a week with us at Birmingham.

I rejoice about your Lectures, but hope you will be able to give them when I am there, though of course you must do what you can.

Have I written to you about our new Literary and Scientific Review? The first number is to come out January 1. There is no pay for writers, but still I might ask you to give some ins and outs of time to an article.[2]

Ever yours affly in Xt   John H Newman of the Oratory

[1] Wood wrote from London on 4 Nov. that he was sending Newman a parcel containing a valuable manuscript for his perusal. Newman replied by asking for further details, not wishing to be responsible for the return of an object whose safety he could not guarantee. Wood wrote on 10 Nov. 'From inquiries at the Railway Station, I infer that the parcel has duly reached you. You are, therefore, in full possession of all the information I could give you on the subject.
You will perceive, that I do not seek a favour: I wish rather to be enabled to confer one.' See letter of 24 Nov. to Wood.
[2] Allies did not contribute to the *Atlantis*.

TO AMBROSE ST JOHN

⌐6 Harcourt Street Novr 12/57⌐

My dear A.

⌐How green an author[1] you are. Leave off thinking about the *sale* — Desine querelarum.[2] You are like me when I [[we]] published St Bartholomew's Eve — running into Munday and Slatter daily, and asking whether any copies had sold.[3] Give it up, and pay your money. All will come right — I will advance you all I can. I only wish Duffy would pay *me*.⌐

I am glad you are unlearning your idolatry for the Hebrew text.

⌐I have nothing to tell you about myself. I suspect they are sending home for Dr Quinn for Pro Vice Rector.⌐

Old Marshall has just been calling. He is coming to see us in Birmingham. He is a very good fellow. He is going to Rome. *He is looking for a vocation.*[4]

Ignatius talks and laughs. How he is I don t know. I find he has written to Stanislas. I am sick about Confessionals, and don't understand your question.

⌐I expect to be home next week — expect me Friday morning (20th)⌐

Ever Yours affly John H Newman

P.S.   Make my condolements to Frederic.[5]

TO SIR ROBERT THROCKMORTON

6 Harcourt Street Dublin November 12. 1857

Dear Sir,

Mr Scott has shown me the letter you were kind enough to write to him about you son.

Our course for Woolwich takes *two* years. I inclose a paper. Probably your son has already advanced as far as the studies which belong to the former of the two, and could begin with the second, if you thought of sending him here.

I trust we should do justice to him. We prepared one young man for Woolwich lately, who acquitted himself respectably. Something must depend on a young man himself. We find it difficult to make some of our students work — though we are anxious to do so.

There is a room in this house which would be ready for your son at Christmas.

Should you require further information, I would direct our Secretary to

---

[1] [[the Raccolta]]
[2] Horace, *Odes*, II, ix, 17, Desine mollium tandem querelarum.
[3] This refers to the first cento of *St Bartholomew's Eve*, the poem of Newman and J. W. Bowden published by Munday and Slatter at Oxford, in 1818.
[4] This was Thomas William Marshall.
[5] Bowles was suffering from a boil.

furnish you with our Calendar. We have two Downside youths in this house, Mr Fraser and Mr de la Pasture, to whom your son might write for information in detail.[1]

I am, My dear Sir, with much respect, Your faithful Servt

John H Newman

Sir Robert Throckmorton Bart.

SATURDAY 14 NOVEMBER 1857   said Mass at Dr Quinn's

TO EDWARD BUTLER

Rough Draft   Nov 15/57

My dear Mr Butler

I thank you for considering and answering the two questions which I had suggested to your Faculty connected with the subject of keeping Terms.[2]

I have not forgotten that you have already passed some resolutions on the general subject. If I have not availed myself of them yet as part of the syllabus of the University; it was not as if I did not feel the importance of the subject or of the suggestions, but because I thought we needed longer time before we legislated on the subject.

As to printing Ornsby's Letter [Lecture], I could not after refusing Dr Lyons this time year.[3]

Nor would such printing answer your purpose. I conceive you wish to make the Faculty of Philosophy and Letters known, as that of Medicine is known.

I don't think you take the right way to do so. At all times I am sceptical about Pamphlets — as they are of momentary effect — but now especially I think we want something more substantial.

I wish we could enlist Dublin more in our favor. Could we do any thing to call attention how we consider Externs as quasi interns, if they are in a Collegiate House during the business hours of the day.

Again Stewart suggested a sort of quasi school (preparatory) such as Dr Quinn's is.

J H N

[1] Sir Robert Throckmorton's third surviving son, John, entered the Catholic University in Feb. 1858.
[2] It was proposed to allow greater freedom as regards taking examinations to those who had completed two sessions at the University.
[3] The Faculty of Philosophy and Letters wished to publish Ornsby's Inaugural Lecture of 11 Nov. at the expense of the University. See letter of 10 Nov. 1856 to Lyons.

TO JOHN J. KELLY

⌜Nov 17/57⌝

My dear Mr Kelly,

⌜I told you yesterday I would write to the Dean of St Patrick's House [[Mr Flannery]] on the subject of his appointment of you to be his Assistant there. On second thoughts I write to you instead, as I think it best, as regards the Dean, to wait for the letter which he is sure himself to send me on the subject.[1]

I understood you last night to say that you were to have formal *classes* morning and evening, of the young men. This seems to me an interference with the office of Professor. I therefore have not unmixed confidence in the success of Mr Flannery's experiment. Also I have spoken to other persons, and they seem to have anxiety on other grounds about the arrangement which you have made with him.

Under these circumstances, I hope you will not think me particular, if I say that while I am ready to give my sanction to his appointment at the moment, I think it safest to limit it to the time between this and Christmas [[as a beginning.]]⌝[1]

I am &c J H N

— Kelly Esqr Dr Quinn's

TO JOHN HUNGERFORD POLLEN

6 Harcourt Street Dublin. Novr 17. 1857

My dear Pollen

It is very kind your thinking of us. I want two men, not to say three, and I have the offer of them, [Edmund] Coffin being reckoned as one. But I can't use them.

Mr Flannery, they say, *is to be* the Co-Adjutor Bishop of Killaloe — [2] but we don't agree, so he is going to put in to his House some one who, I think, won't do. But *while* he is there neither Coffin nor any one else would do, i.e. would not get on with him.

Then I suppose, *when* he goes, then I shall find all those engaged, who at present are open. What a provoking hitch this is! yet I don't know how to set it right. I must be patient and see how things go.

Entre nous, I am much discouraged in finding no increase ⟨⟨Don't tell⟩⟩ in students. I don't think Ireland *has* them. Meanwhile, it is an opportunity for all Anti-Cullenites, to say there would be plenty (which I don't believe)

[1] [[(that is, I suspected he would send me *no* letter, but shuffle the appointment into operation through Mr Kelly's application to me)]]

[2] Flannery was consecrated as Coadjutor Bishop of Killaloe on 5 Sept. 1858.

provided Dr Cullen was away. It does us harm then, not only in the fact itself, but in affording a fallacious argument to the Anti-Cullenites.

Then, I can get neither Vice Rector, nor Pro Vice Rector. They allow me to choose a Pro Vice Rector, if he be a Priest, and there are only four to choose out of, all impossible for one reason or another. So here I am going to Birmingham the day after tomorrow for *months*, with no one to represent me.

Now don't tell all this. I wish England would take us up — but it won't. But if England subscribed £1000 a year and sent youths, then, if the Irish students did not increase, the Arts Faculty of the University might form a College in England, merely going to Dublin for their Degrees. *Please, don't* say a word of this from me — because it is thrown out at the moment.

Say every thing kind from me to your wife — I hope you both are well.

Ever Yrs affly John H. Newman of the Oratory

J. H. Pollen Esq.

TO THOMAS ALDER POPE

6 Harcourt Street Dublin Novr 17. 1857

My dear Mr Pope,

I thank you for your very kind letter — and for the prospect of my forming some arrangement with you about

from France[1]

because I have thrown it out. Be sure it will be equally a pleasure to us, if you come at some other time, when you return

Most truly Yours in Xt   John H Newman of the Oratory

T A Pope Esqr

TO AMBROSE ST JOHN

⌈6 Harcourt Street Nov 17/57⌉

My dear A

I think it cruel that no one has sent me one line about Stanislas, after telling me he was ill. I have been watching every post. You and Henry both said there were lumps in his throat — I asked inside or out — no answer.[2]

The truth is you are bound up in the Raccolta with an attachment which is

---

[1] The lower part of this letter has been torn. What follows is written on the reverse side. Pope wrote on 16 Nov. that he had promised to visit Monsieur Labbé of Yvetôt, but offered to take up work on returning to England. 'It would be a welcome privilege to be a hewer of wood under your direction. Nor have I any curiosity about Emoluments. I believe I may be called poor; but God has given me enough for my wants and for my children's education.'

[2] Flanagan himself wrote on 18 Nov. that 'it was a misuse of the word to say I was *ill*. I was nothing more than seedy and off my oats. I had, it is true, lumps in my throat, *inside*, but they quickly disappeared.'

quite worldly. ⌐I *thought* that article came from the Brompton Oratory and it turns out it did. I said to myself 'the impertinence of praising us⌐ and limiting the praise to *publications*, as if that was our ἔργον.[1] I mean the Review implied that we were worth nothing unless we wrote religious books for the public. The word 'sanctification' when alluding to the Dublin youths was of the same kind. ⌐Don't send me Fr Faber's letters.⌐ I have read *neither* of them. I know they would make me angry.[2] ⌐I think it very impertinent his reviewing you — certainly, his speaking of us and of me.⌐ *Of course* he is getting over you; and you like a goose have let out to someone or other that I am the author of the translation of the Anima.[3]

I don't like your answer to him at all.[4] If you thank him, you are preferring yourself to the whole Oratory — for he is *not* to be thanked for speaking of *us*. What I said to myself was 'Why cannot the reviewer let us alone?' Nor should I say as you do 'more than I deserve;' it is not more than you deserve — but I wish you would not be set on human praise. This I was going to write to you quite independent of hearing from you that the article is Fr Faber's. He is the fox, complimenting you on your beauty, and hoping to get hold of the cheese, which is myself.

[1] 'Employment.' Faber wrote to St John on 14 Nov.,
'I wrote a little notice of the Raccolta in the Register to this week [sic]. Our excellent friend the Editor [H. Wilberforce] has appended a string of fault-findings—so, lest you should know I wrote some of the notice—I wish you to know that *my* notice ended at Felix, faustumque sit, atque fortunatum, and that I never saw or heard of the rest, till the Weekly Register came this afternoon.'
The review of *The Raccolta* in the *Weekly Register*, (14 Nov. 1857), p. 5, began: 'It would be difficult to exaggerate the debt of gratitude we are under to Father St John for his authorised translation of the *Raccolta*. But it is one of many debts we owe the Birmingham Oratory. . . .'
The second paragraph began: 'The work of translation has been most admirably done by Father St John. Many of the prayers and some of them extremely difficult to translate, exhibit great felicity of expression, while all of them are characterised by an unambitious simplicity, which seems to be but a natural expression of the translator's own devotional earnestness. . . .
The third paragraph was as follows: 'To teach devotions seems to be in an especial manner the work of the Oratory, and is but a continuation of that primitive spirit of St Philip, upon which the English Oratory has so ardently endeavoured to form itself. To the Birmingham Oratory we owe Father Caswall's excellent translation of the Hymns of the Breviary, and now this work of Father St John's; while the illustrious Superior of that House is laying the foundations of a great work for the sanctification of the young, by which he also is continuing in another way the work of his great Master and Father St Philip Neri. "Felix, faustumque sit atque fortunatum." ' Cf. letter of 18 Nov. to H. Wilberforce.
[2] Faber had also written to St John on 7 Nov. thanking him for a copy of *The Raccolta*, 'It is a great work to do, and the Anime Sante will have to look after your asthma for it. The sale will no doubt be very great, and we shall of course push it among our own people. . . . I have not been able to get F. Edward's [Caswall] poems [*The Masque of Mary, and other Poems*] any where. I saw them on a table at Arundel, and was much struck and pleased with them, but they had no titleface or publisher's name, and the Duchess pleaded entire ignorance of the matter. I did not read them all; but some I thought *very beautiful* indeed. Please remember me to everybody. . . .'
[3] The concluding part of the review of *The Raccolta* in the *Weekly Register* was by John Morris, and criticised the translation of the *Anima Christi*, which was the work of Newman. 'The translation of the beautiful Invocations of St Ignatius beginning with *Anima Christi* has been made by a friend of Father St John's (p. 116), but it does not please us much.' Cf. *M.D.*, p. 352.
[4] St John proposed to reply to Faber's letter of 14 Nov., 'Many thanks for your kind review, I am sure it is more than I deserve. I earnestly hope you are recovering from your attack.' Faber was suffering from what he feared was 'calculus in the kidney.'

⌐I think you should say no more than 'Thank you for the kindness which dictated your review — I hope you have got rid of your attack.'[1]

I was fuming at the impertinence of the writer praising 'the Birmingham Oratory' and now I find it is Fr Faber! He wishes to sooth us like children who are teething. 'Pretty Dear.'[1]

Ever Yrs affly J H N

I hope to be with you Friday morning.

Depend upon it, you have put your foot into [it] by your letters to F F Faber, and Dalgairns — and they are laughing at you.[2]

WEDNESDAY 18 NOVEMBER 1857   called on Fr Ffrench.[3]

TO MICHAEL FLANNERY, I

[[Novr 18. 1857]]

My dear Mr Flannery

⌐I do not understand from your note whether you are wishing to make any appointment or recommendation of Tutor or Assistant in your House.[4] It is true that Mr Kelly has been speaking to me, but the initiative does not lie with him. As your note stands, I do not understand what your question is. Will you kindly state it?⌐

Yours very truly John H Newman

P.S.   I inclose a letter I have received this morning from Dr Keane with its accompanying account. The cheque I am paying into the Trustee account

[1] St John used these phrases in his reply but added a correction about a part of the review which Faber had not written.

[2] St John replied on 18 Nov., 'Thank you dearest Father a 1000 times for your letter this morning. I read it to the Fathers at recreation for my sins. . . .
I have not *written at all to any one at Brompton* but F Faber. . . . I am not so disgusted with F. Faber as you are, for I believe (I may say I know) Wilberforce asked him to write it, for I had asked H. W. W. for *butter* as I wanted to sell the book. I agree quite that his praise of the Birmingham Orat is impertinence. . . .
May I without vanity send 2 bond copies to Talbot by Laprimaudaye? I want the English in Rome to buy—
Yr most loving goon in St P Ambrose St John'
See also letter of 18 Nov. to Wilberforce.

[3] John Ffrench (1812–73), second son of the third Baron Ffrench, became a Jesuit and was for a number of years President of the College of Tullabeg, Tullamore.

[4] Flannery wrote on 18 Nov., 'If you approve of it, perhaps Mr Kelly who has been speaking to you, might be chosen as the Tutor of this House, *at least for a time*, and until the University will be in a position to supply a young man fitted to undertake the office.' Newman noted, ' "might be—" he does not say *he* wishes it—"might be" is how he might express himself, if his letter was an answer to *my* having said *I* wished it, or at least that Mr *Kelly* wished it. Why does he not ask me to appoint him?'

⌐Nov 18/57⌐

Dear Mr Flannery

⌐In answer to your recommendation of Mr Kelly to the office of Tutor, I write to express my great desire to do any thing which approves itself to you as regards the internal arrangement of your House.[1]

Before however I can concur in the appointment, I should like to know that you mean him to undertake the Tutorial office according to Rule 13 which says 'The Tutor has no part in the College discipline, or any academical authority over his pupils.'

Supposing you wish this portion of the Rule infringed, I should not object to your making him a sort of Sub-dean and general assistant in studies — if you wish it, *without* the title of Tutor.

He tells me, however, that he is to form your inmates into *classes* morning and evening. Formal lectures of this kind seem to me to interfere with the Professorial office. I do not like to make this an obstacle to his appointment — but, as I do not know how it will work, and the Professors may have difficulties about it, I think it best to make his appointment as only an experiment, to end at Christmas.⌐[2]

I am &c J H N

6 Harcourt Street Dublin ⌐Novr 18/57⌐

Charissime,

I am *not* looking out for a Review in the Register of my Occasional Sermons, but, if there is to be one, ⌐I do intreat you,⌐ as you love me, ⌐to let me have a veto first on the Reviewer.⌐ If you do not this, you may be not only inflicting a severe Penance on me, which I shall get merit by bearing, but you will be injuring the Birmingham Oratory. ⌐You are not up to points which may be very important ones — and a praise, based on assumed premisses which I consider false, is of course an offence, doctrinal as well as personal. If I praised you, because I was perfectly sure that you would fight a duel, if necessary, you would not thank me for the officious compliment.

---

[1] Flannery replied at once to Newman's first letter of 18 Nov., 'I am sorry that I have not been sufficiently clear in my note of this morning.

What I intended to convey to you was, that, if you fully approved of it, I would beg leave to recommend Mr Kelly for the tutorship of this House, at least for a time. . . .'

[2] [[The Tutor, according to the Statutes answered to an Oxford *Private Tutor*, and therefore could have nothing to do with discipline or private classes. Mr Kelly was a respectable old gentleman, who, I believe, either had been a master in a school or had coached young men at home etc etc. He could not make himself a quasi-equal or associate with the young men.]]

If I might go further, I would intreat you not to let any one in your Register talk about the Oratory *as such*; — to say that Fathers or Houses of the Oratory are doing this or that good work is merely stating a fact — to say that they are doing a truly Oratorian work or the like, is an opinion or doctrine. All we at Bm [Birmingham] wish, is to be let alone — but there are those who, whether at Rome or at home, will not let us alone, when their sole business and work is with themselves. It is no compliment in any case to talk of the Birmingham Oratory's good works — and there are persons from whom such praise comes with as bad a grace towards the objects of it, as if your friend, who raised the price of your Paper against you with Richardson, and who whispered things against you to the Cardinal, were to take up your cause against Sir John Packington.[1] I trow you would not thank him.[1] It would be bad taste.[2]

I had nothing to say to your questions in your last letter — or would have written

Ever Yrs affly J H N

H W Wilberforce Esqr

P.S.   I mean to go to Bm tomorrow.

THURSDAY 19 NOVEMBER 1857   at night set off for Birmingham

TO EDWARD BUTLER

⌜Nov 19/57⌝

My dear Mr Butler

⌜You may wish to know what I think myself on the various questions which I put before you the other day, so at the risk of tiring you, I write again

1 The *ground* on which I wrote at all was the circumstance that now in the 4th year of the University the number of students in the School of Philosophy and Letters promised to be pretty much what it was in the first year — about 50 — as if it had reached its maximum at once. With this I coupled the fact that experienced persons told me, before we commenced, that there were no youths to be had in Ireland,⌝ in the state *in which things*

---

[1] Sir John Pakington, who was in charge of the Patriotic Fund collected for the victims of the Crimean War, was accused of discriminating against Catholic orphans, and was attacked in the *Weekly Register* and the *Tablet*, in Nov. 1857.

For Wilberforce's enemy see letter of 27 May 1857.

[2] [[NB. All this is directed against Fr Faber, near whom H W W had gone to live, on his going to London]] Cf. letter of 17 Nov. to St John. *O.S.* was reviewed in the *Weekly Register*, (27 March 1858), p. 5. The reviewer remarked that Newman's works, which had been so sought after before his conversion, were now ignored by Englishmen. His connection with the Catholic University was referred to, but there was no mention of the Oratory.

stand at present. The existence yet ill success of the Queen's Colleges both corroborates and increases this misgiving.

2 On this ground, I based my opinion that some thing must be done extraordinary to *change* the existing state or condition of things

3. ⌜Some people say, Get a Charter, get the power of granting degrees. I do not undervalue this advantage at all. It would raise us in public opinion — it would put us somewhat more on a par with Trinity College — but, if youths are not to be had, it will not create them.⌝ It is the plain fact a complaint that youths will not go on to Degrees at the Queen's Colleges, tho' they have the power of granting them.

⌜Others say, 'it is all because the Bishops are not at one.' Well — we cannot help this — but, were they ever so much of one way of thinking, their unanimity would not, ipso facto change, the existing condition of things.⌝

4. I think we must depend on our own selves, and on none other, under Providence. ⌜Affiliated schools will not help us,⌝ that is their conductors will not. The country will not help us, if the Tablet and Nation speak truly. ⌜Every school is for itself and no one else.⌝ We are our own best friends — I mean, though the Bishops, the Schools, the country, the state are *means* through which we are to succeed, still they will not take the initiative, and we must begin by acting upon them, and using them.

5 If then I could get the country on our side, I would do it, though the state were against us. If I could get the state and the Law on our side, I would do it though the country were against us — Self preservation is the first law — and so that we do not do what is wrong, we must simply consult for ourselves, not caring whom we offend, provided we gain by it.

6. If all this be allowed, then I do not scruple to say, feeling withal the vanity of all human prospects, that ⌜it is our wisdom to make Dr Cullen our friend, to stick by him, and please him, not caring what any one else says. I don't think *I* can be of use here. He distrusts English and Scotch — I doubt whether they ever would be *intimate* with him, or get on long with him. I think a person like yourself can — I observe he speaks with great respect and kindness of the Medical Professors. I am sure he likes you —[1] I think it your wisdom to cultivate him — so that you do not get *under him* — else he will treat you without respect, as if one of his curates,⌝ you will have lost your influence. He will respect a layman more than a priest. I think ⌜he likes Ornsby and others — but he will not trust them —⌝ I think he will trust you. I would not care then what people said about our being Cullenites — we are bound in this divided state of things, to take care of ourselves.

7. Next coming to the particular questions which have come into discussion. ⌜If any thing is to be done, it seems to me the most advisable move is, to connect Dr Quinn['s] school with us, as an under school to feed the University.⌝ It has this primâ facie advantage that it is a new movement in

[1] Altered to [[He seems to like you.]]

Dublin before the eyes of all men — so that, as the Register is an act in advance, so this would be. And next, even though it might not increase our numbers at the moment, it would ultimately. It is the most natural way of bringing the youth of Dublin into the University course, and it has the advantage at the same time of not being a new byway, but a continuation and development of what has been from the first.

8. Next, how this is to be done — if it be desirable? I am assuming that the school is just what it is, except that the University both has internal jurisdiction over it, and on the other hand gives it more pecuniary help. I suppose it to have the funds which it has already, and that its staff of teachers etc remain, though re-arranged and completed. The details of the plan it is not [worth] while to discuss, while as yet the very idea of it has to be discussed. It would be a question, however, whether ⌐the school ought not to cease to be a University House as well.¬[1] The advantage of such an arrangement is that the boys by that means melt into University students — on the other hand they are never proper students.

Any negociations on the subject of Dr Quinn's School, would be conducted by the Dean of Philosophy and Letters with the Archbishops and Dr Quinn. The Rector would not come into it except at last.

9 ⌐One thing I think I am clear upon, that, neither as regards St Laurence's or any other House, or the Externs, would I remit the fees and Professors' money — ¬ whatever *compensation be* determined on. The Labourer is worthy of his hire. If the Professors do work, let them have the credit of some little payment to show. The Faculty cost £1800 — if there were 60 students at £10 — this comes to one third of the expense and the Faculty really only costs £1200. I think the Professors will not be wise, if they do not make a point of this. As to the extern's Entrance Fee, you know how we were plagued with Externs coming and going, and our not knowing whether we had jurisdiction over them or not. The difficulty of an Extern is our having jurisdiction over a person who lives at home. Why cannot he choose instead to be a Non-resident Auditor? In that case he would pay no entrance fee, but lecture money term by term, he would be able to go up to the Examinations and he would *not* be under our jurisdiction.[2]

---

[1] [[It ought to cease to be a University House.]]
[2] The draft ends here.

TO MICHAEL FLANNERY

6 Harcourt Street Dublin ⌐Nov 19. 1857⌐

sent Nov 28/57[1]

My dear Mr Flannery,

⌐I meant to draw your attention in my last letter to two points, on which I should have been glad of an answer.

One was, whether Mr Kelly was to have any *jurisdiction or academical authority* over your students.

The second was, whether he was to have *formal classes* of your students.

I myself thought you would answer them both in the affirmative, and wrote accordingly. Will you kindly tell me whether I am right in my conjecture?⌐[2]

Very truly Yours John H Newman

⌐P.S. Since writing the above, I have received the inclosed,⌐[1] and open my cover to send it you. When you have read it, perhaps you will kindly send it to the Dean of the Faculty of Philosophy and Letters.

⌐The Faculty [[of Philosophy and Letters]] hearing it reported that the Gentleman acting, or about to act, as tutor in St. Patrick's House, is appointed to give two lectures a day, on which attendance is enforced on the members of that House, beg to call the Rector's attention to the circumstances, referring to § 13 Rules and Regulations. They conceive this arrangement contrary to the spirit of that Rule, and that there is further a danger of superseding the functions of the *Professors* by those of the Tutor, if compulsory lectures of the latter exist side by side with those of the former.⌐

Extract from Minutes of Faculty of Philosophy and Letters Meeting of ⌐Thursday 19 November — Edward Butler Dean.⌐

D. B. Dunne Secretary

FRIDAY 20 NOVEMBER 1857 Miss French had returned to Bm [Birmingham]
SUNDAY 22 NOVEMBER Mr Aspinall called.

[1] Before this letter was sent Newman received a note from Edward Butler to say that Kelly, rather than be a cause of any disagreement, had resigned. When the contrary proved to be the case, Newman sent his letter. See that of 28 Nov. to Flannery.
[2] Flannery had replied to Newman's letter of 18 Nov. that he merely wanted to use Kelly as a teacher. See Newman's letter of 30 Nov. to Flannery.

TO ROBERT D. LYONS

Nov 23/57

My dear Dr Lyons

It seems to me very important, seeing the matter in itself, that you should avail yourself of the opportunity which offers in the epidemic at Lisbon to prosecute an object so closely concerned with your Professorship; and I will gladly do any thing I can to promote your wish. I say 'viewing the matter in itself,' because I should like the proposal to come formally before me through your Faculty.[1]

Very sincerely Yrs J H N

TO EDWARD BUTLER

⌈Nov 24/57

answered that I should be glad if he attempted and succeeded in the Vice Rectorship.[2]

that he had to consider the difficulties — viz Dr Leahy, my short continuance in the office of Rector etc.

I added that I was making *conditions* [[with the Archbishops]] before I agreed to stop at all — e.g. about a settlement of the University accounts[3]

J H N

[1] Lyons's letter, asking for leave of absence to study the epidemic of yellow fever at Lisbon, is quoted in Newman's letter of 5 Dec. to Robert MacDermott. See the notes there.

[2] On 23 Nov. Butler wrote to Newman, 'With regard to the Vice-Rectorship, would you think it unseemly or injudicious, or unwise on my part, to apply for it to Dr Cullen, on the ground that it would satisfy most parties within and without, although I am fully sensible that many of the requisite qualifications are wanting. The theological faculty might be exempted from the jurisdiction of the lay vice-rector.' Newman added [[vid Dr Leahy's letter of June 1857]] for which see letter of 23 May to Leahy.

[3] Butler replied on 26 Nov., 'It is too bad I should be troubling you . . . I now make bold to send you a rough draft of an application for the Vice Rectorship. . .

I purpose waiting on Dr Cullen with my letter of application; opening the matter to him in conversation and requesting him to consider the ground set forth in the letter. If he refuses to entertain the subject at all, I shall let it drop. Otherwise I shall send copies of the letters to the other three Archbishops.

And then perhaps a letter from you to Dr Dixon might have some effect.

Have you any notion of what Dr Moriarty's views may be on this point? If favourable, he might perhaps act on Dr Leahy'

Newman made a note 'Nov 27 answered that I liked his letter and returned it—that I was likely to stop as Rector but a short time—and I should not acquiesce in his being *Pro* Vice or any thing short of Vice Rector J H N'

See letter of 8 Dec. 1857 to Dixon.

TO A. LISLE PHILLIPPS

The Oratory Birmingham. Novr 24. 1857

My dear Mr Phillipps

This requires no answer. It is merely to tell you that I have been this morning saying Mass for the repose of the soul of your dear son.[1] Nothing, I know well, that others can say, can enable you and Mrs Phillipps to support such a blow. It is the consolation which comes from above, and that alone, which can aid you — and that you have abundantly. And as times goes on, the pain will be less and less, and the light of divine consolation will become brighter and brighter — for you will understand, more than anyone else, how great a thing it is to have a son, secured from the ten thousand temptations of the world, and safely lodged in unchangeable blessedness.

Meantime, be sure you have the deep sympathy of all who know and love you, and their best prayers.

I am, My dear Mr Phillipps Sincerely Yrs in Xt

John H Newman of the Oratory

A.L. Phillipps Esqr

TO THOMAS SCRATTON

Oy Bm Nov 24/57

My dear S

I hope you are about again by this time — but the weather is very trying.

You spoke about Beardwood's bills about 3 weeks or a month ago. and I intended to convey to you that they were to be paid, but I suppose you did not understand me. Beardwood has written to me on the subject.

I sent Broughtons' Bill — does not Anderdon pay half? — I will sign a cheque, if you will kindly send it

Ever Yrs affly J H N

TO THOMAS W. B. WOOD

Birmingham Nov 24. 1857

Sir,

In answer to your question I beg to inform you that your parcel, or what

[1] Phillipps's son Everard was killed at Delhi on 17 Sept. See postscript to letter of 30 July 1857 to Phillipps.

appears to be such, has been received at 6 Harcourt Street, Dublin.[1] Shall I direct the Secretary of the University to open it.[2]

I am &c.

The Oratory, Birmingham Novr 25. 1857

My dear Sir John,

Your letter has just now come, forwarded from Dublin. I very much regret that I have missed you here, and shall miss you there.

I do not know Dr O'Brien well, but I know him quite well enough to write to him about you, and will do so gladly. It would rejoice me indeed if we had a person like yourself in Parliament.[3]

Dr O'Brien is an extremely good friend of the University, and, though Dr Meyler has the reputation of being a Whig, yet he too now is our good friend and I know him very well. Therefore I fear the two are contrary in *politics*, since they seem to me the same way in University matters. I shall be very sorry if Dr O'Brien is a politician of Dr McHale's party, yet I cannot believe it. He is an amiable, calm, well-judging man. All Irishmen are for their own country, and if I were an Irishman, I should be sorely tempted to hate England; but I shall be surprised if Dr O'Brien goes beyond this (loving Ireland).

I would write about you to Dr O'Brien by this post, but that, looking at your letter, I do not see you quite give me leave to do so. I wish I knew any one else in that part of the world. I fear not. The late Bishop spoke to me in the most grateful terms of the Duke of Devonshire, and I should think a number of the clergy felt with him — but you doubtless know much more than I, here.[4]

I am deeply concerned at Mr Morris's accident. Pray remember us most kindly to him.[5]

It is very kind in Dr Döllinger to have taken interest in any book of mine. You do not say which it is. I heard lately from him on the subject of the translation of his own work, in which you are to do the translator a service.

---

[1] In reply to Newman's letter of 11 Nov. Wood wrote on 12 Nov. asking for a categorical reply to the question whether his parcel had reached Newman.

[2] Wood replied that he wished the parcel to remain in Dublin until Newman himself should have an opportunity of opening it. See letter of 15 Jan. 1858 to Wood.

[3] Acton did not succeed in finding a seat in Parliament until he was elected for Carlow in 1859. Dominic O'Brien was the Bishop of Waterford.

[4] Newman first met Nicholas Foran, the previous Bishop, at Waterford on 20 Feb. 1854. William George Spencer Cavendish, sixth Duke of Devonshire (1790–1858), owned large estates in Waterford. He was naturally a supporter of the Whig interest, although his own tastes were literary and artistic, not political.

[5] John Brande Morris, Acton's chaplain at Aldenham, had hurt his arm.

I wanted Fr Darnell to have a talk with you on the subject — but Electioneering duties will, I fear, interrupt literary occupations — but thank you much for your offer.[1]

Most sincerely Yours in Xt   John H Newman of the Oratory

Sir John D. Acton Bart

TO RICHARD STANTON

(not sent)   Oy Bm Nov 25. 1857

My dear Father

I have received your letter — but am sorry I cannot take any part with you in any thing relating to the Oratory here or abroad. I am sorry you asked it.[2]

I am &c J H N

[1] Döllinger wrote from Munich on 5 Nov. giving permission for the translation of *Heidentum und Judentum*, which Darnell had undertaken: 'As you seem to think, that a publisher can be found willing to undertake the risk, and that the translator you have fixed upon, is competent to perform the task, I cannot have the least objection against your proposal; on the contrary it gives me the highest satisfaction. . . .

A revision of the sheets will appear desirable to the translator himself, and as the distance is too great, for myself to do this, Sir John Acton has kindly undertaken to do it, if the sheets will be sent to him successively at Aldenham (Bridgnorth, Shropshire), where he is to reside for the greater part of this year. He is an excellent German Scholar, familiarly conversant with my manner of writing and my ideas, and well acquainted with the matters treated in the book.'

For Darnell's translation, see letter of 7 Oct. 1857 to W. G. Todd.

Döllinger continued, 'If your getting rid of the rectorship of the University gives you greater leisure for literary activity, I would almost find in my heart to hail the event as an auspicious one, for I am convinced that what you may do in the literary way will be of greater importance to the Church in general. Your work on Justification, which I have read twice, is in my estimation one of the best theological books published in this century, and your work on the Arians will be read and studied in future generations as a model of its kind. Pardon me, when I say, that since you have become a member and an ornament of the true church, you have not given to us a work of equal *theological* interest and importance. But I trust, you will do so in time.

En attendant, I look forward with an anticipation of pleasure and instruction to the Essays, you will probably contribute to the periodical, which is about to appear under the sanction of your name. The "Specimen of subjects" I have seen in the papers, is a most promising one.'

Cf. *Ward*, I, pp. 444–5.

[2] Stanton wrote on 24 Nov. that Alfonso Capecelatro of the Naples Oratory was publishing an account of the state of Catholicism in England, and wanted a copy of the Brief making Newman a doctor of divinity. Stanton explained that he would soon be writing to the Naples Oratory and could enclose it. Newman evidently left Stanton's letter unanswered. On the separation of the Oratories see Volume XVII passim.

Capecelatro's book *Newman e la Religione Cattolica in Inghilterra ovvero l'Oratorio Inglese*, two volumes, Naples 1859, spoke as though Pius IX had made Newman and Faber Doctors of Divinity simultaneously, I, pp. 339–40, and in a note there, Capecelatro wrote: 'Abbiamo fatto ogni possibile per ottenere una copia del Breve, con cui Newman e Faber furono dichiariti dottori della S. Sede; ma non ci è affatto riuscito averla. In quanto al Newman ci scrive il St.—Jhon [sic] "E impossibile che io le rimetta una copia del Breve del dottorato del P. Newman, attesochè egli non permetterà mai che si stampi un tale documento durante la sua vita, secondo l'esempio del P. Baronio. Bisogna dunque che ella si contenti del fatto che il P. Newman l'abbia di certo ricevuto, essendo io presente allorchè il detto Breve si lesse dal vescovo della diocesi nella cappella vecchia dell'Oratorio ad Alcester Sbiel [sic] in Birmingham." '

TO LAURENCE FORDE

⌐The Oratory, Birmingham Novr 26. 1857¹

Dear Dr Forde,

I wish I could relieve the difficulty which occasions your letter of this morning; but I fear it is out of my power.² I have been desirous again and again of administering the oath to the Professors, especially last St Patrick's day, but have been hindered by the circumstance that up to this time I have had no official notice from any quarter of the formal nomination of the Professors by the Bishops.

After the Synodal Meeting of Bishops in June 1856, I understood from His Grace the Archbishop of Dublin that they had granted all I asked for, except one or two points which he was so good as to specify. As time went on, however, when I proceeded to act upon this intimation, I found I had misunderstood it; for in fact there was scarcely any of the measures which I had laid before the meeting, which his Grace concurred in my carrying out.

I then thought that I should have to wait for the return of the Decrees of Synodal Meeting from Rome; and that then I should know what had been granted me, and what not. And this is the expectation in which I have been till now — when I am disposed to doubt whether I shall ever hear any thing.

Under these circumstances the only Professors I can recognise are the five who were nominated by the Archbishops at Maynooth in June 1854, as the Archbishop of Dublin distinctly informed me at the time, though I now have misgivings whether here too I may not have mistaken his Grace.

Any how, I am unable to administer the oath to you, and the other Professors, whom I have recommended to the Bishops since June 1854, sorry as I am to decline.³

I am, Dear Dr Forde, Sincerely Yours in Xt

John H Newman of the Oratory

The Very Revd Mr Forde

P.S. Will you allow me to ask you and Dr O'Reilly *for the names of the Preachers* for next month and on?

¹ This letter, of which the autograph is in the archives of the Archdiocese of Dublin, must have been given to Cullen. The holograph copy of it Newman made from his draft, which is practically identical with the letter sent.
² Forde wrote on 25 Nov. that it had at length been arranged that he should open his class in Canon Law on 30 Nov., but that first he must make his Profession of Faith before the Rector of the University, 'both by the general law of the Church and the University Statutes.'
³ Forde replied on 28 Nov., 'With reference to the principal subject of your note in reply to mine—I suppose I shall be correct in considering it as simply expressing your inability, as you apprehend it, to make any arrangements for receiving my Profession of Faith—and very kindly adding the reasons, which induce you to take this view—but not—taking many other circumstances into account—as expressing any opinion on the propriety of my acting in my capacity of Professor of Canon Law.
Accordingly, since under present circumstances—the fulfilment of the rule obliging me

TO JOHN HUNGERFORD POLLEN

The Oy. Bm Novr 26. 1857

My dear Pollen,

Leave Angelo as well as $\dot{\alpha}\nu\alpha\beta\alpha\iota\nu\omega$ by all means, if you will. I only wanted to draw your attention to the matter.[1]

As to the University, first it is only the Faculty of Arts which halts — and recollect that of the London University too Medicine was the sheet anchor for a time.[2] We are prosperous in Medicine. Our Register will give our Science Faculty a name — in Philosophy and Letters we are lame — we always have been. We never have had Irish youths except one or two. Barnewall, Errington, White, I suspect are all. The rest are Burses, English, Scotch, foreigners.[3]

Still, looking to the future — first supposing Philosophy and Letters to perish, quite enough for a University remains. The only hitch is that the Philosophy and Letters costs twice as much as other Faculties, and is made up in great measure of Englishmen. The English party costs £1300; more than the whole of the other two Faculties. You may suppose I don't *say* this, (and tell out only my *thoughts* to you,) but I feel unpleasantly that, for what does good to two or three Irish only, I am making a sort of job in favor of the English of Irish money. I don't say that it really is so — but it is what might be said, and may soon be said.

This it is that makes me so desire that English subscriptions should be given. If England subscribed £1000 a year, it might at any time ship off the Philosophy and Letters Faculty to England, if it thought well, leaving it an integral part of the Dublin University still. This is what I *wish* — £1000 a year from England — but, with lukewarm friends like Sir J.S. [John Simeon] and overdrained friends like Hope Scott and Ward, how can one do anything[4]

Ever Yrs affly, J H N.

J.H. Pollen Esqr.

to the Profession of Faith, previous to teaching is impossible, I shall have no difficulty in considering myself dispensed with, as to its observance.'
Newman wrote on this letter 'Nov 30/57 I mean to send no answer to this—thinking it does not require one.'
[1] This refers to Pollen's article in the *Atlantis*, (Jan. 1858), pp. 129–44, 'Structural Characteristics of the Basilicas.' Newman queried his derivation of apse or absis from $\dot{\alpha}\nu\ \alpha\beta\alpha\iota\nu\omega$, and his spelling of Michael Angelo.
[2] Pollen wrote on 25 Nov. from London, 'I am sorry about the numbers [attending the Catholic University]. Anyone but you would have given up the whole concern I am sure. Indeed as far as *sight* goes I must confess I cannot get any solid comfort for the future, there seem to me such great interests vested in the present state of things in Ireland. I mean in the possession of political and social power by the class who now hold it, and the more the objects of the University come out, the stronger will be the fear of the professors. If I were one of them I dare say I should feel the same.'
[3] With rare exceptions those who held burses intended, after two years in Philosophy and Letters, to transfer to another Faculty. Thus they were not to be taken into account, when discussing the true state of the Faculty. Cf. *McGrath*, pp. 450–1.
[4] On 10 Dec. Pollen wrote his thanks for 'your kind and confidential letter.' He thought

TO MICHAEL FLANNERY

Nov 28/57

Dear Mr Flannery

The inclosed note of mine (viz above of Nov 19) and the resolution of Faculty were made up in a cover for you before I left Dublin. I withdrew them at the last minute and brought them here instead of sending them to you on the information that your negociation with Mr Kelly was at an end. Having this morning learned the contrary I send them[1]

I am &c J H N

TO W. H. SCOTT

The Oratory Birmingham Novr 28. 1857

My dear Scott

I assure you I had been feeling very much for Arnold's anxieties, and (if I may say it) had only been this morning praying for him. He has a great many troubles of various kinds, I doubt not, which he alone can know. I think it affects his spirits, if I judge from his manner.[2]

I heartily wish it was more in my power to aid him than I can — There is no reason, in default of an Intern Tutor, why he should not have University youths to cram — but that does not depend upon *me*. I suppose Mr Flannery does not like to have him, or he would have asked him.

I do not know what you are alluding to in the case of externs. If Externs make themselves quasi-interns by attaching themselves to a house, then indeed we provide tuition — and if our House had five or six such, Arnold could, with your consent, have them, but we have none. And if we had, I suppose that probably they would be preparing for the Artilery [sic], Engineering etc etc and need mathematics, which he might not like to undertake.

Any thing he can suggest, I will turn in my mind — [3]

As to the Vice Rector, there is (between ourselves) some little movement going on quietly just at this minute to get one — and perhaps Dr Dunne and

the Irish and the Irish clergy would support an Ecole Polytechnique rather than a University in the Oxford or Cambridge sense. Pollen added, 'But what is quite new to me and certainly holds out an entirely new hope is what you throw out as to the possible transfer of the Arts department to England.'

[1] See letters of 19 and 30 Nov. to Flannery.

[2] Arnold's anxieties were partly financial, partly caused by his change of religion, to which his wife strongly objected.

[3] See letter of 30 Nov. to Arnold.

Mr Butler have some suspicion of it, and wish to see if any thing comes of it — you might mention this to Arnold.[1]

Ever Yrs affly J H N

TO THE DUCHESS OF NORFOLK

The Oratory Birmingham Novr 29. 1857

My dear Duchess of Norfolk,

Miss French is returned from abroad, and I saw her yesterday for the first time. Knowing the kind interest you have taken in her, I have thought you would let me write you a line about her.

She was first in the South of France, and was much benifitted by the mildness of the weather — this was last winter. Then she went to Lucca — afterwards she was with Mrs Foljambe in the neighbourhood of Rome, where unluckily she caught a fever. However, she has recovered from it — except that such a visitant does not leave the patient once for all, and she has even this last week been reminded of this for a day or two.

She does not feel this cold weather, and I trust is better. But I cannot deny that she looks very delicate — and is still an invalid.

I take this opportunity of thanking you for the kind note you lately sent me, which was far more of a return than the small volume merited — and with my best respects to the Duke, and kindest remembrances to your family circle, (which by now must have got a tall circle, if a circle can be tall,) I am, My dear Duchess of Norfolk, Most Sincerely Yours in Xt

John H Newman of the Oratory

Her Grace The Duchess of Norfolk

MONDAY 30 NOVEMBER 1857   Sir John Acton called

---

[1] Newman copied out part of a letter from Scott, which he thought belonged to Nov. 1857, 'There is a wish among the University authorities to memorialize the Archbishops about a Vice-Rector, and I find a strong wish among the Irish professors . . . for Anderdon

(As to the form)—E.g. If the request were that the Vice Rector should be pro hac vice, considering the emergency, nominated by *you absolutely* and without any restriction as to country or position? Or would it be better to ask for some definite person—and, if so, whom?'

TO THOMAS ARNOLD

Birmingham [30?] Novr [1857?]

My dear Arnold[1]

I have received with the greatest pleasure the announcement of your intention to open a house for the reception of students attending lectures at the Catholic University, under the existing regulations provided in that case by the University constitution. I have only to assure you that I am glad to hear it, and trust that you will soon succeed in filling your house with pupils. For their intellectual progress and the formation of their minds your name is in various ways a guarantee as far as I am in a position to speak without the appearance of interference. From what I know of you, I am confident that you will watch over the moral interests and personal conduct of any young men who may be entrusted to your care, with yet greater vigilance than that which you would employ to further their intellectual progress. I remain

Professor Arnold Catholic Univ.

TO MICHAEL FLANNERY

[[Nov 30. 1857]]

My dear Mr Flannery

⌜Understanding now from you that Mr Kelly will have no sort of academical power over your students, and have nothing whatever to do with the discipline, and that attendance on his instructions [[lectures]] will not be 'compulsory,' I am glad to appoint him on your recommendation up to Christmas on trial.

Should you wish him to share with you the discipline, I am quite ready to allow of it,[1] (provided he has not formal classes for Lectures) ⌜but in that case he will not be a Tutor.⌝

I am &c J H N

MEMORANDUM, THE TRANSLATION OF SCRIPTURE

November 1857

What I think and have thought for some time is this, tho' I don't say it out, because when I have hinted it, I have been thought fanciful —

that the notion of giving me the translation of Scripture was with the

[1] This letter is a draft in Arnold's hand, with corrections and additions by Newman, to make his recommendation stronger. Cf. letter of 28 Nov. to Scott.

intention of the London Oratory doing it, and my chiefly giving my name and general superintendence.

I gathered this from the fact that the Synod which gave it me was held soon after I went to Ireland, at a time when it could not be supposed that I could be more than a nominal translator.[1]

Then nothing is said to me by the Cardinal for more than two years (tho' Dr Ullathorne mentioned it at once to me)[2] when he could not help speaking for by that time the Decrees of the Synod had returned from Rome.

He did not speak to me because not many months after the Synod, just at the very time the Cardinal had sent the Decrees to Rome, our quarrel took place with the London Oratory, and he found the plan marred, and therefore waited to the last minute, hoping things would come straight.

Then after half a year ago I happened to call at Stewart's, and find that Fr Hutchison has been buying of him a set of Bibles, Comments etc bearing on a translation of Scripture.

And now, when I have sent in to the Cardinal the names of Translators etc, and the names of no London Oratorian appears, the London Oratorians have began to coax us, as if the Cardinal put them up to it.[3]

TUESDAY 1 DECEMBER 1857   Mr Eyston called.   M de Bamville dined

TO THOMAS SCRATTON

Dec 1/57

My dear S

I return the cheques signed.

My 'Remarks on the Statute of January 1857' have passed the Council after a careful previous examination of some months — as you must remember. Therefore you must act upon them, certainly.[4]

[1] The Synod was held in July 1855. See Wiseman's letter of 26 Aug. 1857, placed before Newman's of 27 Aug.

[2] Newman made a note at the time in his diary: 'July 1855 NB. For the translation of Holy Scripture 1. Dr Oliver. 2 J B Morris 3 Tierney. 4 Dr Rock 5 Waterworth. 6 Newsham. 7 Canon John Walker 8 Manning 9. Faber 10 de Vere 11 Weedall 12 St John. (who from St Edmund's?)'

Newman later added '(this memorandum was occasioned by Dr Ullathorne's private information that the translation was to be put into my hands—but not acted on, as I did not hear from the Cardinal)'

Newman's tentative list of consultors drawn up in July 1855, when compared with the list of those actually approached, (see second note to letter of 17 Oct. 1857 to Ralph Platt), shows how he always meant to rely on the old Catholic priests. In Oct. 1857 he added several more of these, and dropped only one, Dr Weedall, whose eyesight was failing. Of the five converts in the first list, J. B. Morris, Faber and Aubrey de Vere were dropped.

[3] Cf. letter of 17 Nov. to St John and notes there, and letter of 25 Nov. to Stanton; also letter of 17 Dec. to Faber.

[4] See note to letter of 16 Jan. 1857 to Quinn. Scratton wrote on 30 Nov., 'I really think, if

If the Council chooses to put additional fees on non-residents, it can do so. At present I conceive that none but the Examination fees attach to him — , not the Lecture money, because he does not (viewed as a non resident) attend lectures. Nothing will bring us into worse odour than to charge students for things which we do not really give them. You know how men were disgusted at Oxford at having to pay non-resident Tuition money. The only question is, whether the nonresident's entrance Examination fee should be £1 or £5, and I think it will be fair to charge £5 (for Exhibitioners £5 each).

J H N

P.S.   I keep back the drafts — for query 1. should they not be paid to the respective *Deans* 2 should the whole sum be paid at once, or half yearly?[1]

TO SIR ROBERT THROCKMORTON

The Oratory Birmingham Decr 1. 1857

My dear Sir Robert

A very handsome present of game has just arrived for me with your name inside the basket. I beg to return you my best thanks for it, and feel much pleased at this mark of your kindness

I am, my dear Sir Robert, Very truly Yours

John H Newman of the Oratory

Sir Robert Throckmorton Bart.

TO J. B. MORRIS

The Oratory Birmingham Decr 2. 1857

My dear Morris,

I was very much concerned to hear from Sir John [Acton] of your accident — which I do trust is now almost a matter of history.

He told me too that you are still at your books — and that leads me to ask if you think you could do any thing for our new University Register, of which I inclose a Prospectus. You will see the kind of subject — a tough, dry, learned, unreadable article which would be invaluable, if you could compose such a thing. Alas, we give no pay.[2]

you enquire, that not *one* Professor in the whole University was at all aware of the meaning of the New Statutes when they passed—All (I think without exception) were taken by surprise at the particular sense afterwards attached to them by the Lord Rector.' Scratton wanted to treat non-residents who attended lectures, not as auditors but as externs.

[1] This refers to the payment of the exhibitions of de la Pasture and Keane.
[2] See letter of 11 Dec. to Morris.

192

Can you tell me at what age a Jew (the first born) was formally registered in the family pedigree; — at circumcision? at five years old? on his father's death? — e.g. I turn to Potter,[1] and find at once that Athenian boys were registered at *five* — but I can get no information any where about Jewish.[2]

Ever Yrs affly John H Newman of the Oratory

The Very Revd J B Morris

TO THOMAS SCRATTON

December 3. 1857

My dear Secretary

Will you be so good as to summon the Senate for Sunday 13th December, for the confirmation of my appointment of Examiners for the Exhibitions to be given away at this time, and for other business, which, as well as the names of the Examiners, Professor Butler will specify overleaf[3]

I am, &c &c John H Newman Rector

Thos Scratton Esqr Secretary

FRIDAY 4 DECEMBER 1857   M de Bamville dined

TO ROBERT MACDERMOTT

Dec 5/57

(Copy)

My dear Dr McDermott,

I have been expecting for some days to hear from you as Dean of the Faculty of medicine, on the subject of Dr Lyons's expedition to Lisbon — As I do not, I trouble you with extracts from letters which have passed between him and me.[4]

He wrote to me on November 22 to the following effect:

'I am about to ask leave of absence from you for a brief period under the

[1] John Potter, *Archaeologia Graeca, or the Antiquities of Greece*, two vols., Edinburgh 1804.
[2] Morris replied on 3 Dec. that he had searched in vain for the answer to Newman's question, and guessed that registration took place after twelve years in the case of Jewish boys.
[3] Butler inserted the names of the Examiners, for the Classical Exhibition, Ornsby, Dunne and Scott, for the Mathematical, Penny, Hennessy and Butler. He also proposed modifications of the regulations for the Entrance Examinations.
[4] Scratton wrote privately on 3 Dec., 'There is a general strong feeling of disapprobation at Lyons' Absence. The School of Medicine seems very indignant about it and people in general are very *critical*—'

following circumstances. . . . The most recent accounts of the great Epidemic now raging at Lisbon, concur in describing it as yellow fever of a very bad type. I am extremely desirous of availing myself of this opportunity for investigating the Pathology of this very formidable disease . . . I am annually called on to teach the Pathology and Therapeutics of Yellow Fever and Plague. The present is perhaps the only occasion on which I may have it in my power without passing the limits of Europe to study and investigate the Yellow fever. The French Government has despatched two scientific medical men to Lisbon — no such steps have been taken in this country or in England — but I am myself willing, should you grant me the necessary leave of absence, to proceed to Portugal myself, with a view to a pathological inquiry on the spot. It would be desirable of course that I should proceed at once to Lisbon, and I would propose to spend about the [a] month in that city. As the month of December is in part a time of recreation to students my class would for the present lose not more than some fortnight's lectures, which I propose to bring up by lecturing on additional days upon my return. Trusting that I may receive from you a favorable answer to my application for leave of absence etc.'

I make this extract that the Faculty may know distinctly the grounds on which Dr Lyons's application was in itself, as I think, one which deserved consideration. I replied November 23 as follows

It seems to me very important, *viewing the matter in itself*, that you should avail yourself of the opportunity which offers in the epidemic at Lisbon to prosecute an object so clearly connected with your Professorship — and I will gladly do any thing I can to promote your wish. I say 'viewing the matter in itself,' *because I should like the proposal to come formally before me through your Faculty.*

He answered

'I feel much obliged for the spirit in which you have recognised my mission. *You are already in receipt of a letter from the Dean of Faculty on the subject.* I start tonight for London.'

This is the last I have heard Has any letter from you miscarried.[1]

---

[1] Newman's copy of his letter ends here. MacDermott answered on 6 Dec. that Lyons had applied to the Faculty of Medicine on 23 Nov. and had been referred to Newman. MacDermott understood that Newman had given Lyons leave of absence, and so did not write to him at all. The rest of the Medical Faculty seemed to approve of Lyons's absence. Newman made a note of his reply on 7 Dec. to MacDermott: 'answered that I take for granted he has let the Faculty know that I gave no consent. (I mean to write to Dr Ellis on the subject to say so).'

TO ANDREW ELLIS

The Oratory Birmingham Decr 7. 1857

My dear Dr Ellis

I find a report has got about that I gave Dr Lyons leave of absence. I never should have taken a step so disrespectful to your Faculty without communication with it — nor did I. I should have been willing to do so, had the Faculty told me that his absence would not be injurious to the school. But not till then.

I wrote to him on his application — 'It seems to me very important, *viewing the matter in itself*, that you should avail yourself of the opportunity etc . . . . I say, "viewing the matter in itself," *because I should like the proposal to come formally before me through your Faculty.*'

I expected a letter from your Faculty in consequence of what he said in answer — When I had none, I wrote to your Dean to know, if a letter had miscarried. He replies to me by this morning's post, implying that this is not the case. I wrote no letter to Dr Lyons except the above which I have quoted.

I write this merely to relieve myself from the appearance of disrespect towards you and your colleagues and am My dear Dr Ellis

Most sincerely Yours John H Newman

A Ellis Esqr

TO THOMAS SCRATTON

The Oratory Bm Decr 7. 1857

My dear Scratton

I am frightened to see I owe the University so much for fees.[1] I cannot pay at the moment, tho' I said I would. The truth is the de Lignes did not pay the whole of last year, as I thought they would, and I shall be paying more than I received. Renouf wrote to the Steward or Agent — but I am giving it up as a bad job. Zamoyski too has not yet paid me for this half — and therefore I must, if you please, wait awhile.

It strikes me that, if the wall of your house is beginning to be repaired, it is the time for the University to close with the Blue Coat School people — or the University will build the wall and not get the lease. Would it not be better for Mr Maxwell to write to Dr Leahy (who has sanctioned the rebuilding) to *tell* him the risk the University runs, and to get him to authorize

[1] The de Lignes and Zamoyski, who lived in Newman's House, had not yet paid their University fees.

him in concluding the renewal? Please ask Butler, and if you see nothing better, and he agrees too, you can proceed to write to Mr Maxwell.

Thank you for the trouble you are taking about the de Ligne's £75

Ever Yrs affly J H N

Thos Scratton Esqr

TUESDAY 8 DECEMBER 1857   sang high mass.

TO JOSEPH DIXON, ARCHBISHOP OF ARMAGH

The Oratory, Birmingham Decr 8. 1857

My dear Lord,

You will see that this letter requires no answer — but I write it in consequence of Professor Butler's wish that I should bring the subject of it before you.[1]

He informs me he has been speaking with the Archbishop of Dublin on the subject of his becoming a Candidate for the Vice Rectorship of the University. Of course I am no judge of the propriety or advisableness of the Vice Rector being a layman — though at Louvain this has sometimes been the case — but, viewing the matter apart from that important question, I should say that there could not possibly be a more eligible person than Mr Butler — and, as he wishes me to do so, and I think your Grace will allow me, I feel it a duty to express to you this opinion.

He is wellknown, I believe, to a great number of the Clergy, from his former situation in the Education Staff.[2] He is well acquainted with all our University matters, and, I believe, very popular in the University. He is a thorough Gentleman, a man of the highest religious character, and well judging and moderate in all his views and his mode of acting. He has shown too especial zeal in the University from the first — having giving [sic] up a place more lucrative than that which he holds in it.

However, I have taken up your Grace's time too long, and begging you to excuse me, if I have said more than I ought and begging your blessing I am, My dear Lord, Your faithful & affte Servt in Xt

John H Newman[3]

The Most Revd The Primate

---

[1] Butler wrote to Newman on 7 Dec., 'I have just seen the Archbishop [Cullen] and he received me and spoke to me very kindly. He said he was the party to propose that the Bishops should leave it open to themselves to appoint a layman to the Vice Rectorship. But that at present considering that almost all the Professorships were held by laymen, he thought they were not prepared to appoint a lay Vice-Rector. However he said he would take charge of my application and speak to Dr Dixon and Dr Leahy on the subject. . . .
Perhaps you would now assist me if you were to write to Drs Dixon and Leahy. . . .'
[2] Butler had been a Chief Inspector of the National Board of Education in Ireland.
[3] Newman copied out part of a letter Butler wrote to him on 27 Dec., 'I spoke to Dr Ellis

TO LADY HENRY KERR

The Oratory Bm Feast of the Imm Conc. 1857.

My dear Lady Henry,

I was very glad to hear from you and about you. Several times had I asked others what had become of William, whom last year Lord Henry and you saw on his journey towards India.[1] It is indeed a most fearful awful time for those who have friends in those parts. When the Crimean war began I wondered how friends could endure the mocking tantalizing telegraphs, telling just enough to frighten and unsettle, and then leaving the truth for the slow despatch by mail. But this is a hundred times worse, and in so many different respects that I am quite puzzled to think, how it is that many gentle delicate fragile persons at home, mothers for instance advanced in years, are able to live. I think suspense and the anxiety connected with it one of the greatest of mental troubles. The Greek hero in the Poem was willing to die, so that he died in [a] day.[2] I suppose most men can make up their minds to what is inevitable — but when you do not know with what focus (so to say) you are to look at a thing and are continually hoping and yearning I wonder how any frame can bear it long. It has struck me in this point of view, as increasing the distress, that it is one of the sufferings of human nature which our Blessed Lord could not have — ignorance being one of those four penalties of Adam's sin which He did not share. Of course knowledge has its own incommunicable sufferings but still ignorance has its own too, and these we must bear by ourselves without his experimental sympathy.

You surprise me most pleasingly when you speak so hopefully of Hurrell F.[3] Perhaps I am apt to despond — but I should think it almost a mistake if a youth, like him, took up with the True Faith against his dear Father and the world. I should be frightened to hear it — Yet, even if such good inspirations, as he may have, do not become effectual now, they may be paving the way for his conversion at some future day.

It is very kind of you to have received my small volume in the way you have.[4] I sent it you that you might remember me in your prayers. It is not

about the Vice Rectorship, and he mentioned it to Mr Bianconi. But Mr B. is decidedly of opinion that at present the appointment of a lay Vice Rector would be injudicious, as it would tend to increase the apathy and carelessness of some of the clergy in the matter of the collection.'
[1] Lady Henry's eldest son William Hobart Kerr (1836–1913), was in the Madras Civil Service at the time of the Indian Mutiny. He had been at Harrow School for five years, until he became a Catholic in 1852. He then went to Stonyhurst and Haileybury. In 1867 he became a Jesuit.
[2] Ajax, *Iliad*, XV, 511–13.
[3] Richard Hurrell Froude (1842–1932), was Newman's godson and the eldest son of Mrs William Froude. See letter of 11 Dec. to her. Newman received him into the Church on Christmas Eve 1859. See letter of that day to William Froude.
[4] *Sermons preached on Various Occasions.*

the kind of book to do any one good, as *you* say, but it may serve as a memento of me to those to whom it comes. You speak of your ill health still, which I am much concerned to hear. Thank you for your news of Francis [Kerr]; pray give him my love.

What can you have heard about my thumb? It must be some one else's thumb. Thank God, I have nothing the matter with it.

With kindest messages to Lord Henry and the Hope Scotts

Ever Yrs most sincerely in Xt   John H Newman

TO HENRY WILBERFORCE

ΓDecember 8. 1857

Your ordinary misprints are, as you know yourself, serious things. Why can't you get some convert to whom a small job would be an object, to read over the sheets?Γ1

I think your Register is decidedly looking up. I am told it is known a great deal better in Ireland than is supposed — but your returns are a better guide than any thing I can say. At present, I am hopeful about it, as I never have been before.

By the bye, Father Crowther's letters should be castigated before [being] inserted into your columns. They are written off — but it is somewhat scandalous for a missionary, going to die, to say he could not bear being five or six hours in a tent on the desert, without light reading. The Monks who once inhabited it, meditated day and night[2]

Ever Yrs affly J H N

¹ What follows is on a sheet which has been later dated '1855?' From the reference to Fr Crowther it cannot be earlier than 21 Nov. 1857, and very probably was part of the letter from which Newman copied the above fragment.

² Thomas Crowther, an Augustinian friar, was on his way to serve as a chaplain to troops in India during the Mutiny. He wrote a long letter from Egypt, the *Weekly Register*, (21 Nov. 1857), p. 4, describing his journey with his fellow voyagers across the desert, to join the ship at Suez: 'As we could not all be taken at once, lots were cast who should go first. My portion fell with the late batch, and there for five mortal hours,with no object or aim, no books or amusement, and, worst of all, no pipe, was I doomed to walk to and fro upon that burning sea of sand.' Crowther went on to do missionary work in China and Japan for a while, before returning to England.

THURSDAY 10 DECEMBER 1857   Mr Senez of Cincinnati came into the House — went with him to the Bishop[1]

TO MRS WILLIAM FROUDE

The Oy Bm Decr 11. 1857

My dear Mrs Froude,

Thank you very much for your interesting and pleasant, though painful, details. You have been brought forward wonderfully, and will be brought through. I am very glad you are so open with William — and am sure he will understand the value of it. He will understand how great a thing it is to rely with full confidence that there is nothing unknown to him. What you say about Hurrell is very hopeful — but, while you pray as if immediate success were likely, you must not be cast down at disappointment — There seems a great prospect of your winning them both at last — but you must persevere.[2]

Thank you for letting me see dear Hurrell's letter

Ever Yours affly in Xt   John H Newman of the Oratory

Mrs Froude

TO J. B. MORRIS

The Oratory Bm Decr 11/57

My dear Morris

I am very much concerned to hear how you speak of your arm — but from Sir John's [Acton] account the accident might have been so much worse

---

[1] Peter L. D. Senez (1815–1900), was a French Priest who joined the diocese of Cincinnati in 1844. He appears to have left it about 1860, and in his later years worked in Jersey City. Senez had a letter of introduction from the Archbishop of Cincinnati, J. B. Purcell, to 'Very Revd Dr Newman President Catholic University Dublin':

'Cincinnati 22d Nov. 1857

Very Revd & Honoured Friend

Allow me to introduce to you a very worthy priest of this Diocese, Rev L. D. Senez, who goes to see your Reverence for an object long dear to his heart and to mine. I ventured to name it to you when enjoying your well remembered hospitality in 1851, in Birmingham. It is our united desire to obtain two, or three of the members of the English Oratory, to establish a branch thereof, the first, in the new world. I know you cannot command, but you can advise, exhort, encourage your devout brethren to come and help, to come and save, their brethren in America.

I would fain implore you and them in the name of Jesus and Mary and St Philip Neri not to refuse. There is a wide field for your zeal here which is white for the harvest. Listen then to generous inspirations—Be the docile instruments of the Holy Spirit and let St Philip's name be coupled with the history of the expansion of the faith, which was to go forth into all the earth from Jerusalem, in America—In this new England to which all the heresies of the old were brought, are brought—Cranmerism, Puritanism, Methodism, Mormonism, and its most numerous recruits, and an Anti-catholic Literature, from the land to which we now look for ORATORIANS.

Deign to hear and pray for Yr devoted friend and fellow labourer in Christ

J. B. Purcell Abp. Cin'

See also diary for 14 Dec.

[2] See second note to letter of 8 Dec. to Lady Henry Kerr.

in its consequences, that, now that it has taken a good turn, I will not believe it will not go on happily.[1]

I like your first subject (Job) best, because it is most matter of fact; and should be truly grateful to you for it.[2] When I say 'matter of fact,' you will understand why I prefer you for 'dry' articles. A *Review* has moist, warm, juicy speculations or views — but *we* are made of sterner stuff — at least we aim at being. Give me a good tough unreadable article on Job — and every one will cry out 'astonishing, a walking library — ' If I have any copies of our first number, I will send you one — but I doubt how that will be. We are sending 100 copies all over the continent, and none will be left for home friends.

Ambrose is taking up Hebrew and Syriac again — apropos of the translation of Scripture — and mutters some plan of coming over to your Reverence, and consulting you

Ever Yrs affly John H Newman of the Oratory

The Very Rd J B Morris

SATURDAY 12 DECEMBER 1857   quarant'ore began at 9 a m in our Church   I in retreat

TO THE EDITOR OF THE WEEKLY REGISTER

[December 12. 1857][3]

Sir,

I wonder whether you will allow me to ask a question, which certainly is one of some delicacy, yet I am asking it in no hostile spirit, or with any wish

[1] Replying to Newman's letter of 2 Dec. Morris wrote on 3 Dec., 'My arm is matter of prophecy, rather gloomy, not of history—so I cannot wield books etc . . .'
[2] In response to Newman's request for articles to insert in the *Atlantis*, Morris offered, '1 On the drift and probable date of the book of Job . . .
2. Thomist and Scotist theories of the relation of matter to spirit.
3. Thoughts on the Intellectus agens of Aristotle. . . .'
The article on Job appeared in the *Atlantis*, (July 1859), pp. 378–434.
[3] This letter appeared in the *Weekly Register*, (12 Dec. 1857), under the heading THE CATHOLIC UNIVERSITY. Newman explained its purpose in 'Memorandum about my connection with the Catholic University,' *A. W.*, p. 330:
'Now it happened at the end of the year 1857, that Dr. Cullen expressed regreat that the Professors did not make greater use of the Newspaper Press in bringing the University before the public, and I urged Mr. Ornsby and others to turn their thoughts to the subject. They were willing, and the only question was how to do it. It occurred to me that it would be well to begin some controversy about the University—so, telling no one but Mr. H Wilberforce, the Editor, I inserted in the Weekly Register a very bitter letter signed "Q in the corner". Ornsby replied and I wrote as many as four [three] short letters; but to my disgust I found I was beating him. But what it brought out clearly was the English sentiment. No[t] a word came in advocacy of the University from any English College or centre, and Q's letters were, without disavowal of the sentiments which they contained, attributed generally to this or that English priest. I tried to make it up to the University by writing leading articles for four weeks in its defence; but what came home clearly to me was, that I was spending my life in the service of those who had not the claim upon me which my own countrymen had: that, in the decline of life, I was throwing myself out of that sphere of action and those connexions

to prejudice the institution which it concerns, and shall be sincerely glad if it can be answered. Sometimes it is a real kindness to any such important project or undertaking, to bring together and put on paper the perplexities and misgivings which haunt the minds of sober men concerning it; for it is doing in its behalf as regards those difficulties what the tyrant of old contemplated, when he wished that the Roman people had but one neck, that he might despatch them at a blow. Let me offer myself as the victim whose decapitation, if it be possible, will be the security and triumph of the parties decapitating me.

I assure you, Mr. Editor, I regard the new Catholic University with unfeigned respect and interest, viewed as an Irish institution. It has been nobly set up by the venerable Hierarchy of the Sister Isle, with the sanction of the Holy See, as a bulwark against the encroachments of an insidious Protestant Government, who, as some of your correspondents have forcibly urged, take every opportunity, by building-grants, souperism, national boards, and parliamentary bribes, to circumvent our simplicity. Still it is an Irish University after all, and has nothing to do with England.

Then I say, and others feel, even if they do not say it, why has it got some of our best men from us, who ought to be devoting themselves to English objects — e.g., to the projected new translation of Scripture? We have wants enough at home. I cannot be supposed to feel anything but admiration at the liberality, as well as good sense, of the Irish University itself in securing their services. And men will always go where they are valued and paid, so I do not blame them. And I hear they are quite satisfied with their position, and that there is no truth in last year's report of differences between them and the Irish Professors. But the University has now been set up, I am afraid to say how many years. What has it done for us in England? There are those who feel that it is only embarrassing an existing system of high education which works well. I believe that persons of great weight conceive that if a youth be educated, say at Stonyhurst, and there prepare himself for the London University, he can desire nothing better. Where are morals better guarded than in a Jesuits' College? Where can intellectual proficiency be better ascertained than in London?[1] People are tempted to say, 'Let well alone.' Why is my good friend the respected Rector leaving Dublin? Has not this a meaning?

A second time I deprecate the imputation of unkind feeling towards the University; but surely it is time to speak out. We live in an age when questions must be answered, and if certain of your correspondents, Mr. Editor, make free with proceedings and works of a religious character, sanctioned by

which I had been forming for myself so many years. All work is good, but what special claim had a University exclusively Irish upon my time?'

Newman's other 'Q in the Corner' letters appeared in the *Weekly Register* on 2 and 16 Jan. 1858.

[1] The English Catholic colleges were affiliated to London University and obtained external degrees from there.

prelates of the Church, and based on the repute of miracles,[1] I think it no presumption to ask, with friendly intentions, what good ought we to expect on this side the water from the great institution now rising on the banks of the Liffey?

Your Obedient Servant 'Q in the Corner.'

TO ROBERT ORNSBY

The Oratory, Birmingham Decr 12. 1857

My dear Ornsby

Look at the impudent letter in the Register of today. However, it is most pat for your purpose. ⌈I hope you will answer it. If you do, you must be cautious not to kick the shins of our friends at Stonyhurst. Nor is it necessary, for they do not pretend to be a *University*. The whole question of discipline may be brought in — but indeed you may write on the subject far more than will go into one letter.⌉ This is a point to be attended to — far better write on *one* point, leaving all the rest, than make a long letter; for people will read your one point, if you are short, but not read even one out of all your six, if you are prolix.[2]

Thank you for your letters, which I had intended to answer before this.[3] ⌈I think your Committee may be useful, but can hardly conceive it would wish to act as a censor of what an individual like yourself might write — else, the four members of it bind themselves, and nobody else.⌉ The subject your talk of, 'Oxford and the Middle Schools,' would allow field for a very good article.[4] I don't wish you to overwork yourself — and don't forget you have

---

[1] During Sept. and Oct. a controversy raged in the *Weekly Register* over the genuineness of the apparition of our Lady at La Salette. Ullathorne came forward as a staunch defender of it.

[2] Ornsby's letter, incorporating Newman's advice, appeared in the *Weekly Register*, (19 Dec. 1857), p. 5, signed 'Z'. Ornsby emphasised the importance of University education if English Catholics were to take part in public life. Otherwise they would be competing in 'the unequal battle of native powers against disciplined skill.' The Catholic University offered to English as well as Irish Catholics the educational advantages of the older universities 'unalloyed by danger to the Faith.' Cf. letter of 31 Dec. to Ornsby, who did not know the identity of Q in the corner.

[3] Ornsby wrote on 4 Dec., 'Mr Robertson proposed a memorial to the Archbishops in the matter of the Vice-Rectorship, but the Faculty [of Philosophy and Letters] decided that the Dean should sound the other Faculties on the subject. . . . It is said the Bishops are to appoint a Vice Rector at Christmas, but how far this is true, you will probably be able to judge. . . .
I brought forward my proposal about acting on the press, (which I enclose you); it was favourably received, and a committee appointed . . . to carry out the idea, "but with extreme caution," a condition the necessity of which seemed very decidedly felt. I confess that I rather doubt if the plan can be successfully worked with a committee—it is so tedious a business handing an article to several persons in succession.'

[4] Ornsby added, 'I wrote an article the other day on "Oxford and the Catholic University" introductory to another proposed one, on the recent scheme of Oxford for getting hold of the commercial schools—a scheme which is in principle almost a copy of your own idea of the affiliated schools.'

202

had recently had [sic] so much indisposition — but you can write off articles with very little trouble, and very effective articles. ⌐I should not be sorry if you got attached to the Register.⌐ Wilberforce has so lately got into it, that I suppose he limits his expenses as much as he can, and is not able to engage writers; but ⌐the Paper is certainly making its way,⌐ and if it does succeed it will be well able to pay its contributors. I wonder whether the Editor could engage *after a certain time* to pay those who began now to send regular contributions. Contributors would write up his Paper, and enable him by the increased sale to remunerate them. Or it might be an engagement to begin to pay his present contributors, when his sales should reach a certain figure. But this is a digression — at present his columns are open to any one who wishes to reply to Q.

I have never heard that Dr. Q. [Quinn] has any peculiar views about the education of *laymen* as such.[1] As to clergy, that he should have his own views is excusable, especially as he has the fear of his youths failing at Maynooth. St Columba was failing a year or two ago, on Archbishop Beresford's withdrawing his support — but they said that Mr Hope took it up.[2]

How kind of Mrs Ornsby to think of writing to me, but it was quite unnecessary — I should have been very sorry if she had put herself to the trouble about so small a matter.[3] I hear you have *really* got well. I hope so. The coincidence is curious about the Atlantic and Atlantis. I return your paper, which I quite follow.

Yours affectly John H Newman

TO HENRY WILBERFORCE

The Oy Bm ⌐Decr 12/57⌐

My dear H

Thank you for your letter, and what you say about your paper. ⌐No one can say that it is deficient in writers, but would it be worth while, or possible, to attach some men to it, on the engagement that you would pay them for their articles, when your circulation reached a certain figure?⌐ This I suppose

[1] Ornsby lamented the lack of schools that could prepare boys for the University but thought Dr Quinn might form the nucleus of such a school 'if he had not very decided views about education that I should think would greatly interfere with any such attempt.'

[2] Ornsby wrote in the same letter of 4 Dec., 'I thought the letter you wrote Dr Butler on our general prospects 19 Nov. 1857 most valuable and suggestive; and I think, through the press, the Dublin people might be made to see it would be worth their while sending their sons to us. Whether we could possibly educate them up to the mark of appointments, when we had them, is another thing. The terrible deficiency of solid school education is an ἀνήνυτον κακόν [unending evil], and may go on for a life-time. You may recollect what efforts Sewell made 15 years ago, to establish an infant Eton or Winchester for the Irish Protestants at St Columba's. I heard a report the other day that it is a failure and likely to break up.' William Sewell founded the Anglican St Columba's, at Stackallan, County Meath, in 1843. It survived and eventually flourished.

[3] Newman had sent Mrs Ornsby a copy of *Sermons preached on Various Occasions*.

would not do, as not meeting the difficulty of advertisements — though advertisement would follow circulation. ⌜[[Only]] A *few* writers, though good are wanting in variety — and any one writer must be exhausted by constant demands on him, however fertile he might be.⌝ Even though my suggestion is trite or impossible, it may lead to something. ⌜I suppose you *have* Dodsworth, Wetherell, and one or two others, besides yourself, perhaps de Vere. On what terms are you with Allies? he writes well and eloquently. Again, Ornsby would be most valuable to you, as having got into the knack of Journal writing. Pollen is another. Perhaps Thom[[p]]son already writes for you.⌝ However it is easier to speculate in this free way than to fulfil any one portion of the speculations.

⌜I think I desiderate in the Register a *definiteness* of political view. The separate articles are good and sensible, but no one knows your principles very distinctly. The necessity of your courting Ireland is your difficulty here — but depend upon it, no paper will take which is not bold. I agree here with the Rambler, who says that people *abuse*, but *buy*, a peremptory, lay-down-the law, thick and thin, periodical. I don't think this need imply extravagance of opinion — e.g. Laud was violent with his skimmed milk. This, I suppose, is why Brownson takes so much. He has a view on every subject, I suppose, and keeps to it, stands up for it, knocks down every one who attacks it. Great part of Whately's popularity arises from his dictatorial manner. However, I wasn't speaking of manner, but of thoroughgoing, downrightness of sentiment.

I just recollect, there is a passage in Loss and Gain to the purpose — 'Dr Pusey is always said to be decisive — He says This is Apostolic, that's in the Fathers etc⌝ etc'[1]

Ever Yrs affly J H N

⌜Decr 20. I am glad to see that some persons have taken up Q's letter —⌝ I don't know who they are — but suspect that one at least is a Dublin friend.[2] ⌜By the bye I am much amused at the scare-crow speech of mine that is in your yesterday's — It is as much like the original as a bad photograph. It's my own fault — they asked to put something in and I said 'O *yes* — '⌝[3]

J H N

---

[1] *L.G.*, Ch. XIV, p. 120.
[2] See letter of 2 Jan. 1858 to the Editor of the *Weekly Register*.
[3] On 16 Dec. the people attending the Birmingham Oratory presented Newman with a ciborium, as a congratulatory tribute on his return to them. The *Weekly Register*, (19 Dec. 1857), p. 3, reported Newman as saying: 'When I first heard it was intended to present me so costly an article as that you have now so kindly offered, my first feeling was that I had done nothing to deserve it, and that other and better objects had greater claims upon you. And as it is your desire that I should accept this very beautiful Ciborium, I do not take it as a mark of respect to myself, but more particularly to the other Fathers of the Oratory, who have, in reality, all the burden of the ministry. For myself, I am a simple-minded person, who have no ambition to be distinguished by worldly honours. For instance, I am not ambitious of becoming Lord Chancellor, of receiving the Victoria Cross, or being made a Knight of the Garter. (Laughter). If, however, your kindness induces you to present this to me, I shall ever regard it as a memento of the Providence of God towards me. I have lost many friends of my early life, and I do feel grateful to God that I have gained others in their places, and whom I esteem more because bound to me by the sacred ties of religion. Allow me again to

I suppose Mr Hodges has not been curious enough to preserve any portion of a MS I lately sent you?[1]

SUNDAY 13 DECEMBER 1857 (in retreat)

MONDAY 14 DECEMBER Mr Senez went[2] (in retreat) deposition of Blessed Sacrament John Walker slept here

TUESDAY 15 DECEMBER Mr Law called[3] Fr Raffaele slept here[4]

TO EDWARD BUTLER

Not sent.[5]   The Oratory, Bm Decr 17. 1857

Most Private

My dear Mr Butler,

I write to you in very great anxiety, and for you alone.

I see it is impossible that I *can* be Rector (certainly, without a Vice Rector) at this distance. Misunderstandings will be *sure* to rise between the Professors

thank you most heartily for this affectionate expression of your regard, and earnestly request your good prayers in my behalf. (Applause).'

[1] Nicholas William Hodges, a convert and journalist, joined the staff of the *Weekly Register* in 1857.

[2] See diary for 10 Dec. Before leaving the Oratory on 14 Dec., Senez sent Archbishop Purcell a letter, preserved in the diocesan archives at Cincinnati, in which he described how Newman 'showed his great regard for your Grace by the amiable reception he gave me. There are 9 fathers under him nearly all converts from the Church of England, men truly remarkable for their gentleness, simplicity and perseverance in the mode of life they have embraced. Dr Newman appears to me to conceal a disappointment at the little success his work has hitherto had, for as yet they do not seem to have done much—but one should not judge unfavourably of their Oratory on account of its slow progress, for it may be the foundation of a great and lasting work; they all consider it so and wait with patience. There is no hope of obtaining subjects here nor I fear from London for the foundation of an Oratory in Cincinatti; and if there was, I do no [sic] think they should realize your object and certainly, for all I see about it, they do not answer my wishes for reasons which at my return I shall explain.' Later in his letter, Senez, who was a Frenchman, wrote that from what he had seen of priests in England, he would prefer French ones for his purpose. Senez was in Europe again in 1859 as an agent of the Archbishop of Cincinnati, but appears to have left his diocese soon afterwards.

[3] The Hon. William Towry Law (1809–86), youngest son of the first Baron Ellenborough who was Lord Chief Justice 1802–18, after being at Eton and serving with Army in Greece, went to Peterhouse, Cambridge in 1831, and took orders. From 1839 to 1851 he was Chancellor and Prebendary of the Diocese of Bath and Wells, and from 1845 Vicar of Harborne, outside Birmingham. At first an Evangelical, he was increasingly drawn by the teaching of the Tractarians, and was received into the Church at Oscott on 19 Sept. 1851. Law was twice married and had a number of children. He wrote a memoir of the eldest, Augustus Henry Law, who, after being in the Royal Navy, became a Jesuit, and died on the Zambesi Mission in 1880.

[4] Raphael Gorga, an Italian Passionist working in England and Ireland, who had been Superior of the house of his Order at St Wilfrid's, was at this time Vice-Rector of St Joseph's Retreat, in London.

[5] Newman wrote on the autograph: 'N B This, observe, *was not sent.* I keep it as illustrating *the impossibility of governing at a distance* J H N June 21/72 also the NEED of a *Vice* Rector, for with him, not with the Rector, lay *the discipline.*'

and me. There are two already. And I think I shall keep silence, (unless something from *them* is a call on me to speak,) lest they should blow into something at once.

1. I find that the amendment carried in council was neither moved nor seconded formally. Well — it is an informal act then. Now I *dare* not say this — so I suppose I must keep a dead silence, at least for the present.[1]

2. Then again the Council has not only given its opinion about the offence of the two youths,[2] viz that they ought not to be punished by the consilium abeundi — but it has gone on, and gone out of its way, to do a thing which seems quite *irrevelant* (Now don't, please, as you value our prospects and peace, breathe to any one what I am saying) — The *lesser* punishments *under* the 'consilium' 'are in the hands of the Vice Rector and of the Heads or Deans.' Rule § 17 Now the Council 1. takes the matter out of *their* hands. 2. *invents* a punishment. 3 commits to the *Rector* the executioner's work of administering to the culprits a reprimand. I venture to say this is 1 doing what it should not do, *cannot* do. 2 committing it to an officer (the Rector) whose business it is *not*.

Now, observe, I doubt not the members of the Council would have something to say on their own side in *explanation*. And what is this but the very essence, or at least pabulum, of a difference, viz two contrary views plausibly supported?

Therefore you see, *if I say a word*, at once there breaks out some feeling or other which should not be there, and which is like inflammable gas, ready for the match.

Meanwhile, I fear, I fear, I fear, the *two culprits will escape*. Wait to be reprimanded by me! why the essence of good punishment is, its being *immediate*. Now, please, *be very secret*. We are in most trying circumstances

Ever Yours John H Newman

[1] This was at a meeting of the Senate on 13 Dec. See letter of 5 Jan. 1858 to Ornsby.

[2] O'Reilly wrote to Newman on 16 Dec., 'We had a meeting of the Council yesterday evening, to take into consideration the question of the *Consilium abeundi* in connection with the breach of discipline at St Patrick's. I was requested to communicate to you the following unanimous result of our deliberations. "Resolved that this Council will not advise the Rector to visit the offence of Mr Molloy and Mr Mulholland with the *Consilium abeundi*, but at the same time, the Council considering the grave nature of the offence, respectfully submit to the Rector, that a solemn admonition from the Rector in person should be added to whatever punishment he may deem right to inflict." '

Early in Dec. James Lynam Molloy of St Patrick's House went to an evening party without leave. John Mulholland, another student in his house, induced the servant to leave the door unlocked, so that he could do so, and left a window open so that he could return unnoticed. Molloy said that on his return he spent the night in 87 Stephen's Green, where Scratton had his office, next door to St Patrick's House, 86 Stephen's Green.

Newman, who carefully erased the names of the culprits in the correspondence, made a Memorandum on 11 Dec. 1857: 'It is plain 1. that Mr A. deliberately went out without leave. 2 that Mr B. got the servant to open the door for Mr A. 3 That Mr B. also made provision for Mr A's return without discovery. It is to be observed that they neither of them say that it is a first offence. On the contrary B. justifies it almost, and A. talks of an unaccountable impulse

Whether Mr A. returned, as he says, to Number 87 or not, does not seem to alter the offence, which remains where it was, but it introduces a graver question, which we may pursue, though we do not act upon it. If he did not call up Jones at Number 87, the question

The Oratory Birmingham Decr 17. 1857

My dear Dr Dunne,

I am very sorry that I have not answered your Faculty in writing, on the point which you write about, and that I have put you and Mr Ornsby to the suspense you mention. I forget whether your answer came by your Dean or not, or whether I made a verbal answer.[1]

I lose no time in writing to say that I quite acquiesce in it — and wish you to act upon it.

Hoping you have got quite strong, and returning your greetings of the season, I am, My dear Dr Dunne, Yours ever affly in Xt

John H Newman of the Oratory

D B Dunne Esqr

The Oratory Birmingham Dec 17. 1857

Dear Father Superior,

I have this morning received a copy of Sir Launcelot with 'from the author' on the fly leaf.[2] I thank you very much for sending it to me. Fr Darnell wishes me to thank you for one which he also has received this morning.

I hope your health is better than the last time I heard of it. I am, My dear Fr Superior, Yours affectionately in Xt

John H Newman

The Very Revd Fr Faber D D.

is, *where* did he pass the night? If he called Jones up, perhaps Jones could tell us whether he was dressed for a party or not, if Jones can tell.

Another question has relation to the boy who opened Number 86. Acting as Vice Rector, I could send him off, unless his conduct is satisfactorily explained

As to the two young men, I think decidedly that they should receive the "Consilium abeundi."

The offence requires it. The example's sake requires it. And otherwise, for a long while we have been deeply suspicious of A's character and conduct—and dissatisfied with B. as weak and slippery.'

Jones, the porter, reported that Molloy returned at about midnight. He could not say whether he was dressed for a party.

[1] Dunne wrote on 16 Dec. to ask whether Newman approved of a decision of the Faculty of Philosophy and Letters that students holding Scientific Burses could not enter for Exhibitions. See first letter of 21 Dec. to Ornsby.

[2] *Sir Lancelot: a Legend of the Middle Ages.* A Poem. London 1844, second edition 1857.

TO MICHAEL FLANNERY

Oy Bm Decr 18/57

Sent

My dear Mr Flannery

I received yesterday the following unanimous resolution of Council on the subject of the offence of your two students from Dr O'Reilly who presided.

'Resolved that this Council will not advise the Rector to visit the offence of Mr Molloy and Mr Mulholland[1] with the *consilium abeundi*: — '

I have taken a day to think of what punishment would be suitable, since the Council, doubtless for good reasons, have come to the above judgment.

I have determined that you should from me and in my name inflict on them the following: —

that they should both be sent down home at once not to return till after Easter next, that is, till the the first day of the summer term — with the loss of course of the intermediate term and all disadvantages which that loss involves.

As to the boy who allowed Mr Mulholland to make use of him for the purpose of Mr Molloy's exit from the house, I am willing to hear any thing in extenuation of his offence — but, if nothing can be brought forward, I have no doubt at all he should be sent away[2]

I am, My dear Mr Flanner &c J H N

TO EDMUND O'REILLY, S.J.

[18 December 1857]

Not sent[3]

My dear Fr O'Reilly

I write in some anxiety lest I should seem ungracious to the members of the Council, but I cannot adjust their message to me about the punishment of the two young men with the view I take of the draft of our Rules and Regulations.

I have delayed writing a post or two, from something of dread in having to write at all.

[1] These two names have been scored out, here and later, in Newman's draft.

[2] Flannery replied on 21 Dec. that Molloy had left that day and that Mullholland would go on the morrow. But see letters of 26 Dec. to them. Flannery concurred in the sentence on the two culprits, but extenuating circumstances were found for the boy at the door.

[3] On the short draft of this letter Newman wrote: 'Though not sent, I keep this, to illustrate the controversies which must arise when a Rector is absent from his subordinate officials. J H N June 21 1872'

There are five inferior punishments, in the hands of Vice Rector or Dean — one in the hands of the Council — one in the hands of the Senate. The Rector does not inflict punishment in person in any sense except by concurrence. Now the Council, not contemplating the Consilium abeundi as the punishment of the two young men, necessarily implies that it desires a lesser punishment — but the Rector has nothing to do with the lesser punishments — and if he took them in hand, they would ipso facto cease to be lesser. A reprimand from the Rector not only has no place in the Rules and Regulations, but could not be a lesser punishment if it had.

The Council then seems to force me to remit the matter to the Dean, who appealed to me. I fear I must do this from inability to do any thing else. Any how, the necessary delay which this correspondence involves is a most serious evil. All punishment I think should be prompt — but the Council seems advisably to think the contrary by wishing it to wait over in this case till I am [in] Dublin, that is, probably till March.

I am &c J H N.

TO W. H. SCOTT

The Oratory, Birmingham. Decr 18. 1857

My dear Scott,

I don't suppose any thing which the Faculty of Philosophy and Letters have done, will interfere with my giving leave to Frazer to have the indulgence he wants at the beginning of next term, which I will do, if the Dean (Penny) consents — your assent is already given, I consider.

By this post I hear that Oxenham is willing to come to Dublin — and is coming down here to have a conversation with me.

You then, if you choose it, are free to come here — and I hope you *will* choose it. It is near six weeks since I wrote to the Cardinal about the translation, and he has sent me no answer yet — [1] nor do I think we shall be doing much yet for some months — though of course you could always *find* something to do towards the translation.

I should like to know your opinion of the following plan: — that you should stop at Dublin till Easter — and then come here. Meanwhile that Oxenham should go to Dublin to see the lie of the land, to make acquaintance with the Professors etc and to be introduced by you to the men. The only plan for him I can devise is lodging at Short's at the corner, and taking meals with you. What a great thing it would be for some of the St Patrick's youths, if they were allowed to employ him — but this, I suppose, is out of the

---

[1] Letter of 7 Nov. to Wiseman.

question. (*Entre nous*, if you hear any thing about his ⟨Mr F.⟩ being Coadjutor Bishop, please, let me know.)[1]

Tell me if any thing suggests itself to you about Oxenham, or what you have to say about the whole plan.

Ever Yrs affly J H N

W H Scott Esqr

TO H. E. MANNING

The Oratory, Birmingham Decr 21. 1857

My dear Manning

I suppose you, as others, have your little troubles — I am so surrounded with them that they are my daily food — and one of them now concerns the answer I have to make, (having heard from Dublin) to your kind letter.

I am simply grounded for the moment. To speak in confidence, Scott promised to help us in the Translation of Scripture. He said he would come here for the purpose when I wished. I could not do so, till I got his place supplied at Dublin. When your letter came saying that Oxenham would help us in Dublin, I wrote to tell him so. Now he writes me word 'I have always the feeling that I am of use where I am, and every thing promises that I shall increase what influence I have. I should be disposed now I have become intimate with the men in the house, and know so much as I do of the University, to continue in the same line of work rather than change for an *uncertainty*.'

Now you see I am reduced to a state of discouragement and despondency, which is brought on me by external mishaps continually. I do not see how possibly I should be able able to manage the University at a distance — all sorts of changes will take place suddenly in men's minds without my knowing — and then misunderstandings will take place.

But to return to the case of Mr Oxenham — what can I do?

Ever Yrs affly John H Newman of the Oratory

The Very Revd Dr Manning

P.S. It would be absurd, I suppose, to attempt to engage Mr Oxenham in the translation of Scripture. We want some good scholars.[2]

[1] i.e. the appointment of Michael Flannery as Coadjutor Bishop of Killaloe. This was announced on 1 July 1858.
[2] Nothing came of this suggestion, nor did Oxenham go to Dublin.

TO ROBERT ORNSBY, I

The Oratory Birmingham ⌐Decr 21. 1857

My dear Professor

I beg to accept the decisions, to which you and your Colleagues have come, after the Examinations for the Exhibitions — and in consequence to beg you to be so good as to answer that Mr de le Pasture has gained the Scholar's Exhibition, and that the Student's Exhibition remains vacant.

I think that the Examiners, or you in their name, should seriously impress upon Mr de le Pasture the difficulties you have had in assigning him the Exhibition.¹

I trust I am right in saying that in deciding that Mr Macdermott could not present himself as a candidate, (which I did by return of post on the receipt of Dr Dunne's letter) I only confirmed the decision of your Faculty.¹

⌐I shall be sorry if he does not allow you to make the honorable mention of him which you propose.⌐

Thanking you all for your zealous and successful labours I am, My dear Professor, Sincerely Yours

John H Newman Rector

R Ornsby Esqr

TO ROBERT ORNSBY, II

The Oy Bm ⌐Decr 21. 1857⌐

My dear O

It has struck me whether a prize of books could not be given to Mr Macdermott which would reward his diligence and save our principle.

Surely I have merely *confirmed* the decision of the faculty. I meant to do so.

My dear O. ⌐I am in a sad state of despondency. On the spot I know what you all think, and I can form my judgment and act by the popular feeling — which is indispensable in the case of a person in my place. But here at a distance I am walking in the dark — and may any moment be doing a disservice or committing an offence, when I mean just the reverse.

I assure you I dread *most extremely* misunderstandings arising between the Professors etc and me — *from no one's fault* — but merely from the necessary collisions which take place when men are acting on each other 300 miles off.

I say to myself — How much better to resign now, while people like me — than to outlive my popularity, and leave unpleasant associations behind me. You can't think how this presses on me. Since I have left, two or three very

¹ Hugh McDermott held a burse in Science on the nomination of the Bishop of Achonry. See letter of 17 Dec. to Dunne.

dangerous things have taken place — which, as far as ever I can, I am keeping silence about — but they distress me *for the future*.[1]

To give an instance of what I mean — I don't know how my punishment of the two youths at St Patrick's House is taken — Mulholland [[one of them]] has written me a long letter — will you kindly give me some clue?[1]

Pray for me & believe me My dear Ornsby

Affectly Yours John H Newman

Do you, any of you, wish me to write a letter to the Register on the University?

TO WILLIAM MONSELL

The Oratory Birmingham Decr 22. 1857

My dear Monsell,

Miss Bowles has done her work — and writes to know when she shall get her money. I was surprised to find she was literally unable to pay for her lodgings — it was simple news to me that she was in distress — though I knew she had lost her patrimony.[2]

I answered that it was necessary that her work should pass revision and be published, before she was paid, and she wrote back acquiescing. However, if you thought you could conscientiously advance half the money, it would I know be a great kindness. Her brother here has lent her some pounds for the moment. It is, I know, on your part, a question of *justice*, since it is trust money.[3]

Dr Hayden of our Medical School sends me a letter which I transcribe. I gave him no hope, for I said you were out of office and of the country — however I send you word of his wish.

I trust Sir R. Kane *is* muzzled

Ever Yrs affly J H Newman

P.S. I am about to say some Masses for your Intention about Mrs Monsell.

(Copy)

'At a meeting of the Faculty of Medicine etc, it was proposed to endeavour to obtain for the Faculty the right of giving Lectures on Logic and Natural Philosophy as required by the Army Medical Board. With this view a

[1] See letters of 5 Jan. 1858 to Ornsby, and 5 Dec. 1857 to MacDermott.
[2] Emily Bowles appears to have lost her patrimony when trying to found a Holy Child convent in Liverpool.
[3] Miss Bowles had written a text book for use especially in Irish schools, and Monsell was to pay her from a trust fund given for the Irish poor. He arranged for £12. 10 to be sent to her.

resolution was proposed and passed unanimously. Should it meet your approval, we would take the liberty of asking you to induce Mr Monsell to obtain the necessary recognition from Dr Andrew Smith, who is absolute in the matter. Logic has been made *essential* for medical officers in the Army by Dr Smith, whilst there is at present only one school, out of the six in Dublin, where such a course is given, although all the Lectures given in those schools are recognised by the Army board. Since we have a competent man, there can be no reasonable objection.'[1]

P.S. I have no news to tell of the University. No Vice Rector yet.

WEDNESDAY 23 DECEMBER 1857 Crawley came to begin his Novitiate Mr Restell came for a retreat H. R. [Ryder] (Ignatius) came from Dublin

TO JAMES HOPE-SCOTT

The Oratory, Birmingham Decr 24. 1857

My dear Hope Scott,

ΓI think Lady Henry told me that you open your new Church today.[2] Any how, I have been saying Mass this morning for your intention concerning it. Also, I am glad to call to mind and commemorate by a letter the pleasant days I passed in the North this time five years. Five years has a melancholy sound to me now, for it is like a passing bell, knolling away time. I hope it is not wrong to say that the passage of time is now sad to me, as well as awful — because it brings before me how much I ought to have done, how much I have to do, and how little time I have to do it in. I used to think I should live long — but I don't know what to say to it now. However, at least these are unsuitable thoughts for Christmas Eve — but then I go back again, and begin to speculate how many more Christmas [sic] I shall see — for at any rate they must be within counting.

I was rejoiced to hear so good an account of your health — and of all your party. I suppose you are full of plans about your new property and your old — [3] Your sister tells me you have got into your new wing at Abbotsford — as to the far away region, of which I have not yet learned the name, I suppose you are building there either a fortress against evil times, or a new town and port for happy times. Have you yet found gold on your estate? for that seems the fashion.

---

[1] Monsell replied on 28 Dec. from France, 'I know Dr Smith who is a good Catholic but it might be better to speak to him than to write—' Andrew Smith (1797–1872) was Director General of the Army Ordnance Medical Department, 1853–8. He was a Scotsman and a convert.

[2] Lady Henry Kerr was Hope-Scott's sister. The church which he built at Galashiels was opened on 2 Feb. 1858.

[3] Hope-Scott, who was at Abbotsford, had in 1855 purchased an estate at Lochshiel, in Inverness-shire. Cf. letter of 10 Oct. 1856 to him.

I am thankful to say that we are prospering here with many trials — and at Dublin too. I can't get of the Bishops a Vice Rector yet, and really think I shall have, on many grounds, to resign. It is impossible (to say nothing else) that I can govern 300 miles off without continual little collisions. While I am on the spot, there is a continual action and re-action between all members of the University and myself, which has hindered any thing of the kind. We have hitherto been in most perfect harmony — So we are now — but I despair of its continuing if I am to act in the dark in another place. Then I say, how much better to part, while nothing but pleasant recollections will attend me, than to attempt to do what I cannot, and to die out dishonourably! As to the Archbishops,[1] they have never put any confidence in me down to this day — they never have asked my advice — it has always been a bargaining, and they getting all they can. I am very glad that they don't,[1] (it would put me on a great responsibility,) but ⌐what they ought to say, if they wish me to continue, is, 'Here, have your own way, and do just what you will.'[2]

I wonder whether Badeley is with you — what a strange thing life is! We see each other as through the peep holes of a show. When had I last a peep at him or you?

Give my best and kindest Christmas greetings to Mrs Hope Scott, the children, and your neighbours at the Burn[13]

and believe me, My dear Hope Scott, Ever Yours affectionately in Xt

John H Newman of the Oratory

Jas R Hope Scott Esqr

FRIDAY 25 DECEMBER 1857   Sang mass 5 A M no real midnight mass this year.
SATURDAY 26 DECEMBER   Ignatius went home.   Mr Restell went

TO JAMES LYNAM MOLLOY

Decr 26/57

My dear Mr Molloy[4]

I have no wish to be severe with you or with any one. It is much pleasanter to be indulgent. It gives a person in authority no trouble, and makes him

---

[1] When the autograph was lent to him after Hope-Scott's death in 1873, Newman wrote in pencil at this point, 'This is hard on the Archbishops. J H N'

[2] Hope-Scott replied on 30 Dec., 'What you tell me of the Dublin University is much what I was prepared for, and I would by no means have you yield to men who will not appreciate the sacrifices you make while at the same time they dare not dispense with you —Let me know what further happens—The Vice Rector must be granted or I fear you must resign.'
For the rest of this letter see that of 1 Jan. 1858 to Hope-Scott.

[3] The Henry Kerrs lived at Huntlyburn.

[4] Newman scored out the name in his draft of this letter and of the one that follows. Mrs Molloy, who lived in London, was in great distress at the sentence hanging over her son, and sent Newman a telegram imploring that he might be allowed to remain at the University.

popular. But you must recollect I have an account to give to my own conscience. I have ever regarded the care of young men, in whatever degree it comes upon one, as a heavy charge. At the most anxious season of life, when *their* course for time and eternity may perhaps be fixed, they come under the superintendence of the Authorities of a University. In time to come, they themselves, on whose conduct I had had to pronounce, and their companions too who had been witnesses of it might unite in thanking my memory for what at the time seemed severity, and [not?] in dishonoring it for an unwise unfaithful indulgence.

One of the penalties which usually correct the offender, and which is shared with him by his judge is the suffering which he inflicts on his relatives — I am deeply pained at your mother's distress — but we must do what is our duty, and leave every thing else to a higher power.

The punishment I put on you with Mulholland was not hastily decided on; nor can I say that I at present see grounds for changing it. At all events it cannot be changed hastily. I am willing to receive any consideration you can urge in your favor. I am very glad to hear you say that 'it is the first time in your course that you ever committed a breach of discipline.' I will grant any suspension of the sentence during the Vacation, which Mr Flannery who is on the spot, feels to be consistent with his own sense of duty. So far I will go now, as I understand you to wish to remain just now at St Patrick's (though I was told you had left Dublin)

I am &c J H N

J L Molloy Esqr

TO JOHN MULHOLLAND

Decr 26/57

My dear Mr Mulholland

I have not been unmindful of your letter, though I have not answered it. Were it possible, I should like to hear from you any extenuating circumstances in your case. What you urge that your offence was known mainly through your own avowal I had inquired about some time before I determined on the punishment — but I could learn nothing which was exactly to the point. You mention your diligence during the term. I am open to any representation which the Professors may make about you.

I assure you I have no wish to be severe — but, as I decided on your punishment on definite grounds and with deliberation, so if [I] change it, I must be able to say to myself why I do so. I have a great responsibility in having a number of young men under my charge. I shall have to answer for that charge. I must not act from mere desire to please them, but in order to please Him who at present has placed them under me.

Alas, it is commonly the case that parents have to bear their children's offences; yet I cannot give you any assurance that your punishment shall be changed. All I can say is that I am ready to receive any thing you have to say. It must be considered too that though I may have removed you for a while from St Patrick's, I am not the only person to be consulted in exchanging that removal for another punishment. You must get Mr Flannery to be a party to the exchange

I am &c J H N

John Mullholland Esqr

SUNDAY 27 DECEMBER 1857 sang high Mass
MONDAY 28 DECEMBER Mr Oxenham came

TO WILLIAM KIRBY SULLIVAN

The Oratory Birmingham Decr 28. 1857

My dear Mr Sullivan

I like the appearance of the Number[1] exceedingly, and think it must do us great credit. I understand you to say that the *Postage* of the Register to foreign bodies and editors will be about £5 or £6 a *number*. If so, I think it quite worth while, or rather very desirable, to send it to them. I have nothing to say as to your ample list which must bring our work to the knowledge of all the scientific circles on the continent and in North America. At home I should add the Ashmolean Society, Oxford, and the Westminster Review. In France I should be disposed to add Montalembert's 'Correspondant.'

How about advertising in the newspapers?

Then, for the first number *only*, I think with you that it should be sent to the Bishops of Ireland, and the Professors, chief Public Libraries and Newspapers. I dare say there are some private friends to whom you, as Editor, as well as myself, might like to send it. Besides these I think it would be well to send it to some friends of the University, who are among the associated members. I should say

Cardinal Wiseman,	Professor Fredet Baltimore
Archbishop Hughes New York	Duke of Norfolk
Archbishop Walsh Halifax	Sir John Acton
President of Maynooth	Robert Berkeley Esqr
President of Carlow	M. Errington Esqr
President of St Edmund's Ware Herts	D. Griffin Esqr Limerick
President of Ushaw Durham	J. Hope Scott Esqr

[1] The first number of the *Atlantis*.

216

President of Oscott Birmingham	Thomas Meagher Esqr
Very Revd Abbé Cruice, Paris.	Rt Honble W. Monsell
L'Abbe Maret Vicaire General Paris	Earl of Dunraven
Le Pere Daniel S.J. Paris	Robert Monteith Esqr
Fr Ventura Paris	C.R. Scott Murray Esqr
Mgr de Ram Louvain	Rt Honble More O'Ferrall
Professor Döllinger Munich	James O'Ferrall Esqr
Professor Windeschmann Munich	W.G. Ward Esq
Fr Provincial of the Jesuits Ireland	R. Wegg Professor Esqr

and any others who strike you[1]

Yours sincerely John H Newman

P.S.   The best wishes of this sacred season to you.

WEDNESDAY 30 DECEMBER 1857   a cold — did not say Mass
THURSDAY 31 DECEMBER   Mr Oxenham went

TO ROBERT ORNSBY

The Oratory, Birmingham ⌐Decr 31. 1857⌐

My dear Ornsby

The best wishes of the season to you and yours. I am ashamed to say I forget whether I answered your letter of the 23rd or not. What I feel is that it is better to give Mr Macdermott a prize, as Mr Kelly will have a mathematical prize.[2]

⌐I detected you in Z. and thought the letter a good one.[3] I was glad you promised others. I shall wait myself a little before writing, *if* I write. It is a great thing to hear from Dr Cullen that the University does not want money, not that I am surprised at it. For, if only it goes on, such a set of professors *must* make their way. I think the Atlantis will do us good.

As to myself, recollect I have ever acted, not by formal authority and rule, but by influence, and this power cannot be well exerted when absent. Thank you for all you say — but I am clear that, though I could go on, with a resident Vice Rector in whom I confided, *I cannot go on without one.* And not many weeks will elapse before I shall tell the Archbishops so. I have no wish to separate myself more than I can help from a set of men who have given me such reason to be grateful to them; and, even if I gave up the Rectorship, I should hope still to be connected with them in one way or another — but I

---

[1] Sullivan replied on 5 Jan. that he had sent copies of the *Atlantis* to all those on Newman's list 'and to several other Oxford men such as Baden Powell, Johnson etc.'
[2] Cf. letters of 21 Dec. to Ornsby.
[3] See first note to letter of 12 Dec. to Ornsby, and letter of 12 Jan. 1858 to him.

am rapidly coming to the resolution that I will not go on unless the Arch-bishops treat me better. I very much doubt if three out of the four wish me to go on.[11]

Ever Yours affly John H Newman of the Oratory

P.S. What news of your Greek Testament[2]

TO JAMES HOPE-SCOTT

⌐January 1. 1858[3]

⌐Personal

A happy New Year to you and yours. I write to say, that, if you let me know when your [Church] is opened, I will say Mass for your intention. . .

I write to thank you for your good advice.[4] The truth is, I had done so little, that, when I look back, I can't think *what* I have been doing all my life; and all I have done is unfinished, and at sixes and sevens (whatever that means), and I think of the famous words, as sad as they are real, Heu vitam perdidi, operosè nihil agendo.[5]

I am glad to say that money is not wanting for the University — at least Dr Cullen says it is not. This is an enormous point, for I have doubted whether the annual contribution would stand the trial of apparent failure or little-doing for the first many years. But if contributors are but patient, the Professors are of that *calibre*, that they *must* make their way in public opinion. I told the printer to send you the first Number of the Atlantis, which I trust will act as considerable advertisement and puff. This state of things makes me feel comparatively easy at retiring — provided they don't quarrel, or make great changes, when I am no longer Rector.

What I have said does not diminish my anxiety to have an *English sub-scription organized*. It would be a surprising help to our prospects, if England gave the University £1000 a year, which it could withdraw at any time.

---

[1] [[N B. I suppose the one I thought certainly wished me to go on, was Dr Dixon of Armagh.)]]

[2] Ornsby's edition of the Greek New Testament was published in Dublin in 1860.

[3] Newman wrote at the top of the copy he made of this letter, [[(Henceforth all the letters were from written from [sic] the Oratory, except two or three, which are noted.)]]

[4] Replying on 30 Dec. to Newman's letter of Christmas Eve, Hope-Scott wrote: 'I do not like your croaking. You have done more in your time than most men, and have never been idle. As to the way in which you have done it I shall say nothing. You may think you might have done it better. I remember that you once told me that "there was nothing we might not have done better—" and this was to comfort me—and it did—for it brought each particular failure under a general law of infirmity, and so quieted while it humbled me. And then as to the future—what is appointed for you to do you will have time for—what is not you need have no concern about. There! I have written a sermon. Very impudent I know it is—but when the mind gets out of joint a child may sometimes restore it by telling us some simple thing which we perhaps have taught it. Pat your child then on the head and bid him go to play, while you brace yourself up and work on, not as if you must do some particular work *before* you die, but as if you must do your best *till* you die"

[5] Words of Hugo Grotius on his deathbed.

Think how much more I could have done as Rector, backed up by so large a sum.[1]

TO THE EDITOR OF THE WEEKLY REGISTER

[January 2. 1858][1]

Sir,

It is remarkable with what apathy my letter about the Irish University has been received by your readers. It has excited very little interest. This is what I expected. English Catholics do not care about the University. In one quarter, indeed, it has excited some indignation. I say in one quarter; for three at least out of four letters which you have inserted against me have a family likeness, and smack of Mountjoy Square and Stephen's Green. They all deal with theories, not facts, as far as they deal with anything. I asked, what was the University to us? and in reply, 'Z'. reminds me of the *ancient* idea of a University, 'Anglo-Hibernus' charges me with the *anti-Irish monomania*, my namesake confesses he writes more in the way of question than answer, and 'J.S.' fairly gives the matter up and calls me egotistical.[2]

Now I beg to ask a second time, Is the University an English Institution? If it is, I want to know —

1. Why is it not placed in England.

2. Why none of our Bishops have any share in its management.

3. Why no Diocese dreams of contributing to its support. As to our subscriptions at its commencement, that makes it English as much and as little as our subscription to the Irish famine makes the famine English.

4. Why English Schools and Colleges do not recognize it, or barely so. A few English youths, I believe, have gone to it from Ushaw; but from Stonyhurst, the Catholic Eton, not one. Such is its connection with England! I pause for a reply.

Q. in the Corner.

MONDAY 4 JANUARY 1858   called at Oscott with Robert.   Marshall came

TO ROBERT ORNSBY

The Oy Bm ⌐Jan 5. 1858⌐

My dear Ornsby

Thank you for your kind letter — but ⌐you have not got hold of the *ground* on which I am resolved to bring matters to an issue — and it is so important

[1] This letter appeared in the *Weekly Register*, 2 Jan. 1858.
[2] The letters of 'Z' (Ornsby), 'Anglo-Hibernus,' and 'Another Q in the corner' were published in the *Weekly Register* on 19 Dec., and that of 'J.S.' on 26 Dec.

that that ground should be understood, that I will occupy your time with some words more.[1]

It is not because the Archbishops show me so little confidence. This circumstance is abundantly overbalanced by the confidence shown me by every one else. The Archbishops I seldom see — the Professors daily. I had rather show gratitude to the Professors by remaining, than mark my want of gratitude to the Archbishops by resigning.

This upon the ground of feeling, mere personal feeling. But you must let me ascend to higher considerations.[1] First, my health. I am not at all satisfied with the state of my heart. Last August, a medical man, without my having a suspicion beforehand on the subject, drew my attention to it. It is of the utmost importance to my Oratory that I should live long — even though I could do little or nothing. It is not a case, as regards our Community, in which the saying 'Consummatus in brevi, explevit tempora multa,'[2] can, humanly speaking, be fulfilled. Now *repose* is the one thing necessary for persons who have a tendency to the complaint in question. Recollect I am wedded, in a full sense of the word, to my Congregation. No other duty can come in competition with it. If I attend to other things, they must be but secondary. If my Congregation needs me, I go back to it — and much more, if, as in this case perhaps, by keeping away longer I diminish the time I shall be with it, when I return at length.

But again, ⌐what happened the other day immediately I left and tried to act at a distance, showed how the attempt for me to be Rector *here* of the University *there*, would break down. Depend upon it, we should not pull together, under such a trial. I have spoken to you on the subject before. I must have a Vice Rector, and a Vice Rector whom I can trust. Fr O'Reilly most kindly consents to preside at a meeting of the Senate. All of the Professors wish to show me every attention and kindness — Yet (as far as I can comprehend it) what an utter failure and mistake that meeting has been! how it has stultified itself! If you say that I have not got hold rightly of what was done, I answer 'Well then, that is what I shall *always* be doing. I shall *always* be misunderstanding things, if I am away.' But so it is, what I have heard and taken in of that meeting has filled me with distress and mortification. A resolution was passed — who proposed, and who seconded it? The rule lays down that nothing shall be done in the University 'without the Rector's concurrence', '*nor is any University act formal, except by virtue of his direct participation.*' Where was my participation in that Resolution? *I* proposed one by Dr O'Reilly — it was perfectly legitimate to reject it. I have no

---

[1] Replying to Newman's letter of 31 Dec., Ornsby wrote on 3 Jan. his sorrow that Newman's view of the Rectorship was unchanged, 'It is certainly most natural you should be wounded deeply by the want of confidence and generosity which has been shown, and you may feel that your own dignity requires you to decline from a position where proper respect has not been shown it. The patience you have already shown may be called heroic. . . .' Ornsby thought that Newman could manage without a Vice-Rector.

[2] *Wisdom*, 4:13.

faults at all to find in *that*. I had myself on a former occasion *withdrawn* a proposition, to which in the Senate there was merely an *objection* — much more should I have acquiesced in the rejection of the Resolution on this occasion. But, as if you were resolved into a Committee, you conferred together and passed a new Resolution on the spur of the moment, no previous notice given of it, and no participation on the part of the Rector.[1]

Then I said to myself, 'How plain it is that without a plenipotentiary Vice-Rector, who perfectly understands me, and the state of things, and in whom I confide, it is impossible to go on!' I *can't* govern at a distance — but I *can* commit my power *absolutely* to another, if I CAN TRUST HIM.[2] A man may be an able man, an experienced man, a holy man, yet unfitted to carry on the University — and much more may he be all this, and unable to carry it *on upon another's plan and with the confidence of another*. This proceeding brought home to me clearly *by an example*; and by an example *at first go*, what I already, as a matter of conception; I [sic] felt to be true, that I could not be a non-resident Rector, without a Vice Rector, and one in whom I can *confide*

Now I say *what chance* is there, of this condition being fulfilled? Have the Archbishops, *three* of them at least, one quarter of that confidence in me which would enable them to feel it right to let it be a condition of a Vice Rector that he should have my confidence?[3]

If it were a Vice Rector who [[actually]] had *not* my confidence, the imbroglio would be greater. In addition to all the difficulties of my non-residence, and the continual misunderstandings which would take place, there would be a blundering Vice Rector, putting his foot into it, and making mischief, at every step he took.

Alas, how many have lived too long for their fame! and how much better is it that I should close my Rectorship now with the good will and kind recollections of all, than that I should hazard associations of a less pleasant character!

Try to find some other way in which my name may be connected with the University. The Atlantis suggests one — but don't attempt what is impossible.

I am glad you like the Atlantis. Literary articles, as you say, are wanted — but the hitch is this, there is no pay. In the case of science, it answers for a writer merely to make his name known, if he gains nothing else.[1]

I am concerned at what you say about the certainty of the necessity of you changing your house — but it does not do to get into debt, most surely.

---

[1] Newman's resolution that the Rectorial Council should constitute a committee entrusted with certain functions by the Senate of the University was put aside at a meeting on 13 Dec., and instead an ad hoc committee of eleven was chosen, as Newman describes, to act during the year 1858.

[2] [[November 1872. Is not all this an *unintentional* cut at poor Fr O'Reilly, who doubtless thought himself and was thought a plenipotentiary Vice Rector, in whom I could trust?]]

[3] [[It is plain from what took place in 1852 etc that Dr Cullen's idea of a Vice Rector from the first was, not as an official who would represent me but one who would represent the Archbishop against me, as a regulator of my movements.]] See letter of 13 Oct. 1852 to Cullen, and *A. W.*, pp. 293-5.

It may be a good thing translating Seneca for Bohn. Your difficulties don't seem to me insurmountable.[1] A happy new year & believe me

Ever Yours affly John H Newman of the Oratory

R. Ornsby Esqr

P.S. ⌐You may show this letter in confidence to any one you please.¬

TO THOMAS SCRATTON

The Oratory Birmingham Jan 5. 1858

My dear Scratton,

I return the cheque signed. Please, don't forget to remind me to charge the £108. 11. 4 separate from the University money, when I write to the Bishops. The question is not whether Mr Flannery is to be paid, but who is to pay him. I told Dr Leahy in October that I wished it not to come out of the Rector's quarterly charge.

But I suspect I shall not have to pay any monies long — for I am resolved not to go on acting as Rector without a Vice Rector, and one I can trust.

Thank you for what you are doing about Molloy. Still, I should be obliged by your sounding the Medical people, for Mulholland has to be provided for too[2]

Ever Yrs Affly J H N

Thos Scratton Esqr

WEDNESDAY 6 JANUARY 1858   J. B. Morris came   Marshall went

TO WILLIAM KIRBY SULLIVAN

The Oratory, Birmingham Jan 6. 1858

My dear Mr Sullivan

The best wishes of this sacred season to you and yours — will you convey them from me to Mr Hennessy when you see him, and tell him that Mr Johnson sends me word that — I can't find Mr J's letter, I think it is that he has not yet given his signature to some paper of Mr Hennessy's.[3]

---

[1] Ornsby wrote that these difficulties were, 'the impossibility of translating a passage or two, on the score of purity. But these perhaps I might omit or paraphrase. The second is that many parts of Seneca would read just like Carlyle, and I hesitated whether translating an ancient author could be objected to on this head.'

[2] Scratton had suggested to Molloy that he should 'write a very humble letter to his Dean praying him to consent to receive him back.' Mulholland was the holder of a medical burse.

[3] Manuel Johnson was giving some help to Hennessy in his astronomical work.

My not having spoken about Advertising shows how I forget — [1] I fully intended to have asked you or Fowler the question, and thought I had done so. I will write to Longman. Advertisements in the Irish Papers, and the Times, would be very desirable. I am no judge whether more than this is necessary. Saunders' Newsletter may be one of them, if no one else has a difficulty. I think Longman simply left the matter of sending to and exchanging with Societies etc to us.

In all these matters I wish you, if you please, absolutely to decide. I feel it would be quite worth while, if we had to give away the whole impression. It is no use doing the thing at all unless we do it in the best way.

My great anxiety, however, certainly is about money. I have taken £100 for the first Number from the University Funds. I don't know where the money for Number 2 is to come from. This itself is a strong reason for only bringing it out twice a year at present. I have had far more control of the *details* of the University funds hitherto than I like; and shall not have it in future. Moreover, it is in the highest degree improbable, that I shall continue Rector. I cannot do so unless I have a Vice Rector to whom I can commit every thing — which will not, it seems, be. I owe great gratitude to Fr O'Reilly, who so kindly went out of his way to preside at the last Senate. But things were done, which seem to me distinctly unconstitutional, if not illegal; and the whole affair brought down upon me with the strength of conviction, what I already held on antecedent grounds, that I could not *here* preside over the University *there* — and that I could but be a nominal head; and that I had no right, even if other people wished it, to be that, unless there was a Vice Rector who could simply take all matters off my hands.

I inclose a list of persons to whom the work may be sent in Rome. Others may strike you.[2]

Most sincerely Yours John H Newman

THURSDAY 7 JANUARY 1858 Morris went.

FRIDAY 8 JANUARY Nicholas went to Sir John Acton's Frederic fell ill

TO T. W. ALLIES

The Oratory Birmingham Jan. 8 1858

My dear Allies,

· We shall be very glad to see you and Ward on Saturday and Sunday week.[3]

---

[1] Sullivan wrote on 5 Jan., 'I waited to see whether any numbers of the Atlantis would appear in the booksellers shops, and not having seen one I think it would be desirable to advertise. . . .'

[2] Fr Fitzgerald, a Dominican friend of Sullivan, was taking copies of the *Atlantis* to Rome.

[3] Allies and F. R. Ward wished to discuss the proposed Oratory School. Allies wrote on 7 Jan., 'To put the matter without mincing words, there is not I suppose a

I don't know whether it is worth while to say any thing before we meet but I suppose you understand that I for my part should feel an extreme difficulty in acting against Oscott, nor do I think we need, and I should be ready to face the difficulty, with a determination of over coming it, but not otherwise than by carrying our Bishop and the Oscott people along with us. The obvious mode of doing so is making the terms of the projected school so much higher than those of Oscott that the two interests could not come into competition, that is, as regards the younger boys, for I suppose they are high enough at Oscott for the older. But I must not begin a subject which I should not be able to get through. And I am talking of what I do not know.

The best and kindest wishes of the sacred season now departing to you, Mrs Allies, and all yours. I have heard nothing at all of Basil for an age and have been long contemplating to get some of my *opuscula* bound uniformly for him. He might be interested in some of them now, but unluckily they are not all of a size[1]

Ever yours affly John H Newman of the Oratory

TO WILLIAM KIRBY SULLIVAN

Oy Bm Jany 8/58

My dear Mr Sullivan

Since Longmans give us the choice, would it not be better to do all the work I have asked about ourselves? It would be the beginning of making Dublin *the* (or at least *a*) centre of publication. Would it be possible, I suppose not, to make Fowler's shop a place of sale? I suppose Longmans would agree to it, if asked; but this is premature.

But decide just as you think best — for you will see the expedience of things better than I can.

There is one reason for employing Longmans in the advertising, viz I suspect that (e.g.) the Guardian would not take any advertisement of a book in which I was a writer, unless it came from publishers like Longmans. [2]

Very sincerely Yours John H Newman of the Oratory

W K Sullivan Esqr

convert of Oxford or Cambridge who is not forced into a feeling made up of despair and disgust at the condition of scientific teaching among us, compared with that existing in the best Protestant schools. Now Frank Ward urges me to write to you and proposes . . . that we should come down to you . . . We know well enough the number and the weight of those who will be ready to thwart such a design, but if this school be the greatest want we have, ought it not to be attempted?'
 Cf. letter of 28 Oct. 1857 to Bellasis.
 [1] Henry Basil Allies (1844–97), was the second surviving son of T. W. Allies.
 [2] See letter of 27 Jan. 1850 to Mrs Bowden. Vol. XIII, p. 396.

SATURDAY 9 JANUARY 1858   Fr Fitzgerald called in his way to Rome.

TO JAMES LYNAM MOLLOY

The Oratory, Birmingham January 9. 1858

My dear Mr Molloy

I write at once in answer to your letter, not to keep you in suspense.[1] I could not separate your case from Mr Mulholland's; if I commuted the punishment of one of you, I must of both. I have been waiting for letters from Dublin on the subject, and am still. You may be sure I do not wish to delay my decision

Very truly Yours John H Newman

James Molloy Esqr

TO ROBERT ORNSBY

The Oratory, Birmingham ⌐January 9. 1858⌐

My dear Ornsby

I write a line at once to thank you with all my heart for your most affectionate letter, which I have as yet only had time to look through, but which I shall read at leisure.[2]

⌐I cannot deny that, since I have returned from Dublin, I have been alarmed about myself. I have a hard beating of the heart continually, and my breath is certainly shorter than it was. It is not pain at all as yet — but I know that, if it really be a heart affection, it is incurable and must increase. My medical friend last August bade me avoid walking, and above all ascents. I have been inquiring who are the highest authorities on the subject in London.[3] That it is connected with indigestion, I know — but my anxiety is, lest it should not be caused, but only increased by indigestion. From midnight to 3 A M is my worst time — but at present it is no pain.⌐[4]

R. Ornsby Esqr

¹ Molloy wrote on 8 Jan. that Flannery, the Dean of St Patrick's House, had agreed to receive him back, provided Newman consented. See letter of 11 Jan. to Flannery.

² Ornsby wrote on 8 Jan. accepting Newman's argument that he could only continue in office, if he had a Vice Rector who would co-operate with him. 'I fear therefore the only chance we have of keeping you is the appointment of Mr Butler . . . though the appointment of a layman is not an impossibility, or even violently improbable, still it seems unlikely. . . . I assure you it has gone to my heart to urge you as I have done . . . Your unsparing exertions —in the whole idea and scheme and each point of it, worked out step by step, with nothing to blame yourself for—statutes—lectures—essays—sermons—the church and all its cost and troubles, with the provoking treatment you have sustained, and all this merely the visible points of a whole world of business and vexation; I can only wonder you have not broken down under it long before.'

Ornsby spoke also of his own loss, 'now for three years or more, I have had the continual advantage of your friendship and counsel, besides the great trust of working with you in one of the most important vocations of your life.' See also letters of 12 and 23 Jan. to Ornsby.

³ Ornsby had urged this.

⁴ Conclusion and signature have been cut out.

MONDAY 11 JANUARY 1858   Laurence went for good (*the last of the Brothers*).   Stan. [Stanislas] and Henry went to Rednall

TO T. W. ALLIES

The Oratory Birmingham Jan. 11 1858

My dear Allies,

I don't like to lose your and [F. R.] Ward's visit, but I must in honesty say that I find I am in a few days coming to London, so that I could save you and him the trouble of coming here, if you wished it. I would take a day convenient to yourselves.

Ever yours affecly John H Newman

TO EDWARD BUTLER

[[Telegram]]¹ ⌐Newman,⌐ Edgbaston ⌐to Butler⌐
86 Stephen's Green ⌐Jany 11. 1858

If it turns out as you say,² I go, but I cannot now wish as you wish³ but if you succeed,⁴ I will work it when it is done.⌐⁵

TO ANDREW ELLIS

The Oratory, Birmingham Jany 11. 1858

Private

My dear Dr Ellis,

Will you let me ask you in confidence, what is to be thought of Dr Lyons's prolonged absence. What I have said, is, that 'I will confirm whatever the

---

¹ Butler wrote to Newman on 9 Jan. that the Bishops were to meet on 11 Jan. to appoint a Vice-Rector for the University. Forde had withdrawn 'in consequence, he says, of hearing he would not be acceptable to the Professors,' and it was very probable that Flannery would be appointed.

'We have had much conversation today upon the subject, and I have stated to the Professors present, Ornsby, Stewart, Renouf, Dunne, Arnold, Robertson, how I stand in the matter, and that beyond your good wishes and favorable opinion, and the presumed support of most of the Professors, there is little in my favour, and hardly any chance whatever of our difficulty on this head being solved by my appointment.

So they are of opinion, if you do not object, that I should see Dr Quinn, and explain . . . that they would much rather have him for Vice Rector than others who have been mentioned. . . .

If you have no objection to our urging Dr Quinn to apply for the office, please send me a telegram to that effect. . . .'

² [[i.e. if Mr Flannery is appointed.]]
³ [[i.e. for Dr Quinn's appointment]]
⁴ [[in getting Dr Quinn]]
⁵ Quinn agreed to stand, but the Bishops made no appointment. In April the Professors approached the Archbishops, but with Anderdon as their candidate.

Faculty wishes.' It is just possible that the Faculty may really wish *me* to do this — or that, but not like the responsibility of saying so[1]

Yours most sincerely John H Newman

A Ellis Esqr

TO MICHAEL FLANNERY

Jan 11/58

My dear Mr Flannery

I understand from Professor Butler that you do not object to my commuting the punishment of the two young men to the following — viz that they should reside this term, but be indoors between this time and Easter every afternoon after four O clock, not asking any leave for parties etc etc. If so, I am willing so to commute it, if they will accept it *in writing*. This will be done most easily, their merely *replying by post* to the letters you send to them with the above message from me.[2]

I am &c J H N

TUESDAY 12 JANUARY 1858   went over to Rednall with Ambrose and back

TO ROBERT ORNSBY

The Oratory, Bm ⌐Jany 12. 1858¬

My dear Ornsby

Your most kind and touching letter of the 8th, to which I wrote a few words in reply from grateful feeling on Sunday, cannot be answered at once in detail, things being so unsettled just now, the Archbishops' movements and my own health. I am going up, I suppose in a day or two, to London — and then hope to see my way more clearly about myself. It is curious that a secondary reason of my going is connected with an idea which you throw out at the end of your letter.[3] I shall by going anticipate two friends coming here

---

[1] Cf letter of 7 Dec. 1857 to Ellis, who replied, on 12 Jan., that there had been no official meeting of the Medical Faculty. The absence of Dr Lyons led the enemies of the Medical School to speak disparagingly of it, but no good purpose would be served if serious notice were taken of his absence.

[2] Flannery wrote that he would carry out this decision, and thus the episode of Molloy and Mulholland ended.

[3] In the postscript to his letter of 8 Jan. Ornsby suggested ways of keeping Newman in touch with the University, when he ceased to be Rector '. . . you might possibly do something for us in England. Is it within the scope of the Oratory to be a teaching order? And might you found a house in Birmingham in connexion with the University?

An Oratory here is, I imagine, wished for by many, and I hear is prayed for in the University Church.'

from London — who, to *speak in strict confidence*, were coming to talk to me on the subject of the commencement of what is to be, if it prospers, a large Catholic public school. I am obliged to speak of it confidentially, not only because it is their matter not mine, but also because any premature notice of it would alarm the existing English Colleges, whose authorities they would wish to reconcile to it, if possible.

⌜Wilberforce wishes me to write a series of leading articles on the University in the Register, making no secret of their authorship. I am not against it — but first, I wish the controversy worked out a little more — and certainly do desiderate energy and fulness in the defence of the University in the Register's correspondence. Those writers, who have answered Q, have abused him rather than refuted him. Neither side (Q excepted) quite likes to bring out the truth. I wish you had time to continue your letters, as you proposed. I don't think it fair that (an Editor ⟨a writer of leading articles⟩) should have to take a side in the dispute, instead of arbitrating between disputants — and this he will be obliged to do, unless Q is at least probably answered. I think Q useful — I am glad his letters have been inserted — but I want them vigorously answered. Next — I could not write any Articles without having them first read over carefully by my friends in Dublin — ⌝ which will be a matter of delay. Tell me what you think on all these points.[1]

Ever Yours affly John H Newman of the Oratory

R Ornsby Esqr.

TO HENRY WILBERFORCE

The Oratory, Birmingham ⌜Jany 12. 1858⌝

My dear H W

⌜I quite agree with you that Q's letters are useful — We want routing up. I am sure that *many* agree with Q who do not like to say it. And we are at a great disadvantage, abused in Ireland for being English, and neglected in England for being Irish. I don't go to Q's motives which no one can judge of but that individual himself. I dare say he is not what he seems — but, if I judged of him externally, I should say that he was some disappointed and soured candidate for a Professorship. You speak in your letter of this morning, as if you knew the Author — I thought you told me that you did not; but

[1] Ornsby, who did not know the identity of 'Q in the Corner' replied on 13 Jan., 'I should be glad to shelve "Q in the corner" if possible. He is evidently a very *malicious* writer and would not deal fairly with the controversy. For instance, he simply ignored all I had said, except one, and that not my strongest point. [see letter of 2 Jan.] I think a series of articles from you would be of excellent service, only it would be well they should be clear of the present dispute. I mean that you should not write as if you were yourself taking part in the controversy.' See Appendix I, p. 565.

perhaps you have guessed him — An Editor knows many things behind the scenes, and has the means of making a good guess.[11]

But at present I don't think he has been sufficiently answered. Ornsby promised to do so — but has been very busy — and now all our friends unluckily are absorbed in the meeting of the Archbishops these very days for the appointment of a Vice Rector — which is likely to end in a rumpus. However I should like Q answered pointedly and effectively, before any leading articles (from me)[2] appeared.

I am not at all unwilling that this authorship should be known — but in that case the proof must be seen by some of our Dublin friends. I will try to sketch the subjects of the articles — Of course each would stand by itself — I mean it would not promise another to come, and would be a whole, if it was the only one read.

It is with great reluctance I tell you, and I am so afraid of your being *distressed*, and letting it out indirectly from anxiety, but it is I who want to take advice — and most likely shall come to Town some morning for the purpose.

Ever Yrs affly, J H N

H W Wilberforce Esqr

WEDNESDAY 13 JANUARY 1858   Patrick Dignam came?

TO ROBERT ORNSBY

The Oratory, Birmingham ⌜Jany 14. 1858⌝

My dear Ornsby

It grieves me very much to hear what you say of your own health — and I heartily wish you could at once change your air, and shake off all anxieties.[3] I wonder whether Sir H. Marsh is the best authority — I distrust Court physicians, because they are at the top of the tree and don't take pains. When I say, have your chest examined, it is not to frighten you — but my great maxim is 'Principiis obsta' — I am sure I have saved myself bad illnesses by observing it — and on the contrary I have entailed considerable suffering on myself by not knowing or finding out what ailed me. Just now, I am exemplifying my own rule in thinking about my heart, which is not troublesome to

---

[1] [[N.B All this is fun—for H W W and I knew the author, ('Q in the corner') of the short letters in the Register, tho' the secret was confined to ourselves. They formed the introduction to four leaders by me in the Paper in behalf of the Catholic University.]]

[2] These two words were added, above the line, probably when Newman copied the first paragraph in 1876.

[3] Ornsby wrote on 13 Jan., 'I have never been well since the influenza in the Autumn, and Sir Henry Marsh . . . told me he saw in me a great change for the worse . . .' Sir Henry Marsh (1790–1860) who had a large private practice in Dublin, was made physician in ordinary to the Queen in Ireland, in 1837.

me in any way, and which many a man would take no thought of in my case. And it is the way I treat my Fathers.

⌐How strange you do not seem to recollect that the notion of taking Dr Q's [[Quin's]] school and working it as a feeder of the University was the plan which I suggested, in preference to others, last November and since — and that it is *the only* way which I see, as I told Butler last week, of coming to an understanding with Dr Q. (and thought Stewart ought to work it)⌐1

I have been much interested in your account of your negotiation with him ⟨Dr Q.⟩ — and thank you for it — and be sure, I don't think you are doing too much.[2]

⌐Wilberforce wishes me to write leading articles, *its being known* they are mine.⌐ I don't object to this, but ⌐I would rather it got out as the articles went on — for several reasons. One special one is that I fear you all would think me cold towards the University in the *first* — i.e. I should think it right in leading articles not to play the partizan; and I consider that an argument tells more which begins with great admissions etc etc. I shall send you one or two specimens.⌐

Ever Yrs affly J H N

FRIDAY 15 JANUARY 1858   Frederic went to Mr Eyston's?

TO HENRY WILBERFORCE

⌐Jany 15/58⌐

My dear H

⌐I send you two Articles with which I am very little satisfied. It is very difficult to write easily and forcibly, when you are pulled up. 1st with the thought of what objections can be made to the *matter*. 2nd What objections can be made to the *person saying it*.⌐3

I have no objection to my name *getting out*. Whether I should like it known at first starting, is a further question.

---

[1] See letter of 19 Nov. to Butler. Ornsby on 13 Jan. suggested that Stewart might take over Quinn's school, to prepare students for the University.

[2] Ornsby on 12 Jan. described the interview he and Butler had with Quinn, after the receipt of Newman's telegram of 11 Jan., 'What Dr Quinn said before and after the business of the interview opened amounted to this: that he had resolved from the first to act on your views, whether he deemed them right or wrong . . . from a conversation he had had with you, a long time [ago], he believed that were the office offered to him you would not object. Business difficulties had indeed since arisen between you. All we said as to your views with regard to his candidature was, that we had *no reason to believe* you would object or decline to work with him. The meeting ended in his agreeing to go to the Archbishop. . . .'

[3] [[the *writer*.]]

If you think them worthy to be put into type, and send them me, I will despatch them to Dublin and you shall have them back by return of post[1]

Ever Yrs affly J H N

TO THOMAS W. B. WOOD

Jany 15/58

Dear Sir,

I have just received your letter and write at once to Dublin to request the Secretary of the University to forward to you your parcel according to your wish. As I have not been in Dublin since I wrote to you from this place to inform you of its arrival there, and as you did not allow the Secretary to open it, but wished it to remain there as it came, it returns to you untouched.[2]

I am Dear Sir &c. J H N

T W B Wood Esqr

It will come to you directed 137 Strand, London as I am always anxious about being put in charge with valuable parcels which have to be returned, perhaps you will be so kind as to write a letter to the Secretary 87 Stephens Green Dublin acknowledging its receipt.

TO THE EDITOR OF THE WEEKLY REGISTER

[16 January 1858]

Sir

I will not imitate the personalities of 'X. Y. Z': I will but say that persons who lose their temper seem to have had the worst of the argument. As to the statement of your other correspondent with the long pharisaical signature, who says that 'there are three students at the Catholic University from Stonyhurst,' it is a quibble worthy of a pharisaical 'Lover of Truth.' I said, 'no *English* Student.'[3] All the efforts of such people will fail to make a match between English Catholics and the Irish University. *Ecce signum* in this new month of January.

[1] Newman's leading articles on 'The Catholic University' in the *Weekly Register*, (23 and 30 Jan., 6 and 13 Feb., 6 and 13 Mar. 1858), are printed in Appendix I, pp. 565–83.
[2] See letter of 24 Nov. 1857 to Wood, who wrote on 14 Jan. to Newman that he had sent him on 4 Nov. a manuscript for his perusal. Since then he had received no notification that Newman had seen the MS, and requested that it should be returned immediately.
[3] The letter signed 'A Lover of Truth and a Cordial Hater of Mischief-makers', written from Stonyhurst, and published in the *Weekly Register*, (9 Jan. 1858), p. 7, stated that there were three boys from that school at the Catholic University. In fact all three were Irish.

On the one hand, our Cardinal's Review, in criticising Dr. Newman's recent sermons, does not even allude to their being preached in the University Church.[1] The writer does not omit this circumstance on purpose; but the University is a dead letter to him, Greek, Hebrew, Sanscrit, all goes in at one ear and out at the other.

On the other hand, the University had inserted a long advertisement of itself in its new 'Atlantis.' Take the first instance of it, and consider whether England does not lie in the German Ocean or *Mare Mortuum*, in the reckoning of this 'gem' of the Atlantic.

'The Catholic University of Ireland, though brought into existence by the accidental circumstances of the day, really owes its foundation to the reasonableness or even necessity of the principle, that a country, possessed of intellectual and moral characteristics proper to itself, should not be without some great central school, for the development of the national genius and expression of opinion and sentiment, which belong to it in history and by inheritance. As England glories in her own Universities, as being institutions cognate to her peculiar social temperament, and uses them as abodes and as organs of her peculiar nationalism, so it is natural that Ireland, too, should require some corresponding seat of mental activity, and its establishment when once she began to think and act for herself, was only a matter of time.'[2]

Q. in the Corner[3]

TO HENRY WILBERFORCE

The Oy Bm Jany 17/58

My dear H

Thanks for your letter and information.

I will send back the proof without delay. I sent *two* articles — for *two* weeks — because I hardly liked to send the first to Dublin without the second — for the first is lukewarm

Thanks — Manning takes me in   I will put your case on our prayer list.

Ever Yrs J H N

[1] *O.S.* was reviewed in *DR*, XLIII, (Dec. 1857), pp. 511–14. See fifth note to Memorandum of 20 Dec. 1858.

[2] This is the first paragraph in an advertisement of several pages devoted to the Catholic University, at the end of the *Atlantis*, (Jan. 1858).

[3] Newman made a note beside cuttings of his letters: 'Q in the Corner wrote four letters in H Wilberforce's paper, to act like a chemical test on English Catholic opinion, and to determine whether English Catholics would precipitate one grain of interest in the Dublin Catholic University. His letters decided that they felt nothing at all for it, for they made no reply. Then I wrote some leading articles in the Paper in defence and recommendation of the University—I thought 4, but I find 6.' Newman also mistook the number of his 'Q in the Corner' letters. Only three appeared in the *Weekly Register*, the first on 12 Dec., the second on 2 Jan.

MONDAY 18 JANUARY 1858   Ignatius returned   Bathurst slept here   called on the Bishop   *He* called with Mr Dalton

TO EDMUND O'REILLY, S.J.

Jan 18/58

My dear Fr O'Reilly

Thank you for your letter just received. I am very glad to find that we have the Archbishop's sanction for quietly availing ourselves and our lecture rooms of books which though prohibited, are not like Gibbon, decidedly dangerous, and are necessary for the intended professions of our students.

I will make it known to the persons concerned under an injunction to avoid talking about it.[1]

I am &c J H N

TUESDAY 19 JANUARY 1858   Mr F. Eyston called.   Nicholas returned   Mr B. Wilson and son slept here.

TO T. W. ALLIES

The Oratory Birmingham Jan. 19./58

My dear Allies,

My train gets to Paddington at (I believe) 2.25. I shall leave my carpet bag at Manning's where I sleep, and forthwith come on to Duke Street.

I have written to Mrs Allies to thank her and you for your invitation, and to say that, if you will give me *dinner*, I should be most grateful, though I cannot accept your further hospitality. In that case I should go with you from Duke Street to Abbey Road.[2]

I have further added that I would ask, if *it be possible*, to dine not later than 5½ or 6, as I have some business with Manning in the evening.

Ever yrs affly in Xt   John H Newman of the Oratory

P.S.   Have you observed a letter in the Register? A friend from Dublin wrote suggesting the same thing.[3]

---

[1] This letter is explained by that of 19 Jan. to Butler.
[2] Allies was the secretary of Catholic Poor School Committee, whose office had just moved from John Street, Adelphi, to 17 Duke Street, Manchester Square. He lived at 44 Abbey Road, St John's Wood.
[3] The conclusion of a letter signed 'Britannicus,' in answer to 'Q in the Corner,' ran, 'In a word, if the Catholic University wants English students, let it set up an English school to be its feeder, instead of interfering with the existing colleges.' The *Weekly Register*, (16 Jan. 1858), p. 4. Cf. letter of 12 Jan. to Ornsby.

[19?] January 1858

My dear Professor Butler

. . . In the course of the Christmas recess, Professor Arnold sent me an interesting sketch of the general plan he wanted to adopt for his lectures in English literature. Thinking this a good opportunity of asking for a formal solution of the embarrassment which I had long felt in reconciling his duties with the obedience which a University owes to the Rules of the Index of Prohibited Books, (in which Rules Catholic Universities are recognized as in some sense officials of the Sacred Congregation), I sent the Professor's Letter in question to our Professor of Dogmatic Theology, begging him to consider what the duty of our Professors was generally in existing circumstances. He wrote back as follows . . . . (vid letter of January 8. 1858)[1]

'In reply to your letter of the 6th inst; I would say 1. that there seems to me to be a peculiar awkwardness in the University's *positively* ignoring the index, by a system of teaching which would palpably involve the use of prohibited books; even supposing that an individual in his private capacity might legitimately read such books without leave. 2. The bishops have, I am almost certain, the power of granting leave. 3. It might be a question whether such extensive reading of the books alluded to would not be more congruously provided for by a Roman permission *ad hoc*. 4. There are two opposite mischiefs to be guarded against in any course taken in the matter; one that of *startling* people in this country about the index; the other that of throwing the door too wide open.

If you wish I will speak to the Archbishop on the subject. I do not like doing so without your express consent.'

To this I replied, gladly accepting the offer of laying the matter before his Grace; the more so, as I was myself personally involved in the difficulties which I felt to press upon the Professors, as I was taking young men into my house on the engagement of preparing them for government examinations, in which it was scarcely possible they should acquit themselves as well as other candidates, unless they had a knowledge of books which the Sacred Congregation prohibited.

I subjoin Dr O'Reilly's answer and my reply to him. . . .[2]

'I have spoken to the Archbishop on the subject you wrote to me about. Indeed I spoke to him some days since; but waited for another interview before writing; and having seen him again today, I give you the result. From

[1] The source of this letter to Edward Butler is Newman's draft in which he omitted the text of the letter of 8 Jan. from the Professor of Dogmatic Theology, Edmund O'Reilly. The omission is supplied from the autograph of O'Reilly's letter. He wrote from St Francis Xavier's, Upper Gardiner Street, Dublin.

[2] O'Reilly's second letter, that of 17 Jan., has been inserted in the same way as his previous one.

(See at 18 Jan. Newman's reply to O'Reilly.)

the beginning he admitted the necessity of some books being read which are on the index, and at the same time thought there should be some *permission.* He observed that some decidedly dangerous books, such as Gibbon, should be avoided. He seemed to agree in thinking that too much noise should not be made about the necessity of leave for reading prohibited books in this country. No very definite conclusion however was come to as to the precise mode of proceeding, in our first conversation. The upshot of today's interview was his advising that things should be allowed to go on quietly. Whether any more formal step may be taken hereafter, I do not know; but so far you have his sanction for the proceeding.'

In laying this correspondence before your Faculty my dear Professor Butler, and drawing their attention to the last sentence of my letter to Dr O'Reilly,[1] I will but observe, to avoid the possibility of misconception, that the difficulty which I submitted to him is quite distinct from the question whether the Index is in force in these countries.[2]

J H N

TO ROBERT ORNSBY

Oy Bm ⌐Jan 19/58⌐

My dear Ornsby

⌐There is not *time* to send you the first of my Articles[3]

I send the second — ⌐ send it back as soon as you can conveniently Thank you for your letter

Ever Yrs J H N

R. Ornsby Esqr

P.S. ⌐You must not suppose I am going to submit to *no* appointment of Vice Rector. *I shall retire after February 2 from all business else.*⌐

---

[1] i.e. Newman's letter of 18 Jan.
[2] Two letters from O'Reilly of 9 and 21 Feb. show that Newman continued to consult him, asking whether Protestant books could be set for examination in the philosophy of Religion. Newman's list of books included Butler's *Analogy.* O'Reilly objected to 'the *look* of the proceeding,' but was not prepared to say that such books should be excluded.
O'Reilly wrote his second letter after consulting Cullen who thought 'it would not do to *put them down* in a list for examination. . . . The look of the thing would be objectionable.' O'Reilly did not like 'works by protestants made, so to speak, *substantive matter* of examination in religion.' Before he had completed his letter of 21 Feb. O'Reilly received another from Newman, evidently suggesting that Protestant works could be studied as needing correction and subject to criticism. O'Reilly agreed that this suggestion 'goes some way towards answering not only my objection on the score of *danger,* but also that renewed in my present communication on the score of *appearance*: for the correction and criticizing of a work take off from it's character as an *authority.*'
[3] i.e. the leading articles in the *Weekly Register.*

TO THOMAS SCRATTON

Oy Bm Jan 19/58

My dear Scratton

I was distressed last night to find to my surprise I had not returned to you Dr Forde's draft

I put it in my writing desk for safety and forgot it.

And I now inclose it and my letter

Ever Yrs J H N

Thos Scratton Esqr

TO HENRY WILBERFORCE

The Oy Bm ⌜Jan 19/57⌝[1]

My dear H,

⌜I send you back Number 1 for next Saturday — ⌝[1] (I think it should *not* be headed Number 1) — and propose as follows.

I sleep at Manning's tomorrow (Wednesday) night — now supposing you came to Mass and Breakfast there at half past 8 on *Thursday* morning — I could start with you at 9 for my dentist, who would only detain us a few minutes — and then for Dr Williams. You would then hear the opinion he gave about me — and then could leave me to go to Jermyn Street, in my way back to Bayswater and the Rail.

Or you might join me at the Dentist's (Lintott 23 Wimpole Street) at half past 9. Or you might join me at Dr Williams's Number 49 Upper Brook Street at 10 o'clock.

⌜You will see that my proof of what I inclose, requires careful attention — for I *make no alteration*, only correct according to copy.

There is not time for Number 1 to go to Dublin. As to Number 2 which would appear on Saturday week the 23rd you shall have it back when it returns from Dublin.⌝[1]

Ever Yrs affly J H N

H W Wilberforce Esqr

WEDNESDAY 20 JANUARY 1858 Stanislas returned and went to bed *seriously ill* — *in bed for above 3 weeks.* I went to London — called on Allies — [F. R.] Ward with him, and slept at Manning's (*Bayswater*)

THURSDAY 21 JANUARY went to Lintott — consulted Dr Williams (*in consequence of what Dr Evans said*) — called on Miss Bowles — dined at H W's [Wilberforce] — slept at Manning's — news of Laprimaudaye's death.

[1] Even when copying Newman dated this letter a year too early.

TO AMBROSE ST JOHN

3 Bridges Street Strand Jany 21/58

My dear A

My dentist is keeping me till tomorrow — and here I am wandering about the Town, and not knowing what to do.

You will all rejoice to know, and be as thankful as I am, that Dr Williams, after carefully examining me, pronounces me perfectly and altogether free from any thing like organic mischief in the heart — nor does he think much of the palpitation. He attributes it entirely to indigestion — and has confirmed quite remarkably the conclusions to which my own experience has slowly come, contrary to other medical men. He says I have no complaint to make of my liver — nor have I acidity — but simply, what I more than suspected myself, that I suffer from a want of gastric juice. To meet this difficulty, I have been buying a lot of gastric juice of a calf, with which I am to flavour my meals. It is, he says, not a nauseous acid.

I intend to set off to Bm [Birmingham] by the 2 o'clock train — or by the 3.30. In either case I propose to dine at home

Ever Yrs affly John H Newman

FRIDAY 22 JANUARY 1858   to Lintott — with H W [Wilberforce] and down to Birmingham

TO ROBERT ORNSBY

The Oratory Bm ⌐Jany 23. 1858⌐

My dear Ornsby

Thank you for your criticisms, by which I will do the best to profit.[1]

⌐I have been to London, and I am thankful to say that the medical man I consulted does not think there is any organic mischief in the heart or its neighbourhood — that the inconvenience I suffer is only functional. So far I am greatly relieved — but, to balance it, I find on my return Fr Flanagan in bed — and the doctor seriously alarmed about him. It is an attack of bronchitis, with the great fear of its being only a symptom of deeper mischief. If he gets well, as we trust, off he must go abroad. I don't know whether you know our body well enough to understand how great a blow this is. He has worked harder, and at more things, than any one — treasurer, missioner, workhouse chaplain, confessor, novice master, minister — always ready for any work, and made to do every thing because he has done every thing so well. I don't see how I can possibly retain the Rectorship with this fresh urgent call on me here — I shall not do any part of his work with his perfection and success —

---

[1] They concerned the second of the leading articles for the *Weekly Register*, on the Catholic University.

but I certainly shall be called on to do my part.[11] It is not pleasant to spread unfavorable accounts of the health of friends, so don't repeat my extreme fear that he will not be able to rise from his bed again, and go abroad — or if he does, that his going abroad will be unavailing. Anyhow, he never can be to us what he was.

You have heard Manning's extreme loss, (not to say the Pollens) in Laprimaudaye.[2]

I can't find your letter — so excuse me if I have missed any thing

Ever Yours affly John H Newman of the Oratory

R. Ornsby Esqr

P.S. ⌈I shall show you the formal letter I send to the Archbishops. What has Dr Leahy's accidental illness of a particular day to do with a procrastination which has lasted *since April 2nd* last, when I sent round my letters to the Bishops?⌉[13]

SUNDAY 24 JANUARY 1858   Stanislas in bed for above 3 weeks

TO JOHN HUNGERFORD POLLEN

The Oratory, Birmingham, January 24th. 1858

My dear Pollen,

I know there is nothing which friends can do to relieve so heavy a stroke as that under which you and your wife are suffering. He alone, who in His love has sent it, can enable you to bear it — but it seems unnatural not to write, though one knows that no words can do more than express sympathy.

We too at this moment are in great anxiety. I went up to London, and most thankful I ought to be that, when my case was enquired into, nothing was found amiss about the region of my heart — and there seems no doubt that the palpitation and shortness of breath I have had are to be referred solely

[1] Newman copied out most of this passage in a memorandum of 9 Nov. 1872, headed 'May 1. 1858:'
'What was the primary and *immediate* reason *why* I remained at the Oratory instead of going to Dublin? what was the sufficient obligation? First of all, of course, the Oratorians having *recalled* me to Bm [Birmingham] as by their letter of May 5. 1857 [see letters of 6 May 1857 to St John]—Next,
The following so stated in my letters to Mr Ornsby:—
Jany 23. 1858.   I have been in London . . . to do my part.
Febry 20. 1858.   Fr Flanagan went off yesterday with Fr *Tillotson*.
March 12. 1858.   We are still in bitter anxiety about Fr *Bittleston*.
He has been dying well nigh three weeks. We gave him the Viaticum yesterday.
Fr Bittleston when he got well, went abroad too. I took a good number of their penitents in their absence, and was a great deal in the Confessional all through Lent from February 27 onwards.'
[2] Pollen's father-in-law, Charles La Primaudaye, died in Rome on 20 Jan., of smallpox caught from nursing a student at the Collegio Pio. La Primaudaye had joined Manning's Oblates of St Charles, and was studying for the priesthood.
[3] Newman's formal letter to the Archbishops is the first of 3 Feb. 1858 to Leahy. Ornsby had written on 20 Jan., 'I think it will be *over hasty* if you withdraw action on Feb. 2d. After all Dr Leahy is ill, and they *could not* choose a V.R. (Vice-Rector) by correspondence. . . .'

to indigestion. I know I am not thankful as I ought to be — whereas when I have any trial, I fret over it. Now when I got back from London, I found dear Stanislas in bed, and really we are very much alarmed about him. His strength and voice are gone; he has simply overdone himself — and his medical attendant, I suspect, does not see to the bottom of it more than we. I wanted to have brought him to town with me for advice on Wednesday, but he would not have borne the journey. I believe he will have to go to the South, directly he is able — but our fear is that his strength will go. However, perhaps this is over anxiety. Pray remember him in your prayers, as we will you and yours.

I don't know enough of your wife's family, to know how many children still remain to have their course of life determined.[1] If it was God's will that their father was to be taken away, it has been well, that he took the step of leaving them for the ecclesiastical state — for nothing can have been left unsettled — and except as the ties of affection are concerned, his loss cannot be called sudden. I was extremely rejoiced to be with Manning at the time the news came, and able to say a black Mass the very next morning, with the other priests in his house. You cannot tell what sorrow the news caused here. We are saying Masses for the repose of his soul.

Yours affectionately, My dear Pollen,

John H Newman

J. H. Pollen Esq.

TO HENRY WILBERFORCE

The Oy Bm Jany 24/58

My dear H

I fear I must ask for a *revise* of Number 2. I send also the copy of Number 3 for February 7.

You will grieve to hear that we are in great anxiety about dear Stanislas. You have heard me say again and again, that, in want of hands, he has taken more work than he ought. But don't mention it, for God may be gracious

Ever Yrs affly J H N

TO THOMAS WILLIAM ALLIES

The Oratory Birmingham Jan. 26. 1858

My dear Allies,

I have been trying in vain to find the passage in Cosmos [?][2] containing the reference to some German work on the Philosophy of History, and must

[1] La Primaudaye left nine children, and Pollen had married his second daughter, who was now aged nineteen.
[2] This is the copyists's question mark. Newman probably wrote 'Cantù,' meaning Cesare Cantù's *Storia Universale*.

give up the search. You know better than I that Hegel has a treatise on the subject.

Certainly I do very much wish you to give us an article for July. We are sure to have plenty of science, and good science, but from the nature of the case you cannot expect composition from an experimentalist any more than from a mathematician. The first part of our Register is 'Literary' and it is the most difficult to get supplied, because we cannot pay. Yet even to those who do not get the substantial renumeration which accrues to men of science in the publication gratis of their experiments and discoveries, there is this gain, that they are able to put into print the first draughts or portions of important undertakings which afterwards they may work up into extended treatises. For myself, were I younger, I should like to bring out piece meal and hear criticisms on historical sketches which I might make the basis of something more substantial at my leisure.

By the bye on the physician's table to whom I went (Dr Williams of Upper Brook Street) I saw a printed but unpublished Essay on the Philosophy of History. Of course I did not see enough of it to give an opinion, but the subject seemed carefully divided.

You will be glad to know that the said Dr W. pronounced me quite free from all organic disease in my heart, after a careful use of the stethoscope, which I am very thankful for. What a blow for Manning is Laprimaudaye's death. I am sorry to say Fr Flanagan is seriously ill here, and will have to go abroad.

I was very glad to see you and yours.

Ever yrs affecly in Xt   John H Newman of the Oratory.

TO T. W. ALLIES

The Oratory Bm Janry 28./58

My dear Allies,

I am just back from seeing our Bishop on the subject of the School, and I am much relieved and thankful to find that he has not any objection at all to it, the contrary, and that on the ground which I was prepared for, viz that he hoped it would be the first step towards a division of the lay from the ecclesiastical students. The subject was not a new one to him, for Bellasis had communicated with Estcourt.[1]

---

[1] A copy of a letter from Ullathorne to Estcourt of 24 Jan. is preserved at the Oratory, which shows he welcomed a new school as leading to the separation of the Catholic boys' schools from the seminaries, 'It would be just that wedge in the present system that is wanted.' Ullathorne added, 'Our schools are all full to overflowing, and there is room for another. . . . I should be the first to say to Dr Newman . . . you need have no fear of interfering with us.'

We find there is a good house near us with garden, annual rent £120. I don't know whether things are advanced enough for [F. R.] Ward to move about it. Houses go quickly. There was a very good one to be had last year, which is now gone.

I should rejoice to have your article on Civilization for the July Number, if you will give it.[1]

It was a great pleasure to me to see you, Mrs Allies, and other friends. By the bye I have got the little books in train for Basil.[2]

Fr Flanagan is still abed, though better, directly he can move, he is to go to the South. It is an extreme trouble to us. Never was a harder working fellow, and always cheerful, the more work he had. But whatever happens, I suppose it is his constitution, not his work that is in fault, for his mother died of consumption. A few months will decide it one way or the other. If he is not well by June, I shall despair of him. It is mysterious that so useful a life should be interrupted. Laprimaudaye and R. Wilberforce, great as is their loss, were so much older.

Ever yours affly John H Newman

TO T. W. ALLIES

The Oratory, Bm Jan. 31. 1858

My dear Allies,

I have heard from Bellasis this morning on the subject of the School. He wishes a letter from me by Wednesday next which he can put before an (adjourned) meeting.

Tomorrow I will look at several houses, and shall be able to say something about prices.

At first sight it seems as if Fr Ward's proposition would be feasible — 20 boys at £70. But I can't tell whether more would not be necessary, if there were under 20.

In your message some time ago from Bellasis, he spoke of an annual contribution beyond his boy. I had your letter in my hands a day or two ago, but cannot find it now. Will you repeat what he said? If this were done by several of course it would bring down the charge of the boys.

Perhaps Hope Scott's plan was to supersede this — viz. a sum at first for getting the house ready.

Fr Darnell thinks he could give 4 hours a day to it, e.g. from 10 to 12 and from 2 to 4. We should want a master in the House, who ought to be a public school man. Can you think of any one? I suppose Oxenham would not like it.

[1] See letter of 5 Feb. to Sullivan.
[2] Cf. letter of 8 Jan. to Allies.

Can you give me any suggestions generally We have a Congregation
Meeting on the Purification (Tuesday) and I mean to write to Bellasis after it.

Ever yrs affly John H Newman of the Oratory

MONDAY 1 FEBRUARY 1858 Frederic returned
TUESDAY 2 February Crawley admitted to his first probation as Fr George.

TO EDWARD BELLASIS

The Oratory, Birmingham February 2. 1858

The tenth anniversary of our introduction into England
the ninth of our establishment in Birmingham.

My dear Bellasis

I have brought the subject of the proposed school before our Fathers,[1]
and, on talking it over, various difficulties suggested themselves to us, in the
particular mode of bringing it into effect, (which I mentioned to our friends
when I was in London,) by taking a house near us, and overseeing it from the
Oratory. Mrs Wootten must have a house, or at least apartments, to herself;
but, if so, how could she be present with the boys? — Father Darnell must
be responsible for them, but how, if he dwells, as he must dwell, in the
Oratory? — Then came the question of daily Mass or at least days of obligation in bad weather. And further are we not likely to spend money in adapting,
badly at least, an Edgbaston Villa, to our purpose?

Accordingly the following plan has occurred to us, which we think it well
to let you lay before your meeting tomorrow, if you will kindly undertake to
do so — though we do not like absolutely to commit ourselves to it, without
a second meeting, after we have had time for deliberation. It is the circumstance of your meeting being fixed for tomorrow, which makes us send it you
at once. Your view of it will assist our own final judgment upon it. At present
it is a suggestion offered, we will say by myself, both to your meeting and our
Fathers here.

---

[1] Bellasis wrote on 30 Jan. that at a meeting in his chambers the previous day at which he,
Allies, F. Capes, Dodsworth, F. R. Ward, Wegg-Prosser, and Revd R. G. MacMullen were
present, it had been agreed that a new Catholic school for boys was necessary. It was also
agreed that the plan on which it was formed should be decided by 'the mature deliberation
of some one mind.'

Bellasis continued, 'We further agreed that your connexion with the Catholic University,
and the interest you must necessarily take in the earlier education of youth, point you out as
the person to whom we should address ourselves.

For the reason given above we have nothing further to suggest than that we desire such a
school as shall combine a vigorous intellectual training with the more important element of a
thoroughly Catholic atmosphere,—that we think the school should be essentially a lay school,
and that the annual pensions should be determined not by reference to what is paid at
existing schools, but by what may prove to be required for its effectual support.' Bellasis
then asked whether Newman would undertake such a school, if he were provided with the
necessary funds.

We will undertake a boys' school at £70 a boy, or under, as drawn out below, (with the usual extras for drawing, music etc) and engage to carry it on, if called upon, for as long as 20 years, provided you give us £2000 to start with — and we will provide accommodation for them as follows:

We will set apart and cut off entirely from our House the entire top (i.e. second story) which is light and airy, looking over to Oscott on the one side and to the Clent Hills on the other. We will connect this story and make it approached, by a new building to be built on our own ground in continuation of the line of our House along the Hagley Road and in front of our temporary Church, the available space being in length 80 feet and in breadth 75. We have at present an available play-ground of 200 feet by 24, and a fair ball court; but we will rent (say) an acre and a half of land within a stone's throw, perhaps adjacent to our own ground, and will look out for a cricket field.

We propose that the new building should contain at the end furthest from us, a set of Dame's and servants' rooms, and an infirmary; — and the school rooms, dining room, music room, kitchen — and perhaps some bed rooms; certainly a Father Prefect's room; and that it should communicate, as I have said, with our own upper story, which contains 15 rooms, capable of containing one, two, or three beds apiece, and two corridors, 10 feet and 8 feet broad, and 150 feet and 70 feet long, available for dormitories in part of their length. I think 50 boys could thus be accommodated without our thinking of bedrooms in the new building.

One inconvenience the Fathers will sustain, viz the having the boys over their heads — but this will only be at night, when the boys ought to be quiet. The advantages of the arrangement for the School are such as these — that Mrs Wootten, or the Dame for the time being has access to them from one end, and the Father Prefect from the other, while the two Houses are quite separate. Moreover, our Church being close to the back of the proposed new building, they could go to Mass every morning, and even might have a gallery opening upon the end of it.

We would commence building at once — and I suppose could be ready at the end of the year, making allowances for any inexpedience there may be in using the School rooms etc. without the March wind having blown through them. As to the bed rooms in our own house, they have been dwelt in these six years. I say nothing about any provisional plan by which we could begin at Easter, e.g. taking a house for a year; as this is a separate consideration.

I subjoin a rough sketch of the ground and available spaces — the measurements are pretty nearly right.

As to the question of boys' pension, which I have reserved for this place, as requiring some explanation, I believe it will prove to be our unanimous wish to hinder the undertaking from being a direct source of income to us, an arrangement which, (for myself certainly) I consider most prejudicial to the elevation and maintenance of our vocation. We should desire nothing more than a fair renumeration for the accommodation which we afforded, or in other words a fair interest for the money we have, or shall have expended in brick and mortar, and perhaps £50 a year for the Father Prefect's trouble. Hence we should *wish* to bring down the pension from £70 to £65, £60, £55, according as we reached the number of 20, 30, 40, and 50 boys; though of course we could not pledge ourselves to more than the general principle I have laid down.

In the above plan, I have assumed, what your letter with such kind confidence in me proposes, that I am to have the whole management of the undertaking. In this I see only one difficulty: viz as to the *admission* of boys — Undesirable boys must be excluded; but, in our position here, we should have great difficulty ourselves in keeping out the sons of families of this place who happen to be penitents, or otherwise friends of the Oratory. Would it be possible for the admission to rest with a certain number of gentlemen in London?[1]

I am, My dear Bellasis, Most sincerely Yours in Xt

John H Newman[2]

TO PATRICK LEAHY, ARCHBISHOP OF CASHEL, I

The Oratory, Birmingham ⌐February 3. 1858⌐

My dear Lord,

⌐It is now more than ten months since I signified to their Lordships, the Bishops of Ireland, individually, my intention to retire from the Rectorship of the Catholic University, with which they had honored me.

It is all but three months since the particular day, which in my letters to them I prospectively fixed, as the term of my continuing to hold it.

I have delayed, since the day came, to take an irrevocable step, in the expectation that something might result to hinder it, from the negociation into which the Archbishops condescended to enter with me in the course of last Summer.

I still delay it — but I am sure you will not be surprised at my now informing you, that I have come to the resolution, till things are placed on a

---

[1] A copy of a letter of 7 Feb. from Hope-Scott to Bellasis in reply to this difficulty is preserved at the Oratory. Hope-Scott maintained that Newman must have the sole power of admitting as of sending away boys. If 'Gentlemen in London' nominated boys it would give them more control of the school than was desirable. He added, 'Then with regard to "undesirable boys" as a class—this must mean I suppose the children of people of inferior rank or manners—now the English public schools are open to all who can pay, and I see no disadvantage, but the contrary, in the mixture of classes.' For the particular difficulty Newman raised, 'there is a remedy also known to English schools. Let no boy be admitted except as a day scholar, whose parents reside within 2 or 3 miles of the Oratory.' Hope-Scott insisted, 'if you really mean ever to have a public school you must profess that intention from the first.'

[2] Several copies were made of this letter, and Newman later wrote at the end of the autograph: 'N B. Febry 14. 1863 This is the actual letter which went to Bellasis, and which he returned to me. J H N'

more intelligible footing, to decline, from the date of this letter, to receive any portion of the Rector's salary.[11]

I am, My dear Lord, Your Grace's faithful Servt in Xt

John H Newman of the Oratory[2]

The Most Revd The Archbp of Cashel

TO PATRICK LEAHY, ARCHBISHOP OF CASHEL, II

The Oratory Birmingham Febry 3. 1858

My dear Lord,

The Archbishops' cheque for £2178 has reached me this morning, and I lose no time in thanking your Grace for it. I send it by this post to the Hibernian Bank

I am, My dear Lord, Your Grace's faithful Servt

John H Newman

The Most Revd The Archbp of Cashel

TO GEORGE COPELAND

The Oratory Birmingham Febry 4. 1858

My dear Mr Copeland,

I thank you very much for your kind and valuable present.[3] It is not only valuable in itself, as being rare and curious, but it will be useful to me in my anxious undertaking. I was looking about for such a list of Editions of the Bible — and had intended to get a work, I had heard of, published by

---

[1] For the reply, see letter of 27 Feb. to Leahy.
[2] Newman copied out parts of a letter of 2 Feb., from Edward Butler to himself, 'I showed your letter [[to Dr Leahy?]] to Ornsby and Stewart, and I need not tell you that we regret exceedingly you should have been put under the necessity of taking such a step. [[my not taking any salary henceforth?]] The delay on the part of the Archbishops is to us uninitiated wholly unaccountable, and we feel greatly our anomalous position.

Yet we do not see that any movement on our part by way of memorial to the Archbishops, or deputation to Dr Cullen, would facilitate or expedite matters. We fear much that such a step would be looked upon with great jealousy, might give offence and defeat its own object. With your present feelings and views, and in your position, we do not see what else you can do; and we hope this letter [[to Dr Leahy?]] will bring about a satisfactory arrangement. We feel most grateful to you for your great forbearance, and for the excessive considerateness you have shown to us in all this matter.'
[3] Copeland sent Newman a copy of *Bibles Testaments Psalms and other Books of the Holy Scripture in English*, in the collection of Lea Wilson Esq., F.S.A., etc., London 1845. Only sixty copies were printed, and the author, who was married to an elder sister of Copeland's wife, had presented him with one. Wilson was said to have possessed the largest and most valuable collection of English bibles then in existence. It was dispersed at his death. Copeland asked Newman to accept the book in remembrance of his wife, Selina Bacchus, who died in 1850.

Archdeacon Cotton of Thurles.[1] His account of Catholic English Bibles I have — and most useful it is.[2]

I wish you would let me thank you in person by coming here, and saying as I sign myself that I am

Most truly Yours John H Newman

P S. As you connect your present with a memento, I will say Mass for your intention on the first black day, which (with us) is the 16th inst. February is a time of mementos with us, and, I think, with you. We lost our dear Father, Joseph Gordon, on the 13th. And with me — Hurrell Froude died on the 28th and two near friends of mine on the 22nd.[3]

How your handwriting puts me in mind of your brother.[4]

TO ROBERT ORNSBY

Oy Bm Febry 4/58

My dear Ornsby

I am very much concerned to hear of your various illnesses. As to the tooth, whatever the pain was, I cannot be sorry it is out — for it can plague you no more. Everyone has been having boils.

I inclose a letter for Renouf, as I wish you to direct it for me, or to give it to him.

⌜I mentioned a Pro Vice to the Archbishops in October[5] — and was answered that I might appoint one, so that he was a priest — which made it impossible⌝[6]

Ever Yrs affly John H Newman

R Ornsby Esqr

And I don't know Arnold's direction — so I inclose a letter for him.

[1] Henry Cotton, D.C.L., Archdeacon of Cashel, published at Oxford in 1820 *A List of Editions of the Bible in English from 1505 to 1820, with Specimens of Translations, . . .* second edition corrected and enlarged, 1852.
[2] *Rhemes and Doway. An attempt to shew what has been done by Roman Catholics for the diffusion of the Holy Scriptures in English*, Oxford 1855.
[3] Newman's book of anniversaries had two names entered for 22 Feb., Emma Bowden (first wife of Henry Bowden), 1836, and Walter Mayers ('the human means of the beginning of divine faith' in Newman), 1828. On 14 Feb. appeared 'Mary Copeland 1842.'
[4] i.e. W. J. Copeland, Newman's curate at Littlemore, with whom friendship was renewed in 1862.
[5] [[vid also June 1857]], i.e. letter of 23 May 1857 to Leahy and notes there.
[6] Ornsby was still looking for expedients that would delay Newman's resignation. On 4 Feb. he wrote, 'I confess I was very sorry to hear of your making so very great a sacrifice as that of the salary so long as you can so fairly claim it. However, it is dealing with the case in a *great* manner, and perhaps it will prove a successful way of forcing matters to a crisis. They cannot now, as gentlemen, do other than come to some arrangement.'

TO SIR JOHN SIMEON

The Oratory Birmingham Febry 4. 1858

My dear Sir John

Thank you for your most kind letter just received. I should indeed have been most sorry and troubled to fancy, that I had done any thing to lose the confidence I have hoped that you and others like yourself had in me — and therefore it is most considerate in you to anticipate the chance of my hearing a matter of detail which I might or might not have heard.

But, though you do not make yourself one of the first promoters of the undertaking, for reasons which you are so very kind in making known to me, let me have the full belief that I have your sympathy, concurrence, and good prayers.[1] In so exceedingly anxious and important a work, for which I am making myself responsible, though in many respects so very unfit and though able personally to do so little, I really do need the encouragement of friends. I have no object what ever, as far as I know (what can I have?) except that of doing something towards a great work, before I die. It is a formidable and momentous experiment, if it proceeds. To fail would be to damage English Catholicism exceedingly. And how can I begin except with the co-operation and good auguries of all those whom I love and admire, whether I am intimately acquainted with them or not.

Believe me, My dear Sir John, Most sincerely Yours in Xt

John H Newman of the Oratory

Sir John Simeon Bart.

TO WILLIAM KIRBY SULLIVAN

The Oratory Birmingham Febry 4/58

My dear Mr Sullivan,

Thank you for your complete account of the disposition of the sums of University money, which have passed through your hands. It shall go to the Auditors.

Did I promise you any more? I do not recollect it — and think, if so, I should have taken a note of it. Till yesterday the quarter's money was not paid in, and we were overdrawn at the Bank. I had reserved £100 for the 2nd Number of the Atlantis and £200 for Mr Currie's book — [2] but I doubt whether some part even of this is not spent. I sent to the Secretary yesterday to ask him what would be over after quarterly payments — and, when I know,

[1] Cf. Simeon's letter of 30 April 1857, quoted in note to that of 17 April 1857 to him.
[2] Eugene O'Curry's *Lectures on the Manuscript Materials of Ancient Irish History*, Dublin 1861, was published with a subsidy of £300, allocated by Newman from the University funds.

will see what I can do, but I assure you I shall have great difficulty in doing any thing

Yours very sincerely John H Newman

W K Sullivan Esqr

TO MRS F. R. WARD

Oratory Birmingham Febry 4. 1858

My dear Mrs Ward,

I thank you very much for your letter of this morning, and its inclosure. H's letter is very interesting and amusing too. His astonishment that he should have any sincere friend out of his own family, including of course Godfathers and Godmothers made me smile very much — as well as the pointed way in which he conveys his suspicion that *you* are the friend in question. I have never seen him, but he is in some sort my Godson — so I hope I am his sincere friend, as he seems to take for granted. It is very kind in you to bring him before me, and remind me to perform the duties I owe him, better than I do. I am glad indeed to find that both you and Lady Henry are so sanguine about him.[1]

It was a great pleasure to me to see you the other day — I am sure I may believe, you do not forget me in your prayers. Do ask for me that I may do God's work faithfully and well, whatever He puts upon me. I know He puts nothing on me, which I ought not to be able to do, and which it will not be only my own fault if I do not do; — but at my time of life, when I look back and see how little I have done, I sometimes get out of heart.

Ever Yours, My dear Mrs Ward, Most sincerely in Xt

John H Newman of the Oratory

Mrs Ward

FRIDAY 5 FEBRUARY 1858   Edward went to see his brother off to America[2]

TO WILLIAM KIRBY SULLIVAN

The Oratory, Birmingham Febry 5. 1858

My dear Mr Sullivan,

I have not been neglectful of the Atlantis, though I have not written to you. People speak respectfully of it, as far as I have heard speak. I have one

[1] Mrs F. R. Ward and Lady Henry Kerr were close friends of the William Froudes, and 'H.' is evidently their eldest son and Newman's godson, Richard Hurrell Froude, born 28 April 1842. See letter of 8 Dec. 1857 to Lady Henry Kerr.
[2] This was Thomas Caswall, Fellow of Clare College, Cambridge, until he became a Catholic in 1846.

or two subscribers, not a great many. I have had a talk with Mr Allies about giving an article on civilization contrasted with Christianity, bringing in Mr Buckle's new book and other works.[1] He hopes to have it for next number, but cannot engage to do so. Also I am trying to get Sir John Acton, who is a first rate German scholar, or at least reader of German literature, to do something for us. And I am trying to get something out of Mr Arnold. As to the Waldenses, I had already attempted Mr Renouf, whose both that and Philo are, but he is so busy, he despairs of doing any thing for next time. I don't think I could go on with my own subject next time — but I thought of attempting for Science 'An inquiry into the original tenet of Eutyches — ' the only difficulty is that so much of it would be in Latin, that the *whole* ought to be — and that perhaps is inadmissible.[2]

I am sorry you cannot continue your own article on Language, as I wish to see the argument carried on — but I don't wonder at your wishing to delay it. Mr Currie's will be valuable — indeed your whole list is good; we had better get as much in type as we can, and then select for the next number. Mr Currie's should go to the printer as soon as the type (Irish) is ready.[3]

We must proceed rather carefully about Fowler's part in the publication — I mean, before we actually do any thing, I ought to write to Longmans — but I can't conceive they would object to our getting *subscriptions* in Ireland and serving the copies to subscribers. But I should think they would object to Fowler as a *publisher* except as *their* agent.

Yours most sincerely John H Newman

W K Sullivan Esqr

MONDAY 8 FEBRUARY 1858   Sir John Acton and Bellasis came down on the school matter

TO THE DUKE OF NORFOLK

The Oratory Birmingham February 8th 1858

My dear Duke of Norfolk,

A kind and magnificent present of game has come to me this morning from you. Pray accept our best thanks, and with my best and sincerest remembrances of the Duchess and your family circle

I am My dear Duke of Norfolk Sincerely Yours in Xt

John H Newman

His Grace the Duke of Norfolk

---

[1] i.e. the first volume of Henry Thomas Buckle's *History of Civilization in England*, London 1857. Neither Allies nor Acton contributed articles to the *Atlantis*.

[2] See the *Atlantis*, (July 1858), pp. 330–61 'On the Formula, μια φύσις τοῦ θεοῦ λόγου σεσαρκωμένη, T.T., pp. 328–82.

[3] ibid., pp. 362–92, 'The Sick-bed of Cuchulainn, and the only Jealousy of Eimer.'

Febr 8/58

My dear Scratton

Thank you for your information about the balance. Have you any idea what will be the payments necessary between this and May 1?

I will think over the Auditors' question.[1] I wish I had known they were meeting — for I could have sent in both Sullivan's large account and the Atlantis Account (£100)

Ever Yrs J H Newman

P.S. Stanislas will have been 3 weeks abed come Wednesday. We fear consumption. He is going abroad. He has been overworked.

TO EDWARD BELLASIS

The Oratory Birmingham Febry 9. 1858

My dear Bellasis,[2]

After you were gone, the two Fathers with whom you and Sir John Acton conversed, communicated to me some particulars of what occurred last week

[1] Scratton wrote on 5 Feb. that Bianconi and Errington had just audited the accounts of the University for the half year ending 31 Dec. Their question appears to have been whether O'Curry needed a paid assistant. Scratton also reported that the auditors 'were very savage in re Forde.' His appointment was widely criticised as a 'job.' Cf. second note to letter of 30 Oct. 1857 to Leahy.

[2] Newman made a Memorandum about this letter:

'February 9. 1858
Ambrose happened to go to Town last week on the business of the projected Reformatory, and, in consequence of my suggestion, he called on F. Ward—who, he found, had got quite [a] wrong view of my letter to Bellasis of the 2nd—as if the whole House here were going to give up other employments and turn schoolmasters. He set this right, and the gentlemen in London, whom Bellasis represented, had their adjourned meeting on the day after; on Saturday last, February 6. In consequence of that meeting, Bellasis and Sir John Acton came down here yesterday, when they went over the premises, and talked over the whole plan.

We had no differences, and when they urged getting a number of Catholic names to back me up, I said that now that the Bishop here was for the scheme, I did not care for any thing, except to be right with Dr Weedall [President of Oscott College]. Of course the Cardinal, I said, must be told as soon as possible—that I was not the best man to write to him, since he had owed me an important letter these three months [see second note to letter of 7 Nov. to Wiseman]. Sir John Acton said that the London Oratory had pronounced our proposal here against the Rule.

After they were gone back in the evening, Ambrose told me that at their meeting at London on Wednesday (February 3) when my letter was read, those present had actually declined the proposition of my letter of February 2—and had drawn up an answer to that effect—which was to have been sent me from the adjourned meeting on Saturday, but Ambrose by his conversation with F. Ward on Friday February 5 had turned them all round in favour of my view, and sent Bellasis and Sir J Acton down here.

I should add that after my conversation with them here I hastily wrote down a memorandum, of which I had not time to take a copy to this effect: viz that I was freer to advise than in London, which have altered the view I took in conversation with you yesterday as to the line of conduct incumbent on me relative to the school project.[1]

Knowing the trouble you have taken about it in the midst of your many engagements, I am most unwilling to embarrass or dishearten you, but be sure I do not write this without a good deal of thought or without what I consider good reasons, which are better said to you than written.

I addressed a week ago a letter to your meeting, containing a proposal, which, if agreed to by our Fathers, could not be carried out without involving them in a great sacrifice of privacy and independence. As luckily it has not been answered, I take the opportunity thus offered me of withdrawing it, so far, as not to pledge myself, as that letter implied, to bring it before them again.

I am afraid of going too fast in a delicate matter; but this must not be taken to imply that I do not feel as warmly as before the desirableness of the object to which it relates, or am not as ready to do all in my power to co-operate in its accomplishment.

I am, My dear Bellasis Very sincerely Yours

John H Newman of the Oratory

Mr Serjeant Bellasis

to act, for I could advise abstractedly, but I must act as an Oratorian—advising, I said, no plan could be better than to let the school grow up under the shadow of this Oratory—acting I said that this could not be done in the way of supplying masters—that all we could do would be to supply "superintendence, a Father prefect for a time, and spiritual care—" that the closer it was to us, the more we could do for it, for our work was commonly "on our own homestead—" and that, if it was to be on our own homestead, we never could contemplate the care of more than a certain number of boys. This was the substance of what I said, though put more logically.

But when they were gone, and I reflected over what had been for a time determined on in their London meeting, and that they had been suddenly brought over, I felt the danger of their going back again, after the first excitement, and leaving me in the lurch. I should have all the responsibility and odium, besides seeming bent on carrying on a plan of my own for the sake of filling the rooms of the Oratory and getting rent. Moreover the London Oratory was likely to gossip at Rome on the matter—and, though I had a clear view that it was as little out of the way to take charge of a rich school than of a poor, and that this plan might be entered into by the Oratory, if Reformatories might, and ragged schools, and guilds, yet as it was a new thing it admitted of being misrepresented—and I might be asked for explanations at Rome.'

Therefore next day February 9, I sent Bellasis the following letter.

[1] At the meeting in London on 3 Feb. attended by Bellasis, Dodsworth, Macmullen, F. R. Ward and Wegg-Prosser, to consider the proposal in Newman's letter of 2 Feb., a divergence arose. Some advocated an independent school, over which Newman should have personal control for as long as he thought necessary, others wanted a school connected with the Oratory in the way that the existing Catholic schools were connected with religious bodies. At the adjourned meeting on 6 Feb., from which Dodsworth was absent, but which was joined by Acton, Allies and H. Wilberforce, it was agreed that Acton and Bellasis should visit Birmingham. They discussed the problem with Darnell and St John, who told Newman about the divergence in London. See also Acton's account in his letter of 17 Feb. to Döllinger, Victor Conzemius, *Ignaz von Döllinger, Lord Acton, Briefwechsel, I, 1850–1869*, Munich, 1963, pp. 125–7. Acton was astonished at the opposition of converts to Newman, 'Ich wusste gar nicht dass auch Convertiten so dumm und verächtlich von Newman dächten.' The hope was that the school would raise the educational level of Catholics, and thus lead on to a Catholic university in England.

Oy Bm Febr 10/58

My dear Renouf

Excuse my troubling you — but you have already written to that Agent of the Prince's and therefore I think you can do me this service more easily.

That former application did no good — but that is no matter. *This* he must listen too. [sic] He only sent (thro' Charles de Ligne) £75 in November, instead of £150. Now February is come. If he paid me quarterly (as he said he would and as the £75 implies) I ought to have another quarter, £75 now — but none has come that *I* know of. Perhaps a word to the de Lignes would be enough — If not, I must ask you the great kindness of writing — I think the Agent's name is Hubert.[1]

Don't think I don't covet the articles you gave me hope of — Egypt and Rome — because I did not notice them in my list — but I don't want to be unreasonable

Ever Yrs J H N

Do ask your wife to give and get me some good prayers for Fr Flanagan, tho' she does not know him, you do. We are most cut up

J H N

THURSDAY 11 FEBRUARY 1858   Edward returned   The H Kerrs passed thro to Clifton

The Oratory Birmingham Febry 12. 1858

My dear Bellasis,

Your letter quite expresses what I meant to convey, and better and in fewer words than I have put it myself.[2]

My letter of February 2 is now 'a suggested plan at present withdrawn,' yet, as such, admitting of being 'made use of.'

However, I have the greatest doubts, when it comes to the point, whether the Fathers here will ever consent to it. In a matter so nearly affecting the

---

[1] Scratton wrote on 10 Feb. that de Ligne had brought him a bill of exchange for £75, the previous day.

[2] Bellasis wrote on 11 Feb., 'The fact was we were all agreed that you were the person under whose absolute control the school ought to be, but all had not at first the same appreciation of the advantage of its connection with the Oratory. We are not surprised therefore, when it comes to the point, and you are to ask the concurrence of the Fathers to your plan, that you should hesitate to do so on behalf of persons less anxious than we had hoped, for their consent.'

comfort of individuals, I would not act except with their unanimous consent — and it is impossible to predict that this would be given, when every one with his own ideas and feelings weighed the whole matter.

I do not think the suggestion will be useless, even if impracticable — for the impossible plan may lead to the thought of other plans, which else would not be thought of at all.

What I wish you very much to get men to consider is, *what they propose to themselves to gain*, over existing schools — else, the door is left open to much disappointment.

I wish you did not seem so overworked. It is a shame you should not allow yourself some respite

Ever Yours very sincerely John H Newman of the Oratory

Mr Serjeant Bellasis.

TO MRS GORDON

The Oratory Birmingham February 13. 1858

My dear Mrs Gordon,

To day I have been celebrating a solemn Mass of Requiem as suitable to this day.[1] And in the Memento of the Living, I did not forget to include you and your daughter.

At the end of five years you can bear my speaking of our great Loss — to me it is as great as ever, and his thought is ever in my mind. And be sure, it will remain a perpetual memory in the Oratory, while there are any of us alive who knew him. I hope some day you will come and see the place where he sleeps — We are getting it now nearly as it should be — looking for our own joining him there, one by one, as our own time comes. Only may we be prepared, as he was.

Do not forget to think and pray for me, for us, my dear Mrs Gordon. I did not answer your kind letter, thinking to call on you when I was in London the other day — but the distances from place to place are so great there, that I found it impossible — and I had suddenly to return to Dr Manning, when I was leaving him — from a sudden affliction having befallen him, like that which this day recalls.[2]

With every kind thought to you and your daughter, I am, My dear Mrs Gordon, Most sincerely Yours in Xt

John H Newman of the Oratory

Mrs Gordon

[1] Mrs Gordon's son, John Joseph Gordon, died on 13 Feb. 1853.
[2] The death of La Primaudaye. See diary for 21 Jan.

TO M. KEEFE

[13 February 1858][1]

Dear Revd Sir,

I thank you very much for sending me the Letter of credit in payment of the munificent bequest of the late Revd Mr Moylan to the Catholic University. I have sent it to our Secretary, who will put it into the hands of Mr Flannery, whom the Archbishops have appointed to receive the University Collections

I am &c J H N

TO ROBERT ORNSBY

The Oratory Birmingham ⌐Febry 13. 1858⌐

My dear Ornsby,

⌐I have not wished to renew any negociation with Dr Quinn — much less to appear as one of two parties in an arbitration — and if I could recollect my words to you or Mr Butler, I think I could explain them consistently with this feeling.[2] I think him simply unreasonable — and I have no great hope any thing will come of any new arrangement — but I am quite willing that the Dean or Faculty of Philosophy and Letters should draw up a general scheme for the arrangement of the relations between the University and the Collegiate Houses — and I will give it my best consideration. Also, if Mr Butler will present me categorical propositions from Dr Quinn, I will answer them categorically. The only sense in which I can contemplate what you have called an arbitration, is, that, from a profound sense that nothing will come of any more direct correspondence between him and me,[3] I will answer any questions which any of *you* like to propose to me.⌐

I wish I were able at this minute to suggest a lodger to you — one struck me, who must have occurred to you — but it might be impossible[4] I am glad you are better.

Ever Yours affly J H N

P.S. ⌐In my memorandum which I gave Mr Butler before I left Dublin, I suggested Dr Quinn's school becoming a pure Collegiate House (I think) — [5] If Mr Flannery is going, could he ⟨Dr Q.⟩ move his *University* students to St Patrick's?⌐

[1] On 12 Feb. M. Keefe, a curate at Kilmoyanny, Kilkenny, sent a bequest of £50 from Thomas Moylan, Parish Priest of Windgap in the Diocese of Ossory.
[2] Quinn had said he would defer removing his pupils from the University until Easter. On 12 Feb. Ornsby wrote to ask if an arbitration would be possible.
[3] Newman cancelled here the words 'all I can say is that.'
[4] Ornsby was moving to a larger house, 21 Gardiner Place, Dublin, and so wanted a lodger. In his draft, instead of this paragraph, Newman wrote, 'I suppose Robertson would not become your lodger, or would not be a quiet one.'
[5] See letter of 19 Nov. 1857 to Butler.

TO W. G. WARD

The Oratory Birmingham. Febr 13/58

My dear Ward[1]

Thank you very much for your pamphlet — I can't be supposed to have done more than to read part of it in the few hours during which I have had it, but I have read enough to see that every priest in England who reads it, whether he ultimately agrees with you or not, has reason to be thankful to you for it.[2] I don't scruple to say what looking at it as a practical matter I have a right to say, that you are doing us all a great benefit, which is the more necessary, because priests, as other men when they have been engaged in a work for a long time, get into a routine, and forget the views and lose the feelings, with which they set about it.

For myself personally, I can only say that as a matter of feeling and view, your doctrine is that to which my mind has always turned and turns — and that I think the contrary view methodistical. Also, it is the view I have always supposed to be the Catholic one. When I was at Propaganda they gave me there Busenbaum, and only the other day I turned up notes of mine with extracts from him, in which I find the following 'Non sufficit attritio existimata tantum licet inculpabiliter' 'qui non habet propositum efficax, id est cum quo non possit consistere affectus erga mortale non est sufficienter attritus.'[3]

I have never known the existence of any other doctrine

Ever Yours affly John H. Newman of the Oratory.

W. G. Ward Esqr

TO MRS WILLIAM HENRY BUCKLE

February 14th. 1858 The Oratory, Birmingham.

My dear Mrs. Buckle,

I wish you and Mr. Buckle joy with all my heart on the news you tell me — and do not mean of course to leave your daughter out of my congratulations, whom I have seen so lately. And since I have seen Mr. Athy so lately too, and not so very far off from the time I saw your daughter, I may take the

---

[1] The autograph of this letter is not to be found. On a copy of it, W. G. Ward wrote 'Copy of a letter on a privately printed pamphlet of mine on *attrition*.' This was *Appendix to Five Lectures on Attrition, Contrition, and Sovereign Love*. For the *Five Lectures* see letter of 6 July 1857 to Ward.

[2] Ward propounded the thesis that 'In order to a valid absolution, the penitent must elicit an act of detestation, which shall possess so great a degree of efficacity as to be incompatible with mortal sin.' He then discussed how far such an act was elicited by a reckless sinner who, on the approach of death, sent for a priest.

[3] Newman's copy of Hermann Busembaum's *Medulla Theologiae Moralis*, two volumes, Rome 1844, in the first of which he wrote 'J H Newman Propaganda 1847,' is still in his room at Birmingham. Newman's quotations are in Vol. I, pp. 520 and 521. *Lib*. VI, *Tract*. IV, I, ii.

liberty of congratulating him too.[1] If you will be so kind as to tell me the day when the happy event is to take place, I will say Mass for them upon it.

I hope by this time you have got on some way in your history, you will find the public can bear a second volume at once.[2] It is astonishing how much more is possible now, than was only a few years ago. By the bye, Callista was to have had two volumes, and Burns limited it to one.

Most sincerely yours in Christ, John H. Newman of the Oratory.
Mrs. Buckle.

P.S.   I find on reading over my letter, I have not expressed, which I do now, my sense of your great kindness in going out of your way to tell me what must be so deeply and intimately interesting to you and Mr. Buckle.

TO LADY HENRY KERR

The Oratory Birmingham. Febr 14. 1858.
My dear Lady Henry,

Fr Flanagan thanks you very much for your kind and acceptable present, which just answers what he wants. He will not forget your hints about the respiration.

I have said one of the three Masses and shall continue my first vacant days.

Thank you for what you say about Lady Cecilia. I saw her at Rome and though she may not suspect was much struck with her. I can hardly say why.[3]

Pray for me and believe me to be My dear Lady Henry
Most sincerely Yours in Xt

John H Newman of the Oratory
The Lady Henry Kerr.

TO ROBERT MACDERMOTT

⌐Febry 14/58⌐[4]

Answered that I would forward any application from him to Dr Leahy but that I did not like to go on for 4 years drawing perhaps £30.000 with

---

[1] The Buckles lived at Kingstown. The Athy family came from Galway.

[2] See letter of 9 Aug. 1857 to Ornsby.

[3] Lady Cecil Kerr (1835–66), was the elder of Lady Lothian's daughters. Newman saw her in Rome in 1856. She joined the Sacred Heart nuns in 1859 in France, and died of influenza six years later at Tours.

[4] MacDermott wrote on 12 Feb., 'I am very much pressed by creditors of the School of Medicine for their accounts and fear that if they are longer delayed they may take proceedings against us. . . .' MacDermott apologized for troubling Newman so often about this subject. See also letter of 27 Feb. to Leahy.

but a general leave and without annual audit. If Dr Leahy gave the money, he had the responsibility[1]

FROM CARDINAL WISEMAN

London Feb. 13. 1858

My dear Dr Newman

It was not till yesterday that I was in a condition to reply satisfactorily to your important letter of November 7, 1857. The reason was this. In the private letter accompanying the approbation of our having a new version of Holy Scripture there was added this clause 'cum reservatione tamen finalis approbationis Sanctae Sedi.'

The carrying out of this provision would have most materially interfered with your plan.

In whatever way *final* was to be taken, it involved the sending, before ultimately printing all the version to Rome; whether in sheets, or all together in MS. The Holy See might have sent it to Dr Dixon, or Dr Kenrick, or appointed examiners in Rome—all of which would have caused great delay, and uncertainty; besides the expense and trouble of corresponding for explanations.

If the Holy See intended to name revisors in England, there was the possibility of its appointing some of the very persons whom you might wish to consult, and who without knowing it, might have been first parties and then judges in the case.

I therefore wrote on the subject at length to Rome, explained your plan, and the importance, for economy, of revising sheet by sheet *finally*. Assuming, therefore, that this final revision could only be made in England (for as I explained there were no persons in Rome whose judgment could be preferred to persons previously consulted here, and as being an English work, fruit of a Synod etc, it should not be sent to any other part of the English-speaking world) I respectfully proposed, that the Holy See would *at once* name the person or persons to whom it meant to refer the final revision, empowering him or them to approve etc pari passu with the work, so as to make their final reference or report to Rome, as soon as the work was finished.

The answer to this letter came yesterday, and I enclose it in copy. Allow me however to observe that to facilitate the selection of the Holy See I mentioned the names of persons who I thought would be fit to form the council of revision—as Mgr Newsham, Can. Walker, who advised Dr Lingard throughout his 'New Version'[1] and several others, not mentioning myself, nor my Coadjutor.

You will see, by the reply, that I am appointed Revisor conjointly with the Bishops of Southwark and Birmingham, to whom I send copies of the appointment, but without this explanation. You may have occasion to see the Bishop of B. [Birmingham] and communicate this to him. I shall see them both soon, and will then be able to explain.[2]

I hope that now arrangements may begin for commencing the work, on which I trust that God will send His most copious blessing.

I am ever Dear F. Newman Your affecte Servt in Xt

N. Card. Wiseman.

The Very Rev F. Newman P.O.DD.

[1] John Lingard brought out *A New Version of the Four Gospels with notes*, in 1836.
[2] Cf. letters of 2 and 3 March to Ullathorne.

TO CARDINAL WISEMAN

Febr 14/58

My dear Lord Cardinal

I thank your Eminence for the kind trouble you have been at on the subject of the Revisors of the Translation. I have communicated your letter, as you wished, to our Bishop.

As to the main subject of my letter of November 7 — viz the ways and means — I fear I must modify what I then said so far as this — that I see only two ways of proceeding 1 that I should have the copy right and the whole expenses — or 2 that I should not be pledged to any given sum as the outside of the requisite expense.

I am, My dear Lord Cardinal &c J H N

The Cardinal Wiseman

FROM CARDINAL WISEMAN

London, Feb 15/58

My dear F. Newman

The Bishops will meet in about a fortnight, when I will bring your proposals under their consideration; since it is a matter of synodical origin, and consequently to be decided by them corporately.

Supposing that they adopted the alternative of your having the Copyright, would that mean that the proprietorship of the Text would be entirely vested in you for ever or for a limited period, so that no new issues could be made in any form except by yourself or your legal representatives.

If so must not certain terms be agreed on for such issues etc. Or would a right be established like that of the King's printer in the Ang. Est. [Anglican Establishment] who I suppose regulates the publication himself, without further interference of the ecclesiastical authority.

Or suppose that after publication, further correction were requisite, how could this be made? Would the holders of the copyright be obliged to admit them, say if agreed to in Synod, or would the copyright preclude any such further correction? I should be glad to know your definite plan for the copyright plan.

As to the second plan, could you fix *no* limits to possible expences, nor make an approximative estimate, that we could have examined by a practical printer, here in London.

Suppose, for example that we provided for all the expences definable of salaries to translators, and transcribers, fittings books etc, and all other expences, and then looked ourselves to the mere printing, contracting so as to pay back those first definite expences, could not that be managed?

It will be difficult to induce a number of persons to pledge themselves to an unlimited expence, without power of checking or drawing out. No one will refuse unlimited confidence to your accuracy and care: but people not rich feel very much hampered and uneasy when they do not know what liabilities they may be running into. And I forecast this difficulty here, and I should like to have *an approach to* an estimate at least—say a *maximum* possible.

I am ever Your affecte Servt in Xt

N. Card. Wiseman

WEDNESDAY 17 FEBRUARY 1858 Ash Wednesday

The Oratory, Birmingham Ash Wednesday. Febry 17. 1858

My dear Stewart

I was glad of any thing which gave you a reason for writing — tho' I did not wish poor Berner's death to be that reason.[1] I don't think I have seen him since he was an undergraduate at Trinity — he was my junior — Alas — how time goes and how it ought to make one look out. Nearly all my contemporaries at Trinity, whom I can hear of, are gone — or at least I counted up a good many of them some time ago, whose deaths I had heard of.

Fr Flanagan's illness is so direct a call from St Philip to stay here, that it is as if he wished to put the matter beyond all doubt. Independent of my duties to him as a member of the Congregation he set up, which, tho' not confirmed by a vow, are in my feeling as binding as if they were, still even as Superior of this Oratory, I have a call on me, from my dear brother's illness, which nothing can explain away. Fr Flanagan has simply broken himself with work — there is no one of us who had so many things upon him, and whose sudden suspension from all his functions could cause us so much confusion and perplexity. In some of those functions no one can supply his place, for they are personal; in others I am not the person to do so; but his formal offices in the Congregation I can at least attempt to do in whole or part. So now, Lent beginning, I am going into the Confession — [2] and I am becoming novice-master which will take a good deal of my thoughts, if not of my time — and I am going to take a portion of the duties of F Minister. All this must last at least till his return, which is to be by St Philip's day, May 26. His own absence is not our whole inconvenience — for Fr Tillotson is going too, to take care of him — and though he has not faculties for the Confessional, he is one of our principal preachers, has much to do with the work-house, and is in various ways most useful to us

You will not wonder then that I am likely to have very little time for University matters for the next several months. As to the Translation of Scripture, it is for the present all but put on the shelf.

I don't think that my friends at Dublin would think it a bad arrangement for me to remain a sort of honorary Rector, as I am now, provided only a good Vice Rector could be got. So that, though that is not secured yet, still no step has hitherto been made *in a wrong direction*, which is important.

As to my own health, yes, I have reason to be very thankful. I don't

---

[1] Ralph Berners, third son of the Archdeacon of Suffolk Henry Berners, of Wolverstone Park, Suffolk, was matriculated at Trinity College on 12 Feb. 1820, at the age of 17. He later moved to Magdalen, where he took his B.A.

[2] Before Flanagan's illness rendered it necessary, Newman on returning from Ireland, hesitated as to whether to take on confessional work again. See a paper in which he balanced the pros and cons in the volume of his Oratorian papers.

believe I have any thing seriously the matter with me. It is, I believe, only indigestion. But then it has gone on so long, perhaps 30 years, and for nearly as long (as far as I can remember) somewhat affecting the heart, and now affecting it more distinctly, that I cannot be without some apprehesion, if I cannot alleviate the symptoms or their cause, that there is a tendency to heart complaint in my indisposition. But after all, think of an old man, like me, talking of his apprehension of tendencies to illness!

I am sorry to hear your boy is not well yet. It is quite a long time since his illness. You do not say how you are yourself, and Mrs Stewart.

When you see Dr Dunne, will you tell him I have not forgotten his suggestion about the Philosophy of Religion. At present my hitch is the question of Protestant works on Evidence — how far they are admissible. Not only are some of them good ones, but they have the advantage of being in English. Of course there are difficulties on the other side — I am having a correspondence with Fr O'Reilly on the subject.[1]

My kindest remembrances to all friends.

Believe me, My dear Stewart Ever Yours affectly in Xt.

John H Newman of the Oratory.

James Stewart Esq.

THURSDAY 18 FEBRUARY 1858   Frederic went to London to consult Dr Watson
FRIDAY 19 FEBRUARY   Stanislas and Robert left for Pau. (my letter to Ornsby confirms *this* date. vid below Febr 26 Mar 2)

TO CARDINAL WISEMAN

Febry 19/58

My dear Lord Cardinal

I thank you very much for your clear statement of the primâ facie difficulties which attend upon the alternative which I ventured to submit to your Eminence on the mode of meeting the expenses of the New Translation of Scripture.

As to the wish with which your letter concludes that you should 'have an approach to an estimate at least, e.g. a maximum possible,' an estimate, as you say shortly before, 'of salaries to translators and transcribers, fittings, books etc and all other expenses,' to the exclusion of the 'mere printing,' which your Eminence proposes to leave as a separate matter with the Bishops, I beg to remind you ⟨altered⟩[2] that this was the very subject of my letter of November 7 last year, in which I came to the conclusion that 'the additional expense of the translation (over and above that of merely bringing out an

---

[1] Cf. letter of 18 Jan. to O'Reilly.
[2] i.e. Newman altered this phrase in the letter as sent.

Edition of Holy Scripture, which of course can be made to pay itself by the sale of the copies printed,' would be £1000. I added 'Of this sum, a good part would be ultimately received by the profits of the sale of 20.000 stereotyped copies;' and in this again I have been fortunate enough to anticipate in November another [of] your Eminence's present remarks that the Bishops could 'look to the mere printing, contracting so as to pay back those first definite expenses.'

My maximum then for 'Prolegomena, Books, Desks etc. Transcribers, Purchase of type and compositors, and sundries,' in November was £1000; nor am I prepared at this date to give any other, nor can I answer your Eminence's present question in any other way than I did then.

But in the interval which you have allowed me for consideration it has pressed upon me, that I really cannot attempt to give any maximum estimate at all. This I laid before you in my letter of last Sunday, expressing my sense of its impossibility in the proposal of alternative courses to which it led.

The great difficulty of the problem seems to me to lie in a quarter which I mentioned, but did not dwell on in my letter of November 7 in *the unavoidable preliminary printing expenses.* Transcription is a formidable work when a volume of the size of the Bible is concerned, and when a number of copies is required. And even the best written copy is cumbrous to handle from its size, and difficult to use freely and familiarly, and to master accurately. The Printing then of a preliminary Edition seems almost necessary. Further, if the Revisors receive it only in successive portions, they will not have an opportunity of comparing portion with portion; consequently it is desirable to have type sufficient for the whole edition to stand in type at once. Moreover, in a page of double columns, and of different characters of type, what resetting would not be necessary on the insertion or omission even of a single note! yet how many notes will have to be added, omitted, or altered! If in ordinary printing corrections sometimes make the cost half as much again, what will it be in the case of a number of various judgments acting on a sacred subject matter and on questions belonging or proximate to faith.

Then, as to what I have called Prolegomena, in my letter of November 7. Certainly I should wish previously to get as many judgments as possible, on the principles and the mode of translation as I can. It seems to me quite contrary to the spirit of the commission which has been so condescendingly given to me by the Synod, that I should act as an individual, in preparing my version[,] and not as expressing the sense of the English Church at this time. Even Dr Kenrick, a Bishop of his Church, has not carried his Church with him, when he translated, as he could with propriety do, on his own judgment. Can I wish to produce a translation which would be made on principles, which the Revisors, when they received it, could not approve, or which though they passed, would be so coldly received by English Catholics that it would fall out of their hands, from their want of sympathy in it, except for such formal allowance? I am but the servant of the church, and an unworthy one:

I am no St Jerome, 'in sacris Scripturis exponendis Doctor maximus,'[1] and giving almost a life to the transation. I really cannot act at all except as the representative of my Fathers and brothers in the sacred ministry and the body of the faithful, who have so much more right than I can have, to a judgment on such great matters as I am undertaking. But such Prolegomena, as on this score become necessary, involve an expense which I cannot conjecture, and think others can conjecture as little. Hence I do not see my way to hope much from your Eminence's suggestion, that, if I made an approximate estimate, it could be satisfactorily examined by a practical printer in London.

These considerations made me lean to the other side of the alternative which I proposed; viz that the Bishops should give me the copyright; I was led to it the more from the circumstance of one Bishop stating to me his impression that they would not keep the copyright in their own hands; an impression which seems justified by a remark of your Eminence's of which I quite see the force, that people not rich feel very much hampered and uneasy when they do not know what liability they may be running into.

Considering then that the Bishops would any how dispose of the copyright, I supposed they would feel the necessity of making such conditions with the parties to whom they transferred it, as would serve to secure to them for ever the control over the translation which is ecclesiastically necessary. Whatever hold they retained over it when they placed the copyright in the hands of a publisher, they could retain when they made it over to me. But I have no wish at all for the copyright. I only do not see any other way of solving the difficulties of the case.[2]

J H N.[3]

[1] Traditional title of St Jerome.
[2] To make assurance doubly sure Newman wrote also to Ullathorne on 2 and 3 March. The English Bishops met on 10 March and resolved that the copyright should be reserved to Newman. The official notice of this decision was sent to Newman on 11 Oct. 1858. See letter of 18 July 1858 to Caswall, and also that of 7 Dec. 1858 to P. N. Lynch, Bishop of Charleston.
[3] Newman, now or earlier, made notes about the principles of translation to be followed:
'1. It is for the use of the Catholic public
2. The notes must not be learned, or controversial or spiritual—but simply explanatory of difficulties in the text.
3. Considering it is desirable that the volume should not be unnecessarily large, the notes should be concise.
4 As to the Translation, Latin words must come in, when they have a theological import, therefore justice, and consummated.
5 Ask the Cardinal what *edition* of the Vulgate should be taken—are they all the same? I suppose so.
6 Not to supersede other annotated Bibles but to give the *text*, which [with] only such notes as cannot be helped.'
'1 On how far we may go from the Vulgate.
2. On the *language* of the Vulgate.
3. On the standard text for version—Rheims?
4. Principles, (1) to alter as little as possible (2) to take just one book and then another e.g. Psalms—Gospels—Epistles—Cantica Canticorun—Prophets—Job.'

TO ROBERT ORNSBY

The Oratory Birmingham ⌐Febry 20. 1858⌐

My dear Ornsby

Some Professor lately, I think Dr Lyons, has written to me ⌐on the subject of⌐ your letter of this morning — viz ⌐Lectures to young men of the Middle Class.¹ I referred him to Mr Sullivan;⌐ and for this reason — that, as you must recollect, *he* had a strong opinion against such Lectures from experience, at the time when the application came before the Council last year.²

⌐I agree with him so far, that there is great danger of interfering with the real duties of the Professors and the formal system of teaching, if such Lectures are introduced.

I agree with you in thinking that *in itself* a system of such Lectures is highly desirable.

There is great danger of our making ourselves mere popular Lecturers — and no fruit coming after all from such misapplication of our strength.⌐ A Professor has but a definite store of strength and time, if he gives it to one thing, he cannot give it to another.

⌐I am very sceptical too about the power of attention, of young men, after having been all day in the shops.⌐ I much suspect they will be presenting requests, after the fashion of your Kilkenny friends, for something not 'too dry,' and 'more taking.'³ I don't think we should be able to give them any real education.

⌐At the same time it is a great thing to *employ* the time of young men of an evening.⌐ It is better they should be awake or asleep in a lecture room, than in many other places which they might otherwise frequent. It is better too than that they should go to Trinity College, much better than they should go to the School of Industry.⁴

If any Professors will volunteer, and will make a point of the time they give to these Lectures not interfering with the real performance of their

¹ The Evening Classes had been begun at the same time as the University, in Nov. 1854, but had been discontinued, owing to the small attendance. This was caused partly by the severe winter, and partly because some expected them to be mere displays, rather than occasions for hard intellectual work. Newman tried to set this right in a letter to the *University Gazette*, (April 1855), p. 420. See Volume XVI, Appendix 3, and *Idea*, p. 481.

In May 1857 a spontaneous request was made for the resumption of the evening lectures, and this was still under discussion, when Ornsby wrote to Newman on 19 Feb. that a further deputation of young men had lately appealed to Scratton. They wished to learn 'Latin, English composition, mathematics, chemistry etc etc,' and were engaged in the shops during the day. They offered to pay £1 a year.

² This was on 13 Jan. 1857. On 15 Jan. the statute passed the Senate, which enabled those who attended the evening classes to pass examinations and graduate.

³ Ornsby wrote in his letter that the Kilkenny young men wished him to lecture there, 'but think my subject, (Demosth[enes], Cic.[ero] and Burke) too dry. They ask me to select a more taking subject!'

⁴ Ornsby maintained that if nothing was done for the young men, they would ask Trinity College to provide them with evening classes. Some of them had been to the School of Industry and had been disgusted, having heard attacks on Christianity.

University duties in the received system of study, I think they will be engaging in a very charitable work. I call it charitable, for, however desirable, or even abstractedly imperative, I cannot hope much more from it, (in the case of youths who are engaged all the morning already) than the keeping them out of mischief, and inflicting one or two good principles and useful facts and historical truths on their memory. But perhaps I need to be better informed.

If you are able to do as much as I have suggested, I will gladly co-operate in the work[1]

Ever Yrs affly J H Newman

R Ornsby Esqr

Fr Flanagan went off yesterday with Fr Tillotson

TO JOHN STANISLAS FLANAGAN

The Oratory Bm Febry 21. 1858

My dear Stanislas

You have sent me a sad birthday present — but we must take these things as they come to us, and be thankful.[2]

Your letter is very full and explicit; yet there are some questions still to be answered. I will set them down. First, however, the question is *how* we are to get them answered. Ambrose says that you must go to Dr Watson again; Nicholas that it is worth while to go to some great man in Paris. I incline to a second physician to London. *But in all I say and shall say, recollect, I wish your judgment to be the final one, not mine.* I say this, because, in such a matter, nothing will be done well, which is not your own doing.

I think then, to give my own opinion, that the matter is serious enough to have a second opinion upon it. I do not apprehend any thing of immediate danger — but, as in the case of Nicholas two years ago we had two judgments, or might have had (for I was not here) so I think in your case, there might well be reference had to two physicians. But, mind, not to determine what the matter is with you, (for I take Dr Watson's opinion to a *matter of fact*, as quite decisive), but to determine the *course of treatment* to be adopted towards you, just as we might know Nicholas's *illness*, but might not know *how* to cure him.

Whether then you go to Dr Watson again, or to someone else, or to a French doctor, I want the following questions answered, which I have set down during a conversation with the Fathers.

---

[1] It was eventually agreed that Evening Classes should be given by those professors who were willing to lecture. The Classes began on 15 April with an attendance of nearly a hundred. For Newman's lecture to them, see diary for 2 Nov. 1858. Cf. *McGrath*, p. 459.

[2] Flanagan sent from London the report of Dr Watson on his lungs.

1. For how long you are to be out of England? you do not say — but the mention of Madeira makes us suppose that you are to be *out for a year*. If you are out only till the end of May, I should not think it worth while to take a second opinion, for it matters not (except the trouble) whether you are at Malaga or Madeira for three months. If you tell us you are only to be out of England for three months, you will take an enormous load off mine, off our minds.

2. What is the *ultimate good* of going? Will Dr Watson say that he thinks going to Madeira for a year would have a fair chance of setting you up? If so, then again a load is taken off my mind — for considering your generally good constitution, and the care we have been at to arrest your illness in its beginning, I should have a very sanguine hope that you will come back, please God, well. But if he said only, that it would *retard the progress* of an inevitable complaint, and give it the *opportunity*, if possible, of dying out, if he is doing with you only what is done to so many poor souls, or rather bodies, to worry them about to place to place [sic], and to make them pass their remaining time in exile, among strangers, and in desolation, then of course I should wish you to do as you *would*, but should have no wish that you *should choose* to go away from us.

3 Further, if you are to go to Madeira for so much as a year, then comes the question, Is such a place as Madeira a heavy penance upon you? If you can make up your mind to it, not now merely, but as you anticipate you shall feel through the length of a year, without much effort, I am quite satisfied — but, if you think it is likely to weigh upon your mind to be so far from friends, work, and news for so long, and to be among bad Catholics, and squabbling and fierce Protestants, who both fight with each other and with you, then this is a reason for getting a second opinion about the *place*. I know that *equableness* of climate through the year is the desideratum — and that, I suspect, is not to be found any where in the basin of the Mediterranean — for you would have to shift about from place to place with the seasons. Therefore you must look elsewhere, and few spots indeed are known, which offer what is required. The only other place I have heard of, is Barbadoes — which is much more in the highroad of the World then Madeira — but it is, I believe, almost exclusively Protestant — perhaps with out a Chapel. Fr Frederic, however, mentions St Thomas's.[1]

4. A further question is, whether, if you must go to Madeira, you might stay at Lisbon till May — in which case Robert could stay with you there till then, see you embark, and then return here.

5. As to the said Robert's going with you to Madeira, I have some difficulties — one is whether the climate would agree with him. Supposing it to relax him — I know hot climates are bad for such as he — I have been told so as to India — tho' Madeira has not such heat. This to me is a great difficulty.

---

[1] In the West Indies, one of the Leeward Islands.

6. One other thought strikes me, which I have only mentioned to Ambrose — and that is about F. Frederic's accompanying you to Madeira. I fear I must say that I think he needs such a chance — but I am mentioning him merely for your sake, in order for you to tell me *whether you had rather go alone or with him.*

I have but to add that, if Robert prefers coming down here *this* week, to kicking his heels in London, he can do so.

I should say that Crawley has sent your letter privately as a friend to Dr Charlton of Newcastle, who is a Catholic and has a name for his knowledge of complaints of the lungs, to ask whether he thinks any other place besides Madeira would do for the case as stated in your letter. We shall hear from him on Wednesday

Ever Yrs affly J H N

MONDAY 22 FEBRUARY 1858   Henry in pleurisy — confined to bed   Wingfield came

TO JOHN STANISLAS FLANAGAN

The Oratory Bm Febry 22. 1858

My dear Stanislas

I am sorry to say that Henry is struck down with a pleurisy; and Dr Johnson has just ordered a blister on him.

I am like Job with one trouble after another, and Eliphaz and Baldad saying that it is because St Philip has given me up

Ever Yrs affly J H N

P.S. We put a mustard plaster on him directly, which relieved him. When Dr Johnson came, he ordered him a blister on the same place. Dr J. says it is a sharp inflammation on a particular part. He ⟨Dr J.⟩ hopes that H. will be up on Wednesday — but it is plain, especially with the wind, and coming March, he must not expose himself, and we are in great difficulty, as you may understand, about the Union [Workhouse]. Austin might take it, but then as to his work — I wish you would candidly tell me whether on considering, you think we could do without Robert. I will not let Ambrose take outdoor work extra — nor (I suppose) Nicholas this trying season — then what can Edward do? Please God, I will take as many Confessions in *Church* as ever I can.

Strange that now that we have the Confessionals, we should have no Confessors

The Oratory Bm ⌈Febr 22. 1858⌉

My dear H W

Thank you for your kind remembrance.

⌈My birthday present was a letter from dear Stanislas from London, saying that he was sent to Madeira. This day a second has come, in the shape of a pleurisy which has suddenly struck down Fr Bittleston.⌉

And, I, like Job, have friends, Baldads, and Sophars, who lament so very much, that I am so given up by God and St Philip.

You may think in consequence that I have a good deal of work on my hands. I will send you another article as soon as I can — but cannot promise. ⌈I am nearly well myself — it was a gathering, not a boil.⌉ I have been plagued with such for some years. They are quite an epidemic. So at least they have been in Ireland, and, I see by the papers, in Calcutta. They are a sort of carbuncle — and if bad, would be very serious.

Ever Yours affly John H Newman

P.S. I am quite well. Pray for us, for we are much tried. What are the Penitents of these two Fathers to do, Lent too beginning

Febry 23. Since I wrote yesterday, Stanislas has been to *my* Doctor Williams. He pronounces his lungs to be rather worse than Dr Watson did — but gives a more hopeful prospect of what may be expected. He thinks he may get over it, and in a short time, but his mother died of consumption. He is going to Pau.

Fr Bittleston is better today — ⌈You may think how hard up we are for hands. Thank God, Ambrose is a good deal better — and I quite well.⌉

I don't forget tomorrow.[1]

TUESDAY 23 FEBRUARY 1858 [Henry] better

The Oy Bm Febry 23/58

My dear S

In haste. Thank T.F. [Terence Flanagan] very much indeed for his letter, which was most kind to write. Also you for yours.[2]

---

[1] Wilberforce's eldest son, and Newman's godson, John, died on 24 Feb. 1847, aged eleven.

[2] Stanislas Flanagan and Robert Tillotson were staying with the former's cousin in Kensington. The letters of the two Flanagans described the visit to Dr Williams the previous day. He confirmed that Stanislas had consumption in both lungs, did not think he need go to Madeira, but must go to a warm climate for three months, after which there was a fair chance that he would be quite cured.

We think *Pau*. As the weather gets warmer, you might descend from Pau to the sea, as to Perpignan, if the *physician at Pau approves*, I want you to have sea air.

Robert must go with you.

We can manage the workhouse without him.

Henry, thank God, is better this morning but *I shall not let him* take any work for some weeks

Love to R [Robert]

Ever Yrs affly J H N

I spoke of R's coming *here* for the week, because he said to me 'Had I not better remain in Bm [Birmingham] till the day S. starts from London? I don't know where to go in London.'

WEDNESDAY 24 FEBRUARY 1858   [Henry had] relapse

CIRCULAR LETTER

(PRIVATE)   Oratory, Birmingham, February 24, 1858.

CATHOLIC CHAPEL,
IN THE BIRMINGHAM UNION WORKHOUSE.

Father Flanagan, of the Birmingham Oratory, in asking from his friends the means of relieving him of a debt of £93. 6s. which he has incurred in fitting up and furnishing a Chapel for the Catholic poor in the Birmingham workhouse, offers the following explanation of his application.

The New Workhouse lies beyond the limits of the Oratorian Mission, at Edgbaston, and at the distance of a mile and a half from the Oratory; but, at the wish of the Bishop and Clergy of Birmingham, and with the consent of his Superior and Congregation, he undertook the charge of the Catholics in it, in the summer of 1852, from which date it has continued in the hands of the Oratory.

The Workhouse may be regarded as equivalent to a considerable parish; for, though there may not be more than 150 Catholics there at any one time, (exclusive of children) still, since the population is continually shifting, and consists of persons who generally have been for years absent from their duties, with a proportion of aged and sick far greater than in an average parish, while, from the nature of the case, all are paupers, the ministerial work which it entails is such, as to be exceeded only by that of some of the larger parishes in our more populous towns.

The number of Catholics who pass under the Chaplain's care in the course of the year, as nearly as can be calculated, is 600, involving pretty nearly 600 general confessions.

About 30 are always in hospital, or bed-ridden.

There were 48 baptisms in the year 1857.

The deaths average one a week, or 52 in the year.

Boys and girls under instruction, or in preparation for the sacraments, (exclusive of children under seven years of age), average 30.

From 1852 to 1856 these poor people were accustomed to come to Mass at the Oratory; but there were great difficulties in this arrangement; such as, the distance between it and the Workhouse for the aged and weakly, and the temptation which beset those who had the free use of their limbs, of spending the day in the town instead of going to Church, a breach of discipline naturally involving, as its punishment, the forfeiture of the privilege of attending Mass at all. To these were added the impossibility of any of them going to the Oratory on wet Sundays, their absence from all parochial preaching and teaching, the expense incurred by the Chaplain in giving breakfast to 80 or 90 at the Oratory after Communion on the great festivals, the confusion occasioned in the Workhouse by the early hour of their Sunday expedition, and the jealousy of the Protestant paupers at others having a leave of absence beyond its walls on Sunday which they themselves did not enjoy.

To remedy this unsatisfactory state of things, the Workhouse officials, who have ever behaved with the greatest civility to Father Flanagan, themselves proposed to him the furnishing of a room at home for a Chapel. The proposal was favourably entertained by the Guardians, who, in April 1856, passed a Resolution, which received the sanction of the Poor Law Board in London, to the effect that a suitable room should be set apart in the Workhouse as a place of worship for its Catholic inmates. These proceedings at the same time received the cordial sanction of the Bishop and the Catholics of Birmingham. The Vicar-General wrote to Father Flanagan, that — 'it was a great object to secure Mass for the poor Catholics in the Workhouse, because other large towns might be induced, by the example of the Birmingham Guardians, to grant the same privilege.' He adds — 'I am sure the Bishop and all of us will be very glad and thankful, if you can carry out your charitable design.'

An influential layman added, 'The Chapel should be decently and respectably fitted up, and a subscription should be got up for the purpose.' This gentleman subscribed £5 himself. Other Catholics of the place gave Father Flanagan equal encouragement. The result of these promises is given in the appended list of subscriptions.[1]

In pursuance of the resolution of the Board, a handsome, lofty, and commodious room, capable of holding 100 persons, was given to Father Flanagan, with an adjacent room for a sacristy; with the stipulation, indeed, that the ministers of Protestant denominations should have the right, if they

---

[1] In the first draft this sentence continued, 'Which, considering the few Catholics in Birmingham who are in circumstances to be liberal, is as large perhaps as might reasonably be expected.'

pleased, of assembling there the paupers of their own persuasions respectively, at times when the Catholic Chaplain did not use the room, a stipulation, however, which practically leads to no inconvenience, as the non-Catholic paupers are under the care of the Chaplain of the Established Church, who has a Chapel of his own in the house.

The fittings up of the Chapel consist of sanctuary rails, altar, triptych with three paintings, and carpet; five sets of vestments, and vestment-press; pulpit, font, and confessional: the altar and triptych, with cross and candles being so arranged as to admit of being inclosed under lock and key out of the times of service.

Since the opening of the Chapel, on the Feast of our Lady of Dolours, 1856, there has been on Sundays, in the morning Mass and Sermon, in the afternoon Rosary and Instruction, with from 12 to 20 Communicants every Sunday.

The necessary expenses of books, rosaries, alms, etc., amounting, at least, to £8 or £9 a year, have been borne by Father Flanagan, aided by other Fathers of the Oratory, since 1852.

It need scarcely be said that there is no sort of salary or remuneration attached to the above duties.

As to the expense of fitting up the Chapel, which alone Father Flanagan wishes to meet, it has on the whole amounted to £180.

	£	s.	d.
Of this sum the Bishop contributes	5	0	0
The Very Rev. George Jeffries, V.G.	2	0	0
The Very Rev. E. E. Estcourt	3	0	0
The Rev. B. Ivers	2	2	0
The Rev. J. Sherlock	0	10	0
The Rev. W. Grosvenor	1	0	0
Father Newman	5	0	0
Other Fathers of the Oratory	5	0	0
Father Flanagan, the Chaplain	5	0	0
Friends through Father Flanagan	25	0	0
John Poncia, Esq., the Mount	10	0	0
John Hardman, Esq.	5	0	0
John Poncia, Esq., Gough House	5	0	0
R. Fletcher Esq.	5	0	0
W. Canning Esq.	5	0	0
P. Bretherton Esq.	2	2	0
B. Bretherton Esq.	1	0	0
	£86	14	0

leaving a sum of £93 6s. still to be provided for.[1]

[1] See letter of 15 March to Flanagan. The Circular was first sent to the Birmingham priests and laymen, whose names etc. were inserted before it was sent further afield.

Contributions will be received by the Rev. Father Bittleston, Oratory, Birmingham.

J. H. N.

TO JOHN STANISLAS FLANAGAN, I

The Oy Bm Febry 24/58

My dear Stanislas

Don't be cast down — all will turn out well.[1] Recollect, and let me myself recollect, that from the first it has been my fortune to be ever failing, yet after all not to fail. From the first I have had bad strokes of fortune — yet on the whole I have made way. Hardly had I begun life, when misfortunes happened to my family — then I failed in the Schools; then I was put out of office at College; then came Number 90 — and later the Achilli matter. You talk of 'brilliant success' as not our portion — it is not, because you are all joined to me. When I was a boy, I was taken beyond any thing in Homer, with Ulysses seeming 'like a fool or an idiot,' when he began to speak — and yet somehow doing more than others,[2] as St Paul with his weakness and foolishness. I think this was from some presentiment of what was to happen to me. Depend upon it, we shall be happier and more blessed and more successful in my way then in any other.

Dr Johnson was himself confined to the house yesterday — but he is coming here today. Poor Henry is sadly low, and nothing keeps on his stomach. They say it is the liver. I reckon on his being for a month in his room — when he gets out, what think you of my sending him to you to Pau, and of Robert coming back? He *must* have change of air. This is a middle measure, which might answer. We would shift on till Holy Week — and Robert would come back just to sing the Passion. However, Henry must be better, to say nothing else, before we can decide on any thing.

Then let us be thankful that Ambrose is as well as he is — and that I am so well — You and he cast me down by saying penitents will not come to me. If so, I can't help it — but I am quite desirous to be as useful as ever I can.

I wish you were off and Robert. Give my best love to Robert, and let him pray St Philip to make me useful

Ever Yrs affly J H N

[1] Flanagan wrote in the morning of 23 Feb., 'How wonderful it is that trials should follow so fast one upon the other! Perhaps they are better for us all than a brilliant prosperity would be. I really do not see how you can possibly manage without Robert. . . .'

[2] *Iliad*, III, 219–20. Antenor describes how Ulysses appeared when he stood up to speak at a banquet, before the Trojan War: 'When . . . Odysseus rose, he stood . . . like an idiot; you would say he was a cur and a mere fool. Yet when he spoke . . . no mortal man could contend with him. . . '

TO JOHN STANISLAS FLANAGAN, II

The Oy Bm Febr 24/58

My dear S

By no means ought we to borrow George's money.[1]

I want you and Robert out of the country, *as soon as possible. Get off.*

Henry is not so well — the inflammation is not subdued — and a great deal of water is formed.

I will send a letter for you to the Post Restante Paris

Ever Yrs affly J H N

TO JOHN STANISLAS FLANAGAN

The Oy Bm Febr 25/58

My dear S

This is the last letter I shall write to you there (to London). The next shall be to Poste Restante, Paris.

Henry is somewhat better today, the blister having drawn well, and diminished the inflammation — but Dr J. [Johnson] says that he is certainly in a precarious state — from the circumstance that he seems too weak to throw off the complaint — The fear is, I suppose as in Mrs Philipp's case, consumption.

Did you not take my red Banker's Book to the Bank? Or is it somewhere in your room?

Ever Yrs affly J H N

Revd Fr Flanagan.

FRIDAY 26 FEBRUARY 1858   Stan and Rob. off to Paris (query vid Febr 19)[2]   Wingfield went

TO JOHN STANISLAS FLANAGAN

The Oy Bm Febry 26. 1858

My dear S

I took the 'Workhouse Statement' to the Press yesterday. Your letters have doubtless got safely to George, but I have heard nothing of them yet.[3]

---

[1] Flanagan wrote in the afternoon of 23 Feb., that the novice, George Crawley, had entrusted £1150 to him, for investment, and wondered whether the Oratory might borrow it, at 5 per cent. interest, for building the proposed school.

[2] Newman confused the departure of Flanagan and Tillotson from Birmingham to London, with that from London to Paris.

[3] This refers to the Circular Letter of 24 Feb., and a printed covering letter by Flanagan, which George Crawley was to send out.

If I have an opportunity, I will ask G. before this closes — but I am in retreat today.

Henry has had a better night — if there is any thing more to say after the doctor has come, I will add it. He has been all along incomprehensibly low and weak — as if struck with stupidity and dumbness — though his mind is quite his own. Every thing depends on the strength of his constitution which no one can know. His liver too has been very much out of order.

Dr Watson would say very little to Frederic and F. has either nothing to tell, or won't tell it. I suppose the former. He sounded his chest very carefully but would not say a word — which I thought a bad sign. F. is hoarse, and has not his natural voice. He sang Mass last Sunday without any spirit as if he could not get through it. If I had nothing else to be anxious about, I should be frightened about him — but I suppose there is such a thing as a saturation of anxiety.

I *hope* all this is having the effect of bringing George out and making him more natural — I think he will work clear — and I suppose it is nothing more than what is inevitable.

Love to Robert

Ever Yrs affly John H Newman of the Oratory

The Revd Fr Flanagan.

P.S.   Dr J. [Johnson] has come ⟨Friday⟩. He says that H. is certainly better today than he has seen him yet; that his great malady is the liver — We should not be surprised if he is much yellower today than even he is today [sic]. The Pleurisy subsiding. Whatever danger there is, is from the liver. His lungs would only be affected secondarily thro' the liver. His skin is moist — and he is going on well.

The letters have not come to George yet.

Friday.   I lament to have to tell you that H. is worse — the right side inflamed. Dr J. has just come again — and says it is a very anxious case.

SATURDAY 27 FEBRUARY 1858 [Henry] sinking — anointed   I began to go into the Confessional — *which had been broken off on my going to Dublin several years before.*

TO PATRICK LEAHY, ARCHBISHOP OF CASHEL

The Oratory, Birmingham ⌜Febry 27. 1858⌝

My dear Lord

I thank your Grace for your very kind and explicit answer, in your letter received today, to the inquiry of Dr McDermott about the expenses of the Medical School, which I will act on at once.[1]

---

[1] See letter of 14 Feb. to MacDermott. Leahy wrote on 25 Feb. that he was prepared to take full responsibility for the Medical School payments, 'both because of my entire confidence in yourself,' and because the School could not otherwise continue.

I will also avail myself of what you say of Dr Lyons's journey to Lisbon⌐ to allow him £50 towards his expenses.

What I said to those two gentlemen was that, approving generally of their application, I would forward to you any representation which they thought fit to make with reference to it. I did not mean to give you the trouble of direct correspondence with them.

⌐Your Grace is correct in supposing that my letter of the 3rd was not of an official character. It was meant to refer to my formal letter to the Archbishops of October 16 last⌐¹

I am, My dear Lord, Your Grace's faithful Servt in Xt

John H Newman of the Oratory

His Grace The Archbishop of Cashel

TO EDMUND O'REILLY, S.J.

⌐(sent in substance)

Febr 27 58⌐¹

My dear F O'Reilly

⌐I heartily wish some way may be found by the Council for carrying out the spirit of the Resolution of the Faculty of Science, which I sent you last week. That it is very necessary to call attention to the University throughout Ireland and to excite in the public an intelligent interest in its proceedings and the advantages it holds out, no one can doubt; the question is, what are the *motives* and the *means* by which this is to be done.

I forgot to take a copy of the words of the Resolution [[of the Faculty of Science]] before I sent it to you, but I think it proposed the appointment of preachers through the country to advocate the claims of the University and to make the subject generally popular.² On first blush of the subject, I see one sine quâ non — viz that the measure contemplated should not be one single isolated effort, done and over and not repeated, but should be systematic and annual at least for a period.

[[1. As to the means.]] I do not know whether the Protestant system of itinerancy which is so successful in England, would do for Catholic Ireland. Once a year or two or three persons go on circuit as a deputation from some

---

¹ Referring to Newman's letter of 3 Feb. (in which he said that he had resolved to take no salary until matters were 'placed on a more intelligible footing'), Leahy asked whether he had intimated this resolution to the other Irish Archbishops. 'If not, I should feel it a duty to make it know to them.' Leahy added, 'I should be glad also to be able to say what it is precisely you would convey by the desire you express to see things placed on a more intelligible footing.'

² Lyons sent Newman this resolution, passed on 19 Feb., '*Resolved*, that the Faculty of Science recommend that authorised Preachers be sent to the country to make known the objects utility and influence of the University for the advancement of Catholic Education in Ireland.'

parent society for which they wish to raise money. In each town which they visit, they are received by some resident of name or station — they hold a public meeting, at which they are called on to expound the views of the Parent Society — money is collected at the doors, then on the [[next]] Sunday they give a sermon, with another collection — and they found an association in connexion [[with]] and in support of the London Parent. If this were done in Ireland, or any thing like it, it ought to be held in every place at the time which the Bishop appoints for the yearly collection. Of course the circumstance of a *circuit* is not of the essence of the plan.

Last June year I proposed to those with whom the decision lay, the following plan; — the appointment of a clerical secretary, whose business it would be to correspond with the parish priests throughout the country, to ascertain the Sundays on which the University collection was to be made, prepare for it, print hand bills, put advertisements into the local paper, stimulate the priests when necessary, or when necessary go down and preach on the Collection Sunday — And this to be done annually.[1]

Perhaps the reason why this plan was not thought of was the great difficulty of enlisting the Bishops generally in the plan — it might seem to give the University some rudiments of a jurisdiction in the Dioceses, which would give rise to inconveniences in time to come. Indeed it may be that the very idea or principle of the Resolution of the [[Science]] Faculty is necessarily, on this [[very]] ground, unpalatable to the Irish Clergy, judging by what has happened in the case of the affiliated schools.[2]

For myself, I have all along preferred, as the surer plan, the establishment of a short and frequently recurring periodical; which would answer many other purposes besides.[1] Perhaps the two methods could be combined. As to the ways and means, if a really useful plan, which promised to work and work well, were arranged, I should hope that this would not be a difficulty.

[[2.]] ⌐So much for the method, but when we come to the motives which are to persuade the Irish public to feel an interest in us, I confess I am here in absolute ignorance and perplexity what to recommend. I have no means of knowing or conjecturing how to reach them. In some parts of the country there used to be a great desire after liberal education [[in the lower classes]] — we are told now that the pence table of the National School is more popular than the Latin Grammar.

I am sure nothing will be done successfully, unless we set out with a clear and precise view of how we mean to move the people what inducements we are to offer them as the quid pro quo of their subscriptions. But I am sure of nothing else.[1]

It occurs to me to observe however, first that ⌐if we decide that preaching is to be the means [[of influencing]], then from the nature of the case we have decided also that the motives are to be directly religious ones.

[1] See the end of the letter of 19 June 1856 to the Irish Bishops.
[2] See letter of 13 June 1857 to Scratton.

I will add that the newspapers have lately been talking of the Scotch Universities; and it appears on the one hand that the Universities are well attended, on the other hand that they are great Schools, not Universities and that there are four of them, not one.[1] So far then is plain that the Scotch motive [[which succeeds]], 'a good elementary schooling' cannot be our motive[1]

Yours &c J H N

SUNDAY 28 FEBRUARY 1858   [Henry] better

TO JOHN STANISLAS FLANAGAN

The Oy Bm Febry 28. 1858

My dear Stanislas

If I can find what department Pau is in, I shall send this tonight, to the Poste Restante. You must be most anxious about Henry. He is better.

Yesterday morning at breakfast, George came hastily in, and said he feared he might die at any moment. We at once anointed him. I said to him, 'this anointing is to restore you, not to resign you to death.' He smiled, and has been getting better ever since. Dr Johnson was here three times yesterday. The inflamation has subsided, but the danger was 1. suffocation. 2. exhaustion. We gave him nourishment, wine, beef tea etc every hour. This morning he is even lively. But there is no concealing from ourselves that there may be a relapse — there has been one already — and his weakness is still such that he has nourishment as yesterday. And then, there is the formidable absorption of the water.

I long to hear about your progress — I reckon we may have a letter from Paris tomorrow morning — unless you are still waiting at Dover for the wind to lull. Henry's brother came last night — he has got an India Judgeship.[2]

The bell is put up for Scully to sound, and does its work well. The new confessionals look exteremely well — the names of Frs Stanislas and Henry are posted up on two of them. Frederic was in the Confessional last night. The Workhouse statement is in type; I shall send it round Birmingham first

---

[1] A 'Bill to make provision for the better Government and Discipline of the Universities of Scotland' was introduced on 22 April and received the royal assent on 2 Aug. 1858.

At this period more than a third of the students of the Scottish universities were under seventeen, and more than half under eighteen. The junior Greek classes often began with the Greek alphabet. E. L. Woodward, *The Age of Reform* 1815–1870, Oxford 1949, p. 474. Cf. *McGrath*, p. 458.

[2] Adam Bittleston was appointed Judge of the Supreme Court at Madras in 1858, and knighted on 28 April before leaving England. He wrote to Newman on 13 March to say he was sending 'a small hamper of sherry,' and thanking for his kind reception at the Oratory and the 'unremitting attention' paid to his brother.

— and then send your letters. The Bishops meet on March 11 — when something will be done about the Translation. Wingfield has been here, and is so fidgetty a fellow, that, tho' I suppose he will come I wished he may not.[1]

Love to Robert

Ever Yrs most affly John H Newman

The Revd Fr Flanagan

TO MRS JOHN MOZLEY

The Oratory Bm. February 28. 1858

My dear Jemima,

Thank you for your beautiful pot of marmalade, which came quite safely — and without any loss of its precious contents

How strange it is! — that Pierri was known to us here very fairly well.[2] His daughter is one of our penitents. A very nice good child of about 10 or 12 — and one of us got her to school in a convent at Loughborough, where she still is. She had a bad fever a year ago, and came home to Birmingham — and one of us used to visit her. The fondness of the poor father for her was indescribable. Poor man, I suppose it was his only good point. It is not pleasant to have been near, I suppose, a professional murderer. However, we never liked him — and got a lady to take away her children, to whom he was giving lessons in Italian. Generally, he was very well conducted — but flashes and scintillations of the fire within him came out now and then, sufficient to set us against him. This made us get his daughter away from him

Ever Yrs affly John H Newman of the Oratory

Mrs John Mozley

P.S. At this moment they have got at Oxford one of the triumvirate, Saffi, Mazzini and another being his colleagues.[3] I believe under their reign something like 60 priests were shot at Rome. Saffi is described as a meek quiet person. I might be indicted for a libel for saying this — but I believe there is no doubt of every fact I have stated. But I declare I think you had better burn it, lest it might go off like one of Pierri's grenades. I can't make out there are two Saffis. By the bye, Lord Palmerston said that the Pope's

[1] Wingfield was to help with the translation of Scripture.

[2] Giuseppe Andrea Pieri (1808–58), from the neighbourhood of Lucca, in Tuscany, emigrated to France to escape the consequences of some misconduct, and joined the Foreign Legion. He returned to Italy during the Revolution of 1848 and rose to the rank of Major. Fleeing again to France in 1849, he was banished after the *coup d'état* of 2 Dec. 1851, and took refuge in London. There he became the friend of Orsini, whom he later joined in Paris, in the attempt to assassinate Napoleon III on 12 Jan. 1858. The three bombs used had been made in Birmingham, and killed ten people, besides wounding one hundred and fifty six. Pieri was arrested next day, being found in possession of a bomb, and executed on 13 March.

[3] Aurelio Saffi (1819–70) was, with Mazzini and Armellini, one of the Roman Triumvirate, in 1849. From 1853 to 1860 he was at the Taylorian Institution in Oxford, lecturing on the Italian language and literature.

government was worse than the triumvirate — that poor old man is gone at last, his glory over for ever. I am glad he is gone, but it is most melancholy.[1]

MONDAY 1 MARCH 1858   he [Henry] caught cold — fresh relapse
TUESDAY 2 MARCH   slowly getting better thro' the week   Stan and Rob. off for Pau

TO BISHOP ULLATHORNE

The Oratory, Birmingham In festo S. Ceaddae [2 March] 1858

My dear Lord

I had intended to call on your Lordship and to pay my devotions to St Chad in the Cathedral, in honor of this day – but the weather will not allow me. But besides this, I lament to say, I am writing in Fr Bittleston's room, who has this morning had a third relapse.

I will employ myself then, instead of calling, in writing you some lines, if you will let me give you the trouble of reading them, on the subject of the Translation of Scripture. As the Cardinal has so many engagements, I feel doubtful whether he has quite understood the drift of what I have written to him on the subject; and, if I write to you about it, I shall have the security, in the event of its coming before the Bishops next week, that no misconception will occur.

His Eminence asked me in October to state the probable expenses of the Translation, allowing a large margin for unforeseen additions to them.

I answered him by fixing them, with considerable hesitation, at £1000 — giving him the items, of which that sum would be made up.

In the course of the three months which followed, I had great misgivings whether I had named a sufficient sum, nay whether it was possible to make any reasonable conjecture what the sum would be; and, as luckily the Cardinal had not answered me on the subject of the expenses, I wrote to him about a fortnight ago to state my change of view.

In saying, however, that I could not name a maximum sum, I was *in fact* asking for a carte blanche from the Bishops to draw any sum I pleased. This I could not expect they would give me; therefore I proposed to the Cardinal that they should give me the copyright, (burdened with any stipulations which were ecclesiastically necessary,) and throw on me the responsibility of the expenses. I did this, because I saw then, as little as I see now, any other

[1] Lord Palmerston's Government, after receiving a large majority in the general election, April 1857, was defeated on 19 Feb. 1858, at the second reading of the 'Conspiracy to Murder Bill,' by which (in view of Orsini's attempt on Napoleon III), conspiracy to murder was to be punished as a felony and no longer as a misdemeanour. Palmerston resigned at once, but it was not the end of his glory. He became Prime Minister again in June 1859, and remained in office until his death in 1865.

possible way out of the difficulty. Gladly will I acquiesce in any third plan their Lordships may suggest, but, as the Cardinal asked me for my opinion, I could only speak as the matter presented itself to my mind.

It is true, the Bishops might put the whole matter into the hands of publishers; but that is only what I should do myself, if I had the disposal of it. For my own convenience, I prefer indefinitely that they should do it, but it seemed to me asking them too much, to throw upon them all the responsibility.

Again, it is true they might give me a sum at a hazard, for me to do with it as much as I could, and then come again to them for more, if it was not enough. I would willingly acquiesce in this; but I do not see my way to set down a maximum sum; and I have given his Eminence reasons why I am unable.

I am, My dear Lord, begging your Lordship's blessing

Your faithful & affte Servt in Xt John H Newman of the Oratory

The Rt Revd The Bishop of Birmingham

TO TERENCE FLANAGAN

March 3/58

My dear Mr Flanagan

. . . I cannot deny that your proposal in reference to your Professorship, though perfectly consistent with what passed between us several years ago, perplexes me a good deal at this moment, from the circumstance that University matters are in so different a state from what they were.[1]

I have virtually resigned the Rectorship — I am but holding office, as they say, till my successor is appointed — And especially I have, for some time past, abstained from making any new pecuniary arrangements having wished the accounts altogether to be taken out of my hands.

Another difficulty, pressing on your Professorship in particular, is this — that, tho' I know the trial might have been fairer than it was, yet in matter of fact when we made an attempt to get Engineering Students, we failed. Your having an office in Dublin would I hope ultimately draw them to us, which is very desirable — but I do not think I could give money to carry it on, except in proportion as students came to you. This is the rule I have adopted in other cases; and have maintained it, tho' I have got into trouble for my pains. But what is the greatest difficulty is that the visible, acting person will not be yourself, and especially that he will not be an Irishman.

We have definite wants at the University — E.g. To take an instance we

---

[1] Terence Flanagan proposed that Mr Alexander, an Englishman, should set up as an engineer in Dublin, and act as his deputy in the Professorship of Engineering. Flanagan intended to give him £200 out of the £300 salary.

want a special Professor or Professors for the Woolwich Candidates.[1] If, for instance, you said 'I will definitely take that,' you might reasonably unite it with an office which had another end altogether. But I fear that if an Englishman comes, opens a Civil Engineering office, advertises for and fails in getting University youths as pupils, and receives University money for it, it will not be looked at in the light which we wish it to present, but will deprive me of a principle on which I at present take my stand against various requests which are urged upon me. And the more so, because Mr McCarthy the Architect our Professor of Architecture admits University youths in to his office, taking no emolument.

If it were not for the difficulty of the Englishman — I should not mind giving a sum to aid you in setting off your office in Dublin on the understanding that you were paid a certain sum per head for University students, and the whole Professor's salary when you had a certain number of them.[2]

J H N

TO BISHOP ULLATHORNE

The Oratory Birmingham March 3. 1858

My dear Lord

In order to complete the statement I made to your Lordship yesterday, I will make extracts from my letters to the Cardinal of November 7 and February 19 last.

In my letter of November 7, which inclosed three specimens of types with their respective cost, I said[3]

So far my letter of November 7, on which I have only to observe, in explanation of my choice of assistants in the Translation, that the Cardinal, in his original Letter of August 26, wrote to me, when communicating to me the desire of the Synod, in the following most kind and gracious way: 'The Bishops had agreed, at the time they drew up the Decree, that to you was to be committed the grave and most important work proposed in it, and that you had to select and name the persons whom you would wish to have for assistants in the undertaking. It was understood that most naturally they would be members of the Congregation of the Oratory.'

In my letter of February 19, I took advantage of the Cardinal not having had time as yet to come to any conclusion upon the above calculation, to write to his Eminence as follows: —

[1] The Royal Military Academy at Woolwich, for the Engineers and the Artillery.
[2] Terence Flanagan replied on 15 March, approving of Newman's answer.
[3] Newman proceeded to copy out his letter of 7 Nov., from the second paragraph until the end of the calculation of expenses, omitting a few details.

'In the interval you have allowed me for consideration, it has pressed upon me, that I really cannot attempt to give any maximum estimate at all.'[1]

I am sorry to have had to trouble you with so much reading and am My dear Lord,

Yr faithful Servt in Xt   John H Newman[2]

The Bishop of Birmingham

TO WILLIAM CLIFFORD, BISHOP OF CLIFTON

The Oratory, Birmingham March 4. 1858

My dear Lord,

It was with feelings of a very peculiar kind, which I can hardly describe, that I read the notice of your saintly Father's death.[3] I do not think that you can have any thing but consolation at the event; however, nature will feel it. I have not seen him since I was in Rome in 1846–7; but I know well, as I saw and experienced then, his extreme humility, gentleness, and kindness, united as those graces were with so self-denying and mortified a life and such a perseverance in acts of mercy and devotional practices. How can one be sorry when a soul laden with merit goes to heaven! Yet, though I was never likely to see him again, it made me very sorrowful to hear of his death, as feeling the loss which it was to us all to have a saint the less in the English Church. You may be sure that we, who knew him and have had the experience of his condescension to us, shall not fail to say Mass for him, though we do not think he needs it.

We are in great trouble here. One of our number, Fr Bittleston, has been almost dying of a pleurisy for the last ten days — we trust he is getting better — but he has had two relapses, and even now the inflammation is not entirely gone. Only two days before he fell ill, we had to part with Fr Flanagan, who has gone to Pau for his lungs. Begging your Lordship's blessing, I am, My dear Lord,

Your faithful and afft servant in Xt

John H Newman of the Oratory

The Rt Rd The Bp of Clifton

FRIDAY 5 MARCH 1858   Stan and Robert arrived at Pau

[1] Newman then copied his letter of 19 Feb. from the paragraph beginning 'The great difficulty of the problem . . .' to that ending 'by a practical printer in London.'
[2] Ullathorne wrote on 15 March that the subject of Newman's communications with Wiseman was brought up at the Bishops' meeting on 10 March, 'and it was left to the three appointed to revise [Wiseman, Ullathorne and Grant] to arrange with you. I suppose I ought not officially to state the sense of the Bishops, and that you will hear from the Cardinal.' Wiseman spoke to Newman on 4 July. See letter of 18 July to Caswall.
[3] Hugh Charles, Seventh Baron Clifford of Chudleigh, died at Rome on 28 Feb. 1858.

TO PETER BRETHERTON

The Oratory, Birmm. March 5. 1858.

My dear Mr Bretherton

Fr Stanislas would have begged in person your name for insertion in the list of contributors to the object of the inclosed statement,[1] had he not been carried away to the south of Europe by the advice of his medical attendants.

May I then do so instead of him! When he is able to set down some of the principal Catholics of Birmingham, he means to send it to his friends at a distance.

I am, My dear Mr Bretherton

Sincerely Yours in Xt   John H. Newman of the Oratory

TO JOHN STANISLAS FLANAGAN

(3)[2]   The Oy Bm March 5. 1858 Friday

My dear S

I should have written to you a second time to the Poste R. [Restante] Paris, had I any thought you would remain there so long — and I should have written to you a second time to the Poste R. Pau, whither I sent a letter, last Sunday, but we have had a terrible week and H. [Henry] is not yet out of danger.

On Sunday ⟨last⟩ night Dr J. [Johnson] called H. almost convalescent; on Monday (last) he had a second relapse — I cannot recollect the days after, except to say generally that for a day or two we thought him going, and then for 36 hours, when he lay still, we could not tell whether it was a gradual sinking or rising. However, most thankful am I to say, that he has from Monday improved, slowly indeed, but steadily. This is his best day, and he smiled and almost laughed just now, showing a great increase of strength — but we can not conceal from ourselves that a third relapse is possible — with strength less than when he was first taken ill. He has been supported by Masses and prayers. I have said Mass for him every day, and now Saturday (tomorrow) comes. I ought to fulfil my promise of a Mass for you and Robert, for but one day of the week remains — yet, since he is not yet out of danger, I suppose I shall say it for him.

It is most satisfactory to hear the Doctor say that apparently there is nothing the matter with his lungs, that the water in his side is insignificant — and that the inflammation is going as fast as it can — but, alas, that is very

[1] The circular letter of 24 Feb.
[2] Newman now began to number his letters to Flanagan.

slow, and till it is gone, or even then, he is not safe — not *even* then, I say, because it *had* gone, and returned. His first attack was on his right side — then he had a fierce attack on his left — his third attack, I think, was on his left too.

When he is well enough, we shall send him to you, and dear Robert must return. A sad disappointment that you may not coach him — but it is as much as your life is worth.[1] I have heard from Monsell (as from you yesterday) — he says Dr Andrel summed up thus: — if he is idle for six months and keeps in the south he will recover — if he does not, he will die. Your life depends on this six months. I earnestly trust you will not transgress your rules in any thing. I shall be glad to get R. away from you on this account, lest you talk too much to him, but I rely on his keeping you in order. The Miss Farrants will pay any thing for Henry — that is one good thing. We must coach Robert here — I hope he will gain good from the excursion, though it be a short one. I suppose you have put down on paper Dr Andrel's rules. Monsell gave them much more fully than you had time to do.

Lord Clifford is dead — Ambrose is fussing himself lest I should be bishop of Northampton. They talk of the V.G. [Vicar General] of Birmingham as the person.[2] No great news. Surely we have had our whole Lent already, and are all very tired. Love to R.

Ever Yrs affly J H N

I am sending round today the Workhouse Statement to the Brummagem folk.

SUNDAY 7 MARCH 1858   Henry frightened us from delirium.   Dr Evans called in to assist Dr Johnson

TO EDWARD BELLASIS

The Oratory Bm March 7. 1858

My dear Bellasis

I know you will excuse a short answer on Sunday. We have had such a meeting as we could have, and I send you our answers. Observe, they are merely intended to put you in possession of our views — which is the reason, I consider, why you send them to us. Some questions we could not, or did not feel that it came within our province, to answer. Also, you will observe that our answers are in *undress* — and not intended for presentation to a

---

[1] The Paris doctor forbad Flanagan to give Tillotson lectures in theology. Flanagan had met Monsell in Paris.

[2] This was George Jeffries. William Wareing, the Bishop of Northampton, resigned on 11 Feb. 1858, and was succeeded by Francis Kerril Amherst.

Prince of the Church. I alone am responsible for their wording, which is caused by want of time, as much as by any thing else.[1]

Also I would observe that his Eminence seems to me not clearly to distinguish between a College and a School, a President and a Head-master, though I do not deny we speak of Eton College, Winchester College etc.

We send you our best remembrances. Alas, for a fortnight Fr Bittleston has been lying ill of a pleurisy between life and death. We trust, but cannot be sure, that he is out of danger today. Fr Flanagan who was in bed when you were here, is at Pau, I trust, by this time.

Monsell has a son — who with Mrs M. is doing well[2]

Ever Yrs most sincerely John H Newman of the Oratory

Mr Serjeant Bellasis

QUESTIONS ON THE SUBJECT OF THE PROPOSED LAY-SCHOOL
AT OR NEAR BIRMINGHAM[3]

ANSWERS TO THE CARDINAL'S QUESTIONS[4]

I PRESIDENT

1   Will the Principal or President be a Layman, or a Priest?

I understand 'President' or 'Principal' to mean 'Head Master' and by 'College' a 'school.' This being so, I answer
A secular Priest; — because in the public schools of England, his being a clergyman is in many ways a gain; and that, for his office as such; he is married also, but his wife takes no part in the care of the boys.

2   If the former, will he be married or unmarried?
Answered already

3   Should the latter be optional, would the pupils be under the same roof; or would he have a separate residence?
Answered already.

---

[1] Bellasis wrote on 6 March that he, and Sir John Acton had applied to many converts and old Catholics, asking if they would join in a request to Newman to consider opening a school. They had received many replies, all of them favourable. W. G. Ward wrote on 15 Feb., 'Quite certainly there is no one of our present English colleges or schools to which I could dream of sending my son.' He thought 'every one of them as bad as bad can be; and that the religious education is almost as low as the intellectual; though such a feat might seem almost impossible.' About the projected school, however, W. G. Ward added, 'The only matter on which I should doubt, would be whether J H N would give sufficient prominence to definite religious *teaching, instruction,* in fact *theology,* as distinct from *training.*'
Bellasis and Acton had also approached Wiseman, who was non-committal, but had just sent them a paper of forty-one questions which they forwarded to Newman, asking for his advice as to how to answer them. See enclosure at the end of this letter.
[2] Monsell's only surviving son, Gaston, was born on 5 March 1858.
[3] These questions are printed from the original in Wiseman's hand, which he sent to Bellasis on 5 March 1858.
[4] These are printed from Newman's draft.

4   If a priest, would he be a Secular or a Regular (in the widest sense)?
    Answered already

5   In either case, who would have this nomination?

6   How could he be removed?
    Answered already, so far as is implied in saying he is a secular priest.

7   For what causes?
    offences against faith and morals, scandalous conduct, unfitness for his office

8   What, and from what source would be his salary?
    no answer.

II PROFESSORS

9   How many professors or masters will there be?
    as many as the number of boys requires. On the whole an average of one master to 30; but, if the school is under 200, the average of masters must be much higher.

10 All laymen, or some ecclesiastics?
    ecclesiastics or lay, as it may be.

11 How will they be named?
    by the headmaster or President.

12 Under what discipline, e.g. as to rising, prayers, and common duties? Will they have the same rules for these as the boys?
    under no discipline, with the explanation that the masters during the school hours, or when the boys are in their houses, keep discipline. They are not under the same rules as the boys.

13 Will any live out of the house?
    All may live out of the school building but the head master.

14 Will the same persons be teachers and master of discipline— prefects in playground, chapel, refectory, dormitories etc? Or will there be distinct staffs for the two?
    The office of master of discipline is distinct from that of teacher, though the two offices may be accidentally united.

15 Who will dismiss any of them?
    Head Master or President

16 What scale and mode of remuneration is proposed
    no answer

III RELIGIOUS INSTRUCTION

Understanding that *for a time* the Fathers of the Oratory undertake the spiritual care of the House, the following questions apply to the time when a permanent arrangement is made.

17 Will one or more priests *reside* in the house, for the spiritual direction of the scholars.

17–22 no answer

18 Will any of them have free access to him beyond stated times for confession, for advice etc?

19 Will he have full power to regulate communions and spiritual reading etc. for each student, without interference?

20 What will be his (if more than one their) position in relation with the President?

21 Who will name, and who remove?

22 Beyond the stated and fixed religious instruction as catechism, and instructions, what means are proposed for forming and training the minds and hearts of the students to habitual piety, and deep religious sentiments?

IV DISCIPLINE

23 Will the internal discipline differ materially from that of our existing Colleges?
the internal discipline will be that of the existing Colleges, except with those changes which are implied in the idea of school.

24 If so, in which direction, in greater strictness, or in greater laxity or freedom?
In both directions, for the regime of a school is different in kind from that of a College.

25 Will there be any difference in the system of rewards and punishments?
I suppose so, inasmuch as a school is different from that of a College

26 What will be the machinery for the enforcing and preserving discipline?
The Birch.

27 Will the President alone have power of expulsion?
The Head Master or President alone.

V STUDIES

28 On what plan or system will these be arranged? According to *forms* or *classes*?
Forms, with classes for subjects out of the regular course of study.

29 Is it intended to give preponderance to classics, or to science, or to neither over the other?
classics.

30 Will as much be given to modern languages, history etc as in our present Colleges?
    we do not (know) enough of the present College system on that head.

31 Will the system of teaching be by private tuition, or by classes, or by lecture;
    and if by all, in what proportion: e.g. will each boy have a private tutor, whether
    master or senior boy?
    Each form would have its own master, but any boy might have in private prepara-
    tion for the lessons of his form.

32 How many years will the course occupy, if fully gone through?
    as many years as he is there

33 Does it comprise what we understand by a philosophical course? If so, of how
    long a period?
    certainly not.

VI GENERAL MANAGEMENT

34 Who is to be responsible for the property at the College, its rent, or interest on
    borrowed money, if necessary to start it, taxes etc.
    34–38 [no reply]

35 Should the site and house be purchased, or the latter built, in whom will it be
    invested, and under what Trusts?

36 What will be the power of Trustees, in the management of the house, in its
    internal finance, studies etc?

37 Should the Establishment not succeed, how will it be disposed of, or at any rate,
    will such a conclusion be come to by its not answering as a commercial specula-
    tion, by the Trustees?

38 What will be the power of the Bishop, as to visitation, correction, removal of
    chaplain and spiritual supervision?

39 At what age will pupils be admitted?
    at any age.

40 What guarantee will be required for the morality of those admitted?
    none

41 Will the education have reference to any subsequent teaching; e.g. the Dublin
    University, or will it be complete in itself?
    It will have reference to such a system as the Dublin University, but will be as
    complete as a mere school can be.[1]

---

[1] Before answers to these questions could be sent to Wiseman he wrote on 8 March to
Bellasis that he had no right to put them. See last note to letter of 12 March to Bellasis.

The Ory Bm ⌐March 7/58⌐

My dear H

⌐I do trust we may today pronounce Fr Bittleston out of danger — but I dread to be sure,[1] after what happened last week.

⌐He got steadily better after he had been anointed.⌐ On this day week evening the doctor pronounced him almost convalescent. From imprudence he got cold in the night, and on Monday morning he had an attack on the left side. It was unattended with fever, and not a bad one — that was the gain — but then 1. he was weaker than he was originally — 2. His side, being flayed with the blister, would not bear a second — and so he lay the whole week — good part of it with one being unable to say whether he was sinking or improving. However he has slowly got to the point he was this day week. After such a reverse, however, we dare not boast.

The doctor has been most careful of severe remedies — but where would he have been without his blisters! ⌐When we hastily anointed him he seemed going, and the doctor said he *might* go any minute.⌐ The Sacrament then was a real cure, which was undone by imprudence, but which I hope has been got over

⌐If possible I shall send you an Article for this week — and then shall stop.⌐[1]

Monsell has got a boy which with Mrs M. is doing well.

⌐We have not heard of Stanislas from Pau yet. He is to be out till September — ⌐ and then to return cured — so says a famous old French Doctor, who also says he will die, if he neglects himself during that period

Ever Yrs affly J H N

Sunday.   We are still not easy about Father Bittleston

Who are the three persons named by the Chapter of Northampton? I have a reason for asking.[2]

MONDAY 8 MARCH 1858   the two physicians came twice daily for a week or ten days

[1] The last of the leading articles on the Catholic University in the *Weekly Register* appeared on 13 March.
[2] See end of letter of 5 March to Flanagan.

TO SIR JOHN ACTON

The Oratory Bm March 8. 1858

My dear Sir John

I shall be much pleased to see you tomorrow as you propose. The Cardinal's questions puzzled me. I sent Bellasis our opinion of them — but I cannot conceive his Eminence making his approval turn on details.

Thank you for the trouble you have taken for me with Dr Döllinger.[1] Do give us your prayers, for we are in sad anxiety here — not only have we been obliged to send off Fr Flanagan to Pau — but Fr Bittleston has been lying ill of a pleurisy and between life and death for the last fortnight, and now the complaint has taken another form which is so critical, that we are watching him hour by hour

Yours most truly in Xt   John H Newman of the Oratory

Sir John D. Acton Bart

P.S.   Pray say every thing kind from me to [J. B.] Morris, whose new affliction I saw in the Newspapers.

TO DANIEL WELPLY

March 8. 1858

My dear Sir

Excuse my delay which was unavoidable in answering your very welcome letter of March 1 — [2]

I am much flattered by your wish that I should receive your Son into my house — but I am sorry to say I have not at this moment any definite prospect of room in it before November.

If you will allow me a little longer time, I will write again

I am, My dear Sir Yours very faithfully J H N

TO HENRY WILBERFORCE

⌈March 8/58⌉

My dear H

I don't think I shall please myself with my new Article enough to send it you this week.

---

[1] See last note to letter of 25 Nov. 1857 to Acton.
[2] Daniel Welply of Upton House, Innishannon, Cork, wanted his son who was at school at Oscott, and aged seventeen and a half to come to Newman's house at the University. Newman noted on his draft the names of those then at his House: '2 de Ligne's, Zamoyski, Bethell, de la Pasture, Frazer, Segar, Errington, Throckmorton.'

ᒥDear Fr Bittleston's complaint has taken a new turn — or rather a new complaint has taken its place — delirium, which, if not subdued, will be fatal. It alarmed us, as I was sending you my letter last night. He is better than yesterday — ᒧ but we cannot get him today to sleep — though he has taken a large opiate. He exerts great command over himself, and is very obedient — but how long this will last no one can say. ᒥIt now must be decided one way or the other in a day or twoᒧ

Ever Yrs affly J H Newman

WEDNESDAY 10 MARCH 1858 Henry frightfully beside himself. would not eat   better at night

TO ROBERT BEVERLEY TILLOTSON

4   Oy Bm March 10/58

My dear R,

Your letter of Saturday the 5th[1] came last night. Thank you for it. I have written two letters to Poste Restante, Pau, the second last Friday the 5th.

I must not delay longer writing again — but, alas, it is to impart to you the great distress in which we are ourselves. Henry is alive — but we know nothing of the future. This morning we all thought ourselves out of the wood, and I was half inclined to say a mass of thanksgiving. Again, we are rolled back, and should despond, except that by God's grace, I intend to go on hoping and praying till He in His infinite mercy declares His will. Suspence and disappointment are very trying.

Henry got stronger and stronger all through Saturday — nay on *to this time!* but on Friday (perhaps) rose a silliness of manner which annoyed us — but we thought it weakness or opium. Dr J. [Johnson] said it was the effect of the calomel; and spoke very satisfactorily of him, though he did not sleep. He still had nourishment every two hours. By Sunday (the 7th) this sort of semi-delirium increased — and, when they called me into his room Sunday afternoon, he did not know me. Mrs Wootten was so urgent, and had been so through the week, in pressing the Miss Farrants' wish he should see another physician, that we got Dr J. to bring Dr Evans with him Sunday night. They pronounced him cured of the pleurisy — but with beginnings of a nervous affection which could only be called delirium tremens. We were not to leave him by himself a minute. The great thing was to get him sleep. A strong dose of opium (which would have made Dr E. sleep for 24 hours) had no effect on him — a stronger on Monday night had no effect either. Both Doctors have

[1] A slip for '6th.'

been twice a day since Sunday night. Meantime I should say that he was asleep when the Doctors came Sunday night, and slept for 5 hours, and they thought he would take his food, go to sleep again and sleep himself well — This hope, as I have said, was disappointed, in spite of the two great doses of opium on Monday morning and Monday night. They gave him a day of rest on Tuesday (yesterday) — trusting to nature, and he ate almost voraciously through the day to our great delight. The doctors every day pronounced him better. Last night he fell asleep — and has slept at intervals in the night (say) five or six hours. I thought him *well* — Dr Evans had said that sleep would be a cure.

After Mass this morning, Wm [William] comes to me to beg me to come, that H. is singing, halloing, throwing himself about. We could do nothing with him. Providentially, it was close on the time of the Doctors coming. They pronounced him (at the *moment*) deranged; nothing physically the matter with him — his pulse, heart, lungs, side etc good. They gave him chloroform. This at once restored him, and they inflicted on him two cups of beef tea, brandy etc. Since then he will not eat — and his derangement has returned. We have sent to the doctors. They told us not to press him — but to leave him quiet and then let John Smallwood bring him a chicken as a matter of course at 5 for his dinner. As I write ($\frac{1}{4}$ to 5) in comes William with a message from Henry to ask my forgiveness for disobedience and to know whether he may eat the chicken. I have not yet given him leave — for he has already played the same game. My fear is, he will consent till the moment the chicken comes to his mouth; then he will shut his teeth resolutely and nothing will persuade him   I will let you know.

J H N

5 oclock. He is eating the fowl with knife and fork perfectly sane!

THURSDAY 11 MARCH 1858   [Henry] received the Viaticum, seeming to be sinking
FRIDAY 12 MARCH   better, but still no sleep.

TO MRS T. W. ALLIES

The Oratory, Mar. 12. 1858

My dear Mrs Allies,

Such letters as yours do me good, for they make me feel that people may keep up kind thoughts of me, who do not see me, and sometimes give me their prayers.

We need them here now. We have been extremely tried since I was at your House.[1] When I got back, I found dear Fr Flanagan in bed. He remained

---

[1] See diary for 20 Jan.

there a month, and then was sent off to Pau with another Father to take care of him. The day but one after he left us, Fr Bittleston was struck down with a pleurisy. He has been in bed three weeks, and had the Viaticum yesterday. I think he is kept alive by prayers, and that, when the hands of Moses get tired and fall then he relapses. For his ups and downs have been trying beyond expression. He has had three, four, or five relapses. I can't count them. The morning before last I felt half disposed to say a Mass of thanksgiving for his being quite out of the wood. Yesterday we gave him the Viaticum, now he is better than he has been for many days, but *so* weak and worn. This day eight years he was received into the Congregation, and he is determined St Gregory shall cure him.

I meant Basil to have Loss and Gain, and Callista, and must inquire of Burns why they are not sent him.

With every kind thought of Mr Allies, who I hope, has got comfortably into his new Office by this time.

I am, My dear Mrs Allies, Most sincerely yours in Xt

John H Newman of the Oratory

TO EDWARD BELLASIS

The Oratory, Birmingham March 12. 1858

My dear Bellasis,

I should not have delayed to answer your two letters, but for the great anxiety and suspense we are in about Fr Bittleston. We gave him the Viaticum yesterday — Our distress has been one long ague, with hot and cold fits, hopes and fears fiercely succeeding to each other. You may understand how wearing this is.

In answer to your remarks, I observe,

1. The Oratory consists of simply secular Priests. All of us are secular Priests living in Community, and nothing else. Therefore, when I said in my first answer 'Secular Priest,' I included Oratorians. Is this what your question means?[1]

2. We never contemplated pledging ourselves to the School for good, if it were only for this, that it might be hard on our successors. The utmost I ever said was in my letter to you of February 2nd — 'for 20 years.' This is far longer than I should prefer to say.[2] However, I do not see any objection to calling it our school absolutely, it being understood that we may give it up, as any schoolmaster may give up his own school — with this understanding,

[1] Bellasis wrote on 8 March about Wiseman's questions, 'What do you mean by your answer to the first question, that the head master will be a "secular Priest"? Is an Oratorian one? or do you mean that if the Oratory gave up the school there should *then* be a secular Priest at the head of it?'

[2] Bellasis went on to ask why Newman spoke of the connection of the Oratory with the school as temporary.

that, properly speaking, the school would be mine and Fr Darnell's, not the Oratory's. As we may have a Father taking care of a Ragged School, a Reformatory, a Workhouse, or a Guild, so (much more, for our Brief speaks of the 'Nobiles etc') may Fr Darnell have the school on his hands as his work. It must be understood too that we have not the temporalities of the School upon us.

3. As to 'the same roof' I said in my letter of February 2 that the two *families* would be cut off from each other; but I much doubt, when it comes to the point, whether our Fathers will give up their upper story to boys.[1]

Very sincerely Yours John H Newman of the Oratory

Mr Serjeant Bellasis

TO JOHN STANISLAS FLANAGAN

5   The Oratory, Bm March 12. 1858

My dear S

I wrote to R. [Robert] I think on Wednesday the 10th bringing up events to that evening — but I am so very tired that my memory gets confused. Yesterday morning, (Thursday) though he had had very little sleep ($\frac{3}{4}$ of an hour) in the night — he was quite himself — when, after breakfast, I was told he was dying. When I came he could not speak — hardly nod. We determined to give him the Viaticum, while we could — for, when I say 'dying' his feet indeed were cold, and there had been a sudden great change in his face, but we did not think his last moments were close at hand, not so *close* as when we gave him Extreme Unction. He rallied after the rite, and all delusion had gone from early morning. He ate and took his physic with great gusto and conscientiousness — and I took heart. Last night they gave him an opiate — yet he has slept barely two hours — yet the doctors pronounce him better today. He declared himself well, and wants a Te Deum on St Gregory's day. He is not wandering — all through he has been 1. most hopeful, 2. most queerly devoid of fear — though he could not hear the sacred name without

---

[1] On 7 March Bellasis sent Wiseman Newman's letter of 2 Feb. and other papers about the proposed school. Wiseman replied by return, and on 10 March Bellasis wrote to Newman: 'The Cardinal replied . . . that . . . perceiving that it was to be essentially a lay school, under not only Oratorian management but under the same roof as the Oratory, and at Birmingham it appeared to him that he had no right to put any questions on the subject, and that it would be unbecoming in him to hazard an opinion upon it.

He concludes by suggesting that it may perhaps be necessary to refer to the Holy See for permission that females should be under the same roof as Oratorians, because he says, if the Dame and the Fathers have both access to the school from their respective ends of the house they may be held to be under the same roof. However, he goes on, all such difficulties may no doubt be provided for.'

tears coming into his eyes — and even in his worst delirium kissed his relic of the True Cross with intense devotion. He is now living on valerian, beef tea, turtle, yolk of egg, and brandy. I should say, they gave him another opiate this morning, which has as yet only had the effect of stopping his cough — which cough is beginning to alarm us. It is a miracle, if he gets well — yet every one is praying hard for him.

Of course Monsell let you know of Mrs M's happy confinement.

The Bishops are holding a meeting in London. The Cardinal declines to give an opinion about the school plan, 'since it is to be under an Oratorian roof — ' but that is not the case; however he says 1. that Bm [Birmingham] is a bad place. 2. that we ought to get a dispensation from the Holy See for having women so near us. I *won't* get one — but would give up for this, if for no other reason, any thing which was against the Canons. I have been looking at my letter to Bellasis. I said nothing about women being accessible to the Oratory — on the contrary. I said it was to be *cut off* from the school.[1] However, 'under the same roof' may be a technical phrase — tho' abroad, when they live on floors, roof cannot stand for house or home, as with us. It seems that a number of persons have given in their adhesions to the school plan — several Bishops connected with Oscott (not ours) were to speak against it in the Synodal Meeting. I fear Dr Weedall is hurt — we have not seen him since you left.[2]

I hope you have got over your fatigue, which did not surprise me. I shall not be sorry if it inflicts on you that in no sense of the word must you *work*. Your life depends on your not working Love to R

Ever Yrs affly J H N

March 12! 1000 people skating on the reservoir today! Henry has had ¾ of an hour's sound sleep, and is now employed in giving to the servants an order for a bowl of gin punch in honor of St Gregory. He insists on their [sic] being benediction this evening.

P.S. Your letter of March 9 just come. *Make Robert give up his reading if necessary.*[3]

[1] Letter of 2 Feb.
[2] Bellasis wrote on 10 March, 'We heard however that the Bishops interested in Oscott (not Dr U.[Ullathorne]) intended to offer some kind of opposition.' For the names of laymen who supported the proposal for a new Catholic school see letter of 13 April to Bellasis.
[3] Tillotson was unwell.

TO WILLIAM MONSELL

The Oratory March 12. 1858

My dear Monsell,

I must delay no longer to congratulate you most warmly, as I have in my heart ever since the receipt of your letter on the good news you reported to me so kindly and so speedily.[1] I had been looking out for it with great anxiety, and should have not let a post pass without writing to you, except that I wished to send you news of Fr Bittleston, as you asked, and we have been, and are, in such a state of cruel suspence, or rather alternation of hope and fear, that I have had nothing to say definite.

Nearly three weeks have passed since his first attack, and day after day seems to bring a crisis and does not, and our frequent disappointments hinder us having confidence in any improvement which occurs. He was attacked by a pleurisy in his right side and was to be out of his bed in two days — when a second attack came on in his left. He got so bad we thought him dying — so did the doctor — water formed in his side, which threatened to choke his lungs, and his weakness itself seemed about to kill him. We administered Extreme Unction, and he got almost convalescent in the course of two days. Then from imprudence he caught some cold and had a third attack. He then seemed to lay [sic] between life and death for some days, and we could not tell whether he was sinking or gaining ground. However, at length there was no doubt, that he was surely, tho' slowly, making progress, when he was attacked by delirium, and we were again in disappointment. He had not slept for the whole time of his illness, and his medical attendants, for he had now two, did all that art could do to get him rest, — and at length succeeded. He had a long sleep, and when he woke in the morning, we thought he had at length broken the complaint and that we were out of the wood. It seemed so certain that I half thought of saying a Mass of thanksgiving for him. Alas, an hour had not passed when his delirium returned with frightful increase. Well, it was subdued, and he seemed getting right, and at length quite right, when suddenly, yesterday morning, he seemed dying again of exhaustion — and we gave him the Viaticum. Since then he has got better, but now we are getting anxious about his lungs. He has been kept alive by prayers — and I will not despair — but you may think how we are worked both physically and mentally.

I was exceedingly obliged to you for your valuable letter about Stanislas.

I trust mother and child are going on as well as when you wrote and am My dear Monsell

Ever Yrs affly John H Newman

[1] The birth on 5 March of a son and heir.

TO ROBERT ORNSBY

The Ory Bm ⌐March 12/58⌐

My dear Ornsby

I am sorry you are still ill.

⌐I have written to you and to Mr Butler various letters about Dr Quinn's House, containing proposals on my part. I think it better that these should be distinctly *put aside*, before new beginnings are attempted.

E.g. I think I said in my last that if (e.g.) Mr Butler put down [[on paper]], as from the Professors, Dr Quinn's proposals categorically, I would reply categorically.[1] Thus Mr Butler, you, and the other Professors, would have something definite to consider.

I cannot directly negociate with Dr Quinn. We fail to understand each other.⌐

We are still in bitter anxiety about Fr Bittleston. He has been dying well nigh three weeks. We gave him the Viaticum yesterday.

Ever Yrs affly J H Newman

SUNDAY 14 MARCH 1858 last night [Henry] had 10 hours sleep — turning point of illness

TO T. W. MARSHALL

March 14/58

Answered that I had thought of Paley already, and on a former occasion in relation to the University, when he had given me no encouragement.

that I feared I could not avail myself of him now 1. because we should begin in a small way. 2. because I was thinking of others before him.[2]

J H N

MONDAY 15 MARCH 1858 [Henry] from this moment better.

[1] See letter of 13 Feb. to Ornsby.
[2] Marshall wrote on 13 March, suggesting F. A. Paley as a master in the proposed Oratory school. Newman made a note on his draft, which he did not include, 'N.B. I have thought of Allies, Pollen, Woodward, E. Coffin, W. Palmer, Arnold.'

TO JOHN STANISLAS FLANAGAN

6   The Oy Bm March 15/58

My dear S

I really trust we have turned the corner. One hardly knows how to believe such good news — we must be very thankful, and I hope we shall not fail in being so.

I told you about the Viaticum on Thursday. His delusions left him that morning, and he *changed*. We thought him sinking. After the Viaticum, he gradually rallied. I told you about St Gregory's day. Every time the doctors came, they had said he was stronger — and this was the fearful thing when he was not himself, that he had nothing physical the matter with him — his pulse was quite regular. Hence they whispered the word 'mania.' But to return; he went on eating heartily — but the opiates *would* not send him to sleep. However, they calmed him — and the doctors continued to say he was better. On Saturday he was well enough for them to give him tonics. And on Saturday night he slept 10 hours! What news it was yesterday (Sunday) morning! I should have written at once — but feared to be disappointed again. But today I write. He had not much sleep last night — but after all, *three* hours which is *health*, compared to his former state. It seems an age since yesterday morning — it seems an age of ages since the Viaticum, which was only last Thursday. It is three weeks today, since Ambrose broke into my dressing in the morning, with the news of his illness. What an ocean of time! but I trust we are safe now; tho' the doctors do not deny that he is still so weak that he may talk himself back into delirium. But I trust that He who has hitherto been so merciful, will be merciful still to us.

My Brummagem answers to your Statement must come in slow — so that your letters have not yet gone out.[1] But I think you will be pleased with your success hitherto. The Bishop £5 Vicar G. [General] £2 Mr Poncia £10 Mr Fletcher £5. Mr Canning £5. Mr Gough House Poncia £5. Mr Ivers £2.2. Estcourt £3. Mr Grosvenor £1. Mr Sherlock 10/ Mr P. Bretherton £2.2 making £40.14 already. The Vicar General who was here today said that there must be additional collections, if enough did not come into you — so you are sure of the money.

I suppose we shall soon hear from you. Love to Robert. He won't get back by the Passion — because Henry won't be ready to take his place. But we shall see about it after Easter. Don't let him fatigue himself with reading. The eclipse was *just* seen today thro' the clouds, which did instead of smoked glass.[2] The school plan progresses well

Ever Yrs affly J H N

[1] See Circular Letter of 24 Feb., and letter to Flanagan of 26 Feb.
[2] This was an annular eclipse of the sun, visible as a partial eclipse at midday on 15 March.

TO EDWARD BADELEY

The Oratory Birmingham March 16. 1858

My dear Badeley

Thank you for your most pleasant arrangement. The dentist cannot see me till next week. I hope this will not disturb it. I will let you know the day. Tuesday or Wednesday I believe

Ever Yours John H Newman

E Badeley Esqr

FRIDAY 19 MARCH 1858 Crawley announced his intention of leaving us. *Crawley went.* Edward went to Mr Lambert at Peterborough[1]

SATURDAY 20 MARCH Walker came for some weeks. Edward returned

TO HENRY HENNESSY

The Oratory, Birmingham March 20th. 1858

My dear Mr. Hennessy,

I wish I could promise you £400 for the physical Observatory. Could you do anything for that small sum worth spending it? And at what distance of time must the money be forthcoming? Even if I got together that sum, I certainly could not hold out the promise of anything more. Will you consult with Mr. Sullivan on the subject?

Yours very truly, John H. Newman

H. Hennessy Esq.

TO WILLIAM KIRBY SULLIVAN

The Oratory Birmingham March 20. 1858

My dear Mr Sullivan

I have not forgotten your wish to have a further grant — but I really cannot do more, or at least as much as you named, without distinct application to the Archbishops. I will tell the Secretary to draw a cheque for £50, if that will satisfy you.

You see I have no possible means of ascertaining *what* the subscriptions will bear. I only know that the Bishops have tacitly allowed my request of £5000 + the interest of the funded money for definite purposes, as the Professors' salaries. Within the year some anxiety was expressed even about one of these salaries, by one of the Archbishops.

---

[1] i.e. John Lambert of Salisbury, whose mother came from Oundle.

I want to do something towards the physical observatory. I wish you would advise Mr Hennessy how best to begin it. What I should like would be to promise him £400 which I would get by hook or by crook. Yet I don't like to commit myself to so large a sum. However, if I *could* promise it, could any thing be done for it worth the doing?

How will the new Government affect your relations with Sir R. Kane, and your position at the Museum?[1]

Can you recommend me two works for presents in Natural History, Geography, Meteorology, or other physical subject not over technical or mathematical. Works of the day, or just published, would be best — and in English better than in French — not in German. The one should not exceed £10 *bound* — nor the other £5 *bound*.[2] Excuse this trouble and believe me

Most truly Yours John H Newman of the Oratory

W K Sullivan Esqr

TO ROBERT BEVERLEY TILLOTSON

(7)   The Oy Bm March 20/58

My dear Robert,

Certainly I have been disappointed at not hearing from one of you since your letter of last Tuesday week the 9th — and have been watching the post for some days. I wanted to know if you were in lodgings yet. Did I find you (i.e. S. [Stanislas]) settled and tolerably well, I should have asked you to get back by Palm Sunday — Now that is impossible. I am not without fear, from your not writing that S. is not so well — but any how I think you should have written. Only think this is the seventh letter I have sent you. I sent three in one week. And you are *idle*, I busy.[3]

Henry gets stronger every day. He sits up for some hours — Monday or Tuesday he is to leave his room. He says some Office. I do not see why he should not go to Stanislas in Easter week.

What an odd world this is! George [Crawley] is leaving us forthwith. He has been making up his mind for a month past, and at last told Ambrose to tell me. But, for his own convenience, he wishes to stay in the non descript character of neither Father nor novice till over Easter. Meanwhile his Bishop in the North was aware of it at least a fortnight ago, i.e. at least 10 days before I heard a word about it, and told the person who told me what he meant to do with him when he went back. It is an odd world. His reason is merely that

[1] Lord Derby's second ministry took office in Feb. 1858. J. W. Henley succeeded Lord Stanley at the Board of Trade, which controlled the Industrial Museum in Dublin.
[2] These were probably presents for the Birmingham doctors.
[3] Flanagan excused himself on the ground that they were looking for lodgings at Pau, in the end successfully.

he finds his present position so dull compared with the mission — he having left the mission in order to have some rest and read theology. On February 2nd he declares before us all, that he means to remain till the end of his life, and by the 18th (for it is a month ago) he has had trial enough of us to begin bringing before his Confessor the question of leaving us. And he pressed himself on us — and after 17 months deliberation made a retreat and flung himself forthwith into faces, without giving us time to answer his letter announcing his coming. A very odd world.

March 21. Another day without a letter. It is incomprehensible.

Henry says 'send for Robert conditionally on Stanislas not being ill. He will at least get here by Good Friday.' But I want to be the judge myself Love to S

Ever Yrs affly J H N

P.S. Stanislas must keep strictly in mind the French Doctor's words, as Monsell reports them, 'If he does not remain for six months *idle*, he will go into a consumption. If he does, he will get well and go to work.'

All my 4d stamps are out — so this will be my last letter for a time.

TO T. W. ALLIES

The Oratory Birmingham March 21. 1858

My dear Allies,

I know that moving does not conduce to literary work, but I hope it is over now, and I write from a great desire that you should not fail in your good intentions to give us an article for the July number of the Atlantis.

We have been in great trouble here, two of our Fathers in the midst of their work, have suddenly been arrested and laid up. Besides the extreme anxiety about their lives, you may think what additional work it has thrown upon the rest, and the work of nursing too, which is not slight. It has been most merciful, that I was not tied by the leg in Dublin. What should I have done if it had been two years back! I am now employed in keeping together their penitents, and in any other use I can be of.

Fr Bittleston is, I trust recovering, Fr Flanagan is at Pau where he must be for some time. And I suppose B. will join him.

Will you let Mrs Allies know of Fr Bittleston's recovery? I wrote her a doleful letter, as far as I remember it.

Ever yours affectly in Xt   John H Newman of the Oratory

The Oy Bm March 22/58

My dear Child

God will be sure to prosper, guide, and reward so strong and pure a resolve.

The self command you go on to speak about, by which the mind rules itself to believe, I consider in the highest degree meritorious, and sure of a reward — but I don't *word* it as you do.

It is not, that faith is an act of the *will* — but the will obliges the *reason* to believe. Nor is there a want of faith and of acts of faith in the *reason*, in the case you put — but a languor of the *imagination*. For I consider the 'realization' you speak of is to be as distinct from faith, as *emotion* is. It is a state of the imagination.

Ever Yrs affly John H Newman

Sister Mary Philip.

I shall say a Mass for you once a week for some time

TO J. R. BLOXAM

The Oratory Birmingham March 22. 1858

My dear Bloxam

I am ashamed to think that I have not acted on your kind permission of last year to send your name to the publisher as a subscriber to our new Periodical.[1]

All I can say in my defence is, that our commencement was then a long time off — and that I did not place your letter where it would have at once turned up, when I wanted it.

If it is not too late, I should like to repair my mistake now.

You have had a great many losses in Oxford, since I wrote to you, which must to residents alter the place, as removing familiar faces. And one always fears, that such deaths are tokens of the probable loss of others too, who may be contemporaries of those who are gone and about whom one has not heard for some time.

Ever Yours affly John H Newman

The Revd Dr Bloxam

[1] See letter of 3 July 1857.

The Oratory, Birmingham March 22. 1858.

My dear Lord Henry,

I have never thanked you for your kind letter and its inclosure of last month. I sent it at once to Fr Flanagan who ultimately decided on Pau, where he is now as I trust improving.

My silence was owing to the great and more urgent trouble which came upon us when he had hardly left the house. Fr Bittleston was taken with a pleurisy, and for those weeks lay between life and death. He now is out of all danger, I trust, and sits up for some hours every day. It has been a most extremely trying time for us.

Francis [Kerr] passed through as you know the other day. He is grown out of knowledge.

My kindest remembrances to Lady Henry who I rejoice to hear is better.

Yours most sincerely in Xt   John H Newman of the Oratory

The Lord Henry Kerr.

TO THOMAS SCRATTON

The Oy Bm March 22/58

My dear S

I have again made a careful search through all my Dublin letters, which since November, when I left, I have kept in one place all together. I can't find any draft — and what is stranger, I can't find any letter from you dated February 26, speaking of the draft.

I infer, either that the letter *never reached me*, or else that I have put both it and the draft in some safe place suddenly, (e.g. if I were leaving my room close upon receiving it) and have forgotten all about it. As to the latter hypothesis, I have hunted through my table drawer, my writing desk, and three other parcels of letters in vain.

At present I can say no more — but that I am much annoyed about it —

My own *first* impression was that I had received it from you and returned it

Ever Yrs J H N

Monday ⌜March 23 [[1858]]⌝

My dear Mr Butler,

I inclose a letter of Scratton's. ⌜Myself, I think it quite a dream that we should get a charter from Government — but I would not for the world put any difficulty in the way — Perhaps you and Dr Dunne, who seem the Professors most decided and sanguine on the subject, might call on the Archbishop⌝ who returns to Dublin tomorrow (Tuesday,) and ask him about it.

I shall send you, perhaps tomorrow, some remarks on your Mark scheme. It is carefully done — and promises well. I wish you *not to give my remarks any weight* beyond what you yourselves feel to be their due. They are not meant as objections, but suggestions

Ever Yours John H Newman

Edwd Butler Esqr

WEDNESDAY 24 MARCH 1858 went to town — to Lintott — then to Badeley who found me a bed   Hope-Scott and Acton to dinner — Manning called

THURSDAY 25 MARCH Lintott — called on Bellasis, T. Flanagan, Monsell, Burns, H. W. [Wilberforce]   Bowyer to lunch at Badeley's — came down to Bm [Birmingham] with Sir John Acton[1]

TO SIR JOHN ACTON

The Oratory Birmingham March 26. 1858

My dear Sir John,

I shall be very much pleased, if the list which I inclose should suggest any subject, on which you will write for the Atlantis. What you said to me yesterday, encourages me to send it to you.

We should be very grateful either for

1. A literary article on some *definite subject*, embracing notices by the way, of German works.

2. A literary article bearing on the *literary history* of Germany in some particular department of learning.

[1] 'I have had a long and very satisfactory talk with Newman on matters connected with the *Rambler*. He hopes before long to make the *Atlantis* a quarterly. Will not that diminish our chance of being able to set up a quarterly?' Acton to Simpson, 25 March 1858, *Gasquet*, p. 12. For Acton's account to Döllinger see Victor Conzemius, *Ignaz von Döllinger, Lord Acton, Briefwechsel*, I, p. 141.

3 A historical notice (in smaller type, for the last pages of the Number) of various German works *on one subject*.

4. Separate *unconnected* notices (in smaller type) of various German works.[1]

Very sincerely Yours in Xt   John H Newman of the Oratory

Sir John D. Acton Bart

TO EDWARD BADELEY

The Oy Bm March 26/58

My dear Badeley

First, my profound thanks for your careful hospitality. Next, the words of our decree —

'Cum multi sint in Ecclesiâ Dei, qui audiendis monialium confessionibus aut dant operam, aut dare optime possunt, proptereà, ne quis *ab instituto* Congregationis nostrae *proprio* possit *abduci*, statutum est, ne nostrorum aliquis *se obliget* aut *dedat* confessionibus audiendis, moribus reformandis, rebusque earum gerendis. Idem dicimus de Seminariis, Collegiis Congregationibus, Societatibus,, *aut aliis Universitatibus*, rebusque earum, *sine gravi necessitate*, tractandis.'[2]

The question is, if a Ragged School, or a Reformatory is not a Universitas, is a School for gentlemen's sons? *or is a* Ragged School a Universitas?[3]

Ever Yrs affly John H Newman of the Oratory

E. Badeley Esqr

Private

P.S.   I put it down on paper distinctly, that I was not in any way sounded by any one as to my willingness to undertake a translation of Scripture before the Synod at which my name was mentioned was held. I heard it quite to my surprise *afterwards* in private from our Bishop — and then when two years passed by, I thought and expected, as well as hoped, it had come to nothing — when last August the Cardinal wrote to me on the subject.[4]

---

[1] Acton never contributed to the *Atlantis*. See his letter of 29 July placed before Newman's of 2 Aug. 1858.

[2] *Instituta Congregationis Anglicae Oratorii S. Philippi Nerii*, Rome 1847, Decretum LXX, p. 30.

[3] Decretum LXX had been the occasion of the breach with the London Oratory, and Newman wished to be quite sure that he would in no way infringe it. Badeley replied on 29 March, 'I have looked at the meaning assigned by writers on Canon and on Civil Law to the word "Universitas," and I cannot find anything which leads me to the conclusion that either a School for Gentlemen's sons, or a Ragged School, comes within it.' See also letter of 12 Jan. 1862 to Hope-Scott.

[4] See letter of 27 Aug. 1857 to Wiseman. Badeley commented, 'Your Postscript about the

The Oratory, Birmingham. March 26th. 1858

My dear Mr. Hennessy,

I am not surprised, however sorry I am, that you cannot make a good job of the £400 — and, as I could not scrape together that sum (if I could do it at all) without great inconvenience, I think it best not to offer it to you.

I was influenced in writing to you by an additional motive. The Auditors had been making enquiries about Lectures delivered, and I think it will be necessary before long for you to make some statements as to the work of your Professorship. It struck me then, that if you really could shew that you were making observations, and could publish, if called upon, their results — it would have been an easy way of meeting public opinion, which I fear is being turned to the subject. But I know how expensive the apparatus is which physical pursuits require, and, reluctant as I am, I submit to what I cannot help.

Yours most truly, John H Newman.

H. Hennessy Esq.

TO D. B. DUNNE

⌐(Sent in substance)¬

⌐March 27/58¬

My dear Dr Dunne

⌐I have just received your painful letter,¬ which, however, you are quite right in thinking I should have been sorry not to have had, the circumstances being what they are — for the pain is in the facts, not in the notice of them. As you speak of being 'the medium' of the news, I consider you write in the name of other Professors, (perhaps (virtually) as the Secretary of your Faculty)¹

Translation of the Scriptures surprised me—They seem to have treated you very coolly, and, I cannot help thinking, not very properly.'
    For Acton's account to Döllinger of the confusion and lack of interest among the bishops in the subject, see Victor Conzemius, *Ignaz von Döllinger—Lord Acton, Briefwechsel*, I, p. 141, letter of 5 April 1858.
    ¹ Newman copied out the relevant parts of Dunne's letter of 25 March:
    'Last night the "Historical, Literary, and Aesthetical Society" had a lecture, open to the public. Mr Robertson was the Lecturer. The audience included the Lord Mayor, Lady Mayoress, Dr Ellis, Dr Hayden, and many ladies and gentlemen of high respectability. The lecture was delivered in the Lecture room generally used by Mr Butler. The students were collected standing in a body at the end of the room—Mr McDermott (student) in the chair —Augustus Bethell (President of the Society) was in the first rank of the collected students. I am ashamed to say, that, from the commencement to the end of the Lecture, the conduct

11

(The disgraceful disturbance you inform me of is owing, initially I suppose to the want of a Vice Rector, and immediately to the influence, which is so catching of the Trin: [Trinity] College rows.)[1]

⌈I observe that Mr Quinn, who was foremost in the disturbance, is of Trin: College — that Messrs Hanly, Hobart, and Dolan are externs, (if I am not mistaken,) and not really specimens of our youths. As to Zamoyski and White, their conduct must be inquired into.

I also observe that it was not a University Lecture, but one of the Aesthetic Society.

Now I am writing by return of post, and therefore I have not very carefully considered what is best to be done, but I think, if the Professors have my first impressions, they may improve on them or use them as suggestions for something better.

1. Since it was a private Lecture, and the Professors guests I hardly think the University can directly interfere. The Professors laid aside their Professorial gown, when they attended it, and cannot resume it to punish. It must be thrown on the gentlemanly feeling and good sense of the members of the Society — Who form the Committee or Governing body? they ought to make a private though distinct apology in the name of the Society to the Lord Mayor etc — and they should strike off the rioters from their lists. And one or other of them might be told confidentially that I had thoughts of suppressing the Society altogether[1] (for it certainly *would come* to that) ⌈by way of stimulating them.[1] If they have not legal power to expel, then let them dissolve the society, and divide the books (if it is not a great loss) and then form a new society to the exclusion of these riotous members. And let them know that the University *could* expel any rioters, if *they* can't. I say this in

of the body of students (and unfortunately they included most of the students of the University) was so bad, that worse could with difficulty be conceived. The Lord Mayor, by gestures, repeatedly expressed his deep dissatisfaction: and Mr Ellis, in seconding the vote of thanks to the Lecturer, was compelled to remonstrate with them on the way in which his own observations were received.

1. There was a rambling sound of voice kept up perpetually, mocking the inflections and emphases of the Lecturer's voice . . .

2 Pocket handkerchiefs were knotted and used as flagella .. .

3 Students were knocked down . . .

4 The door of the room was (creaked) for minutes together .. .

5 A perpetual jostling, shuffling and humdrum chatting . . .

6. Towards the close of the Lecture a great crash . . .

7 These disturbances caused no small merriment to the "young lady" portion of the audience.

8 Mr MacDermott's expression of deep gratification etc at the close was literally *crushed down*.

Foremost among the disturbers were Messrs H. H. and D. The names of—and—of St Mary's House have also been mentioned. Conspicuous was a Mr Quinn (who 18 months since was at St Patrick's House, and now is a student of Trinity College) I cannot say too much of Augustus Bethell's conduct His demeanour alone ought to have reduced the rioters to order.'

[1] Newman put this paragraph in brackets, and presumably it was omitted in the letter as sent.

order to give them an argumentative protection for strong acts on their part.[1]

⌐2. I think it is a great opportunity, coincident as it is with the report of their sympathising in the Trin College rows, to ask earnestly of the Arch-bishops a Pro-vice-rector; under the strong apprehension that the University is going to pieces for want of one. I wish the whole body of the Professors could be got to take part in this formal application.[2]

3. I am not sorry that an opportunity occurs of putting an end to a practice which I have ever disliked, and which has shown its evil before now — viz the Professors lecturing in the Undergraduate Society. Mr McDermott, the President, is for the moment the Superior of Professor Robertson. I shall ask the professors' leave to put an end to his unseemly proceeding.[1]

Ever Yours affly J H N

P.S   Pray give my best and kindest regards to your wife. You have heard perhaps what great trouble we have been in here. First Fr Flanagan in bed for a month — then Fr Bittleston for 3 weeks, in great or extreme danger the whole time.

I wrote to Augustus Bethell lately about the Philosophy of Religion   Ask him to show you the letter.

TO THOMAS SCRATTON

The Ory Bm March 27/58

My dear S

I have just learned that no Mass is provided in my House in Penny's absence. I should be very much obliged by your getting me a Priest, if it be possible, to supply his place in this respect. I have usually given £1 a week

Ever Yrs J H Newman

Thos Scratton Esqr

---

[1] Robertson wrote on 5 April that the noise was only made by six or seven students, and after the lecture, during the speech of the President of the Aesthetic Society. 'The students have disowned the conduct of their six turbulent associates by offering through their President, an apology to the representative of vice-rectorial authority, Mr Butler, and by calling, (as they intend to do to-day for the same object,) on the Lord Mayor himself. Further the six riotous students will each be subjected by the Aesthetic Society to a heavy fine, tantamount to the penalty of expulsion.' See also *Centenary History of the Literary and Historical Society of University College Dublin 1855–1955*, Tralee n.d., edited by James Meenan, pp. 9–11.

[2] [[The Vice Rector was by the Statutes charged with the *discipline of the University*]] Butler wrote to Newman on 23 March about a report in the [Protestant] *Dublin Evening Mail*. The students at Trinity College had clashed with the police on the occasion of the entry of Lord Eglinton as Viceroy earlier in March. The *Mail* of 19 March stated, 'It is, we are assured, a certain fact that the sudents of the Catholic University offered to make common cause with those of Trinity College in case of the occurrence of any further outrage on the part of the Police rendering active resistance necessary.' Cullen demanded an inquiry, and Butler was able to write to the *Mail* that it had been misinformed and that the offer of an alliance had not been made.

SUNDAY 28 MARCH Palm. I celebrated, and through the week. fully occupied in the Confessional

TUESDAY 30 MARCH Robert returned from Pau

TO ROBERT ORNSBY

The Oy Bm ⌐March 30. 1858⌐

My dear Ornsby

Thank you very much for your long and valuable letter.[1] ⌐Be sure that the success of the University is, after this Congregation, the nearest object of my heart. And also let me say that I have no kind of doubt, in spite of our present discouragements, of its continued wellbeing. All commencements are experiments — we must throw out our lines in every direction, and not be annoyed at loss of toil. For myself, I have no hesitation in altering any thing which ought to be altered, and in following up any new opening which promises well.

But the first and immediate necessity is a Vice Rector or Pro-Vice-Rector. I am kept here [[the Oratory]] by simple duty — ⌐ and it is providential — for it saves me further deliberation. ⌐But,⌐ were I at *liberty* to come to Dublin, the grave question would present itself whether I *ought* to do so, *till* a quasi-Vice-Rector is appointed. ⌐*I* am not Vice Rector. It is unfair to me to make me undertake responsibilities which do not immediately attach to me. Our one necessity, imperative and instant, is a *Vice Rector*, or one who will act as such. As I am not exactly in the position I was in October, when negociations were going on for my continuing two years more, I should not feel obliged to make objection to any one who should be named by the Archbishops. Not that I have been ever in circumstances leading me to do this, but I mean that I should *not* do it.

A Vice Rector is a first necessity, and I think the Professors should respectfully make the Archbishops understand this.[2]

You may show this to whom you will⌐

Ever Yrs affly John H. Newman[3]

R. Ornsby Esqr

[1] Ornsby's letter of 28 March described his efforts to persuade Dr Quinn to send more students to the University. Quinn asked for increased financial aid. See letter of 12 April to him. He also regretted that the students at the University were allowed so much freedom, and that those who were church students read the classics rather than seminary philosophy.

[2] Ornsby wrote on 11 April that the Professors were unwilling to approach the bishops, and feared to give the impression of dictating to them. Cf. letter of 12 April to Ornsby.

[3] Newman preserved the draft of this letter, and wrote on it 'sent in substance but shorter and more guarded.' There were only slight differences in the first paragraph. The rest was as follows: 'But the first and immediate necessity is a Vice Rector or pro-Vice-Rector. And I do not move till that necessity is supplied. I am kept here by a strange disposition of Providence, for I cannot move, were there ever so many strong reasons for moving. But I conceive it is my actual duty not to show myself in Dublin, till the Archbishops do what ought to have been done six months ago, or rather several years ago. It is treating me with extreme

TO BISHOP ULLATHORNE

The Oratory Bm March 30. 1858

My dear Lord

In the greatest hurry I ask your leave to send you a very few illarranged words about our school plan, about which two Gentlemen are, I believe, to talk with you tomorrow. I wish your Lordship to know, that this Congregation is not committed to it yet, though I have promised to interest them in it.

I do not even myself go beyond the idea of *such* a relation on the part of our body to it, as we might have to a Ragged School, Reformatory, or Workhouse — I mean, the assigning one or two Fathers to the *superintendance* of it. These two would be Fr Darnell and myself. Fr D's connection with it would be based on the circumstance of his being a Wykehamite [sic], and his having a good name as a disciplinarian. My own connection would be merely that, which arises from my late position in Ireland.

As to the *spot*, I have wished that it should be close to us, even on our own ground, because we can take part in its work better, if close to it, than if at a distance.

As to the *period* of time, during which we shall be connected with it, it has one or two necessary limits — 1. the size of the school — we could not undertake more than 50 boys, as things are. 2. the health and strength of Fr Darnell — for we have no one to take his place. What we have been asked to do, is to '*nurse*' the School, while it is in its infancy.

Our *Congregation* has settled nothing; — not time — not place. It is certain that none of our existing body, except Fr Darnell, has the qualifications or taste necessary for the work.

I have said all this to Sir John Acton and Serjeant Bellasis — but I think it best, however hastily and imperfectly, to say it to your Lordship.

Fr Bittleston, I thank God, is quite convalescent, and more

Begging your Lordship's blessing I am, My dear Lord, Your affte friend & Servt in Xt

John H Newman of the Oratory

The Rt Revd The Bp of Birmingham

unfairness to put all the work on me, and make me responsible for duties not mine. I am not Vice Rector, and will not do the work of a Vice-Rector. I cannot undertake the discipline, if it were merely on this account that it is not my line, and I could not exercise the office. And, since I am now in a different position from what I was in last October, for then a negociation was going on for keeping [me] which has come to nothing, I do not feel it a duty to object to any one whom the Archbishops wish — not that I have ever done so in any formal way in any instance, but I mean I would now have no opinion on the matter.

You may show this letter to whom you will — and I certainly think that the Professors should petition for a quasi Vice Rector

J H N'

WEDNESDAY 31 MARCH 1858   Bellasis and Acton came down about the School Plan.

Oy Bm March 31/58

My dear S

Will you pay this into my account at the *Hibernian*.

£8 . 10 of it belongs to you for which I send you a cheque

Ever Yrs affly J H N

TO EDWARD BELLASIS

The Oratory Bm April 1. 1858

My dear Serjeant Bellasis

I am sorry to say that our Bishop has spoken to Fr St John so strongly today on the subject of our school plan, that it is impossible to proceed without some explanation.

He has, apparently, been frightened by the Cardinal — who has been put up to it by others.

What I think is absolutely necessary is for you to ascertain what position our Bishop wishes to take — The Cardinal tells him that he (Dr U.) will have the whole *responsibility* — now you wish him to have no responsibility at all — only to allow, or not to veto, the plan,.

Don't you think then you could write to him to say, that you, and Sir John considered the result of your conversation yesterday to be this — that, though he (the Bishop) could not take on himself the responsibility of the project, if he had been asked to do so — yet, since he was *not* asked this, but only informed that such a plan was projected and that it was, as a matter of duty, submitted to him before commencing it, he did not object to it under this aspect.

If he answers in the affirmative and we have the correspondence in black and white — it will be something to appeal to — but it will never do to have it said (*which will otherwise be said*) that we, you and ourselves, began against the expressed wish of the Bishop of the diocese.[1]

Excuse this hasty letter and believe me

Most sincerely Yours John H Newman of the Oratory

Mr Serjeant Bellasis

[1] Bellasis wrote at once and received a satisfactory reply. See letter of 6 April to him. Acton, who had interviewed Ullathorne with Bellasis on 31 March, wrote to the latter on 6 April, 'As I undoubtedly considered the upshot of his [Ullathorne's] remarks to us a declaration of war his letter seems more satisfactory than could have been expected . . .
I am afraid that when Newman says the Cardinal was "put up to it by others" there can

SUNDAY 4 APRIL 1858   Easter Day

TO J. D. DALGAIRNS

The Oratory Birmingham Easter Day 1858

My dear Fr Bernard

A Happy Easter to you, and to all your Community.

I have just received your article on the German mystics, which I take for granted is your gift.[1] Thank you for it — I know well the subject must have been done justice to by you — and I shall read it with great interest

Yours affly John H Newman

The Revd Fr Dalgairns

MONDAY 5 APRIL 1858   Thanksgiving Mass for Henry's recovery

TO SIR JOHN ACTON

The Oratory Birmingham April 5. 1858

My dear Sir John

I quite forgot at the right time to speak to you the other day on the subject of your contributions to the Atlantis, as you so kindly offered them. I write now merely to supply my omission, by saying, that I perfectly agreed to what you proposed in your letter, and shall be very glad to receive what you are to send

Very sincerely Yours John H Newman

Sir John Acton Bart

TO JOHN STANISLAS FLANAGAN

The Oratory Bm Easter Monday 1858

My dear S.

As I have one stamp over, which was intended for Monsell, but he came to London, I send my Easter greetings with it — but I shall be stingy for a

be no doubt as to whom he means.' i.e. presumably the London Oratorians. See also Acton's letter of 20 March 1858 to Döllinger, Victor Conzemius, *Ignaz von Döllinger—Lord Acton, Briefwechsel*, I, p. 134. The school plan had been so much discussed that it could not be abandoned without damaging Newman's position and influence. Acton claimed to have talked with all parties in London. Faber was personally friendly, but opposed the projected school and was playing a roll which did him no credit. He had won over to his side Wiseman and the Duke of Norfolk. For Ullathorne's opposition see Acton's letter of 5 April to Döllinger, *ibid.*, p. 141.

[1] *The German Mystics of the Fourteenth Century*, London 1858, reprinted from *D R*.

time, and borrow the letters of others to say a word in. We have had a thanksgiving Mass for Henry today, very well attended. Robert got here soon after Nicholas's letter went to you. We thought him looking very well — Poor fellow, I fear he was rather disappointed at having to return, but he has been *very* useful to us, and I originally *said* (as soon as *you* were not allowed to coach him, and *Henry* was taken ill) that he should come back by Palm Sunday.

I don't want you to write very often, if you have nothing to say — but, when we wondered you did not write, recollect, Robert had given an uncomfortable account of you, which we *hoped* was to be explained by the fatigue of your journey, but we could not know for certain till a second letter came — and I *could* not tell Robert to come home, till we did know.

Somehow I am sanguine that a spell of trouble is going to be taken off us, but I cannot tell.

The Cardinal has washed his hands of the school plan, and has pointedly told our Bishop that *he* will have the whole responsibility. Our Bishop (post or propter I know not) has advised us strongly against it because it is sure to be a failure, yet, when he gives reasons, they are so unintelligible, as to show they are not his real difficulty, whatever it is. Bellasis and Acton, who have been here again, are writing to put to the Bishop this question 'Does your Lordship wish to have the giving of your *formal sanction* to a lay school and you don't give it, or do you think it simply a case of *veto* or no-veto, and you do not veto?' If he answers the former, we have nothing to do with it of course — if the latter, we do. The plan is now, to return to our original plan, and rent a house with boys under 11 for two or three years as a trial. I suppose it will be settled, whether we take it or not in a few days.

The Congregation has determined to unite the two departments of music under Fr Frederic. This has never been yet, and I am sceptical of the possibility of their being united, without one or the other being sacrificed — however, it has had the good effect of making apparently a considerable change in Fr Frederic, who seems desirous to come [out] of his isolation — and actually proposed today to go to Rednall, which he has never seen since it was a green field. I shall make a great effort, (and I hope you will keep in mind this intention of mine with peculiar interest and diligence) to get more intimate with him, and to make a change in him, for such slovenly unoratorian ways as he has pursued must not go on — or he will lose his vocation. You know how his omitting to say Mass has annoyed me.

Ambrose is sorry he has not told you before that Mrs Cantifer is dead. Cantifer bears it well.

Ever Yours affly J H N

P.S. I suppose Henry will set out in a day or two. You shall know.

The Oratory Birmingham April 5, 1858.

My dear Mrs Froude,

Thank you very much for your long and welcome letter. All in time will go right, I trust and believe — tho' it may be a long time. What is going on, what is done, is a ground for great thankfulness and hope.

More thanks, for remembering me in your prayers. We have had and have much trouble. Fr Flanagan, one of our most important and dearest members, has been ordered to Pau for fear of consumption. Hardly had he left the house, when Fr Bittleston was seized with pleurisy, and was in *great* danger for three weeks. Thank God, this very day we have had a thanksgiving Mass for him. He is going out to join Fr F. at Pau — so I have a vast deal of work thrown on me, as they had so many penitents and other engagements.

Now don't suppose I am not most deeply interested in all the details of your letter because I say so little. Please, do not deprive me of such news, when you can give it, and believe me,

with best Easter greetings to you and yours, Ever yours affly in Xt

John H. Newman of the Oratory.

Mrs Froude.

TO WILLIAM KIRBY SULLIVAN

The Oratory Birmingham April 5 1858

My dear Mr Sullivan

I am exceedingly concerned to hear of your accident — which was news to me when Mr Hennessy mentioned it a day or two ago. He said that you were nearly well.[1]

I told the Secretary to send you the Fifty Pounds — I will do my best, but I cannot promise, to get you the other Fifty after May. You will have to give in an account to the Auditors as before.

Sir John Acton will do something for the Atlantis — but I fear not by July, Mr Allies is uncertain.

It seems to me that, as might be expected, the non-existence of a Vice Rector is weighing with most serious effect upon the University. Cannot the Professors see their way to bring it before the Archbishops? I have opened the subject to one or other of them again and again.

Very sincerely Yours John H Newman of the Oratory

W K Sullivan Esqr

[1] Sullivan had burned himself with naphtha.

TO EDWARD BELLASIS

The Oratory Birmingham April 6. 1858

My dear Bellasis

We think your correspondence with the Bishop quite satisfactory — and shall commence operations with a solemn Novena to St Philip, in which our people, without being told our intention, will take part.[1]

I am glad the Bishop has brought out to you his real difficulty, for he mystified the matter to us. If he means I am not in *practice* a good disciplinarian, I quite confess it. I have it as little in me to be a good schoolmaster or Dean, as to be a good rider or successful chess player. But this does not hinder my feeling the *need* of strict discipline for boys — for many a man approves what he cannot practise.[2]

Then perhaps people about him or in London have told him stories about our goings on in Dublin, which, though not so exact and well managed as I should like them to be, are not what some good people represent them. Here too I may say, first, that it does not follow quite logically, because I think that in matters of discipline a University should *not* be like a school, (which I *do* think) that *therefore* in those matters a school *should* be like a University. Moreover, as to any defect of our academical discipline at Dublin, it must be considered that, not the Rector, but the Vice Rector is the officer of it — and I *never* have had a resident Vice Rector allowed me by the Bishops, and at this moment there is none even nominally. Deans too are hard to be got — they are either as strict as Prefects in an Ecclesiastical Seminary, or they are indulgent and lax. Difficulties such as these are only temporary, but they are serious at starting. Under our circumstances, I wonder we have got on so well.

Probably there are other reasons given, to suggest distrust and hesitation

[1] In his letter of 2 April to Ullathorne Bellasis wrote: 'As the school, altho' essentially a lay school would probably be placed in your immediate neighbourhood it was thought to be a duty to inform your Lordship of it, and to submit the plan to you before commencing it, we had however no notion of committing your Lordship to an approval of it or of putting you in the position of being in any way responsible for it.

We understand your Lordship to approve so far as the plan tended to effect a separation between Lay and Ecclesiastical students, but to have considerable doubts as to our means of commanding that degree of discipline and school management which is to be found in existing schools. Your Lordship's advice on this will probably materially affect the ultimate arrangements, but we did not understand that you intended to put any veto upon the school itself and should be glad to be certified that we have not misunderstood you in this respect.'

Ullathorne replied on 4 April: 'Your letter of the 2d Inst expresses accurately the views which I conveyed to you and Sir John Acton, at our recent interview.

You are correct in stating that, subject to the remarks which I then offered, and which are resumed in your letter, I am in no wise disposed to offer any opposition or discouragement to the contemplated experiment at Edgbaston.'

When enclosing Ullathorne's letter. Bellasis wrote on 5 April, 'His idea is that you, and the fathers of the Oratory generally, as well as all converts are under the impression that the existing rules of discipline at Catholic Colleges are too strict. . . .'

[2] Ullathorne himself is said to have 'had little idea of managing boys.' Cuthbert Butler, *The Life and Times of Bishop Ullathorne*, London 1926, I, p. 24.

in co-operating in our school plan, and these feelings can only [be] removed by time and experience of us. We are on the best terms with our Bishop — and his fears will gradually give way. I do not think much would come from trying to persuade him by compulsory or compendious means. So I propose to let him alone, though keeping him au courant of our proceedings.

I should like very much if there were two or three persons, such as Hope Scott, whom we might privately and confidentially consult on the details of our plan of proceeding. The only point of *principle* on which we should differ from the Colleges, is that we should aim at doing every thing above board — and abjure espionage, listening at doors etc. The question of opening letters has to be considered here — but certainly I should desire such honesty and openness in our conduct to the boys, that they would have no temptation to *distrust* us.

As we want to write to Fr Flanagan before commencing the Novena, it will not begin till next Sunday, to finish on the 19th. Meanwhile we shall be looking after houses

Ever Yours most sincerely John H Newman of the Oratory
Mr Serjeant Bellasis

TO W. J. O'NEILL DAUNT

The Oratory Birmingham April 6. 1858
My dear Sir,

I have only this morning received your letter, and hasten to reply to it. Gladly would I give you any information about Clondalkin, if I had had any knowledge of it when I was in Ireland — but this was never granted me.[1] Your account about your son interests me very much — how anxious you must be to do what is best for him![2] I do not know what the terms are at Ushaw, but every thing I hear of that school is good in those points to which you refer — the *charge* against the place being that there is too much danger of the boys finding ecclesiastical vocations there! I say this without meaning any disparagement to Oscott or St Edmunds, which are under the presidency of most excellent men — whom no one can know without revering and loving.[3]

[1] Daunt wrote on 3 April to Ask Newman's advice about the education of his son, aged eight and a half, whom he wished to be 'a pious, holy, fervently attached Catholic.' He wondered whether to send him to Mount St Joseph Seminary, Clondalkin, near Dublin.
[2] Daunt wrote of him as 'extremely intelligent, wild, idle and impetuous, learns, despite much carelessness and inattention; shows dashes of very strong Catholic feeling, strangely mixed with precocious scepticism on the subject of the Trinity; has a great propensity to fun and mimicry; and, on the whole, has in him the makings (according to his training and associations) of something very good or very bad.'
[3] i.e. Weedall and Weathers.

As to ourselves, it is true some attempt at a purely lay school is in contemplation here — but it has not yet assumed any very definite form. The experiment will be necessarily expensive — and the terms at first must, I fear, be high[1]

Yours, my dear Sir, with much respect, Very truly in Xt

John H Newman of the Oratory

W J O'N Daunt, Esqr

TO THE DUKE OF NORFOLK

[7 April 1858]

My dear Duke of Norfolk

Fr Bittleston has shown me your most kind letter to him, inclosing so liberal a contribution to the workhouse, that Fr Flanagan, to whom he sets out tomorrow, will be filled with consolation on hearing of it from him in his exile at Pau[2]

Most sincerely Yours in Xt   John H Newman

FRIDAY 9 APRIL 1858   Henry went for Pau

TO MISS M. R. GIBERNE

April 9/58

My dear Miss Giberne

There is not much news to tell; and what there is, I suppose Ambrose has given you. The weather this Easter week has been atrocious. Our Atlantis is getting on famously and Ambrose is hard at Hebrew.

With our best Easter greetings

Yours affectionately in Xt   John H Newman[3]

SATURDAY 10 APRIL 1858   called on the Bishop who was out.
SUNDAY 11 APRIL   beginning of Novena about the School plan

---

[1] Daunt wrote, 'The pension at Clondalkin would just suit my means, which are very small. The charge is somewhere about £22 per annum . . .' See letter of 13 April to Newsham.
[2] Newman enclosed this note with Bittleston's letter of thanks.
[3] This note was written at the end of a long letter from St John to Miss Giberne.

TO ROBERT ORNSBY

The Oratory, Bm ⌈April 12. 1858⌉

My dear Ornsby,

Thank you for your important letter just received. I am truly sorry to hear of Mr Butler's illness: pray give him my best remembrances, and, when he is fit for business, the inclosed letter, which I have written to Dr Quinn in answer to his propositions received by me this day. The letter is for you, Stewart etc.[1]

⌈As to what you say about the Vice Rector,[2] I don't think the Archbishops *can* be unmindful of the words of the Synodal Meeting, 'Nominandum decernimus Vice-Rectorem, *qui consilio et auxilio* PRAESTO *sit Rectori.*'[3] Nor can they urge against me my own Rules and Regulations, (vid my Report of last year) which expressly say, '*The Vice-Rector has, when the Rector is* PRESENT, *the routine administration of the University.*'⌉[4]

Ever Yours affly John H Newman

R. Ornsby Esqr

TO JAMES QUINN

(Copy)   The Oratory, Birmingham April 12/58

My dear Dr Quinn

Though I shall have the pleasure of seeing you tomorrow, I think it best to

[1] See next letter. Ornsby wrote on 11 April, 'Dr Quinn you will have heard from. He proposes to call on you at Birmingham on the subject of his own house, with a proposition I believe for 40 burses being founded. He could sent 30 students next term if there were.'
[2] After saying that Butler was against asking the Bishops to appoint a Vice-Rector, Ornsby continued: 'He is inclined to think the Bishops may be putting the matter off till the bulls arrive for Fr. Flannery, so as to save his *amour propre*, and not to seem to pass him over [in the choice of Vice Rector. He was about to become Coadjutor to the Bishop of Killaloe]. I suspect too, from Butler's surmises, that there must be some hitch about the office of Vice-Rector itself. "They would say, why does not Dr Newman reside? If he resided, there would be no need of a Vice Rector, because by the statutes they have given us, he has no duties whilst the Rector is in residence. There is a Dean of the University for discipline." Such is my note of part of the conversation. Butler remarked in another conversation that Dr Cullen had sent for Fr. Flannery on occasion of the late dispute as to whether the University students had got mixed up in the Trinity College disturbances. Now if they are dissatisfied on the question of what the Vice Rector's office really means, this may be why they are keeping it open in the way they do.'
Newman commented, [[Dr Cullen from the first considered Mr Flannery *the* Dean of the University. I never recognized him as more than Dean or Head of St Patrick's House. The Vice-Rector by the Statutes was the officer of *discipline*. That the Archbishops wished *to force* that office upon me, was one of the reasons which hindered me going to Dublin, while there was no Vice-Rector. Nov 18. 1872.]]
[3] *Campaign*, p. 89, among the decrees of the Synodal Meeting of 18 May 1854.
[4] *Campaign*, p. 107, 'Scheme of Rules and Regulations.' April 1856, §7.

put on paper my answer to your letter of this day, because it will be a record of what I thought I had already said in substance in conversation with you and others, on the subject of your house.

I am sure it is unnecessary for me to assure you here, how much I wish to retain your establishment in connection with the University; and therefore any propositions, which came from you, would be read by me with great interest. However, I am obliged to add most reluctantly, that in those you now make you seem to be carrying me beyond those bounds, within which I have ever wished to confine my University proceedings.

Your first proposition is this: 'That the University should endow St Laurence's House with the same amount and for the same purposes as it has endowed St Patrick's; the endowment to be given at the rate of £10 for each student to the number of 40.'

This proposal seems to me founded on a misapprehension of the state of the case as regards St Patrick's House, and the part I have taken in what I certainly should not myself call its 'endowment.' My own view of it is this: — I found the House in possession of the University before I came to Dublin and furnished it at the Archbishop's wish for the reception of students. I found it already burdened with a large annual sum for rent, rates, taxes etc. When Students came, they were not numerous enough to meet the expenses of house-keeping. The first year there was an excess of expenditure to the amount of about £500, and there was the prospect of a like excess in subsequent years. I had nothing to do with incurring this great expense. All I did was to attempt to turn it to account. I said, 'If this large sum *must* be spent, it is better we should get something for it than nothing.' I considered, that, if there were additional students, receiving burses, and paying (after the deduction of their burses) a certain number of pounds each, they would not increase the existing annual expenditure. So I aimed at nothing more than at getting ten Medical Students at a low pension into an almost empty house which was already charged with rates, taxes, etc, whether they were there or no. I considered that in this way I was increasing the students of the University, and laying the rudiments of a superior medical school, without any additional charge on the University. I did not ask the Bishops for a single penny for the establishment of St Patrick's, which would not otherwise have been demanded of them by the very fact of their being responsible for the House itself, open for the reception of students.

If, in like manner, I had found St Laurence's in the University's possession and costing an annual £500, I should have tried to do the same with it. But I can as little take the initiative in giving a large annual sum to St Laurence's, as I have done in giving a large annual sum to St Patrick's.

I am sorry then to be obliged, however I may regret it, to decline entertaining your first proposition.

Your second proposition is this: — 'That the University advance £6000 for the purchase of a house and land in Upper Leeson Street, the money to be properly secured and repaid on the principle laid down in the land improvement Act, viz 6 per cent for 22 years.'

It is not very long since I attempted myself without success to borrow of the University Trustees £2000 to pay therewith pressing debts incurred in building my own Church in Stephen's Green, though I offered security and interest. It is not wonderful then, that I should not feel encouraged just now to meddle with transactions of this nature. Nor have I sufficient knowledge of business to be a judge of the bearings of your proposition. And therefore I am obliged most unwillingly to decline it as well as the former.

However, I will gladly submit your letter to the consideration of the Faculty of Philosphy and Letters, if you wish me to do so.

I am, My dear Dr Quinn, Very faithfully Yours

(signed)   John H Newman of the Oratory

The Revd Dr James Quinn

P.S.   I will send a copy of this to Mr Ornsby.[1]

TUESDAY 13 APRIL 1858   Dr Quinn called

TO EDWARD BELLASIS

The Oratory Birmingham April 13. 1858

My dear Bellasis

Thank you for your kind promise about the prayers. It is a shame I did not propose it to you — but I was thinking of our own people here. For their sakes we have made the *necessary* prayers as few and easy as possible — a Pater, Ave, and Gloria — [2] Your list of names is very good, and I am glad to have it.[3] You shall soon hear about houses. One great difficulty is this — As far as I see, children and boys take in religion principally through the eye. Either we ought to make a handsome chapel *in* or *close* to the school house,

[1] The text of this letter is taken from this copy sent to Ornsby.
[2] Bellasis on 12 April asked what prayers were to be said for the Novena about the school, 'I would participate in them and make others do the like.'
[3] Among the laymen who supported the proposal for a new Catholic school were, the Duke of Norfolk, Viscount Campden, Viscount Feilding, Lord Henry Kerr, Lord Charles Thynne, Sir John Acton, Sir Robert Gerard, Sir John Simeon, Sir Robert Throckmorton, T. W. Allies, Edward Badeley, W. Bagshawe, Serjeant Bellasis, Robert Berkeley, Henry Bowden, William Dodsworth, John Arthur Herbert, James Hope-Scott, Edward Jerningham, William Jones, T. W. Marshall, William Monsell, Robert Monteith, R. Biddulph Phillips, C. R. Scott-Murray, S. Nasmyth Stokes, Stephen de Vere, F. R. Ward, W. G. Ward, F. R. Wegg-Prosser, H. Wilberforce. Later, Thomas Gaisford.
Bellasis wrote, 'All of these unless it be with one exception are decidedly friendly, and some of them (but not many) will help pecuniarily.'

or we must alter and improve our own. And in both plans there are great difficulties.

The Cardinal must be exerting himself against us, in order to give to the Bishop of Newport the representation you mention. I suppose he said the 'married men and their families' were to be under our roof.[1]

As to F. Ward's wish, it seems very hard not to consult for the wishes of so warm a friend of the plan; but then it must be recollected, if the present plan is to go on for three years, before any building commences on our own ground, that his son now 12, will then be fifteen — and up to that age in a kind of nursery. How is this to be got over?[2]

I will write again

Ever Yours most sincerely John H Newman of the Oratory

Mr Serjeant Bellasis

P.S. Mrs Bellasis with all the young Catholics indoors must pray — a diapason and more is it not?

TO CHARLES NEWSHAM

The Oratory Birmingham April 13. 1858

My dear Dr Newsham,

The good Catholic whose letter I inclose has from time to time corresponded with me, though I have not the pleasure of his personal acquaintance.[3]

He asked me whether we were not going to set up a school here. I told him that we were not likely to do any thing which could rival what he would find elsewhere — and mentioned Ushaw to him. My only fear is, that he wants a school where the expenses are lower than they can be at the Colleges. Ours would be far higher still.

I was about to write to you on the subject of our school, but the necessity of sending on Mr Daunt's letter anticipates my time of mentioning it. I cannot conceive its interfering in any way without [sic] Ushaw or the other Colleges. I suppose we shall begin with admitting none but boys under eleven. A Lady will take care of them — though they will have masters to take the supervision

[1] Bellasis added: 'I saw the Bishop of Newport [Thomas Joseph Brown] whilst in Wales, he had been told by the Cardinal that it was proposed to have married men and their families living in the school house etc etc. When I explained the matter to him he authorized me to say that he approved of the experiment being tried.'
[2] The plan as it then stood was to admit only small boys, and after three years to build accommodation for older boys. F. R. Ward's sons, Francis born in 1846 and Richard in 1848, were among the first boys to come to the school, when it opened on 2 May 1859.
[3] i.e. O'Neill Daunt. See letter of 6 April.

of them in the playground and in their dormitory. The persons, who have set it on foot wish lay boys to be kept distinct from ecclesiastical — and our Bishop is as strong for ecclesiastical being kept apart from lay. What I feel anxious about myself, and our Bishop is anxious about too, is whether a lay portion can be kept religious without the element of ecclesiastical. But we are beginning in so humble a way that, if we fail, it will soon be discovered and no harm, I trust, will have come of it. Begging your good prayers, I am, My dear Dr Newsham,

Affectionately Yours in Xt   John H Newman of the Oratory

The Rt Revd Dr Newsham

TO E. B. PUSEY

The Oratory Birmingham April 13. 1858

My dear Pusey

I should have answered you before this, had I not been more busy than usual from the illness and absence of some of our party here. Gladly will I do any thing I can to make Philip at home at Madrid — give him my love — but I don't know what I can do, till I try, which I will do at once.[1]

Thank you very much for your permission to keep the readings of St Athanasius. I am very sorry I have had them so long without knowing it — but I began about six months ago to 'put my house in order' — and then turned them up.[2] It has sometimes struck me that, had I time, I should like to translate my notes on St Ath. [Athanasius] into Latin. This I could not do without your leave, but I do not suppose it would at all interfere with the sale of the English — in that case they would be appended to the Greek text, and so the various readings would be used. But with my engagements and at my age this is one of those dreams which flit away when steadily looked at.

As to the revision of the Douay, I suppose I shall have to do it, though the undertaking is quite unsuited and unwelcome to me. I had not a hint before hand that it would be put upon me, and now it comes to me from a synod confirmed at Rome. But the work is so great and will perhaps be so expensive, that I cannot say it practically presses on me at the moment, though it troubles me in prospect. I shall be truly glad of any suggestions or help from you. Ambrose St John, for whose nephew you so kindly provided a studentship,[3] is hard at the Psalms — and I am told [J. B.] Morris is to help

<hr>

[1] Pusey's son Philip evidently proposed to visit Spain.
[2] Cf. letters of 11 March and 21 April 1854 to Pusey.
[3] This was Richard St John Tyrwhitt (1827–95), son of Ambrose St. John's elder sister Catherine. He was a Student of Christ Church 1845–59, and from 1858 to 1872 was Vicar of St Mary Magdalene, Oxford.

me in Job — [1] But at the moment I really do not know where I stand or what I want — but I will remember your kind offer.

As to geology, I am the worst person to consult possible, and so I think is any correligionist of mine — and for this reason — because so little is determined about the inspiration of Scripture, except in matters of faith and morals. There is an old traditional feeling in favour of many views, which may not in the event prove more tenable than that of the sun going round the earth. I think that in Galileo's time a shock was given to the Catholic mind which never can be repeated. And then too I cannot help thinking a lesson was given to ecclesiastical authorities, which they will never forget, of not *seeming* to mix, what in fact they did *not* mix up, questions of theology and questions of science.

Then on the other hand I have a profound misgiving of geological theories — though I cannot be sure that facts of considerable importance are not proved. But in the whole scientific world men seem going ahead most recklessly with their usurpations on the domain of religion. Here is Dr Brewster, I think, saying that 'more worlds than one is the hope of the Christian — ' and, as it seems to me, building Christianity more or less upon astronomy.[2] I seem to wish that divine and human science might each be suffered in peace to take its own line, the one not interfering with the other. Their circles scarcely intersect each other.

I say all this as an apology for not being able to answer your question. I am ashamed to send what is perhaps hardly to your friend's purpose, and so strange in shape, yet I think it worth while to send you, what *may* suggest some things to him — so I shall put it into the post. It has appeared since delivery in the Dublin 'University Gazette' — but I have not been able to find a copy at the moment. I don't want back what I send[3]

Ever Yours most affectly John H Newman

The Revd Dr Pusey

WEDNESDAY 14 APRIL 1858   slept at Rednall first time

FRIDAY 16 APRIL   Penny came

SATURDAY 17 APRIL   Penny went to Ireland

MONDAY 19 APRIL   end of Novena about the School plan.   Pollen came down about enlarging the church

TUESDAY 20 APRIL   Pollen went

---

[1] Cf. letter of 9 July 1858 to Sullivan.

[2] Sir David Brewster (1781–1868), who began life as a Presbyterian minister, and was later a zealous member of the Free Church, devoted himself to scientific studies. From 1859 until his death he was Principal of Edinburgh University. In 1854, in reply to Whewell's *Plurality of Worlds*, he published *More Worlds than One, the Creed of the Philosopher and the Hope of the Christian.*

[3] This was the lecture delivered on 10 Dec. 1855, 'On the General Relations between Theology and Physical Science,' published in the *Catholic University Gazette*, (3 Jan. 1856, pp. 2–14), *Idea*, pp. 428–55.

TO WILLIAM KIRBY SULLIVAN

The Oratory Birmingham April 20. 1858

My dear Mr Sullivan

I opened your letter with a bad conscience, for I owed you a letter — yet I had a good reason for my delay — and was on the point of writing to you to say what it was. I did not like to write without answering your question, whether I could send any thing for the July Atlantis myself. So I set to — and I have just broken the neck of a few remarks on the Eutychian doctrine, or rather a point connected with it. It will cost me a great deal of trouble and reading, from the subject and my name between [being] put to it, with (I fear) not any corresponding result — for I have not said much which has not been said before me. However, there it is, or will be — if you like to have it for the *Scientific* part of the number.[1]

By all means get Mr Kelly's paper, if you can.[2] I have had a portion of Mr Curry's sent to me by Fowler, and was very much pleased with it.[3] The Irish type is a very beautiful one, but I do not understand its merits, and my praise is worth nothing.

Whether we can say that 'the *University*' gives the Atlantis, is a difficult question. What would the Council say to it? Perhaps the 'Rector and Council' would consent to give it — would *this do*?

Make any arrangement you think good in details — such as circulars etc. I am glad our prospects are so good. I don't expect Mr Allies's article will be done in time for July — Sir J Acton's will not be ready till the Autumn — but he wished to send some short reviews — I hardly know what, for July. I rejoice to hear of Mr O'Hagan's paper.[4]

Thank you for talking with Mr Hennessy on the subject of the Observatory. Between ourselves, I am seriously afraid I shall be asked how far his Professorship is available for present University purposes. He can't help it if there are not enough young men to want him, but still I ought to find some work for him. I talked about £400 — how I am to find the money, I don't know. I could not all at once, and don't know what credit he could obtain of the people he employed. Of course I am taking no salary now — so, while I remain Rector, there is £400 a year available. The July Atlantis will take the May quarter. August and November quarters will give £200 for the Observatory, and I must take my chance for the rest. But *I want a good job done*, as I

---

[1] The *Atlantis*, (July 1858), pp. 330–61, On the Formula, μία φύσις του θεού λόγου σεσαρκωμένη, *T.T.*, pp. 329–82.
[2] John Kelly's paper, 'On the Carboniferous Rocks of Ireland, and chiefly on the Yellow Sandstone, and its relations with the Coal Measures and other groups,' appeared in the *Atlantis*, (Jan. 1859), pp. 221–76.
[3] Eugene Curry, 'The Sick-bed of Cuchulainn, and the only Jealousy of Eimer,' the *Atlantis*, (July 1958), pp. 362–92.
[4] John O'Hagan's article on Joan of Arc was the first in the *Atlantis* for July, pp. 245–83. Neither Acton nor Allies contributed.

have told him. That is, one which *will enable him to work*. And therefore in any thing I say to you or him on the subject, I wish this, if you please, taken into account; that if I give a certain sum of University money, it is to *effect a purpose* — not to do a thing *good in itself*. A telescope or microscope or air pump is a good thing in itself — but nothing may come of it after all.

And now for your letter of this morning. First I am very much obliged to you for the trouble you have taken on the subject — at the same time I do think a Vice Rector absolutely necessary to us, and, with the engagements of the Archbishops, you cannot expect they will act unless they see the Professors feel strongly on the subject. I cannot fancy their taking it ill, that the Professors should show such natural zeal for the welfare of the University — It seems a simple act of duty which the Archbishops will be the first to appreciate.[1]

As to Mr Anderdon, it never struck me that he *could* be thought of, (while I was Rector) for the reason you mention, that he is English; still, I am very much pleased that he should have come into the minds of some of the Professors. He has very considerable qualifications for the office — the only point on which no one can perhaps speak to them, is, how he would stand as Vice Rector *relatively to the Professors*. If I beg to speak to you in *perfect confidence*, it is not because I have any thing to say, but merely because my mooting the point might be mistaken, if others knew it, to my having a meaning, which really I have not. Now the Vice Rector not only will act upon the public, and upon the young men, but upon the Professors — and when you take upon yourselves to recommend a person, you are implying that you will like him yourselves. I think well that you should all narrowly look at the appointment in this aspect. For myself, I certainly think it would be productive of great good — I should not wonder if he came down upon the young men with a vigour, which they both deserve and require — and that he would do much to make the University popular in circles where at present no interest is felt in it, I am perfectly sure.

It would remove all difficulty in the circumstance of his being English, if (to harp on an old string) Dr Moriarty or Dr Leahy of Dromore could be a nominal Rector, I retiring. But it would be a bad move if I made way for (in confidence) Mr Flannery. Still, is there nothing I could have which would keep up my connection with the University, yet allow of an Irish Rector?

Any thing I can do to forward your proceedings I will gladly do — and *you* must be the judge whether there *is* any thing. Perhaps the less I do the better, having thus shown you my feeling generally.

I should be glad of a Charter, and think that there is some hope from the present Government — but what would be the Quid pro quo? One has struck me which Lord Derby, as Chancellor of Oxford, would like very much — but the Bishops and Jesuits of England, I fear, would oppose it — viz to get the

---

[1] Sullivan wrote that several professors thought Anderdon had the necessary qualifications of a Vice Rector and proposed to memorialize the Archbishops.

Pope to engage that Catholics would not set up a College in Oxford or Cambridge

Ever Yours most sincerely John H Newman

W K Sullivan Esqr

P.S. I hope the effects of your accident are all over.

WEDNESDAY 21 APRIL 1858 determined in Congregation to attempt the school[1] — went to Rednall and slept there

TO SISTER MARY IMELDA POOLE

The Oratory. Bm April 21/58

My dear Sister

Had I not been very busy, I should have written to return your Easter greetings — especially to your Mother Prioress and those of your Sisters whom I know. Thank you for your Prospectus which I am very glad to have, and which supplies what I should think must be much wanted.[2]

We have been in great trouble — and, had I not been so busy in consequence I should have written to you and others to beg you to give us prayers, though I know we had them, for others wrote to you, and have to thank you for their success. One of our Fathers is I trust recovered, but we are still very anxious about dear Fr Flanagan. Have you, have others these troubles? We have lost three members while we have been a Congregation, all of them real losses, some of them great. I suppose every Community which God loves, is blest and tried at the same time. We have many blessings, and trials too, — God who sends them knows them.

I wish I could do something to deserve more than I do the interest of those of you whom I know. Shall I say a Mass a week for some time for S . . . and her undertaking? or any other object Mother Prioress wishes. And then when I am again in trouble I shall feel I have some claim on you, to have recourse again to you.

I have lately had, or rather am having some correspondence with Dr Pusey. He is as kind and affectionate as ever — the misery is that he so little recognizes any serious difference between him and me, that one hardly dare take and return his affection lest it should increase this insensibility.

Ever yrs most sincerely in Xt   John H Newman of the Oratory

To Sister M. Imelda

[1] See letter of 22 April to Bittleston for the text of this unanimous resolution of the Oratorians at Birmingham.
[2] Mother Margaret Mary Hallahan and her nuns at Stone had just opened a girls' school.

TO E. B. PUSEY

Rednall. April 21/58

My dear Pusey

I want merely to acknowledge and thank you very much for the collations.[1] From what you say, I very much fear that I have been the cause, by mislaying the others, of your not publishing St Athanasius yourself. As to what you say about [J. B.] Morris, I quite assent. The whole task is so vague at present, that no plans can be really formed (about the translation of Scripture) The first thing I shall do is to try to get a clear view of the object of it, and the principles on which it is to be conducted.

I quite feel what you say about Buckland's Reliquiæ.[2] It has made me distrust every theory of geology since; and I have used your words 'Why take the trouble to square Scripture with facts and theories, which will be all changed tomorrow, and be obliged to begin over again?'

To-day is the anniversary of my going up to Littlemore in 1842. I write from our burying place, where we have a small cottage and nice garden. Our dear brother, John Gordon, lies there, close to where I am writing, and there I suppose I shall myself lie. My friends in New York sent me a present in money some years ago, after I had been in trouble, and I bought this place with it, which is not far from Hagley.[3]

Ever Yours affectly John H Newman

The Revd Dr Pusey

P.S. If you come upon Heyse's letter, it will be very kind in you to lend it to me. But it is not worth while to hunt for it.[4] The two works I had *wished* to undertake, in what remains of life, were an argument for Theism and a review of the mythical theory of the Gospel History — but, alas, I shall have time for nothing.

TO THOMAS SCRATTON

Oy Bm April 21/58

My dear Scratton

Can you in confidence give me any information about the inclosed? A[5]

---

[1] Pusey sent Newman further collations of readings of St Athanasius. See letter of 13 April.
[2] William Buckland (1784–1856), the geologist whose lectures Newman had attended in 1819 and 1821, published in 1823 his *Reliquiae Diluvianae, or Observations on the Organic Remains attesting the Action of a Universal Deluge.*
[3] See letter of 12 July 1854.
[4] This refers presumably to a letter from K. W. L. Heyse (1797–1855), the German philologist, perhaps dealing with the origin of languages.
[5] Scratton replied on 22 April that he knew nothing about 'A', but thought he could find out if Newman allowed him to ask questions in Dublin.

I will draw up the letter to the Archbishops directly, if you will send me the items. The Medical £200 is an extra etc.

I inclose the drafts signed, and Dr Russell's letter etc.

Ever Yrs affly J H N

Thanks for your, Mr E's [Errington] and B's [Bianconi] contributions to the Workhouse. Considering Stanislas's friends have given so much money themselves, and that the poor poor [sic] have no consolation but the sight of a well decorated Chapel etc, and Mr Hardman's express wish it should be so, Mr B's observations about 5 sets of Vestments is superfluous.[1]

Give de Vere at the rate of what Pollen had.[2]

TO JOHN WALLIS

The Oratory Birmingham April 21. 1858

My dear Wallis

I meant to have acknowledged your Post Office order before now, not for safety's sake, but by way of thanking you — but my engagements of various kinds have made a great heap of letters, I am sorry to say, rise up upon my table. Also, I was sincerely concerned at your mention of your sister's illness — for I understand well how serious an affliction it must be to you, and to your Mother. I had hoped to have said a Mass for your intention before now, but have not had a vacant day. I hope early next week to do so.

We hear[d] from Fr Bittleston who is with Stanislas yesterday. I don't know that his account ought to make one anxious — still it disappointed me. He has not lost his hoarseness, which was his one bad symptom, and though he eats, he seems to have no appetite. I have all along said to him, 'nil actum est, till your hoarseness goes.' He has been six weeks at Pau — perhaps one is impatient. He is not to return, till he has been six months from home.

Ever Yours most sincerely in Xt   John H Newman of the Oratory

J. E. Wallis Esqr

P.S.   I was very much pleased by the article in the Tablet on Universities last week — and thought it very telling.[3]

---

[1] Errington and Bianconi each gave £1 for the Birmingham Workhouse chapel. The latter thought five sets of vestments (for the liturgical colours) extravagant.

[2] Aubrey de Vere gave two public lectures, on 21 and 22 April.

[3] The Tablet, (17 April 1858), pp. 248–9, contrasted the attitude of Catholics in England and Ireland with those in Prussia: 'The Prussian Catholics insisted that they are entitled to have a seat of Catholic learning on the same footing and with the same privileges as the Protestant universities, and they omit no opportunity of forcing their claim on the Government, and of familiarising the public with the reasonableness of their claim. We don't remember having heard the Catholic University being ever mentioned in Parliament as entitled to have its degrees recognised. . . .'

THURSDAY 22 APRIL 1858   unpleasant letter about Stanislas's health from Henry

TO HENRY BITTLESTON

The Oy Bm April 22/58

My dear H

I have just got your second letter — It is a great mercy you are with S. [Stanislas] He is, I must say, very imprudent. His doctor must limit him in talking — and he must comply under obedience — say, one or two hours a day. Then one of his physicians, I think the Paris one, expressly said that he must not take stimulating things as coffee and wine. And behold he is taking them! *I much doubt if snuff is good for him.* He will not realize how dangerous his state is. In the coffee and wine I have hit a distinct blot, and it will be some time before I can trust any thing he says about himself, and does towards himself.

This will be the 14th letter I shall put into the post today. I have just come from Rednall, walking to Barnt Green and from Moseley here. The weather is very hot.

Yesterday we decided on taking the School. I will transcribe our Decree. 'That the Congregation gives its sanction to Fr Nicholas Darnell's being Fr Superior's representative in undertaking, at the instance of friends in London, the establishment and formation of a school for lay boys of the upper classes, of the nature of such public schools as Winchester and Eton, his relation to it being not materially different from that which a Father of the Oratory would bear towards a Ragged School, Reformatory or Workhouse, and the other Fathers of the Congregation being in no way connected with the boys except as having their direction in spiritual matters and in ecclesiastical functions and devotions.'

What trials we have. We ought to be very thankful about your recovery — God grant we may not be wanting in our continued prayers for Stanislas. Mr Bowen, who has just been here, bids me tell him he shall say Mass for him tomorrow morning.[1] We intend to enlarge and decorate the Church and charge the interest on the boys of the new School. Pollen has been down here — the roof will, not be raised, but opened with a lantern where the two diagonals cross in the sanctuary with the monogram — an aisle added between the nave and the house's long wall —, and, as Nicholas and Ambrose wish, the south wall of the Church carried on beyond the apse as far as the long House wall, the apse destroyed, and a baldacchino put instead, the high altar remaining where it does, with a chapel of the Blessed Sacr (as a lady chapel) beyond — between which end or lady chapel and the high altar will be the choir of Fathers *behind* the high altar — a second end-altar being where the

[1] Charles Bowen, the priest at St Peter's, the church in Birmingham nearest to that of the Oratory.

entrance now is from the plough and harrow lane, being the altar of a chapel for the boys school, which chapel will stretch down towards the part at present under the gallery — the gallery removed and the way from the apse *end* of the Sacristy into the Church along the passage were the cochins [?] were. All *this* alteration seems to me indefinite in expense but Heywood's estimate has not come in. The alterations *in nave* and for *new aisle* won't reach £450. Love to S.

Ever Yrs affly J H N

Dont read S the objurgatory parts.

TO EDMUND O'REILLY, S.J.

The Oratory Birmingham April 22. 1858

My dear Fr O'Reilly,

Though you had so little success in persuading the members of the Council to meet some two months ago, I fear I must once more trouble you to make the attempt. The want of a Vice Rector is ruining the University. The best rules of discipline will do nothing, unless there is some one to enforce them. I do not consider this to be the Rector's duty; and I feel that it is as little *my calling*, as you (most intelligibly) felt it to be yours.

Now in the absence of this most necessary office, what is to be done? I can think of nothing better, than that the Council should give their authority to a set of rules, which they should *impose* on the Deans. You cannot expect the Deans to act without some one to fall back upon. They must be able to say to the members of their Houses, 'we are obliged to do so and so.'

Now what I think best is this — for a small committee to be appointed, consisting of the Deans, (who practically acknowledge the authority of the University in their Houses) viz Mr Flannery and Mr Penny, (Fr Bennett I am told has hardly any of our students just now) with one or two of the Professors of the Faculty of Philosophy and Letters with (say) Dr McDermott etc (but I am not suggesting of course, only illustrating what I mean) — and that they should draw up some rules to submit to the Council — and that then they should come out with the Council's authority.[1]

I have great dread of this long summer term. I hear that some of the students skip dinner, and dine in Coffee houses. There are the long evenings too. On these and other accounts, considering there is no chance of a Vice

[1] O'Reilly replied on 7 May, 'The committee we project (for the purpose stated by you) is as follows. Messrs Flannery, Penny, *Quinn*, Stewart, Dunn, Ornsby, McDermott.' This list was submitted to Newman as containing the name of Quinn, which he had 'studiously omitted.' Although Quinn was less concerned with discipline, since he had a strict system in his own house, it was thought advisable to include him.

Rector before the Long Vacation, I feel I should be wanting in a duty, unless I wrote to you this letter

I am, My dear Fr O'Reilly, Most sincerely Yours in Xt

John H Newman of the Oratory

The Revd Fr O'Reilly

TO ROBERT ORNSBY

The Oratory, Birmingham ⌐April 22. 1858⌐

My dear Ornsby

I have received the lecture list for the fresh Term, and think it very imposing — but ⌐I can take pleasure in nothing, while I know so perfectly well that we are suffering perhaps irreparably by the want of a Vice Rector. We have *ever* suffered from this want — but it shows itself more now.⌐ Renouf's table of contents too is splendid.

Scott is still discontented, and, as far as I see, with some reason, about the Cicero. The Professors oblige candidates to take up certain books — *why?* — in order to oblige them to attend their lectures. But how do they become practically obliged, unless the Professors lecture in those books bonâ fide? If they do not, they merely limit arbitrarily the choice of books, which should in that case surely rest with the Tutors.

I hope you are well, and Butler better

Ever Yours affly John H Newman of the Oratory

R Ornsby Esqr

TO THOMAS SCRATTON

Oy Bm April 22/58

My dear Secretary

Will you put the inclosed with the former from the same gentleman, in some safe place for the Vice Rector, when he shall be appointed

Ever Yrs John H Newman

TO EDWARD BELLASIS

The Oratory Birmingham April 23. 1858

My dear Bellasis,

We have decided to commence the School — but I will inclose our Decree that you may see exactly what it is we are undertaking.[1]

[1] See letter of 13 April to Bellasis, and for the Decree that of 22 April to Bittleston.

We have come to this decision in consequence of the wish expressed by the noblemen and gentlemen, whose names you sent me. We do not think it any presumption in us to undertake it with the sanction of such friends. Nor have I any great fear of the attempt failing, while they support us. I think it will succeed, if we begin with, and keep up for a certain time a fair number of boys, say thirty. But I do think it important that we should have a fair number promised to us, both for the appearance and to clear the expenses, and moreover in order that we may have a sufficient number of patrons and advocates in the Catholic body through the country; for we are sure of having to encounter much prejudice, opposition, criticism, adverse whispering, and ready belief of tales told to our disadvantage.

The question is, how to secure the *continuance* of such interest and support on the part of a number of influential persons during the first years of this arduous undertaking. The most obvious expedient is one which is on its own grounds the most necessary — viz by making them responsible for the first expenditure and risk of expenditure which will be incurred.

As far as board goes, every boy ought to meet it with his pension day by day, and there is no great risk of loss here; but there are other expenses which must be incurred on starting, before a single boy comes — and these are either once for all and necessary for the outfit — or in advance.

The *outfit* is for furniture, which will cost (say) £500 and for alterations (say) £100 — £600. This we should wish our friends to undertake, having the ownership in the furniture.

The outlay *in advance* consists of such expenses as house rent etc. These will amount to about £1000.

viz House rent, rates, and taxes — (say)			£200
Masters — Head Master	—	£100	
Latin Master	—	£300	
Prefects of play ground and bed rooms		£200	£600
Servants —			£100
			£900

These expenses would be covered by 30 boys at £70 Thus

Half the Pension, for board, washing etc

The other half from the above £1000 — i.e. 30 × 35 = £1050

But what if there be less than 30 boys?

1. The pension at first might be set at £80 not £70, or

2. Our friends might guarantee the deficit.

Besides these expenses we consider we must enlarge and improve our

Church, since the Church must be one main instrument of religious and moral training. We mean to lay out £1000 upon it, and we ask our friends to lend us that sum, for which we will pay £4 per cent, obtaining it (when and as far as we can) out of the boys' pensions.

Should there be (safe) profits from the school, if considerable, we should lower the pension — if the over-plus were small, we should lay it out in candles, flowers, etc etc for the devotional objects in Church.

On the whole then we ask our friends, 1. to expend as much as £600 in furniture and alterations. 2. to guarantee the expenditure arising from deficiency of numbers. 3 to lend £1000 at 4 per cent.

I send this to you as a first sketch, to be shown to one or two, whom you select, but not as our final proposal till I hear what you say to it.

Most sincerely Yours John H Newman of the Oratory

Mr Serjeant Bellasis

P.S.   I have kept this some days, hoping to send you some information of our proceedings — but I have nothing to tell and do not like to keep it longer.[1]

April 27. 1858

TO THOMAS SCRATTON

April 23/58

My dear Scratton

I have sent the cheque to Dr Leahy — altering it by £50, for since I did not ask the Bishops for Sullivan's £50, I must screw it out of the £5000 and £1200.

As to Mr Manly's fee, certainly I returned a portion myself of Mr F Kerr's pension, and therefore Mr Flannery may do the same in this case. I don't think the University £5 should be refunded.

---

[1] Bellasis acknowledged this letter on 28 April. He explained that Acton, Monteith and Scott-Murray were abroad, and that he was very busy with the Shrewsbury Peerage case. This correspondence about the school was not resumed until the end of Nov. Newman made a memorandum: 'N B. May 19. 1858

I think it impossible that the scheme of a lay school can progress, unless the Gentlemen who are interested in it appoint some one to act for them in gaining promises of support, in raising funds, in securing pupils, etc and in transacting business with the Oratorian Fathers.

However, that is their business, not mine. *We* are only concerned in making our own proposals to those Gentlemen — and those proposals are contained in my letter of April 23 . . .

The object of these stipulations [at the end of that letter] is, not only to set us free from the chance of loss, but also in order to interest the Gentlemen above referred to in the project in some especial way, by making its success an object of personal concern to them. . . .

J.H.N'

The letter of 23 April was eventually withdrawn. See postscript to letter of 4 Dec. 1858 to Bellasis.

I am truly glad to hear that the Evening Lectures are so popular, and willingly consent to the £10 — the *Examination* will be the test. And you may spend the £10 on Mr Mc Carthy's desks.[1]

I should be much obliged if you could (quietly) inquire about the person mentioned in the Letter A I sent you.[2]

Fr O'Reilly surely has not taken his salary *for several quarters?* Did I tell you that I should not take mine this May?

Ever Yrs affly J H N

TO FRANK SCOTT HAYDON

(Sent in substance) April 24/58

My dear Sir[3]

Your letter as you are aware, involves an objection to religious evidence as wide as it is deep — and I am not the person to undervalue it, though I utterly disallow it.[4] That it is not irrational in me thus to speak will, I hope, appear, from the one position I am about to offer you on the principle of controversy which you wish examined. You ask 'Must there not be an infallible evidence for an Infallible Church?' I would rather word the question thus, 'Can I be certain that God is true and that God has spoken?' And I prefer to

---

[1] Nearly a hundred students were expected at the Evening Classes, and £10 was required to light two more of the University rooms with gas. J. J. McCarthy, the Professor of Architecture required large desks for architectural drawing.

[2] See letter of 21 April.

[3] Frank Scott Haydon (1822–87), eldest son of Benjamin Robert Haydon the historical painter, worked in the Public Record Office, and was responsible for 'Calendars of Documents' included in the deputy-keeper's reports. He also edited *Eulogium Historiarum* for the Rolls Series in 1868. He published *Benjamin Robert Haydon Correspondence and Table Talk*, after his father's death. Both the father and the son ended their lives by suicide.

[4] Haydon wrote on 12 April that although he was not personally acquainted with Newman, he had been greatly interested in his works, and wrote to him now 'simply for the satisfaction of doubts.' He enquired, 'in what authoritative work I can find the grounds of the Infallibility of the Church in matters of Faith stated and demonstrated? And if there be no such demonstration how any such property as that of Infallibility can be known to exist?' He thought infallibility useless unless it could be infallibly proved.

Newman's reply is not to be found, but on 20 April Haydon wrote: 'I am much honored by your very kind and very clear reply to my question. I am quite willing to admit that the argument "Infallibility must be infallibly proved" applies with as great force to the Bible as to the Church. . . .' He went on to explain that 'tho' externally a member of the Church of England . . . I am sadly and to myself painfully unsettled on the most fundamental questions . . . tho' of course I admit that "God's Word" is infallible, I cannot conceive the possibility of such word being communicated to . . . men in such a manner as to convince, without the barest possibility of doubt, every human mind of the infallibility of the communication . . .

I would go even further than this and say that I do not see how mathematical proof itself can escape the taint of probability—for mathematical demonstrations have been erroneously executed and not very infrequently . . .

What you say about the connection between belief and will, I admit with a modification. Indirectly belief does depend upon will, for belief depends upon evidence directly (real or apparent) and evidence upon examination and a man may *shirk* evidence . . . But I cannot think that the act of believing is directly voluntary . . .'

put it in this shape, because I understand what is meant better, while I think it is the real interpretation of any thing which I hold myself about the Church's infallibility.

In considering then whether there is any antecedent impossibility in our being certain that God is true and that God has spoken, I am disposed to allow what you advance that not even mathematical proof itself escapes the taint of probability; but there I make a distinction between the judgment of the mind about the cogency of a conclusion and the state of mind consequent on that judgment. There may be this objection raised to the Euclid i. 47[1] that it implies a comprehension at once of a number of previous propositions in the memory, and that the memory is fallible — In my *judgment* then the evidence is not simply demonstrative — but *certainty* is a state of mind, and in spite of this *judgment*, I suppose we are *certain* without any sort of fear of mistake, that the proposition in question is true. At the same time I think that state of mental certainty depends ultimately on the will — and that the will could so act upon the mind as to lead it morbidly to make that microscopic objection an occasion of doubt in the truth of that proposition. In like manner when I say that the proof of a certain person or body being the oracle of the God who can neither deceive nor be deceived is sufficient to lead to certainty, I mean no more than that it is such that certainty is the state of mind to which it legitimately leads, and will lead unless an act of the will interferes to hinder it. How often do we say 'I cannot prove it, but I firmly believe it,' that is, 'though I cannot draw out proofs to which no logical objection is possible, I am sure there is enough to give me grounds in reason for believing.' I surely may take it as a law of the human mind that 'proof, speculatively incomplete is sufficiently for (not only practical but) speculative belief;' or again that 'objection and doubt are not correlative ⟨(connatural?)⟩ ideas.'

Am I not certain that England is an island? am I not certain that I shall die? let us try to make out a demonstration of either proposition. Well then, am I to doubt of the truth of the laws of the human mind? If so there are no laws of *reasonings*. Am I to go on till I am sceptical of my own scepticism, and, though I practically conform to what is probable or what is safest, may *rationally* have speculative doubts whether I live or feel?

This, however, you will say is a mere reductio ad absurdum, and not a positive answer to your difficulty. I am aware of it. And I must leave it so, though for myself, I have an answer which satisfies myself. Many persons indeed will think it a greater assumption than any other which I could possibly make. But it is my first principle, and first principles must be assumptions, and if it be a first principle which approves itself to me, it may to another. I assume then the being and presence of a Moral Governor of mankind, and I look at every thing which comes to me as coming from Him. The question simply is, What are the laws of thought, of belief, of conduct under which

---

[1] Pythagoras's Proposition, that in a right-angled triangle the square on the hypotenuse is equal to the sum of the squares on the other two sides.

my mind lies? if I can find them, they are His imposing. He might have willed that, as the Angels, I should need no middle terms at all; and now that He teaches me by means of inferences in reason, He may will that they should not be infallible ones. The means of knowledge which I find are his instruments by which I am to do my duty to Him. ⟨I may have clear information of His will, in [?] the law of my nature   I can [?] have clear intimations from a diligent scrutiny into human life and human affairs⟩

If it is not impertinent thus to refer to myself personally, I would say that this sense of God's presence is the only protection (which I have had to keep me from unlimited scepticism, though an overabundantly sufficient one) and that I expressed it in the first book I wrote. In my work on the Arians, after speaking of the apparent unreality of all phenomena, I added 'Though on the mind's first mastering this general principle, it seems to itself at the moment to have cut the ties which bind it to the universe [and] to be floated off upon the ocean of interminable scepticism, yet a true sense of its own weakness brings it back, the instinctive persuasion that it must be *intended to rely on something* and therefore that the information given, tho' philosophically inaccurate must be practically certain; — a sure confidence in the *love of Him* who cannot deceive, and who has impressed the image and the thought of Himself and of His will upon our original nature,'[1] — as to which I must explain that by 'practically certain', I meant, more correctly 'practically sufficient for speculative certaintly.' Eleven years after in a University Sermon, I said the same thing: — 'Should any one fear lest thoughts such as these should tend to a dreary and hopeless scepticism, let him take into account the Being and Providence of God, the Merciful and True — and he will at once be relieved of his anxiety. All is dreary, till we believe, what our hearts tell us, that we are subjects of His governance — nothing is dreary, all inspires hope and trust, as soon as we understand that we are under His hand, and that whatever comes to us is from Him, as a method of discipline and guidance. What is it to us whether the knowledge He gives us be greater or less, if it be He who gives it? What is it to us whether it be exact or vague, if He bids us trust it? Why should we vex ourselves to find whether our deductions are philosophical or no, provided they are religious?' etc etc.[2] I do not know what others will think of such a view of the matter, — but for myself I can only say that in matter of fact, from this abiding conviction, though I am as keenly sensitive as anyone to objections in any part of religion, of doubt in religion I have never known any thing at all.

Now I will suppose a powerful sceptical system brings out forcibly the 'taint of probability' attaching to mathematical demonstrations. In such a case, I don't think it would be preposterous in any one who felt them keep him from prosecuting the study, to repel them by a strong act of the will and to make an act of faith in the truth of Euclid's or Newton's conclusions, and

---

[1] *Ari.*, p. 76.
[2] *U.S.* xv, 'The Theory of Developments in Religious Doctrine,' pp. 348–9.

that on the broad principle that objection does not ipso facto involve or demand doubt. And in like manner I think it possible to have such evidence that the Church is the organ of the Almighty for certain purposes as to make it a duty towards Him to believe it, under the conviction that He would not have afforded proof of such a quality, though not demonstrative, unless He had meant thereby to convey to us the objective truth of the conclusions to which that proof points, and this something in the way that I understand a Superior's signs and signals, whom I know well, though they cannot [be] put into formal sentences.

Excuse this long letter, which nevertheless is, I know, most imperfect for its arduous subject.[1]

TO ROBERT D. LYONS

The Oratory Birmingham April 26. 1858

My dear Dr Lyons

Thank you for your suggestion, which seems a very good one. Mr Butler mentioned it to me, I think from you, and I wrote him word the same opinion about it which I now send you. I think it should be brought before me in some formal way, on which I might act. In Mr O'Connell's case Dr Leahy was the mover.[2] I have moved very little or at all in any money matter myself, except in asking a sum generally for the yearly expenses of the University

Very sincerely Yours John H Newman

A D Lyons Esqr M D

WEDNESDAY 28 APRIL 1858   went and slept at Rednall
THURSDAY 29 APRIL   returning, found Wingfield here, who slept here

---

[1] Haydon replied at length on 8 May, unable to agree that Newman's 'first principle — credible though it be, and satisfactory alike to the intellect and the heart — removes the proof of Infallibility out of the region of "probable matter".'

[2] Daniel O'Connell's grandson received a free place in the University. Lyons suggested a similar favour for the son of John Hogan the sculptor, who died in Dublin on 27 March 1858. However, on 25 May, Archbishop Leahy wrote to Newman, 'It is on my mind that Hogan, the Sculptor compromised himself some how in the late revolution in Rome. I may be in error.

If he did so, you could not well think of paying a tribute to the memory of such a man by giving a free place in the University to his son. None but a distinguished Catholic could be so honoured.' See letters of 1 June to Scratton and 8 June to O'Reilly.

Hogan, who was born in 1800, left Cork for Rome in 1824, to complete his education as an artist. There he remained until the Roman Revolution was put down in 1849, when he returned to Ireland. 'It was erroneously supposed that because he left Italy during the revolutionary period his departure must have been attributable to political reasons. This injurious suspicion, Mr. Hogan fancied, made him be regarded with a certain coldness on some occasions when he fully expected to meet with a cordial reception.' 'Hogan the Sculptor,' by S. A. [Sarah Atkinson], the *Irish Monthly*, (July 1874), p. 397.

The Oratory Bm ⌜April 29. 1858⌝

My dear Ornsby,

You are a capital fellow for keeping one au courant, and I am very much obliged to you for your letters, which I have read with great interest.[1] ⌜I have no kind of doubt that the University is steadily making way, under all difficulties, some or other of which we must undergo, if we are to do any real and good work.⌝

I am writing this at our Cemetery at Rednall — where your papers are not — but I hope to inclose them, when I get to Birmingham.

I am very glad you are getting up a Conversazione.

⌜As to Dr Quinn's house, recollect I said in my letter to him that I would take into consideration any thing that the Faculty put before me. *I never have given away money.*⌝ Though the case of St Patrick's had *not* been alluded to, this fact would remain the same. ⌜When the Bishops met in 1856, they asked me *what I wanted*⌝ *for the routine expenses of the University?* When they asked, I answered — and what they asked, I answered. Nothing more.[2]

I have no doubt that your Lectures at Kilkenny, Navan etc. will do the University a great deal of good, and am very glad to hear what you tell me of them. Thank you for the Newspaper.

As to Scott, Zamoyski, and Cicero, I still am not satisfied — for this reason — the rule was *in order* to bring the students to the Professors' lectures. According to your own showing, it does *not*. Therefore you put a restriction on the student, without doing any good to the Professor.[3]

Ever Yours affly John H Newman of the Oratory

R Ornsby Esqr

P.S. I thought your move on the Archbishops very well done — and it has succeeded. Thank you for the kind way, which I do not disown, in which you speak of me.[4]

[1] Ornsby wrote on 23 April, 'You will see . . . that we [the Faculty of Philosophy and Letters] have at length taken the great step of addressing the Archbishops on the subject of the Vice-Rectorship. . . . Meanwhile another movement was being got up by Sullivan and Hennessy among the professors generally. . . .' Ornsby and Robertson presented an address from the Faculty of Philosophy and Letters to Cullen, and copies of it were sent to the other Archbishops. This was followed up by a second address signed by many of the Professors as individuals. Ornsby continued, 'I have no idea whether any individual is contemplated by them [the four Archbishops] for the office of Vice-Rector. I think there are professors who would like if Mr Anderdon were chosen. There was a rumour the other day that Dr Quinn had been elected, but I have heard nothing more of it. It was proposed at the council meeting [of the University] to have a conversazione of professors like that which you used to have . . .' Ornsby then described the success of the Dublin evening classes, and of others he had given elsewhere, of which he enclosed a newspaper report.
[2] Referring to Newman's letter of 12 April to Quinn, Ornsby wrote on 25 April, 'I would perhaps have wished that St Laurence's case had been stated on its own footing only, without reference to St Patrick's.'   [3] Cf. letter of 22 April to Ornsby.
[4] In his letter of 23 April Ornsby described the address to the Archbishops from the

The Oratory, Bm. April 29/58

My dear Sister

Thank you for your most kind letter. Gladly will I give your Revd Mother a Mass for as long as I can. I wish it were in my power to promise a weekly Mass, without limit of time — but my intentions are much engaged. At present the one I hope to give her will be the fifth weekly one engaged, and this without taking into account any one of the needs of our own Congregation. I rejoice to think that you are going to give me your prayers. Should you want Masses at any time for any particular intention, I know how glad our Fathers will be to give them.

What you say about Mother Prioress' troubles is a great lesson to me — [1] but the Oratory is a body unlike any other (at least Congregation of *men*) in the Church. Since it is local and isolated it does not want novices except like so many drops now and then falling upon it. But since it has no vows, it cannot well part with those who at length by long trial and habit have become knit into it. Here emphatically 'the old are better,' a dozen novices could not (humanly speaking) make up for one Fr Flanagan. In the loss of dear Fr Gordon five years ago, we suffered what was irreparable. If it be God's blessed will to take Fr Flanagan that again would be an irreparable blow — but He who gave eyes to the blind and limbs to the maimed can supply for bereavements even as great as these — , but it must be almost as miraculously. Fr Bittleston has been saved by the prayers of the faithful and I trust Fr

professors. These stated 'with reference to yourself, their high sense of the importance of your government of them, that notwithstanding distance you entered into the minutest details, as well as developed the principles of administration; then spoke of the necessity of a Vice-Rector that even when the Rector was present, that office was obviously a most essential complement to the organization and system of the University. And that when the Rector was absent, his functions devolved on the Vice-Rector who then became practically the executive authority of the University.'

Ornsby wrote again on 25 April to say he had received a reply from Archbishop Leahy. 'The other Archbishops have not written. It would appear from Dr Leahy's note that the appointment is already made; and Fr Flannery told Fr Penny that it was so, and that the person selected is one who had not been much talked of . . . who made a great sacrifice in accepting the office, and who would be likely to give general satisfaction. . . . I cannot see how the second of these attributes applies to Dr Quinn, and would infer that it must be somebody from Maynooth. I saw a good deal of Dr Quinn this morning, and . . . I thought he hoped for the appointment, and even believed he had it, but that, if he is appointed he does not know the fact. He enquired if we had named any one in our address or only recommended it to the Archbishop's consideration.'

On 26 April Ornsby wrote, 'I heard today from Dr Dixon. He says: "For my own part I am long convinced that the subject of the memorandum demands the prompt attention of the Archbishops . . ." He has written to the same effect to Hennessy, in acknowledgment of the general address. Dr Leahy has also written to Hennessy in reply to the same, and says that an appointment has been made, but that he does not yet know whether it has been accepted . . . An opinion prevails that *Dr Moriarty* is the individual who has been appointed . . .' On all this see letter of 28 May to Monsell.

[1] Sister Imelda wrote on 25 April of the severe losses by death in the early days of Mother Margaret Hallahan's nuns, who now numbered forty-seven professed, and seemed likely to continue increasing.

Flanagan will be so also. Our accounts of him might be worse than they are, but they are not satisfactory.

Ever yrs most sincerely in Xt   John H Newman

TO THOMAS SCRATTON

The Oratory Bm April 29. 1858

My dear Scratton

I gladly give my approval to the list of Preachers.

I am very glad to hear the Evening Classes are so promising. Thank you for taking Frazer's Pension for me.

Ever Yrs affly John H Newman of the Oratory

T Scratton Esqr

TO BISHOP ULLATHORNE

⌐April 29/58

[[P S of a letter to Dr Ullathorne]]

P.S.   Serjeant Bellasis showed me a correspondence which he had with your Lordship on the subject of the proposed school. I gathered from it, what I gathered from your conversation in February, that you approved the object, and without directly forwarding did not disapprove of the experiment.[1]

J H N[1]

TO HENRY WEEDALL

The Oratory, Birmingham April 29. 1858

My dear Dr Weedall,

We have determined within the last few days to superintend an undertaking, of which you have doubtless heard, but about which I did not write to you, because it was as yet only in contemplation.

There are various Catholic gentlemen who wish to send their children to

---

[1] See letter of 6 April to Bellasis.

a purely lay school; and they mentioned the wish to me last January, with the inquiry whether Fr Darnell of our Congregation would undertake it. I spoke at once to the Bishop, who entered into the idea with much interest, from his wish to encourage the principle that the ecclesiastical education should not be combined with the education of laymen. After various suggestions, we have determined to take boys under (about) eleven, placing them in the care of a lady of experience, with whom we are intimately acquainted, and who already has been a great friend of our Oratory. I cannot conceive that such a school will have any tendency to hurt the time-honoured institutions for the purposes of education already existing — but it will supply a want which many people feel, and will ultimately be of service to the Dublin University.

Nor do I conceive that (since the undertaking any how would be commenced,) it could be commenced with feelings more respectful and deferential towards St Mary's and other Colleges, than now that it is connected with us.

Certainly, as far as I am concerned, those feelings, if I can promise any thing of myself, will never alter either towards the College, or especially towards yourself, than whom there is no one I more revere or love in the whole Catholic body[1]

Ever Yours, my dear Dr Weedall Very afftely in Xt

John H Newman of the Oratory

The Rt Revd Dr Weedall

FRIDAY 30 APRIL 1858   Wingfield went.   De Vere came — slept

TO HENRY BITTLESTON

Oy Bm. April 30. 1858

Private

My dear H

Your letter of the 27th is just come. I have written to S. [Stanislas] on the other side. Tear it off and give it him, while you read this.

Your letter has confirmed my worst fears. I for one never feared anything *immediate* from the blood. All your efforts have been to show no more than this. On the other hand, instructed (I suppose) by Dr de C. [Castro][2] you talk of S. being not being [sic] fit for work for several years. That means, he will die. I don't like to say so, lest we should relax in prayer. If we had

---

[1] Weedall replied on 3 May that Oscott and the Oratory School fulfilled different needs, and would consist together without the one interfering with the other. He also thought that the lay element would have to remain in the old Catholic colleges, in order to provide them with financial support.

[2] The English doctor at Pau.

desponded in your case, we should have lost you. But my enormous fear from the first has been this — that dear S. would be tormented by exile for his last 2 or 3 years, and *we* should have the great suffering of his absence. What I said to Dr Johnson was 'if he does not come back materially better, I shall give him up.' I say so now. If he is not *materially* better when September comes, let him come back and die in peace. I have seen so much of the worreting about of poor invalids, of whom there is no hope. I only so fear our leaving off to pray. I am trying to make a great union for prayer among his penitents etc. God's will be done — but I am a better judge than you —- because I am older and at a distance — and I repeat it — there must be a great improvement and no mistake by September; else let him come back and die. To me his want of care about himself is incomprehensible. You don't attempt to defend the black coffee, which is far worse than the wine.

We have tried to know God's will about the school — but the great blows we have, whenever we attempt any thing, leaves me in a state of great and dark suspense whether we are following His blessed will or not. Stan. seems a great element in the school, in people's minds. Bellasis, now that I have said that we must have at least 30 boys, seems backing out — I don't mean improperly — but he is occupatissimo, and he seems to me to shrink to be *answerable* for the 30 — and who *is to be whipper in?* that is the point?

Ever Yrs affly J H N

TO JOHN STANISLAS FLANAGAN

The Oy Bm April 30/58

My dear S

Ellen Mulligan says you promised her a Rosary; she wants it. Tell me the price and I will get her one for you. Black Patrick is gone, having twice been guilty of an offence, the most unsuitable to a night porter. It *developed* itself in not turning off the gas burners and spilling oil all over the house. Don't forget at your leisure to dictate to Henry the history of our property, and the places where our deeds etc are lodged — for my memory in these things is so bad, that I must have it written down to get hold of it. At last I have written to Drs Weedall and Newsham to say that we intend a school — and, as soon as I have done it, the difficulty commences which (I suppose) we here all of us foresaw — that, when it comes to the scratch, there is no one to get the actual *promises* of boys to come — without which we should be taking a house for nothing. What would you and H. [Henry] think of our hiring a man like F. Ward to be a sort of Mr Hayter, a man of business to act for, i.e. in reality instead of, the heavy paternal matter thro the country, and to be its form[1] promised him £100 when the school would bear it. *He* is interested in it, as having sons. Think of this and improve on it. I thought I spoke of the opening

---

[1] The page is torn and two or three words are missing here.

of the Church roof — it was the come-off instead of raising it, which Nicholas did not like. *I* don't like the East end plans. Ambrose is very far from well. We are very much tried. I feel like Abraham, but I ought to feel his consolation too. Noli timere Abram, Ego protector tuus sum et merces tua magna nimis. Dixitque Abram, Domine Deus quid dabis mihi? ego vadam absque liberis — [1] Can you make any thing of Mr Pope?[2] Tell Henry that he is dement [?] to fancy I supposed he was to return by St Philip's day. Let him remain till you are to move from Pau, and then we will see about it. There is enormous talk of a Vice Rector now, and the Archbishops say that it is someone who will make a sacrifice etc, who has not been spoken of before — who won't consent etc etc. Some think it Dr Kelly of Maynooth, some Dr Moriarty. It's odd not a word have they said to me — nay, tho' Dr Leahy wrote within this week on other matters. However, the University is looking up somewhat — and I ought to be thankful instead of grumbling. There is a real talk of a charter — the quid pro quo? the quid pro quo? *I* say that the Pope should consent to give up the permission of Catholics going to Oxford and Cambridge, which would be a bait to Lord Derby; but one speculates and then un-speculates. Nothing yet about the Reformatory. Not a word from the Cardinal yet about the expenses of the Bible Translation. I wrote to him November 7. May 7 is approaching.[3]

SATURDAY 1 MAY 1858   De Vere went.

TUESDAY 4 MAY   The Diocesan Synod — no Sermon — dined at St Chad's with clergy accident to Wm [William] and Ign [Ignatius] in chair — horse killed — Wm bruised —old man wounded[4]

FRIDAY 7 MAY   better letter about Stanislas

TO WILLIAM MONSELL

The Oratory Birmingham May 9. 1858

My dear Monsell,

Your triumph in the House showed me you had come back from Paris, and I was going to write to you — but have lately been most uncommonly busy.[5]

---

[1] *Genesis*, 15: 1–2.

[2] Thomas Pope had been staying at Pau since Nov. 1857, with Pierre Labbé, superior of the Petit Séminaire of Yvetôt in Normandy. Flanagan replied on 10 May that he could not judge whether Pope, who had left for England, would be useful for the school, but that he was very easy to get on with. Cf. letter of 17 Nov. 1857 to Pope.

[3] There is no conclusion to this letter. For the reformatory see letter of 21 May to Pollen.

[4] See letter of 13 May to Flanagan.

[5] Monsell, who was now in opposition, brought forward a motion on 26 April in the House of Commons, to retain the open competing examination for entry into the Royal Military Academy at Woolwich, of those who wished to obtain commissions in the Royal Engineers or the Royal Artillery. The Government wanted to confer a monopoly on the Royal Military College at Sandhurst, and to insist that all future officers should first enter there. Monsell's motion was carried by 217 votes to 177.

That triumph will make me fear you will think yourself a bad negociator in the University matter — but, as you do not say any thing on this head, I hope my fear is unfounded.[1]

How strange that the Archbishops that is, Dr Cullen and Dr Leahy, should keep me in such utter ignorance of all their proceedings! but so it has been from the first. They never on any one occasion have asked my advice even, which would not have obliged them to follow it — and, when I have on various occasions gone out of my way to give it, I have got no answer.[2]

There is no doubt we are getting on, in spite of all disadvantages. We have lately started evening lectures — and have got 90 Dublin youths to attend. Of course there is a good chance of their falling off again — but for the moment they do us good. I think my absence too has done considerable good, by putting the Professors on their mettle — and making them advertise themselves etc. There can't be a set of men with a better spirit or more zeal. What we want urgently is a Vice Rector — I cannot get one appointed. I wrote in the beginning of February a private letter to Dr Leahy to say that I could take no salary from that time till that appointment and other improvements were made — nor shall I stir from this place till it is. As yet I can get nothing done. The state of the young men is suffering considerably — and this is our real evil, though we try to remedy it.

But coming to your questions, I really do not see what I have to say in answer — and I bow to your decision when you say you 'must do as the Archbishops desire' you. They seem to consult no body.

I will write privately to our Secretary for a return in answer to the questions you ask, — if you wish — but the account of the number of students in past years will not be satisfactory.

As to *how* you are to approach the Minister, I am tempted to throw out what may be a foolish idea. Would it be possible to tempt him, as Chancellor of Oxford, with the bait of our giving up the right to a position in the English Universities? I suppose there is a great chance of our ultimately having the power, with other religious communions, of setting up Halls there. Could the grant of a Charter to us be given on condition of our losing this right? You yourself, and other Catholic gentlemen, might not like this — but there is no one else to dissent. The English Bishops would go with the Holy See — and they know how strong the feeling is at Rome just now against the English

---

[1] Newman feared that Monsell would not be *persona grata* with Lord Derby's conservative ministry. Monsell wrote to Newman confidentially on 8 May: 'I received this morning with some surprise a letter from Dr Cullen requesting me on his own part and on that of Drs Dixon and Leahy to apply for a charter for the Catholic university to Lord Derby. I of course must do as they desire me, tho I am rather puzzled to know how to approach his Lordship.

Could you without inconvenience tell me in a few words what I should say to him. Have you any document which shews the progress of the University from the first. The number of pupils in each year. The names of the Professors and the subjects and character of the Examinations.

I see no harm in the application about to be made, except whatever may consist of evil in labour fruitlessly expended. Will you tell me whether this is your view.'

[2] See also notes to letter of 28 May to Monsell.

Universities. Within this two years I think the Cardinal has received a letter from Propaganda against allowing Catholic youths to go to them.[1] Perhaps the Jesuits would not like this deprivation.

While I have some apprehension you may fear to undertake the negociation with Lord Derby, I cannot help thinking it is worth attempting it. The Whigs are doctrinaires — the Conservatives, if pledged to any thing, are pledged to discourage mixed education, though Sir R. Peel founded the Queen's Colleges.

Is there not any way of getting at Lord Derby through Gladstone, or some one still better?

By the way, would not the chance of success be greater if some Irishman, and not I, were at the head of the University? It would then be a boon to Irish Catholics, not to English Apostates. It might any how be said that I was holding the place of Rector provisionally. To tell the truth, I think the Archbishops *would* dispense with me, as soon as they had got the Charter.

Ever Yrs affly John H Newman

P.S.   I am glad to hear so good an account of Mrs Monsell and the little child.

We have been alarmed about Stanislas — he spat blood — but the inclosed account is an encouragement.

Miss Bowles wishes you to see *one chapter* of her little book — to see whether it meets what you want.[2]

I wish I could come to London to talk to you about the school — but I am tied by the leg with Stanislas's and Henry's penitents. I almost think I could come some Wednesday to return on Thursday, if you would give me *dinner*.[3]

J H N

MONDAY 10 MAY 1858   still better letter about Stanislas

TO THOMAS SCRATTON

May 11/58

My dear Scratton

I am quite knocked up with something I am attempting for the Atlantis. I can but say that I should like to have done about the placard when [what]

[1] Letter of 16 May 1856. Archives of Propaganda, *Lettere*, Vol. 347, f. 252 v. Wiseman wrote to Ullathorne about the matter on 2 June 1856. His letter is preserved at the Birmingham Oratory. See also Newman's letter of 12 March 1856 to Barnabò.

[2] Emily Bowles was writing a history text book for use in Irish schools. Cf. letter of 22 Dec. 1857 to Monsell, who replied on 13 May, 'I shall be delighted to see Miss Bowles and her chapter any morning she can call on me. Montalembert is here and was thinking of running down to pay you a visit.'

[3] Monsell wrote in his letter of 8 May, 'I hope that your school project is prospering. I am charged by Bellasis to look out for pupils. Is there any chance of your coming to London soon?'

the Deans of the Faculties like.[1] Should Scott's name be down, not being a Professor?

Ever Yrs J H N

<small>THURSDAY 13 MAY 1858</small> Seager came and slept here

TO JOHN STANISLAS FLANAGAN

The Oy Bm May 13/58

My dear S

Your letter just come — sad weather here for Ascension day. What a shame no one should have written to you about W's [William's] accident. Robert told me he *had* — what an odd way of telling! he thought — he thought — he thought of course that someone or other in the air, a bird I presume, would have told.

While we were all at Synod, Ignatius gets leave, against Ambrose's grain and mine, to drive in basket Wm (on business) to Rednall. At Chad Hill horse runs away — drives against a donkey cart — cuts open an old man (of 75)'s head, who goes to hospital (for some days Wm's great apprehension was an inquest) pitches out all of them, runs off, breaks his leg with the shaft, is shot — William's hip bruised, his nose cut, various lesser injuries, while we are all in Synod. William was six days in bed — is up now — went to Rednall with N. [Nicholas] to [in] Mr Poncia's brougham yesterday — was in Sacristy today.

I have half a hundred things to write to you and Henry about — messages from penitents or questions — but my hand is very cold, and I can't recollect them. I inclose something for Henry. I am told Ellis is a very pretty girl — so much the worse — she has, it seems, come to me to confession several times — but I have not learned yet to distinguished one person from another — which is a great trouble to me, and will be for a while. I dare not seem to give them an hypostasis, lest I should mismatch different confessions. I have been overwhelmed with writing a few pages for the Atlantis — and have almost been getting weak, but it has gone off. I sent off all but a few pages of the end yesterday.

They *say* that Dr Kelly of Maynooth has been offered and refused the Vice Rectorship — and now that another is actually appointed. The evening classes have brought in as many as 90 fresh members! If a Vice Rector really appears, alas, I shall have to go over.

We keep St Philip's day on the *26th*. A grand high mass, perhaps the Bishop celebrant — a Procession with the relics and St Valentine — like C.C. [Corpus Christi] a collation with water and chocolate ices, and other delicacies

---

[1] This refers to a lecture list.

in the fasting way — set out in the Oratory, and then the afternoon to ourselves.[1]

The last account of you cheered us — thanks for your news of Henry, which I am glad of. The weather here is most mournful.

The school plan is at a stand, for want of the London agent — I think of going to Town for a day to remove the hitch. The aisle will be covered in by the end of this month.

Thanks for your letter — I wish you would say (by Henry), if anything strikes you as to raising the definite £1000 for the Church enlargement, which Wm and I are to pay the *interest* of.

Ever Yrs affly J H N

If you say some prayers for me, it will make up for every thing. Ambrose bears the loss of his pony very well, poor fellow.

Keep up your spirit, my dear Fellow — we are all in very good heart.

TO MICHAEL FLANNERY

May 13. 1858

Dear Mr Flannery

You must not suppose I have been an uninterested witness of the deprived condition of St Patricks House since the Long Vacation. If I have not interfered, it has been because by my letter to you, I think of last July, I left the Tutorial arrangements of your House to you, for reasons I then stated.[2]

In answer to the question contained in your letter of the 7th instant, I reply that I have never objected to your engaging an external teacher for your young men, but I thought and think that you should try to obtain one from the list of the Professors[3]

I am &c J H N

TO JAMES STEWART

The Oratory, Birmingham May 15. 1858

My dear Stewart

Thank you for your welcome letter, and the news you give of the evening classes. I hear on all hands that they are very popular, and they come in very happily now to put all parties in good spirits, when there was so much to

[1] See diary for 26 May.

[2] Letter of 23 May 1857. On 7 May 1858 Flannery asked for permission to engage an extern teacher, since he had been unable to find a competent resident tutor.

[3] As a result of this letter, Flannery engaged Thomas Arnold, who wrote on 15 May to thank Newman 'for this piece of good fortune, which will be the greatest possible assistance and relief to me . . .'

discourage our friends. Another ground of satisfaction is, that this has been done in my absence. The more the Professors are put on their mettle, and made to rely on themselves, the more people will see their real merit. No set of men has more in them, than they have — and it is well that it should be brought out.

The only misgiving I have is about the *future* of the evening lectures. You know how apt things are to take at first, and then to be put aside. A system of examination with a diploma, such as that we once talked of, seems to me necessary to clench the measure.

I am glad you are beginning a conversazione. It was very much wanted, and will be in many ways useful.

I suppose you hear far more reports about the Vice Rectorship than I do — and they are contradicted, before they reach me. One of the last I have heard is, that the person you speak of, whoever it is, (for I do not know more than you) has declined. The Archbishops seem as if they were in real earnest now, and all I can say is 'better late than never at all.'[1]

TO WILLIAM KIRBY SULLIVAN

The Oratory Birmingham May 15. 1858

My dear Mr Sullivan

I am glad we are so well prepared for the July Atlantis. As to putting all the Articles in pages, I fear that Mr Scott's and mine must wait till Fr O'Reilly has looked at them. And I think there might be some alteration in Mr Arnold's — though perhaps it would not be worth while.[2]

I quite understand your difficulty about the arrangement of articles. It is taken, as you know, from the Genevan periodical.[3] Any other you like better will be sure to satisfy me. You know so much more of such works than I do, that you must be able to name some other periodical, which we might follow. We shall have to recollect the 'wes' and 'Is'. Mr Scott's is set up partly in 'wes' and partly in 'Is', he wrote to me about it, and I wrote him word yesterday, since he seemed in a hurry, for it was his second letter, that it ought to be 'I' — but perhaps you will be so good as you pass Fowler's, to suspend the change till we see our way.

I am quite content with the order of the 14 articles you mention, if you think it best. It is in fact to decide to keep physical and mathematical science *together* — is it not? and no more.

As to the difficulty about discoveries being anticipated, this applies to other subject matters — e.g. to Mr Renouf's Egypt or Persia. In like manner

---

[1] Conclusion and signature have been cut out.
[2] Scott's article had to be postponed. See letter of 25 May to Sullivan. Arnold's was on 'The Genius of Alcibiades.'
[3] See letter of 9 Sept. 1857 to Sullivan.

I had thought of taking up some time the question of the new work of Hippolytus — about which fresh conjectures are ever being made abroad — or of St Ignatius's Epistles; — in which nothing would be more likely, if what I said was true, than that another might say it before me.[1]

Yours most sincerely John H Newman of the Oratory

P.S.   I suppose I did not look at that Genevan work enough — but what I did see surprised me so far as this, that the Literary part seemed *light reading* — too light for our purpose — which will be a reason for abandoning it as a pattern.

TO JOHN HUNGERFORD POLLEN

The Oy Bm May 16/58

My dear Pollen,

You must wonder you have not heard from some of us in answer to you; but

Imprimis. Wm [William] was thrown out of the basket, the horse killed, a man taken to the hospital with a broken head — himself bruised in the hip and cut on his nose. He was confined to his bed a week, and still limps.

2. We could not agree what was best to do

3. There was a hitch about the money. However Heywood is inclosing the aisle. We are not quite certain whether to open the roof or not — the cross beams in the lantern are a great difficulty.

As to the additions at the upper end, Heywood seems to allow we could not do them under £1000, and scarcely any accommodation room gained.

So what we think of is to turn the Sacristy into a (temporary) Chapel of the Bs. [Blessed Sacrament] and to decorate it; and to cover over the small court with a sky light and make it the Sacristy.

Anyhow you see we want three altars for the aisle — and decoration for the whole — tho' we shall reserve as much as we can for the Sacristy. There is a German artist here who might do some cartoons under your directions, and you might think of alabaster etc.

Perhaps if the plan be adopted, it will be best not to have all the Altars in the *Aisle* new — but to make that in the Sacristy one of the best — and I don't like to have so many altars as we now have. Our Lady's where the image is, will remain, only thrown back (what do you say to a sort of Louvre over it, to throw light into the aisle?) that at present in the Sacristy would do for a second in the aisle. So only three new ones would be wanted.

Ever Yours John H. Newman

J H Pollen Esq.

[1] The *Philosophoumena* of Hippolytus was first published in 1851, at Oxford. Newman wrote 'On the text of the seven Epistles of St. Ignatius,' completed in 1870, *TT.*, pp. 92–135.

MONDAY 17 MAY 1858   The additions and alterations of Church began about this time Query? the day after St Philip?[1]

The Oratory Birmingham May 17. 1858

My dear Capes

I heard lately that you had altogether retired from the Rambler, and that on such good authority, that, tho' the news surprised me as well as caused me regret, I could not doubt it.[2] What qualified my concern, was, the thought that it would be a great relief to you — but then this thought suggested another, viz that that relief might be necessary to you, which grieved me again.

Any how, I think the Catholic body in this country owes you much gratitude, from the animus and object of your undertaking, the devotion you have shown to it for so long a time, and the various important benefits it has done us. But it is well for us, my dear Capes, that we do not look out for any reward for what we do in this world, for, whether we do or not, we are sure not to get it here — for what we do imperfectly or wrongly affects the public ten times more than what we do well, even though the good may be ten times as much as the amiss. But this is God's merciful dispensation to oblige us to look up to Him, and lay up treasures above, whether we will or no.

I should have written before, had I not been so busy — but accept these few lines, for the sake of their intention, from

Yours affectionately John H Newman of the Oratory[3]

J. M. Capes Esqr

[1] Newman added last six words in pencil later.

[2] Capes, who had resigned the editorship in Oct. 1857, afterwards sold the *Rambler* for £200. Simpson became the editor, and a half share in it was bought by Acton, a quarter by Simpson and a quarter by Frederick Capes. The new management took control early in 1858.

[3] Capes replied on 18 May, 'Your kind and sympathising letter has given me great pleasure;' and explained that to continue as editor would have been the ruin of his health. He went on to say he hoped that the *Rambler* had 'done some little towards propagating a love for *truth* and *justice*, virtues not very common among Catholics.' He ended by saying that he heard occasional news of Newman, most recently 'from that very nice fellow Acton . . . You must have had pretty clear proofs during the last few years, and *months*, of the difference between people's professions and performances . . . . We have learned a good many things since this time 13 years ago, when (at least it only wants a month to that date) I came down to see you at Littlemore, and you told me you had begun to think better of Dr Wiseman and showed me a letter you had received from him, and therefore advised me to choose Oscott as the place for being received at. And so it will be to the end.'

The Oratory Birmingham May 17. 1858

My dear Pusey

I do not know whether you happen to be able to tell me where I can find an answer to a question connected with the Jewish registers of genealogy; but as it is one which for some months has been in my mind, and to which I am not able to find an answer, I will ask you.

It may be an hypothesis, which fails as soon as it is examined, but I should like, if I could, to find a reason other than that of date of birth, for our Lord being said in Luke 3 to be ὡσεὶ ἐτῶν τριάκοντα ἀρχόμενος. It seems to me, as commonly interpreted, to be a great chronological difficulty.

What I wish to do is this — first, to consider it as part of the genealogical table — that is, that St Luke is as little answerable for it, as for the variation or omission of any names in his and St Matthew's tables. It really does seem the beginning (as far as matter goes) of the formal document; and since the genealogies have already considerable difficulties, to add this particular difficulty to them, is to get rid of a *head* of difficulty.

Next, I wish to make out that the Jewish children were registered, say at 5 years old, and that the 30 years counts from the registration.

Or again that the names were entered in the formal register, only where persons came to be the representatives of the line — i.e. on their fathers' death. Which would mean in this case that our Lord was thirty when St Joseph died.

If it were not for the ὡσεὶ, I should like to interpret, 'he was thirty years, at the commencement' (i.e. the commencement of His ministry) as ἀρχόμενος εἶπον Thuc. iv. 64 τελευτῶντες in Thuc. Herod. and Plato. And the meaning would be 'He was of the *legal* age for ministry'. (vid. Numbers iv. 3 In Chron xxiii, 3 the words '*numerati* sunt' look like a catalogue. Gen. xli, 46, 2 Sam. v, 4) and it would imply, not that He was *only* thirty, but *full* thirty, thirty and more.

The Fathers seem to have had no tradition of chronology, and never to have cultivated the science themselves. Do they not consider our Lord's ministry to have lasted only one year? The only real tradition (i.e. professedly such) is that of St Irenaeus — which makes our Lord older than is commonly held — and seems to agree best with modern scientific examination[1]

Ever Yours affly John H Newman

WEDNESDAY 19 MAY 1858   Nicholas went to Town about the School plan

[1] Newman was concerned with Scott's article for the *Atlantis*. See letter of 25 May to O'Reilly. For Pusey's reply see letter of 7 June to him.

TO JOHN STANISLAS FLANAGAN

The Oy Bm. May 19/58

My dear S

While I think of it, do you wish me to give any money in charity to any penitents of yours, or to others? — or does Henry? let me know.

Austin grumbles that Henry won't dream of paying for his confessional — and wishes me to appropriate it, that he may get the money for Hooper. Shall I do so?[1]

Amherst, Bishop elect of Northampton is to sing High Mass, on St Philip's day, *the 26th* — the Bishop to assist pontifically — and perhaps Manning to preach. The procession is impossible, since the Guild cannot attend. There is to be a lemon ice collation after it.

Perhaps Amherst will gain St Philip's favor for us, better than I have been able, who hitherto has [sic] sung the High Mass every year since we were a Congregation. He seems to have cast me off. I should call it cruel, except that, did I see behind the scenes, as he does, I doubt not at all he would be able to sustain a successful defence against my impeachment. I never have, nor have had, (thank God) any temptation to murmur against His dispositions — for, *whatever* I receive of good, (and I receive not 'whatever' but infinite good) is ten thousand times more than I deserve — but I do not ask any thing for *myself* of St Philip, and I sometimes fancy that I have deserved something of him (tho', I repeat, I doubt not he would silence me, if I were behind the said scenes) — and he has struck me some blows so piercing, that I am tempted to say, Et tu Brute — or rather Nunquid oblivisci potest mulier infantem suum? et illa oblita est.'[2]

I think we have decided as follows: — the Aisle will be done in a week's time — then, to leave the existing Church utterly alone — (except in the way of painting and decoration) — to turn the Sacristy (pro tempore) into a Chapel either of St Philip or of the Blessed Sacrament — to break arches into the two small sacristies — to break the window of the small baptistery into a door into the small court — to cover over the court with glass and floor it, making it a pro tempore) Sacristy — to break a door through the window out of the court in the opposite side into what was lately Fr Frederic's music room — and make that a low mass sacristy connecting by a door (already) existing) into the aisle. To decorate highly the (real) Sacristy — to decorate the Sanctuary and Apse — to lay out as little money as possible in paint upon walls and ceiling here. To place four altars in the aisle — 1. the one next the West and (Baptistery altar) with font before it — (an existing altar.) 2. next to it, the Altar of St Valentine, (say, a new Pollenian altar). 3. the altar of the Sacred Heart — (the present high altar) 4 the present image etc of our Lady. Two

---

[1] Each Oratorian was paying for the cost of constructing the confessional box he used in the church.   [2] *Isaiah,* 49: 15.

more new Pollenian altars, with marble, alabaster and spar for the high altar and St Philip's altar in Sacristy. All Heywood's work is to be done by middle of July. The Church to be shut up say from July 1st to Assumption.

When do you leave Pau? the middle of June? I think H. [Henry] might come back then, and perhaps Ambrose take his place. Perhaps he would go as far with you as Venice.

Ever Yrs affly J H N

TO HENRY BITTLESTON

The Oy Bm May 21. 1858

My dear H.

The office and Mass of St Philip are on the 31st. We can't alter this.

I can't think what possessed me to write to Stanislas a doleful letter a day or two ago, knowing as I do that anxiety is a bad thing for him. It struck me just after I had sent the letter. We have ten thousand things to be thankful for. (However, *don't read it out*, but I am going to be a little doleful. Nicholas went to Town yesterday to see why the school matters flagged — and has just given me in his report. I really do think the whole plan is at an end. Our friends cannot raise the money for what may be a losing concern — and I suspect they are throwing the blame on me 'for not striking when the iron was hot last January.' I wrote to Dr Newsham only about three weeks ago, and to the Bishop at the same time, saying we were going to undertake it — Thus I have *just* committed myself *in order* to fail. This is a fresh great mortification to me, and I hope I shall bear it well. But it is plain I am being put aside in all hands as in some way or other unpractical and unsuccessful. Don't tell S. [Stanislas] *all this — but* tell S. that)

The hitch of money is operating on the school plan. And, between ourselves, (for I shall not say it to the Fathers, lest I should discourage them) I don't think it will come to any thing. I cannot be sorry. We have many ways of serving God and St Philip. Only the other day I was saying that I wanted to know God's will *clearly*. The misery is the beginning *in twilight* — Well, I had rather a thousand times *not* begin it, than be in doubt whether He wished it or not. I shall dismiss it from my thoughts. It is never difficult to *reconcile* one's mind to any thing — the trial is the being in *suspense*.

William is still very lame, but he *says* he is getting better daily. I trust the old man is more than convalescent. Ambrose lately ascertained (by accident) as many as *650* frequenters of our Church (this was not a *full* list) — I think it good. What we want is *diversity*. I am startled, compared with Alcester Street, at the number of young women in the confessional. I know I now have yours and S's — but still the difference is great. I have very few old, very few men. By the bye, old Mrs Brennan found me out the other day. It was very different in Alcester Street.

J. Walker is trying hard to let me allow him to attempt a noviciate. I am

352

so out of heart, that I cannot make up my mind to it. (Of course as a first step I should send him to the Bishop to get leave. I think I ought to have done this in Crawley's case, and should have, but for Crawley —) I wish you and S. would try to find out God's will. His ways are not as ours. Both from dislike of W. and from despondency, I am no fair judge. He ought to have joined us ten years ago, and I should have been glad. Now, he gives us the dregs of his life when he *cannot amalgamate* with us. Moreover, he comes when he is disgusted with the Bishop, and having tried Montgomery.[1] So it is no *drawing*. Yet he would be useful in many ways. I wish to do simply what the Fathers wish. We certainly want *hands* very badly[2]

Ever Yrs affly J H N

Some parsons have been poking about Mrs Dee's angle, who is said to be dying. Is it grumbling to fear that our next blow will be a schoolmaster's house on it under our nose?[3]

TO JOHN HUNGERFORD POLLEN

The Oratory Birmingham. May 21. 1858

My dear Pollen

Nicholas missed you yesterday — and now I write to tell you something' which, as regards our decoration plans, is for the moment a great hitch. *You must not repeat it*, but I *give up* the expectation of a school, from what N. reports to me of his visit to London. Now we are decorating *because* of the school. Else, we should lay out the money in a very different way. E.g. we talk of a Reformatory, and we should give to it, what else we would have given to the decoration. How far this will affect us, having got so far, I do not know. I don't think it will affect the *Altars* — but will write in a few days. N. took your sketches to town with him in order to talk with you. We liked them, and did not then fear the dearest of them, but I can't say more now.

I am sorry to have put you to so much trouble — but I am inclined to go on — So I inclose one front for an idea, which I want from you.

1. Your four windows have quite *beautified* the end of the new aisle — and I want four more windows at the end of the *nave* position. Will that do?

2. Next, I want *under* the two sets of windows, so as to inclose the two doors, a sort of porch or vestibule. Your porch at Rednall is much admired, and though this vestibule will be too *long* for any such structure, yet I should be much obliged for your devising one for these two doors. We have plenty

---

[1] John Walker, now forty-two years old, worked in the Birmingham diocese, as the priest at Kenilworth. He had lately been assisting the priest at Wednesbury, George Montgomery, a convert like himself.

[2] St John wrote on Newman's letter, 'What a grumpy letter this is! Bellasis is full of the Shrewsbury job and that is the reason of N's [Nicholas] failure yesterday. They will never let the school drop. The Father is overworking in the Confessional that is the mischief. He has not been out for 3 weeks; but he is well and so are we all. . . .'

[3] This refers to a site close to the Oratory.

of bricks from the walls that are demolished, and so without much expense it might be done. It ought to be 10 feet broad at least, with a good deal of light, that people might not loiter about it, beggars and the like. Opposite the great nave door it should be bricked up, that, when there was an Exposition of the Bl. S. [Blessed Sacrament] the B. S. might not be seen in the street on opening the said door. It should be so high as not to hide the windows.

Ever yrs affly J. H. Newman

J H Pollen Esq.

P.S.   Perhaps you will think it better to put windows in the porch than in the nave end. In that case the said porch would be higher. But we must not make the porch a *great* job.

There is nothing to determine how far the vestibule might run on to the *left*. You might think it look better to go as far as the side wall. Another reason for bricking it opposite both church doors, would be to keep out the wind from the inside of the Church.

P.S.   Are you disposed to come down for next Wednesday St Philip's day? Of course we will give you a bed, and your fellow Goth Mr Amherst celebrates.

TO THOMAS SCRATTON

May 23/58

My dear Scratton

Since you press it, get the Press[1]

Ever Yrs J H N

P.S.   I almost rejoice I am not in Dublin, for I think all persons are put on their mettle, and the University advances indefinitely more, by showing, as *I* know full well, how much there is in you all. It brings it out.

No decisive accounts of Fr Flanagan

TO THOMAS SCRATTON

May 24/58

My dear S

As to the fees of Dr Quinn's students, as we don't pay him his £200 or whatever it is for students, it is broad as it's long — isn't it?[2]

Ever Yrs J H N

TUESDAY 25 MAY 1858   Amherst came, in order to celebrate tomorrow

[1] This was wanted to hold the professors' gowns and papers at the University House.
[2] Scratton wrote on 22 May, 'Is anything to be done about the fees of Dr Quinn's students? Not one has paid a single farthing this year.'

TO EDMUND O'REILLY, S.J.

The Oratory Bm May 25. 1858

My dear Fr O'Reilly,

I do not like to delay answering you, and thanking you for your congratulations to us on St Philip's feast, which I do cordially in the name of all our party — but, considering the bustle of all kind which precedes, in a usually quiet house, a Mass celebrated by a Bishop elect before the Bishop of the Diocese, with the addition of decorations of all kinds in Church and out of Church, you must excuse me, if both my handwriting and my sentences run disorderly.

Thank you for your criticism on Mr Scott's article. The truth is, it should not have been sent to you without my orders, as I meant to have written to you with it.[1] I like the end as little as you do, and till there is some way of commenting on St Luke more reverently than he has done, I think the first part, which I do like, should not be published. The unlucky thing is (quite in confidence) that he is rather proud of the end portion, which to me is as illogical as it is uncomfortable. And thus, *I* think, he has damaged in your mind the bulk of his article altogether, which *on its own merits*, and prescinding the question of St Luke, I think is valuable.[2]

I made a distinction of this kind, which I suppose you will not admit. As to Luke ii, 2 it would be no shock to my feelings to find the Evangelist mistaken in a *secular* date. Why is a sacred writer to be inspired in profane history, when it does not actually come in his way? Where were the registers of Proconsulates and Procuratures kept? Why should the Roman annals be more familiarly known by him than the motions of the heavenly bodies? I am not arguing, but showing you what my view of his article was.

As, however, to Luke iii, 23, the case is very different — for it relates to *our Lord's life* — and I was trying, I hope not wrongly to make good a theory of *this* kind — viz: that the verse was virtually part of the genealogy, which it heads, and was taken *from* the genealogy, and meant what the *genealogy* in Jerusalem *meant it to mean*. Next, I wanted to make out 1. either that it meant '30 years from the *registration*,' and that the registration took place (say) at 5 or 7 years old — so that our Lord would really be 35 or 37 at the time of His baptism — or 2. that the names were formally entered and recognised, *when*

---

[1] For O'Reilly's criticism of Scott's article 'On the Dates of the Nativity and the Crucifixion,' see letter of 25 May to Sullivan. O'Reilly, in his letter of 23 May, also complained that the hypothesis was 'put forward as tenable, and recommended to the reader—that St Luke made a mistake, and wrote what is false. The elaborate explanation of *how* he made the mistake, so far from diminishing, rather, I think, increases the unfavourable impression produced.'

[2] The conclusion of Scott's article was that the date of the Nativity could not have been later than 8 B.C., nor that of the Crucifixion earlier than A.D. 33. The only objection to this was the statement in Luke 3: 23 that our Lord was about thirty at the time of His Baptism. Scott's explanation of the difficulty was omitted when his article appeared in the *Atlantis*, in Jan. 1859, and an editorial note added. See also letter of 7 June 1858 to Scott.

their owners became the head and representative of the line — so that the meaning would be '30 years on the death of St Joseph,' which might have occurred some years before; which would bring our Lord's age to some years past 30, as before.

3. A third hypothesis would be to say that St Luke specified our Lord's *legal age* for *ministerial offices* — vid. Numb. iv, 3. 1 Paralip. xxiii, 3. cf. Gen. xli, 46. 2 Kings v. 4. The ὡσεὶ is the difficulty to this interpretation.

I say all this to show you that I was quite alive to the anxieties of the Article, and did not mean to let it out of my hand. But by accident it has burst like a shell before I discharged it.

I have written to Dr Leahy about young Hogan — tho' I have been so busy that I delayed.[1]

Thank you for your kindness about my own article. I suppose you will get some more of it, before this reaches you[2]

Yours most sincerely John H Newman of the Oratory

The Revd Fr O'Reilly

TO W. H. SCOTT

The Oy Bm May 25. 1858

Private

My dear Scott

I am sorry to say that Fr O'Reilly has plucked your article. Unluckily Fowler sent it to him without express directions from me. I meant to have written to him about it, and made a distinction between the *hypothesis* at the end, (which I have never admitted,) and the *bulk* of the article.

He does not say any thing about your *view* of our Lord's age itself — but he says of the *ending* 'Its publication would injure the University. It is hard to say when Mr Scott or you would hear the end of it.'

I suppose we must lie on our oars for the present. And take time to think. The *hypothesis* about St Luke's 'error' I think is certainly impossible now

Ever Yrs affly John H Newman

[1] See letter of 26 April 1858 to Lyons.
[2] See note to letter of 25 May to Sullivan.

TO WILLIAM KIRBY SULLIVAN

The Oratory Birmingham May 25. 1858

Private

My dear Mr Sullivan

Fr O'Reilly has spoken so strongly against Mr Scott's Article that we cannot publish it with out the certainty of its damaging us greatly. The *end* of it I certainly have never liked — and am sorry that Fowler sent it to Fr O'Reilly without my formally telling him to do so — for I hoped to have written an ending myself with explanations. However, we certainly must not venture on it in this number.

He says 'I consider its publication in the Atlantis would be fearfully offensive, and would injure the University. Passing by the theory about our Lord's age, which might unpleasantly startle many' (*This* portion of it, and it is the *bulk* I thought very valuable) 'I confine myself to Mr Scott's hypothesis to explain St Luke;' — (well, this I certainly did not like.) He adds 'I think it *ought* not to go down, and I am quite certain it *would* not. It is hard to say when Mr Scott or you would hear the end of it.'

The 'I' or 'We' is a great difficulty. I must say a word about it in the Postscript.

Will you then suggest some fresh arrangement. I suppose we are in no want of matter — and I almost think that you reckoned that the excess of pages in Number 1 would enable us to be short of the full number in Number 2.

I am glad to say that Fr O'Reilly has passed the ticklish part of my own article — and it is ready for the press as soon as it is wanted. (Fowler is pressed for Greek type, and had better print off part first.) He says of me 'Without pretending to pass any judgment, I like your view and have no objection to make.'[1]

Excuse great haste

Yours most sincerely John H Newman

W K Sullivan Esqr

P.S.   I do not see it is possible to dispense with a division of the Number into three.

1. Compositions or discursive articles which will use 'we', and have the writer's name at the end. (as yours last time and mine last time)

2. Scientific ones of which Literature is the subject matter — (as Mr Scott's — or Mr Arnold's — or my own this time.)

[1] Newman's article was that 'On the formula μιά φύσις . . .' The 'ticklish part' was that at the beginning about the inadequacy of language to describe revealed truth and the reluctance of the early fathers to use scientific terms.

3 Mathematical and Physical etc.

There need not be the first or second head in *every* number. *This* number will have none of the *first* head.

WEDNESDAY 26 MAY 1858 Kept St Philip's day, tho' Ember — gave the Priests dinner ⟨a dejeuner viz in midday⟩ — *a dejeuner for Edgbaston people* — *Mrs Fletcher*

TO THOMAS SCRATTON

26 May/58

My dear Scratton

I write a hasty line amid the festivities of this day to thank you for your handsome £3 and the additional two.

Let me know when the half yearly Audit is coming off.

I inclose the cheque signed

Ever Yrs J H N

THURSDAY 27 MAY 1858 *began additions and alterations to Church* (*in aisle, and raising the nave.*)

TO WILLIAM MONSELL

The Oratory Birmingham May 28. 1858

My dear Monsell

You must have wondered I did not write to you — but many things, I can't tell what, have hindered it. One was, I expected to go up to London and avail myself of your hospitality. But this has gone off. Stanislas's direction is '15, Rue Henri iv, Pau, Basses Pyrenées — ' I was concerned to find you were disappointed — for the letter I sent you was much the best we have had. I have never concealed from myself that his illness is very serious — he had been aging all through last year, his spirits, voice, and energy failing him — and then his mother dying of consumption. He pleads hard to come home for the *summer*, and I am not quite against it. We have heard nothing of his health since that letter — whether this is good or bad news I do not know.

I could not help being rather for the Tories against all you oppositionists in the last struggle — first from the merits, as I thought them, of the question itself, next from my extreme distrust of Lord Pam [Palmerston] and Lord John [Russell]. But all the Catholic peers almost voted for them.[1]

Monsell wrote on 13 May, 'So long as there is any hope of your coming [to London] I will not go into the question you start about terms for the charter. I must lie on my oars until we see the results of Cardwell's motion. I hardly think him wise in going on now for he will have but a narrow majority, if he has one at all, and that means a dissolution.'

I am glad there is a chance of your coming down here. If you do, we will have some talk about the school plan.

The Vice Rector, who was *coming*, has vanished in fumo — [1] I suppose you have not thought of doing any thing with the Ministry.[2]

Ever Yours affectly John H Newman of the Oratory

The Rt Honble Wm Monsell M P.

TO JOHN HUNGERFORD POLLEN

Oy Bm May 28/58

My dear Pollen,

The inclosed is from your own pencillings.

Heywood wants *at once* the details of the *stone* work — i.e. sizes, mouldings etc etc, from A to A.

I am sorry to trouble you when you are so busy.

Please when you write send back the inclosed.

Ever Yours J H Newman

Edward Cardwell on 13 May moved a resolution in the House of Commons, against the Conservative Government, for making public a despatch to Lord Canning, the Governor General of India, in which he was blamed for his minatory proclamation to the landowners of Oudh, after the Mutiny. Many liberal Englishmen, including John Bright, approved of the policy of clemency now that resistance had ceased. After four days of debate Cardwell's motion was lamely withdrawn on 21 May, and represented a signal triumph for the Government, which was led in the House of Commons by Disraeli. A similar motion in the House of Lords was defeated by 167 votes to 158. More than a dozen Catholic peers voted with the Liberal minority against the Government.

[1] Archbishop Leahy wrote to Newman on 25 May: 'Mr Kelly of Maynooth months ago was appointed Vice-Rector. He declined. The Archbishops met on the subject about three or four weeks since. He was then willing to take the office. So we commissioned Dr Cullen to say in our name that we were satisfied.

Yesterday I had a letter saying he declines again on the score of health. We must, therefore, think of some one else. It is time.

Dr O'Reilly was appointed as well. He too declined.

It is very difficult to get a fit person.'

Newman commented in 1872, 'Nothing can show more clearly how little chance Dr Cullen thought there was of my remaining, than the utter abstention the Archbishops observed all along from making me au courant with the search for a Vice Rector. I was not only not consulted, but not informed of what was going on. Dr Forde knew at the time, Mr Flannery knew — but I knew nothing — I was not in the Archbishops' confidence. They had given me up, or at least Dr Cullen had.'

[2] Monsell wrote on 6 June, '*Private* I have seen Disraeli about the charter. He entered into the question with interest, was extremely civil and agreeable but of course did no more than promise to take the matter into consideration.'

28 MAY 1858

TO THOMAS SCRATTON

Oy Bm May 28/58

My dear S

I approve of the Preachers for June.

I grieve for the O'Connells — and beg you if you have the opportunity, to convey my respectful sympathy on their great bereavement.[1]

Fr Jones S. J of Gardiner Street wants a Burse for a Medical Student. Will you, on his calling, 1. consult with him what Bishop he had better apply to. 2. explain to him *precisely how* much a Burse-Student pays each year, and what his obligations of the Scholarship are etc etc.

I shall send you some papers for the Auditors, when I know the day.

I am told that *Dr Butler* of Limerick is the Bishop of Killaloe's coadjutor. Is it so?[2]

Ever Yrs affly J H N

TO WILLIAM KIRBY SULLIVAN

The Oratory Bm May 30/58

My dear Mr Sullivan

Mr O'Hagan's article has come to me this morning. I like the look of it very much, and I am glad you are putting it first.[3]

I think it either has 'we', or nothing at all. Arnold's too has 'we' — These two then, I suppose, will be the *discursive* or literary articles. (I am somewhat disappointed in A's — It has so little point.)[4]

Then, the 'Critical' articles will follow Had they not better begin a *fresh page?* to show the division.

I suppose 'The records lately edited by M. Quicherat' should be left out from the heading of Article one, and 'John O'Hagan' should be at the end of it — and 'Thomas Arnold' at the end of Article 2.

My own article is ready as far as Fowler's Greek type has allowed it to be. And Fr O'Reilly has passed it.

There are some false prints still in Article 1. e.g. one in note at page 281

Very sincerely Yours John H Newman

W K Sullivan Esqr

[1] John O'Connell (1810–58), third son of the Liberator, died on 24 May, leaving a widow and eight children.
[2] George Butler became coadjutor to the Bishop of Limerick in 1861.
[3] O'Hagan's article was 'Joan of Arc, followed by Arnold's 'The Genius of Alcibiades.'
[4] Acton wrote on 6 July to Simpson, 'Neither Hagan nor Arnold is up to the mark, but we could cry up Newman's paper by way of compensation.' A. Watkin and H. Butterfield, the *Cambridge Historical Journal*, x, (1950), 'Gasquet and the Acton-Simpson Correspondence,' p. 84.

MONDAY 31 MAY 1858   Nicholas went to Rednall for his month

TO JOHN STANISLAS FLANAGAN

The Oy Bm May 31/58

My dear S

Your letter of the 28th has just come. I was going to say what your letter wishes, that you had better come home with Henry. The weather here at this moment is hot to melting. Of course it mayn't continue. I suppose you would find Rednall too hot. Would you in the kitchen? or is it damp? Perhaps you think being so near us would make you anxious. I doubt it — unless we were inconsiderate as I was in my letter to you.[1] But however, whether you are at Bath, Rednall or Kingstown, is an after consideration. As you and H. are to travel together, I shall not send him Testimonials. I will, if he writes again. As to money, say what you want and how it is to come, and Nicholas shall send it. What a shame you should talk of your expense! Tell H. I fear that the additional money which the Miss F's [Farrant] have given is gone to pay old bills, but I will ask Nicholas. Would not the Bankers at Pau for expedition lend you the money to start with? As H. is coming so soon, I shall not do much about his almsmen.

The whole matter of the school has so blown away from my mind, that I have forgotten it. I am not in suspense. Henry mistakes me when he fancies I complain of having to begin without seeing endings. It never tried me, *that*. Nor has St Philip any thing to do with it. It has been my lot all through life. The thing I do feel are the falling off of friends, and the like. Mrs Bowden sent me some weeks back what even Ambrose confessed was an unkind letter.[2] H Wilberforce is doing all he can and straining every nerve to show that he does not forget what I was, and to be as loving as possible. It is not till a peg is loose that there is such effort. [W. G.] Ward, Lewis, and a number of others whom I know more or less, are in the same way. But even this is not what I call a stab — but, when I have said it, I have said it, and there is an end — and I assure you, nothing has made me *unhappy* — and I dare say, if you were near us, you would have less anxiety about our matters, than if you were away. Suspense there is none. The Atlantis is becoming, I think, a decided hit. The evening classes flourish, and rise to a hundred youths. I really think the University is growing and will grow. I don't like to boast, but I am better in health then ever. Yesterday week, I, first went in the confessional for an hour and a half, then sung high mass — then went into the confessional — preached in the evening — took the novena — gave benediction, and then

[1] i.e. that of 19 May.
[2] Mrs Bowden, whose letters were now infrequent, sent on 29 March the barest account of herself and her family, with all of whom Newman's ties had been so close.

into the confessional till 10, with out any inconvenience. It is no disappoint-ment whatever to me, perhaps a relief, the school's failing, if it fails.

Ignatius is going on well — I don't know whether it will last, but he is quite cheerful after his tonsuring. I proposed to him today to help Robert at the Union Workhouse, or Edward with the little Oratory, and he smiled in a way which is perfectly new to his face. Patrick Dignam is going on capitally.[1] We talk of a brother from Belgium. Delinquencies have been found out which seem likely to lead to Charles's going. I should be glad to be rid of all of them. I said to you in a former letter that I trusted the spell of ill luck was broken. I think so still. Henry's recovery is St Philip's good act — but tell Henry, when he abuses me, that Fr Prever once put St Joseph out of window; I think suspended him by the neck.[2] St Philip has hit me so hard, I have a right to hit him — and, though he will have the best of it, yet I don't know, for all that, why I may not have it out with him. It is better than desponding, and really I don't think my complaining is desponding.

We now talk of *raising* the Church also. I *hope* the arches of the Sacristy will be seen half down the Church — for the wall running from the sacristy door to our Lady's altar comes away. I think we shall then have done all that will be done in our time — and that it will be a pretty picturesque Church. Were even £10.000 left us, it would go before a penny could reach a new Church. £7.000 debt — £2.000 Miss Bowden, and £1000 William's and my outlay now.

Nicholas is gone to Rednall for a month to get on with his translation of Döllinger.[3] I for one shall not (please God) go away for a day, and I am up to any work.

Love to Henry

Ever Yrs affly J H N

TO EDMUND O'REILLY, S.J.

The Oratory Birmingham May 31. 1858

My dear Fr O'Reilly,

Thank you for the trouble you have been at about the Council.[4] It pleases me very much to think you are interested in my article, and I am much obliged for your looking over it.

I don't like the idea of the Requiem Mass, and think it had better drop.[5]

Yours most sincerely in Xt, John H Newman of the Oratory

[1] A young Irishman, who hoped to become a laybrother.
[2] Giambattista Prever (1684–1751) was a priest of the Oratory at Turin. The incident Newman describes is not mentioned in his life, published in London in 1851. Bittleston told Newman he should work for St Philip without seeing results.
[3] See letter of 7 Oct. 1857 to W. G. Todd.
[4] The Council was to consider rules of discipline drawn up by a committee, as a result of Newman's suggestion in his letter of 22 April to O'Reilly. See also letter of 8 June to him.
[5] It had been suggested that there should be a Requiem Mass at the University church for John O'Connell, in consideration of the merits of his father.

31 MAY 1858

TO WILLIAM KIRBY SULLIVAN

The Oratory Bm May 31/58

My dear Mr Sullivan,

I hope no great harm will come of Fr O'Reilly's criticism of Mr Scott's article, except the delay. At least, he is quite open to having the matter argued — tho' he *will* object (and I think rightly) to the concluding portion of it. And I am glad that Fowler was not the *mover* in the Article going to him — because he has acted without orders before now, and it seemed a repetition of what ought not to be.[1]

I approve of all the plans detailed in your letter, and have nothing to say, except that I prefer the 'wes' to go first (with the author's name at end) altogether rather than to mix 'Is' and 'wes' up. Go on with the printing.

What you say about the state and prospects of the exchanges is very good.[2]

Mr Hennessy's article seems a good one, as far as I understand it.[3]

From what Longmans said in the letter which I think I sent you, I don't suppose they would object to any Dublin publisher, who was respectable — which we should wish also — They named one or two, did they not?

I do not answer you in detail, because I wish you to carry out the various suggestions you have made, if you will take the trouble — knowing with what zeal and judgment you will do so

The number seems to me to promise very well.

Yours most sincerely John H Newman

W K Sullivan Esqr

P.S. Mr John O'Hagan writes me word, that you and he had been talking together about the University's position and prospects. I need scarcely say how interested I should be in hearing the results of your conferences.

TO THOMAS SCRATTON

The Oy Bm June 1. 1858

My dear Scratton

I must trouble you to write a circular to the Professors, in preparation for

[1] Sullivan had told Fowler the printer to send Scott's article direct to Fr O'Reilly, in order to save time.
[2] Sullivan wrote on 29 May that exchanges with other learned periodicals would reach more than one hundred and fifty after the appearance of the second number of the *Atlantis*.
[3] Hennessy had two articles in the *Atlantis* for July, 'On a Uniform System of Weights,

363

the next Audit. It is too delicate a matter to print. It will entail on you the trouble of one to each Professor. *I* will fill it up to each, and sign it. I have written it over-leaf. I fear your thoughtful proposition about John O'Connell's second son is impossible. The first has not done us credit — and as Hogan's son has not passed the Trustees, it would seem like a leaning in politics. At all events, it must come from another quarter.[1]

Ever Yrs John H Newman of the Oratory

T. Scratton Esqr

Each *Professorship* must have one, e.g. Mr Sullivan will have *two* — and Mr Butler, etc. And none will be sent to those who have no salary. Those who have a salary assigned, but do not take it, must have one.

1. Fr O'Reilly Dogmatic	13 English Literature
2. Professor of Canon Law	14 Italian and Spanish
3 Surgery	15 French and German
4 Anatomy and Physiology (Hayden)	16 Ancient History and Geography
5 Anatomy and Physiology (Cryan)	17 Modern History and Geography
6 Practice of Medicine	18 Geometry
7 Medical Chemistry	19 Logic
8 Materia Medica	20 Catechist
9 Medical Jurisprudence	21 Mathematics
10 Greek and Latin Literature	22 Natural Philosophy
11 Greek and Latin Language	23 Physiology
12 Irish Archaeology	24 Physical Chemistry

1st Page

My dear Professor —

At the request of the Gentlemen who are kind enough to undertake for me the office of Auditing my accounts, I must request of you to do me the kindness of filling up as far you are able to do so, the table overleaf,

I am, My dear Professor — Very sincerely Yours

Measures, and Coins for all Nations,' and 'On the Distribution of Heat over Islands, and especially over the British Isles.'

[1] Scratton suggested on 28 May that John O'Connell's second son, aged sixteen, should be given a free place in the University, like the eldest son Daniel. The Irish Archbishops, the trustees of the University, had just objected to the granting of a free place to the son of Hogan the sculptor, on account of the latter's supposed connection with the Roman revolutionaries. See letter of 26 April to Lyons. John O'Connell had been a supporter of the Whigs and an enemy of the Young Irelanders.

3rd Page

Professorship of
1. Name of Professor   —
2. Date of appointment   —
3. Annual salary   —
4. Date of first payment —
5. Date of first Lecture —
6. Average number of Lectures —
7. Average number of students —
8. Amount of last payment —

TO JOHN HUNGERFORD POLLEN

Oy. Bm. June 2/58

My dear Pollen

I don't know whether it is worth while to say to you that perhaps you may carry the porch *higher* than 12 feet — or rather that all that you have to think of is to get *under* the 12 new windows of the aisle — i.e. to take in the *small* doors of the aisle shutting up the *windows*. We are still talking of raising the roof of the nave.[1]

Ever yrs affly John H Newman of the Oratory

J. H. Pollen Esqr

TO JAMES STEWART

The Oratory Birmingham June 2. 1858

My dear Stewart

I rejoice very much at the intention, of which you inform me of your publishing a Handbook of Memoranda etc.

I wish too we had some plan for turning publishers. And, if you come into the notion, I wish you would talk with other Professors on the subject. Mr Sullivan, I suppose, would have an opinion upon it. I am already pledged to find money for Mr Curry's book. Now I wish to know how I (i.e. the University funds, or rather the 'Cullen and Newman account' at the Hibernian) could manage to undertake the publication of any work of a Professor if suitable. (All this depends on your not having already provided yourself with a publisher.).

What I should like would be a University Press Board — consisting of four or five persons, who would take the management of all publications, and

[1] The copyist reproduced Newman's sketch here.

365

recommend (in confidence) to me such works as come to them for printing. If I had the decision and responsibility, it would relieve them of any odium. I should say, for instance, Dr Ellis, Mr O'Hagan, Mr Sullivan, Renouf, and Fr O'Reilly, as representing the five faculties. The terms with the writer might be such as London publishers offer, 'half the profits.' Now the question is, what capital would be required to start a scheme of this kind?

I will gladly promise from the University income £10, as you propose, for fee for the 10 evening classes — £1 a piece.

Ever Yours affly John H Newman

James Stewart Esqr

THURSDAY 3 JUNE 1858   C C. [Corpus Christi] procession
SATURDAY 5 JUNE   Monteith called
SUNDAY 6 JUNE   procession
MONDAY 7 JUNE   Church shut up for alterations. *Oratory room used (the present boys refectory)*

TO E. B. PUSEY

Oratory, Birmingham June 7/58

My dear Pusey

Thank you very much for the trouble you have taken, and for the light you have thrown upon the subject about which I wrote.[1]

I suppose I may keep Dr Scott's note. He only refers to Acts i. 22 etc. I had fancied there was a passage in the Septuagint of Job in which ἀρχόμενος was used for 'at first' — but I cannot find it. What would you say to ἀρξάμενος αὐλίσθητί Judg. 19. 6? but I do not see why the classical passages I gave are not enough — especially τελευτῶντες.

Yours very affly John H Newman

TO W. H. SCOTT

The Oratory Bm June 7/58

My dear Scott

What I propose to do about your Article is this — to keep in type all which is *positive* on the subject of the Christian Era — i.e. the bulk of the Article — but not to make use of the *explanation* of Luke ii and iii. I had intended to

---

[1] Pusey wrote in substantial agreement with Newman's interpretation of Luke 3 : 23 in his letter of 17 May 1858. He also enclosed a letter of 31 May from Robert Scott (1811–87), Master of Balliol 1854–70, joint author of Liddell and Scott's Greek Lexicon. Scott preferred to translate ἀρχόμενος etc as 'at the commencement of his ministry.'

have sent the former portion first to Dr O'Reilly, and got it provisionally passed before I sent your *explanation* — which I myself never thought would pass a censorship.

I had sent Fr O'Reilly my own conjectural interpretations; and to Pusey, to see if he could throw light on the subject. I inclose you his answers which have come this morning, and you will see he takes my view of ἀρχόμενος — I do not take it ἀρχόμενος ἀπό as in Acts i. but like τελευτῶντες in Thuc. [Thucidydes] or as ὡς ἀρχόμενος εἶπον in Thuc. Isocrates etc. Also I take 30 to be put down as the *legal* age — and the ὡσεί merely to state the fact, not *what* our Lord's age was, but that it was the *legal* age.

I had intended, if Fr O'Reilly passed the bulk of your article, and not the rest, to have added an *Editorial* note to this effect — 'To the above erudite etc dissertation this objection may be made, that it runs counter to Luke ii and iii. As to Luke ii in so obscure a point of history, upon which ancient authorities and chronologists differ, it is enough to say that it is not of that vital importance to the inspiration of St Luke it [to] make it of consequence to decide upon it — but Luke iii certainly does concern a point of sacred history, and here etc' giving the above interpretation.[1]

I advise you to break up the type of your *explanation* of Luke ii and iii, (taking as many copies of it as you choose) *leaving* in type all the rest, including the paragraph about St Irenaeus, for Atlantis Number iii.

Please return me the two letters I inclose.[2]

As to your wish of coming here, we could not let you or Anderdon enter into a *bargain* with us.[3] You must come for *us* to decide on you, and no one else. *Lay brothers*, as their name implies, are not ecclesiastics, nor have they a formal noviceship; and at Rome they are sometimes persons of a higher class. But we cannot let you bargain with us — you come, if you come, in that *recognised* way, which our body admits, and submit to the rules *proper* to the recognised capacity in which you come.[4]

Ever Yrs affly John H Newman

[1] See the editorial note at the end of Scott's article, the *Atlantis*, (Jan. 1859), pp. 71–4.

[2] Those from Pusey and Robert Scott.

[3] Scott, who was to assist with the translation of the Bible, wrote on 5 June, 'Anderdon recommends me to ask you to receive me at the Oratory—but says I *must* go as a layman, and declare positively that I have no thought or intention of entering the Novitiate. Can you have me on such conditions?'

[4] Scott replied on 8 June, 'By the way, I ought to say that when I mentioned Anderdon's name I did not mean to imply that he was in any way addressing you through me, or intended to do so. It was as my spiritual adviser, that he gave me counsel on the subject—and not in any other way.' See also letter of 26 June to Patterson.

TO JAMES STEWART

The Oratory, Birmingham. June 7. 1858

My dear Stewart

Thank you for your return   I shall send the Auditors also the letters the Professors in Philosophy and Letters sent in to their Dean last November[1]

I am very glad to see Mr Cheyne's Sermons, and Fr Caswall has seized on them with much gout — [2]I will say Mass for your intention respecting him on the 15th which is the day, (a lesser event,) on which our gracious Sovereign visits the town of Brummagem.[3]

Since you have inadvertently got the fine edge of the wedge in, I suppose you must have £1 for each of the Classes — but I cannot promise it another time.

I can easily fancy the scheme of Examination for the Evening Classes will take time to digest and accomodate to the circumstances of the case — but I shall be much obliged if the four you mention S.A.B and yourself would undertake it.[4]

As to the question of commencing the classes in October, it is altogether a question for the Professors to do what they think best

Ever Yours affly, John H Newman of the Oratory.

J. Stewart Esqr.

TUESDAY 8 JUNE 1858   Stan [Stanislas] and Henry left Pau for England   Ambrose went away for two months

TO EDMUND O'REILLY, S.J.

The Oratory, Birmm. June 8. 1858

My dear Fr O'Reilly

I did not thank you for your last letter, telling me of the meeting of the Council, since I had written to Mr Butler about it.

On second thoughts, however, I write to you — principally to suggest (what doubtless has occurred to all already) that we must take care not to be *uncivil* to the discipline committee — but, while we put aside their suggestions,

---

[1] Cf. the latter part of the letter of 19 Nov. 1857 to Butler.

[2] Patrick Cheyne, *Six Sermons on the Doctrine of the Holy Eucharist*, Aberdeen 1858. Cheyne was condemned at an Episcopalian synod, on 15 June 1858, for teaching in these sermons that Christ 'is really, truly, and substantially present in the Eucharist,' and was deprived by his Bishop, of the incumbency of St John's, Aberdeen, which he had held for forty years. See H. R. T. Brandreth, *Dr Lee of Lambeth*, London 1951, pp. 28–34.

[3] Queen Victoria and the Prince Consort visited Birmingham to open Aston Park.

[4] i.e. Sullivan, Arnold and Butler.

must thank them for them as respectfully as we can. I don't like the suggestions, and I do like the Council's ammendment.[1]

As to the want of a sixth member good part of the meeting, I really do not know enough of such matters to answer the difficulty. However, since the Council only recommended to me, what I could statutably do myself, I don't think it matters.

I doubt whether there should be moving and seconding in the Rectorial Council. By which I meant that I did not mean there should be — being unfeignedly unwilling you should merely go by what I *meant*.

I have sent a letter of Dean Meyler's as well as Dr Lyons's to Dr Leahy about Mr Hogan.[2]

Most sincerely Yours in Xt   John H Newman of the Oratory

TO ROBERT ORNSBY

The Oy Bm ⌐June 8/58⌐

My dear Ornsby

Thank you for the papers, two of which arrived safe.[3] I saw what work you must have been at to produce such Lectures. You must give the whole Vacation to getting well.

⌐What you say about the Meath feeling as to the University is only what Marshall exemplified in its fulness.⌐[14] But such things will not touch its

[1] The Committee (Dunne, Flannery, MacDermott, Ornsby, Penny, Quinn, Stewart) appointed to draw up rules of discipline, (cf. letter of 22 April to O'Reilly), settled these at a meeting on 30 May. They consisted of a system of penalties. Dunne wrote to Newman next day, 'Mr Flannery is, I believe, the only one who cordially approves of them; Dr MacDermott seems to *accept* them as the decisions of others: Stewart takes them through a sort of desperate feeling that to do something is imperative: Penny views them all with grave misgiving . . . Dr Quinn considers that such a system of management is not in harmony with the views which presided over the formation of the little collegiate bodies—like families . . . I do not think them prudent or adapted to our actual circumstances . . .'
The Rectorial Council rejected the suggestions of the Committee on discipline and proposed instead that Newman should write to the Deans of Houses insisting on the observance of the Rules and Regulations of the University.
Penny had written to Newman on 27 May, about the need for discipline. 'Some of the youths are extremely troublesome and irregular. The Princes [de Ligne] follow in the wake of the Count [Zamoyski], and White keeps at least pace with them . . . the latter gentleman . . . this term has strangely altered for the worse—he seldom goes to lecture, e.g. last week he appears to have been only once . . . the four above named, on Monday last . . . went to some races . . . and came back about 8 . . . [they then went out lawfully to get dinner in the town, but] did not make their appearance till twelve . . . Errington too . . . is not quite what he was —Segar not much altered. Charley [de la Pasture] and Augustus [Bethell] the same excellent fellows that they always were. . . . Throckmorton goes on much as usual.'
[2] See letter of 26 April 1858 to Lyons.
[3] These gave an account of Ornsby's public lecture at Navan in County Meath, where Dr Cantwell was the Bishop.
[4] Ornsby wrote of his visit to Navan, 'I cannot say that much cordiality was expressed towards the *University*. One priest I met entered into considerable details on the subject— said the University had not answered the expectations of the people . . . that a strong impression prevailed that it was Dr. Cullen's pet institution that he had the whole control of it; that his policy, (in repressing the political action of the priests) was against the liberty of the

progress, the causes of which are quite independent of Dr Cantwell or Dr MacHale, so long as there is elsewhere in Ireland the means of an annual collection, which there seems to be. ⌐The Anti-Cullen influence has done its worst, for it has withheld its money, yet without deficiency of the resulting income of the University. While the funds allow of the Professors to teach, their talent and energy will carry the day¬ against whatever amounts of agrarian opposition, which, I say, simply will not touch them.

Your evening classes, though one cannot yet prophesy their continuance, are at the moment a great stroke; and nothing shows more the real life of the University, than that, as I really think, it is advancing more in the absence of Rector and Vice Rector, than in their presence. The Atlantis too, I trust, is likely to be a hit. I am sanguine about it. ⌐I think there is far more chance of a Charter now, than when the Whigs were in; both because there is no Lord Clarendon to back up the Queen's Colleges, and because the Tories are deeply pledged to the leaders of the Separate Education system in Ireland.¬[1] Altogether I am very hopeful.

⌐I shall be very sorry if Dr. Q. [Quinn] is the new Vice Rector — which is the more likely because I mentioned his name among others to the Archbishops last October, when they asked for a list; — but things have changed very much since then.[2]

I am dissatisfied at the little that appears in the Catholic Periodicals about the University.¬ I sent the Weekly Register the List of Public Lectures with my initials — but it has taken no notice of it — and this, after my remonstrating and its repenting of a similar omission a year ago.

Ever Yrs affly J H N

TO AMBROSE ST JOHN

The Oy. Bm ⌐June 8/58¬

Charissime,

Ignatius has just come to me to ask to go home. He would like to go from now to our meeting again, say July 15. I said I did not see any difficulty at first sight — but would ask you. My notion is that we ought to let him go, (*not to return* except with a full understanding that he can proceed in his real noviciate — but I throw this out.) Answer, if possible, by return of post.

⌐An incident

1. On Sunday last I wrote first a¬ much stronger ⌐paper for the Chapter,¬

people; that if the University were to prove successful, it could be represented at Rome as an evidence of *his* success in Ireland, and that in consequence people were not disposed to send their sons to, or to help an institution, whose prosperity could be used as an argument in his favour. This he stated as the feeling in Meath.'
    [1] Monsell wrote to Newman on 6 June that the Government were deeply committed to the Irish Church Education Society.
    [2] Ornsby wrote that he felt sure Dr Quinn would be the Vice-Rector.

than that which I read. ⌐On Monday reading it over, I thought it injudicious, tore it up⌐ (I almost always *burn*) ⌐threw the bits upon my grate,⌐ [[and wrote another,]] writing ⌐what I read to the Fathers.¹

2. Most of the pieces fell upon the coals and wood — some few bits dropped on the fender. I said to myself 'I don't like this,' and I intended to take them up, and throw them into the grate, when something called away my mind.

3. A few hours afterwards looking, the bits on the fender were gone! I said to myself 'I could all but swear they fell there — nay, I *could* swear. I meant to have mentioned the matter to you, and forgot.

4. Just now, passing along the corridor, I see Charles's fuel box, and in it⌐ (he persists in *refusing* to get brown paper) ⌐I saw bits of letters torn up. I looked at them and saw a bit about a scapulary, etc etc. I told Austin.

5 Austin inspected the whole — and has discovered a whole letter of Sister Mary Ph. [[Philip]]² to me, a good bit of a letter of Nicholas's, some other letters, a receipt to you from Mr Page for £20.2 — *my bits which I had lost from my fender* et id genus omne.

Verbum sap.⌐

Ever Yours affly J H N

WEDNESDAY 9 JUNE 1858   Fr Frederic left

TO AMBROSE ST JOHN

The Oy. Bm. June 9/58

My dear Ambrose

It seems selfish to inflict my troubles on you during your holy day, but I gain more by it than you lose — and perhaps I am saying nothing but what you expect. A letter from Henry has just come with de Castro's formed opinion about S. [[Stanislas]] which is too bad for me to tell except in confidence to you.

1. there is a dull sound at the apex of the lung under ⟨above⟩ the right collar bone. 2. this marks the presence of a tubercle. 3 This is corroborated by his hoarseness, loss of strength, haemorrhage, loss of appetite etc. 4. Tubercles sometimes stop in their first stage for years — they never go. 5 His regularity of pulse, good digestion are in favor of the disease not proceeding — his constitutional tendency is against it. 6. If it proceeds, it suppurates, and eats the lungs out. If it is arrested, it still makes him an invalid for life. 7 This is a very critical time for him. No one can foretell how he may be

¹ This Chapter Address on reserve in dealing with boys will be included in the volume of Newman's Oratorian papers. Cf. *Trevor*, II, pp. 182–3.
² i.e. Catherine Anne Bathurst.

in three months. If the disease is not arrested, its progress will be very rapid, and he would sink soon.

On the other hand *he* writes me word, 'I laugh in my sleeve when I go to a doctor, as I have all the appearance of as bluff, hearty, and stout a working man as you ever laid eyes on.'

Dr de Castro wishes him to go through the summer in England from house to house, and then in September to take advice again. *My* advice would be to remain quietly in Birmingham till that time, all messages and letters from his penitents etc coming to him through me.[1]

Edward is evidently patronizing Walker's candidateship. I wish I knew what my reluctance to it is worth; how far from despondency, how far from personal disaffection towards him, how far from real insight into him.[2]

Ever Yours affly John H Newman

TO W. H. SCOTT

[9 June 1858]

My dear Scott

The only difficulty of your keeping the end in type is the expense of locking up type.[3] Fr O'Reilly's objection, I fear, is decisive against it. My own objection to it is the tenableness of the view; his the religiousness of it.

You may be quite sure that what he feels the whole body of religious people will feel — and, as he says, if we published it, we should never hear the end of it.

As to my objection, I can only say, that, if you get any half a dozen persons to agree with you, I will give it up. I speak especially of the explanation of Luke iii. I don't think Fr O'Reilly sees the force of it (quite independently of the theological question) more than I do

Ever Yrs affly John H Newman of the Oratory

W H Scott Esqr

THURSDAY 10 JUNE 1858 Ignatius went to Rednall, thence to go home. Austin went, his mother calling

[1] As to the account of Flanagan's health, St John replied on 11 June that it did not increase his despondent feelings, and added 'Well, Father, whatever comes while you are at the helm I don't care because you always come up to the scratch croak as much as you will beforehand.' See Newman's comment in his letter of 13 June.
[2] See end of letter of 21 May to Bittleston.
[3] Scott wrote on 8 June that he was sorry his article could not be put in the *Atlantis* at once, and hoped the whole of it could be kept in type, because the six months' interval might produce some confirmation of his hypothesis.

The Oy. Bm. June 10. 1858

My dear Pollen,

We like your porch very much, and only wish you to complete and detail it. I wanted William to send you a sketch, but he takes his drawing paper, and begins something too large almost for a luggage van — so I hope you will excuse the inclosed.

The front of the nave externally is 32-6. The aisle (I think) 19 feet. To the spring of the aisle roof and to the string course (going the whole 32.6 × 19), is 19 feet.

The windows in the aisle commence at 12 feet from the ground, and they commence at 4 feet from the junction between nave front and aisle front. The nave is to be raised 10ft, so that it is 28 or 29ft from ground to new spring of nave roof.

We submit as follows to you

1. (A) Four windows, something like those in aisle front, (B) for the nave front, above the string course.

2. (C) Your porch, but without a roof, and leaded flat, just above its ceiling, i.e. (say) at 12 feet high. Your facade (D) or whatever it is called forming a sort of parapet or balustrade, of such height as you think right — the higher the better, if it does not kill the windows of the aisle front, and thus a place formed for keeping flower pots for the Altar or other purposes.

3. A staircase at E, leading not only to the flat leads, but to a door F, which will be *the* way into the organ gallery, without going through the Church.

4. This door to be hid by a sort of turret G.

5 The porch to be entered along the nave front (32.6) and 4 feet on each side, i.e. from a little beyond the external new pier on the garden side, (which the turret will hide) to the windows of the aisle front. The left first division of the porch containing the staircase.

6. The number of divisions or openings according to your judgment — six (as I have put it) will not do, as bringing an upright clean across the great church door.

7. I have defeated your plan of lighting, which was so good. Would it be possible to do so from the *end* (H.) of the porch?

All this is very impudent. Your idea we like very much — as being neither pretentious (considering our poor building) yet not mean.

Ever Yours John H Newman

We think of opening the Church to the road having part of the present screen wall, as a foreground or frame to it.

TO AMBROSE ST JOHN

Oy Bm ⌐June 10/58⌐

My dear A

⌐If £200 is not lying at Jones, Loyd and Co from me for Mr Heywood by June 20, my acceptance will be dishonoured, and unknown consequences will happen.

Therefore, since the money is to be paid to *you*, you must (please) drop a line in the Bm Banking Company stating the particulars I inclose, and telling them *when* the money is paid in to your account, at once to send up £200 to the London Bankers aforesaid.⌐

Also you must tell them to advertise *me*, that they have done so

Ever Yrs affly J H

Mrs Mills of Covet Hall ⌐[[Austin's mother]] has just been here⌐ and I have been expatiating on Baronius's picture in the Refectory.

FRIDAY 11 JUNE 1858 Ralph Kerr called. F. Gaynor called

TO WILLIAM MONSELL

The Oratory Birmingham June 11. 1858

My dear Monsell

Miss Bowles wishes the little book off her hands. Therefore will you kindly send it back, if you have done with it, and give her directions what you wish done? Is she to finish it and send it to Dr Cullen, or to whom? I have looked over part of it, and will gladly to do [sic] again, but I am not the formal reviser, nor can well be. As to Duffy, I suspect he never answered her note at all; any how, I know he acted very remissly.[1]

You will see Stanislas in a few days. Alas, you must not believe his account of himself — tho' it is not good to tell him so, for his great chance of life is to be kept from anxiety. So critical do I believe his state to be, that I shall claim his return here at once, being quite ready to give him up, if he finds this place does not suit him. He shall be kept from all work, and amuse himself as he will. I much fear it will be the last months I shall have of him. But keep this to yourself, because bad news spreads so fast, that, if happily I am wrong, I shall have raised an alarm for nothing

Ever Yours affly John H Newman of the Oratory

The Rt Honble Wm Monsell M P

---

[1] See fifth note to letter of 9 May to Monsell.

SATURDAY 12 JUNE 1858 extraordinary rain and thunder. Mr Walker of Scarboro' called

TO THOMAS HAYDEN

[13 June 1858][1]

My dear Dr Hayden,

I am truly distressed that you should think that Mr Sullivan has not treated the Medical School with respect in his editorship of the scientific portion of the Atlantis, for, believe me, I fully understand, as you say, that it is on public grounds as a matter of principle and justice that you write to me, and not merely in consequence of any personal disappointment, though a disappointment to you it also must be. And, I assure you also, with great sincerity, that I am very grateful to you for letting me know your feeling on the matter, for it is a great kindness, in the Professors putting me in possession of what goes on in the University in my absence, and giving me an opportunity frankly to give my opinion, as things occur.

Let me add that I heard with great pleasure that you are going to give the Atlantis an article, and am disappointed at what has happened to prevent it.

But I fear I must say, though unwillingly, that I cannot with proper delicacy interfere in what is Dr Sullivan's special department — I think you will see in what great difficulties I should involve myself, if I did so. I judge from what I should feel myself, if the Bishops, for instance, instead of the considerate confidence they have placed in me as Rector, had interfered with my proceedings in the University. I should have judged it an inconsistency in them to fill up an office, and then to be doing the work themselves. And I feel somewhat in the same position towards Mr Sullivan.

Moreover, even could I interfere, I feel it is too late to make alterations in the number now.

I am confident you do not estimate high enough the position to which the Medical Faculty has already attained, when you think that it will excite surprise that two numbers of the Atlantis have appeared without a scientific article from the Medical School.

I write this, having no knowledge whatever of the matter except from you — I earnestly hope that you will not continue to entertain the painful feelings which have[2]

[1] On 11 June Hayden wrote angrily to Newman because his article for the July Atlantis had been postponed.

[2] The draft ends here. Hayden replied on 14 June, 'I am deeply indebted to you for your kind and considerate letter of yesterday. I admit the force of your reasoning . . . I am willing to dismiss the matter entirely, and in deference to you, all further recollection of it . . .' See also letters of 16 June to Sullivan and 1 July to Hayden, whose article appeared after all in the Atlantis, (July 1858), pp. 476–90, 'On the function of Sömmering's Yellow Spot in producing unity of visual perception in binocular vision.'

TO AMBROSE ST JOHN

⌐The Oratory. June 13. 1858⌐

My dear Ambrose

⌐The whole house and mission seems to have lapsed to me today — though Nicholas came in yesterday for some hours, and Edward has taken the 11 o'clock Mass. The day before yesterday I was summoned to the Workhouse on a sick call. The same day F. Gaynor came[1] to see Fathers and Brothers — ⌐the Fathers were taking holyday, but where were the Brothers? [[he asked]] and he named them — [1] In evening recreation in stalked Ralph,[2] having come with his troop to attend on the Queen. Where were the Fathers? I thought he probably had come for confession — poor fellow, [[if so,]] there was no one here (I suppose) he cared to go to.⌐ We told him Nicholas was to come in as yesterday, and he promised to come and see him — but I suppose the deluge, of which you will hear hindered him.[3] ⌐Then he looked about for the brothers. Where was Laurence? Charles? Thomas? I shuffled — Unhappy Charles lay in wait for him to present to him his whiskers.[4]

Now all this has brought strongly upon me one thought. It is in vain for us to say to ourselves, what is most true, that each has gone on his own reason, and that we can quite account for each case. *To the world* it will seem as if there was something rotten in the state of Denmark for so remarkable a phenomenon. Depend on it, we have good friends who emphatically announce the fact — and are much surprised and distressed — as that good weak soul Miss   ,[5] was.

And then again, it almost seems a scandal for a religious house to be served by secular and hired people. I do think we *must* have lay brothers — and I feel this so strongly now, that I will frank your journey to Belgium to look out for one or two.⌐ But I will write more about it in another letter, after you have answered this.

⌐I do not see your logic, when you say that, *though* I croke [sic], I come up to the scratch [[after all]]. To me it seems as inconsecutive [[to say so]] as if you said, that, though I slept at night,[6] I eat my breakfast heartily in the morning. To let out one's feeling[7] is a great relief, and I don't think an

---

[1] Francis Gaynor had been a servant at Alcester Street. See diary for 10 and 25 Sept. 1849.

[2] Newman carefully erased the name when this letter was returned to him, and put only a dash when copying. The diary reveals it. Lord Ralph Kerr was an officer in the 10th Hussars. For Queen Victoria's state visit to Birmingham, see letter of 7 June to Stewart.

[3] See diary for 12 June. At this time Bittleston and Flanagan were still abroad. Bowles, Mills and St John were away, Darnell was at Rednal; so that the only priests at home, besides Newman, were Caswall and Tillotson.

[4] Charles was working as sacristan, but was no longer a lay brother. See diary for 28 June 1858.

[5] Again Newman erased the initial or name.

[6] [[though I could not sleep at night,]] See first note to letter of 9 June to St John.

[7] [[sorrows]]

unlawful one. I don't speak to the whole world, but to you, Stanislas, and Henry. Job too had three friends — and he let out to them — yet he was the 'most patient of men.' I think you mistake between complaining and having a vivid conception of inequalities.[1] What is so common in the Psalms and Jeremias, as the sentiment, 'Just art Thou O Lord, yet will I plead with Thee'? Yet for myself I know too well, how infinitely more I have from the Giver of all good than my deserts, to have any [[even]] *temptation* to complain. But, when I think of St Philip, I argue thus — 'There is just one virtue he asks for "detachment;" [[which at the same time he prevents me having.]] now the only external thing which keeps me from being perfectly detached,[2] is that I have made myself *his* servant. What wish have I for life, or for success of any kind, except that I have got his Congregation upon my hands?[3] *He* has implicated me in the world, in a way in which I never was before, or at least never since my sisters married and my mother died. For his [[St Philip's]] sake I have given up my liberty, and have as far as the temptation [[and trial]] of anxiety goes, done almost as much as if I had married.[4] The one thing I ask of him is to shield me from the temptation to extreme anxiety; and the only way by which I can reconcile myself to the notion that he is doing what I feel I might expect is that he sees in me some very great offences against him.' And, when I complain, I utter inarticulate cries about something too deep for words. I now, (considering our disorganized state, and the malign action of St Philips own people, my sons, upon us,) so far, pity poor Father Dalgairns in his restlessness here, from understanding it better —[5] though I trust I shall never be so unfaithful to St Philip as he was to me. Please God, and I hope not from pride, I will be faithful to St Philip, and then God will reward me, though St Philip does not.

And therefore you see I am going perhaps to bottle up my thoughts — and to fancy St Philip saying to me what a French conducteur once by gestures said, when I looked to see if he had put up all my luggage safely, 'Who are *you*? what's it to *you*?[6] why do you put in *your* jaw? won't you be off? who, I say, are *you*? save your eyes, who are *you*? I say?' I fancy St Philip thus speaking to me — dimitto auriculas, et oculos.

⌐Obmutui, et non aperui os meum quoniam tu fecisti.[7]

The words of Job are ended

Ever Yrs affly J H N[1]

---

[1] [[I think you don't discriminate between complaining and realizing.]]
[2] [[There is just one thing which hinders me being detached]]
[3] [[except so far as, and because I have this Congregation on my hands?]]
[4] [[become as secular almost as if I had married.]]
[5] [[The one thing I ask of him is to shield me from the extreme force of this trial; and the only explanation I can suggest to myself why he does not do so is that I have in some way or other greatly offended him.' And, when I too cry out to you, it is not in complaint, but as signifying inarticulately feelings which are too deep for words. And considering this, I pity, so far, poor Fr Dalgairns in his restlessness here, from understanding better what distressed him;]]
[6] [['It's my business, not yours.']]
[7] *Psalm* 38:10.

P.S. I hear today gossipping, and laughing in the kitchen — how long is this state of this [sic] to go on?

⌐4½ P M. I have just baptized after beating off [[the ceremony]] for 2 hours and a half in hopes of a rescue from Edward or Robert. It is to me misery. I am sure to get scruples.⌐¹ ⟨(I have never recovered Mrs Phillipps' when I said Spiritui for Spiritus)⟩¹ ⌐The water was exhausted out of the abominable shell before I made the three crosses — ¹ and I made a hash of it. ⌐I do hope it was good ⟨valid⟩ — but I assure you it is quite cruel to [[leave]] me [[to do it]].⌐¹

The words of Busenbaum are these — 'forma cum qualunque primâ ablutione, Baptismum constituit.'

I lost half an hour making out whether a girl might have a Patri*nus*. And then it turned out that both parents were Protestants. I really will not solemnly baptize again.²

MONDAY 14 JUNE 1858   called on H Fourdrinier's sister (Mrs Plant?)³

TO MRS COPPINGER

The Oratory Birmingham June 14/58

My dear Madam⁴

Will you kindly forward the inclosed to your daughter? I do not know how to address or direct to her, since the initials affixed to the Preface are E.D.M. I am sorry my acknowledgment comes so late

Very truly Yours John H Newman

Mrs Coppinger

TO THOMAS SCRATTON

Oy Bm June 14/58

My dear S

I don't forget about the Fees. I will pay in, £30 I think it was, by the Audit, if you will give me notice of the day.

---

¹ Newman conditionally baptised Mrs Phillipps on 17 March 1850.

² St John replied on 15 June, 'Truly you are Job, and truly are we like Job's Comforters —thinking of self and not of their friend. Well if you have lost your first sons is not this perhaps that you may have more and better afterwards? St Ignatius's first companions forsook him. I am sure that you must have St Philip's blessing, working as you do . . .'

³ Antoinette Sarah Fourdrinier, was Newman's first cousin once removed, grand-daughter of his uncle Henry Fourdrinier and daughter of his first cousin Charles. She married the Rev. S. Plant, Weston-on-Trent, Staffs.

⁴ The Coppingers were an ancient and numerous Irish Catholic family from County Cork. Even with the aid of the *History of the Copingers or Coppingers . . .* edited by Walter Arthur Copinger, Manchester 1883, it has not been possible to identify Newman's correspondent.

Also, will you the kindly tell me the state of my youths' payments to me? I see in my Bank of Ireland book, 'May 1 £75' — this I conjecture is Zamoyski. Also 'February 20 £75' — is not this de Lignes paid in by *you*? Then you have paid in several into the Hibernian. The *rest*, I believe, are unpaid.

The billiard room account is capital[1]

Ever Yrs J H N

Most anxious accounts of Stanislas. He re[turns][2]

P.S.   You had better keep the two inclosed, which Dr Leahy has sent me. I have already had letters from both writers, and have answered the male one.

TUESDAY 15 JUNE 1858   Fr Frederic returned   bad thunderstorm at night

TO ROBERT D. LYONS

The Oratory, Birmingham June 15. 1858

My dear Dr Lyons,

I have read with great pleasure and interest the Report of your Faculty — and will gladly accompany it with a letter of my own — but I think it would hardly be respectful to the Bishops to *print* my letter.[3] I would send the report to Dr Cullen, with it in writing, and then perhaps he would grant permission to lithograph or print it. However, this is a question of detail, which may be decided this way or that.[4]

Have you shown the Report to Mr Flanagan? that he is not now drawing an income from the Funds of the University, and offering his talents and experience to such few Students as choose to avail themselves of him, is simply owing to his great forbearance, for which I am very grateful.[5] I suspect he has lost by the University, for I brought him from Lisbon, and wished him to open an office — but he preferred the good of the University to an arrangement which would be an immediate gain to himself. For this reason, I should be sorry, if he had not an opportunity of concurring in the acts of his Faculty. I am assuming you do not know his direction, and therefore have not had an opportunity of consulting him. His address is 'Terence Flanagan Esqr, 4 The Terrace, Spring Gardens, London, S.W.'

[1] The billiard room Newman had constructed (see letter of end of June 1855 to Flanagan), made a profit of £20 for the University, a return of 10 per cent on the outlay.
[2] The page is torn here.
[3] Lyons was Professor of Physiology in the Faculty of Science, and the Report outlined the needs of the Faculty, with proposals for remedying them. Lyons wanted Newman to write a letter recommending these proposals to the Archbishops, which could be printed with the Report. See letter of 17 June to Cullen.
[4] For Lyons's reply see the letters to Cullen and to Lyons of 28 Sept. 1858.
[5] Terence Flanagan was Professor of Civil Engineering.

The only other remark I have to make is, that, as to the important and true observation at p 15. I wish it could any how be suggested that, were the emoluments of the Scientific Chairs adequate, the Professors who hold them would retire from their existing duties in other Faculties.

I am, My dear Dr Lyons, Very sincerely Yours John H Newman

P.S. I inclose the copy of Dr Meyler's letter, thinking you may wish to make use of it.

TO JOHN O'HAGAN

The Oratory Birmingham June 15. 1858

My dear Mr O'Hagan.

If I have not answered your letter of the sixth before this, I am very sorry for it, and do so now. I liked very much your proposal of 'expanding the ideas' you mention, into a paper, which Judge O'Brien, etc. might approve of, and enable me to present to the Bishops — and I trust and believe that the delay of my answer has not interrupted the course of your thoughts with reference to its execution.[1]

I do not know what I have more to say, except that I am very desirous the Bishops should have the plan set before them, even though they did not adopt it quite at once

Yours, My dear Mr O'Hagan, Affectionately in Xt

John H Newman of the Oratory

John O'Hagan Esqr

TO AMBROSE ST JOHN

The Oy Bm ⌐June 15/58⌐

My dear A

Your keys came safe, and I have strung them with your green door key, and put them in one of my pigeon holes, for (I fear) Edward lost his watch from his room last night.

I have received by good luck my banker's account ⌐from the Bank of Ireland, and find my balance is £260.⌐ This consists of money I shall have to pay for the expenses of Harcourt Street before the end of Session. But ⌐it is

[1] O'Hagan was Professor of Political Economy.

available for the moment. So I shall write to have £200 sent up to Jones, Loyd and Co for Heywood.

As to the Poncia matter, let it wait.[1] When we originally talked of them, I thought there was to be *no* security — that was your hope. And at that time I *told* you the interest was too high.

If I am right, you would lose under £5 if you sold out your India Stock just now — but still £5 per cent is good — and I think we had better cogitate [[before you part with it]]. Meanwhile, take the Poncia matter cool, it will last till you return; for Heywood[1] need not be paid any thing more for this month to come. At the same time, ⌐how to get the money *is* a difficulty.

I dare say that India Stock will decline, and all stock. Things look more like, I won't say war, but troubles than they have since the peace [[in 1856]][1] — and the Indian revolt is not over — but still you get £5 per cent — which is good interest. If we give you £4, you lose £10 a year on £1000. Then again ⌐we shall have *any how* to pay 'Tom's' [[Poncia]] bill — which is a great nuisance. So don't let us make it large. If ultimately the *Poncias* decline the mortgage, well and good.⌐ 'You have no more papers to grant.' That's your position. Don't write to Canning, don't run up a bill.[2] ⌐These are my impressions, tell me what you think of them. I suppose I could raise a £1000 on my Dublin Church, if necessary.⌐

Ever Yrs affly J H N

TO AMBROSE ST JOHN

The Oy Bm June 16/58

My dearest A

S [Stanislas] and H. [Henry] cross the water today. I have sent your letter to lawyer Poncia with a (civil) letter of my own, I *hope*, to the effect that I want back your deeds to show them to Stanislas who is just returning — and that you wish no further *legal step whatever* to be taken without fresh authority from you. He is running up a bill. Let old Mrs Poncia pay it, if she has a fancy for lawyer's bills — but don't you incur one. The money is no great catch — let them take the security they find, or none at all.

I will write more about the lay brothers. I do think the absence of such is a scandal. The servants seem to me to get worse and worse. I would keep John a while merely for our convenience — but we certainly should get a brother who *can* cook; so that we may have two strings to our bow. I shall not be happy till John goes. I go into the kitchen just now for something — there are two or three of them lolling on the tables and chairs and chattering together — perhaps eating. I submit to all this in silence as a great infliction.

[1] Thomas Poncia, the solicitor, required certain deeds before drawing up a mortgage.
[1] Canning was the lawyer who was to alter the mortgage, so as to include in it stock belonging to St John.

The House is no longer ours, but given over to seculars. Better that we should turn cooks and porters ourselves (with Baronius) than suffer this.[1]

I think it would be as well to write *at once* to two or three Priests, M. Bouquéau, Canon (I forget his name) at Brussells [sic], and I think another, to see how the land lies before you go. I could write to Mgr Malou, Woodward, and the Abbé Maes at Westbury.[2] But I am bent (please God and St Philip) on getting lay brothers. I am quite indignant at these fellows.

One of your Italians came to me to Confession Sunday morning to my great misery — I did not like to reject him when he had entered, but I was so afraid I might make some mistake, that I determined with myself not to send him to Communion any how, nor did I. But there he was at my Mass, $\frac{1}{2}$ an hour after.

Ever Yrs affly John H Newman

P.S. If you go to Belgium, you had better send back home first all your correspondence with the lawyers.

TO THOMAS SCRATTON

The Oratory Bm June 16. 1858

My dear Scratton

I cannot deny I stand a chance of being hard up for money — and I think I had better pay you, lest I should delay it still further.

One payment, I think, I must take off.[3] When you put down the 2 de L. [de Lignes] and Z. [Zamoyski] as £15 on March 17, 1857 (we have talked of it before) it implies the three were entered in *November* from the beginning of the Session. Now this is so little the case, that Z. *wished* to take advantage of a quasi November entrance, to go up for his examination next month, and it is given against him — and I do not see why they or I should pay money, for which they have not the quid pro quo, and I have not received. It will make some confusion in your books, but one quarter must be entered per contra as wrongly charged — this takes off £7. 10 from the first £15 (of March 17. 1857).

Accordingly, on finding you agree with my calculation, I shall send you a cheque for £45—£7. 10=£37. 10s — groaning I think I shall still have another £15 to pay for them at the end of the session — is it not so?

How I am to make both ends meet, now I have not any Rector's Salary,

---

[1] In the beginnings of the Oratory at Rome the Fathers took turns to cook, that of Baronius coming so frequently that he chalked up 'coquus perpetuus' in the kitchen.
[2] Félix Boucquéau had visited Oxford in 1841. See letter of 19 Aug. 1863 to St John. Mgr Malou was the Bishop of Bruges. For Maes see letter of 20 June 1858 to St John, who did not think it worth while to write to Canon Donet at Brussels.
[3] What follows refers to lecture fees.

I really do not see — and I am full of difficulty what to do for the year 1858–9, which will close my lease of Mrs Segrave's House. I have the greatest doubt whether Penny will undertake the speculation, or whether I could recommend him to do so.

I forget the *list* of inmates in my house. I take it for granted *all* have paid me up to March 17 — after that date it stands thus: —

Thro' T.S. [Scratton] at Hibernian from April 1 and onwards

(1)	Throckmorton	—	83.	10.	0
(2)	Errington	—	50.	0.	0
(3)	Frazer	—	50.	0.	0
(4)	de la P. [Pasture]	—	50.	0.	0
(5)	Segar	—	50.	0.	0

at the Bank of Ireland. May 1. (6) Zam. — 75. 0. 0

There remain to pay

(7.8)	the Lignes two *quarters* up to the end of Session	—	150.	0.	0
(9)	Bethell	—	50.	0.	0

I suppose this exhausts my list. For the de Lignes money (which comparing the two former quarters I had come in June 15. £75 and August 20. £75) I must wait. But I should be much obliged to you to dun Bethell.

Ever Yrs affly John H Newman

TO WILLIAM KIRBY SULLIVAN

The Oratory Birmingham June 16. 1858

My dear Mr Sullivan

I know too well myself the complicated troubles which come on an Editor from Publisher, Printer and contributors, to wonder that there should have been any momentary misunderstanding between Dr Hayden and yourself. And I only write this from anxiety, which I dare say is superfluous, for you may have anticipated what I am going to suggest.

He has written to me a very kind and considerate answer to what I observed to him, for which I feel much obliged to him.[1] And this leads me to think that you may have an opportunity of saying some conciliating words to him with good effect. There are few persons, to whom it would not be a disappointment

---

[1] See letter of 13 June to Hayden.

to be working at a composition with a notion it was to come before the public on a particular day, and then to find the publication was put off for six months. In saying this, I repeat what I began with, that I know too well an Editor's multiplied annoyances, and Dr Hayden has most clearly and candidly stated how you came to postpone his article; — and having said my say, I leave it to you to do what you think best or possible.

I send the name of a German work on languages, which a friend told me you had not referred to in your article in Number 1.

Yours most sincerely John H Newman of the Oratory
W K Sullivan Esqr &c &c.

TO EDWARD WALFORD

The Oratory Birmingham June 16. 1858
My dear Walford

Last night I had a request from our Faculty of Philosophy and Letters, that you should be engaged for the Licentiate (B.A.) examination. It is late in the day to apply to you — for the Examination begins some day (I do not know what day) next week.

It is the first B.A. Examination, and will be important, as ruling a number of points. Not above three or four are presenting themselves; some of them go up for honors, and are sharp fellows. On the other hand they are young, and cannot be expected to come up to the standard of an Oxford man of 21 or 22.

If you do not give up the idea at once, please to write, for the sake of expedition to 'R. Ornsby Esqr, 21, Gardiner's Place, Dublin — ' I am sorry to say I don't know your direction — so I send this to Burns for you.

Your Colleagues will be (I *think*) Fr O'Reilly, Professor of Dogmatic Theology, Dr Macdermott of Trin. Coll. Dublin, Professor of Materia Med. [Medica], and Fr Kelly, S.J. You are the *extra*-ordinary Professor, which the Statutes prescribe for the B.A. Examination if possible.[1]

I am, My dear Walford, Sincerely Yours in Xt
John H Newman of the Oratory
E Walford Esqr

---

[1] Walford accepted this invitation. See letter of 14 July to him.

TO ARCHBISHOP CULLEN

The Oratory, Birmingham, June 17th, 1858.

My dear Lord Archbishop,

The Dean and Faculty of Science have sent me their Report on the wants and requirements of the Faculty, with a request that I would submit it to the Archbishops and Bishops of Ireland, with such recommendation as I might think fitting.[1]

As they suggest that it should be laid before the next Episcopal meeting, I feel I am best giving expression to their wish by addressing myself, as I now do, to your Grace as the formal President of the *Coetus Episcoporum*.

No remarks which I could offer on their Report would be in themselves of any value, considering the matters of which it treats; but, since I am *still* Rector, there is both a fitness in the Professors addressing the Archbishops and Bishops through me, and a call on me to declare my full concurrence in the step they have taken, founded on my intimate sense of the claim which the Faculty has on the zealous and munificent patronage of those who, like the Archbishops and Bishops of Ireland, have come forward in the sight of Europe as the founders of a great University. I am encouraged in this strong expression of opinion by the recollection that when I was in Rome two years since, persons there of the highest consideration urged upon me the duty, under which I lay as Rector, of furthering to the best of my power the interests of Physical Science.

I am, my dear Lord Archbishop, With profound respect Your Grace's most faithful servant in Christ,

John H. Newman of the Oratory.

His Grace the most Rev. the Archbishop of Dublin, etc., etc.

SATURDAY 19 JUNE 1858   Fr Brady O.P. called   Ignatius came in from Rednall

TO JOHN HUNGERFORD POLLEN

The Oy Bm. June 19/58

My dear Pollen,

Your Front or Facade is splendid — and is in Heywood's hands. How did *your* hands sustain so terrible an accident? It is wonderful to me. It is wonderful to me, the accident still being so serious, how you can write so well.

Nearly every one is away, taking advantage of the closing of the chapel.

[1] See letter of 15 June to Lyons.

I have not only to say Mass, preach, confess, but have had to visit the work-house, to baptize, and to take an Italian's Confession — I suppose the grace of the Sacrament inspired me with a knowledge of Italian. Nicholas is deep in the translation of Döllinger at Rednall, and Ambrose deep in the Hebrew Psalms at Deal. Stanislas and Henry are now in London on their way here; I wish I could say we were not anxious about the former.

I hear most flourishing accounts of our new University City Schools. We have above 100 students in them, with a great deal of zeal, and desire of prizes. And the next Atlantis will be a prodigy. Also Dublin people tell me that there is a feeling there, outside of the University that this Ministry is really not unlikely to give it a Charter, if they can hit off conditions acceptable to both parties. Two other projects are in agitation, the foundation of a law school and the erection of museums by McCarthy. All this shows the spirit and good heart with which they are proceeding, if it shows nothing else.

The Protestant Church near us was struck by the lightning two or three nights ago — the storm was tremendous. Two or three days before, the rain burst the drain, and managed to flood our hall with its contents.

My kindest remembrances to your hosts, and believe me,

Ever Yrs affly John H Newman of the Oratory

J H Pollen Esqr

P.S.   What does 'Pembridge' mean?[1]

TO SIR JOHN RATCLIFF

The Oratory, Birmingham June 19. 1858

Dr Newman presents his compliments to Sir John Ratcliff, Mayor of Birmingham, and thanks him for the two tickets he received from him for admission to the Town Hall on occasion of her Majesty's visit to Birmingham.

He has to apologize for the accident which has been the occasion of this acknowledgment being delayed.[2]

The Mayor of Birmingham

---

[1] In 1858 Pollen moved to 11 Pembridge Crescent, Bayswater.

[2] Sir John Ratcliff (1798–1864), rich manufacturer, and Mayor of Birmingham 1856–8, was knighted in the Town Hall on the occasion of the royal visit of 15 June. Newman was not present. He only once saw Queen Victoria, and that was in Sept. 1834, before her accession.

TO THE EARL OF DUNRAVEN

The Oratory, Bm June 20. 1858

My dear Lord Dunraven,

It would be a great pleasure to me to grant what you so kindly urge as a personal favor. As far as I am concerned, no difficulty shall be interposed to your having dear Fr Flanagan next winter at Adare.[1]

But I must tell you in confidence (which no one out of this House knows) that the Pau doctor fears tubercles — and *therefore* I have had him back here, for it is a bargain between us, that he does not leave home, if it appears God's will to take him from us. Again, when winter comes, mild as your country is, the medical men may object to it. And further, he has been forbidden to say Mass, for a time said Mass only on Sunday, and now only twice a week. Moreover, he is warned against any exertion, any anxiety. He is not allowed to have any penitents, or even to read, and much less to teach the junior Fathers, theology.

All I can say is, that, if there is a fair prospect of his life, and if the Doctors allow it, I should feel the greatest gratitude to you to accept the charge of him in so mild a climate as Adare for the winter

Believe me, My dear Lord Dunraven, Most sincerely Yours in Xt

John H Newman of the Oratory

The Earl of Dunraven

TO AMBROSE ST JOHN

⌐The Oy. Bm. June 20. 1858⌐

My dear A

⌐Give up the notion of Belgium — and don't affect Turin and Verona. 'Twill be a failure.[2]

I have two suggestions.

1. Keep seculars [[servants]] from all but the public rooms. Let none go upstairs. Let [[tall?]] Patrick take the first and second floors — For the public rooms, i.e. the ground floor, Get a butler a married man, from a *distance*, and give him good wages — or take Tom Ford and give him 50 guineas a year and let him marry. Then you would have two married men, he and Scully, for the public rooms. On this arrangement, you might have a female cook.

---

[1] Lord Dunraven met Flanagan at Paris in the middle of June, as he was returning to England, and wished him to act as chaplain at Adare. Flanagan told Newman his preference was to remain at Edgbaston.

[2] St John wrote on 19 June that Canon Louis Maes, the Belgian chaplain at Westbury, held out no hope of finding laybrothers in Belgium. St John added, 'The Benedictines here at Ramsgate tell me . . . that they are obliged to go to Italy for lay brothers, and find them very good. They have no English or Irish. I think I shall write on spec. to *Turin*, I should say also Brescia and Verona but Austrian subjects would hardly get leave to come.'

2. Get youths who would take a five years vow (renewable yearly, if they pleased) of chastity. This would prevent them from being too intimate with our people. It is not unoratorian, 1. because the Brothers are not part of the Body. 2 because the vow is not to the [[our]] body, but to chastity, and [[3]] because the Fathers too, as priests, are under a vow of chastity, a perpetual one.

I throw out these suggestions, because they may lead to others. One thing alone I see — that we cannot go on as we are.

Lawyer Poncia has brought back your deeds, and so the matter stands till your return[1]

Ever Yrs affly J H N

Stanislas is at 4 The Terrace Spring Gardens London SW
Ignatius is gone home, i.e. going.

MONDAY 21 JUNE 1858 Edward went for his Holyday. Dr Moriarty called—went with him to Workhouse and convent and to Mr Hardman
TUESDAY 22 JUNE Henry returned from abroad

TO ROBERT ORNSBY

The Oratory Birmingham ⌐June 22. 1858⌐

My dear Ornsby

Thank you for your letter of information.[1] ⌐I don't think it worth while spending time on your Committee about the Charter, and hope nothing I have said has (against my intention) led to the subject being mooted.⌐[2] If there is a difference of opinion among the Professors, it does not matter just now. I can't help thinking, ⌐if a Charter was actually offered, even those [[of the Professors]] who do not approve it, would, when it came to the point, accept it; nay, consent to ask for it, if they knew they could get it for the asking.

I have always despaired of a Charter with the Whigs — I don't with the

---

[1] Ornsby described a meeting of the Professors on 20 June, to discuss the question of a charter. Ellis and Ornsby proposed that the Professors should address the Irish Bishops on the subject, through the Rector. Lyons wanted the University to assert its independence and to confer degrees at once on the authority of the Holy See. He disapproved of looking towards the English Government. Quinn complained of lack of information on the subject, and suggested that what the University needed was not a charter, but the remedying of other defects. He then moved that a committee should be named to report on the nature of a charter, and its effect on the University. This was carried by the casting vote of the chairman.

[2] Ornsby was able to reassure Newman but, in his reply of 26 June, wrote, '. . . with regard to your last letter, certainly I would have done nothing if I had thought your feelings were *against* a charter, but I concluded what you said seemed to indicate the time was favourable for acting.' See letter of 29 June to Ornsby.

388

Tories   I write the above under the notion that *I* may be the cause of your moving — if the Professors agitate it proprio motu, very well.[1]

Ever Yrs affly J H N

R. Ornsby Esqr

TO JOHN STANISLAS FLANAGAN

The Oratory Bm June 23/58

My dear S

You are a very bad fellow to take my letter as an injunction, and to sit with a sheet of letter paper before you.[1] I wrote chiefly to put you au courant — and if you will not suffer this without thinking you are at once to plunge yourself into responsibilities, you won't be able to stay here. As if I were going to let you resume the F. Ministry,[2] or any thing else.

Stay in London, as long as ever you like.

Ever Yrs affly J H N

P.S.   This is not for you to think over, but to read and dismiss. Wm [William] gave £2090 for his Irish property, and *clears* 7 per cent — if he got for it £4000, he could offer to invest in the public funds, which give 3½ per cent.

You must have been cool with Fr Faber, that he refused to see you the second time.[3]

TO CHARLES RUSSELL

The Oratory Birmingham June 23. 1858

My dear Dr Russell,

I hope you will not think me tardy in acknowledging your kind present.[4] When the book first came, one of our Fathers took possession of it, and when he brought it back, I did not like to acknowledge the gift, till I had had the pleasure of making acquaintance with it.

It is indeed a very delightful book, most interesting and suggestive, and full of information. I cannot say I have read it continuously, but I have had it on my table, and profited by it, when I had leisure during the day.

I trust it will have a very good influence on our Protestant brethren. It is

---

[1] Flanagan had tried to write his views as to the best solution of the lay brother problem, and then given up.

[2] i.e. act as Father Minister, or bursar. Flanagan spoke of doing his 'ordinary work.'

[3] Flanagan wrote on 22 June, 'I went to the Oratory with him [Lord Dunraven] on Sunday . . . Faber preached, and, on enquiring after mass, we found he was too ill to see us. *I* had already paid my respects with Fr Henry. I saw almost all the other Fathers.'

[4] Russell sent a copy of his *The Life of Cardinal Mezzofanti*, London 1858.

so singular as to startle the common reader, and most impressive as a lesson, to see such gifts as Cardinal Mezzofanti had, united, not only to such simplicity and amiableness, but to such deep piety, such cloudless intimate faith, and such devotion to the See of Peter.

One of our invalid Fathers returned last night from the continent, I trust, restored — for this we ought to be very thankful The other, Fr Flanagan, is still a cause of deep anxiety to us. I hope you are all well at Maynooth. So you would not give us a Vice-Rector.¹ For me, I have been more tied here lately than months ago — Yesterday I was the only Priest with faculties in the House

Ever Yours affectly in Xt   John H Newman of the Oratory

The Very Revd Dr Russell &c &c

P.S.   If you happen to be able to answer the following questions, will you do it in one line — 1. Where can I find a resumé of the Hippolytus controversy, with the theories, arguments etc which have been put forward, *in English*? is there not some North American theological, which does this kind of thing? 2. Do you know of [if] any comment on the Rule of St Dominic — or history of, or dissertation on the Order — e.g. Marchese etc. have treated of it in respect to its *artists*. What standard books are there besides, Quétif, Malvenda, Touron, and the Bollandists?²

TO AMBROSE ST JOHN

⌐The Oy Bm June 23/58⌐

My dear A

Henry is back and looking well. *When is Charles's month out?* answer me this at once.³ I have taken a copy of your letter, and sent a few lines of my own, as you had not answered Mr S.F.P's question categorically.⁴

⌐The building does not get on as fast as I could wish. I was the only priest with Faculties in the House yesterday. Dr Moriarty was here good part of Monday. Mr Mann on Saturday. Pollen has nearly cut his fingers off.⌐

Ever Yrs affly John H Newman

¹ See second note to letter of 28 May 1858 to Monsell.
² Domenico Marchese, *Sagro Diario Domenicano*, Naples 1668; Jacques Quétif and Jacques Echard, *Scriptores Ordinis Praedicatorum . . .*, Paris 1719; Tommaso Malvenda, *Annales Ordinis Praedicatorum*, Naples 1667; A Touron, *Histoire des hommes illustres de l'ordre de S. Dominique*, Paris 1743.
³ St John replied that he had given Charles notice on 31 May.
⁴ This concerned a matter about which St John wished to consult Manning.

The Oratory, Birmingham June 24. 1858

My dear Miss Giberne,

Father Caswall, who is away from Edgbaston for his holyday, will be very much pleased to hear of your kind information that you have written to your lawyer to ask him to forward the sum of £10 for Smethwick — which is Fr Caswall's work. As to paintings, you know how we value yours, but we are somewhat exhausted by the carriage payments, especially the £15 for the scene of the Nativity which M. Szoldatics with so much kindness gave me at your request.[1]

Thank you for your inquiries after Fr Flanagan and Fr Bittleston. The latter returned here the day before yesterday, to all appearance perfectly restored to health, and has begun his work. Fr Flanagan is to come home tomorrow, and though his case is a more anxious one, yet I am thankful to hear that he has gained in flesh since he was away. I smiled at your wishing me away from the University on the ground that the authorities did not value my presence — If we waited, if *I* waited till people valued what I did, I should do nothing at all — because, I suppose, the very precept of the gospel, which we all have to practise, is, to 'do good, hoping for nothing thereby,' for thus we become the sons of the Highest. If we do a good work, it does not become 'odious,' because God has to reward us, and not man. I am glad to find you are not overpowered by the heat, which has been very great here. The Thames is said to have become simply poisonous, and a man, who had been plying on it, died, yesterday or the day before, of pure Asiatic cholera, and no mistake — in a few hours. This has increased an alarm which before existed that the Thames has become worse than the Pontive Marshes. Thank you for your zeal in recommending people to come and see us, but I somehow think that Fr St John did not speak in jest last summer, when he said 'Leave us alone — say nothing about us, for praise or for blame.' Somehow I have ever thought that that is the highest boon we could ask of St Philip, or receive from Catholics. Fr St John is away at Deal, taking his holyday — his tendency to asthma does not interfere with his reading, and he gives a good many hours, contrary to his usual habits, to sedentary employments. He has got a room upon the beach, and enjoys the shingles. There is a lady there too, who is almost one of his converts, and with her he takes tea. It is a great thing we have got from this new ministry, and what there seemed no chance of getting from the Whigs, that Catholic chaplains in the army are to be as numerous as Protestant (proportionally) and as well paid. *Now* the difficulty will be *ours*, viz to find the men; for it is a great question with the excessive demands upon us, whether, even from Ireland, we shall be able to secure the

[1] See letter of 15 Oct. 1856 to Miss Giberne.

necessary numbers to supply the requirements of the Catholic soldiery, who are said to be a third part of the army. But I am interrupted by the business of the house, and, hoping you will take care of yourself during the hot weather, I am, My dear Miss Giberne,

Yours affectly in Xt   John H Newman

Miss Giberne

TO THOMAS SCRATTON

The Oy Bm June 24/58

My dear S

By this post I send some circulars.[1] At the moment I can't find more. By the bye, I hear some surprise that the meeting which was called about the *Charter*, had 'the Charter' printed — was it so? Is it not too secret?

I inclose a cheque for £45 − £7. 10 i.e. for £37. 10, which clears me

Ever Yrs affly John H Newman of the Oratory

T. Scratton Esqr

P. S.   Badeley's address is 'Paper Buildings, Temple, London.' I congratulate you on having got thro' such a number of circulars.

We are a month off the end of term — I suppose we can't well send to the Archbishops for a fortnight or more to come.

When you talk of my expenses, you must recollect that my furniture cost over three hundred pounds, my new buildings over £300 — that I lost the first year when my house was not full — that I lost during the month of the scarletina — and that I have yearly bills of wear and tear etc, etc. which you would know nothing of in the short time you had my youths. Besides I give wine — you too had them in the summer when coals are not burned. But any how I have had to make up an outlay of perhaps £800, as I have stated above. Then I have made payments for tuition, over what the University gives.[2]

FRIDAY 25 JUNE 1858   Stanislas returned from abroad

[1] Prospectuses for the University.
[2] Scratton in his letter of 17 June argued from his own short experience, that Newman's house ought to have made a profit.

TO AMBROSE ST JOHN

⌐Oy Bm June 25/58⌐

My dear A

1. ⌐Go and look at Lady Olivia's [Acheson] grave at Chelsea, when you are in London.

2. Mind do not speak one word about this Oratory, or about me, or about the University or about the Translation of Scripture, or about our alterations in the Church, or about the ⟨Nicholas's⟩ Boys' School, or about Stanislas and Henry, or about any thing else, to Fr Faber, *for he will get something out of you*,[1] or [[again]] to *any of* the Fathers at Brompton or to *Henry Wilberforce*, for it all goes to Fr Faber — do observe this. *Poor Henry does not deserve* we should treat him with any *confidence*, whatever *love* we have for him. Don't be melted — he in turn loves us, but does not trust. Don't let out to Mrs H.W.[2]⌐

Ever Yrs affly J H N

⌐Henry is looking remarkably well. Stanislas, thank God, has gained nearly 5 lbs in weight.⌐

P.S. No objection has been made to the 5th of July.[3]

Thanks for your Mass

⌐Stanislas just come. He looks thin and is hoarse. I have not heard an opinion, but by the looks [[faces]] of everyone I think they feel as I.⌐

SATURDAY 26 JUNE 1858   Austin returned from his holyday.

TO JAMES LAIRD PATTERSON

The Oratory Birmingham June 26. 1858

My dear Patterson,

I thank you very much for your friendly letter of this morning. Scott and ourselves are very good friends, and I wish there could be some such arrangement as he proposes. His health makes it very uncertain whether he could follow out an Oratorian vocation, though his time here passed so pleasantly

[1] [[for he will be sure to make something of it.]]
[2] St John wrote on 1 July, when he was staying with the Henry Wilberforces at Onslow Square, Brompton, near the Oratory, 'All here are very kind, but they are evidently so very thick with the Bromptonians that I feel on tenterhooks. I believe really I have been as little communicative as I could, but indeed I have had little temptation to be otherwise. F. Dalgns [Dalgairns] and F Stanton were with me one morning when I breakfasted there. F Dlgns affectionate F. Stanton cold. F Faber is at Glasgow. They are almost rebuilding their church and all but 6 fathers are away.'
[3] St John wanted permission to use Rednal on that day for the outing of the women's guild.

both for him and for us last year, that I am not without good hope that he would succeed.

Of course, if he came to try his vocation, he would have to enter the noviciate, for he could not become a member of the Congregation without having been a novice. But we should require a considerable trial of him, before we let him take the habit, i.e. enter into the noviciate — and he would be a novice three years before the question of his taking holy orders came into consideration. Even then, though it is our rule that Fathers of the Oratory should be in Holy Orders, I do not see why such a rule should not have exceptions. However, in his case, I think, if he had health to be a Father, he would have health to enter into Holy Orders, leaving the Priesthood as a still further question.

I can't quite understand what his Confessor can mean by his coming *but not* as a novice — [1] Does he mean that, while with us, he could retain his present Confessor, who would decide whether he should stay with us or not? This is impossible. He cannot join us without the 'animus permanendi semper usque ad vitae obitum,' as the Rule says. And not only must he have an 'assignatus confessarius,' when he has *entered* the Congregation, but he must *have* been, in *order* to admission, a frequenter of the Oratory, and 'solitus alicui ex nostris Sacerdotibus saepius confiteri.'[2] In a word, he puts himself into our hands to decide whether he has a vocation or not — and it does not seem a great deal to ask him as much as this.[3]

If you ask me what I should think best for him, it would be that he should come and stay with us, as he did last Long Vacation, definitively resigning the office in the University which he has been so kind to me as to undertake. He is so amiable a fellow, that I should have the greatest hope of his going on happily, and enabling us to recommend him, at the end of six months or more, to put on the habit and become a novice. There is just this difficulty (to speak to you in confidence) — he might possibly get impatient — urge his being received at once — fancy he was trifled with — and even go on to be suspicious that we were using him ill, imagine that we were whispering about him, and having an understanding with each other about him, purposely insulting him etc etc.[4] This makes it the more necessary to begin by stipulating

[1] See letter of 7 June to Scott.
[2] *Instituta Congregationis Anglicae Oratorii S. Philippi Nerii*, Rome 1847, Decretum xxxvi, Decretum lvii, Decretum xxxiv, pp. 21 and 26.
[3] Newman omitted at this point a paragraph that was in his draft: 'Did the run of his letter allow of it, I could fancy his Confessor was alluding to something else I said to him. I said that the only inmates of our House who had not a formal noviciate, though they *have* a quasi noviciate too, are the lay brothers, who (at the Chiesa Nuova) are sometimes of a higher class, and are rather persons retired from the world than charged with servile offices. I do not know what our Fathers would say to the introduction of such a description of persons into our body, though I see no insurmountable difficulty myself. But, if he were one of these, tho' he wore the habit and attended our chapters and exercises, he would never be one of the Fathers, or have a voice or vote in the Congregation.'
[4] Newman again omitted from his draft: 'On the other hand we might find there was no difficulty in his belonging to us as a *quasi lay-brother*, but that he was not certain of perseverance enough to be more (for of course the tie to us of such a lay-brother would not be so

that we must be the judges, not he, *whether* he is to join us, and *when* he is to join us and, when he *has* joined us, whether or not he has a *vocation*; and, if we think he has a vocation, whether he should be in minor orders, holy orders, or present himself for the Priesthood. It is in his power to come here, or not to come, but, when here, he is in our hands, not in those of any Confessor at a distance. In the hands of *some* confessor he *must* be, whether he will or no, and obedience to Santa Communità is especially the Rule of the Oratory.

Excuse this long letter; — and again thanking you for your kindness,

I am, My dear Patterson, Very sincerly Yours in Xt

John H Newman of the Oratory

The Revd J. L. Patterson.

MONDAY 28 JUNE 1858 Fr Frederic went for his holyday Charles Goderich left. ⟨? his putting off habit is mentioned some time before I think he remained as lay sacristan⟩[1]

TO THOMAS SCRATTON

The Oratory Birmingham June 28. 1858

My dear Scratton,

Both our Invalids are back. As to dear Stanislas, who is our anxiety, we have this great encouragement, that he has gained nearly 5 pounds in weight since he went abroad — which is real proof that disease is not making way. On the other hand he is still hoarse — showing that the seat of the disease is not yet as it should be. What we fear is incipient tubercles, but there seems no imminent danger, though his most candid and anxious adviser considers these next three months most critical.[2]

As to Walford, look to see what he had when he came over before — and let the Dean of Philosophy and Letters determine the sum he should have now, with that as a basis.[3]

John O'Hagan has read, I suppose, 6 Lectures — He has taken great pains with them, and he has had nothing for his Professorship I think he ought to have £7 a lecture, which will be 40 guineas.

Ever Yrs John H Newman

T Scratton Esqr

strong as that of a Father of the Congregation) — but any how, to avoid disappointment on his part, we must begin by stipulating . . .'

[1] The part in brackets is a pencilled addition. See diary for 29 April 1857.
[2] See letter of 9 June to St John.
[3] Walford, who was examiner in July 1855, now received £15.

TO WILLIAM KIRBY SULLIVAN

The Oratory Birmingham June 28. 1858

My dear Mr Sullivan,

The Atlantis came yesterday morning, and gratifies me very much. Not of course that I am able to understand the greater part of it, but I see well how much there is in it, and what an extensive field of thought it covers. I cannot help being very sanguine about its present and future effect upon our prospects.

Did I tell you I had sent two addresses of subscribers to Fowler? He has somewhat startled me by his yesterday's letter thanking him [me] for making him 'agent.' I meant no such thing — but that, as he sent out the work to Scientific etc Bodies already, so he should send out these two copies — and I pointedly referred him to you. Please, let there be no mistake here. I mean, don't let him use *my* authority for any thing he does. Do what you think well yourself — and what others of our friends wish.

I am glad to see that Dr Hayden has an article in the number after all.

By the bye, I should say that Hope Scott's copy must be sent, not to Abbotsford, but to 44 Parliament Street, London. Will you tell Fowler so?

What do you think about strangers writing in the Atlantis? I mentioned Sir John Acton, because I thought his name would do us good, and I fully believe he will give us a good article. But there is another person, Dr Logan, who once was Vice President of Oscott. He has the reputation of being a first rate mathematician and metaphysician; and, when the University commenced, his friends applied to me to give him a chair.[1] Besides other difficulties, there was the state of his eyes which made reading and writing hopeless. A friend of his has now applied to me to get me to write and ask him for a mathematical paper — saying that some one or other, who ought to know, said that Mr Penny's paper was nothing to what he can do.[2] The difficulty is that he may send a paper which no one can understand and no one can give an opinion of. This difficulty is in addition to the question of *principle*, i.e. whether we ought to admit writers external to the University and to Dublin.

Yours most sincerely John H Newman of the Oratory
W K Sullivan Esqr

TUESDAY 29 JUNE 1858 Austin went into retreat at Rednall.

[1] Cf. letter of 8 Dec. 1854 to Countess Granville.
[2] Penny's paper in the July *Atlantis* was 'On the Inequality of long period in the motions of the Planets Jupiter, Saturn, and Uranus.'

TO EDWARD CASWALL

The Oy Bm June 29/58

My dear Edward

I condole with you about your boils, which are sad nuisances. Let me know at your leisure (on your return) what the 'course of medicine' is — for you know I have been from time to time a sufferer too.

Fr Henry seems equal to any work, and you may safely stay out for as long as you like. At the same time, if you resolve to come and go again, you can do it with great ease, for the Church will be a long while finishing. In this case you will see both Henry and Stanislas.

Stanislas seems to me thin and hoarse. He certainly is weak. But it is a very good sign that he has gained nearly five pounds. There can be no active mischief going on while he gains flesh.

You give me no direction but 'Devizes', to which I send this note[1]

Ever Yours affly John H Newman

TO ROBERT ORNSBY

The Oratory Bm ⌐June 29/58⌐

My dear Ornsby

I am quite puzzled to think how I can have led you to suppose that I am against a Charter. 1. I never have thought there was a prospect of one from *the Whigs*. 2. I never have expected any immediate *direct* benefit from one. But I think our chance very fair with the Tories — and I think to succeed is of great importance from the fact that it *will* be success. Accordingly, I have written to several of the Professors urging it, *provided* they thought it well.

I am not at all in the Archbishops' confidence, and suspect, from what you tell me of Dr Cullen, that he is annoyed at their counsels having *got out*. (This may be a fancy.)[2] I have heard something of what you tell me from *another* quarter, but, having been told in confidence, I keep silence about it.[3] This much I will say, that ⌐I have done nothing *myself*, beyond expressing my opinion to Professors and others, when asked,⌐ as I am doing now to you.

⌐I am concerned to find that Dr Quinn is taking so strong a line — ⌐ Between ourselves, ⌐I don't think he has much chance of being Vice Rector.[4]

---

[1] Caswall was staying with his mother.

[2] Ornsby wrote on 26 June that the Professors had learned from Bishop Moriarty of Monsell's interview with Disraeli. Moriarty had telephoned to Cullen at Monsell's request for the latter to be authorized to treat with the Government for a charter, but had not yet received a reply. Moriarty was in favour too of a deputation of Professors approaching the Government.

[3] See last note to letter of 28 May to Monsell.

[4] Quinn, at meetings of the committee of Professors to consider the application for a charter, was strenuously opposing it. He argued that the University would lose its independance, become a mere state affair, and forfeit the support of the Irish people. He spoke

Also, I think that if the Irish members asked for a charter, they would get it.[1] Also, I have no objection, if the Professors ask me, to take any part in urging them to do so. But they ought to act at once.

However, ⌐if you ask the *principle* I wish observed in speaking of me, it is this: (which, if you please, must be your key note) — I feel the utmost delicacy of my opinion being used in the discussion *as an argument*. I wish you to decide the matter on its own merits and your own judgments. But, at the same time, I can't deny I should be very glad if we got a charter [[from the fact that it would be *success*]]¬, and would take part with the Professors in moving for one. But ⌐I (personally) could not take the Maynooth oath — of course I could take the Oxford oath of allegiance without hesitation.¬

As to prizes to the University classes, I should like it more carefully considered. I like the plan of Professional *examinations*, and only fear that the prize will look like a school reward to the best boy

Ever Yrs affly J H N

R. Ornsby Esqr

TO THOMAS HAYDEN

The Oratory, Birmingham. July 1 1858

My dear Dr. Hayden,

I was very glad to read what you tell me in your letter of this morning about Mr. Sullivan. I assure you his calling on you etc. was entirely his own act.[2]

I know something was said, on the subject of the relation of the Demonstrators to the Professors in the Faculty, by Dr. Ellis and myself, at the time when the former was appointed. Of course I should like to keep to what was said then.[3]

---

slightingly of the teaching in Protestant Universities. He also urged that the University was already chartered by the Holy See, and should exercise its degree-giving powers. Further he thought the English Professors were anxious for a charter from the English Government, in order to have their position in the University secured. Eventually Quinn was overruled, and it was agreed that a deputation of Professors should ask the Irish Archbishops for a decision as to the expediency of a charter.

[1] O'Hagan pointed out that if a charter were granted, the Professors would have to take an oath of allegiance. The Maynooth oath denied the 'indirect power' of the Pope. The Oxford oath was simply one of allegiance. See letter of 28 June 1854 to Monsell.

[2] See letter of 13 June to Hayden about the intended rejection of his article in the *Atlantis*. He wrote on 30 June, 'Dr Sullivan called on me about ten days ago to explain, in consequence of some intimation you were kind enough to make to him. . . . our relations are on their former footing again.' Newman perhaps forgot that he had written on 16 June to Sullivan that he might 'have an opportunity of saying some conciliatory words.' Or he may have felt that Sullivan's action went much beyond what he, Newman, had hinted to him.

[3] Hayden wrote on 30 June that he and Cryan had been discussing the question of the Demonstrators in Anatomy. 'It is of the utmost importance to the well working of the anatomical department that the Demonstrators should understand that the professors of Anatomy and Physiology are to prescribe their duties to them, and that to them alone in the School—except when the professors chose to take the advice of the faculty—they are accountable . . . that the professors of Anatomy and Physiology should have the exclusive right of nominating the Demonstrators, and dismissing them . . .' See letter of 26 July to MacDermott. Hayden also asked for an increase in the salaries of the Demonstrators.

I fancied certainly that the Rector appointed and parted with them, as it seems reasonable, since they have salaries as other officers of the University, and the Bishops lay down in the fundamental statutes, that all the officers, except Vice Rector, are in the appointment of the Rector i.e. as subject to their own formal nomination.

I should hope the increase of salary, of £50 apiece to two, instead of £85 between three, would not be a difficulty.

I am, My dear Dr. Hayden, Very sincerely yours,

John H. Newman of the Oratory.

Thos. Hayden Esqr. M.D. etc. etc.

TO THOMAS SCRATTON

The Oy Bm July 1. 1858

My dear S

As to the de Lignes, they have to pay £300 for the Session.

They have never put money into my hands, or by letter, I mean during this Session.

They are accustomed to pay quarterly by £75s.

I find in my Bank of Ireland Book —

Zamoyski's ⟨1857⟩ — Nov 2.	————————————	75. o. o
15	————————————	75. o. o
Zamoyski's ⟨1858⟩ — Febr 20	————————————	75. o. o
— May 1	————————————	75. o. o

This is all I know of —

You can send Frederic to the Hibernian to ask if £75 has been paid into my account *there* since February 20 — but I have heard nothing of it, and it is scarcely possible.

I have always given receipts, as you have — which ought to corroborate the above.

From my Banker's Book, as above, it appears, they have paid only £150, and owe the other £150.

As to the Audit, are there any more acoounts I owe to send you?

I can send the Reports of the Dean and Professors of Philosophy and Letters for last year, if they would like to have them

Ever Yrs affly J H N

FRIDAY 2 JULY 1858   Ambrose returned after his holyday—

TO THOMAS SCRATTON

The Oratory Birmingham July 2. 1858

My dear Scratton,

As to the inclosed, *who* can have promised that the £5 should be returned? Mr Flannery had not the *power*. I don't understand the letter.[1]

It would be good that a notice should be printed on the Paper of Fees, that they were *not* to be returned. Nothing need be said about the Pension.

After all did Butler enter from November last, the names of the Freshmen in the Register, according to the formal leave I sent? If not, I will send another — for they must be entered. The day on which I was to have entered them, and you were taken ill was Tuesday November 17 last. They ought to be entered in *each* Term.

Ever Yours affly John H Newman of the Oratory

T. Scratton Esqr

TO JAMES STEWART

The Oratory Birmingham July 2. 1858

My dear Stewart

I am glad your expedition to Armagh turned out so well — especially since there was some little hesitation last year. When other schools see the various advantages which will attend such visits, they will become jealous and will follow the lead.[2]

As to your book. I should be very sorry that it should not be published, on various accounts — but what I wanted you to talk to Sullivan about had reference to that very point. I do not know how to take responsibility myself, but a Board of Professors might do so, if a definite sum was put into their hands. When the Atlantis is out, perhaps Sullivan will be at leisure. Dr Macdermott would be a good person too to take the matter up.[3]

Ever Yrs affectly John H Newman of the Oratory

James Stewart Esqr

---

[1] A lady claimed the return of £5 for University fees, alleging the authority of Professor Butler, who denied having said anything of the kind.

[2] Stewart had gone as an examiner to St Patrick's College, Armagh.

[3] Stewart consulted Sullivan, and wrote on 9 July that the latter gave his full approval to the plan of a board of professors, who would arrange for the publication of literary and scientific works. Sullivan wished professional and especially medical works excluded 'otherwise we should be flooded with medical works.' He thought that between £200 and £300 would be sufficient for the scheme. See also letter of 12 July to Stewart.

SATURDAY 3 JULY 1858   Austin returned from Rednall

SUNDAY 4 JULY   went over with Ambrose to Oscott for Dr Amherst's consecration

MONDAY 5 JULY 1858   Guild party at Rednall   Bishop [Ullathorne] and Dr Mullock of Newfoundland called.[1]   Mrs Amherst etc called

TO WILLIAM MONSELL

Oratory Bm July 5/58

My dear Monsell

The inclosed has just come to me.[2] Please, let me have it back. I send it to you, to ask your advice, if you will kindly give it.

Dr Moriarty is at the bottom of it. Dr Cullen, I *suspect*, does not like *openly* to commit himself — but I may be wrong.

Would it be possible to have a deputation of Irish members and one or two Irish Professors to Disraeli?[3]

Ever Yrs affly John H Newman

The Rt Honble Wm Monsell M P

TUESDAY 6 JULY 1858   Nicholas returned from Rednall

WEDNESDAY 7 JULY   storm, lightning and rain

TO C. R. SCOTT MURRAY

July 7. 1858

My dear Mr Scott Murray

I have waited to see Mr Monsell, who is passing through this place, before answering your truly kind letter.

I should rejoice to have your sons at the projected School here, if it comes into operation, and I beg you to accept my best thanks for the offer you make of a contribution towards its establishment.[4]

[1] John Thomas Mullock (1807–69), born at Limerick, became a Franciscan, and in 1847 was consecrated in Rome as Coadjutor Bishop of St John's, Newfoundland, succeeding to the See in 1850.

[2] Ornsby sent to Newman on 4 July, an address, drawn up in his hand, and signed by eighteen of the Professors of the University, announcing 'their adhesion to the principle of a Charter,' and expressing the wish to hear that 'negotiations were proceeding between the Rector and the proper quarters . . .'

[3] Monsell replied on 6 July, 'I hope to see you on Thursday and to talk to you about the charter—my opinion is that you and the Professors should prepare and sign a document stating the early history, present position, and objects of the Catholic university and praying the government to grant it a charter after the form of that which has recently been granted to the University of Quebec— This document should be drawn up in the tone that persons would adopt who were asking for a thing, which, as a matter of course, would be granted.— I would then send the document with a letter from myself to Disraeli—'

[4] Scott Murray wrote on 5 July, promising £100 towards the Oratory School. He also thought the pension 'should never be less than £70, which I consider with my protestant ideas *very* low indeed.' His two sons were aged eleven and ten.

I gave Serjeant Bellasis a rough sketch of what I supposed would be its initial expenses.[1] I do not think they need be more than a school of thirty boys would meet; but till it reaches that number, there will be serious risk of loss. I rather dread beginning and creeping on with a few, and thus incurring a debt, without securing any of the advantages, or even coming up to the idea, of a school.

It has seemed to Bellasis and Monsell, as well as to myself, that the gentlemen who are interested in the scheme should depute some one to represent them, whose business it would be to correspond with me, and to get as many promises as possible of money and boys. I had hoped a professional man like Mr F. Ward would have undertaken this; but he feels it impossible. There is one friend I have thought of, but do not know what he would think of the proposal.[2]

When I have any thing more to say, perhaps you will let me write to you

I am &c J H N

THURSDAY 8 JULY 1858   Monsell passed the day in his way to Ireland.   A. Bethell came in his way home from Ireland

TO SIR JOHN ACTON

The Oratory Birmingham July 8. 1858

My dear Sir John

I thank you very much for your kind and confidential letter, and wish I were able to write you such an answer, as it deserves.[3]

Certainly I should like very much to see the Dublin in your hands, and I

---

[1] Letter of 23 April 1858.

[2] Evidently J. H. Pollen. See letter of 20 Aug. 1858 to him.

[3] Acton, now aged twenty-four and a half, wrote on 6 July from Aldenham, 'I have just been informed that a circular has appeared announcing that the Dublin Review is given up, and I am asked whether I would take it in hand myself. I do not entirely reject the idea, because I think it would be a pity that it should cease to appear, or that it should pass into the hands of unsatisfactory persons. In particular I recollect that when you spoke to me so kindly about the Rambler you said that you were disposed to regret that I was not rather connected with a Quarterly Review. But I have written to say that I can give no answer until I know what your wishes are with respect to the Atlantis. If you propose converting it into a quarterly it will more than answer all the purposes I should have in view for the Dublin.

On the other hand the contributors to the Atlantis are, I suppose, limited in number, and as in one case scientific articles predominate in the other there would be a political department instead. Again it would ensure harmony of view and tone in our three principal periodicals. Will you allow me to put the matter before you rather for your decision than for your advice, and to assure you that I have no wish or will in the case but your own?

I have written to Simpson to know how he considers that it would affect the interests and position of the Rambler, if I should at the same time conduct another review. . . .'

Bagshawe sent Newman a copy of his circular, dated 25 June, announcing his retirement from the editorship of *D R*, and suggesting that it might be kept going by 'competent persons.'

don't think you would be without sufficient assistance, and that of a quality such as you would wish — and I do not see at the moment how you would get over the one great difficulty, which is the cause of failure of many other periodicals besides the Dublin, the expenses of it.

No periodical is on a satisfactory footing which does not pay its contributors fairly, and as a matter of business. There must be a sort of contract between Editor and writers; the latter sending in their compositions by a fixed day, and the former as punctually paying for them. Else, I think you will be short of hands, and will have no control over those who offer themselves. They will promise you articles, and disappoint you, and at almost the last moment you will have to sit down and write articles yourself.

Some years ago I tried to raise an annual sum to be put into the hands of the Editor of the D.R. [Dublin Review] but the attempt failed.[1] I fear the publication must be considered to cost £1000 a year — thus:— 64 sheets at £8 apiece to the author=£512; Editor's salary=£100. Printing=£400. The cost of the Atlantis printing (Number 1) was about £100; sheets only 14, but the composition heavy; which gives £400 for the year. In this estimate there is no allowance for advertising, or for books; but I do not see why any thing should be allowed for the latter. Nothing was ever paid for books to the Editor of the British Critic; on the contrary, more books were sent to him by publishers than he knew what to do with.

Against this £1000 are to be put the profits from the sale. I *think* the British Critic sold 1400 copies, and the publishers rather lost by it than otherwise. The publisher was brother to the Printer.[2]

Do you know any thing of Richardson as a publisher? The late Editor speaks well of him in his Circular, and I am not presuming to hint any sort of want of confidence; but it is always right to seek testimonials or references. Do you know Mr Wilberforce enough to consult him? *I* could — he has had extensive dealings with the Richardsons[3]

Very sincerely Yours John H Newman

TO EDMUND O'REILLY S.J.

Private   The Oratory, Birmingham July 9. 1858

My dear Fr O'Reilly

I should like to know what you, Mr Butler, Mr Sullivan and Dr McDermott think of the following plan. I select them, as belonging to distinct Faculties, and as having experience of other Universities and Schools besides our own.

---

[1] See the letters to Russell in the Autumn of 1850.
[2] The *British Critic*, which Newman edited from 1838 to 1841, was published by the Rivington brothers.
[3] For Acton's negotiations about *D R*, which broke down at the end of Aug. 1858, when Bagshawe returned as editor, see *Gasquet*, pp. 30–4, *Altholz*, pp. 72–3, and *MacDougall*, pp. 32–4.

But you may put your veto on it, if you will, and burn this letter, without consulting them upon it. But, any how I write the letter in confidence as regards yourself and them.

I have been all along dissatisfied with the Examination system — it being an old idea of mine, of near 30 years standing, that the Examiners, at least *some* of them, should be permanent, paid well, and an influential element of a University system. Want of money, and the difficulty of a plan, have prevented me attempting anything hitherto.

But now, considering the existing paucity of our students, I think something might be done, in the way of retrenching Professors, or turning them, (if they will consent to be turned,) into Examiners. At the moment there are to [sic] many Professors for the students

Further, some of the Professors are underpaid; and others, though not overpaid *as Professors*, have not a great deal to do.

I am contemplating at present only the Examinations in Philosophy and Letters. And I should propose three permanent Examiners (not excluding others, such as are at present, for the occasion or the session, with a small remuneration) — one for the Classics and English Literature — one for History and Philosophy (i.e. all history, Logic, Political Economy etc) and one for theology, metaphysics, ethics, and mathematics (the mathematics being not any great things in the Philosophy and Letters School) —

I should try to prevail on two of the existing Professors of the Philosophy and Letters School to undertake two of these Examinerships, giving up their Professorships, and handing over their province to other Professors, who, under the existing paucity of students, might not think it unfair to them to have this additional charge. (As I have not yet sounded particular Professors, I cannot tell what difficulties would arise in *fact* — here I am only concerned with the *principles* of the arrangement.)[1]

For the third, I should try to obtain a Priest. I will say no more at present.[2]

Ever Yrs most sincerely John H. Newman

---

[1] Renouf informed Newman on 6 July that the Queen's University spent annually about £1450 on examiners.

[2] O'Reilly replied on 21 Aug., 'The substance of what I have to say is, that all the persons whom you wished me to consult, were of opinion, and I agreed with them, that the plan you proposed, tho' having it's advantages, was not advisable, at least at present. The objections were various. One which weighed much with me, and which I hinted to you at once . . . was that the public would not view favourably the payment of large salaries to persons appearing to have little to do.' O'Reilly also pointed out that to reduce the number of the professors would suggest that there had been too many of them before. See letters of 21 Aug. to MacDermott and 23 Aug. to O'Reilly.

TO WILLIAM KIRBY SULLIVAN

The Oratory Birmingham July 9. 1858

My dear Mr Sullivan,

Mr Monsell left us last night for Dublin. He hopes to find you out and make your acquaintance — and I shall be very sorry if he misses you. He has taken great interest in the steps we are taking for getting a charter.

Mr Morris has sent me an article for the Atlantis on Job. He is one of our best Hebrew and Syriac scholars, and I doubt not his article is a good one, though I have not yet had time to read it. On dipping into it, I somewhat fear it will offend like Mr Scott's; but I will try to set that right before it is actually offered to the Editors.

By the bye, the only criticism I have heard on our work is the want of homogeneity in its articles. There is truth in this. I had fancied that it would have been somewhat softened, by heading the articles with a general title; i.e. in this number 'History' would have headed the two first — 'Antiquities' would have introduced Mr Curry's —- 'Criticism' mine etc. But any how it is a difficulty. I am almost inclined to recur to our original plan — of three or four discursive articles, on any subjects whatever — and then a break — i.e. the rest of the page blank — And then with a new page to begin strict Science of whatever kind. Or again, perhaps we are strong enough in experimental etc. sciences, to confine the work to subjects which fall under them. Any how, I think the juxtaposition of (e.g.) Mr Curry's and my articles is harsh.

July 11. I have kept this back that I might be able to send you Longmans' answer, which I inclose

Yours very sincerely John H Newman of the Oratory

W K Sullivan Esqr

TO SIR JOHN ACTON

The Oratory Bm July 10. 1858

My dear Sir John

From your answer to me I find I have created in you an impression that I am simply opposed to the notion of your undertaking the Dublin, which is not *at all* the case.[1] As to the Atlantis, the Dublin would not even tend to

---

[1] Acton wrote on 9 July, 'Your very kind letter was most welcome and useful to me. I gather from it that on the whole you do not think it worth while to run the risk of another failure, and unless I see my way more clearly than at present I do I am ready to acquiesce in your opinion.' Acton then proceeded to give reasons for thinking that *D R* could be undertaken successfully. He concluded, however, by saying that if the *Atlantis* 'is to become a quarterly, and the contributors are not confined to the Professors of the University, I see no reason at all why the Dublin should exist. It is clear that Politics are much better dealt with in monthly than in quarterly articles, and political questions are the only ones which the Dublin would discuss which are not discussed in the Atlantis. The literary wants of our Catholic public are unfortunately easily satisfied.'

interfere with it — and to make the chance of any mutual interference still less, I wrote on receipt of your letter to a friend in Dublin, to express, what I had on other grounds felt, viz the desirableness of the Atlantis contracting its range of subjects, and of even confining itself to scientific.[1]

If you see a plan, by which you could without risk of loss, carry on the Dublin for two years as a trial, I should be very glad. It would be a great thing to get it out of Richardson's hands — or rather an imperative necessity. You would then know what the *real* state of the case was. But I fear he would ask a large sum for the property. However, I am arguing without sufficient facts here — for you may know what his price is.

Nothing can be better than the scheme of Burns's purchasing it.[2] If so you would only have to stipulate with him for due payments to the Editor and contributors. I cannot tell what the worth of a 6/ book is to a *publisher* — but, if I recollect rightly, I found that, in the case of a book *I* published with Longmans, *after* paying the printing expenses myself, only one *third* of the sum realized by the *sale* (to the public) of an Edition of 1000 copies, was paid over to me: e.g. 1000 copies of the Dublin at £1. 4. each = £1200 — of which a fourth, £400 (profits of sale), would have to be set against the printing, which, as I have calculated in my former letter, would be just £400 — leaving nothing for contributors. But I cannot lay my hand upon my papers, and I know well that the cost to a publisher bears no resemblance to the cost to an author.

As to the effect of your taking the Dublin on the Rambler, so far I should anticipate — that you would not have time, thought, and zeal sufficient for both, and that, if the Dublin gained, the Rambler would lose.

Very sincerely Yours John H Newman

SUNDAY 11 JULY 1858   Nicholas went to the North

[1] On 11 July Acton quoted this sentence to Simpson as follows: 'As to the difficulty with regard to the Atlantis that foolish old man Newman writes to me this morning: "To make the chance . . . scientific." Of course he must be rebuked for this, but it shows his animus towards the plan . . .' *Gasquet*, p. 31, corrected from A. Watkin and H. Butterfield, the *Cambridge Historical Journal*, x, (1950), 'Gasquet and the Acton—Simpson Correspondence,' p. 85. Acton appreciated Newman's wish to support him over *D R*. See letter of 14 July to Acton.
[2] Acton wrote in his letter of 9 July to Newman, 'Now I understand that Richardson is willing, or even anxious to give up his connexion with it [*DR*], and I strongly suspect that Burns induced Allies to write to me about it. . . . He was anxious to make a quarterly of the Rambler if the Dublin should come to an end. If he does not entertain the plan now the reason is, most likely, that he has a strong (commercial) dislike for Simpson, and thinks that he makes so many enemies that no Review could succeed, as a speculation in his hands. I have reason to believe that the Cardinal [Wiseman] intimated to him that he would bestow his countenance on the Rambler only on condition that my name should appear alone in the Editorship. Burns has been urging this upon us for some time, and meeting with very little encouragement . . . I set so high a value on Simpson's vigour and activity that I should not think of entering into any arrangement from which he should be excluded.'

TO ROBERT ORNSBY

The Oy Bm ⌐July 11/58⌐

Private

My dear Ornsby

⌐I send a *first* draft of the letter of the Professors to Disraeli, which will be presented to him by two members of Parliament.

Let your Deputation to the Archbishop see it — and let me have it back with their opinion and remarks, before the body of Professors see it. *I don't wish* the Archbishop to see it, unless (which is unlikely) he should press — but it will enable you to tell him the general purport of it.[1]

It does not commit the Bishops — nor the University as a body.[2]

Ever Yrs J H N⌐

MONDAY 12 JULY 1858   Lord Lovat called.   Northcote called

TO JAMES STEWART

Ory Bm July 12/58

My dear Stewart

I forget whom I named for the Printing Committee — but I can do nothing, till after the quarterly payments when I shall see what balance I have.

Certainly all but *academical* works should be excluded. I mean whatever belongs to a profession, e.g. books of ceremonies, treatises on moral theology, Meditations, catechisms, contingent remainders, remarks on cerebral congestion, works on civil engineering, etc etc.[3]

Ever Yours affectly John H Newman of the Oratory

J. Stewart Esqre

TO HENRY WILBERFORCE

The Oy Bm ⌐July 12.1858⌐

My dear Henry,

There could not be a more acceptable offer than that of a visit to Boffin[4] to any poor Priest who had to make holiday — and it would, I am sure, have

---

[1] Ornsby wrote on 9 July that Cullen had agreed to receive a deputation from the professors on the subject of a charter.

[2] For the proposed letter of Disraeli see at 19 July. The professors found it most satisfactory. Ornsby returned Newman's draft at once, since Cullen was absent from Dublin.

[3] See letter of 2 July to Stewart. Stewart published *Memoranda of Greek Grammar with a complete system of accentuation*, Dublin 1859, and *A Latin Grammar for use in schools and Colleges*, Dublin 1860.

[4] This was the island Wilberforce had bought, off the west coast of Ireland.

been caught at by one or other of our party, had we our vacation before us —
but we are all out on holiday at present, or have been so already — and we
are expecting our Church to be ready in a week or two — when we have
agreed to be here, and to begin work again with as much zeal and devotion
as we can work up.

⌐Of course you will make use of my house in passing through Dublin — ⌐
the term ends on the 22nd — when it will be free for your party. ⌐I shall
write by this post to Frederic[1] to prepare him.⌐

Thank you for your kind thoughts of me — I take it to mean that you
don't forget me in your prayers

Ever Yrs affly John H Newman, of the Oratory

H W Wilberforce Esqr

TUESDAY 13 JULY 1858   went to Rednall and slept there

WEDNESDAY 14 JULY   returned with Ambr. [Ambrose] to Bm [Birmingham]   Stans
[Stanislas] and Robert went to Rednall

TO SIR JOHN ACTON

The Oratory, Birmingham July 14. 1858

My dear Sir John

Certainly, I should be very sorry if the Dublin were given up — and I
should much like to see it in your hands. And you would be sure to succeed
if it paid contributors fairly. As to my writing or not for it, my not writing
would not be from want of will — but I could not promise for a great many
reasons — and you would get an abundance of writers without me.[2]

But capital is indispensable. Would not Burns make the attempt, say, for

---

[1] i.e. Thomas Godwin. The Wilberforces passed through Dublin on 24 July, and made
use of Newman's house.

[2] Acton wrote on 12 July, 'The feeling that the kind interest you take in the plan I consulted
you about may lead to a modification of the Atlantis troubles me exceedingly and makes me
fear that I did wrong in putting the matter before you as I did. I earnestly hope that you will
not allow your good wishes for our proposed undertaking to induce you to make a change
which though it may not affect the circulation of the Atlantis will bring a great loss upon the
Catholic public. The only thing which could compensate for the diminished number of
literary papers in the Atlantis would be your consent to give the Dublin Review or the
Rambler some of the crumbs that fall from your table. At any rate nothing would so much
increase our chance of succeeding. . . .

I shall rejoice at the present confused and melancholy state of our periodical literature if it
results in inducing you to break your resolution of not contributing to any of the Reviews.'

two years? But I do not know who would wish to have any thing to say to it, unless it were absolutely out of the hands of Messrs Richardson

Yours most sincerely in Xt   John H Newman of the Oratory

Sir John Acton Bart

P.S.   I hear a great deal of an article of yours in the Rambler, but have not yet seen it.[1]

TO THE EARL OF DUNRAVEN

The Oratory, Birmingham July 14. 1858

My dear Lord Dunraven,

I know perfectly well, how well dear Fr Flanagan would be cared for at Adare — and I wish I might trust he will be able to avail himself of your kindness. At present, one can only hope in God s extraordinary mercy. Fr Bittleston was saved to us, as I believe, by prayer — when, humanly speaking, he was gone. And now, our people are praying very hard and patiently for Fr Flanagan. Judging of him according to the natural course of things, I should have no hope. I should expect him to be better and worse, always ailing, and gradually declining, till his state left no doubt how the end would be; but I think his case is just such at present, that a grazia might be shown him, which either might restore him altogether, or at least for years. And such grazie prayer gains. You may think what a trial it is to us.

I wish I could gather from your letter that your own particular trial is less.[2] Pray give us your good prayers

and believe me ever, My dear Lord Dunraven Most sincerely Yours in Xt

John H Newman of the Oratory

The Rt Honble The Earl of Dunraven

TO ROBERT D. LYONS

The Oratory Birmingham July 14. 1858

My dear Dr Lyons

I thank you for your letter giving me your views on the subject of a Charter and our granting degrees. I was glad to receive them, and think them

---

[1] According to *Gasquet*, pp. 16–25, none of the articles in the *Rambler* for July were written by Acton. He contributed literary notices, and also wrote an introduction for Simpson's article on 'Mr Buckle's Thesis and Method,' which is perhaps the one to which Newman refers.

[2] Presumably his wife's disapproval of his having become a Catholic.

entitled to great consideration. No one can feel very sanguine that our present application to Government will be successful — but most of us seem to think it ought to be made.[1]

As to the course to which you incline, so bold a line of policy would, I think, succeed, and be advisable, were Ireland united in political action — but, taking things as they are, it seems to me safer, if we can, to make Government our friend

Very sincerely Yours John H Newman of the Oratory

R. D. Lyons Esqr &c &c.

TO JOHN O'HAGAN

The Oratory Birmingham July 14. 1858

My dear Mr O'Hagan,

I ought to have written a line before this in answer to your last letter. Thank you for agreeing to add the Professorship of Jurisprudence to your present Professorship.

Will you tell me if it will be what you expect and are satisfied with, if I consider your regular salary of £200 to begin with the opening of next Term i.e. the first payment to be due on Decembr 21

I am, my dear Mr O'Hagan, Very sincerely Yours in Xt

John H Newman of the Oratory

John O'Hagan Esqr

TO EDWARD WALFORD

The Oratory Birmingham July 14. 1858

My dear Walford

I have been waiting before answering you and thanking you for your double letter, private and public, to hear from Dublin about the final result of the examination — but I have heard nothing except vaguely that my own youths did well.[2]

I was quite prepared for your report about de la Pasture. He is a most exemplary fellow — but he has been badly grounded at school — and there

---

[1] Lyons wrote on 8 July from Dublin that in his opinion either the University should grant degrees at once, in virtue of its papal charter, or else secure Government recognition of its degrees. He strongly favoured the first course.

[2] Walford wrote privately about his work as examiner in Dublin, and also enclosed a copy of his formal letter to the examiners.

He awarded honours to Bethell and Keane, and a pass to de la Pasture. See also letter of 21 Aug. to MacDermott.

is not, and never will be any help for it — He will always risk breaking down incomprehensibly, and, after going on in a way quite to deceive an examiner, committing some appalling blunder in gender or concord.

Thanking you for your services in Dublin, I am, My dear Walford,

Sincerely Yours in Xt John H Newman of the Oratory
E Walford Esqr

TO HENRY HENNESSY

The Oratory, Birmingham. July 15th. 1858

My dear Mr. Hennessy,

Thank you for your letter. Mr. Monsell told me it was arranged that Mr. Maguire and Mr. De Vere, as representing two sections of Irish Politics would kindly go to Mr. Disraeli on the subject of the charter.[1]

I sent a letter addressed to the latter and to be signed by the Professors to Dublin for approval at the beginning of this week, and your signature will be wanted.

Mr. Maguire and Mr. De Vere, who are undertaking this delicate matter, shall have our letter for presentation as soon as it is signed.

Yours most sincerely, John H. Newman of the Oratory
H. Hennessy Esq.

P.S. Of course you will take care not to seem to be deputed by the University — which would create embarrassment.[2] You are not likely to do anything that could be by mistaken — but a man like Disraeli, with a great deal on his hands, might not be accurate in his impressions.[3]

TO WILLIAM HOUGHTON BEARDWOOD

[16? July 1858]

Dear Mr Beardwood

I am obliged to you for informing me of your intention of beginning the wall of 87 Stephen's Green. As you are acting strictly under the order of the

---

[1] John Francis Maguire, Member of Parliament for Dungarvan, was the leader of the Independent Irish Party, now giving support to the Tory Government. Stephen de Vere, sat in Parliament for Limerick, 1854–9, as a Liberal. In the end Aubrey de Vere left the Professor's letter for Disraeli. See letter of 25 July to de Vere.

[2] Hennessy wrote about 14 July that Maguire had just sent Disraeli a private letter urging him to grant a charter to the Catholic University, and enclosing a statement of the reasons in favour of it, drawn up by Hennessy, who was in London.

[3] Hennessy replied on 16 July that he had not committed the University. Maguire's letter was a confidential one and referred to the support he had given and proposed to give to the Government.

Archbishop of Cashel, you had better write to him on the subject. I think you told him what it would cost.[1]

TO JOHN HUNGERFORD POLLEN

The Oratory Bm July 16/58

My dear Pollen

I have been writing to you daily, but have waited till we were far advanced enough.

Have you the measurement of the Predellas of the Altars? As time has gone on changes have come over us, of course. And I doubt whether you can do much without coming here. We wish to consult you about various details. We can tell you much better now than before, what we want, because we know how the money stands. I wish the Altars put in hand, but think you should see the place as it is. St Valentine's Altar will be on a predella seven feet long. It will be in the new aisle, which they are now tiling. The tiles will be hard in about a week, so as to walk on and put down the platform of altar which is made.

William agrees with me in thinking you should come. Could you come in a week? To ask you for Sunday (week) is scarcely a compliment, we are in such disorder. But what say you to it? say, come Saturday week the 24th?

Ever Yours sincerely John H Newman of the Oratory

J H Pollen Esq.

TO JOHN STANISLAS FLANAGAN

The Oratory July 17. 1858

My dear S

Thanks for Mrs Hope's money. We will think about it.[2]

Henry and Robert tell me you think that you cannot well be *idle* except with your friends in Ireland. Since then I do not think it right to keep you longer in Edgbaston. I think you ought to get off to Ireland as soon as you like

Ever Yrs affly J H N

P.S. I inclose a Registered Letter.

SUNDAY 18 JULY 1858   Dr Duke called in evening   Walker left today or yesterday

---

[1] Newman's draft is unfinished. These repairs were the concern of the University church, which the Irish Archbishops had accepted from Newman. Cf. letters of 31 July and 16 Oct. 1857 to Leahy.
[2] Cf. letter of 6 May 1856 to Dalgairns.

TO EDWARD CASWALL

The Oratory Bm July 18. 1858

My dear Edward

I always have an idea that, when persons are travelling, they never get their letters — and, as I did not know how long you would make Cobl. [Coblentz] or any other place your head quarters, I did not write, and especially as there were no letters to send you. Now, however, I answer your letter of yesterday without delay, lest you should be desirous of knowing how we fare.

After Stanislas had been here a fortnight, I proposed his going to Rednall for a fortnight. There he is at present; but, since I have just heard from Robert that he wishes to go to Ireland, I have told him by all means to go to Ireland. It is of the first necessity that he should in a matter of this kind have his own way — so I fear you will not see him on his return. He has said distinctly to Robert 'The only way of making me well is to send me to Ireland.' This I do not follow in my own expectations, but I cannot withstand a wish, so expressed, and Henry and Ambrose agree.

We are not in any part of the Church yet. The nave is covered in — the transept is uncovered tomorrow. The plasterers are at work in the nave. I suppose we shall get into the whole Church by the Assumption — but there will be the Sacristy to do *then*.

When the Cardinal was down at Oscott for Dr Amherst's consecration he said that the Bishops had put the whole matter of the Scripture into my hands to make the best bargain I could with a publisher. Dr Clifford was to send me a formal letter, which I suppose I shall have in good time.[1]

Walker is going away tomorrow on a visit to Bernard Smith. Then he is going into retreat at Beaumont Lodge[2] to make up his mind, whether he shall offer himself to us.

---

[1] Cf. letter of 3 March 1858 to Ullathorne, and 19 Feb. 1858 to Wiseman. Amherst's consecration was on 4 July. Bishop Clifford wrote on 11 Oct. 1858: 'Mr Wingfield has reminded me of a very great omission on my part. I have never sent you a copy of the Resolutions passed at the Bishops' meeting relative to the translation of the Bible

They are as follows.

March 10th 1858.—"The Cardinal read Dr Newman's letter upon the New Version of the Bible, and explained that he (the Cardinal) had asked His Holiness to consider how the revision was to be conducted.

His Eminence also read a letter from Propaganda appointing the Cardinal Archbishop and the Bishops of Birmingham and Southwark to review the New Version on their own responsibility.

Dr Newman having proposed two alternatives respecting the expense of publishing a Translation of the Holy Scriptures, it was agreed to allow the copyright to be reserved to Dr Newman, and his legal representatives; and the Reviewers appointed by the Holy See were requested to arrange with Dr Newman the conditions and duration of the copyright." '

For the sequel, see letter of 7 Dec. 1858 to P. N. Lynch, Bishop of Charleston.

[2] The Jesuit house near Windsor, now Beaumont College.

The Professors of the University are presenting a letter to Disraeli to ask for a charter — it can do so no harm, and may do good.

The Tablet and Dublin Review are both hoisting signals of distress, and want to begin again.

Young Sweeny is in the Hospital, and was to have an operation for the stone on Friday. The Doctors have put off the day once or twice, and I have not yet heard if it has come off. It is a large stone — and one in twenty die — but I am sanguine he will be brought through. I have said Mass for him, poor boy, twice.

We have promising news of two more lay brothers.

Fr Frederic and Nicholas are at their brothers' houses.

And now I have told you all the news I can think of. Enjoy your holyday, and return the stronger for it

Ever Yrs affly J H N

TO JOHN STANISLAS FLANAGAN

The Oy Bm July 18/58

My dear S

Thank you for your affectionate letter.

1. You are unjust to Robert and Henry — My conclusions which follow are from my own premisses.[1]

2. I have never doubted you must be away for the winter — whether at Adare — Torquay, or abroad. That is, I dare not go against a consensus of doctors.

3. I do not think you ought to stop in *this house* now, for above (say) three days running — for I have *observed* that congregational matters try you.

4. I don't think you are likely to read *as little* at Rednall as I wish — not from any fault of yours, but from your nature.

5. Since then you cannot be here now, and since there is a danger of your doing too much at Rednall, if you do any thing, I think it safest that you should go to Ireland

Ever Yrs affly J H N

MONDAY 19 JULY 1858   called on the Bishop.   Mr Hardman called

[1] Flanagan wrote a long letter from Rednal on this day, regretting that Tillotson had passed on the conversation they had had together.

TO BENJAMIN DISRAELI

Copy[1]

Dublin July 19. 1858

To the Rt. Honble. B. D'Israeli M.P. &c &c

Sir,

We the undersigned, being the Rector, Professors and others in office and authority, of the University established some years since in this Metropolis by the Roman Catholic Bishops of Ireland, beg to address you in behalf of the Institution, in which we are thus immediately and intimately interested. And we hope you will pardon the informality, should we be troubling you with a matter which is foreign to your own department of State affairs, and that you will do us the favour of making known our application in the proper quarter.

The Institution of which we are members, originating, as is well known, in a conscientious reluctance to systems of mixed education, which is also felt by other religious communities in Ireland, has for its one direct object the intellectual culture of Roman Catholic youth, both Irish and English, who, after leaving school, desire to carry on and complete the education, liberal or professional, to which their earlier years have been devoted.[2]

It has been founded, and is supported, by the Heads of our Church, on the conviction, that cultivation of mind is at once a protection to religion, and a momentous social and political benefit; and that the widest pursuit of scientific and historical truth never can interfere with even the most zealous acceptance of Revelation; — a conviction, of which both they and their flocks have given practical evidence, by the large sums, amounting to many thousand pounds, which, under their sanction, have been collected, and are annually collected, in Ireland, in furtherance of their object. Indeed, we much question, whether, in any other part of the world, a voluntary effort can be pointed out, so considerable as this, which has now been made for some years, and by the humbler classes of the community, for the encouragement of those literary and scientific studies which constitute University Education.

We further beg to submit to your consideration, that our University embraces the Five Faculties of Theology, Law, Medicine, Philosophy and Letters, and Science, of which four are in active operation; that the Medical Faculty is in possession of a large Medical House, containing under its roof theatres, laboratory, and dissecting rooms; that the same Faculty is in possession of a library of 5000 well selected volumes, many of them of great rarity,

---

[1] There are two drafts by Newman of this letter, which is printed here from the fair copy in Ornsby's hand. This differs in only a few minor details from Newman's second draft. See also letter of 20 July to Butler.

[2] In the drafts Newman made an addition here, which he cancelled: 'and which at present they can only hope to obtain by the establishment of colleges professing their faith in the English Universities.'

and in seven languages; that during the present Session it has had 80 students in lecture, with a prospect of increase, as time proceeds, and that it has commenced a system of lodging houses for their accommodation; that the Faculties of Philosophy and Letters, and of Science, support a periodical for the advancement of the subjects which they respectively profess, which is gradually obtaining for them the recognition and correspondence of learned bodies in Great Britain, the Continent, and the United States; that above 100 young men of Dublin, who are engaged in business during the day, attend with great interest and regularity the evening lectures of the Professors of Philosophy and Letters, who at the same time are lecturing the matriculated students, distributed into four Collegiate Establishments, in the higher classics, in the Antiquities of Egypt and Palestine, in English and foreign literature and Modern History, in Irish Archaeology, in Logic, Metaphysics and Mathematics; and that, on the whole, the University has had as many as 249 Students in its various classes during the present Session.

Under these circumstances, we hope we may without presumption ask for that recognition from the State, which we are continually obtaining from the centres of learning and science in Europe and North America.

In referring to the Charter lately granted by Government to the Roman Catholic University of Quebec, we both explain what we venture to anticipate, and assign our reason for anticipating it.

We have the honor to be, Sir, Your obedient humble servants[1]

TO WILLIAM MONSELL

The Oy Bm July 19/58

My dear Monsell

I kept back the Letter to the last post (Saturday 3 o'clock) and then despatched it for signatures to Dublin, *the Professors separating for the Vacation this day.* So I could not profit by your corrections received this morning.[2] I have received it back signed this morning, with a letter from Fr

[1] This letter was left at Disraeli's house on 28 July by Aubrey de Vere. Disraeli merely acknowledged it, but a second application was made to him in Jan. 1859 by Irish Members of the House of Commons. In March 1859 he received a deputation from them, which put the case for a charter, on the lines of the letter of 19 July. Disraeli promised to bring the matter before the Cabinet. There was a general election in April, and in June the Derby Government was succeeded by that of Lord Palmerston. Cf. *Campaign*, pp. 385–90, and E. R. Norman, *The Catholic Church and Ireland in the Age of Rebellion 1859–1873*, London, 1965, pp. 58–9. Negotiations for a charter were resumed in 1865–8, but broke down, the Irish bishops insisting on a certain control over the professors, the Government that the University, although denominational, must be independent and self-governing. E. R. Norman, *op. cit.*, Chapters five and six.

[2] Monsell wrote on 17 July that it would be better to send Disraeli the Professors' letter after Parliament had risen. Concerning the passage about the pursuit of scientific and historical truth not interfering with the acceptance of revelation, Monsell suggested, 'would it not be better to put more general words such as "best fits men to discharge the duties

O'Reilly scrupling to sign it lest the Archbishops should not approve of it. Accordingly I have told him in *confidence* what I have told to no one else, that the Archbishops applied to you in May, to go to Lord Derby about a Charter. And I have sent the letter back to Fr O'Reilly asking him, after signing it, to send it to you.

Mr de Vere and Mr Maguire, will they not be leaving town immediately after Parliament is up, if not before? would it not be best to send it to Disraeli at once? but you know best.

Ever Yrs affly John H Newman

The Rt Honble Wm Monsell M P

TO THOMAS SCRATTON

The Oratory Bm July 19.1858

My dear Scratton

I should have liked to have had the money for the Burses from the Bishops, if I have to pay it, certainly; and this made me ask you when sending the letter to Dr Leahy. Before I sign the draft for Mr Flannery, I should like to see what we have over for the Long Vacation, after paying all bills and salaries now. Therefore I have kept the said draft back

Ever Yours John H Newman

P.S.   I have puzzled my brains in vain to recollect 'M.J. Fitzpatrick £30.' So I have entered it. I send back 25.
P.S.   (Private) When did Dr Dunne begin lecturing in the Medical School.[1]

TUESDAY 20 JULY 1858   Robert went to Holywell

TO EDWARD BUTLER

The Oy Bm July 20. 1858

My dear Mr Butler,

I *trust* that I have persuaded Fr O'Reilly to sign the Letter — and I can say to you as much as this, that the movement for a charter does not originate in myself.

which devolve on them as citizens of a free state"—Qui excuse s' accuse and the words as you have put them seem to presuppose an impression on Disraeli's mind that mental development is hostile to Catholicism—' Monsell added, about the penultimate paragraph, 'Is it wise to admit that the granting of a charter is an act of recognition on the part of the state? would not facilities be a better word?'

[1] Dunne began on 17 June. See letter of 30 July to him.

On receipt of the letter to me of the Professors of July 1, which, (in consequence of what I had written to several of their number,) was a request to me to turn 'my attention to the subject of asking Government for a charter,' I wrote to Mr Monsell, with whom I had already been in communication about it.

He wrote back on the 6th saying he should see me in Birmingham on the 8th, and would then talk with me on the subject.

His advice was, not a deputation of Professors to London, which I had suggested in consequence of what I had heard from Dublin, and that on the ground that it might rouse the Orange Party, but an address to Disraeli to be signed by the Professors.

I took several days to draw this document up, as I wanted to do it with deliberation. On Monday the 12th I sent a draft of it to Monsell and to Ornsby, begging them to let me have criticisms upon it. I forget how I worded my letter to Ornsby, but I think I shall be found to have asked for any remarks he could get from the Professors.[1] At the same time I did not mean that my *own* copy of it, though corrected thro' Ornsby, should be signed — but that it should *ultimately* leave my hands as a rough copy, tho' (as it were) in *revise*, and that the body of Professors should have the *last* word upon it, and that the Secretary should transcribe it, and that it should be sent back to me by them for signature.

This intention of mine was defeated by Monsell leaving Tervoe without telling me, and delaying to return my draft of the letter till the day week after I send it to him, and Ornsby writing me word that Monday last ⟨(yesterday)⟩ (the 19th) would be the last day that the Professors would be all together in Dublin. I kept back the Letter till the last possible post (3 P.M. Saturday) and then sent it transcribed and signed by myself — to save loss of time on Sunday — but I think I said in my letter to Ornsby that, if the Professors liked to add or alter and transcribe, I would sign the transcription.

I cannot help thinking, (but it is only my surmise,) that the Archbishops do not wish to commit themselves in the movement one way or the other — so that I do not think I could have signed the Letter, had it been added, (what you suggest) 'that the application was made with the cognisance of the Bishops.'[2]

---

[1] Cf. letter of 11 July to Ornsby. Butler wrote on 19 July that he had not signed the letter to Disraeli because he had not seen the draft in Ornsby's possession until the previous day: 'I do not mention this with the intention of blaming any one; only to account for the difficulty I had in making up my mind yesterday. Had I seen the document earlier, I should have suggested a few alterations; e.g. Some more formal mention of the Lectures of the Faculty of Science; of the Natural Philosophy courses; of the Physical cabinet.'

[2] Butler's letter continued: 'I should also have suggested the insertion of a clause stating that the application was made with the cognizance of the Bishops. The absence of a clause to this effect has been my great difficulty, especially as there has not been as far as I know any intimation semi-official or unofficial that they are parties to the transaction.'

Mr Monsell said, I think, that, before he left town, he had suggested, or made arrangement, that the Letter should be presented to Disraeli by Mr Maguire and Mr de Vere.

I think you cannot do better than make the arrangement you suggest, for the examination in Science.[1]

Ever Yrs sincerely John H Newman of the Oratory
E Butler Esqr

P.S.   I have received, neither directly nor indirectly, any message from the Archbishops on the subject of a charter.[2] Thank you for the sight of Mr Hennessy's letter, which I return.

TO ROBERT ORNSBY

ΓJuly 20. 1858

I sent the Letter back to Fr O'Reilly yesterday, hoping for his signature˙ I return the signatures you sent me. Scott too wants to sign. Fr O'Reilly will send it to Monsell

J H NꞮ

FROM ARCHBISHOP CULLEN

Private[3]

Dublin, July 20/58

My dear Dr Newman,

Some persons connected with the University have informed me that the professors have signed a memorial to Mr Disraeli asking for a Charter for the University.[4] A short time ago, at the request of Drs Dixon and Leahy, I wrote to Mr Monsell on the same subject, and begged of him to learn from the Government whether a Charter would be granted if applied for by the Bishops. I took it for granted when writing to Mr Monsell that it was to the Bishops the Charter was to be granted, and at their request. It appears that Mr Monsell spoke to Mr Disraeli and was very graciously received.—I have not seen the Memorial of the Professors, but as I am informed that you are to present it, I mention what has already been done, lest any unpleasant complication should arise, or that there should appear to be any opposition between the Bishops and Professors, or that the object of their petitions should be different. I do not presume, however, to say any thing regarding the Memorial of the Professors, as I have not seen it. I merely suggest that as the Bishops founded the University, their opinion should be heard as to the terms of the Charter before any thing final be decided on. But you will best understand what is right to be done, and I shall be perfectly satisfied with any steps you take.

[1] Butler wanted Dunne to be appointed as one of the examiners.
[2] In May Cullen had asked Monsell to apply for a charter for the University, but without saying a word as to informing Newman, who only knew of the matter from Monsell's confidential letter of 8 May. See second note to letter of 9 May to Monsell.
[3] This letter was written by an amanuensis, and signed by Cullen.
[4] See letter of 21 July to Sullivan, and notes there.

You will excuse this trouble I give you. I wish merely to put you in possession of the facts.

I regret exceedingly that we have been so long deprived of your presence.[1] I fear that when you were here we troubled and annoyed you—but you may be assured that we all revered and respected you. I wish you could arrange matters to come to live among us continually.

Not being in good health, and suffering from want of sleep, I have not been able to write as I should wish, or to explain myself sufficiently.

Hoping you are quite well, and wishing you every happiness, I remain, with greatest esteem,

Your devd Servt ✛ Paul Cullen

Very Revd Dr Newman.

TO ARCHBISHOP CULLEN

The Oratory Birmingham ⌐July 21. 1858⌐

My dear Lord,

⌐I assure you I feel most deeply your Grace's continued indisposition, and I pray God that your great labours and anxieties may be met by a corresponding abundance of bodily, as well as spiritual, succour from Him.

As to the Charter for the University, we are doing nothing which will at all prejudice the prerogatives of the Bishops, or interfere with any movement of the Archbishops respecting it.

We are not definitely and formally asking for one, but opening negociations. We should not dream of proceeding without referring to your Grace.[1][2]

I feel much obliged by your Grace's kind allusion to my connexion with the University, and am,

My dear Lord, Your faithful Servt in Xt

John H Newman of the Oratory

His Grace the Most Revd The Archbp of Dublin

TO JOHN HUNGERFORD POLLEN

The Oy Bm July 21/58

My dear Pollen

I am glad you can come on Saturday. You had best see the space once more before you actually order the Altar. About the Baldacchino, for instance, we rather fear that you will not take into account the position of the windows

[1] Newman commented in 1872, [[This is a simple ignoring of the correspondence with the Oratory, of my *terms*, of my actual holding the Rectorship conditionally, and my taking no salary since February.]]

[2] In the draft Newman wrote, 'We are not definitely asking for a Charter, and we should not dream of proceeding in any negociation for it without referring the matter to your Grace. We are merely taking a preliminary step.'

in the Sacristy. Had we money to face the altar and the Sacristy with Alabaster, I should like the Derby man to come here at the same time to give an estimate — but our £1000 is running very low.

I have told Heywood to meet you here on Saturday. I shall be glad to hear your account of Colonel Gaisford.[1] Scott Murray has written a kind letter to me about the school. Else, in statu quo.

Ever Yours John H Newman

J. H. Pollen Esqr.

TO WILLIAM KIRBY SULLIVAN

The Oratory Bm July 21. 1858

My dear Mr Sullivan

I am sorry to say that Fr O'Reilly has got the subscribed Letter — but I have written for it at once. I shall send it at once to Mr Maguire.[2]

I am fully of opinion, and have been, that the Bishops only wish not to be committed. When Dr Quinn plumply asked Dr Cullen about the Charter, he could but return one answer. I think it was a false step referring to Dr Cullen at all.

Yours most sincerely John H Newman

W K Sullivan Esqr

P.S.   As I have not Mr Hennessy's direction at hand, will you ask him to send me without delay the direction of Mr Maguire and his christian name.

THURSDAY 22 JULY 1858   Scott came in evening

[1] Thomas Gaisford, eldest son of Thomas Gaisford, Dean of Christ Church 1831–55, had recently become a Catholic. He was a Captain, not Colonel, in the 79th Highlanders.

[2] Sullivan wrote on 20 July, 'I hope you have already sent the letter to Mr D'Israeli and that the matter is in full train . . .

There cannot be the slightest doubt that every bishop and priest in Ireland would be glad we got a charter,—nothing could do us more service. But there is not the slightest hope that the Bishops will ever combine to get one. The only chance that remains is the step you have so judiciously taken.

For some reason which I cannot fathom Dr Quinn has given a good deal of opposition which has I regret led me to believe that he is not a man of much discretion. He went to the Archbishop and apparently represented to him that we were acting very precipitately and he got him to write to me deferring the interview we were to have had with him, and intimating that we ought to consult the bishops [See letter of 11 July to Ornsby] My view of this matter is simply that the Archbishop would like that we got the Charter but would rather that he was not suspected to have been instrumental in the matter. Dr Quinn compromised him by going to him and forced him to make an observation which he did not care to make.'

On 23 July Ornsby wrote to Newman that 'Dr Forde, though he declined to sign the letter, wished it God-speed, and hoped we might get a Charter.'

421

TO THOMAS SCRATTON

Oy Bm July 22/58

My dear Scratton,

I inclose the cheque for Dr Flannery.

If de Ligne does not pay me, I must borrow the £150 from the University Balance, till he does.

You said he would pay in a week. Frederic[1] is waiting in Dublin to pay my bills which I can't do without money

Ever Yrs John H Newman

SATURDAY 24 JULY 1858   Robert returned   Pollen came.   Fr Frederic returned.

TO EDMUND O'REILLY, S.J.

The Oratory Bm July 25/58

Confidential

My dear Fr O'Reilly,

My own belief is that the Archbishops, wishing a Charter for the University will be very glad for any assistance the Professors can give them in getting it, provided we do not interfere with their perogative, as founders and owners of the University, to settle the terms — In other words, they wish us to petition, but, 1. they don't wish to *know* we petition, and 2. they don't wish us to imply that we are the ultimate authority in the matter.[2]

The facts which lead me to this view of the matter are such as these —

1. Mr Monsell's words already quoted, under date May 6. [8] that the three Archbishops had 'requested him to apply for a charter.'[3]

2. A subsequent letter of his, in which he says, 'Subsequently Dr Cullen sent me a *paper, which I gave Disraeli,* in which the form (of treating on the subject with Lord Derby) was, as well as I recollect, 'the Irish R.C. Bishops.'[4]

[1] i.e. Thomas Godwin.
[2] O'Reilly wrote to Newman on 23 July to say that he had signed the letter to Disraeli, but feared it went far beyond the wishes of the Irish Archbishops, although he explained that he himself had had no communication whatever with them on the matter.
[3] In an earlier letter to O'Reilly Newman had quoted from Monsell's letter of 8 May. (See second note to letter of 9 May to Monsell.) On 23 July O'Reilly wrote, 'The terms "to apply for a charter" are wonderfully strong. Could Mr Monsell have mistaken what was meant by Dr Cullen? There is a great difference between *applying for a charter* and merely *feeling one's way.*'
[4] In an undated letter, on which Newman has written in pencil 'July 1858,' Monsell wrote from Cromore, near Coleraine, 'It was Dr Cullen that asked me to go to Lord Derby telling me that the Archbishops of Cashel and Armagh were favourable but that Dr McHale would probably not be. Subsequently he sent me a paper which I gave Disraeli in which the form used was as well as I recollect "The Irish R.C bishops." '

3. A letter which I have received from Dr Cullen, *since* the letter which Dr Quinn obtained — [1] in which he says, 'I mention what has already been done, lest any unpleasant complication should arise, or lest there should appear any opposition between the Bishops and Professors, or that the object of their petition should be different. *I do not presume, however, to say any thing regarding the memorial* of the Professors, and I have not seen it. *I merely suggest* that, as the Bishops founded the University, *their opinion should be heard as to the terms of the Charter*, before any thing *final* be decided on. *But you will best understand which is right to be done, and I shall be perfectly satisfied with any steps you take.*'

All this certainly sets me quite clear, as far as my own view of the matter goes.

On the receipt of the last letter, I did two things. 1. I wrote to Mr Maguire to tell him that there must be no mistake, that *the Bishops* were the ultimate negociators, and I am writing the same to Mr De Vere. 2. I wrote to Dr Cullen as follows, and as he has not replied, I consider he is satisfied. 'We are doing nothing which will at all prejudice the prerogative of the Bishops, or interfere with any movement of the Archbishops on the subject of a Charter. We are not definitely and formally asking for a charter, but opening negociations, and we should not proceed in them without referring to your Grace.' ⟨N.B. I think it would have been better to have introduced a clause 'Salvis juribus Episcoporum etc' but I don't think there can be a mistake.⟩

Yours most sincerely John H Newman of the Oratory

The Revd Fr O'Reilly S.J.

P.S. I don't think myself we *shall* get the Charter this time. But it is a good thing to try.

TO THOMAS SCRATTON

The Oy Bm   July 25/58

My Dear S

Thank you for the cheque. I inclose the receipt (and the cheque, if you will kindly send it to the Bank.) Should the Prince not send me the money soon, I really must get you to dun him in the name of the University. I will write again.

As to the state of Dr Quinn's youths, really it is so anomalous, that it cannot last, Are they on the *books* or not? If not, they could not go up, or *have* a test number. If they *are*, we must make an account of what Dr Quinn *might have* had for the youths, setting against it their entrance and scholarship

---

[1] i.e. Cullen's letter to Sullivan, saying that the bishops should be consulted. See note to letter of 21 July to Sullivan.

fees. I suppose the balance will be in his favor. We shall pocket it, if he does not come to an arrangement with us.

I am much surprised I hear nothing of the Licentiate. Please, write an official letter from me to the senior Examiner, saying that I am waiting to be informed of the result of the Examination, and that I happen to know that some of the candidates are waiting in some suspense to know whether they shall receive testamurs, and *have* them, if they have deserved them.

As to Dr Mc Dermott's pay, £30 seems a good deal, since he has had twenty already. Fr O'Reilly and Kelly don't take any thing, I think, but is it not *out of proportion* to what the other examiners have had? will you tell me *what* have been the payments for examiners throughout the year?

Don't you come this way this Vacation?

Ever Yours John H Newman

T Scratton Esqr

TO AUBREY DE VERE

The Oratory Bm   July 25. 1858

My dear Aubrey de Vere,

Inclosed is our Letter to Disraeli — with a letter from Monsell to him.

Monsell says 'Perhaps the best thing you can do would be to send your Letter to Aubrey De Vere and to tell him to have it presented to Disraeli in the way he thinks most advisable.'

Here is the whole of it then — if you will kindly undertake the job. Dont forget we are to see you again here

Ever Yours most sincerely

John H Newman of the Oratory

A de Vere Esqr

P.S.   You can add your name to the Letter.

I should be very glad, if you would write a few lines yourself, to say that, in petitioning for a Charter, we do not forget *that the Bishops, not the Professors, are the ultimate negociators* — lest Government should mistake. I think there is some nervousness in some quarters, lest we should be, superseding the Bishops.[1]

MONDAY 26 JULY 1858   Stanislas went to his friends   Pollen went.

---

[1] Aubrey de Vere wrote on 29 July that he added his own signature to the Memorial and wrote the covering letter for which Newman asked. These and the letter from Monsell he left at Disraeli's official residence.

(copy)

The Oratory Birmingham July 26. 1858

My dear Dr Dunne

Thank you for your letter, which I am glad pleases you.[1]

I write a hasty line merely lest thro' any negligence of mine you should misunderstand me. Certainly, I did not mean, as you have thought, that my silence should be an assent. Nor am I able to see that you have any direct claims on the University for *pecuniary* recompense for your various services to it as Secretary to your Faculty etc. while I fully acknowledge with much gratitude the great zeal and cheerful energy which you have ever exerted in the cause of the University, and especially the warmth of feeling which you have ever shown to myself.

Gladly would I increase both your own salary, and that of others, were it at the moment in my power. And I do hope, as the University proceeds, it will be able to make such an acknowledgment which is the only one in its power, to those who will have been the real authors of its celebrity and success — but I should be wrong, if I suffered my silence to mean what it really does not mean — and this I should be doing, if, after your letter, I did not write these few lines in explanation.

I earnestly hope you will get up your health in the Vacation, and that the pleasure we have in witnessing your exertions for the University may not be alloyed with the thought that you have been impairing your bodily strength or vigor in your devotion to its interests

I am, My dear Dr Dunne, Yours affly in Xt   John H Newman

D B Dunne Esqr

July 26. 1858

My dear Dr Mc dermott

In acknowledging your letter of this morning on the subject of the position of the Demonstrators in the Medical Faculty, I feel it natural to express in the first place my sense of my inadequacy, which is most obvious, to the office of entering upon it.[2]

[1] Newman evidently meant, 'from which I am glad to see that mine pleases you.' See also letter of 30 July to Dunne.
[2] There was dissatisfaction with the Demonstrators in Anatomy. On 21 July MacDermott wrote that Hayden and Cryan, the Professors of Anatomy and Physiology, claimed the right to settle all matters relating to the Demonstrators, and only to consult the Faculty of Medicine as a matter of courtesy. See letters of 1 July to Hayden and 31 July to MacDermott; also Newman's letters of 24 Sept. 1858.

When I was lately asked as to the relation which they were to bear towards the two Professors you speak of, two questions occurred to me as requiring a previous answer, 1. what had I determined when the Demonstrators were first appointed, and 2. what was the practice in other Medical Schools. As far as I could recall to my memory what perhaps I have on paper in Dublin, but of which I have no record here, I think I said at that time the Demonstrators 'were to be practically under the jurisdiction of the two Professors (though formally and constitutionally under the Rector) —' and next, on inquiring what the practice was in other Schools, I found that there also they were considered as subordinate to and dependent on the Professorship of Anatomy.

Before then I comply with your request, that I should decide on a question, on which I find there has been a difference of opinion in your Faculty, might I ask whether I am right in what I have been stating as a fact, as regards other schools; if it be such, on what grounds the Faculty desires to change in its own case a practice which generally obtains, and what is the exact explanation it gives to the term of its proposal, as contained in your letter, that 'in all important matters the opinion of the Faculty should be taken,' and 'changes *communicated*.'

I am &c J H N

TO ROBERT ORNSBY

⌐July 26. 1858

I agree with you and Mr Sullivan that the Archbishop did not mean to stop our Letter. So I sent it, with the addition, besides the signatures you sent me to attach, of Pollen's and de Vere's. I wrote to Mr Maguire to say, that we must not be supposed to compromise the Bishops, who had the decision of the matter.

I don't much expect we shall succeed — but we shall certainly have done ourselves good.

J H N

TO THOMAS SCRATTON

The Oratory Bm July 26. 1858

My dear Scratton,

Dr Dunne tells me that he has delivered 12 Medical Lectures. I think he should have 3 guineas apiece for these. So much for this term, but *instead* of this in future, I think it is fair his income should be increased by £50, and his name will appear on *two* Faculties, £200 being his salary in Philosophy and Letters, and £50 in Medicine. The first payment of the increased salary will be in December 1858 for the quarter beginning November 3.

Ever Yrs John H Newman

P.S. I think I shall have to borrow Bethell's £50 as well as de Ligne's £150. Indeed I meant the cheque to have been drawn for £200. Frederic is to inquire my balance, but I suspect it is on the wrong side.

TUESDAY 27 JULY 1858   Walker returned about now.

TO SIR JOHN ACTON

The Oratory Birmingham July 27. 1858

My dear Sir John,

I am very glad you are progressing in your negotiations about the D.R. but you have considerable difficulties, as you say, still. It is very kind in you to make so much of my writing in it.[1] I wish I could promise, but I have quite the *will* to send you some kind of an article, but you cannot conceive how much time I lose in finding subjects. At length when I get one, I spend perhaps a good deal of time on it, and after all cannot please myself, and throw it up — nor do I find afterwards that I have been wrong in discarding such — on the contrary I have had such proof that I should have made some great mistake, had I persevered, that I never can get myself to carry on to the press any writing about which I have this secret misgiving.

I understand from you that Burns will take the Review out of Richardson's hands — that is very good — but *how* can the Dublin and the Rambler be united? it is simply bringing the R. to an end, is it not? or in other words

---

[1] Acton wrote on 26 July, '. . . . The Cardinal and Dr Russell have expressed themselves relieved from a considerable difficulty by my proposal to conduct the Dublin, and are ready to make it over to my management unconditionally and with a promise of support. Burns has also made up his mind to his part of the work . . . I hope to begin in January. . . . Two great difficulties remain. The Cardinal and Dr Russell wish to have the Rambler merged in the Dublin, which might be somewhat modified to receive it, and Burns asks me to name Allies, who evidently expects it, assistant editor. I have explained to Dr Russell why the Rambler had better be continued and have written to Burns that I cannot agree to Mr Allies' appointment because I have already committed myself to Simpson. This last difficulty is very annoying, and it was unjustifiable in Burns meddling in the affair. Simpson's name will frighten him, and there is just a chance that he may give up the whole thing in consequence, and the difficulties elsewhere will be still greater. It would have been almost treacherous to the Rambler to separate myself from it to conduct the Dublin, and the union of the two reviews is only complete if Simpson is engaged in both. I do not think you can have a doubt of Simpson being the most [sic] competent of the two, and I am persuaded he has energy enough for both reviews, and will be greatly improved by the restraint it will impose upon him.

I cannot make up my mind to begin without the hope of your aid at first. An occasional half hour during the next four months would enable you to give us a paper, which, however short, would settle the question of success at first, and a good start is a great thing.'

427

purchasing the copyright of the R. If you are Editor, you must have a Sub Editor, with whom you are absolutely familiar and at your ease, and intimately one in opinion. He must be your choice, and (I should say) you must pay him — Burns pays the writers and the Editor, but not the Sub editor. This is what seems to me right, else there will be a double government. And you must have the absolute decision what articles are to be inserted; the Publisher not having even a Veto. I don't see the good of being Editor, without sovereign power and undivided responsibility.

I am very much obliged to you for your thinking of me so prominently in connexion with Dr Dollinger's visit to you, and wish it were possible for me to accept your kind hospitality.[1] But I have just declined the invitation to Ushaw, on the ground I never went from home, and I fear I must keep my rule, or I shall get into difficulties on various hands.[2] I hope you will let me catch Dr D. on his way through Bm [Birmingham] Will you thank Morris much for his poem. I shall thank him with my own hand in the course of a day or two[3]

Ever Yours sincerely John H Newman

THURSDAY 29 JULY 1858   Scott went

TO MISS HOLMES

The Oratory Birmingham July 29. 1858

My dear Miss Holmes,

A state of suspense is so uncomfortable that I am glad you at length see your way to make up your mind to return to England. From every thing I have heard of Mr Gainsford, I should consider he was a very zealous Catholic — but I have not the pleasure of knowing him. I have heard your account of yourself with great interest, as always — but, as I have have [sic] not infrequently 12 letters to write a day on necessary matters, sometimes more, you will easily understand that it is a great trouble to me to take pen in hand, and that, if there is one thing more than another which is first an impossibility, and next a penance, it is the writing letters without being absolutely called on to do so.

The Vincentians are at Sheffield — and they have a good name every

---

[1] Acton wrote on 26 July, 'I go abroad (next week) to fetch Dr Döllinger over to England. He has promised to remain from the 6th to the 18th September at Aldenham, where I am anxious to bring together as many of his friends as possible. I need not say that you have the first place among them. . . . I am sorry to say that Badeley cannot come because he is off to Rome, and Mrs Hope expects an event in September which will prevent Hope from joining us. Morris is rather nervous about Job.'

[2] The celebration of the golden jubilee at Ushaw College on 19 July was attended by two hundred visitors, including Wiseman, Manning, Talbot, Herbert Vaughan, and a number of bishops. See also note to letter of 2 Aug. to Acton.

[3] See letter of 2 Aug.

where, though it be a different one — for they are called Lazarists in France, and Fathers of the Mission in Italy. There is a great deal of Catholicism in Sheffield, I believe — from the Duke of Norfolk's influence there[1]

FRIDAY 30 JULY 1858   Sister Mary Philip (*Miss Bathurst*) went to London for retreat Fr Frederic went to S. Sulpice (*query Beaumont? vid Aug 27*)[2]

TO D. B. DUNNE

July 30/58

My dear Dr Dunne

I have not time to look out your letters out of the great pile of Dublin letters I have received since April — but the following is my own interpretation of the point in what has passed between us to which you refer.

I said that I would gladly offer you one additional £50, for past services if you could find definite grounds for it; and I waited to hear from you those definite grounds *on the receipt of which* I *could* grant that sum — When you did not, as I consider, produce them, I thought the whole matter was at an end — and I had no idea whatever you did not understand this — and still think you do not produce grounds in your letter of this morning so definite and intelligible as to enable me, to the satisfaction of third persons such as the Auditors, to make a difference, such as you desire, between you and others.

Then, still wishing to show my sense of your services to the University, I caught at the fact that you have begun your Medical Lectures, to begin again making it a ground for a permanent increase of salary. Instead of offering you one £50 for the past, I rejoiced to have a real ground for offering you a permanent £50 per annum in future. I was glad to be able to do much more than I hoped and I thought you were rejoicing with me — I had no notion that there was any thing in question In order that you might not even have one term of this Session without a remuneration, I allow you 3 guineas a lecture, for your Medical Lectures in June.[3]

On the principle of a quid pro quo I can act intelligibly.

I am very sorry I should not have better made my meaning clear to you.

I now have said all that it occurs to me, all it is likely will occur to me to say on this matter

Yrs affly J H N

[1] The conclusion of this letter has been cut off. Miss Holmes was going as a governess to the family of R. J. Gainsford, Darnall Hall, Sheffield. The Duke of Norfolk was the chief landowner at Sheffield.
[2] Newman was uncertain where Bowles, who was hesitating about his Oratorian vocation, went to make a retreat.
[3] See letters of 19 and 26 July to Scratton.

TO THOMAS GODWIN

Oy Bm July 30/58

My dear Frederic,

I send you a cheque for £111. 11. 11, which is more than the bills etc by £8, which I have added for the Servants on account of the Vacation. Thus

House Bills	270.	7. 11
Extra bills	32.	4. 0
On account for Servants	8.	0. 0
	£310.	11. 11
July 26	199.	0. 0
July 30	111.	11. 11
	£310.	11 11

And now I suppose there is nothing to hinder your coming directly — and I shall be very glad to see you to thank you for your care. Say every thing kind from me to Mrs Grady and Mary. Fr Stanislas is going to his friends, and you won't see him. He is in Scotland

Yrs affly John H Newman

Mr Godwin

TO WILLIAM MONSELL

The Oratory Birmingham July 30/58

My dear Monsell

A. de Vere has sent the application to Disraeli, with a letter of his own, saying, at my suggestion, that the Bishops were the ultimate negociators, not the Professors — This was necessary.[1]

What do you think of my getting at Mr Henley through Denison, who is (*is he not?*) his son in law? Also, I *could* write to Lord John Manners. Would it do any good for me to write to Gladstone? I don't know what his relations are towards the Ministry — and certainly I have no reason to suppose he would feel any interest in receiving a letter from me. Both Lord Malmesbury and Sotheron Estcourt are Oriel men, but I hardly knew the latter, and was

---

[1] Monsell replied on 1 Aug. from Tervoe that he had received a bare acknowledgement of his letter to Disraeli, which Aubrey de Vere had sent in with that of the Professors. See also letter of 25 July to de Vere.

not on the best terms with the former. Estcourt, our Bishop's chaplain, is cousin of the latter, and might forward a letter of mine addressed to him (the Priest) to Sotheron E.[1]

De Vere says — 'The pressure should be kept upon the Government, and perhaps the members of Parliament, who have already spoken to the Government on the subject should be urged to follow up our memorial by writing or speaking again on the subject at once.'

Ever Yours affly John H Newman of the Oratory

The Rt Honble Wm Monsell M P

TO ROBERT MACDERMOTT

Private

July 31. 1858

My dear Dr Macdermott

I suppose I am right in interpreting your answer to my first question to mean that I am not correct in stating that in other Schools of Medicine the Demonstrators are altogether subject to the Professor of Anatomy, as my inquiries led me to believe.

Of course, if this be so, one of the grounds on which I came to the decision ⟨⟨query 'determination' vid letter of July 26⟩⟩ which I signified to Dr Hayden, does not exist. Would you have any objection to my sending to him so much of your letter as relates to this head?[2]

As regards the other ground, viz my decision on the subject at the time

---

[1] Monsell replied on 1 Aug., 'I think it would be very well to get Denison who is Henleys son in law to explain the question of the charter to him. It would also be a good thing for you to write to Lord Malmesbury as he is not, I imagine, a bigot and he would be anxious to conciliate Catholics. If you write to him it would, I think, be better to get some one else to write to Lord John Manners. Ambrose Phillipps knows him and is one of his constituents and supporters. If you were to write to many ministers I should be afraid that they might be frightened and might fancy that they were pressed to do some great act, whereas our line is to ask for what we want as a matter of course piece of common justice. It will be a great point to make old Henley see the justice of our claim, for, I really believe him to be an honest man —as to most of the others they will simply calculate the party results of the act they are asked to do.

Estcourt is not in the Cabinet and therefore will not be consulted. It could do no harm if his cousin spoke to him.'

George Denison was a Fellow of Oriel College from 1828 to 1838, when he married Georgiana, eldest daughter of Joseph Warner Henley, who joined Lord Derby's cabinet in March 1858 as President of the Board of Trade. See letter of 2 Nov. 1858 to Denison. Lord John Manners, who had been a Young Englander with Disraeli and was generous in his treatment of Catholics, had become First Commissioner of Works and sat in the Cabinet. The Earl of Malmesbury, went up to Oriel in 1825, where Newman was his tutor. See letter of 15 Sept. to Ornsby.

Thomas Henry Sutton Sotheron Estcourt (1801–76), went up to Oriel in 1818, and took a first in Classics. In March 1858 he became President of the Poor Law Board.

[2] MacDermott wrote on 3 Aug. partially retracting his answer to Newman's first question. See also letter of 18 Aug. to MacDermott.

when Dr Hayden was appointed one of the Professors of Anatomy, I will admit that at that time the Faculty did not exist, which of course is a material point in determining what is advisable now. I will admit also that even then I laid great stress on the necessity of the Rector having a real control in the appointment etc of the Demonstrators; and this I did with the express intention that they should not be simply under the Professorship of Anatomy; and, since (as I have observed) the Faculty was not appointed at that time, I could not do more.

Would the Faculty be satisfied, if, in consideration of the impossibility of the Rector practically exercising any control over the appointment etc of Demonstrators, as being not a medical man himself, I made it a rule that he should always consult the Faculty, and listen to the representations of the Faculty, on those points which your letter specifies?

I am &c J H N

MONDAY 2 AUGUST 1858   Ambrose a bad attack of Asthma at Rednall

FROM SIR JOHN ACTON

Aldenham Park Bridgenorth July 29th 1858

My dear Father Newman,

Your letters have been throughout my greatest encouragement in the affair of the Dublin Review. I will leave the matter of your writing, without further importunity, to you, with perfect confidence in your kindness towards us.

I have had a letter of 24 pages from Mr Bagshawe which does not promise to facilitate arrangements, as he offers to continue editor himself, and wishes to keep Richardson, and suggests several things I cannot agree to. I have answered that my engagements with my friends make it impossible for me to accept conditions, and that if there is any difficulty in making it over to me unconditionally I shall at once retire to make way for an arrangement more to their satisfaction. I added that if I was to accept the trust at all I should consent to share neither the responsibility nor the power. I gather from your letter that you will not disapprove of this. What you say about the choice of a sub editor comforts me greatly, as you seem not to condemn the appointment of Simpson, who is the only person who fulfils the conditions you mention. The agreement with Burns will be substantially what you recommend. The 100 a year will go to Simpson. My merit is my cheapness. There will be no question of stopping the Rambler. I have already explained to Dr Russell that that cannot be.

It will very probably be thought adviseable [sic] to have a theological counsellor and referee. May I hope that you will consent to be the person? No other person would have at once public and private authority, so as to satisfy our readers as well as ourselves. The mere use of your name would be invaluable and your occasional advice and censure more precious than I can say. It will be the only way to make Simpson's theology no longer dangerous, as he will submit unreservedly to your judgment. And I see no other way in which so inexperienced a person as myself could hold his own as Editor over the contributions say of some of the older clergy. I need hardly give you the assurance that there is no intention in any one of making the Dublin what the Rambler has been, a party organ. Even if we should not have the benefit of your assistance and advice I should aim at keeping to a line such as you would, I think, approve.

I can by no means give up so easily the hope of seeing you at Aldenham. It would be so great a disappointment to Dr Döllinger not to find you here that I venture to hope you will reconsider your decision. The comparison with Ushaw, I beg to say, does not hold good. For we are very near neighbours and that was a journey. Aldenham is in fact only a little further than your villegiatura. Certain visits to Abbotsford might have been quoted by your Ushaw friends, and may I hope be quoted in favour of Aldenham.[1] This would in fact be a visit of rest and quiet, instead of a ceremonious festival. Nothing can show you better than my impertinence and presumption how sorry I should be to lose the pleasure of seeing you.

I must ask your indulgence about my German historians. Unless they are wanted to stop a gap in January I am afraid I shall not be able to finish them without great haste and hurry by which the article would suffer.[2] The business attending the new start of the Dublin will take up a great deal of time this Autumn, besides the Rambler, and I work very slowly.

Ever faithfully Yours J D Acton

TO SIR JOHN ACTON

The Oratory Bm August 2/58

My dear Sir John,

I am glad to hear you are progressing. Did I say any thing on the scheme of one Editor being for both periodicals? I am afraid it would not work. A Review or Magazine is an absorbing work — it demands, if not a man's whole time, yet his whole interest and his continual thoughts. I think, even though one man were physically up to the work, one or other publication would suffer. And then again, a periodical has a sort of identity, and part of its interest with the public consists in its individuality. When it was known that only one idea was represented in two works, one or other would cease to attract attention. This is what I can't help thinking. The *object* of the two is practically one and the same. Now there is a sort of impropriety, which we naturally recognise, in two organizations, having precisely the same work. This is what has puzzled me, e.g. in the Collegio Pio at Rome, which, whatever its original purpose, seems to have become the English College over again.

As to your kind wish, that I should be theological censor, it requires serious consideration. I am no theologian.

I wish I could promise myself the prospect of accepting your most kind wish that I should visit you at Aldenham — but I assure you, I can't get over the difficulties which are in the way

As to Simpson, he is one of the cleverest writers of the day — but I shall be surprised, if you succeed in making him sub-editor against the Cardinal.

Ever Yours most sincerely John H Newman

[1] Aldenham was thirty miles from Birmingham, Rednal seven. For Newman's visit to Abbotsford see note to next letter.

[2] This refers to the article Acton had promised Newman for the *Atlantis*. See *Gasquet*, p. 19, and letters of 26 March and 5 April 1858 to Acton, and 5 Feb., 5 and 20 April and 28 June to Sullivan.

P.S. I explained to Dr Newsham the case of Abbotsford — it was six years ago — and my last visit any where — Nay, I will say my solitary one — as I said to him, for so many years that I can tell how many — and it was taken simply on obedience to the Cardinal, when I was out of health, and he said I must choose between St James of Compostella and Walter Scott.[1]

TO J. B. MORRIS

The Oratory Bm August 2/58

My dear Morris

I wish I had time at the moment to write to you on the subject of the poem you have so kindly sent me, and of your MSS, as they deserve.[2] As to the Poem, I shall show it to Fr Caswall as soon as he returns, for I am sure he will be pleased at any thing so much in his own way. You have added a very interesting and ingenious dissertation, as far as I have read it, which, as all you write, is full of thought.

Your paper on Job is very valuable and I hope you will let us use it for the Altantis. The fault is that it consists of two parts or subjects, which can hardly be united under one categorical proposition. Also, the style is not dry enough, or grave enough, for such matter of fact business like people, as we are. We have of course to pass a censorship on what comes out from the University — and since I have been there, a paper of mine has been plucked, and a friend's paper sticks in the passage, though I hope we shall ease it through. As for you, you will take wings and sail aloft over the sacred congregation and its familiars. I make no doubt.[3]

Ever Yours affly John H Newman of the Oratory

The Very Revd J B Morris

[1] Newman stayed at Abbotsford from 17 Dec. 1852 until 25 Jan. 1853, at a time when he was exhausted from overwork and the anxieties of the Achilli trial. Wiseman insisted that he must go away, either to Spain or to Abbotsford. Cf. Vol. XV, pp. 209 and 245. This he explained to Charles Newsham, the President of Ushaw College, when refusing the invitation to attend the golden jubilee celebrations and to deliver a short address during them. For the Aldenham meeting, cf. letter of 18 Oct. to Allies.

[2] The manuscript was that of Morris's article on Job for the *Atlantis* and the poem was his *Taleetha Koomee: or the Gospel Prophecy of our Blessed Lady's Assumption. A drama in four acts*, London 1858. At the end of it was a Latin dissertation, 'De Hostiis Aeternis,' in which Morris argued for the doctrine of the Assumption from the miracle of the raising of the daughter of Jairus. Morris was Acton's chaplain at Aldenham, and the latter wrote on 25 July to Simpson, 'Jack Morris' poem is out, full of atrocious theology,' A Watkin and H. Butterfield, *art. cit.*, p. 86.

[3] 'An Essay upon the Date of the Book of Job,' appeared in the *Atlantis*, (July 1959), pp. 378–434, with the theological section omitted. See letter of 7 Sept. 1858 to Morris. For Newman's paper that was plucked, cf. letter of 10 Oct. 1857 to Sullivan. The paper that was being eased through was that of Scott 'On the Dates of the Nativity and Crucifixion.'

TO JOHN HUNGERFORD POLLEN

August 2/58

My dear Pollen

We like your altar very much — and think it happy and effective. We criticize

1. The 4 circles at the four sides of the large one in the middle compartment, as something wanting in invention, like neighbour Flamborough's family picture, with each child with an apple in his hand.[1]
2. We fear the two twisted pillars will be expensive, but you are the judge.
3. We think the sopraltare should *rise* somewhat under the Tabernacle, and come forward an inch. What say you? The mysteries of art come in here, for what I know.
4. We doubt about a tabernacle altogether, since we must cover it with a veil. We almost think you had better leave a place for it, and leave us to get a temporary wood one here.

I hope the change of air will soon set right your family troubles.

Ever Yours John H. Newman of the Oratory

J. H. Pollen Esq.

FRIDAY 6 AUGUST 1858   Henry called to London by Miss O. Farrant's death[2]

TO MRS WOOTTEN

The Oratory Augst 6/58

My dear Mrs Wootten

I am sorry to say we heard very anxious news about the Miss Farrants this morning — and Fr Henry went to town in consequence. Fr Austin called on you to-day about it — but I have just learned that he did not find you at home. When you come here this evening, will you send for me

Yrs affly in Xt   John H Newman

SUNDAY 8 AUGUST 1858   First Mass in enlarged church. I said it, being the only Priest in the House. 3 Priests with ⟨counting⟩ me all duplicating, Austin at Alcester Street, Robert at Workhouse

[1] See Oliver Goldsmith, *The Vicar of Wakefield*, chapter XVI.
[2] Octavia Farrant died of apoplexy on 5 Aug.

not sent The Oy Bm Augst 8/58

My dearest H

Thanks for your sad letter.[1] How heavily the Hand of God weighs upon us — never in my life till this last year have I felt it any thing of a difficulty even for a moment to feel resignation. It is hard one should go back. I felt it at Robert Wilberforce's death.[2]

Ambrose has got rid of his asthma — (I find a young Catholic girl has just died here of it, by suffocation) but he has got something else the matter. He sends this morning from Rednall for Walton — being unable to move. He thinks it a strain from the emetic — I think it may be gravel — All day long have we been waiting for Walton, and for news — but no news comes — Wm [William] is gone, a second messenger, after Walton. We don't know whether he has gone and returned, or not gone, or any thing about it — At dinner, no one — but Walker besides Robert — poor innocent Walker, but it is a great irritation to me his being in the house — and some how he does not go.[3]

It is so helpless, as if I had not the use of my limbs, thus to be left alone. I said the first Mass today in the enlarged Church, the only priest in the House! Austin, Robert and I, all duplicated — Austin has gone to Alcester Street, Robert to the Workhouse.

Meanwhile the state of servants is an additional irritation. I am helpless — there is no one to do any thing. Goodrich and George in the kitchen, which is against rule. John most unsatisfactory. I know what I should do, if I had any will — I would send him to the right about this night.

Wm has just returned — Walton has gone to Rednall, and not returned. He hoped, before he went, it was lumbago

Ever Yrs affly J H N

I said one of my Masses today for the living Miss Farrant.

MONDAY 9 AUGUST 1858 Went to Rednall — opening the Sacristy began *the throwing two small rooms into St Philip's chapel began.*

TUESDAY 10 AUGUST Nicholas returned or tomorrow

[1] It was an account of the death of Octavia Farrant.
[2] 3 Feb. 1857.
[3] Cf. letter of 21 May to Bittleston.

TO J. M. CAPES

Rednall Augst 10/58 (The Oratory, Birmingham)

My dear Capes,

It is little to the purpose to say how exceedingly your paper shocked me —[1] and how difficult it is to me to conceive that any such objections as it contains should not have struck you, been mastered by you, and disposed of by you, thirteen years ago, considering that they are some of the most obvious in controversy; or what possible new light can have been shed upon them by any experimental acquaintance you have had, since you became a Catholic, with the mode in which Catholics hold them.

In my own case, the three mysteries which you have noted under your 2, 3, and 4 heads, were not even difficulties to overcome before I entered the Church — for two of them, the Holy Trinity and Eternal Punishment, I have held, held (I believe) with a divine faith, ever since I was a boy — and the remaining one, the Real Presence, I have believed these twenty five years.

As to the objections to these three, definitely made in your paper, all I need say is, that you assume various propositions as undeniable, which seem to me simply untrue, and which certainly ought to be proved, before they are to be admitted. For instance:—

'The presence of wholeness in one place implies its absence from all other places.'

'Every phrase and word employed in the enunciation of a doctrine must have a meaning of some kind or other, comprehensible' (in all respects?) 'by the mind.'

'How can a person merit an eternal hell, who cannot merit an eternal heaven?'

I do not mean to say, that you do not throw these and the like positions into different shapes, and say the same thing in fresh sentences, which *you* may feel to be the proof of them — but to my apprehension your conclusions

---

[1] On 7 Aug. Capes sent Newman a printed paper containing his objections to Catholicism, ranged under the four heads which Newman mentions in his reply. In a covering letter about these difficulties Capes wrote, 'For a long time I thought that I might see my way out of them myself . . . But the longer I have waited the more unassailable the difficulties have appeared to me, and for a considerable time past they have assumed to my mind the certainty of an actual demonstration.

. . . The worst of it is that there are so few persons who are capable of entering into subjects of this kind; still there are some, and I am quite prepared to find that I have been arguing all astray. . . .

Do not hurry yourself inconveniently to answer my letter . . . though I find the STRAIN on the mind quite intolerable.'

Already in June Capes had written to Acton, in order to ensure that he could put his difficulties to Döllinger, when he visited England. On 2 July Acton wrote to the latter that Capes was goaded on by some of the utterances of Wiseman and Faber, and did not properly appreciate Newman. Victor Conzemius, *Ignaz von Döllinger—Lord Acton Briefwechsel*, I, p. 149.

and your premises are so closely one and the same — that they are only verbal explanations of the meaning of each other, and whole paragraphs are nothing beyond respective expressions of categorical assumptions without proof.

Lastly, as to your first heading on the Infallibility of the Church, here again the arguments you profess to overthrow are so different from those which have brought conviction to my own mind, that I do not feel capable of entering into them. My own proof of it would be such as this:—that our Lord set up a Church in the beginning which was to last to the end; that it was to retain His revelation faithfully; that the present Catholic Church is that destined continuation of it; that therefore primâ facie it teaches now in substance what it taught then; that its early vague teaching is to be explained and commented on by its later and fuller; and, as to Infallibility, that, to say the least, there is nothing in its early teaching of a *positive* nature to hinder the interpretation of the early teaching on that point which is contained in its later teaching.

I have not delayed my letter, as you half wish me to do, because, whatever be the force of your arguments, none of them are new, and because I am not likely to require or to find better answers than those which I have been accustomed to use. I am,

I am, my dear Capes, Yours very affly John H Newman[1]

TO MISS HOLMES

Rednall August 10. 1858

My dear Miss Holmes,

I condole with you with all my heart — I know what it is to lose a mother — and, though so many years are past since, my remembrance is quite fresh of that time of great trial. I will say a mass for your mother's soul (that is, for your intention) the first vacant day I have.

Don't forget to pray for me. We all must have trials in this life — they are for our good, or rather they are simply necessary to us. I have had accumulating trials for several years, and I expect that they will increase rather than diminish. But on the other hand, so great and many mercies, that the troubles are as nothing by the side of them.

I have nothing more to say, except that I am,

Yours affectly in Xt   John H Newman of the Oratory

Miss Holmes

[1] See also letters of 22 and 27 Sept. and 1 Oct. to Capes.

Rednall Augst 10. 1858

My dear Pollen,

I am much concerned at what you tell me of yourselves — but trust you are all recovering. I have come over to see Fr St John, who has had the worst attack of Asthma he has had yet. There must be something in the weather unpropitious.

As to what you say about the sopraltare, I think it will be quite satisfactory. Ditto about the Baldacchino. As to the Tabernacle, I think we still scruple. For myself I have had so great a dislike of a square tabernacle with curtains not coming to the top, that the Fathers put a false top on our Alcester Street one, to pacify me. However it is a shame, I feel it to be so, to thwart you, as we do, at every turn — and I shall be quite satisfied if you do what you deliberately think best.

Yours affly John H Newman of the Oratory

J. H. Pollen Esqr.

P.S. As the arches (with granite pillars) are in course of formation during this week, we could give the walls of the Sacristy their proper colour, if you would tell me what it should be.

WEDNESDAY 11 AUGUST 1858 returned from Rednall with Fr Ambrose
THURSDAY 12 AUGUST Henry returned or tomorrow

⌜sent in substance⌝ ⌜The Oratory Birmingham Augst 12. 1858⌝

Private

⌜My dear Plumer,

There is no one who can value Capes's services in his long Editorship of the Rambler more than I do. He has borne a great deal in every way, and had no thanks. Gladly would I take part, if it depended on myself, and there was a prospect of success, in such a scheme as you so thoughtfully recommend. And his domestic sorrows are always in my mind.[1]

---

[1] Plumer wrote on 9 Aug. to Newman, suggesting that a subscription should be organised for Capes, on his retirement from the editorship of the *Rambler*, to show appreciation 'of his persevering efforts for so many years in the Catholic Cause.' Plumer, who lived at Woodchester like Capes, explained that he was in financial straits and intended to move into lodgings, 'which Invalid as he is, with a blind and invalid wife and growing up family would subject him to many disadvantages.'

But I really do not think there is the chance of even a few score pounds being collected for it. Capes has made many enemies, and frightened those whom he has not alienated.[1] Any one who takes a line of his own pays this penalty, that he stands by himself. And no one knows, till he tries, how difficult it is to raise money, where money is so scarce, as it is among Catholics. We at the Oratory have wanted lately to raise £200 to furnish a chapel in our workhouse — a great object, for there is no other workhouse, except Manchester, any where which allows of it — but we have only got a portion of it after a good deal of effort. Lucas's subscription, I think, was a failure, though he was so popular in large classes of the Catholic body.[1][2]

I am afraid I must say something more. I have above used the words 'if it depended on myself.' I am sorry to have reasons, which I cannot mention, which hinder *me* moving. I say all this in confidence.[3]

If you are ever ten minutes in Birmingham, waiting for a train, do let me have the benefit of it; — or if you ever want a bed, we can give you one

Yours most sincerely in Xt   John H Newman of the Oratory

J. J. Plumer Esqr

TO WILLIAM KIRBY SULLIVAN

The Oratory Birmingham August 12. 1858

My dear Mr Sullivan

I trust you are on the spot. No one will be able to manage the step indicated in the inclosed letters better than yourself. But if you are away, perhaps you will write to Ornsby, and get him to undertake the matter with the Archbishop. I think both of you were on the deputation which went to him[4]

Yours most sincerely John H Newman of the Oratory

W. K. Sullivan Esqr

[1] Acton wrote to Simpson on 2 July, 'Capes's letter [about his religious doubts] explains in a way I was hardly prepared for the anomalies which it was impossible not to observe in his life and conversation. . . . What struck me most was his contempt for everything ascetical, and his dislike for prayer under the guise of weak health. Intellectual contempt for fellow-Catholics has brought many men, within my knowledge, to nearly the same pass. . . . I vote that we in particular should be very careful in our communications with him . . .' *Gasquet*, p. 29.

[2] For the workhouse see circular letter of 24 Feb. 1858. There was a subscription for the family of Lucas after his death in Oct. 1855.

[3] Newman cancelled this paragraph in the draft, and omitted it when copying for his collection of letters and papers 'In Re Rambler 1858–1862.'

[4] See letter of 18 Aug. to Sullivan. Ornsby and Sullivan were members of the deputation which proposed to approach Cullen in July about a charter for the University, and with which he communicated by letter. See note to letter of 21 July to Sullivan.

SATURDAY 14 AUGUST 1858   Edward returned   Sister Mary Ph. [Philip] returned from London

SUNDAY 15 AUGUST   First High Mass in enlarged Church (at Altar in Aisle) (*St Valentine's?*)

MONDAY 16 AUGUST   The young Phillipps in Edgbaston

TO ANDREW ELLIS

The Oratory Birmingham August 16. 1858

My dear Dr Ellis

I always feel your kind services, and in the interest you show in the Atlantis, you give only an additional instance of the zeal with which you have promoted the well-being and advance of the University from the first.[1]

I am sure what you send will be valuable, and cannot doubt but Mr Sullivan will gladly have it, as being a judge of its merits, which I cannot be as a professional man is. He is the scientific Editor, and though I am at present Editor for the Literary portion, this is only for a time. I think from what you say, you quite understand what it is that we want.

When the Medical School got on so well, there was some anxiety felt in some quarters, lest I was throwing the *School of Philosophy and Letters* into the back ground. Especially, the great publicity of the meeting in the church for distributing the Prizes, with the gold medals, was mentioned to me.[2] I could not grudge the success of the Medical School, and rejoiced to know that it arose from the zeal of the Professors who belonged to it; however, I saw that equal publicity ought to be given to the Faculties of Philosophy and Letters and of Science — or zealous and able men, who wished to serve the University, would fret at not having the opportunity of doing so. This was a principal reason for the establishment of the Atlantis, which is for those two Faculties, pretty much what the Medical House is for the Medical Faculty, though it will be some time before its expenses, great as they are, will equal those of the purchase of the buildings in Cecilia Street.

Accordingly the two great divisions of the Atlantis are into Literature and Science, as being respectively the provinces of the Faculties in question. Your article, from what you say, will be done in Science, but of a popular character. Will you tell me how many pages you wish to have? My dear Dr Ellis,

Most sincerely Yours John H Newman of the Oratory[3]

A Ellis Esq

[1] Ellis on 15 Aug. offered to write an article for the next number of the *Atlantis*, and asked if he could count on its insertion, provided Newman approved. He said he did not contemplate writing an abstruse medical article, but one more acceptable to the general reader.

[2] See diary for 16 July 1856.

[3] See letter of 22 Aug. to Ellis.

TO PATRICK LEAHY, ARCHBISHOP OF CASHEL

The Ory Bm ⌐Augst 17/58⌐

My dear Lord

I have received letters from zealous friends of the University who say we shall not succeed in gaining a Charter from the Government, unless the Irish liberal members move in our favor at once, and that they will not move without the Archbishops urging them.

I write then to suggest to your Grace['s] better judgment, the importance of taking some step at once in this direction. It is with much regret that I hear so discouraging an account of Dr Cullen's health, that I have not thought it right to trouble him on the subject — but I am sure the matter cannot be in better hands than your own and the Primate's.[1]

⌐As I am writing will you let me ask you when it would be convenient to the Archbishops to give effect to the arrangement made this time year for the purchase from me of the University Church.⌐ Could it be completed by November 1?[2]

⌐The terms which the Archbishops agreed to purchase it on were these, which I quote from my letter to you of July 31. 1857

'Of the whole sum (which it cost £5600) £2400⌐ should be paid to me at once; that, in lieu of the remainder I and my heirs should receive from the Trustees £120 a year, to remain as a first mortgage upon the Fabric (or a first charge upon the congregational collections) and to cease absolutely if ever it ceased to be a Church, and to be applied by me and my heirs, while I receive it, to some University purpose or purposes to be approved of by the Coetus Episcoporum or the Archbishops.

I am &c J H N

TO ROBERT ORNSBY

The Oratory Bm ⌐August 17/58⌐

My dear Ornsby,

⌐I have written to Dr Leahy to take up the matter of urging on the Irish Members — and think it would be very good if some of the Professors also wrote to him and to Dr Dixon. The Government will do nothing unless they are pressed hard.[1]

Of course it is not pleasant to have one's name associated with Saffi's —

[1] i.e. Archbishop Dixon. Leahy wrote on 25 Aug. agreeing that Members of Parliament ought to bring pressure on the Government, and promising to speak to the bishops as Newman wished. He also reported that Cullen's health was very much improved.

[2] Leahy replied on 25 Aug. 'There is no reason why the arrangement for the purchase from you of the University Church should not be completed by the 1st November. I will remind the Archbishops of the matter with a view to their concluding it by that time.'

but I don't see where to draw the line, if you make this a ground for not writing in the Dictionary in question.[1] Would you let your name appear in the List of a volume published by subscription, if his were on it? Would you sell out your shares in a railroad if he bought in?

I hope you are recruiting

Ever Yrs affly John H Newman of the Oratory

R. Ornsby Esqr

WEDNESDAY 18 AUGUST 1858   Henry went up to Miss Farrant at Windsor

TO ROBERT MACDERMOTT

Oy Bm Aug. 18. 1858

My dear Dr Macdermott

As Dr Hayden allows me to make use of the inclosed, I think it best to ask your remarks upon it.[2]

If I were to give an opinion, not on the question of custom but of expedience, I should say that the Extract from the Report of the late Government Commission of inquiry into the Queens' Colleges comes to me with great force; and that, first from the reasonableness of their proposal, and next from their authority.

They say, 'We think that the appointment to the office of Demonstrator should be placed at the disposal of the Professor of Anatomy, subject to the approval of the College Council, and that the Demonstrator should be removable at the pleasure of the Professor.'

I spoke to you in my last letter of the Rector having the control with the *advice of the Faculty*. It seems a more simple arrangement to give it to the Rector in Council

I am &c J H N

TO WILLIAM KIRBY SULLIVAN

The Oy Bm Augst 18/58

My dear Mr Sullivan,

1. I think you have done a good deal in reference to the point I wrote to you on, tho' Dr Cullen, I fear is too ill to move in it. I have written to Dr Leahy on the subject.[3]

---

[1] Ornsby had been asked to contribute to the *Imperial Dictionary of Universal Biography*, for which Aurelio Saffi, who had been one of the Roman Triumvirs with Mazzini, was also writing. See letter of 28 Feb. 1858 to Mrs John Mozley.

[2] Hayden sent Newman conclusive evidence against MacDermott's view. See letter of 31 July to him.

[3] See letters of 12 Aug. to Sullivan and 17 Aug. to Leahy. Ornsby and Sullivan called on Cullen on 15 Aug. to urge that the Irish Catholic Liberal Members of Parliament should be approached about the petition for a charter, but he was unwilling to commit himself.

2. I have told Fowler to divide his Atlantis bill into two — for Number 2 and Number 3 — for it comes to £170! I fear I can't give above £30 more for the next Number. I see Fowler sends a circular in his own name. Of course he has got your leave. Shall I write to Allies for an article next Number — or how do you stand?

3. Did you, as Dean of Science 1856–7 give in any Report to me? or was Dr Lyons Dean that year? Dr Leahy has written to me for a Rector's Report, and I must get materials.[1]

Yours very sincerely John H Newman of the Oratory

W K Sullivan Esqr

Augst 23. I have luckily just found this letter, which by accident fell down among some bills[2]

FRIDAY 20 AUGUST 1858   Henry returned

TO JOHN HUNGERFORD POLLEN

The Oy. Bm. Augst 20/58

My dear Pollen,

I have put Mrs Charlton's letter into Nicholas's hands, who will answer it.[3] Thank you for your news about the continued agitation about the school — of which but for you, I should hear nothing. I have wished you would consent to be the Agent at (say) £100 a year — but it depends on yourself on the one hand, on Bellasis and Co on the other — not on me.

The arches are now done, and promise very well. We will screw up £28 for altar, but can't go a penny beyond. I suppose the carriage won't cost many shillings. ⟨Has the Altar wings? i.e. side supporting sopraltare? If not, we must add them in wood.⟩ I wish you could devise something in wood or plaister by way of ornamenting the six square windows I inclose. What will you do with the space between their bottom line and the line of the

---

[1] Sullivan was Dean of the Faculty of Science for the 1856–7 Session, and Lyons for that of 1857–8.

[2] i.e. this letter of 18 Aug., which went at the same time as that of 23 Aug. to Sullivan.

[3] Mrs William Henry Charlton (1815–98), was evidently enquiring about the proposed Oratory school, to which she later sent her sons. On 13 July 1858 she wrote to Mrs Bellasis, 'My daily prayer is for the speedy success of Dr Newman's proposed school . . . Our own Colleges and Convents are so undeniably behind the times, in all things relating to education, it would distress me, to have my boys put under the care, of wellmeaning, but, untutored "ecclesiastical" ploughboys. A good manner is a sweet ingredient of religion!—in respect to which, we can only look to the aid of Converts, for the prosperity of the old Faith.'

cornice above the arches. I suppose it is too narrow for frescoes. What I should *like* would be to have arches and pillasters or half pillars flung round the windows not flat arches however, but in character with the three large ones.[1] I inclose the measurements. Perhaps you will [do what] you think it best to decorate it in paint, not by wood or plaister.

Ever Yrs John H. Newman

J. H. Pollen Esq.

P.S. Thank you for your account of yourselves. I hope you have no more anxiety now

TO ROBERT MACDERMOTT

The Oratory Birmingham ⌐August 21. 1858⌐

⌐Sent in substance⌐

My dear Dr Macdermott

I am sincerely concerned at what you say about Dr Cullen — but I trust that, as it is not the first time he has been attacked by this most serious malady, he may still manage to get free from it.[2]

⌐As to the announcement of the result of the Examinations, I feel that the Examiners have other duties, and that the University ought to be very much obliged to them for undertaking the office in addition to the ordinary calls on their time and thought.[3] And perhaps Dr O'Reilly will now feel more kindly disposed to *some* or *other* project of putting our Examinations on a more systematic basis than he was several months ago, when I sent him one project which I think he showed to you.[4] The Examination system is the key to the whole University Course, and the Examiners should be as formal Officers of the University as Professors.

This being premised, I will own to you that the silence of the Examiners as to the result of the late Licentiate Examination did and does perplex me — It was the most important act we have had — the termination of the Under-graduate Course — yet not a word was said to me what the award of the Examiners was. I sent several times to inquire in vain; at last I formally

---

[1] The copyist reproduced Newman's sketch here.

[2] MacDermott wrote that Cullen was suffering from almost total sleeplessness.

[3] MacDermott, who was one of the examiners for the Licentiate Examination, (see letter of 16 June to Walford) wrote on 20 Aug. to say that he had been shown by Dr O'Reilly an angry letter from Augustus Bethell. He made grave complaints against the University examiners for delay in announcing the results, for not giving them proper publicity, and for failing to distinguish sufficiently the merit of the candidates. The examiners had said of Bethell and Keane, 'Satisfecerunt egregiè,' and of de la Pasture and Molloy, 'Satisfecerunt.' MacDermott explained that the examiners had found difficulty in agreeing as to the merit of the candidates. See also letter of 23 Aug. to O'Reilly.

[4] See letter of 9 July to O'Reilly.

445

applied through the Secretary to the Senior Examiner.[1] Meanwhile the University Session was ended, and the candidates went down without even a testamur or certificate that they had *passed*, to which they had a right the very hour after it was settled, to say nothing of the question of honors.

To this minute, I doubt whether a formal paper has come to me from the Examiners,— though I may be wrong here.

If before the young men broke up, (and the examination was in *June*,) a paper had come out signed by the Examiners and been posted up, with nothing more than the word egregie *printed*, not written in at top, I think there would have been no complaint. One thing more I should have recommended, viz that the three names had been arranged in order of merit. On this I [[as Rector]] should have written to the successful candidates, and to their friends, to congratulate them — they would [[upon that]] have received the congratulations of their friends in Dublin — the list would have been published in the Freeman, Tablet etc. and, I think, all would have been well — even though they had already left the place; — but the delay both irritated, and raised expectations — and hence Bethell's letter.

Between ourselves, when it first came to the Secretary, he in confidence showed it me. I thought it *an extremely improper one*; so improper, that I had better not be known to have seen it.

I speak under correction, for you are on the spot; but I am not disposed to recommend you to do more than this:— to be silent during Vacation — and the Secretary's answer will be, if any second letter comes, that 'it is Vacation time,'— when Term begins, to post up a printed paper (if the Examiners think well,) in order of merit with the three names, and let it be put into the papers. Whether and what the Secretary is to write back then to Mr Bethell, is a matter of further consideration — but I don't think the *Examiners* ought to take notice of his letter.[1]

What you are so kind as to observe on the whole subject in your letter, which I must own Mr Bethell does not deserve, has been taken into account by me in what I have written above; but ⌜for distinctness I will add two things — 1. though there was a difference of opinion between the Examiners, I think the matter should have been decided before the end of three weeks, when the Session closed — that it was not, I attribute, not to the Examiners, for whose anxious exertions I feel most grateful, but to the inconvenience to which I have referred above, that the Examinership is hardly a substantive offer [[office]]. 2. It was, as you say, impossible to have *classes* of merit — but still I think the names might have stood in *order* of merit. [[e.g.]] Nobis Examinatoribus egregie sese commendaverunt, or whatever the words are,[1]

Augustus Keane
Augustus Bethell
Carolus de la Pasture, or however they would run.

[1] Scratton wrote to Newman on 22 July, "The Licentiate youths have certainly passed but beyond that fact I can get nothing from the Examiners.'

I thought it best to send you Dr Hayden's statement. I suppose you saw my letter with it

Yours most sincerely John H Newman

TO ANDREW ELLIS

[22 August 1858][1]

My dear Dr Ellis

Thank you for your kind proposal about your Article for the Atlantis, but I think from one thing you say you would like me to explain more fully the object which I have had in setting it up.[2]

I wished the Professors of Philosophy and Letters and of Science to have the same opportunity of showing their attainments which the Professors of Medicine have in the establishment of the Medical House. We have so few students, and of such comparatively low attainments in those faculties, that it is not fair on the Professors to have no other way of exhibiting their qualifications for their respective departments of literature or science. Thus the very idea of the work implies compositions, not addressed to the general reader, not popular, not like those of a Review or Magazine, but hard and dry articles, the result of study and labour, communicated for the sake of the learned or scientific at home or abroad, and adapted to advance the province of speculation, observation experiment or research to which they respectively belong.

From this it follows that, paradoxical as it may seem, I am obliged to decline the kindness of friends writing articles simply *for the Atlantis* — for they ought to be the result of previous research or discovery.

Coming then to your proposed article, I have no hesitation in saying that if you have it in view to throw light on some obscure subject or confute some received error I shall be very grateful to you for it. But much as I should value and like to insert any thing whatever of yours, I could not well take a paper from you of any other character, without risking the introduction henceforth of compositions which would change the tone and the object which it ought to preserve.

---

[1] Dated by Ellis's reply the following day.

[2] Ellis wrote on 18 Aug. that he hoped his article for the *Atlantis* would be 'a biographic sketch of some celebrated British physician or surgeon; consequently there will be nothing *scientific* in the article I intend to write.' Sullivan wrote confidentially to Newman on 20 Aug., '. . . somebody who in the end of August proposes to look for a subject over the wide range of British Medical Biography with the intention of finishing off an article before November could not contribute anything very new. Again of all subjects in the world biography requires new matter or new views to entitle it to come within our programme. . . .

If he has any scientific results not absolutely professional—the Atlantis would of course be a proper vehicle. . . .'

I was very sorry to hear from you of Dr Hayden's indisposition. I hear alarming news of Dr Cullen.

Thank you for the pains you have been at to get me information about the Demonstrators.[1]

MONDAY 23 AUGUST 1858   Ambrose went to Rednall for the week

TO EDMUND O'REILLY, S.J.

The Oratory, Birmingham Aug. 23, 1858.

My dear Father O'Reilly,

I am glad to hear that you thought my reasons sufficient for proceeding with the Letter to Disraeli. It requires being backed up with representations to the Government from the Irish members, and on this subject I have lately written to Mr Sullivan. It is with the deepest concern I hear bad accounts of Dr Cullen's health.

As to Mr Bethell's matter, I wrote last night in answer to a letter of Dr Macdermott's.[2] I hope you will not think it strong. I wrote it twice, knowing that words written are so different in effect from words spoken. And how I hope you will take care that it is understood that to Fr Kelly, who has so kindly taken part in the examination, and who could have nothing to do with anything but the drudgery of examination, as he is not a member of the University, we owe simple gratitude and nothing else. Nor is any one to blame, but the system, or rather want of system, which my late letter to you on the subject of examiners, to which you allude, was intended to remedy.[3]

On the other hand, I think Mr Bethell's letter so very unworthy of him, so extremely unbecoming, that I should not like to be known to have seen it.

Ever yours most sincerely in Xt   John H. Newman of the Oratory

[1] Newman's draft has no conclusion. Ellis replied on 23 Aug., willingly abandoning his plans for an article in the *Atlantis*.

[2] O'Reilly in his letter of 21 Aug., which crossed Newman's of that day to MacDermott, admitted the shortcomings of the examiners, 'You have seen Mr Bethell's letter to Mr Scratton. The latter says you seemed to wish it should be laid before the Examiners. . . . What is to be done? The heads of complaint are . . . 1. The testamur is insufficient in form and matter. It has no solemnity. . . . 2 There is no classification . . . 3 There was no notice put up . . . much less a publication . . . 4 . . . negligence etc on the part of the Examiners. . . .

Dr MacDermott will probably have written more fully to you. Bethell's letter is no doubt *strong* and annoyed Dr MacDermott considerably. Fr Kelly was also dissatisfied with it. However, I am disposed to make allowances.'

[3] This was the letter of 9 July to O'Reilly.

The Oratory Birmingham August 23. 1858

Private

My dear Mr Sullivan

I wish I had thought of sending to some one a hint about Mgr Talbot, the Pope's Cameriere, who was in Dublin yesterday. It would be very important that he should take back good impressions of the University. He used to be a friend of mine, though never very near me, but he has lately taken a somewhat strange position, so I do not think I could *personally* do much good with him. If any one courted him and the Cardinal on their return to Dublin, and showed them deference and attention, it would be a good thing for us — Else, we might suffer somewhat. Who is the best man to do this? — They should be taken to the Medical School, Church etc etc. The Secretary is officially the proper person — but I fear he is away.[1]

Your letter, which I inclose, is very good — but I fear the Members of Parliament would not like us to write something for them — however, you are the better judge here. I am writing to Dr Moriarty, as I wrote to Dr Leahy, to beg him to do his best that Dr Cullen's illness should not prejudice the movement.

Would not Mr Maguire be the best man to take up the matter? I do not know him, but he has shown great interest and already moved in it. Monsell and Bowyer, whom I know, would not be the men. By the bye, a letter has been lying here for Mr Hennessy some days, I did not forward it, thinking that it showed he was coming this way. It is just possible it is from some one who writes on University business, and so sends it through me. I inclose it.

Do you know Mr Maguire well enough to send him your draft of letter?

Yours most sincerely John H Newman of the Oratory

W K Sullivan Esqr

WEDNESDAY 25 AUGUST 1858   N. Stokes to dinner

FRIDAY 27 AUGUST   Frederic returned from Beaumont Lodge?   vid supr July 30

---

[1] Talbot was in Dublin at the time when Wiseman visited Ireland to preach at the opening of St Michael's church at Ballinasloe. Wiseman landed at Kingstown on 23 Aug. and the visit became a triumphal progress. For his reception at the University see letter of 31 Aug. to Sullivan, and for his tour generally, *H.S.* III, pp. 255–6 and W. Ward, *The Life and Times of Cardinal Wiseman*, 2nd ed., London 1897, II, pp. 289–320.

27 AUGUST 1858

TO PATRICK LEAHY, ARCHBISHOP OF CASHEL

August 27/58

My dear Lord

I will have a copy made and sent to your Grace of the letter which the Rector and Professors lately sent to Mr Disraeli in respect of the University.[1] The step did not originate with myself, though I considered I saw good reason to give my assent and assistance to it. The Archbishop of Dublin asked and received explanations about it. As the three Archbishops did not mention to me[2] their own application to Disraeli, I considered that they did not wish to be committed to any such similar proceeding as in imitation of their Graces we might think it desirable to take ourselves. You will find we did not speak as if we had the ultimate decision of the question, and I took care to request Mr Maguire and Mr Aubrey de Vere who took charge of our Letter to make this point clear to Mr Disraeli and to remind him that the decision lay with the Bishops

J H N

SATURDAY 28 AUGUST 1858   Ambrose returned from Rednall

TO ARCHBISHOP CULLEN

The Oratory Birmingham August 31. 1858

My dear Lord,

I have just received your letter of the 28th, and write by this post to Dublin to the Secretary to request him to give you the information which your Grace requires.[3] As I have before now anxiously inquired into both of the points you mention, I cannot doubt the answer you will receive will be satisfactory to you.[4]

[1] Leahy wrote on 25 Aug., 'It was but the other day I learned that the Authorities and Professors of the University had in their own behalf taken some steps in the affair of the Charter. That is all right and good. To secure unity in the views and movements of us all, would it not be well for us Bishops to know what you have said and done? Have you any objection to favour me with a copy of such documents as you have drawn up on the subject of the Charter?'

[2] In the draft Newman added after this word and then erased 'the Rector.'

[3] Cullen wrote in his own hand on 25 Aug., a letter now in the Dublin diocesan archives, to ask for some receipt to show that in 1854 he had paid £1350 for the purchase of the Cecilia Street Medical School. He thought the deed had been 'drawn up in favour of some person in London to conceal' the identity of the purchasers. He also asked for a receipt for £200 which he had paid into the Cullen and Newman Account on 28 Sept. 1855, and which included a donation of £50 from Lady Fitzsimon to the University church. Cf. letters of 16 Nov. 1856 to Murray and St John. Cullen in his letter of 25 Aug. said he wanted 'a proof that the money was properly applied.'

[4] Scratton wrote on 2 Sept. to Cullen in a letter also preserved in the Dublin diocesan

450

It was with great pleasure that I heard from Ireland an account of the improvement of your general health.

I am glad to hear that the Bishops are to have a meeting on the affairs of the University, the success of which is always in my thoughts and my prayers.[1]

I am, My dear Lord, begging your Grace's blessing Your faithful Servt in Xt

John H Newman of the Oratory

The Most Revd Dr Cullen Archbp of Dublin &c &c.

TO AUGUSTUS HENRY KEANE

Aug 31/58

My dear Mr Keane

You have certainly a claim to be considered in the new arrangement of St Patrick's House — but in a matter of this kind I should act with the Dean, and, though I doubt not Dr Flannery will resign, he has not yet signified it to me.

archives, '1. The School of Medicine Cecilia Street is now vested in the joint names of Your Grace and Dr Newman by a Deed which Mr Maxwell has in his possession. I am writing to Mr Maxwell to beg he will immediately give Your Grace an opportunity of perusing the Document, and further take your instructions as to the transferring of the Property to the Trustees [of the University, the Irish Archbishops].

2. With regard to the £200 . . . the whole sum appears in the General Balance Sheet of the University Accounts ending December 1, 1855. In a subsequent Account audited by Messrs Errington and Js. O'Ferrall (8 Oct. 1857) Dr Newman acknowledges the receipt from the above Fund of £50 as the bequest of Lady Fitzsimon.'

[1] This same day, 31 Aug., Cullen wrote to Cardinal Barnabò at Propaganda about this meeting of the bishops, '. . . . The University will fall to the ground if we don't give a hand to sustain it. The rector has not been in Ireland at all this year, and things cannot go on without someone in charge. Furthermore Father Newman has organized things in such a costly manner that they cannot be supported from the collections, and while the students are few, he has nominated very many professors who have nothing to do. Moreover there are complaints regarding discipline. Father Newman kept a kind of boarding school for a dozen young men in his house, and some of these went to dances and kept horses for hunting. Father Newman justifies this system by saying that there should be more liberty at university than in the secondary schools, but the people reply that collections are not necessary to educate young men in dancing and hunting. I spoke repeatedly about these matters, but it seems that Father Newman so greatly admired the university of Oxford, that he could not bring himself thus to condemn practices which are in force there. But he should have remembered that in Oxford they have to do with a great institution richly endowed, while in our case we are trying to set up a university with the contributions of the poor. However that maybe, things are now in such a state that they will result in collapse if some remedy is not applied.

For this purpose it seems absolutely necessary to have a meeting of the bishops, but I am not sure that things will go well in it. Some bishops were never much in favour of the university, and will not now take any trouble over maintaining it; and as for Archbishop MacHale, I am persuaded that he will seek to increase the difficulties. He has lately shown himself in bitter temper . . . Being in such a mood, it is clear that he will avail himself of the mistakes of Father Newman to justify the opposition which he has given to the university, and to attack the Archbishop of Dublin, who took a principal part in inviting Father Newman to govern this institution.' S.R.C., Irlanda, 1857–60, ff. 762–3, translated and quoted by J. H. Whyte in D R, (Spring 1960), 'Newman in Dublin,' p. 36. See also his comments on Cullen's letter, pp. 38–9.

I do not consider it would be advisable in any case to admit you to the full office of House Tutor except gradually.[1]

I take this opportunity of congratulating you on your honours

Very truly Yours J H N

TO JOHN HUNGERFORD POLLEN

The Oratory Birmingham August 31. 1858

My dear Pollen,

I inclose a cheque for £200. Can you form any guess, *when* either of the Altars will be sent down

Ever Yours John H Newman

J H Pollen Esq

TO WILLIAM KIRBY SULLIVAN

The Oy Bm Augst 31.1858

Private

My dear Mr Sullivan

Do you in Ireland know more than I know here, of the meaning of the great demonstration at Ballinasloe? The Cardinal used to be a great friend of the University — I can't tell if he is now; but if the Professors have an opportunity, a very little will kindle the latent fire — and he might be got to conciliate the Archbishop of Tuam.[2] I am glad to hear that the Secretary is back, and that the Professors mean to do what they can.[3]

The more you can do with Mr Maguire the better.[4] Do you suppose the

[1] Keane, who had just obtained his Licentiate, applied on 28 Aug. to be made tutor in St Patrick's House. Thomas Arnold, who had been acting as tutor, was unwilling to relinquish the post. Newman, while leaving the final decision to the new Dean, suggested that Arnold and Keane should share equally the work and the emolument.

[2] Sullivan replied on 17 Sept, about the enthusiastic reception of Wiseman, that 'the demonstration at Ballinasloe was a mere accident and I think without any plan in the first instance though it has assumed a considerable degree of importance from the results which have grown out of it.' John MacHale of Tuam was the celebrant at the opening of the Ballinasloe church, and made an eloquent speech at the banquet which followed.

[3] On 7 Sept. Wiseman visited the Catholic University at Scratton's invitation, and was accompanied by the Lord Mayor. Wiseman was received by Fr O'Reilly, Dr Quinn, O'Curry, Ornsby, MacDermott, MacSwiney and Scratton, all in academic gowns, and was given lunch in the library. 'He was shown through the lecture halls, library, museum, etc., and highly admired their several arrangements. He next proceeded to visit the beautiful interior of the University Church, and appeared much struck with the excellent taste displayed in the splendid decorations. . . . Before taking his leave he made several inquiries concerning the University, and expressed himself highly gratified at the progress which it had made.' *The Sermons, Lectures and Speeches delivered by his Eminence Cardinal Wiseman, Archbishop of Westminster, during his tour in Ireland in August and September* 1858 . . ., Dublin 1859, p. 225.

[4] Bowyer wrote to Newman on 24 Aug., 'I wish I had known what was going on. For Monsell and De Vere are names likely to indispose the Government as they are *incurable* Palmerstonians . . .

Bishops of Connaught have any definite plan, short of the University against the Queen's Colleges? In what I saw of their Synodal Address, they avoided mention of it. If they, now allied with Cardinal Wiseman, kept aloft [aloof] from the University, we should not, I suppose, induce the Irish M.P.'s to take our part with Government.[1]

I want some kind of a report, if you please, of the Science Faculty from 1856–1857 I should print any fact it contained in the Appendix to the Rector's Report for that Session, which a letter from Dr Leahy has just now put me on sending in.

Do think about the ways and means of the Atlantis. I find the last Number (taking out what stands over for Number 3) cost £150! I am attempting some safeguard to Mr Scott's article. Mr Morris will have to write his again. Would it be well to have more than one article from an extern? I wish I could continue the Benedictine article — I have been at it for this six weeks — but I have no time, and get on so slowly that I cannot prophesy whether I shall be ready for next Number. I am glad you are to finish yours on Physical Geography etc. Your news of the progress of the Atlantis abroad, translations etc is very encouraging.

As to Mr Curry's Lectures,[2] I should like to know what the *cost* of printing will be; on this will depend the number of copies. Of course I wish it to have the widest possible circulation.

Most sincerely Yours John H Newman of the Oratory

W K Sullivan Esqr

P.S. Have you any thought who would be a good Dean for St Patrick's house, instead of Dr Flannery?

WEDNESDAY 1 SEPTEMBER 1858   Mrs Wootten ill   Henry went to Miss Farrant

FRIDAY 3 SEPTEMBER   Mrs Wm Froude and her daughter in the evening   Henry returned

You may depend upon it that D'Israeli will pay very little attention to their representations —though the name of Maguire will have weight.'
   [1] Sullivan replied, 'I do not think the Connacht Bishops have any definite plans.' MacHale and the bishops of the province of Tuam had just met in synod and issued an address on 16 Aug. denouncing 'mixed'education and the Queen's Colleges in strong terms, but without mentioning the Catholic University. The *Weekly Register*, (28 Aug. 1858), p. 5. The occasion of the protest was the proposal of a Royal Commission to set up a new network of 'mixed' schools in Ireland.
   [2] *Lectures on the Manuscript Materials of Ancient Irish History*, Dublin 1861.

answered Sept 3 [1858][1]

that she would be surprised if she knew how small my annual income was, far less, I would venture to say than hers, and with not fewer claims upon it. Indeed I never could get thro any one year, except by such casual additions to it, as I have no reason to expect will be made to it, as years go on.

Under these circumstances, of course it is a difficulty to me to know whether to answer or not — and, if it was painful to her to receive no reply, she ought to see that it was painful to me to have to make an explanation so personal as this was

J H N.

SATURDAY 4 SEPTEMBER 1858 Sir John Acton and Döllinger called in evening
SUNDAY 5 SEPTEMBER First High Mass at high altar. Sir J. A. and Döllinger in evening

TO W. H. SCOTT

The Oratory Birmingham Septr 5. 1858
My dear Scott,

There are two books, one of which you have read, I think, but both of which you ought to see, before your article appears — one is Tholucx on the difficulties in St Luke, referred to by Allioli in his new translation of the Scriptures into French — the other is San Clemente's work, referred to by Fr Perrone — The latter work, if not both, I ought to see myself — can you tell me where to find it?[2]

Thank you for your letter of yesterday. I fear I have driven you up into a corner about 6 Harcourt Street, but time is so getting on that I am frightened — and, if I don't hear from you soon, I shall write to Scratton or to some one else to suggest to me means of getting out of my difficulty. Meantime, I certainly should avail myself of giving your name, as you let me, as *possibly* going on as Tutor — for I am sure any one would be glad of it.[3]

I don't see why you might not come here without going to Beaumont

[1] Mrs Bellamy wrote a begging letter from 34 Portland Square, Plymouth, on 23 July and again on 1 Sept. She was a convert and a widow with children. Although she had a sufficient income to support herself and them, she found herself with debts of £100.

[2] Frederick August Tholuck (1799–1877), German Protestant theologian. Newman probably refers to his reply to Strauss's Life of Christ, *Glaubwürdigkeit der evangelischen Geschichte*, published in 1837. Joseph Franz Allioli (1793–1873), a German Catholic exegete, translated the Bible, Landshut 1838. In 1853–4, a French translation from the German, was published at Paris, in ten volumes. Henry Sanclemente, Abbot General of the Camaldolese, wrote on the chronology of the life of Christ, *De Vulgaris Aerae Emendatione*, Rome 1793. Scott replied, 'Sanclemente I have never been able to get (not even in Trin. Coll. Dublin)'.

[3] Scott, who had thought of taking charge of Newman's house, agreed to this suggestion.

Lodge, and talk over the whole matter. You know how pleased we should be to have you, but on both sides for the good of both the matter must be carefully examined and understood.[1]

As to the plan of a school, it progresses, but slowly — we should not begin till we had a good number of boys secured to us

Ever Yours affly John H Newman of the Oratory

W H Scott Esqr

P.S. Of course I shall remember your wish to be borne in mind at Mass etc.

TO JOHN WALLIS

The Oratory Birmingham Septr 5. 1858

Private

My dear Wallis,

I have long been wishing to show my real and grateful interest in the Tablet, to the conductors of which, since I was a Catholic, I have owed at various times much in the way of encouragement and help. But I have done nothing, at a time, when, if ever, I might show it, first from the fact of my poverty, or rather, straitened circumstances, and secondly because I did not wish to do any thing which would look unkind to my old friend Wilberforce. No one could be more sorry than I was that he engaged in Newspaper literature, but he is the judge, not I, and, since it is his choice, of course I should be most sorry to do any thing which would seem in the eyes *of the public* to reflect upon his judgment.[2]

Under these circumstances I wish you to be so good as to keep what I am going to say secret — but, if I may ask this favour, I will also ask you the favour of your putting down my name for £10 in Tablet shares, (I don't mean *my own name*, but some initials say A B or the like to represent me) with the understanding that you will let me send you the money at my own convenience, which I fear will not be very soon.[3]

Why do you not sometimes come this way in your passage to and fro?

Yours most sincerely John H Newman of the Oratory

J E Wallis Esqr

[1] Scott wrote on 3 Sept. of his wish to offer himself to the Birmingham Oratory as a novice. He thought this might make it unnecessary for him to make a retreat at Beaumont Lodge, which he had been urged to do.
[2] Henry Wilberforce was proprietor and editor of the *Catholic Standard*, (which became the *Weekly Register*), from 1854 to 1863. Wallis was about to transfer the *Tablet* back to London from Dublin.
[3] Wallis replied gratefully on 7 Sept., and considered there was room both for Wilberforce's paper and his own. Wallis had wanted to further Newman's work at the University, 'But I found the best I could do was to do as little harm as possible.'
On 8 Sept. Ornsby wrote that Wallis was about to relinquish the proprietorship of the *Tablet*, but would remain its editor.

MONDAY 6 SEPTEMBER 1858 Godwin went to his home. Mrs Wootten better. Mr Slatter to dinner[1] Sir Robert Throckmorton called. Ignatius went to Beaumont Lodge

TUESDAY 7 SEPTEMBER 1858 Nicholas went to Sir J Acton's. Manning came

TO J. B. MORRIS

Rednall Septr 7. 1858

My dear Morris

I have read your Paper with great interest and consider it to be able, and (as far as I can judge of it) good — at the same time the feelings about it which I expressed in my former letter are confirmed.[2] And perhaps I ought to have set before you with greater minuteness what the sort of composition is which is suitable for the Atlantis;

The Atlantis does not admit of theology, as such — at least not of revealed — Thus the idea of the supernatural, as such, does not come into its field of view.[3] The Holy Trinity, e.g. could not be spoken of, except as the object of a conception which in *fact* is generally entertained and worshipped by a body *historically* called the Catholic Church. The subjects of the work are either literary or scientific — and theology will accidentally find its way into its pages, as history, as philosophy — and in similar ways. I do not conceive a single supernatural fact, or supernatural principle can be *assumed* as true by any writer *for the purposes of argument or proof.*

This remark has a direct bearing upon the important portion of your article contained in pp. 37–70 — which is theological. It is also controversial, as speaking against Protestants and Infidels — and that, without proof in each particular case, of the propositions you set down — and again, as containing various other unproved propositions, e.g. 'Ex supremo dominio potest Deus torquere etc.'

This, I conceive, to be the great difficulty in the availableness of your dissertation for our purpose and as it stands.

The main defect of the article as a *Composition* is that it is on the 'drift and date' etc — for drift and date are absolutely distinct subjects, having (as I think) no direct connexion with each other.[4]

As soon as I return to Birmingham I will send it back to you — not knowing whether you will consent to trouble yourself with the necessary recasting.[5]

[1] This was perhaps one of the sons of William Slatter of Iffley. The eldest son John, who went to Lincoln College in 1835, was Perpetual Curate of Sandford-on-Tyames, 1852–61, the second son William, was an Exhibitioner at Lincoln College 1843–9.
[2] See letter of 2 Aug. 1858 to Morris.
[3] Morris, who made several disapproving annotations on this letter wrote here, 'the deuce!'
[4] Morris annotated, 'Pity you did not say so at first.'
[5] Morris annotated, 'or rather total absorption of it.'

I consider 1. *one* and but one proposition should be *stated* (e.g. the date is so and so) and then 2. *proved.*

Thank you very much for the trouble you have already taken and believe me

Ever Yrs affly in Xt   John H Newman

TO ROBERT ORNSBY

The Oy Bm ⌐Sept 7. 1858⌐

My dear Ornsby

⌐Since last July year the three Archbishops have [[ever]] negociated with me by themselves. And they three sent in their proposals to Disraeli.[1]

I think we are but following their lead in writing to three only, and I think you will not do good by writing to Dr Machale. At the same time, if Dr Cullen *told* you to do so, I suppose you must. But if so, I think he will take your letter as worded, almost as an insult. However, I don't know him, and cannot speak — only I know on a former occasion, he flared up on my putting Dr Cullen's and my own names together, and your letter contains both; 'in pursuance of *his* suggestion and *our Rector's*, to *invite* your *Grace!*' etc If you can, you had better leave him alone — Don't rouse a sleeping lion.⌐ [2]

Ever Yrs affly J H N

R. Ornsby Esqr

WEDNESDAY 8 SEPTEMBER 1858   Manning went.   I went to Rednall till Saturday

TO ROBERT ORNSBY

Rednall Septr 9. 1858

My dear Ornsby

The matter cannot be better than in your and Sullivan's hands.[3]

Are you sure that Dr *Leahy* wants a draft? If you said that Dr Dixon suggested one, it would explain the matter. But I see you *have* done so over leaf. I cannot help hoping that the letter of the three Archbishops *must* tell

Ever Yrs affly John H Newman

R. Ornsby Esqr

[1] Ornsby had written to Dixon of Armagh and Leahy of Cashel, asking them to approach the Irish Catholic Members of the House of Commons on the question of the charter. He wondered whether he ought to write to MacHale, whose name Cullen had also mentioned.
[2] See note to letter of 3 May 1856 to Cullen. Ornsby decided not to write to MacHale.
[3] i.e. the business of the charter. Dixon suggested that Ornsby should draw up and get Leahy's approval of a circular which the Archbishops might send to Members of Parliament.

FRIDAY 10 SEPTEMBER 1858   Nicholas returned
SATURDAY 11 SEPTEMBER   returned from Rednall — found Seager at the Ory. [Oratory]
MONDAY 13 SEPTEMBER   Seager went?

TO ANDREW ELLIS

The Oratory, Birmingham Septr 13. 1858

My dear Dr Ellis,[1]

Before I decide on the question which the Medical Faculty has put before me, I should like to have your judgment, in the absence of Dr Hayden, whether I take a right view of the various facts, as to the position of Demonstrators in other schools, which have been supplied to me.

On these facts it is natural I should lay great stress in making up my mind; for the usages and change of usages in other bodies of a like character are my best guide in a question of expedience.

1. In Trinity College the Demonstrators have been appointed and removed solely by the Professor of Anatomy, who has been responsible for the performance of their duties, as if those duties were his; that is, he has provided and employed the Demonstrators. In the ensuing Session, however, it is anticipated that they will be made independent of him, that is, he is not to provide or appoint them.

2. In the Queen's Colleges they have been paid by private arrangement with the Professor; that is, he employs them; which implies that he provides them, or in other words, appoints and dismisses them (as is expressly stated in the case of Cork and Belfast,) — subject of course to the supreme control of the College itself.

3. The recent Commission recommends that they should be placed in closer connexion with their College, and assigns them £100 a year. That is, it wishes to transfer them from the pay and employment of the Professor to the service of the College. At the same time it would place their appointment and removal in fact in the hands of the Professor, subject of course to the supreme control of the College.

4. In the Carmichael School they are (apparently) paid by the Proprietors; and appointed by them also, i.e. by their representatives, such Lecturers as are share-holders.

5 In the Original School the case is the same, though the salary goes through the Professor (if Mr O'Doherty belongs to this school.)

6 In Dr Stevens's they are appointed by the Professor; nothing is said about control; though, since there is a government grant, I suppose it exists.

7. In the Royal College of Surgeons, the Demonstrators used to be appointed and removed by the Professors of Anatomy; but since 1851 by the

---

[1] A duplicate of this was sent to MacDermott.

Board, though they are still under the care and governance of those Professors.

8. In the Queen's College Birmingham, they have been lately raised to the status of Professors of Practical Anatomy; that is, they have been taken from the service of the Chair of Anatomy, and brought into as close and as recognised a connexion with the College as the other Professors.

Am I right in gathering from these instances the following?

1. There is no instance of the Medical Faculty or Board having any relations with the Demonstrators except that of the Royal College of Surgeons.

2. They have been universally or almost so, under the jurisdiction of the Professor of Anatomy, as contrasted with the Medical Faculty or Board.

3 There is a concurrent movement, in such bodies as are the best able to act freely and command the greatest consideration, to raise their position, and more or less to transfer them from the service of the Professor of Anatomy to that of the whole body to which they belong.[1]

I am, My dear Dr Ellis, Most sincerely Yours, John H Newman

Andrew Ellis Esqr M D

P.S.   I have sent a duplicate of this to Dr Macdermott

TUESDAY 14 SEPTEMBER 1858   Sir R Throckmorton and his son called.

WEDNESDAY 15 SEPTEMBER   Ignatius returned from Beaumont Lodge.   Dr Wayte and Mr Okely came *for a week*.

TO ROBERT ORNSBY

The Oy Bm ⌈Septr 15/58⌉

My dear Ornsby,

I ought before now to have returned your satisfactory inclosure,[2] and to have thanked you for your news. I am going to write a letter to George Denison for Mr Henley his Father in Law in whose department the Charter granting is.[3] We shall not succeed without agitating, but with it we have a very fair prospect. I wish I had not so unmercifully snubbed Lord Malmesbury when he was in Lecture with me — or I could have written to him. I have not seen him this thirty years.[4]

---

[1] Ellis replied on 15 Sept. accepting Newman's first and second conclusion, but not his third. MacDermott accepted Newman's letter as substantially correct. Both were satisfied with Newman's eventual decision in his letters of 24 Sept.

[2] This was Leahy's letter of 7 Sept., agreeing to help in the approach to Members of Parliament about the charter.

[3] Letter of 2 Nov. See also letter of 30 July to Monsell.

[4] James Howard Harris, third Earl of Malmesbury, who had been at Oriel College under Newman, was now Foreign Secretary. Years later in *Memoirs of an Ex-Minister. An Auto-*

⌐I think Dr Leahy's last paragraph contains somewhat of a hint that we had better not act again without the Archbishops. He said *something* of the kind to me, and I defended myself manfully for what I had done, on the ground that the three Archbishops had originally written to Disraeli without saying a word to me.¹ ¹ So his sentence to which you refer is a promise on his part as well as a wish as to ourselves.

Ever Yours affly John H Newman

R Ornsby Esqr

P.S. Your letter of yesterday has just come with Sullivan's which I return. I think he wrote to me about the Burses. I gladly will do any thing. What seems to me the most natural is to ask the Bishops when they meet to give them away by concursus.² I am very sorry about Mrs Stewart's accident.³

I think you had better get back the Greek Testament and offer it to Burns.⁴

TO J. R. BLOXAM

The Oy Birmingham Septr 18. 1858

My dear Bloxam

I am much obliged to you for the thoughtfulness of your letter just received — its sad announcement grieves me very much.⁵ If you have an opportunity, pray be so good as to let his brother and Stevens know how much I sympathise with them.⁶ I suppose, however, they were quite prepared for the event — as I have heard so much of his slow sinking — and, if he was in that hopeless state which I have heard of for some time past, I do not know how they could wish to keep him longer with them. At the same time such

biography, London 1884, i, 18, he described Newman as a bullied don. This drew a public protest from Frederick Rogers, Lord Blachford, that 'Mr Newman's conduct to the undergraduates and theirs to him was absolutely the reverse of what Lord Malmesbury describes.' Cf. *Trevor*, ii, pp. 620-1.

¹ The last paragraph of Leahy's letter of 7 Sept. to Ornsby and Sullivan ran: 'The movement on the part of the University Authorities and Professors, the Members of Parliament, and the Bishops, should be simultaneous. Being simultaneous, it would be all the more effectual.' Newman's letter to Leahy was that of 27 Aug.

² The nomination to burses in Medicine and Science lay with the Irish Bishops. Ornsby wanted the annual grant raised from £80 to £100. A fragment of a letter of 19 Sept. from Newman to Ornsby is printed in *Campaign*, p. xxxviii, 'I am glad you have moved *in re bursaria*. I have put it into my report.'

³ She and her children were in a car that overturned.

⁴ Duffy had been procrastinating over Ornsby's edition of the Greek Testament. Duffy eventually published it in 1860.

⁵ i.e. that of the death of Charles Marriott on 15 Sept. 1858. He never recovered from a severe stroke of paralysis on 30 June 1855, when he was found lying on the floor, in his rooms at Oriel College.

⁶ The last three years of Charles Marriott's life were spent at Bradfield, where his brother, John, was curate. The Rector, Thomas Stevens, was the founder and first Warden of Bradfield College, 1847–81. Stevens, an Oriel man like the Marriotts, sent to Bloxam on 22 Sept., his and John Marriott's '*cordial* thanks' for Newman's sympathy.

departures are very trying when they come, however we may be prepared for them, and however little they really add to the substantial bereavement.

I shall not forget him in my Mass tomorrow

Ever Yours affly John H Newman

The Revd Dr Bloxam

TUESDAY 21 SEPTEMBER 1858   Dr Wayte and Mr Okely went.

TO J. M. CAPES

The Oratory Birmingham Septr 22. 1858

My dear Capes

I am very glad to hear from Fr Bowles that you have let your house and are going abroad. Sincerely do I trust that your health will gain that advantage from it which you require and deserve. You know how highly I think of your labours, so long and so unrequited.

I am constantly thinking of you, since your last letter[1] — three times a day, I think I may say, your name is in my mouth. But I cannot stomach such formal cartels of defiance, as printed papers of the nature you sent me, which to me are as strange as the subjects mentioned in them are to the composers of them.

Ever Yours affectly in Xt   John H Newman of the Oratory

J M Capes Esqr

TO THOMAS SCRATTON

Oy Bm Sept 22/58

My dear S

Will you kindly send me the *copy* from which the Proof of the Prospectus, which you have sent, is printed.[2] I have not it here and this Proof puzzles me.

Dr Flannery has given me no notice he is leaving St Patrick's. Can you find out somehow for me?[3]

I consider that you take possession of Number 6 on November 3 —

[1] See letter of 10 Aug. to Capes, and also that of 27 Sept.
[2] The Prospectus of the University was being reprinted.
[3] Flannery had been consecrated as Coadjutor Bishop of Killaloe on 5 Sept. Scratton replied on 23 Sept., 'The Porter tells me that Dr Flannery in taking leave of the servants said to them "I have now nothing more to do with the house" "It is entirely in Dr Newman's hands." Will this suffice to act upon? I think it ought, but otherwise what can be done except to write to Dr Flannery and ask him the question?'
Flannery wrote to Newman on 30 Sept., 'I fear I have delayed too long in sending in my formal resignation of the Deanery of St Patrick's Collegiate House.
Now, however, I beg to do so; and at the same time I wish to offer to you the expression of my grateful thanks for your great kindness to me during the time that I discharged (however imperfectly) the duties of that office.'

not that you will not (I trust) receive it from me before that, but I say it, since you may like to know[1]

Ever Yrs affly J H Newman

Thos Scratton Esqr

THURSDAY 23 SEPTEMBER 1858 Mr Colthurst came, for several days
FRIDAY 24 SEPTEMBER William went away for three weeks, or yesterday?

TO ANDREW ELLIS

Sept 24. 1858

My dear Dr Ellis

I inclose a copy of a letter I have sent to the Dean of the Faculty of Medicine. I am truly sorry to hear of your late indisposition &c &c

J H N

TO ROBERT MACDERMOTT

⌐Septr 24. 1872[2]

My dear Dean of Medicine

It has taken a long time to answer your letter of July 21, written to me in the name of your Faculty on the subject of the position of the Demonstrators in it, but I cannot accuse myself of having unnecessarily delayed it.[3]

Your question was contained in the following sentences. 'The Faculty most earnestly disclaims the idea that etc' . . . . down to 'upon this point.'[4]

In answer to this question I observe that it seems to me a duty incumbent on the Rector to carry out two principles. 1. to place the Demonstrators under the ordinary care and direction of the Anatomical department. 2. to see that that department, as every other, does its duty.

I mean then to observe the following Rule,— till there is reason to supersede it.

The Rector will have the confirmation of the appointment of Demonstrators, as made by the Professors of Anatomy, in Council, and the times of their demonstrating, not later than a month after their names and hours are given in to him. He will in the interval communicate on the subject with the Faculty, being open also to representations from the Faculty about their qualifications and conduct at other times.

I am J H N[1]

---

[1] Scratton was to take over the running of Newman's House, St Mary's, 6 Harcourt Street, and Anderdon was to be its Dean. In the summer Newman had consulted Renouf as to the suitability of Dr Logan for the latter post.
[2] This error for 1858 shows date at which Newman copied out his draft.
[3] See Newman's letters to MacDermott from 26 July onwards.
[4] 'The Faculty most earnestly disclaims the idea that it desires anything like constant interference in the government of the anatomical department, but it considers that in all important matters, such as appointments, hours of demonstrations qualifications etc, their opinion should be taken, and the proposed changes communicated. . . . I would feel glad to have your decision upon this point.'

Sept 24. 1858

My dear Mr Tyrrell

In answer to your letter of August 5, I have to express my hope that the following regulation which I am today sending to the Dean of Medicine will be satisfactory to you.

I have always had the best of reports concerning your ability and diligence in the Anatomy School — and the report has come to me of course from the Professors of Anatomy

'The Rector will have etc' (from letter of this date to Dr Macdermott, Dean of Medicine)

I am &c J H N

SATURDAY 25 SEPTEMBER 1858   Godwin returned from his home
SUNDAY 26 SEPTEMBER   Lisle Ryder came

TO J. M. CAPES

The Oy. Bm Septr 27. 1858

My dear Capes

I am conscious of the most affectionate interest in you and your thoughts, and of nothing else; but really, if you saw your packet of August 7 with my eyes, you would not wonder that I wrote with very little display of feeling.[1] To give me the first news through a printed paper, was, (putting a grave matter on a merely *personal* ground,) pretty nearly what it would have been to send me a letter by means of the Times or Tablet: — it was as surprising as it would have been to you, if I had sent you a printed answer to your letter. When you had got so far as to print, it was a sad thing to reflect that leaden types have no feeling, and to express feeling would have been impertinent. But there is a higher ground — and, if it was a serious act to print categorical sentences of disbelief, (for printing is necessarily a kind of publishing,) still more startling was it to find that you headed your paper (simply unnecessarily, as far as I can make out) 'A *Catholic* has serious difficulties etc.' Then again, I think there was not a single syllable in your letter asking for prayers — you seemed to challenge dry argument.

Let me add that I have so expressed myself in my *last* letter, that you have misunderstood me. I do not dream that your clear mind does not

[1] Capes wrote on 23 Sept., 'I was excessively glad to get your note this morning, for I confess I was not a little pained and disappointed both at the matter and the tone of your reply to the letter I wrote some little time ago. [See letter of 10 Aug. to Capes.] And even now your implying that I know nothing about the subject on which I consulted you in confidence, shows how little you realise what the subject has been to me.'

understand the difficulties of the case perfectly well. I suppose it must be my word 'strange', that has been the mistake — what I meant by the word was 'incomprehensible —' but I thought it would be rude to use it — I wished to express, that your proceedings were as incomprehensible to *me* as any of the doctrines, animadverted on in your printed paper, were to *you*.

As to the question of certainty, to which you refer, it is both a very interesting one, and, as I think, a difficult one.[1] As far as I can make out, our conclusion in reason (about the truth etc) is not demonstrative, but goes so far towards absolute proof, that it is our duty by an act of the will to believe it *as* firmly as if it were;— somewhat in the same way, that (as *I* should say) we (personally) have no *demonstration* that *we* (personally) shall *die* — but a man would be a fool who did not hold it certain.

I have not said a word about any thing but the *tone* of my first letter (not the *controversial* part) because the *tone* has hurt you, for which I am very sorry.

Ever Yours affly John H Newman

TO JAMES HOPE-SCOTT

The Oratory Birmingham September 27. 1858

My dear Hope Scott

I rejoice at the news which Sir John Acton conveys to me from you — and beg to offer my congratulations to Mrs Hope Scott also — and to Mary Monica, who I hope is not put out that she cannot, in addition to her own pretty names, have Margaret Anne besides.[2]

You have heard from Dollinger all the news here. We are laying out a good deal of money on our Church, and must live on bread and cheese in consequence. Pollen is rearing some wonderful altars. As to Ireland, the

---

[1] Capes's letter continued, 'It was only the other day that I turned up a letter of your own to me which first set me thinking afresh on the difficulties which lie at the root of the whole question of an infallible Church, and to which I have been vainly seeking an answer *ever since*. [See letter of 27 Jan. 1850 to Capes.] It was in reference to a passage in my "Four Years' Experience etc," in which I had implied that religious belief is only a matter of *probability*. I assure you that up to that time it had never occurred to me that the Catholic idea of "certainty" meant anything more than distinctness, clearness and completeness of statement, as contrasted with the variations and vagueness of Protestantism, the whole question *in its basis* being still a question of mere historical criticism.' See also Newman's letter of 1 Oct. 1858.

[2] Acton and Döllinger were the guests of Hope-Scott at Abbotsford. In his letter of 25 Sept., arranging to bring Döllinger to visit Newman, Acton announced the birth of Margaret Anne, Hope-Scott's second daughter, who died on 3 Dec. 1858.

Bishops are to meet next month and take the University seriously in hand. We have some chance of a charter from the Derby ministry. You can't help us with any of them, I suppose? A charter would be my own εὐθανασία.[1]

Badeley is, I suppose, on the continent.

Ever Yours affectly John H Newman of the Oratory

J R Hope Scott Esqr

TO JOHN HUNGERFORD POLLEN

The Oy Bm Sept 27/58

My dear Pollen,

Accept my hearty congratulations for yourself and Mrs Pollen on your announcement.[2] I had not heard about Mrs Hope Scott; — since you wrote. I was made anxious by hearing that she had the whooping cough.

Miss Farrant, who is here, wishes, in fulfilment of her sister's wish, to give us an Altar of the Sacred Heart. She has great notions of red and white marbles, pillars etc etc. I don't know to what extent, and at the moment she is poor. She wants to put a sum into your hands to make the most of — This is what I hear — but I don't see that any thing can be done without your seeing her. Are you coming down with the Altars? I don't know how long she stops — but we lost £200, with the same object, from her some years ago by (unavoidable) delay — not that she has any such sum in her hands now for it.

Fr William was fairly knocked up at last — and I sent him away for three weeks, though our rule is that all vacations are over by September 29. I am thankful to say we have good account of Stanislas.

Ever yours John H Newman of the Oratory

J. H. Pollen Esq.

P.S. I have inquired and cannot afford the price of your novels. If you have them and could lend them, you might be moved to send them to Burns's to be sent down here in a parcel which is coming.[3]

[1] 'Happy death.'
[2] The birth on 21 Sept. of Pollen's eldest son, John Hungerford Pollen, who became a well-known Jesuit and died in 1925.
[3] See letter of 8 Oct. to Pollen.

TO WILLIAM KIRBY SULLIVAN

The Oratory Bm Sept 27. 1858

My dear Mr Sullivan,

I think your move was very happy at the banquet — and your speech was admirable. It touched me very much that you should so speak of me. I have never coveted the very shadow of popular fame — but it is most exceedingly pleasant to me to find I evoke [?] the kind feelings of any one who knows me personally.[1]

As to Mr Curry's book, the expense takes me quite by surprise.[2] I cannot give above half of the sum you mention — but I will write to Dr Leahy, and I think he will certainly take it up. Fowler has sent me some papers, but you or Mr Pigott had better managed [sic] the whole.

Thank you for your report of the Science Faculty, which is sent to press.

Whether I shall produce any thing for the Atlantis this next Number, I cannot tell. I am half through a continuation of the Benedictines, but days on days pass without my being able to write a line or read a page — and I assure you putting aside the composition, and the thought, the reading alone is a very anxious matter in a portion of history which I have never got up or written upon.[3]

Yours most sincerely John H Newman of the Oratory

W. K. Sullivan Esqr

P.S. Mr Morris's article will not do. I hope Renouf's is forthcoming.

[1] Sullivan wrote from Waterford on 17 Sept., 'I made an effort to serve the University here which has succeeded beyond my expectations. I succeeded in getting it put upon the list of toasts at the banquet to the Cardinal. [14 Sept.] It came after the "Hierarchy of Ireland" I assure you I cannot convey an idea of the enthusiastic way in which it was received and in the few remarks which I made in Answer to the toast I endeavoured to connect the Cardinal by a compliment with the University. He paid the most marked attention to what I said and expressed himself to the Mayor very much pleased.' Sullivan added, 'The effect of this public compliment to the University has told well upon the Priests . . .' For the reception of Newman's name, see last note to letter of 7 Oct. to Ornsby.
The toast of the University was proposed by the Mayor of Waterford. 'Professor Sullivan, of the Catholic University, returned thanks. It was a curious coincidence, he said, that at a meeting to do honour to an illustrious Prince of the church and a distinguished scholar, the toast of the Catholic University should for the first time have been proposed in Ireland. There was a point connected with the Catholic University to which he wished to allude. The origin of it had been attributed to the circumstance that other colleges had sprung up, but the fact was that it was established as an inevitable necessity in the country, no matter how many colleges were established, for five millions of people could not remain in receipt of the intellectual outdoor relief which other colleges afforded them. He considered the time was come when, as a matter of right, the people of this country should demand the recognition of its university, which would so much contribute to its success and to the development of the intellect of the country. *Cardinal Wiseman's Tour in Ireland*, p. 345.
[2] The cost of printing two thousand copies of O'Curry's *Lectures* was estimated at over £300.
[3] Newman's article 'The Benedictine Centuries' appeared in the *Atlantis*, (Jan. 1859).

TO WILLIAM HENRY ANDERDON

The Oy Bm Septr 28/58

My dear Anderdon

A thought has just come into my head, which would not have occurred to me unless you had to my surprise, but great pleasure, undertaken the care of St Mary's House, and thus seemed to show an intention of stopping some little time in Dublin.

If you take a lease of several years of the University Church, you are quite at liberty to make any alterations in it whatever, which Pollen does not disapprove — e.g. the alteration of the pipes. And I would sell it to the Bishops with the condition of the lease being recognised by them[1]

Ever Yrs J H N

TO ARCHBISHOP CULLEN

The Oratory Birmingham Sepr 28. 1858

My dear Lord,

In reply to your Grace's letter of yesterday,[2] I beg to say, that, when the Professors of the Faculty of Science in June last sent me their printed Report, and begged for a letter from me to your Grace, for an Episcopal meeting then close at hand, I willingly wrote it. When they further expressed a wish that my letter should be printed and prefixed to the Report, I made that depend on your Grace's plea[sure].[3]

Dr Lyons, the Dean of Faculty, then wrote me word as follows:

'As time is running short, I send you a proof of your letter to his Grace by return of post; but I shall await your instructions and his Grace's, before using it further.'

---

[1] Anderdon replied on 1 Oct. that he would like a long lease, but his chief concern 'would be our possibly misapprehending each other's meaning.'

[2] Cullen wrote to Newman on 27 Sept., 'A letter which you had the kindness to address to me on the 17th June last was left here yesterday together with a printed report of the Dean and Faculty of Science of the Catholic University. The report is marked "proof," but I believe copies of it are already in circulation.

As far as I have been able to read the report, it appears to appeal to the Bishops to increase the number of Professors in the University, and also to add to the expenditure. I fear that such an application would not be judicious at present as the expenditure already exceeds the income, and there are complaints that the number of Professors is more than proportionate to the number of students. For my part, I think it will be necessary to curtail the expenses very considerably to prevent us from getting into debt. Under these circumstances, I doubt whether it would be prudent to publish the report, as it would only attract attention to wants which cannot at present be supplied.

I am leaving Ireland and expect to be absent for some weeks. I will send your letter and the report to Dr Leahy (Thurles) and beg of him to correspond with you on it.' Cullen left Ireland on 28 Sept. and returned on 1 June 1859.

[3] See letter of 15 June to Lyons.

He drew a line under the words, which I have so marked.

I am surprised to find my wishes have not been complied with, and will make inquiry at once on the subject.

I am, My dear Lord,

Your faithful Servt in Xt   John H Newman of the Oratory

His Grace the Archpb of Dublin

TO ROBERT D. LYONS

⌐Sept 28. 1858⌐

My dear Dr Lyons

⌐I have just received a letter from his Grace the Archbishop of Dublin, in which occur the following sentences.

'A letter which etc' (from Dr Cullen's letter of Sept 27) He adds 'I doubt etc'

You wrote to me June 18 as follows

(quote 'As time etc' the above letter)

Will you kindly write to the Archbishop to explain this difficulty[1]

I am J H N

TO JOHN O'HAGAN

Oy Bm ⌐Sept 28/58⌐

Private

My dear Mr O'Hagan

⌐I have just received a letter with the following passage from the Archbishop of Dublin. I am deeply anxious lest it should throw serious difficulty in the way of my fulfilling my engagements with you as to your Professorship.[2] It takes me quite by surprise. It is the first hint he has thrown out since I was Rector of the necessity of reducing the expenditure.

'The expenditure already exceeds⌐ the income; and there are complaints that the number of Professors is more than proportionate to the number of students. I think it will be necessary to curtail the expenses very considerably to prevent us from getting into debt.'[3]

I am &c J H N

John O'Hagan Esqr

[1] Lyons wrote on 1 Oct. to Newman explaining that copies of the Report had been printed in view of the meeting of the Bishops that was expected in the summer. Copies were sent to some of the Bishops and to some friends and supporters of the University, but it was not 'in any sense published.'

[2] See letter of 14 July 1858 to O'Hagan.

[3] See letters of 11 Oct. and 14 Nov. 1858 to O'Hagan.

TO J. B. ROBERTSON

⌐Sept 28/58⌐

Private and Confidential

My dear Mr Robertson

⌐I am sorry to have received this morning a letter from the Archbishop of Dublin with the following passage⌐ in it about the University

⌐"The expenditure already exceeds the income —⌐ and there are complaints that the number of Professors is more than proportionate to the number of the students. I think it will be necessary to curtail the expenses very considerably to prevent us from getting into debt.'

⌐You see, my dear Mr Robertson, I had reason to be cautious in what I said to you in answer to your request for an increase of your Salary —⌐ for this abrupt announcement from his Grace leads me to fear a curtailment of it or a suspension

I am &c J H N

J B Robertson Esqr

TO WILLIAM KIRBY SULLIVAN

The Oratory, Bm ⌐Septr 28. 1858⌐

Private

My dear Mr Sullivan,

I have just received, apropos of the Science Report, the following abrupt announcement from the Archbishop of Dublin⌐:—

I have no chance of money from the Archbishops for Mr Curry; and I must either give him no part of my share towards the expense of printing, or can give nothing to the next January Atlantis. Will you turn this in your mind?

Extract —⌐'I fear that such application (as is contained in the Science Report) would not be judicious at present, as the expenditure already exceeds the income, and there are complaints that the number of Professors is more than proportionate to the number of students. I think it will be necessary to curtail the expenses very considerably to prevent us getting into debt.'⌐

I am, My dear Mr Sullivan, Sincerely Yours

John H Newman of the Oratory

W K Sullivan Esqr

WEDNESDAY 29 SEPTEMBER 1858   read (*in a lecture*) the yearly review of year.[1]

TO WILLIAM KIRBY SULLIVAN

The Oy Bm Septr 29/58

My dear Mr Sullivan

I wrote to you a somewhat anxious letter yesterday.

This morning, I am glad to say, comes a letter from Longmans stating that the profit on Number 1 Atlantis is £22.2.4. This will go towards the expense of Number 3 It is good too as a promise of a fair sale.

Would it be impossible to get subscriptions in Dublin etc as you once thought? I am out of heart about England, for I tried a year ago and failed. But I think you must bring down the expense to within £100 a number. The expense of Number 2 was £130 — putting this sum from Longmans against it brings it down to £110

I send *you* the Account, because the whole account must soon be in your hands.

Yours very sincerely John H Newman

W K Sullivan Esqr

THURSDAY 30 SEPTEMBER 1858   Lisle went?   Dollinger and Sir John Acton came, went with them to Rednall — they went away in evening.

TO THOMAS SCRATTON

[End of September 1858?]

Private

My dear S

I believe Dr Cullen will *not* be at the Episcopal Meeting, *and* that our *expenses* will be entered into. So be you ready.

There are frightful rumours of retrenchment. I should not be surprised if we found it difficult to keep even the £5000 — cutting off all extras.

Ever Yours John H Newman

T. Scratton Esqr

P.S.   Whyte owes Frederic £5 when he went away — perhaps you would not like to add that in your letter to the Father?

---

[1] The review of the year had previously been the work of Caswall. On 6 Oct. Newman transcribed his address, and the manuscript is preserved at Upholland Seminary, Wigan. It was published in the *Catholic Gazette*, (Nov. and Dec. 1923).

Newman spoke of the publication of Caswall's *The Masque of Mary and other Poems*, of St John's translation of the *Raccolta*, of the illnesses of Flanagan and Bittleston; also about the various schools under the care of the Oratorians, about the confraternities, and about the reconstruction of the church.

TO J. M. CAPES

The Oy Bm Octr 1. 1858

My dear Capes,

As it seems to me, your objection about certainty is more to the point than any thing you have printed. My only wonder is that you should not have felt long ago that it is the great philosophical difficulty in Catholicism.[1]

For myself, half my Oxford University sermons are on the subject, and I have a chapter on it in my Essay on Development.[2]

When I came to read Catholic theology, I found that it was solved in a way which I felt to be satisfactory.

It is a property of the human mind, to be certain *speculativè*, not *merely practicè*, in certain cases in which no complete proof is possible, but only proof that the point in question 'demands our belief,' or is *credibile*.

I have no demonstration that I shall die — but I am as speculativè certus of it, as if I *had* demonstration. For the evidence is such and so much, as to make it clear to me that I should be a fool not absolutely and implicitly to believe it.

It has a claim on my speculative belief that England is an island, even though I have no demonstration of it. Reason goes just so far, not as to prove it, but to tell me it is but common sense in me to order my mind to believe, or to direct my mind to believe it. I do not merely say to myself, 'It is *safe* to act as if I believed it.'

I am speculativè certain that intemperate habits lead to loss of health;

---

[1] Capes wrote on 29 Sept. 'As to the possibility of certainty in matters of religion, I cannot see how the method of *forcing* a certain belief, by the method you refer to, and which is so incessantly recommended, is otherwise than logically absurd and morally wrong. If it is a fact that the knowledge of revelation *is* surrounded with argumentative difficulties which cannot be cleared up by pure reasoning, surely religion towards God requires one to be contented with that fact. To *will* to believe as certain that which the *understanding* knows is uncertain, appears to me simply destructive of all truth and religion together. It shocks my whole moral and intellectual nature.

To *act* upon an uncertainty is a totally different thing, and involves nothing absurd or morally false; supposing of course you are obliged to act one way or another. It is the simply adopting *as expedient* that which is the more probably desirable course of action.

As then a man is a fool who is not practically content with probabilities in human affairs, so—it seems to me—a man is most religious towards God who is content with that merely probable religious knowledge which is all that can be logically attained; content, I mean, not only in action, but in the uncertainty of religious faith which it involves. If all that I can conclude is that it is more probable than not that the Christian revelation is true, it is wise to *act* on the hypothesis of its certain truth; but to profess that *one is certain that it is true*, is to utter a direct falsehood and nothing less.

Speaking for myself, I am (or wish to be) as satisfied with what God does not, as with what He does. I used, when much younger, to have the usual longing for religious certainty; as I get older, I am more content as a matter of feeling with whatever is the fact as to the amount of certainty which God has made possible to humanity. I get less and less to refer religious opinion and faith to my own personal feelings, and wishes and habits, as being mere sources of delusion. My own confidence in God increases as my confidence in man and myself as a man diminishes. I see more and more that the feelings, the imagination and the will must be strictly subordinated to the pure reason, if I am *to act as a reasonable and responsible being* towards that God whose existence and nature I know only by reason.'

[2] *Dev.* 1st ed. Ch. III, Uniform ed. Chs. II and III.

and that, in consequence, not of my having direct proof of it, but in consequence of my having just enough evidence to show me that I *ought* to believe it. Say, a temptation to drink comes and obscures this clear conviction, and in consequence I do *not* believe it. Here, it is not, as you seem to say, that, when I believe it, my will 'forces' my mind to believe, reason disapproving, but that, when I do not believe, my will, reason disapproving, keeps my mind *from* belief.

I cannot see that induction is ever a demonstration — but it makes the conclusion 'credibile' — viz 'claiming belief.'

I cannot understand the state of mind which can love our Lord really with the feeling upon it, 'After all, perhaps there is no such person.' It is loving a mere vision or picture, and is so unreal as to be degrading. I cannot fancy (you will say perhaps from an idiosyncrasy) this existence of devotion without certainty. I could not throw myself upon any one here below, of whom I had the suspicion, 'Perhaps he is not trustworthy.' On the other hand, I daily control and direct my mind into a firm belief, or speculative certainty, of truths which I cannot prove, on the ground that I should be a fool not to believe them, or, that reason bids my will to bid my mind to believe. *How* it is that we are so constituted as to be bound by our reason to believe what we cannot prove, is a question which I do not pretend to solve.

I am, My dear Capes Yrs affly John H Newman

SATURDAY 2 OCTOBER 1858 Palmer came

TO AN UNKNOWN CORRESPONDENT

The Oratory Birmingham Oct 2nd 1858

My dear Sir,

I do not like to delay longer my answer to your very kind and flattering letter. I had hoped to have heard your chorale before this, and put it into the hands of a friend at once for this purpose. This I have not yet effected however but, though I should have been better pleased to have been able to thank you for the music as well as for the compliment, I am glad to acknowledge the latter. I willingly give you permission to publish the words with my name.

I do not see that you need go beyond the first four stanzas.[1]

I am, My dear Sir Sincerely Yours   John H Newman of the Oratory

[1] Newman's correspondent was perhaps John Bacchus Dykes (1823–76), Canon of Durham and musical composer, who later composed tunes for Newman's hymns, and corresponded with him.

TO PATRICK LEAHY, ARCHBISHOP OF CASHEL

The Oratory Birmingham ⌐Octr 2. 1858⌐

My dear Lord,

I think your Grace will like to see the inclosed letter to me of Professor Sullivan's, to whom I wrote saying I did not know how I was to find money for the publication of the Atlantis, and of Mr Curry's volume.[1]

⌐May I ask your Grace to be so good at the approaching Episcopal meeting as to allow me through you, respectfully to remind their Lordships, that, since November 14th last, I have been holding the Rectorship only provisionally until a successor is appointed, and that I should be very thankful to them, if they proceeded to the appointment of a new Rector⌐ [2]

I am, my dear Lord,

Your faithful Servt in Xt   John H Newman of the Oratory

The Most Revd Dr Leahy, Archbishop of Cashel

SUNDAY 3 OCTOBER 1858   Palmer went

FROM PATRICK LEAHY, ARCHBISHOP OF CASHEL

Thurles, 3 Oct. '58.

My dear Dr Newman,

At the meeting of the Archbishops held last week—no—on Friday last week—we confirmed the previously made appointment of Rev. Mr Kelly, of Maynooth, who now says his health is equal to the duties of the Vice-Rectorship of the Catholic University.[3]

At the same meeting the Revd Mr O'Loughlin, for many years Prefect and Dean of the Irish College of Paris, was appointed to succeed Dr Flannery as Head of St. Patrick's. We presumed he would be acceptable to you. He is a subject of mine—and from a long and intimate knowledge of his character, I can vouch for his fitness for his new situation.

At the same meeting I proposed to bring to a close at once the yet pending, or rather unsettled, University Church question, about which I had previously written to Drs Cullen and Dixon. There was a difficulty—(so they said)—in the way of it's immediate settlement, namely the want of money. Not money enough, nor I believe any, to the credit of the University in the current account with the Hibernian Bank. We should draw upon the money in the Funds, and then would arise a new difficulty—Dr MacHale might, most probably would, refuse his consent, and so no portion

[1] See letter of 11 Oct. to Sullivan.
[2] When copying in 1872 Newman noted, [[If Dr Leahy received this before his of October 3, it is incomprehensible that his answer should have been, as it was 'Reside as before,' etc etc. unless he had meant me forthwith to resign.]]
[3] The meeting which confirmed the appointment now announced to Newman was held on 24 Sept. On 23 Sept. Scratton wrote to Newman, 'I hear that Mr Kelly of Maynooth has accepted the Vice Rectorate.' Kelly fell ill again and died on 30 Oct.

473

of the money in the Funds could be liberated. He has not as yet positively refused, but I fear he will.

Dr Cullen before leaving Dublin wrote to me on the necessity of your residing in the University as before, or at least for some time, some considerable time, each Session.[1] Indeed, I believe your presence for a much longer time than you gave last year necessary to the success of the University.[2]

Dr Cullen has sent me the accompanying Letter for you.[3]

I remain, my dear Dr Newman, Yours Very Sincerely, ✝ P. Leahy

The Very Revd Dr Newman, The Oratory, Birmingham

TO WILLIAM HENRY ANDERDON

October 5. 1858[4]

My dear Anderdon

I am obliged to you for your caution in speaking to Mr O'Ferrall.[5] The difficulty you mention of his being a Parish Priest is one which I felt myself, and thought would be almost insurmountable. However, I have another reason to be glad of it and a most unexpected one. I have just received to my great surprise a letter from Dr Leahy mentioning the name of a Priest whom the Archbishops wish to be Dean of St Patrick's. I do not know how I can refuse their express wish, though the Episcopal Statutes confirmed at Rome, certainly give the appointment to me. They run as follows:[6]

I am &c J H N

[1] Newman noted, when copying this part of Leahy's letter, [['This corroborates my Memorandum, (above August 13. 1857) [See last note to letter 8 Aug. 1857 to Leahy.] that Dr Cullen always stickled for, never really granted, partial residence. In this message to me both he and Dr Leahy forgot the "trial of nine weeks a Session" (August 25. 1857), unless they by "Session" meant "Term". If so, there was another misunderstanding. But vid. his letter of October 5, in which he recognizes the distinction between "Session" and "Term."]]

On 5 Oct. Leahy wrote: 'There is now no reason to think there will be a meeting of the Bishops of Ireland this Year. There is reason to think the contrary. That being so, what will you have me do respecting the Rectorship?' [[They seem to have thought that by not calling the Bishops together, they *forced* me to stay in spite of my having given warning.]]

'Your separation from the University will be a very serious blow to it. As you value it, and have laboured so much for it, consider the possibility of your spending some time in Dublin each Term for the next Session or two, until it gets out of it's present critical position.' [[I was quite ready to do so,— so was the Oratory,—if the Archbishops would grant my conditions, which were not unreasonable. If they wished me to stop, *why* did they not grant them]] [[Is it not *wonderful* too, that, whereas I had just said to him in my letter of October too [2] 'Since November 14 last (1857) I have been holding the Rectorship *provisionally*, *till* a Successor is appointed' (and without salary), he should, ignoring this, say 'You must come to/Dublin.'!]]

[2] Newman noted, [['For my answer to this, vid below November 12. I delayed my answer nearly six weeks.]]

[3] This was a duplicate of Cullen's letter of 27 Sept. to Newman, quoted in note to that of 28 Sept. to Cullen.

[4] Newman kept a draft of this letter and those of this day, to Kelly and Leahy, headed 'Letters consequent on Dr Leahy's letter of October 3.'

[5] Anderdon wrote on 2 Oct. that he had spoken about the possibility of becoming the new Dean of St Patrick's House to Timothy O'Farrell, Parish Priest of Skerries. The latter hesitated to relinquish the position he already held, unless he had some assurance that he would be appointed. Anderdon wrote, 'he seems to be the man you want. He is very good and conscientious, a thoro' Irishman, hearty and yet priestly.'

[6] Newman then quoted the Latin text, as in his letter of this day to Leahy.

TO MATTHEW KELLY

Octr 5 1858

My dear Dr Kelly,

It is with the greatest pleasure I hear this morning of your appointment by the Archbishops of [to] the Vice Rectorship of the University. My only regret is that I am not in office with you. I have been only holding on, without salary, till a successor was appointed since the winter, and I have lately begged the Archbishops to name the person. I shall be very glad to hear that it is you[1]

Yours most sincerely J H N

Revd Dr Kelly Maynooth

TO PATRICK LEAHY, ARCHBISHOP OF CASHEL (I)

The Oratory Birmingham ⌐October 5. 1858⌐

My dear Lord,

⌐I am very glad to be informed in your Grace's letter of this morning that Mr Kelly of Mayhooth is appointed Vice-Rector of the University.⌐ My only regret in the matter is, that I have not the satisfaction of acting with him, as I trust the Bishops at their approaching meeting will take into consideration the request I have made to them in my letter to your Grace which has crossed yours of this morning.[2]

⌐As to the Archbishops' appointment of Mr O'Loughlin to the Deanery of St Patrick, I beg to lay before your Grace an extract from the Statutes of the University, as contained in the Decrees of the Synodal meeting of May 1854, and confirmed by the Holy See.

'In praesentia,⌐ et donec aliter visum fuerit coetui Episcopali, nominationem Secretarii aliorumque omnium Academiae officialium pertinere ad Rectorem decernimus. *Eidem jus erit* instituendi sumptibus academicis, de

---

[1] Kelly replied on 7 Oct. from Maynooth, 'Your kind letter has added still another difficulty to the many I felt in accepting office in the Catholic University. As those who know you and me best can assure you, I had always resolved to be true to you, and to sustain your views whenever I could do so, if Providence should place us in the same establishment. Should the Archbishops accept your resignation, which I hope they will not, you will not it is true have left us without a guide, so long as we have your publications on University education, but you will make my position uncomfortable, and endanger, I fear, the success of the University. My earnest wish would be that every one should know I was in perfect harmony with you, which I fear cannot be, if you retire immediately. . . .'

[2] i.e. Newman's letter of 2 Oct. which crossed Leahy's of 3 Oct.

consensu Episcoporum incurrendis, ⌜Collegia seu Paedagogia, *quorum praesides nominabit* et congrua statuta ordinabit.'⌝ [1]

I am, My dear Lord Your Grace's faithful Servant

John H Newman of the Oratory

The Most Revd The Archbp of Cashel

P.S. I inclose a copy of a letter I sent to the Archbishop of Dublin in answer to a duplicate of the letter which you sent me from him. [2]

TO PATRICK LEAHY, ARCHBISHOP OF CASHEL (II)

Oct 5/58 [3]

My dear Lord Archbishop

Your Grace will, I am sure be so kind as to take charge of this letter, which I wish laid before the Bishops of Ireland, at their meeting which, I understand, is soon to take place in Dublin.

I now have continued superintending the affairs of the University nearly a year after the time which I set down for my retiring in a letter which I addressed to their Lordships individually in the beginning of April 1857. [4]

I am sure they cannot consider it more satisfactory than I do myself, that I should be acting as Rector at this distance from Dublin. For myself all I can say is, that my time has been absolutely occupied with correspondence and other matters of the University ever since I left it in the beginning of the winter, and, that I have taken no salary since I ceased to reside. But I know perfectly that a resident Rector is indispensable.

Under these circumstances I humbly and earnestly intreat their Lordships to proceed to appoint the new Rector, and thereby to set me free from

---

[1] *Campaign*, p. 90.

[2] This was a copy dated 5 Oct. of Newman's letter of 28 Sept. to Cullen.

[3] Newman left two drafts of this letter, which was not sent, for the reasons which Newman noted at the time at the end of the second draft, that printed here. Newman's note follows immediately in the text.

[4] Newman's first draft was somewhat different and continued as follows, 'In the intermediate summer, the Archbishops of Dublin, Armagh, and Cashel condescended to enter into a negociation first with my Congregation here and next with myself, on the subject of my continuance in the University. After some correspondence your Grace wrote me word that the above mentioned Archbishops would "try for one Session" a plan which my Congregation had wished me to mention to him, by which I should be released from permanent residence in the University, and you asked my own and my Fathers' consent to this proposal. [Letter of 25 Aug. 1857 from Leahy.]

I had no difficulty in this plan myself, if certain conditions were included in it, which I thought absolutely necessary. The principle of these was the appointment of a Vice Rector. [Newman then quoted to that effect from his letter of 16 Oct. 1857 to Leahy.] And I did not on my part assent to the proposal, since no Vice Rector was as yet appointed.

As no Vice Rector was appointed, nor the other matters arranged which I though necessary for the success of the plan proposed, I considered the negociation at an end, and I wrote to your Grace on February 3, to say that I continued holding the Rectorship since November only in expectation that something might result from the negociation to hinder such a step, but that, till the point I referred to was decided I did not intend to receive any portion of the Rector's salary.' Cf. letter of 12 Nov. 1858 to the Irish Archbishops.

responsibilities to which I am not equal, and to condescend to accept the great inconvenience to which I have put myself during the last year as a token, insufficient though it is, of the gratitude which I shall always feel towards them for the honor they have done me in choosing me for their first Rector, and the great kindness they have shown towards me in my time of office.

N.B. On second thoughts, I think it will be best for me to write nothing, and wait to see what the Bishops do at the meeting. I have already sent by Dr Leahy a message to them to the effect that I hope they will be so good as to appoint my successor and relieve me of my responsibilities.

If they answer me by 'requesting I would just come for a term or two and set Dr Kelly off,' I can answer 'I will, if *Dr McHale* as well as the rest ask me,' or 'if the request is unanimous.' The *handle* for doing this is afforded me by Dr Leahy's letter of this morning, who for the first time speaks of Dr McHale as dissenting. He says the Archbishops cannot buy my Church because *Dr McHale* will dissent — Well, if this dissent tells against me, by hindering my getting the money, it will tell for me, by enabling me to refuse my consent to being longer Rector. I can *notice* in my letter that I am now *drawn* to *the fact of Dr McHale's* keeping aloof *by* this reason for not buying the Church

J H N

FROM PATRICK LEAHY, ARCHBISHOP OF CASHEL

Thurles, 8 Oct. 1858.

My dear Dr Newman,

You are right in thinking the appointment of the Dean of St. Patrick's belongs to you, as the Rector. At least such is my interpretation of the passage quoted in your letter from the Statutes of 1854.

You would have every reason to consider the appointment of Mr O'Loughlin as nothing less than an *empietement*, an encroachment upon your rights as Rector, could the proceeding of the Archbishops be supposed for a moment to arise from any cause other than simple inadvertence. Let me assure you it was owing simply and solely to inadvertence.

It remains to consider how best to provide against the rather awkward results of the step taken. As one of the parties concerned, I would in my own name, and I may add, in the names of the other two Archbishops, request you to nominate Revd Austin O'Loughlin Dean of St. Patrick's, as if nothing had been done by us.[1]

Will you excuse me, my dear Doctor Newman, if I venture to throw out a suggestion which has often presented itself to my mind as an easy means for providing for the interests of our University and same time, at least in part, for the necessities of

---

[1] Newman summarised at the top of this letter his reply of 11 Oct. (which is no longer to be found), 'answered saying I had *mentioned already* the Deanship of St Patrick's to someone.' See letter of 5 Oct. to Anderdon. When copying in 1872 parts of Leahy's letter, Newman noted: [[I answered that I had already offered the post to some one else. It was not an act of 'inadvertence.' Dr Cullen *never* considered that Deanship a mere headship of a house, but that the occupant was 'Dean of the University:' and in his gift, as much as the office of Sub-rector]]

your own Community. It is the establishment of your Oratory, or a branch of it, in Dublin.

The Oratory in Birmingham, important an object as it confessedly is, dwindles (forgive me for thinking so) to a small thing in comparison with the Catholic University, for which as I once took occasion to remark to you, it is my belief that Providence was preparing you long years before your secession from the Church of England.

I return Professor Sullivan's Letter. It would be a sad falling off to interrupt or delay the publication of the Atlantis or Mr Curry's Book. No effort of mine shall be wanting to procure the necessary funds.

I remain, My dear Dr Newman, Very Sincerely Yours,

✠ P. Leahy

The Very Revd Dr Newman The Oratory, Birmingham.

TO T. W. ALLIES

The Oratory Birmingham Oct. 7. 1858

My dear Allies,

How many, many times have I been writing to you about your promise for the Atlantis. But I had forgotten your direction, and am quite exhausted with letter writing, which is a sort of *instantia mea quotidiana*, caused by my engagement in Dublin. My head [hand] aches so now, as to make it difficult for me to write.

But now, October is not far from December. Can you give it us.[1]

I hope you will give me a good account of Mrs Allies and of all of you.

Ever yours affectly John H Newman of the Oratory

TO JOHN STANISLAS FLANAGAN

The Ory Bm Octr 7. 1858

My dear S

We want you the first fine day to go to Dublin on the business of the Congregation. There is my house and servants, if you have no where else to go to.

The Archbishops (among other uncivil things, which it boots not to plague you with) have declined to buy the Church, — virtually.

So we think of purchasing the longer lease of Number 87 of the Blue Coat School Trustees, — in my name.

Scratton will give all information, and is zealous about the purchase, and will be pleased to be made much of — I will tell you what I can recollect.

Mr Hughes M.P. (or ex M.P), at the instance of Scratton, got me the offer from the Trustees of a lease of (say) 50 years, on condition I kept the house in condition (*which is an undertaking*, for it needed a new wall, price £100, at once) and an increased rent.

I could not accept it, since the Bishops said *they* would take the whole

---

[1] See letter of 18 Oct. to Allies.

concern, and I made over the proposal to *them* — nothing was done, except that this summer they have built the wall, without asking for the lease.

I have built my Church on the *garden* and I underlet the *house* to the University — and (I suspect) have in consequence charged them with a portion of the fine which I paid for the existing lease to Mr Carmichael(?)[1]

We should have 1. to agree to the increased rent. 2. to pay, instead of the University, for the new wall. 3 to pay the portion of the fine which the University has paid. 4. to pay the lawyer's bill. When I say 'we *should*', I mean it is for you to consider whether in justice we are not bound to do so, and relieve the University?

The lawyer is Mr Maxwell (Kelly and Maxwell) — I suspect Scratton has the whole matter at his finger's ends.

I think you should mention only ME, and act for *me*, not as if the Congregation of the Oratory had any thing to do with it.

How we are to get the *money* which will be necessary, I do not know.

The sooner this can be arranged the better. I could tell you a host of things, but am pretty nigh worn out. My trouble is having to write an article for the Atlantis, and having an hour or two for it every week and no more — and this *exhausts me.*

I thank God for your good account of yourself

Ever Yrs most affly J H N

The Revd Fr Flanagan

TO ROBERT ORNSBY

The Oy Bm ⌜Octr 7. 1858⌝

My dear Ornsby

Thank you for the Freeman.[2] Stewart must think it odd I have not written to him, but I have had both nothing and too much to say, and no time.

Will you in confidence tell me what Duffy offered you for your New Testament? I have to adjudicate a similar payment, and the knowledge would guide me.[3]

Private

⌜I am in great anxiety about University matters. The Archbishops are simply taking a new line, and you may expect great changes at the Episcopal meeting.

---

[1] James Carmichael held the lease of 87 Stephen's Green.

[2] This was a copy of the *Freeman's Journal* containing the long and favourable reply of John Burke, M.P. for Waterford, to Archbishop Dixon's circular letter to Catholic Members of Parliament, asking them to support the request for a charter.

[3] See letter of 11 Oct. to Russell. Ornsby replied on 8 Oct. that Duffy offered him £50 for his Greek Testament with notes for the use of schools.

Dr Cullen has told me to reduce the number of Professors, — I forget his exact words.

The three Archbishops have peremptorily (and abruptly) told me to come into residence. Which is impossible, so that, I suppose, my resignation is imminent.

Also they have abruptly, and without any notice, taken the nomination of the new Dean of St Patrick's out of my hands, tho' the Decrees, confirmed by the Pope, give it to me, and appointed a person whom I never heard of.[1]

All this is for yourself. I must have some thought before I can say what is to be done — but *don't tell* — it will make mischief. Several persons know about the *retrenchments*, but nothing more

Ever Yrs affly J H Newman

R Ornsby Esqr

⌐P.S. Since writing the above, a letter comes from Dr Leahy, informing me that most probably there will be *no* meeting of the Bishops!

I do not see how I can get out of the difficulty of resigning. The Archbishops have told me I must reside a considerable time in Dublin — I feel a Rector ought to do so. *I can't.* Resignation then is all that remains.⌐[1]

2. P.S. Your letter has just come. I know nothing about Mr Walpole, and don't know who does.[1]

I am truly glad that Duffy is getting alive. I can't recommend about the new Draft — It is a very delicate document to word — one ought to know the relations of Dr Dixon to the Liberal members. I feel the desirableness of his writing to them.[2]

In what humour is Butler?[3]

What you tell me of the reception of my name at Waterford is most exceedingly pleasing to me. I have very rarely such encouragements — and, tho' I do not court them, I am grateful for them.[4]

I can't write for cold.

⌐I have since I wrote this, written to John O'Hagan, and told him what I have told you.⌐[1]

[1] Spencer Horatio Walpole, Home Secretary in Lord Derby's Government, was about to visit Dublin to look into the subject of education, and there was thus an opportunity to approach him about the charter.

[2] Ornsby wrote on 6 Oct., that it was a mistake not to have sent the circular appeal on the subject of the charter to Liberal Members of Parliament, instead of confining it to the Catholic ones.

[3] Butler had been hurt at not being sufficiently consulted over the letter to Disraeli. See notes to letter of 20 July 1858 to Butler.

[4] See letter of 27 Sept. to Sullivan, who, in his speech at Waterford, in reply to the toast of the Catholic University, had referred to Newman. Ornsby wrote on 6 Oct., 'at this dinner, on his mention of your name, all the people rose up, and cheered enthusiastically. So you see, after all, your long absence has not diminished your popularity with the public.'

The Ory Bm Octr 7/58

My dear Stewart

I should have written to you before this, were I not exhausted with letter writing, and am weary in hand and head.

Your question was no use — I answered you directly because you wished it — but I thought it would not reach you in time, that you would not get an interview if it did — and that it would not succeed, if you got an interview.

Dr Cullen has written to me to say that some Professors must be struck off — I don't recollect his wording.

That is, ever since I was in Dublin, they won't answer any question about finances, won't commit themselves to anything, and then suddenly come down upon me, when I am committed to the Professors.

They suddenly tell me they have no money, having gone on to honor my cheques up to this date. Really I am not at all easy that I shall get my cheque signed for November — both on account of what I have said, and because the only three trustees in Ireland are Dr Dixon, Dr MacHale, and Dr Cantwell.

I am truly glad that Duffy at last is bestirring himself.

Dr Kelly is the new Vice Rector and a good appointment.

Yours affly John H Newman of the Oratory

J. Stewart Esqr

TO WILLIAM KIRBY SULLIVAN

The Oratory Bm Septr [October][1] 7. 1858

Private

My dear Mr Sullivan,

I don't know that it matters writing to you at the moment, but, while I think of it, I state my perfect conviction that the Atlantis must in some way or other support itself. I am at the moment in great doubt whether I shall ever get the money for the November Salaries.[2] It seems very hard, when I have from the first protested against having to put my hand, as it were, into a bag, and draw out what I would, and asked for some definite round sum, and to know the limit of what I might draw, and what I might promise, that suddenly without notice they should come down upon me, as they have done, and say, You have too many Professors, you spend too much money.

I don't see a chance for the Atlantis. What will be said to Mr Curry's book, which stands on different grounds and is one definite undertaking, I cannot

[1] The contents of this letter make its date clear.
[2] Newman copied down part of Scratton's letter of 9 Oct., 'I think with you that the quarter's salaries are in jeopardy,—that is, if we depend upon the Trustees. We might pay them from the Cullen and Newman from the balance' The Balance in that account was £1104.

481

say, but, if I am to take what is said literally, their purse is empty, — putting aside the funded money, which they don't mean to touch.

For myself, I am £2500 out of pocket with my Church, after allowing for £3000 and more which I started with — and I cannot get them to buy it, though they have promised to do so, nor to lend me my debt on interest. So, I suppose they *have* no money, and had better not have promised it.

Dr Kelly of Maynooth is Vice Rector, which is a good thing — but I doubt whether I can go on being Rector longer, and not resident.

Yours very sincerely John H Newman of the Oratory

W K Sullivan Esqr

TO JOHN HUNGERFORD POLLEN

The Oratory Bm Octr. 8. 1858

My dear Pollen,

Thank you for the novel. What a shame you should buy it for me — I thought it was a 3 volume work. I have not yet had time to read it — but I looked at the beginning, and one thing touched my fancy so much, that, after I was in bed last night, I am ashamed to say, I burst out laughing, and, when I woke in the middle of the night I began laughing again.[1]

As to your coming down next week I find that Miss Farrant stops here till next month for certain — therefore take your choice of coming down as you propose, or when the Altars are ready.

Ever yrs affly John H. Newman of the Oratory

J. H. Pollen Esq

MONDAY 11 OCTOBER 1858 Dr Masfen came

---

[1] Cf. postscript to letter of 27 Sept. to Pollen. What was the novel? Pollen was a close friend of Thackeray, but Newman needed no introduction to his novels at this date. Can the novelist have been Trollope? His popularity was only beginning, and he came to share with Thackeray Newman's predilection.

In 1855 Trollope published *The Warden*, and in 1858 *Dr Thorne* and *The Three Clerks*. Newman appears to have had no copy of this last, and his editions of the two former novels were published in 1860 and 1859 respectively. In Aug. 1859 Pollen lent him a copy of *Dr Thorne*. On the other hand *Barchester Towers* was first published in 1857 and the one volume copy still in Newman's room at Birmingham was published in 1858. Several things could have touched his fancy in Chapter I, 'Who will be the new bishop?'

TO JOHN O'HAGAN

The Oratory Bm Octr 11. 1858

My dear Mr O'Hagan

Thank you for your most kind letter.[1] — On the contrary, I have experienced nothing but kindness and attention, of which I am quite unworthy, from every class of persons in Ireland, whom I have come near. I make no exception, except Dr Cullen and Dr Mc Hale. To all the other Bishops I feel exceedingly grateful — If I don't use the word 'grateful' about the Professors, it is because I should use much warmer and more intimate terms in speaking of them. I submit to it as a mortification, intended to wean me from this world, that I am bound by duty here, and by my years, to separate myself from persons I love so much and from a work to which all my human feelings so much incline me.

Excuse my horrid writing but my fingers are so tired, I can't direct my pen

Ever Yours affly John H Newman

John O'Hagan Esqr

TO ROBERT ORNSBY

The Oy Bm ⌜Octr 11. 1858⌝

My dear Ornsby

Thank you for your letter — thank Stewart for his, if you see him. I thought your draft very good — I only meant that in *matter of fact* I was not a judge how an Archbishop should address Protestant MP's — not knowing their relations to each other.

⌜It is simply impossible I can remain Rector.[2] I had already begged Dr Leahy to get the Meeting of Bishops to appoint some one in my place. And after this, comes the letter calling on me to reside — It never would do to disobey such an injunction — *and I cannot reside.* That is the long and short

[1] Newman copied out part of John O'Hagan's letter of 9 Oct., 'All that you mention is hard and trying in the last degree. I fear your associations in connexion with Ireland will dwell very unpleasantly in my [your] memory, as a country that never understood or appreciated you. Well—so far as regards the Irish Professors in the University (I speak of those whom I know as laymen) it is quite the opposite. We have always felt that you only wanted power and freedom of action to make the institution march. It is painful not to be able to do anything beyond expressing sincere sympathy.'

[2] Ornsby wrote on 8 Oct., 'Whatever conclusion you arrive at I am sure will be the best the case admits of. . . . it is indefinitely better for us to have you, even absent, than perhaps any individual who could be named. . . . I am much mistaken if any successor could complete your work, according to its idea, at this stage. . . . You know I have always thought the real solution of the difficulty would be the founding of an Oratory here. . . . As to the nomination of the Dean of St Patrick's, one would think you could only accept it under protest, saving your right as Rector.'

of it. I am wanted here — *not* wonderful that a head and body cannot be separated longer than three, four, five years.[1]

I don't see my way through the difficulty of the Greek text quite — but I don't think you need to follow the Mai Edition's bad *spellings*, which are not really different *readings*.[1]

Ever Yrs affly John H Newman of the Oratory

R. Ornsby Esqr

TO PETER LE PAGE RENOUF

The Oratory, Birmingham Octr 11. 1858

My dear Renouf,

I was very glad to hear from you. Döllinger had gone, and a Vice Rector appointed, however, before your letter came.[2] Dr Kelly of Maynooth is the Vice-Rector, a very good appointment, and Döllinger would not accept, I am sure, a mere Upper-deanship. I wish he could be Rector — he would have consented seven years ago, I think — not now. I don't suppose I can be long Rector — the Archbishops have peremptorily called me into residence, and that is impossible.

I hope you have been busy for the Atlantis during the Vacation, and are with your wife well — say every thing kind from me to her. I wish you would break your Dublin journey at Birmingham — but I should not wonder if I am at Dublin before you.

Anderdon is to be Dean of my house, Penny Mathematical Tutor, and Arnold classical.

I wish you would do me a favor. The two Princes have owed me £150 since March 17 — and I can't get it. It is very hard. If you thought you could write the man of business, Hubert (is that the name?) at Brussels a line in my name, it might do me some good. You know, I never was paid properly the *first* sum — but I have passed that over.[3]

---

[1] Duffy the printer wanted Ornsby's work to be 'Cardinal Mai's Greek Testament with notes by Professor Ornsby,' but the Vatican MS reproduced by Mai had much peculiar spelling, which would have to be altered. It would thus cease to be Mai's edition.

[2] Renouf wrote on 4 Oct. a letter marked '(Private)',

'Dearest Father

Döllinger is in England as you are no doubt aware. Would it not be possible to get him as Vice-Rector? . . . I cannot think his appointment would be so difficult as might be supposed. Every Englishman or Irishman would meet with greater opposition than a complete stranger. Dr Cullen would be guided in this a good deal by Cardinal Reisach, who would certainly be favourable. I dare say you would not wish to have any direct hand in the business, but indirectly I dare say you could do a great deal.

Döllinger has not the least notion of what I am proposing.'

Reisach had been Archbishop of Munich before becoming a Cardinal in Curia.

[3] This refers to Princes Charles and Edward de Ligne. Scratton wrote on 23 Oct. to say that M. Hubert, who had been absent in Austria, had sent a bill of exchange for £150.

My hand is so tired with writing, that you will hardly be able to read this. I have no news for you

Ever Yours affly John H Newman of the Oratory
P.L.P. Renouf Esqr

TO CHARLES RUSSELL

Private   The Oratory Birmingham Octr 11. 1858

My dear Dr Russell

You are ten times as good a judge as I am what should be paid to Mr Abraham.[1]

The course of my thoughts has been as follows: —

1. I got £80 for 280 octavo pages of the translation of St Athanasius, in which I had to translate, transcribe, and put notes, besides various dissertations.

2. I got £50 for my Essay on Ecclesiastical Miracles, which I had to compose, transcribe, and put notes to — pp 216 octavo.

3. I think I got £27 for my Essay on Miracles in the Encyclopedia Metrop. [Metropolitana] 60 pages large duodecimo, composed, transcribed and notes.[2]

Protestant publishers pay higher than Catholic.

I have heard of a projected edition of the Greek Testament with notes, for which a Catholic publisher pays £50.

I think £30 was offered me for my Callista; composition, and transcription, besides reading necessary for it. pp 296 duodecimo

If these data are just, I think £30 would be handsome remuneration for Mr Abraham. At all events my facts would be useful to you.

Should the weather and my engagements let me cross the channel, could you receive me on Sunday the 31st at Maynooth to take Dr Kelly back with me to Dublin?

Ever Yours affectly in Xt   John H Newman
The Very Revd Dr Russell

---

[1] George Whitley Abraham had edited for Duffy *The Christian Classics, for the use of Colleges and Schools, being Extracts from the Historians, Fathers and other Writers of the Church,* Part I, Greek, Part II, Latin, Dublin 1858. His remuneration was left to be decided by Russell and Newman. After receiving this letter, Russell recommended £20 for the Greek and £15 for the Latin volume.

[2] This was published in 1826, the two previously mentioned works in 1842.

TO WILLIAM KIRBY SULLIVAN

The Oratory Birmingham Octr 11. 1858

My dear Sullivan,

A letter just come from Dr Leahy says — 'I return Professor Sullivan's letter — I[t] would be a sad falling off to interrupt or delay the publications of the Atlantis or Mr Curry's book. No effort of mine shall be wanting to procure the necessary funds.' It would be very good if *you* could correspond with him, and with Dr Dixon, if possible.

Yours most sincerely John H Newman

W K Sullivan Esqr

TUESDAY 12 OCTOBER 1858   Scott came

WEDNESDAY 13 OCTOBER   Dr M. [Masfen] received

THURSDAY 14 OCTOBER   William returned.   Bellasis came.   Dr Masfen went

FRIDAY 15 OCTOBER   Bellasis went?

TO ROBERT ORNSBY

The Oratory Birmingham ⌐Octr 17. 1858⌐

My dear Ornsby

⌐As you have heard that the Bishops could not have gone further, consistently with their dignity, in the advances they made to you [[me]], I send you Extracts of the correspondence between them and me.¹¹ Do not let the paper go out of your hands.²

⌐From it you will find, that a middle plan, suggested by Dr Cullen and Dr Leahy separately to me last May year, was acceded to by the Oratory, viz that I should continue Rector for two years at 9 weeks [[residence]] a year. But both the Archbishops and I had difficulties about this plan, pure and

¹ Ornsby wrote on 13 Oct. urging that this particular moment would be a painful time for Newman to resign, and wondering whether a compromise could be arranged. Then in the postscript Ornsby added, 'I heard, now a long time since, a man who knows Dr Leahy well, say something like this—that the bishops had made all the advances to keep you which were consistent with their dignity—that they could not do more without compromising it. Are you sure you exactly have their point of view? Dr Cullen, I think, oftener than once in our interviews with him, asked whether you were coming to reside, and I should think he was really anxious for it. Your resignation at present, one would think, would be embarrassing to them. I only mention this, not to conceal from you anything that could at all help you in making up your mind.' After writing this postscript Ornsby read in *The Times* the announcement of the appointment of the new Dean of St Patrick's House. He told Newman this and commented, 'The situation certainly is excessively puzzling . . .'

² The extracts were from Leahy's letter of 20 July 1857; the Fathers of the Oratory of 8 [6] Aug. 1857; Newman to Leahy, 8 and 17 Aug. 1857; Leahy to Newman, 25 Aug, 1857, I; Newman to Leahy, 26 Aug. 1857; Leahy to Newman, 25 Aug. 1857, II; Newman to Leahy, 16 Oct. 1857; Leahy to Newman, 24 Oct. 1857; Newman to Leahy, 30 Oct. and 1 Nov. 1857; Leahy to Newman, 2 Nov. 1857; Newman to Leahy, 3 Feb. 1858; Leahy to Newman, 25 Feb. 1858; Newman to Leahy, 27 Feb. and 2 Oct. 1858; and Leahy to Newman, 3 Oct. 1858.

simple. The Archbishops proposed one year instead of two. This I did not object to — but I made a *Vice Rector* a condition of it.

Was it the appointment of a Vice Rector which would have been 'the *advance* which their dignity could not stretch to'? For this is what they did *not* give.

This was not the *only* condition I made — but it was the chief — and even *it* was not granted me. Accordingly I never came in to the arrangement.[1]

I don't see any difficulty in what you ask about Mai's text, except the ἔπεσαν etc.[1] Is it uniformly so? What would scholars say? is it likely to be the true reading? If Mai has brought into theological literature the true dialect, you can't say that you follow him, yet omit one of his characteristic (what may be called) discoveries. But I speak under correction.

⌐You must give up the notion of my continuing at Dublin. Dr Cullen has no notion at all of treating me with any confidence. He grants me nothing — and I am resolute that I will have all I want, and more than I have yet asked for. He has treated me from the first like a scrub,[2] and *you will see he never will do otherwise.* I have wished to organise a method of collection by which we should have money enough — he never has done any thing but take my letters, crumple them up, put them in the fire, and write me no answer. And so with every thing else. The Archbishops *formally promised* to buy my Church, as soon as the papers could be made out, last August year, thanking me for the liberality of my terms; now they refuse, under pretence of Dr McHale not coming in to it. So Dr McHale is to be brought in as a bugbear, when it suits them. Dr Cullen rides over the Episcopal Decrees, and puts in a Dean in St Patrick's without saying a word to me. These things must cease, and be reversed, or I could not do good, if I were ever so willing to stay. I say this to you, not to the world⌐[3]

Ever Yrs affly John H Newman

---

[1] This was the spelling in Mai's text of Codex Vaticanus for ἔπεσον.

[2] 'a hard-worked servant, a drudge.' *O.E.D. McGrath*, p. 471, misreads 'scout.'

[3] Ornsby wrote on 21 Oct. asking to keep Newman's paper of extracts a little while longer, and concluded, 'I cannot help thinking when once things are set a going for the present term, with a Vice Rector, you will find all go on much easier than before.'

On 25 Oct. he wrote again with the news that Dr Kelly was too ill to be Vice-Rector. 'One would think there was really no end to the difficulties which successively arise . . . I return you the extracts, thinking you may want them at the moment. Certainly your letter of October 16. 1857, above all, ought to have had a real consideration, and nothing can be more embarrassing than to be expected to conduct business on such a footing as has long existed. At the same time, (as things are,) I really cannot see how you *can* dispossess yourself of the office of Rector till the meeting in June next year.'

Ornsby wrote again next day, 'Nothing can be more provoking than the whole state of things which has long existed, nothing more natural than that you should feel more than hurt at it. Perhaps any other man in your position and with your antecedents, would have thrown it off long ago. Still one would hope you will not lose the fruits of so much endurance, when the occasion for it may not last much longer. Another thing too, often strikes me that much is to be explained by the peculiar habits and way of doing business of the class with whom you should have to deal; their habituation to a rigid system of government; their little experience of the world at large; above all, their difficulties with each other, and, in the question of the Vice Rector, the intrinsically difficult and embarrassing nature of the choice under the most favourable circumstances. I know all this is little to the purpose as regards the extreme

The Oratory Birmingham Oct. 18 1858.

My dear Allies,

Much as I rejoiced to find that you are getting ready lectures for Dublin, I have not yet mustered sufficient resignation to be easy under your passing by the Atlantis. At the same time, I know well, how out of the question it is to attempt to force oneself to write on a given subject. Still, I am disappointed that I am not to have some criticism on Mr Buckle, or at least on his theory; the more so, because without mentioning your name, I said to a person the other day that we were to have some remarks on the subject in the Atlantis.[1]

I should have liked to have met you at Sir John Acton's, who kindly asked me.[2] On full deliberation I did not go. People are strange to say, so watching me, that I find I must be most cautious, for every thing I do is known. I had declined going to Ushaw on the ground (which is true) that I have not been out anywhere for years, and for this reason I felt I could not accept Sir John's invitation, and I have since found reason to rejoice in my determination.[3]

As to Ireland, I have been only provisionally Rector since last November,

annoyance of the want of confidence shown by Dr Cullen, and his general conduct to you throughout. But . . . you can at least always get a *reply* from Dr Leahy . . .'

Newman commented: '[[As to their difficulty in finding a Vice Rector, since January 1857, nearly two years[,] it must be recollected that I from the first, from 1852, earnestly asked Dr Cullen to let *me* have the appointment—and that he merely kept silence, and decreed it, without a word to me, otherwise. Who asked them to do what *they* felt to be so difficult? Why did they not let me do, what they did not do themselves?

As to the general question, why I did not delay my resignation for half a year, I answer, because I know that, whether I proposed to resign in 1859, 1860, 1861 etc etc I *always* should have had the same kind of battle, and should have left things in the same kind of confusion. J H N. Nov 15. 1872]]'

[1] See letters of 28 Jan. 1858 to Allies and 5 Feb. 1858 to Sullivan.

[2] For Newman's invitation to Aldenham see letter of 2 Aug. to Acton. Allies at Aldenham 'was encouraged by both the German and English historian to proceed in his labours [on Christian history]. Father Faber, whom he consulted, somewhat discouraged him.' Mary H. Allies, *Thomas William Allies*, London 1907, p. 108.

[3] The theological meeting at Aldenham took on the aspect of a seditious plot. On 30 Oct. Talbot wrote from Rome to Wiseman 'the spirit was most detestable that was manifested in it. The only subject of conversation was abusing your Eminence, the Bishops, all Ecclesiastical Superiors, and ridiculing old Catholics.' Quoted by *Altholz*, p. 75. Wiseman inquired of Bellasis whether Newman had been at Aldenham; see next letter and Memorandum of 20 Dec. 1858. Capes wrote at the end of his letter of 29 Sept. to Newman, 'I had a great deal of confidential conversation with Döllinger at Acton's. It is impossible not to respect and also like him in a very high degree.' But when Capes's doubts became public property, the wildest rumours became current, and as Acton wrote to Döllinger on 25 Nov. the popular view was that a crowd of converts had sworn, half of them to apostasiren, the rest to remain outwardly Catholics, in the hope of doing further damage by means of the *Rambler*. 'Ueber unsere Reunion in Aldenham laufen die sonderbarsten Gerüchte, zu denen Capes' jetzt nicht mehr ganz verborgener Zustand Veranlassung gegeben. Die populäre Ansicht ist dabei eine Menge Convertiten sich verschworen haben, die Hälfte zu apostasiren, die Uebrigen zu bleiben in der Hoffnung, als Schein Catholiken durch den Rambler noch mehr zu schaden. Der Cardinal selbst hat sich an verschiedenen Orten darüber erkundigt, besonders ob Newman dabei gewesen.' Victor Conzemius, *Ignaz von Döllinger—Lord Acton Briefwechsel*, I, pp. 156–7.

and have taken no salary, nor have resided. Now however the Archbishops have peremptorily called me into residence, which, if nothing else, will involve an immediate resignation.

I cannot be sorry that you did not accept the editorship of the Dublin. You would have found yourself sadly entangled.

Give my kindest remembrances to Mrs Allies. I am very sorry indeed, and taken by surprise, to find you are still in anxiety about her. I had heard nothing so long which led me to think it, though I knew how unwell she *had* been.

Ever yours affecly in Xt   John H Newman

At any time ask me for Masses for Basil. Don't forget.

TO JAMES HOPE-SCOTT

Private[1]   The Oratory Birmingham ⌐Octr 18. 1858⌐

My dear Hope Scott

⌐Give us your advice about the boys' school. I will try to put a case before you.

Left to myself, I should not wish it — It increases anxieties, responsibilities, and enemies.

There are various reasons which make me stir in it. Among others, 1. the need. 2. Fr Darnell's both wish and capacity to undertake it.

1. My original idea was to begin with a few children in a private way — which would lead to no remark; and let it grow, and the fact of its existence grow on people's minds.

2. When various gentlemen took up the notion in the Spring, it necessarily changed to a formal intention, and a sort of recognized, public undertaking.

3. It has now subsided again into something like its original state — and if we began it, we should begin it with a few children without show.

4. But now, it having been made public, it will be measured, not by what it is, but by those greater ideas which were to come after, and which have been divulged.

5. Further — when a number of respectable names were likely, so as to set it off, *then* I was personally protected. I was answering a call. Now I am, on my own responsibility, a priest in this diocese, setting up, what has been bruited as a great plan, against Oscott, Ushaw, and Stoneyhurst. This I don't wish at all.

6. Moreover, I know people are looking at me very sharply just now. The Cardinal inquired of Bellasis 'whether I had been at the theological gathering

---

[1] Newman wrote later in pencil on the autograph 'This letter was returned to me by Miss Hope Scott.'

at Sir John Acton's.'[1] I have no friend whatever at Rome (except the *Pope*); and the Cardinal, Mgr Talbot, and Dr Cullen *not* friends.

7. It may be represented at Rome, that I am setting up a convert school and perpetuating a convert spirit and party.

8. I have no taste, nor time, nor money, nor strength, for journeys to Rome to explain

Now, as my friend, what would you advise me to do?

I hope you can give a good account of Mrs Hope Scott and the little child[1]

Ever Yours affly John H Newman of the Oratory

James R Hope Scott Esqr

ᴘP.S. I should add that our Bishop is not against us; but, if left to himself would be for us — but I fear that otherwise the feeling is against the plan in the Coetus Episcoporum.[12]

TO WILLIAM MONSELL

The Oratory Birmingham Oct 18. 1858

My dear Monsell,

Dr Cullen is the only one of whom I have cause to complain — Drs D. [Dixon] and L. [Leahy] do but record his decisions. *He* has been, and is, ruining us. He will do nothing, let us do nothing; he will give no answers to questions, or imply he grants and then pull you up when you have acted. He is perfectly impracticable.[3]

---

[1] Newman later made a note in pencil on the autograph, '(It was a few friends at a country house to meet Dollinger. I was *not* there. J H N)' When copying he noted, [[There was a party at Sir John's, to meet Dollinger. I was not there.]] See also letter of 30 Nov. to Sullivan.

[2] Hope-Scott replied on 21 Oct., 'You seem to have two kinds of difficulties—1 Those which must attach to a plan under any circumstances—2 Those which have arisen from the discussion and delay.

The latter I think little of. They relate to prestige and opinion, which cannot much affect a project for which a crying necessity exists, and that among a definite number of people who know and trust you. Those who will send pupils will not care for anything but the hope of getting for their children that which they *know* they cannot find elsewhere.

As to the other branch of the subject, I do not see that the difficulties are greater now than they were at first. Indeed it seems to me that the publicity which the scheme has already undergone must have exhausted the feelings of hostility which it was likely to produce. So much has been said, and that openly, of the *want*, that people must feel satisfied that sooner or later an attempt at supply will be made . . . its [the school's] actual institution will now appear the smallest part of the mischief.

I say then, go on by all means. If you have your Bishops's *permission* only, you are ecclesiastically safe—and if the general question of Converts etc arises, why we must send a round robin to the Pope, and tell him how the matter really stands.'

[3] Monsell wrote on 12 Oct. from Tervoe, Limerick, 'I was very sorry to hear the news which the last portion of your letter contains—I have been spending two days with Dr Leahy at Thurles. He is very unhappy indeed about the prospects of the University and was much grieved at a letter he has received from you refusing to remain, but he spoke of you in such a way that I am surprised that he should have had any part in the usurpation of the appointment

But now, in his absence, I wish I could stimulate Drs Dixon and Leahy to allow us to do something which I have attempted this two or three years past, but in vain. And I write to you, because you would have weight with Dr Leahy, and might stir him up.

We must interest the country in the University, if we are to keep up the collections. Various plans have been proposed for the purpose for years — one was a continuance of the University Gazette — another sermons — a third a Secretary and organization for that special purpose — a fourth public meetings — a fifth indulgences from Rome, which *have* been got. Dr Cullen all the while silent, impenetrable to me, and at last himself adopting the last plan.

I do not see that *all* might not be entered upon — but one leads to another, and it might be well to begin with one. At the moment I am led to suggest public meetings, as the most ready, and most effective in our present circumstances. The difficulty is that the ecclesiastical authorities in some of the principal cities would not take us up.

I trust we should get leave at Belfast and Waterford. Could not we get leave at Limerick? *perhaps* at Cork — not, I suppose, at Galway. Let a deputation of Professors etc go down — and be assisted by the local M Ps etc, make a collection and organize a plan of subscription.

If you approve, perhaps you would write to Dr Leahy — any how, write to me, and let me know about your sentiments on the plan.[1]

Thank you for your Lecture in the paper which I was very glad to see, and your audience, I am sure, must have been very glad to hear.[2]

I expect to be in Dublin for a day or two soon.

Ever Yours affly John H Newman of the Oratory

The Rt Honble Wm Monsell M P

TO ROBERT ORNSBY

⌜Oct 18. 1858

Dr Dixon under date of October 8 says there will be an Episcopal meeting. Dr Leahy, dating October 5, tells me there will not be.

J H N[13]

of dean—Dr Cullen is very uneasy at the pecuniary aspect of the University and I suppose that this is the cause of the Economy as to professors.—If they proceed to disband the staff you have got together I suppose we must look upon the whole thing as gone. Still I can hardly bring myself to believe that it will go—After the failure is announced, if it does come, the amount of jubilation and scoffing among the Protestants will be terrible to look upon.'

[1] Monsell replied on 24 Oct. that he thought that a large meeting could be organised at Limerick for the University only if it were for the sake of demanding a charter.

[2] Monsell was giving literary and historical lectures in Ireland, for which Newman had supplied information about guilds.

[3] Newman copied out part of a long letter from Leahy dated 20 Oct.,
'With every respect for the opinion of others, I for one have little faith in the project of

TO THOMAS SCRATTON

The Oy Bm Octr 18. 1858

My dear S

1. I opened my eyes wide when I saw your words 'You seem to understand that I was making inquiries of you as to the amount of Dr Kelly's salary. I can hardly see how the mistake arose — but I never dreamed of such curiosity etc etc' And I have not a dream of what you mean. The thought never entered into my mind. Do not make mystifications where there are none please.[1]

2. I wish you had taken my offer when I made it to you, to make your income in part depend on a percentage on the fees — I did so, *looking forward* to the future. I can't *do* it now — tho' I don't mind *recommending* it if you wish. Many is the time when I have wished to do a kindness *prospectively* in the matter of salary to you — and you have thwarted it by not seeing what I was at.

3. Will you, please, let me know who the Deans of 1857–8 are — who the new Deans are — and *when* they respectively come into their office.

4. And also *what* Bishops have, and what have not, availed themselves of the Medical and Scientific Burse.

5 Stewart says he thinks Stanislas looking thin — that was my impression when I saw him here. What do you say? He has gained flesh, but perhaps he has only gained *upon* his previous loss.

Ever Yours affly John H Newman

Thos Scratton Esqr

P. S.   If on second thoughts you *fear* to take my house for the whole year and will take it for two quarters, that is till May 2, do so,

2. P. S.   I have just heard from the Princess [de Ligne] that Charles does not return — but that Edward does.

Will you answer the inclosed, as far as it concerns you?

sending Missionaries through Ireland to preach up the University.—I have been spoken to and written to about it . . . A meeting, a speech, a sermon, to be of advantage in the way of bringing in funds should be held or made immediately before, or very soon before, the holding of a Collection in any particular locality. Now, the Collections being for the most part simultaneous, how can you find a sufficient number of persons to carry out the preliminary proceedings? . . . .
. . . To improve the prospect of the University Collection, you say, "Something ought to be done at once—" . . . Allow me to point to the "something." It is to remove the apathy towards the University which exists in a portion of the Bishops, and a larger portion of the clergy of Ireland. How is this to be done? I have always thought, By frequent, or at least annual meetings of *all the Bishops* . . . Give all the Bishops a part in the management of the University—they will at once take a lively interest in its welfare . . . Again and again have I urged this on Dr Cullen. I had hoped etc . . That hope is now disappointed . . . There is no prospect of a meeting of all the Bishops on this side Christmas'
[1] Scratton had apparently asked what pension Dr Kelly would pay, if he lived in St Mary's House. Newman in his next letter remarked, 'I have not a dream what Dr Kelly's salary will be.' Scratton on 15 Oct. then wrote the sentences which Newman quotes.

The Oratory Birmingham Octr 20. 1858

My dear Lord Dunraven

I could not answer your letter at once, and now I extremely regret to say I cannot answer it favorably.

Fr Stanislas had gone to Dublin to consult Dr Stokes, and we did not hear about him till yesterday afternoon.[1] Dr S. not only thinks the South of Ireland too wet for him to winter in — but has ordered him out of the country as quick as he can go. He says he must not be in a damp climate, and he sends him *abroad*.

A great trial it is to him and us any how, his not being with *us*. But if he was to be away, it would have been an enormous gain to have had him under your roof — where we should be sure he would be happy and carefully watched. But to go abroad again is most forlorn. I shall make an attempt for Hastings or Torquay, but I fear it will not be granted.

What is so very trying, and it was not difficult to fear it from the first, is that in so many cases of the kind the disease is suspended only *while* and so *long* as the patient is away from his home; and, whenever he comes back, he comes to die. Every one agrees that Fr Flanagan's lungs are touched, but there seems as little doubt that the disease is suspended and that there is no active mischief at present — but damp, cold, poverty of fare, anxiety, and the like would infallibly rouse it into activity. The hope is that it may in time be so far subdued that no ordinary influence of weather etc. would affect it — but even then he is not safe — for Dr Stokes seems to imply that he will never get back to his work as before — And I am desponding enough to think this means, that his life henceforth will be the precarious feeble living on of an invalid.

I sincerely regret he cannot be of service to you, as I had hoped, in your present great anxieties — and I know in turn that you will feel and pray for us.

Ever Yours, My dear Lord Dunraven, Most sincerely in Xt

John H Newman of the Oratory

The Earl of Dunraven

P.S. I have just heard from Stanislas himself — his Cousin wrote yesterday — It is a *somewhat* different account, but not materially so. He intreats not to be sent abroad, but to come here.

---

[1] William Stokes (1804–78), Regius Professor of Physic in the University of Dublin from 1845 until his death, one of the leading physicians of Europe. He was an authority on diseases of the chest.

TO JOHN STANISLAS FLANAGAN

The Oy Bm Oct 21/58

My dear S.

Excuse the greatest possible hurry.

I have no intention of selling the Church for so little as £2500 as heretofore. The offers to the Bishops and Anderdon are past. I think we are content to let the £2000 take their chance — since we get very high interest now, and there seems no moral insecurity in the investment.[1] Anderdon talked of taking a *lease*, or I talked of it to him — not of *buying*, for this year or two years past. If he took a *lease*, he would find it his interest to associate some one in the work so that, if he fell ill, he would have some one to supply his place. Therefore I should be *glad* of his taking a lease at £200 a year.

In answer to your letter, I have to say that we abide by Maxwell's opinion *not* to take the longer lease, but to leave matters as they are.[2]

I fear I shall have to pay the building of the new wall of Number 87 and Maxwell's bill, which together came to near £100.

We think on the whole you had better go to Lord Dunraven's — but not *make any bargain for money*.[3] If you could say Mass daily, it would be a different thing — but we are decidedly of opinion you must not say a word about money.

I expect to be in Dublin Monday morning next — unless the weather is bad. Perhaps you won't be gone

Ever Yrs affly J H N

TO THOMAS SCRATTON

The Oy Bm Octr 22. 1858

My dear Scratton

The inclosed seems a shameful charge. What would Fr Murphy say to it? I suppose he must decide.[4]

Thank you very much for all your kindness. I have nothing to say but to assure you that I am,

Yours ever affectly John H Newman of the Oratory

Thos Scratton Esqr

---

[1] This refers to the loan for the University church from the Birmingham Oratory. See letter of 16 Nov. 1856 to St John.
[2] See letter of 7 Oct. to Flanagan.
[3] i.e. Flanagan must not take a regular post as chaplain.
[4] This refers to the expenses of the choir at the University church, which the Jesuit Francis Murphy helped to organise.

MONDAY 25 OCTOBER 1858   Mr Robertson and his youth came

TO JOHN STANISLAS FLANAGAN

The Oy Bm Octr 25/58

My dear S

You had better stay in Dublin for the present. Whether I come or not, I don't know. I dread *two* journeys, if I come now — for I doubt whether the term is advanced enough for me to do what I wish to do. If I was sure of calm weather a month hence, I certainly should put it off.

As to A. [Anderdon] he always has jibbed at the notion of a lease. *He* perhaps would say 'That Father keeps me so to the *letter* of my engagements, and is so prosaic; and would come down upon me, if I could not adduce written words in justification of what I was doing — and I certainly say 'That A. is ever incroaching and riding over every thing, without regard to any one else, and if it is in black and white then I shall nail him.'[1]

Ever Yours affly J H N

The Revd F. Flanagan

P.S.   Will you see for me what is right to do about wages in the case of my servants. I proposed to Frederic [Thomas Godwin] to give them a month's warning and wages — which ends *now*. But if they seem to think it shabby, I will give more. F. *seemed* contented. *I* want Mrs Grady as our cook here — but it is a thing so concerning the Fathers generally, that I don't press it — so I suppose we shall lose her, from every one dawdling.

TUESDAY 26 OCTOBER 1858   went to Dublin with them [Robertson and his youth] in mid day Mrs Hope Scott died

WEDNESDAY 27 OCTOBER   Stanislas called on me

[1] Newman made a note, 'N B. Oct 28/58 Things are changed since I offered A. a lease of my church some weeks back, for *then* the Bishops were to take it off my hands at once—now they have withdrawn their promise. In offering a lease then, I was doing him *a favor*.

Now the effect of a lease is just this—on the one hand to hinder me taking the building into the market and *selling it* for what I can get—which *I might do*—and on the other hand binding A for a definite time and so securing a *rent*.

I am against any Lease now—and so I propose as follows:—

'that he should hold it year by year, giving me half a year's notice, if he quits, and vice versa'

Newman added various other conditions, which were revised by Flanagan.

TO JOSEPH DIXON, ARCHBISHOP OF ARMAGH

Dublin. ⌜Oct 27. 1858⌝

Private.

My dear Lord,

⌜I am sorry to say, I hear from Dr Russell that Dr Kelly's state of health is such, as to make it impossible for him to enter upon his duties as Vice Rector with the beginning of the session

If your Grace sees no reason to the contrary, I propose to avail myself of the words of the Decree, 'nominationem secretarii aliorumque omnium Academiae officialium pertinere ad Rectorem decernimus,'[1] to ask Mr Anderdon's consent to be Pro Vice Rector, for the present emergency⌝

I am &c J H N

⌜I am sending a duplicate of this letter to the Archbishop of Cashel.⌝[2]

The Most Rev the Archbp of Armagh.

TO CHARLES RUSSELL

6 Harcourt Street Dublin Octr 27. 1858

My dear Dr Russell

Here I am after all — I found, if I did not come now, I might not be able to come at all. And your account of Dr Kelly was so sad, that it led me to doubt if he would be fit for such conversation, as I had proposed with him, for a long time.

Therefore, if you please, I will come over to you now — and will bring my dear brother, Fr Flanagan, of our Oratory, with me.

As to the day, since I have only just come, and don't know my engagements yet, I cannot say. It will either be Friday or Saturday — If they allow me to stop with you Monday, I shall not be able to come till Saturday. If I

---

[1] Decrees of the Synod of the Irish Bishops, 18 May 1854, *Campaign*, p. 90.
[2] [[Dr Cullen was in Rome]] Dr Dixon replied on 29 Oct., 'I think you can, by all means, appoint Mr Anderdon pro-Vice Rector in the present circumstances. If it should please God to restore Dr Kelly to health before the end of the year, this appointment would still leave it open to him (Dr Kelly) to enter upon his duties as Vice Rector.' For Leahy's reply see letter of 12 Nov. to Leahy.
Newman also preserved a note of an earlier letter of his, on 22 Oct. to Leahy, in which he said, 'For myself I cannot comply to Dr Cullen's wish for my return—I do entreat etc.'

come on Friday I shall leave you after Mass on Monday. Excuse this freedom, and believe me

Ever Yours affly in Xt   John H Newman of the Oratory
The Very Revd Dr Russell

THURSDAY 28 OCTOBER 1858   packed up   saw Professors etc

TO JAMES HOPE-SCOTT

Dublin Octr 28/58
My dearest Hope Scott

Your news is some of the saddest I ever heard. You have my deepest sympathy. I shall say Mass for her soul tomorrow morning — and for your intention every day through the week. I only got your letter today[1]

Ever Yrs most affely John H Newman
J R Hope Scott Esqr

FRIDAY 29 OCTOBER 1858   made calls etc etc

TO ISY FROUDE

Dublin Oct. 29/58.
My dear Child,

I have just got your letter.[2] Since I saw you, I have been remembering you in my prayers several times a day, — you and your brother especially.

I think it would be good, as you propose, to offer to let Papa talk to you — but you must pray God earnestly before it, and during the conversation, for grace to do in all things His holy will.

I think your letter is a very natural one, and therefore a very good one. I think you *should* send one.

And now I believe I have answered your questions, though I am writing in a hurry to save the post.

Ever yours affectly John H. Newman

[1] Hope-Scott's wife, Charlotte Harriet Jane Lockhart, grand-daughter of Sir Walter Scott, died on 26 Oct., leaving three small children. 'Her husband's disposition never allowed him to believe in misfortune till it had really come, and, almost up to the last hour, he had failed to see what was plain to all other eyes; the parting, therefore, with him and with her little daughter Mamo (who could scarcely be torn from her) was sad beyond expression.' Robert Ornsby, *Memoirs of James Robert Hope-Scott*, London 1884, II, pp. 152-3.
[2] Isy Froude was making up her mind to follow her mother into the Church, which she did the following May.

SATURDAY 30 OCTOBER 1858 went over with Stanislas to Maynooth.   News of Dr Kelly's death as we started

TO JAMES HOPE-SCOTT

Maynooth Octr 31. 1858

My dear Hope Scott

Fr Flanagan who is with me, and all our Fathers, have said, or will say, Mass for your intention.

I could not find words to use, when I wrote to you the other day, nor can I now.

God is so good in His heaviest visitations. You have one of the most enduring afflictions which *can* be — but it is the pledge of the most enduring mercies on you and yours. You will have one in heaven to watch over you all, with that peculiar affection, which can be hers alone.

Well may we say, God's will be done — for His will is so loving. You must know this; though I, who have lived longer, know it more.

He will support you, though no one else can. We, who love you, can but beg Him to do so — but that I do continually,

Ever Yours most affly John H Newman

J R Hope Scott Esq

TO LADY HENRY KERR

Maynooth. Octr 31/58.

My dear Lady Henry,

What most sudden heavy news! tho' you were somewhat prepared for it. Do, please tell me something about your dear brother. I have written to him in answer to his extreme kindness in writing to me — but what *can* I do except say Mass for him and pray for him through the day, which I do!

O what an extremely wonderful trial which will get greater and greater — and so enduring — but He who sent it will carry him through it.

I am so sorry to think that I might have seen Francis [Kerr], if he had known I was in Dublin, or I known where to find him. As to Miss H [Holmes] she is very clever and very good. I have no news to answer your question *well*, but the Leighs who value her very much and with whom she was some time, would answer me, I dare say, any questions you asked, which were *definite*. All *I* should have to say, is, that she had seldom kept steadily to one place or one thing, and seems to me to change her mind. But it may not be her fault.

She is at present with Mr Gainsford. I do not know her direction, nor how long she stays. I missed her when she passed thro' Birmingham.

Fr Flanagan, who is here, sends all kind messages (he is much better,

498

thank God). He and all the Fathers at Birmingham are saying Mass for your dear brother's intention.

All kind remembrances to Lord Henry and believe me My dear Lady Henry

Yours most sincerely in Xt   John H Newman of the Oratory

The Lady Henry Kerr.

TO ROBERT ORNSBY

⌜Maynooth Oct 31. 1858

My dear Professor Ornsby,

I have to acknowledge the receipt of the Address inclosed in your envelope;[1] and beg you will express to the Professors from whom it comes my thanks for the kind language which I am sure I shall find it to contain.[2]

As I have come to Dublin on express leave from my Congregation, and, as you tell me in your private letter that the Address has reference to the subject of my resignation, I have thought it my duty to send it to the Oratory at Birmingham. On my return thither, I propose to read it with our Fathers assembled in General Congregation, and to return to the Professors such an answer as they shall advise.[3]

I am,[1] My dear Professor, with the warmest feeling of attachment, Yours affectly

⌜John H Newman⌝ of the Oratory

R. Ornsby Esqr &c &c.

[1] This Address of 31 Oct. begging Newman not to resign, is placed before Newman's reply of 6 Nov. It was signed by twenty-one Professors of the University and by three Deans of Houses. Ornsby in a covering letter of 31 Oct. wrote 'I have been commissioned by a numerous meeting of the professors, to forward you the enclosed copy of an address to you which was unanimously agreed upon by all present. If the address meets your approbation, they would respectfully request you to name a day on which it might be presented to you by a deputation.'

[2] When copying in 1872 Newman noted, [[N.B. I received the Address of the Professors and Professor Ornsby's Letter accompanying it, at Maynooth, where I was attending Dr Kelly's funeral. The request contained in the latter of the two put me into great difficulty. It would be most ungracious and awkward to return to a deputation of Professors, when standing face to face with them, a blunt negative to the request which I well knew the Address embodied. To meet a deputation was to yield something, as regarded my withdrawal from Dublin, and I could not, as a subject of my Congregation at Birmingham, yield any thing, nor did I wish to yield. So I wrote to Professor Ornsby as follows, [letter of 31 Oct.] writing also to Fr St John, the Dean of the Birmingham Oratory.]]

[3] Letter of 6 Nov.

TO AMBROSE ST JOHN

⌐Octr 31/58

My dear Dean

I send you an Address from the Professors and a letter from Professor Ornsby to me, with my answer to the latter. When I return, I propose to bring them before the Congregation.

Ever Yrs affly J H Newman[11]

[[To Fr A. St John
    Dean of the Oratory]]

TUESDAY 2 NOVEMBER 1858 Dr Kelly's funeral. Stanislas returned before it — I in the afternoon *to Dublin* and dined at Mrs Flanagan's and gave lecture to the evening classes[2]

TO GEORGE ANTHONY DENISON

Maynooth Nov 2. 1858

My dear Denison

I do not think you will dislike my writing to you on a subject, on which we agree in principle, and in which my own object, if attained, would promote interests to which you are attached yourself.

We have been for some years attempting a University in Dublin with considerable promise of success. The time has now come, when we think we may fairly ask Government for a charter; and I suppose it is only a matter of time as to when we get it. However, I had rather have it at once of course; and your near connexion with Mr Henley, the President of the Board of Trade, with whose department charters lie, make [sic] me feel that you could so far help me, if you thought right, as to lay my representation before him. The matter has been before the Chancellor of the Exchequer this six months

The argument in our behalf, which I think worth your consideration, is this: —

In proportion as our Dublin University prospers, so will it become the Alma Mater of Catholic youths, who otherwise will go to Oxford. As things

---

[1] St John wrote on 3 Nov. to say how pleased the Oratorians were with the Address. 'It is everything that ought to be said, most affectionate and most true. . . . I only want you to carry it to Rome and lay it and your resignation at the Pope's feet. . . . You can't go on being bullied for ever, you must be free to act if you are to continue to be useful to the University. Oh why is there nobody to represent things as they are at Rome either for us or for the University?'

[2] 'Discipline of Mind,' *Idea*, pp. 480–504. This and the lectures delivered on 3 and 4 Nov. were first published in *Lectures and Essays on University Subjects*, London 1859, dedicated to Monsell, *Idea*, p. 243.

are, a residence in Oxford would be found to weaken their faith in Catholicism. In consequence, if many Catholics went there, a movement is sure to take place for obtaining Catholic halls or colleges. There are parties, who are aiming at this, I am sure, though I do not sympathise with them from my great dislike of mixed education.

At present Propaganda at Rome is strongly opposed to mixed education; but I should fancy the authorities there yielding to strong representations in its favour, especially if our Dublin experiment fails.

This consideration seems worth the attention of those, who desire the supremacy of the Established Church. It concerns its prospects in Ireland as well as in England; for, in proportion as we succeed, will the cry for opening Trinity College, decline.

If we had a charter, I do not doubt that in process of time we should make our University in Dublin as attractive to Catholic youths, as Trinity can be, or even Oxford.

If you cannot do for me what I ask, do not think more about it, but pardon my giving you the trouble of reading this, and believe me &c

J H N.[1]

WEDNESDAY 3 NOVEMBER 1858   gave lecture to Philosophy and Letters[2] dined with Mrs Flanagan[3]

THURSDAY 4 NOVEMBER   gave away Medical Prizes and gave Lecture[4] — off for Birmingham in evening (*never been to Ireland since — Sept 3. 1874*)

FRIDAY 5 NOVEMBER   got to Oratory at 8 AM found Walker there and Miss Bowles

[1] Denison replied on 6 Nov., from East Brent, 'My dear Newman
The sight of your handwriting after so many years has moved me much.
It seems to me that if the Roman Catholic citizens of England ask for a Charter, there is nothing in the social policy of England as respects forms of Faith to warrant a refusal, but everything not only to warrant, but to induce the grant of it.
But as I am persuaded that that policy—not as regards yourselves only, but as regards *all*— is wholly wrong; and that England's boast—the unrestricted exercise of the right of private judgement in matters of Faith—is her dishonour and her sin, I could be no party, directly or indirectly to the obtaining of such Charter.
For that right of private judgement, however you may—as I do—denounce and condemn it, would be her warrant for granting what you ask.
Will you let me add that I do not think you would advance your case in the quarter you name by any private or personal advocacy—
    believe me very Sincerely Yrs G Denison'
Newman evidently replied to this letter for Denison wrote again on 10 Nov., 'I will not "thank" you for your letter. "Thanks" are a very poor word in answer to it.
I bless GOD that there is between us this bond of Charity when others have been severed.
To what you say so kindly towards the end of your letter let me reply in all sincerity that I believe the true account of the matter to be that in the times you speak of you were "Sober minded" and I was not.'
[2] 'Literature,' *Idea*, pp. 258–94. Arnold wrote on 6 Nov., 'I was very sorry that I could obtain no more than one or two hurried glimpses of you, while you were in Dublin. But if you had been divided into twenty individualities you could not have satisfied the eager desires of all who wished for an interview or interviews with you, so I must console myself that I did not fare worse than others. I must tell you how greatly I enjoyed your lecture to our faculty. It threw a broad illumination over a field of thought which I myself have often essayed to enter.'
[3] Mrs Stephen Woulfe Flanagan, who lived at 20 Fitzwilliam Place, Dublin.
[4] 'Christianity and Medical Science,' *Idea*, pp. 505–19. Dunne, who sent Newman a resolution of 'admiration and gratitude' from the Faculty of Philosophy and Letters for the

6 NOVEMBER 1858

[31 October 1858]

To the Very Rev. J. H. Newman, D.D.
Rector of the Catholic University of Ireland

Very Rev. Rector,

We, the undersigned Professors and other officers of the Catholic University of Ireland beg leave to congratulate you on your return amongst us again; and at the same time to express the extreme regret and even alarm, with which we have heard a rumour, we trust unfounded, that you contemplate an early resignation of the office of Rector. We trust that we shall be able to state reasons which may induce you to change this purpose, if it be intended. But before entering on such reasons, we cannot help saying that we feel a kind of shame in urging upon you the continuance of those weighty responsibilities which you have for so many years so nobly sustained. If it were possible, no motive that might bear even the semblance of selfishness, would induce us to press you to stay with us, loved and honoured though you are. We would rather see you in that peaceful and religious repose after which you have so long yearned, surrounded by the affection and respect of a holy community, pursuing undivided duties, vexed by no cares of this world, looking back to the recollections of an exalted life, looking forward to the reward we hope and believe is laid up for you in heaven. You may claim this indulgence as a right from us whom you have taught to value you, however painful the severance may be, come when it may. We also most fully admit that your community, whilst they naturally feel as we do, are bound to you by closer ties than we, and have therefore claims upon you which we cannot have. We are sensible that we already owe those excellent men a debt we can never repay for having spared your services so long. When therefore we say that our affection and gratitude towards you, and our sympathy and regard for the Oratory would lead us, in spite of ourselves, to consent to your going, the reasons must be strong that can induce us to ask you most earnestly to re-consider this step, if contemplated. They are these:

The catholic university of Ireland is an institution on which the Holy Father has set his heart. It is one the success of which comes home to the hearts of the prelates and people of Ireland; for which the humblest classes have shown a zeal which would have done honour to those of the most refined education, and in which the interests of the Catholic faith for generations to come, are deeply concerned. The task of laying the foundations of this important structure was confided to you by the Holy See and by the Episcopate of Ireland, as one peculiarly qualified for this great trust, than which it is not too much to say that none greater appears in the history of the Church since the days of Bede and Alcuin.

You have shown yourself during these long seven or eight years fully equal to the task imposed upon you. You have thrown out ideas; you have propounded laws; you have almost organized a society; you have written volumes which we and our successors shall cherish as the record of your experience and wisdom in the conduct of the higher education. And you must perceive already that results have been attained, if not yet complete in themselves (else we should not be here with this request), still in some

lecture of Wednesday, also wrote on 6 Nov., '. . . the close of both your addresses—on Tuesday night and on Thursday—has saddened—I might say dismayed—many of us, not only professors, but others remotely connected with the University. I earnestly pray that the calamity, which your words seemed to foreshadow, may not come upon us.

There are many here more useful, and who have better and more faithfully corresponded with your views, than I have: but I am sure there is none more attached to you. From the first moment of my connexion with the University I have looked up to you rather as a father than a superior— and I have had good reason. Hence, for myself personally, I cannot conceive anything that could cause me greater sorrow than to see a stranger in the place, to which I have so long looked with veneration and love. Whatever comes, I trust you will remember me in your prayers; as your memory can never be absent from my heart.'

large measure encouraging, as full of promise commensurate with the talents and pains you have bestowed so unsparingly. To mention two great leading departments of our University: in one, the youth of Dublin of the middle class, the rough strength and vigour of society, have been gained to the higher culture bestowed by institutions of this kind; in another the great professions of medicine and science have been rescued from peculiar dangers, and subjected to the training and the influence of Catholicity.

But whilst we feel thus encouraged, we cannot conceal from ourselves that all this real success is not only balanced by as real causes of depression, but also that its consolidation will be most materially endangered if your hand is withdrawn at the present critical moment. It would be as if some great machine, scarcely brought to act even by its projector, were suddenly left either to itself, or to untried hands, and surrounded by persons only too ready to cry it down as a chimera. With the fullest reliance on the wisdom of authority, we suppose none will deny that the selection of a successor would be a most delicate and difficult task; and meanwhile the institution, in some important functions very unformed and unsteady, will, just when there is a chance of its becoming firmly knit, be exposed to the danger of a rickety growth, if not of failure. A few months of uncertain or untried government might now make all the difference between brilliant success, and, to say the least, a very disappointing issue. Add to which, the importance in the eyes of the world at large of your celebrated name, and the loss of the *prestige* which accompanies it, is a thing not to be lost sight of, in many points of view. For example, the success of the Charter may be much affected by this, as it would be by any of the elements of failure which would be involved by your withdrawal at this moment.

We could say much on the disadvantages which to natural feelings would be great, of your retiring from the work with which your name will ever be associated in the history of the Church and of Ireland, before that work is finished. We know that greater considerations have always guided you, and will guide you in this decision. But if the completeness of a name ought to you to be as nothing, we are confident that you cannot but deeply feel the completeness of a mission. You have been singularly marked by the hand of God for a special vocation. We allow it cannot but be a trying one, as all divided vocations must be; but we earnestly hope that you will not leave this mission till it be accomplished; and in this hope it is our firm belief the whole country would join, were this the occasion of giving popular utterance to its high sense of your merits. We must not lengthen this already too protracted address, except to take this opportunity, whether you stay or depart, to express, as a body and as individuals, our most affectionate confidence in you as our Rector; our great gratitude for all the blessings of which you have been to us the instrument in that capacity; and our fervent prayers, that you and your excellent community, (in whose prayers and good works we would wish to be ever associated) may receive, each for the sacrifices they have made or may make, an eternal reward in the blessedness of heaven.

We remain, Very Rev. Rector, With great respect, Your faithful & obliged Servts

L'abbé Schurr
  professor of French & German
Edward Butler
  Professor of Mathematics
James Stewart
  Professor of the Greek & Latin
  Languages
Henry Tyrrell
  Demonstrator of Anatomy
Robert MacDermott
  Professor of Materia Medica
Robert Cryan
  Professor Anatomy & Physiology

A. C. Marani A.B.
  Professor of Italian and Spanish.
Andrew Ellis
  Professor of Surgery
Thomas Hayden
  Professor of Anatomy & Physiology
Eugene Curry
  Professor of Irish History and Archae-
  ology M.R.I.A.
Robert Ornsby
  Professor of Classical Literature.
Laurence Canon Forde,
  Professor of Canon Law.

S. M. MacSwiney, M D.,
    Professor of Forensic Medicine.
Francis B. Quinlan,
    Demonstrator of Anatomy
John O Hagan
    Professor of Political Economy &
    Jurisprudence
J. J. McCarthy
    Professor of Architecture
Robert D Lyons
    Professor of Medicine Pathology &
    Physiology
William K Sullivan
    Professor of Chemistry

Edmund J O'Reilly S.J.
    Professor of Dogmatic Theology
Thomas Bennett D D
    Dean House B L of Mt Carmel
W H Anderdon,
    Dean of St. Mary's House.
D. B. Dunne
    Professor of Logic
Henry Hennessy
    Professor of Natural Philosophy
James Quinn D.D.
    Dean of St. Lawrences's House[1]

TO THE PROFESSORS, DEANS, AND OTHER OFFICERS OF THE UNIVERSITY

⌐The Oratory Birmingham November 6. 1858

My dear Professors, Deans, & other Officers of the University[2]

It is rare indeed that a man has so speedy and so large a reward of responsibilities which he has taken upon himself in any important work, as I have in the knowledge of your feelings towards me as Rector, which are expressed in your Address. Those feelings, indeed, I am conscious, are far beyond what I can fairly claim by my actual services, and so far ought rather to humble than to rejoice me; but, if my right to their possession is to be determined by my own feelings towards yourselves and my zeal for the object which has associated us in common labours, then certainly I will allow that your attachment is not undeserved and its expression most welcome.

And I have to thank you also, in the name of my brethren here, for your consideration towards them. It would be strange indeed, if they were not touched by the allusions you have made to the selfdenial, with which for the sake of the University, they have so long and so silently borne this discouragement, which during the last year you have sustained yourselves, of the absence of their head. And I thank you for it most sincerely myself, for you could not have done me personally a greater kindness, than you have laid me under by thus showing that there are those who enter into the past difficulties of my brethren, and acquit them of unreasonableness in at length recalling me to Birmingham.

I wish it were as easy to solve a very arduous problem, as it is thus to express gratitude for the extreme kindness of your letter, and to feel a real and deep sympathy in the perplexities which have occasioned it. I will say a

---

[1] Arnold did not sign the Address, because, as he wrote to Newman on 6 Nov., although there seemed 'hardly a word in it I did not sympathize with . . . I thought that you must know your own affairs best . . .'
[2] This letter is printed from Newman's fair copy, which he retained.

few words, first on my own position, then on that of my Congregation, relatively to it.

1. For myself: — the following message has lately come to me from the Archbishop of Dublin through the Archbishop of Cashel.

'Oct. 3. 1858. Dr Cullen, before leaving Dublin, wrote to me on the *necessity* of your residing in the University *as before*, or at least for some time, *some considerable time*, each Session. Indeed I believe your presence for a much longer time than you gave last year *necessary for the success* of the University.'

But on the other hand my Congregation had expressly written to the Archbishops fourteen months ago, in answer to a communication from them, as follows: — 'August 8. [6] 1857. We conceive we do not mistake in interpreting your Graces to mean, that you wish to gain our consent to our Father Superior's residence in Dublin, *as during the last three years*, for an indefinite time to come. Now we are sanguine that we shall be able, by a statement of the circumstances of the case, to carry your Graces with us in the conclusion, to which we have come ourselves, that such a further leave of absence from the Oratory, to be granted to our Father Superior, is *simply incompatible with our duty to St Philip*, and that we cannot with a clear conscience make ourselves partners to it.'

And in the previous May I had received at Dublin from the Oratory the following notice: —

'Congregatio Generalis May. 5. 1857. Whereas by Decree of May 6. 1852 we gave permission To our Father Superior to accept the office of President of the Catholic University, and whereas the time has long since expired which we contemplated for his absence, when we gave him that permission, and whereas we find we cannot continue longer this great inconvenience arising from his protracted separation from us: — We hereby unanimously determine in General Congregation assembled, that his leave of absence shall end, and that, in virtue of obedience to St Philip, he must return to us.'

Under these circumstances, bound by duty to be here, bound by honor to residence in Dublin, as a necessary condition of the Rector's office, a condition which my own judgment accepts, and yours also, *what is left to me* but to *resign* it [[that office]]?

2. As to my Congregation. Our Fathers here wish me distinctly to bring to your knowledge, what you may not have heard, that, far from bidding me relinquish the office of Rector, or from precluding me from any residence whatever in Dublin, they wished, in a correspondence with the Archbishops last summer year, of which I have already extracted a portion, to come to a compromise or middle measure, by which I was to be allowed, for the two years then to come, to reside in Dublin for some weeks in every term of the University Session. This proposal, which was with difficulty entertained by their Graces, and then accepted only for one year on experiment, came to nothing, from no fault of our Fathers, but from some difference of view, after

it was out of their hands, in the negociation which followed upon it between the Archbishops and myself.[1]

From these statements it would appear that the solution of the difficult problem which is in question does not rest with *me*, for their Graces exact of me what my Congregation prohibits; nor with *my Congregation*, for it has made a concession of which their Graces have been unable to avail themselves.[2]

Nothing now is left to my Fathers or myself than to offer our prayers to that Wise and Good Providence, who brings to an issue what He has begun, that He would deign, as He doubtless will, to find a remedy for difficulties, which, however anxious at the moment, belong to those [[such]] undertakings, which are at once great in themselves and have the sure promise of eventual success.

I am, my dear Friends, Yrs affectionately & gratefully in Xt

John H Newman of the Oratory[1]

The Professors &c. of the Catholic University

SUNDAY 7 NOVEMBER 1858   sang high mass

TO MISS HOLMES

The Oratory Bm Novr 7. 1858

My dear Miss Holmes

Your letter followed me to Maynooth, and thence I have brought it here. I was so fully employed hour by hour, that I had not time even to read it. You may think how the news which led you to send it shocked me. I had heard from Mr H.S. [Hope-Scott] only a day or two before, saying his wife has got safe to Edinburgh. He was not alarmed — but his sister,[3] who also wrote to me, was very anxious. Mrs H.S. had had a bad cough for near a year. And, when it would not go, they hoped change of air would remove it. My only wonder is, that she has lived so long. It is a most dreadful blow to him. He is going with his children to St Leonard's, I believe. The little infant is a much stouter child than the others. The succession (male) to Sir Walter depends on the little boy born last year.

I should have written to you before this, but[4]

MONDAY 8 NOVEMBER 1858   Miss Bowles went

[1] i.e. the silence as to Newman's request for a meeting of the Archbishops or their representatives once a term to deal with University matters, and of his request for a Vice-Rector. See second letter of 16 Oct. 1857 to Leahy, and that of 18 Nov. 1858 to Butler.
[2] [[vid my letter to Mr Butler below. November 18]]
[3] Lady Henry Kerr.
[4] The second half sheet of this letter is missing.

TO THE EARL OF DUNRAVEN

The Oratory Birmingham Novr 8. 1858

My dear Lord Dunraven,

I am very sorry to say that the view I took of Fr Flanagan's arrangements for the winter, in the letter I last wrote to you, is that which must be carried out; and that he must go abroad, instead of following the course which would be far more agreeable to him, and far pleasanter for us to recommend, a stay under your roof.

Since I wrote my letter to you, Dr de Castro, whom he saw at Pau, wrote strongly urging him to go southwards. The hitch then was his own dislike to go abroad, and the expense — and this led us to give up the notion. Unexpectedly, the expense has been met by a friend who most earnestly begs that a precious life should not run any risk, now that hopes are so much better than they were.

I am very sorry indeed to disappoint you, and hope you will pardon what seems perhaps like disrespect — but my own view from the first has been decided, — and only resisted, from his own great anxiety about what that view would involve — Now, however, that such difficulties as stood in the way are removed, I feel bound in duty to carry out what I could not with a safe conscience, now that it simply depends on me, put aside.

I really hope you will put yourself in my place and excuse me, and believe me,

Ever most sincerely Yours in Xt   John H Newman of the Oratory

The Earl of Dunraven

TO ROBERT ORNSBY

The Oy Bm ⌜Novr 8/58⌝

My dear Ornsby

Thank you for your letter.[1] ⌜I am very glad our letter has been so well received by the Professors. If you go to Rome, you must reckon on the Fathers

[1] Ornsby wrote on 7 Nov. about the reception of Newman's reply of 6 Nov. to the Professors' address, 'There was not a regular meeting, but I read it to all present after mass . . . No opinions were expressed publicly today, but I think your reply, that is the feelings expressed in it, gave great pleasure, as they could not but do. And on the whole, I think they were glad to be put in possession of the facts, and that it is as well as the case admitted of. As far as I could judge, they were not disposed to take a gloomy view . . . and that the tendency will be to view the case as much altered by the fact that there is practically at present a Vice-Rector, that your old difficulty is thus overcome [see letter of 27 Oct. to Dixon]; and that we ought to petition the Holy See to make you stay. If the latter, I should say, to give you your discretion as to the time and duration of your residence . . . I suppose Fr Anderdon will preside next Sunday as Pro-Vice-Rector . . . I am very glad to find that our address gave you pleasure, and also that the Oratory were pleased. I have long felt that their position had not been duly appreciated . . .

here being on the look out and going to Rome also. Also, you will have to settle it with the Bishops of Ireland.[1]

I am most gratified to find you all liked my Lectures.

Ever Yrs affly J H N

R Ornsby Esqr

P.S.   I have just had a letter from Archdeacon Denison very discouraging to the chance of *my* doing any thing with ministers as to a Charter — and I really think it will have more chance if I am kept out of sight, or if I was not Rector[1]

TO R. CUSSEN, VICAR GENERAL OF LIMERICK

Oy Bm ⌐Novr 9/58⌐

Dear Very Revd Sir

⌐I thank you for your letter, which came here this morning.[2]

You will be relieved to know that I have never made any objection at all, as you suppose, to Mr O Loughlin as the new Dean of St Patrick's House, though I cannot take to myself any share in his appointment.

I believe he is now at the post where the Archbishops have placed him[13]

I am, with great respect &c J H N

FRIDAY 12 NOVEMBER 1858   sent to the Archbishops my *formal* resignation of Rectorship (*seven years to a day from my appointment.*)

By the way your lectures have given *very* great satisfaction, and, as to the last, I have never known anything you have done meet with greater applause. [[they were delivered in the first week of November, and are contained in "University Subjects"—J H N]]'

[1] Monsell wrote on 3 Nov. about the difficulty of interesting the Irish bishops and clergy in the University 'as long as Dr Cullen is considered to be the sole external director of its movements and policy—But on the other hand how could its government be in the hands of the whole episcopal body? It seems to me that the first step to be taken is to require an answer from the Government as to the charter—whatever that answer may be it may be turned to account.

I hope that your resignation may not be known until we have the Government reply.' Cf. postscript to letter of 12 Nov. to Ornsby.

[2] Cussen wrote on 4 Nov. a letter, marked 'strictly private,' 'I have heard with deep regret that you object to the appointment of the Revd A O Loughlin to the place vacated by the Coadjutor Bishop of Killaloe.

If your opposition is not personal—or to the person—but to the mode or to an invasion of your authority I have no observation to make. You are the best judge of your position and its rights and I will be silent.

If your opposition be to the person so named by the Bishops, and recent events of deplorable notoriety make me apprehend this source of objection—I beg to state most respectfully that Revd Mr O. L is known to me thoroughly for many years . . .' Cussen, who thought the objection to O Loughlin might be connected with the recent troubles of the Irish College at Paris, then proceeded to vouch for him.

[3] [[I never heard Mr O'Loughlin's name, before the Archbishops appointed him to an office which by the Decrees was simply in my hands. Nov 23. 1872]]

TO THE ARCHBISHOPS OF IRELAND

(*Copy*)[1]   The Oratory. Birmingham November 12. 1858

My Lords,

I have lately received a letter from the Archbishop of Cashel, dated October 2, in which the following passage occurs: —

'Dr Cullen, before leaving Dublin, wrote to me on the necessity of your residing in the University as before; or at least for some time, some considerable time, each Session. Indeed, I believe your presence for a much longer time than you gave last year, necessary for the success of the University.'

On the other hand, I beg to bring before your Graces the words of the Fathers of my Oratory in this place, written to three of your Graces as much as fourteen months before the Archbishop of Cashel's letter, as follows: —

'Such a further leave of absence from the Oratory is simply incompatible with our duty to St Philip, and we cannot with a clear conscience make ourselves partners to it.'

Before proceeding to the only solution left to me, of the difficulty in which I find myself relatively to your Graces and my Congregation, I beg to observe: —

1. that I signified to the Bishops of Ireland individually, full nineteen months ago, my intention of resigning into their hands the trust with which they had honored me.

2. that at the same time I named the day of my intended resignation, viz; last November 14th.

3. that a negociation, which three of your Graces opened with me better than a year ago, for some compromise between continual residence on my part in the University and no residence at all, came to nothing, in consequence of their not granting the requests which I ventured to make to them in my letter dated October 16. 1857

4. that, accordingly, in the beginning of the present year, February 3rd, I wrote to the Archbishop of Cashel on the subject of my resignation, with a reference to the requests made in my letter of October 16. 1857, as follows: —

'February 3. 1858. I have delayed to take an irrevocable step, in the expectation that something might result to hinder it, from the negociation into which the Archbishops condescended to enter with me. I still delay it: but I am sure you will not be surprised at my informing you, that I have come to the resolution, till things are placed on a more intelligible footing, to decline, from the date of this letter, to receive any portion of the Rector's salary.'

5. that, in consequence, since February 3 last, I have been holding the

---

[1] This letter is printed from the copy Newman made and sent to Ornsby. See letter of this day to him.

office, which I had given notice of resigning so long before, only provisionally, without salary, and waiting for a successor.

6. that, in so doing, I have done all I could do, not denying the duty of a Rector's residing in Dublin, but being unable to reside from my duties in this place.

7. that now I receive a letter from the Archbishop of Cashel, conveying and concurring in a message from the Archbishop of Dublin, by which, without other words, the duty of residence is simply and absolutely urged upon me.

Under these circumstances one course alone is in honor left to me.

I hereby resign into your Graces' hands the high office, the duties of which have occupied my mind now for seven full years: and, begging you to pardon all my shortcomings in fulfilling them, during the time for which I have had so distinguished an honor.[1]

I am &c (signed) John H Newman

Their Graces The Archbishops of Ireland

TO JOSEPH DIXON, ARCHBISHOP OF ARMAGH

Oy Bm ⌐Nov 12/58⌐

My dear lord,

⌐It is with great sorrow and reluctance that I send you the inclosed — but after Dr Cullen's message through Dr Leahy, nothing else was left to me in honor, especially since I concurred in the principle which it enforced.

I beg to offer your Grace my most sincere thanks for the kindness which I have ever experienced from you; and indeed I owe the same in one degree

[1] Newman made a memorandum on 23 Nov. 1872:
'I ought not to have undertaken the Rectorship without
1 having *all* the Archbishops of Ireland distinctly with me. (It must be recollected that Dr McHale did move formally in the Committee for my nomination)
2. without the Bishops of *England* formally taking part in the establishment.
3 without stipulating that the accounts should be in the hands of laymen
4 without settling the number of weeks in a year I should be in Dublin
5 without more distinctly stating the number of years for which I was to be Rector'
Cf. *McGrath*, p. 124, whose footnote, however, is superfluous, since, owing to faulty transcription, he has inserted a 'not' in the bracketed sentence thus, 'MacHale did not move formally.'
William Neville copied out another note of Newman's:
'Dr Cullen was dissatisfied with me for
1. not residing continually
2. for taking to the young Ireland party.
I resigned
1. because of Dr Cullen's impracticability
2. the needs of my own Oratory
3. because the hope of the University being English as well as Irish was quite at an end.'

or other to Dr Leahy, and the Bishops individually, whom the Board of Archbishops represented.[1]

I am &c J H N

P S. ⌈I have also to thank your Grace for your ready compliance with my proposal that Mr Anderdon should act as Pro Vice Rector in place of the lamented Dr Kelly.⌉[1]

TO PATRICK LEAHY, ARCHBISHOP OF CASHEL

Oy Bm ⌈Novr 12/58⌉

My dear Lord,

⌈I had already written my letter of resignation, which I inclose, when your kind letter came.[2] You will see I am in no position to make any reply to your notice of Vice Rector. I have to thank your Grace for your compliance with my proposal of the provisional appointment of Mr Anderdon as Pro Vice Rector.

Nothing was left for me after your Grace's letter conveying Dr Cullen's message with your own comment upon it, than to resign. I have waited six weeks, since your letter of October 2, that I might not act hastily, and that I might open the term.[3]

J H N

---

[1] Dixon replied on 15 Nov., 'As you think that no other course was left to you in honour, I shall say nothing to induce you to reconsider the matter . . . . I shall ever consider it one of the greatest honours of my life to have been permitted to cooperate with you—little as that cooperation was—in that great work. For it is in many respects a great work, although it has not attained all that development which its friends desired for it; and none more ardently than its Rector, as there was none, who laboured more strenuously than he, to give it that development. I shall ever indeed remember with affectionate gratitude the kindness which on all occasions I have received at your hands.'

This was the end of Newman's correspondence about the University with Dixon. For the friendship between Newman and this Archbishop, who was remembered for his simplicity and sanctity, see Thomas O'Fee, *Seanchas Ardmhacha*, III, (1959), 'Some Letters of Newman to Archbishop Dixon of Armagh,' pp. 390–2.

[2] Leahy wrote from Thurles on 10 Nov., 'The interests of the University will not suffer under the direction of Mr Anderdon

Why I did not say so much before the receipt of your last Letter [that of 27 Oct.] you may judge, I had rather not say. This, however, I will say—that you are one of the last in this world towards whom I would be guilty of any discourtesy.

Dr Dixon and myself consider Dr Gartlan, the Rector of the Irish College of Salamanca, a fit person for the Vice-Rectorship; and we reckon upon the concurrence of the other Archbishops—at least of Dr Cullen. Have you any objection to Dr Gartlan?'

[3] Leahy replied briefly on 14 Nov., 'You have my concurrence in the appointment of Revd Mr Anderdon as provisional Pro-Vice-Rector.

With no small regret I have received your Letter of Resignation.'

TO ROBERT ORNSBY

The Oratory Bm ⌐Nov 12. 1858⌐

My dear Ornsby,

⌐I send you a copy of my Resignation which the Professors may see. I think it right that they should know my precise grounds for the act, and not be at the mercy of rumours and reports, as I find from you they have been.

I have told the Primate that I have sent you a copy of it.[1]

I fear you must not indulge the idea that it is not a final act — for I do not think the majority of the Archbishops at all disposed to grant what, even were I at liberty to make terms, which I am not, I certainly should require, for the good of the University⌐

Ever Yrs affly John H Newman of the Oratory

Robert Ornsby Esqr

P.S. ⌐What I hear, on sounding a friend, is, that any personal or private interference of mine with members of the Government, would do the prospect of a Charter no good.[2] Indeed, I am convinced that an *Irish* Rector would be a gain with Government. I wish you could get Dr Moriarty.

However, I leave it to you to determine how far my resignation should be made known, and to whom. Only, recollect the scrape you got into last June and July.[1][3]

SUNDAY 14 NOVEMBER 1858   Edward went to funeral of his wife's trustee

TO JOHN O'HAGAN

The Oratory Birmingham Nov. 14. 1858

Private

My dear Mr O'Hagan,

The other day I wrote out a statement for Mr Anderdon, which he is to deliver to his Successor, in which *in* the £5000, allowed the Rector hitherto for the Professors etc annually, £200 is included for yourself, £100 as Professor of Political Economy and £100 as Law Professor.[4] I sincerely trust, and I *believe*, Dr Cullen will not alter this arrangement; I am led to hope that his letter to me about the expenses was written under the influence of the severe

[1] Newman must have added this to his letter to Archbishop Dixon as sent.
[2] Cf. letter of 2 Nov. to Denison. Ornsby replied on 14 Nov., 'I consulted with Sullivan as to what you said about the effect of your continuance in office on Government. He differed from your informant as to its probably effect.'
[3] i.e. when Ornsby was showing round the draft of Newman's letter to Disraeli.
[4] See letter of 28 Sept. to O'Hagan, and Appendix 2, p. 584.

indisposition which has made him so anxious and distressed about his heavy duties generally, and that, when he comes back, he will see reason to withdraw what he said to me. I therefore do earnestly hope you will not desert the University. I inclose a letter as a memorandum which you may keep

Begging your good prayers, I am, My dear Mr O'Hagan,

Affectionately Yours in Xt   John H Newman[1]

John O'Hagan Esqr

MONDAY 15 NOVEMBER 1858   Walker went

TO THOMAS SCRATTON

The Oy Bm November 15/58

My dear Scratton

Under the circumstances, I don't mean to sign more drafts — what I will do is, to put a large sum, say £500, into the hands of Anderdon, which may last till February 2nd or such time as ends his provisionary rule of the University[2]

Ever Yours affly John H Newman of the Oratory

Thos Scratton Esqr

TO JAMES STEWART

The Oratory Bm Novr 15. 1858

My dear Stewart

I do not know in what words to thank you for your kind letter. It is far more than a reward, (as far as I ought to look for one here) for whatever trouble and care I have had at Dublin, to meet with such affection from those without whom I could have done nothing at all.[3]

---

[1] Newman copied out part of O'Hagan's reply of 18 Nov., 'There is no use in saying any thing, I suppose, on the subject of your resignation. Every thing (as you once wrote to me) has no doubt its reason; but I cannot help deploring your loss, as a calamity to the coming generation of Irishmen.'

[2] See letter of 11 Dec. to Scratton.

[3] Stewart wrote on 13 Nov., 'Though I did not like to give Dr Dunne a great disappointment by claiming to myself the privilege as Dean of the faculty of writing to express the gratitude and affection we all bear towards you, still I think I may write a note to thank you for consenting to publish your lecture at our solicitation and to express to you how sincerely I concurred in the vote of my brother professors. All this looks very like taking leave—I am sure it would break all our hearts to think it possible you were not to come back to us again—I am sure I pray most earnestly that our University and ourselves may be spared such a blow. However come back to us or not, I shall never cease to feel a glow of gratitude come over my heart whenever I hear your name.'

In a postscript he added 'Mr Anderdon presided at the Council on Wednesday and so well.'

Considering my age, it is impossible that I could anyhow have been much longer in Dublin — and, when ever I went, there would be real reasons for my not going.

I feel the stress of work, and am not so strong as I was — and I want to be quiet and collect myself — I repeat, you want a man in the prime of life and in vigorous health to carry the University on. Don't be sure, by the bye, that you would have Anderdon for any long time

I hope my Lecture will read as well as you seem to expect.

Ever Yours most affectly John H Newman of the Oratory

Jas Stewart Esqr

TO WILLIAM HENRY ANDERDON

[[Novr 16. ⟨?⟩ 1858]]

My dear Anderdon

I thank you for giving me information about the Proceedings of the Professors, and for taking the trouble to transcribe for me some of their resolutions at last Sunday's meeting.[1]

I understand their third Resolution, to which you call my attention to be addressed to you, who are the acting Rector. You will be cautious what you do before giving it your sanction — for there is an impression in various quarters that the Bishops do not like our acting in the matter. Perhaps Dr Leahy would privately give you a hint. On the other hand they would be very glad of our moving in the matter, provided we succeeded in it. ⌐As a member of the University I shall be sure to approve of what you do. Pray command

---

[1] 'At a meeting of the Professors, Heads of Houses, etc. held in the University Library on Sunday November 14, 1858, (pursuant to a notice issued by direction of a similar meeting on the Sunday preceding)—the Pro-Vice Rector in the Chair; the following resolutions were proposed, seconded, and carried:—

1. Proposed (as an amendment) by Dr Forde, seconded by Dr Sullivan, That the Pro-Vice Rector, Professors etc. of the University lay before the Rector their deepest regret for the last step taken by him in regard to his office in the Catholic University.

2. Proposed by Professor Renouf, seconded by Dr Sullivan, That a memorial be presented to their Graces, expressing the hope entertained by the members of the University, that such arrangements may be come to by their Graces as shall continue to the University the benefit of the Rector's invaluable services.

3. Proposed by Professor Hennessy, seconded by Dr Ellis. That with the sanction of the Rector, a Committee be appointed to communicate with Mr Blake and the other members of Parliament who take an interest in forwarding the question of the Charter, with a view to furnish them with information.

4. Proposed by Professor Marani, seconded by Professor Hennessy, That in the event of the Rector sanctioning the Resolution Number 3, the following Committee be appointed to carry it out; namely, Very Rev. Pro-Vice Rector, Dr Ellis, Prof. Sullivan, Dr Dunne, Prof. De Vere, Prof. Hennessy.

5 Proposed by Professor Sullivan, seconded by Dr Hayden, That the Pro-Vice Rector, the Deans of Faculties, and the Rev. the Dean of St Patrick's House, form a committee to carry out Resolution Number 2.

W. H. Anderdon, Chairman'

me at any time if there are questions on which you want an opinion or a testimony.[1]

I can't agree with you as to the effect of my retiring on our prospects of a Charter — I wished to approach one of the ministers thro' a friend, and received for answer that the less *I* did, the better — ⌐

It is a grave question whether the Archbishops will let you have any thing to do with the money. I send you the scheme of payments as a document[2]

I am &c J H N

TO ROBERT ORNSBY

Oy Bm ⌐Nov 16/58⌐

My dear Ornsby

Thank you for your letter, which interested me much.

⌐I *never said a word* in my letter of October 16/57 about laymen.[3] It is just an instance of the system I speak against, that *nothing is said to* ME, and whispers *about* me circulated by the Archbishops to defend themselves. I send you my words for any one to see. But if they mistook me, why not *answer* me, and so get it cleared up, instead of saying nothing? The board I wished to sit was just for the purpose of obviating in one point this miserable and intolerable *silence*.

It is not likely that any thing will make me submit to this, for it is impossible a Rector can fulfil his duties, while he is groping in darkness.

I cannot answer Resolution 3,[4] for I am *not* Rector — and the Archbishops must clearly understand I am not playing at make-belief — which Dr Quinn and others will be sure to suspect. I shall write Anderdon what I *think* of the Resolution.

Dr Leahy has answered me, accepting apparently my resignation, with regret.

I have some doubts whether Dr Moriarty will like to be committed. Perhaps his friends at Allhallows can answer your question better than I.[15]

I should be much pleased at your reviewing my Article on Cicero, if they

[1] In copying Newman substituted [[information]]
[2] This is printed from Newman's autograph, as Appendix 2, p. 584.
[3] Ornsby, in the postscript to his letter of 14 Nov., wrote, 'Butler remarked to me when I showed him your letter [of resignation], that the Bishops "considered your name of great importance and worth any sacrifice that was consistent with what they considered their rights." He seemed to think one great point was the financial committee. There was jealousy between the lay and clerical element in the country. He thought the Bishops would not concede a lay committee. It would be better were it as Dr N wished, but if that were impossible, why not concede it?' See also notes to letter of 1 Dec. to Ornsby.
[4] [[about applying for a Charter]] See the previous letter.
[5] Ornsby wrote that he decided it was better not to mention at the meeting of the Professors, Newman's suggestion in his letter of 12 Nov. that Dr Moriarty should be asked to be Rector,—it would have been thought premature, 'Because recollect you are still rector, till your resignation is accepted . . . If Dr Forde is right, the Archbishops cannot act for the University, except when they meet for that purpose . . .' Ornsby asked, 'Do you think it would do any good, if as an individual I wrote to Dr Moriarty . . . suggesting his being Rector as a solution to the difficulties . . .'

will take it — but you must recollect I wrote it in a great hurry, when I was almost a boy; well, 23.[1]

Ever Yrs affly J H N

THURSDAY 18 NOVEMBER 1858   Pollen came   Stanislas came from Ireland

TO EDWARD BUTLER

not ⌐sent — but in substance — viz less fierce, and more minute in detail — and more exact in sequence.⌐

The Oratory Birmingham ⌐November 18. 1858⌐
My dear Mr Butler

⌐Ornsby tells me you have heard that one of my conditions, presented to the Archbishops, on which I would continue Rector, was the appointment of a *lay* committee of *Finance*.[2]

This is not the case. What has led Dr Cullen to misunderstand me I don't know — but I know that, if, instead of observing an impenetrable silence, he had answered the requests I did make, he would at once have found out that it was not the case — and that he misunderstood me.⌐ But though he did not speak to me, he can, it seems, speak of me to others.

⌐In 1856 indeed at the meeting of the Bishops, I did ask a lay committee for receiving and entertaining money requests from the Rector. (I understood Dr C. [[Cullen]] *generally* that this [[with other things]] was granted [[to me]]. When [[afterwards]] I asked him to let me therefore act upon it, he kept silence. Had I had a dream that he did not approve it, I should have dropped the question etc etc)[3] I should not have urged my request a second, and a third time in that year, as I did, had I had any sort of intimation at all, that Dr Cullen did not like it — ⌐ or had I conjectured it.

However, all this, though the ground, I suppose, of the misapprehension, is nothing to the purpose.

⌐What I *did* propose, as a condition of my coming to an arrangement with the Archbishops, was a year *after* the meeting of the Bishops, viz in 1857,⌐ and was conceived in my letter of October 16 of that year in the following words: —

⌐'5. that a step be taken by the Archbishops,⌐ which is of such importance to the interests of the University, that without it I do not see how we can go on any longer, viz that the *Archbishops, or persons they appoint to represent*

---

[1] i.e. the article written for the *Encyclopaedia Metropolitana* in 1824, *H.S.*, I, pp. 239–300. See letter of 14 Feb. 1859 to Ornsby.

[2] [[This statement, whether from the Archbishop or not, is the only answer which, as far as I know, was attempted to my Letter to the Professors of November 6. above]]

[3] Newman first wrote instead of the sentence in brackets, 'To this proposition I never got any answer, good, bad, or indifferent—when a single word "No" would have satisfied me.'

them, sit once in every term in Dublin, to receive questions or applications, whether from the Rector himself or from the Deans of Faculties.'

⌐Here is nothing about lay men — and nothing about Finance.

And I distinctly say, the Archbishops, or their representatives. [[when I ask for a meeting once a term in Dublin.]]

The truth is, that the drift of it is[1] to put an end to that reign of impenetrable silence, which I felt to be such an evil, that, as I express it, 'I did not see how we could go on any longer' under it.⌐

(added that ⌐it was the fact of conditions at all, not this or that condition which broke off the negociation)⌐[2]

Excuse this explanation, and believe me,

Ever Yours most sincerely John H Newman of the Oratory

E. Butler Esqr

FRIDAY 19 NOVEMBER 1858   Baldacchino put up in St Philip's Chapel
MONDAY 22 NOVEMBER   Pollen went

TO JAMES STEWART

Oy Bm Novr 22/58

My dear Stewart

I have cut the inclosed out of the Evening Mail It shows that Degrees can be prepared for by the aid of Evening Classes.[3]

The Press, I see, *denies* that we are to have a Charter from Government

Ever Yrs affly John H Newman

---

[1] Newman substituted [[The truth is I wished to put an end]]

[2] Butler's mother was ill and died on 12 Dec., so that he did not reply until 20 Dec., when he wrote, 'I never said that I had *heard* "that one of the conditions of your continuing Rector, was the appointment of a lay committee of Finance." I was *under the impression* such was the case and said so. But I never heard anything about any conditions except what you were kind enough to communicate to me yourself, until Ornsby showed me a few days before the receipt of your letter, the copy you sent him of the conditions you had made. Dr Cullen never spoke to me on University matters except wherein I was personally concerned and applied to him about them, and never made the most distant allusion to negociations.

I need not say how deeply I regret the step you have felt called upon to take. Your retirement from the office of Rector is a great blow to the prospects of the University under existing circumstances, when all is experimental and tentative, and in a very unsettled condition. It has been felt as such by the Catholic Laity especially. . . .

Believe me dear Dr Newman to remain with deep feelings of gratitude to you for your past kindness to me, and of sorrow at your departure from among us. . . .'

[3] This was a letter in the *Evening Mail*, praising the Evening Classes at King's College, London, and showing, from the testimony of the writer of it, that it was possible thus to obtain a B.A. degree, while still continuing to work for one's living.

TO WILLIAM KIRBY SULLIVAN

The Oratory Birmingham Novr 23/58

My dear Mr Sullivan

I am very sorry to be late with my Article, but there is a vast deal of work necessary for it, I have not much time, and just now the weather is so cold, I shirk being in the Library more than I need be. I send a good deal for paging tonight, and hope to send the rest tomorrow.

As to Mr Scott's, I have never had my Note back from Fr O'Reilly, tho' he brought it with him and talked it over with me, when I was in Dublin.[1]

(Private) I get anxious lest there should be some hitch. It would be well if you dropped him a line as a matter of course saying the Printer wished to put the Note into pages, and that you, as Editor, wrote to ask him to have the kindness to send it back. I know there *are* things I am to leave out, but I don't know how much. I won't detain it above a post.

My article will be called 'The Benedictine Centuries — ' Scott's is 'The Dates of the Nativity and Crucifixion — ' but till Fr O'Reilly sends back the proof, I don't know how to promise it.

I am very much annoyed to hear this morning that the Church has been denied you for the Science Lecture. I made a distinct stipulation with Mr Anderdon, that it should be open for such purposes, and I cannot conceive how it has happened — except that there is a report that the Vicar General has interfered — but how did he come to do so?[2]

Yours most sincerely John H Newman

P.S. I quite concur in your arrangement of articles.

TO EDWARD BELLASIS

The Oratory Birmingham Novr 25 1858.

My dear Bellasis

Will you give me your opinion of the inclosed, on the *whole* — and again in *detail*.[3] I will write another, if you wish one on a different type.

I think of having a number printed and sent to friends

Ever Yours most sincerely[4]

Mr Serjeant Bellasis.

---

[1] This was Newman's note at the end of Scott's article, the *Atlantis*, (Jan. 1859), pp. 71–4. See letters of 25 May and 7 June 1858 to Scott. Newman's own article 'The Benedictine Centuries' is now in *H.S.*, II, as 'The Benedictine Schools.'

[2] Ornsby wrote to Newman on 22 Nov., 'Sullivan and Hennessy are *excessively* angry about the refusal of the church for the inaugural affair of the Science faculty. I think Fr Anderdon acceded to the request, and then Dr Yore [Cullen's Vicar General] forbade it. Meanwhile they had invited numbers of professors from Trinity College etc.'

[3] This was a prospectus about the opening of the Oratory School. See letter of 4 Dec. to Bellasis.

[4] The signature has been cut out.

TO LORD CHARLES THYNNE

The Oratory, Birmingham Nov. 25th. 1858

My dear Lord Charles,

I do not know how to thank you enough for your most kind letter. As to your daughter, pray convey to her my best thanks, when you write, for her message, and assure her of the pleasure it would be to me, if ever it were in my power to avail myself of it, and to make her and Lord Castlerosse's acquaintance at Killarney, I should not say, Lord Castlerosse's, for I already owe him a great kindness, when he was so good as to give me the countenance of his presence on a trying occasion.[1]

At the same time I feel as if I should never leave home again, now I have once got released from my engagement in Dublin — I am getting old, and my duties are urgent here, and moving about does not quite suit me.

As to yourself and Lady Charles, certainly if any thing took me to Clifton or to London, when you were there, I should make a point of calling on you. I did not know you were in Town, when I was there for a day last March, till it was too late, or I should have called then.[2]

What you say about one of my books being known at Eton, is remarkable, and very grateful [sic] to me.[3] I hope to be able to send you a sort of Prospectus of our new school very shortly.

When you write, pray remember me to Frederic,[4] and believe me, My dear Lord Charles,

Most sincerely yours, John H Newman

The Lord Charles Thynne

[1] Lord Charles Thynne's only daughter, Gertrude Harriet, married Viscount Castlerosse on 28 April 1858. He was the heir of the Earl of Kenmare whom he succeeded in 1871, and the family seat was at Killarney. Lord Charles Thynne wrote on 22 Nov. 'My daughter Lady Castlerosse wants so much to know you and wishes you would propose to pay her a visit at Killarney.' Lord Castlerosse was present in court, when Newman was sentenced at the end of the Achilli trial. See diary 31 Jan. 1853.

[2] See diary for 24 March 1858.

[3] Thynne wrote 'When I was at Eton a little while ago, one of the tutors (Johnson) a very clever man enquired about you spoke nicely and properly of you and said that both Tutors and Boys owed you a great debt for your lectures on the University; that nothing was ever equal to it; that it gave them a new feeling about universities altogether; and that no book had ever come out which created so great and good a sensation amongst the Boys and men at Eton.'

William Johnson (1823–92), was a master at Eton from 1845 until 1872, in which year he assumed the name of Cory. During the same period he was a Fellow of King's College, Cambridge. He was a poet as well as a brilliant tutor, and considered himself a disciple of Newman, whose course he followed with interest. See Faith Compton Mackenzie, *William Cory*, London 1950, pp. 47–56.

[4] i.e. Lord Charles Thynne's eldest son, who after a few weeks at the University in Dublin, during April and May 1855, had entered the army. His father wrote on 22 Nov. 1858, 'Lady Charles and I often speak of you Your kindness to our poor wayward boy will never pass out of our memories. We wish we could see you.'

TO THE DUCHESS OF NORFOLK

The Oratory. Birmingham Novr 26. 1858

My dear Duchess of Norfolk,

This of course requires no answer. An announcement I have just seen in the Paper leads me to write.[1] And I write to send you our truest sympathy in your bereavement, and to say that we will each of us say Mass for your intention.

I am, With the greatest respect & attachment, Most sincerely Yours in Xt

John H Newman of the Oratory

The Duchess of Norfolk

TO JAMES STEWART

Ory Bm Nov 26/58

My dear Stewart

You must not suppose I have any knowledge of what is going on, except what you, Ornsby etc tell me. I had not heard about the matriculations. I am very glad of them. Certainly any thing which will create a greater stir about the Charter will be good.[2] You will have a difficulty in getting a Protestant to a *degree*.[3]

Ornsby wrote me that there was some hitch about the Church for Hennessy's Lecture.[4]

Anderdon has quite enough to do without writing to me. He has not once, and need not

Ever Yours affly, John H Newman of the Oratory

J. Stewart Esqr

TO JAMES GARTLAN

⌜Nov 30/58⌝

My dear Very Rev Sir[5]

⌜I thank you for your kind note — at the same time I am not able to respond to its courteous and friendly advances, as I am no longer Rector of

[1] The first Lord Lyons, father of the Duchess of Norfolk, died at Arundel Castle on 23 Nov. 1858. He served in the navy against Napoleon, and commanded the Mediterranean Fleet during the Crimean War.

[2] Stewart wrote on 24 Nov. that a deputation of students from the evening classes wanted to go to London to represent to the Government 'what great things our University is doing for the education of the middle classes in Ireland.'

[3] Stewart wrote that a Protestant youth wished to enter the University.

[4] See letter of 23 Nov. to Sullivan.

[5] Ornsby wrote to Newman on 28 Nov., 'I dont know whether you will have been apprised of the fact, but to our great surprise "the coming man" made his appearance yesterday. A

the University, having resigned my office into the hands of the Archbishops several weeks ago[11]

I am &c J H N

TO WILLIAM KIRBY SULLIVAN

The Oy Bm Novr 30/58

Private

My dear Mr Sullivan

I have today heard from Fr O'Reilly.

It is quite clear that we must not have Mr Scott's article or my note in the forth coming Number.

If Fr O'R. scruples, who will not?

He considers the publication of it will hurt the University.

Also, for myself — I have found lately that some good friends of mine are taking great liberties (at least in their thoughts) with me — and are looking at every thing I do in the way of theology, and I feel certain I shall be whispered about at Rome, if it appears.[2] At my time of life, with so many things to do, and so many interests to protect, I have no wish for a new controversy and quarrel, in addition to the many in which I have been engaged.

It is most provoking, after all the time which has been spent upon it — but at least it cannot appear, as I think you will agree with me, in the forthcoming number.

Most sincerely Yours John H Newman of the Oratory

W K Sullivan Esqr

P.S.   I hope Mr Curry's book is getting on — I know that the Auditors will be disposed to make a row, if they have not the printing bills soon. I owe them a great deal for the trouble they have taken for me, and it is fair that they should in consequence be peremptory.

Mr Gartlan, late Rector of the Irish College at Salamanca is to be the Vice-Rector. . . . you have an idea of him, if you imagine a very *large* face and head . . . He has been in Spain I understand, for 40 years . . . He has been in this country since July last. . . . My impression . . . is that if matters end in your resuming the office of Rector, you will find him not difficult to deal with. Of course Anderdon's powers as Pro-Vice-Rector merge in Dr Gartlan's . . .'

[1] James Gartlan, the newly appointed Vice Rector, wrote to Newman on 29 Nov., 'I have the honour to inform you that in conformity with orders to that effect received from the Lord Primate and the Archbishop of Cashel I reported myself on Saturday at the University, and in your absence proceeded to carry out the views and wishes of those Prelates in concert with the Revd W. H. Anderdon in reference to our respective positions as Vice-Rector—and Pro-Vice-Rector. . . .

Availing myself of this occasion to place myself at your disposal unreservedly . . . with eager wishes for your early return . . .'

[2] See letters of 18 Oct. to Allies and Hope-Scott, and Memorandum of 20 Dec. 1858. Newman ended by inserting Scott's article 'On the dates of the Nativity and the Crucifixion,' in the *Atlantis* for Jan. 1859.

2nd P.S.   Since writing the above I think you must give me twenty four hours to see if I cannot devise some expedient for being [bringing] in Mr Scott's article after all.

TO ROBERT ORNSBY

The Oy Bm ⌈Decr 1. 1858⌉

My dear Ornsby

You must not think me ungrateful to your two welcome letters,[1] because I have not written — but I have been quite oppressed with the Article I am printing in the Atlantis, and I have been not quite well since I returned here. It seems indeed as if I have returned from Dublin when I ought. I certainly want rest, and propose to lie fallow the whole of next year.

Do you see that the Prior of Downside, though I believe he is one of those who inveighed against our discipline, has threatened the London University, that, if they proceed with their innovations, he and the other Catholic authorities will leave them?[2]

Ask Stewart privately, if any thing can be done with the *address* which the young men of the Evening Classes made me — as a middle plan, instead of addressing ministers. ⟨(I mean, making it known in some influential quarter)⟩ I am uneasy that nothing more is doing about a charter — I wish I was in the way of speaking to any of the ministers — but my first attempt has succeeded so ill, that I am afraid to make a second.

⌈I am amused at the Vice Rector appearing as a Deus è machinâ — If I had resigned this time year, I suppose he would have appeared just as promptly. I suppose they had no objection at all to let me have the whole work, while I would, dimittens auriculas meas.[3]

As to Butler's objection, which Scratton endorses, that the Trustees would have granted me any money without conditions or need of an audit,[4] it is well

---

[1] Those of 22 and 28 Nov.
[2] Of the Prior of Downside, James Sweeney, Scratton wrote to Newman on 16 Sept. 1858, 'the Prior I know has a very sinister view of the [Catholic] University.' Downside and other Catholic colleges were affiliated to London University. Under its new charter of 1858, the B.A. Examination was to be revised, and as the *Weekly Register*, (27 Nov. 1858), reported this was objected to, because it would include an 'examination in mental philosophy, which implies really principles of religion in which Catholics could not submit to an examination from non-Catholic examiners.' Prior Sweeney defended the ability of the Catholic colleges to teach mental philosophy in their own way, 'they had known the secret, and had practised it for centuries.' He hoped that the Senate of London University would not, by insisting on the new regulations, 'force the Catholic colleges to give up their connection with the university.' See also Henry Tristram, 'London University and Catholic Education,' *D R*, (Oct. 1936), pp. 269–82.
[3] Horace, *Satires*, I, IX, 19–21. Ornsby wrote on 28 Nov., 'The Bishops having acted in this way shows that Dr Ford's statement must be unfounded, about its being impossible for them to act in affairs of the University, unless all four of them are assembled for that purpose.'
[4] Ornsby wrote on 22 Nov., 'I have showed the extract of your letter of October 16th 1857 to Butler and one or two others Butler's notion was that the Bishops did not like to be

to talk in the case of another person, but I am sure none of you yourselves would have liked on your own responsibility to have spent £30,000, without *even being told* that you *might* do so — without its being *said* even, 'Dr Newman, there is no need of your stinting yourself.'

On the contrary, so far from this only being wanting in fact, in fact there was the distinct protest of *one* of the Four Trustees the other way, *refusing* to sign my cheques, *refusing* to be responsible for my acts, in actual letters written to me.

Moreover, another Trustee (Dr Cantwell) so shaky, that I dared not apply to him — and, when I did apply, taking occasion to read me a lecture apropos of my conduct to Dr MacHale.[1]

And then comes the third fact, which you mention, that a third Trustee, when I actually *do* build a Church proprio motu, though I had mentioned to him every step I took from the first, refusing me not the money to pay for it, but even the *loan on interest* of a third part of the money.[2]

And then fourthly the same Trustee, when I propose to appoint a Professor of English Literature, refuses to give his assent for half a year, on the ground of money.[3]

And then suddenly, after a dead silence, of a year more, suddenly bids me destroy some of the Professorships and contract my expenditure.[4]

Very like unlimited trust, this — I should like to see a cautious man like Butler, doing himself what he recommends to me.

And this is all independent of the question of *silence* — which extended to every matter whatever, not to money matters only. E.g. I was *encouraged* to attempt to get some of our Professors into the Stephen's Green Hospital — and I committed myself to the promise of doing so.[5] Then, when all seemed clear, I was suddenly met by the Archbishop with an absolute silence,[6] which no means I could take would shake. I went on trying to find out what the matter was for six months, and then gave it up in despair. To this day I have not a dream what the hitch was.[1]

As to the resumé you kindly think of, I am so tired of the whole matter, I could not enter into the notion.[7] And I doubt its prudence. ⌐You should see

plagued, and that you would have done better in *assuming more responsibility*, and in expending money which he was sure would have been allowed when you presented your report. He quoted the example of the Education Board which exceeded their funds by 20000£, which Government allowed. Of course the answer was obvious, to refer to your outlay of the Church. [[as to which Dr Cullen would not even lend me a penny, though I offered interest.]] But he did not seem open to arguments . . . . My own notion is that you have had to contend with insurmountable difficulties, and that it is only astonishing even with your powers you have effected all that you have. . . .'

[1] See letter of 20 Feb. 1857 to Cantwell.
[2] [[a third part of the cost.]]
[3] See second letter of 21 March 1857 to Cullen and letter of 30 Oct. 1857 to Leahy.
[4] See letter of 28 Sept. 1858 to Cullen.
[5] [[vid May 7. 1856]] i.e. the letter from Mac Namara quoted in first note to letter of 29 July 1856 to him.
[6] [[vid July 29, 1856 July 31 etc]] i.e. the same letter to Mac Namara, and the last note there, quoting his reply.
[7] Ornsby wrote on 22 Nov., 'Would it be a good thing to make a résumé to the Archbishops of the whole history of your administration, and of *the* great difficulty [as described by Ornsby

the letter of a Munster *priest* I suppose, in the Irishman paper No [November] 20. The drift is the turning out all the English Professors — [1] I sent my copy to Scratton — but you should get one for yourself. ⌈It is well written.⌉ It is no time for squabbling. If Government saw that letter, I think it would help our Charter.[1] If Mr Seymour Fitzgerald is in Dublin (the Papers say he is) I should be very much tempted to write to him and inclose it, and to send him the Address of the Evening Classes.[2]

And as to the 'Extracts,' I say the same. I doubt whether it is good to keep up a controversy.[3]

Ever Yrs affly J H N

Rt Ornsby Esqr

Excuse my miserable writing — my hand aches, and my fingers won't form letters.

TO SIR JOHN ACTON

The Oratory Birmingham December 2. 1858

My dear Sir John,

I have been thinking over your proposition respecting the Atlantis, and I will tell you what difficulties occur to me at first sight.[4]

First — the Atlantis ever must be an Irish publication — it is to represent the Literature and Science of the Catholic University, and, to say nothing else, while just now it covets the contributions of persons not connected with the University, I don't think even now it would like so many of them as to destroy its character, I doubt whether in time to come it would wish to have any. And as its conductors wish it to be Irish or at least Academical, we on our side ought to aspire to something English. Thus there will be a difficulty on both sides.

Then again any thing of a practical character, every subject of the day, is

---

'that the Rector was not supreme, that in some way or other he had to refer to the archbishops, but that this supreme power was not come-at-able.'] you have had to encounter? You have never, as far as I can see, ever remonstrated with them on the *principle* of it, as rendering administration hampered at every step; yet it could not but be admitted in fairness.'

[1] This was a letter, signed 'A Munsterman,' in the Belfast newspaper the *Irishman*. It maintained that the Catholic University was un-national and even anti-national. See also letter of 12 Dec. to Ornsby.

[2] William Robert Seymour Vesey Fitzgerald (1818–85), was matriculated at Christ Church in 1833, but moved to Oriel in 1835, taking a second in Classics in 1837. He was Under Secretary of State for foreign affairs in Lord Derby's Government, Feb. 1858–June 1859.

[3] These were the extracts from his correspondence with the Irish Archbishops, which Newman had sent to Ornsby on 17 Oct. and which had been returned. In his letter of 22 Nov. Ornsby wrote that he would be glad to have them to keep.

[4] Cf. letters of 8 and 10 July 1858 to Acton.

excluded from the Atlantis — and, though I think great caution ought to be used in the admission of such topics, even though you had a periodical of your own, you would be altogether forbidden them in the arrangement you are contemplating. Politics, ecclesiastical matters, theology would be impossible.

A third difficulty which I do not see my way to solve is the question of remuneration to the writers. There is none at present — and for this reason — it is the interest of men of science to get their experiments and their results printed for nothing — and so of literary research too, especially since just now it is a great point for the Professors, whose chairs are somewhat insecure, to show that they are worth their salary, as they are abundantly. But, if some articles are paid and others not, a confusion will arise which I do not see our way out of.

Please, write to me if you have any remark to make on the above.[1]

I have been exceedingly interested by Döllinger's Article in the new Rambler.[2] I have to acknowledge the great kindness of a notice of myself in another article.[3]

Yours most sincerely John H Newman

Sir John Acton Bart.

---

[1] Acton's letter of 10 Dec. is placed before Newman's of 16 Dec.

[2] 'The Paternity of Jansenism,' the *Rambler*, (Dec. 1858), pp. 361–73. See letter of 31 Dec. to Acton.

[3] This was in a review, *op. cit.*, pp. 407–15, of H. L. Mansel's Bampton Lectures, *The Limits of Religious Thought examined in Eight Lectures*, London 1858. Simpson was the reviewer and he imagined Mansel was indebted to Newman not only for the whole gist of his argument, but for the details of his proof, which had 'been wrought with much greater artistic completeness and beauty by that master-mind than by the Bampton lecturer.' For Mansel's defence see letter of 11 March 1859 to Simpson.

Among Simpson's references to Newman, the following paragraph, pp. 411–12, occurs:—

'We have had occasion once before, in criticising Dr. Newman's style and method, to point out the side where his powers are limited. [The *Rambler*, (June 1853), pp. 484–95. Cf. Volume XV, pp. 380–1] He gives us colossal fragments, but he does not usually construct a finished edifice. He is like Homer, from whom all the Greek philosophers took their texts, as St. Thomas culls the principles of his science from Scripture. The systematiser who comes after him, and who selects and arranges some portions of his boundless wealth, naturally gets much of the credit that should fall to the creator of the store. But if Mr. Mansel has not rendered honour where honour was due, perhaps we are not those who should throw stones at him. The judicial oblivion to which Dr. Newman has been consigned in the communion which he has left has found too faithful an echo among ourselves; and the consequence has been, that Dr. Newman has almost ceased from literary production. A priest has a higher vocation than a mere artist. An artist creates to satisfy his instinct of creation, and forms beautiful objects for the mere love of beauty. But the priest is a man of action; he must husband his forces, and use them, not to create beautiful objects, but to convert souls. His conscience will not allow him to spend all his time in literary work, unless he sees that work produce the fruits he seeks for; and how shall he measure this fruitfulness but by the reception his works meet with? A cold welcome freezes the stream, and the fountain forms another channel for its waters. It is not praise that we ask for Dr. Newman; it is the recognition of his influence. There is nothing easier than flattery, and nothing more uncommon than well-merited praise. Undistinguishing laudation is much worse than satire; this sometimes leads men to mend, but no one was ever surrounded with unmixed praise without being spoiled, as Poggius says. To be praised by those who show no discrimination in their admiration, can be no encouragement to Dr. Newman: first, he must doubt their sincerity; secondly, he must mistrust the competence of their judgment, even when they praise him at all, which is seldom enough.'

TO ROBERT ORNSBY

The Oratory Bm Decr 3/58

My dear Ornsby

I have not heard a word from Anderdon or Scratton — or from any one but you.[1]

I cannot interfere as Rector, for I am Rector no longer. I do not write to the Vice Rector lest he should assume I write as Rector. I do not write to Stewart for the very reason that he is Dean of the Faculty.

But I write *as the friend* of the two poor youths — and *I demand* that they be righted according to the statutes of the University.

I do not ask that they shall be recalled — I suppose they would not come. But a stigma attaches to them, and I beg you to be so good as to see that matters are put in train for its removal. The matter must come before the Council.

The Dean of St Mary's had quite a right to remove them from his house — but he could not let them quit his roof till he had brought the matter before the University; whereas he let them go into the town, and go away, without, as I understand from you, the University knowing.

I conceive it was no great offence speaking against Scratton. He is no authority of the University.

His presiding at Table in Harcourt Street was so far unknown to me that I did not think he dined there at all, except by accident. I am so far to blame that the day I dined there he *did* preside — but, as I never presided myself, I believe I considered he was saving the Dean trouble.

I expressly begged him, when he undertook the honor, to keep himself in the background

Ever Yrs affly John H Newman of the Oratory

R. Ornsby Esqr

P.S.   I did not *mean or wish*, nor do I, the address to *me* to be sent, unless the petition to *Government* is *not*.[2]

---

[1] On 27 Nov. Count Zamoyski, after he had been out hunting, returned to St Mary's House in red coat and top boots, too late for dinner. He dined in his room, which was contrary to the rules, and when wine was not forthcoming, sent to ask for it. This Scratton refused him, and Zamoyski, when he met him on the stairs said, 'There goes a screw,' or similar angry words, and then 'It is too bad to speculate on our stomachs in this way.' He was called upon immediately by Anderdon, the Dean of the House, to apologise to Scratton, and said he would if Scratton would do the same. Zamoyski was instantly dismissed from the House by Anderdon. When Prince Edward de Ligne heard what had happened he told Anderdon he perfectly agreed with Zamoyski, and also left the House. The two remained at a hotel in Dublin for a few days, and then went to Belgium. Meanwhile the affair had in no way been brought before the University. Ornsby, (who reported all this, at secondhand), Arnold, and others were very anxious lest the future prospects of the two young men should be imperilled. See also Newman's account in his letter of 5 Jan. 1859 to Flanagan. Scratton was the lessee of St Mary's House, but not its head, nor with a position in it recognised by the University.

[2] Newman had suggested that the students of the Evening Classes might present an address to him, as being less difficult for them than an address to the Government. There was no need to do both. See postscript to letter of 10 Dec. to Hennessy.

The Oratory, Birmingham Novr [December] 4. 1858[1]

My dear Bellasis

I am amused at your and Hope Scott's lawyer-like caution, in cutting off every unnecessary word from my manifesto.[2] Alas, it has been my fault through life to have spoken out. Without it, I should neither have had the hebdomadal judgment on Number 90, nor old Campbell's ineptiae.[3] I do really believe it arises from an impatience of not being above-board. I wish I could take to myself the comfort of the sacred lectio, 'Deridetur justi simplicitas; hujus mundi (that is, the lawyers') sapientia est, cor machinationibus tegere, sensum verbis velare etc' etc[4] I think I shall reform, as old Demea, at the end of life; and, as he got liberal, so on my part become close.[5]

This leads me to say one thing. It has only been just now brought home to me what hard and wrong things are said of me, by those who ought not.

---

[1] Both autograph and draft of this letter have 'November,' but above the date on the latter Newman has written 'Dec?'. It is clear from Bellasis's letters that December is correct.

[2] Bellasis wrote on 29 Nov., 'Hope Scott and myself are delighted that you are going to make a start,' but they made excisions in the draft Prospectus for the proposed School. Newman drew it up thus:

'Father Newman, of the Birmingham Oratory, intends with the blessing of God, to commence on May 1 next, a School for the education of boys, not destined for the ecclesiastical state, and not above 12 years of age on their admission.

He takes this step at the urgent instance of friends, and with the concurrence and countenance of a number of Catholic gentlemen whose names have been transmitted to him.

Their object in this application is, as he conceives, that of the establishment of a School, which, while securing the high religious benefits of Catholic training, is founded under a sensitive apprehension, and conducted with a direct contemplation, of the needs and circumstances of the day. [Bellasis excised this paragraph, as he wrote on 29 Nov., because it 'implies, or may be conceived to imply that existing schools are not "founded" and "conducted" etc—and affords a point of attack.']

For himself, his own recent engagements in the new University, which has excited so much interest in Great Britain as well as in Ireland, have naturally suggested to him the expediency of some system of education for boys, which might be in harmony with the University course, and might look towards that course as the complement of the teaching carried out in its own classes. [Bellasis excised this paragraph, because 'it will allow people to say that the school is a mere feeder to the Dublin University.']

He feels confident, that the firm and recognised position, the *status*, the high repute, and the overflowing numbers of the existing Colleges, will of themselves be sufficient to protect him, without any explanation of his own, from any appearance of disrespect towards those time-honoured establishments, or interference with their object, in the prosecution of his own design, which does but contemplate a scheme of education suitable to youths whose duties are to lie in the world. [Bellasis excised this paragraph on the ground that 'Qui s'excuse, s'accuse.']

The undertaking is commenced with the approbation and good will of the Right Revd the Bishop of the Diocese.'

The Prospectus went on to explain that a suitable house had already been taken within five minutes walk of the Oratory. Newman's 'This house will be managed by ladies residing in it,' was altered to 'The house will be committed to the managements of an experienced lady, as Matron,' because Bellasis and Hope-Scott thought the term 'ladies' 'might be conceived to imply "religious," and so cause observation.'

Finally, the Schoolroom and its masters were to be superintended by Darnell.

[3] The Hebdomadal Board at Oxford condemned *Tract XC* in March 1841. Lord Campbell was the judge at the Achilli trial.

[4] St Gregory, *Libri Moralium*, x, xxix, on Job 12:4.

[5] Demea is a character in the *Adelphi* of Terence.

Now I have no intention to increase a scandal, which is none of my making, which on the contrary I have done all I could to hinder.[1] The wrong words said against me may tend seriously to involve the prospects of the school; and, when I am fully embarked in the undertaking, and the inconvenience is felt, friends may be tempted to say, that I am bound for the sake of the school to answer them. I do not mean to do so: — first, because on the long run falsehood refutes itself: — secondly, because to speak out would retort the blame on those who throw it, and who can bear it less easily than I — thirdly, because spiritual books tell us, that, except when accused of unsoundness in faith, (though this, to be sure! may follow in time,) it is best to let imputations rest on one's head, without shaking them off; and fourthly, because I am too proud and indolent to move even my finger in the matter.

Still, it might be said, when the school is once begun, 'This is a public matter now, — not a personal; you are bound in duty to speak — ' and this I could not do without a great sacrifice, and an extreme distress. Therefore, I think that all those who are earnest in the plan of a school, should carefully think over these contingencies first, and see their way clearly as regards them.[2]

Another thing I have to mention, is, the subject of money. We think of engaging Arnold, if we can get him, as second master. We cannot offer him less than £300 a year. The House etc will not be much under £200. Here is £500 and of course for a *term* of years. This is an anxious undertaking. Before putting one's foot into the stream, the anxiety presents itself with more force than ordinary.

I often think, why should I be so busy? Why did I engage in the new University, bringing on me indefinite trouble and care, and taking up so many years? It was no business of mine. And now, scarcely am I rid of it, when I am putting my foot into another responsibility, when I might sit under my own vine and fig-tree in peace, for such years as Providence still gives me. Is it really the will of God? Shall I not, as time goes on, wish I had nothing to do with an undertaking which has only brought me anxiety and mortification?[3]

P.S.   I send a proof for your last criticisms. Please, return it.

Will you burn, or return to me, the paper I sent you last (I think) *April*, containing a project for the School, which is now superseded.[4]

---

[1] See the Memorandum Newman drew up on 20 Dec. 1858, listing the proofs he had of 'wrong words said against him.'
[2] See second letter of 21 Dec. to Bellasis.
[3] The conclusion has been cut out.
[4] This was the letter of 23 April to Bellasis.

TO CHARLES RUSSELL

The Oratory, Birmingham Decr 4. 1858

My dear Dr Russell,

⌐Thank you for your friendly letter.[1] I had already answered Dr Gartlan who most kindly announced to me his arrival in Dublin.

It is now 20 months since I acquainted the Bishops of Ireland individually of my proposed resignation of the Rectorship, naming the day, November 14, 1857

I kept it on a year longer to give the Archbishops time to make arrangements. I resigned absolutely last November 12.

If you care to see the state of the case, Mr Ornsby will give you a sight of three documents of mine, which are in his possession.⌐

I am, My dear Dr Russell, Yours affly in Xt

John H Newman of the Oratory

The Very Revd Dr Russell

MONDAY 6 DECEMBER 1858   Baldacchino removed into Church *to high Altar*

TO ROBERT ORNSBY, I

Decr 6/58

My dear O

⟨(of course all this is modified by your letter — but it will show you what I am aiming at) I only want no stigma to rest on the two youths.⟩

If I were asked what is the *simplest* way of getting out of the scrape about those two youths, it would be for the Vice Rector to write a letter to the Prince de Ligne and to the Countess Zamoyski to say that no sort of punishment has been inflicted by the University on the youths, that there was a disagreement between them and the gentleman who rented the house, that the Dean of it felt he could not keep them in it — but that they were hasty in not going to the Vice Rector, and, instead of that, of going away.

Ever Yrs J H N

[1] Russell wrote on 2 Dec., 'I am greatly distressed by the intelligence in your letter to Dr Gartlan, and he is still more so. I trust that what you say only amounts to this that you have offered your resignation, and that it is still possible to arrange so that consistently with your personal engagements and your avocations in your order you at least for a time retain your place as Rector. This is Dr Gartlan's most anxious wish. He begs me to say that he will do anything and everything to carry out this object and that his first and last wish is to act in every way in accordance with your views and wishes. He is a man whom I know you will like and understand and who will make it easy and agreeable for you to act with him. He is one of the honestest and most unselfish of men.

I will on my part do everything with the Primate and Dr Leahy to get this arrangement carried out. I feel strongly that if the University has a chance of being well settled it is in this way it must be done.'

18   529

P.S. I wrote by the first post to the two mothers, to assure them I was certain, that, whatever was the cause of what had happened, I was sure that their sons had done nothing inconsistent with their characters as gentlemen etc.[1]

P.S. Your letter just come.

1. If Anderdon says he told Z [Zaymoski] and de Ligne that he was *not* dismissed etc. it QUITE answers what I mean.[2] *But* it has ever been usually [sic] at Oxford, for the Tutor etc to write to the parents to state this fact. This has not been done in the case of Zamoyski. If a letter had been sent to me, for his mother, I could have forwarded it. I now send the mother's direction. 'Countess Zamoyska, 26 Quai de Béthune, Paris.'

I certainly did not mean you to *show* my letter. I say this, because the *tone* might have been offensive to them. But n'importe.

I protest against Scratton having any place *in* the House. It is no *gain* to me, for, as to the rent, the *furniture*, which is mine, would cover it.

There is no need of summoning the Council, if there is nothing but what can be explained by letter.[3]

I have never doubted Anderdon had a right to send a youth away from *his house*. But (entre nous) it *does* seem *cruel* to cast off two youths into the town.

Ever Yrs affly John H Newman of the Oratory

R Ornsby Esqr

P.S. You must be very much on your guard, please, lest you say things from me so, as if I were claiming *authority*. Scratton writes to me as if I had interfered as *Rector*. This is not *your* fault, however.

The Nation is very civil.[4]

The question is to be asked, whether Scratton should not give up the House at the end of the half year. I am *quite willing* — only I ought to know soon.

[1] The Princess de Ligne, née Hedwig, Princess Lubomirska, wrote from Beloeil, near Mons in Belgium, on 6 Dec., to thank Newman for his letter and 'for all your kindness for my children,' but was perplexed how to complete her son's education.
[2] Ornsby in his letter of 5 Dec., said that Anderdon had told Zamoyski clearly that he was being dismissed from St Mary's House, not from the University. De Ligne was not dismissed, but said that if Zamoyski went, he would go too.
[3] Ornsby requested Anderdon on Newman's behalf, to summon the Council, and gave him Newman's letter of 3 Dec. to read. Ornsby feared he might have acted rashly. See letter of 8 Dec. to Anderdon.
[4] Ornsby had sent Newman on 5 Dec. 'a copy of the *Nation* containing an exceedingly obliging reply to the attack in the *Irishman*.' See the end of Ornsby's letter of 1 Dec. The *Nation*, in its leading article on 4 Dec. defended the Catholic University from the accusation of being anti-national, by pointing out how numerous the Irish professors were, and how indispensable the English ones.

The Oratory Bm Decr 6/58

My dear Ornsby

I write this merely as a record. When I gave Scratton the House, I begged him not to put himself forward. I said that he should have the virtual appointment of Dean and Tutors — he could not have more than the virtual, by the Statutes. It really was mine.

I never supposed he would have taken any *place* in the House.[1] I gathered from him (rightly or wrongly) that he was still going to live at Kings town. I thought he will be like Sherrick in the Newcomes.[2]

I dare say there was incaution on my part, as there often is, knowing Scratton's ways. But, had he said I am going to take a place *as lessee*, I should have never allowed myself to make agreement with him. I should *not* have objected to his being Tutor, because Tutor is a recognised position.

I certainly think the University would have great right to complain of me, if I had knowingly brought into a collegiate house an authority who is not recognised by the Statutes. As far as it is my fault, I am very sorry. If the University interferes and undoes the arrangement, I shall not suffer by it.

In a letter just received, Scratton says 'Having undertaken it, I consider myself master of it, and I certainly must say that I think the master's place is head of his own table.'[3]

Ever Yrs affly J H N

TO P. N. LYNCH, BISHOP OF CHARLESTON

Oy Bm Dec 7. 1858

My dear Lord

I have to thank your Lordship for your obliging letter and the Document which accompanies it.[4] I cannot at the moment make a more suitable answer

---

[1] Ornsby in his letter of 5 Dec. reported Anderdon as saying that he and Scratton had conjointly discussed Zamoyski.

[2] *The Newcomes*, Chapter XVI, Sherrick, the Jewish landlord, controlled his lodgers from a distance.

[3] Newman made a note on his collection of letters from Scratton: 'N.B. While I could do any thing for Scratton it was "My dear Father," "I hasten to close with your kind offer"— "Your excessive kindness confuses and overwhelms me"—"You have been much kinder to me than I deserve" "Yours very affectly"

But when I had left the University, it was "Dear Dr Newman" "do me the favour to send me a receipt," "Most faithfully yours." [See letter of 16 Jan. 1864 to Scratton]

At the same time, while I was at Dublin, I grant he served me most faithfully—but—as it seems to me, it was for hire. I doubt whether he ever heartily took my part, as Ornsby did.
                                                                                        J H N'

[4] The Bishop of Charleston sent Newman a printed copy of Resolutions passed at the Ninth Provincial Council of Baltimore on 8 May 1858. Archbishop Kenrick of Baltimore

to it than by explaining to you and the other Prelates of the Province of Baltimore the relation in which I stand to the great work which the 2nd Synod of Westminster proposes, and the circumstances which have brought me into that relation.

I esteem it a great honor to hold it, and a great honor also to be made the subject of your Lordship's letter and of the Resolutions of your Rt Revd Brothers, and for my name to be associated in such a matter with your Archbishops

Soon after the 2nd Synod of Westminster, held at Oscott in July 1855, while I was in Dublin in my then duties in the new University, on my return here for the Vacation, my Diocesan, Dr Ullathorne, said in the course of confidential conversation 'we have put into your hands the duty of preparing a new translation of Scripture,' or words to that effect. The information simply took me by surprise, as I had not turned my thoughts that way, and I supposed I should have heard of it officially in a little while. This anticipation was not fulfilled for a reason to be stated presently and in consequence the subject passed from my mind, nor did I take any one step towards it.

So matters rested for above two years — when (under date of August 26. 1857) I received the following most gracious communication from our Cardinal Archbishop — ' I beg to call your attention to the ninth Decree of the 2nd Provincial Synod of Westr [Westminster] p 30, "De Versione canonicarum scripturarum." You will easily understand, how it would have been inconvenient, not to say unfair, to have inserted the names of any persons in a Decree subject to approval or disapproval, in substance and in details, by a higher authority. And therefore no persons were named in the Decree itself. But the Bishops in reality had agreed, at the time they drew up the decree, that to you was to be committed the grave and most important work proposed in it, and that you had to select and name the persons whom you would wish to have for assistants in the undertaking. . . . But further, in the Letter, explanatory of the Decrees, which I forwarded to the Sacred Congregation of P.F. [Propaganda Fide] with the Acts of the Synod, I explained who were the "viri docti" contemplated in this decree, that is, yourself and your Colleagues. So that the approbation of this Decree has been granted by the Holy See with the cognisance and approbation of this circumstance. . . I now therefore, in behalf of myself, and my episcopal brethren, request you to accept this expression of the confidence reposed in you by the English Episcopate, and to undertake etc.'

---

had already published a translation from the Vulgate of the New Testmanet, the Psalms and Sapiential Books, while his translation of the rest of the Old Testament was prepared for publication. The Council proposed that Newman should be asked to co-operate with Kenrick in producing a joint version that could be used in all English speaking countries. The Bishop of Charleston in his covering letter of 11 Nov. explained that the rest of the American Bishops concurred with those of the Province of Baltimore. He hoped Newman would not find 'any serious difficulty' in the proposal. Wiseman and Barnabò had also been asked to approve.

On receiving this letter, I requested a copy of the Acts and Decrees of the Synod, and found, at p 30, the following Decree: —

'Ut versio accurata Sacrae Scripturae ex vulgatâ Latinâ quam primùm habeatur, Patres censuerunt committendam esse viris doctis ab Eminentissimo Archiepiscopo eligendis ejus confectionem, servatis tamen regulis Indicis etc (quoad operis revisionem, notas apponendas ex SS Patribus et piis scriptoribus desumptas, et permissionem et approbationem lectionis ejusdem.)'

Considering the great confidence and the great honor shown to me in this act of the united Episcopate of England, the authority of a Synod, and my duty as a priest to concur in its decisions, (to say nothing of the concurrence of the Holy See) and on the other hand the extreme ungraciousness and ingratitude of declining so high a mark of its consideration, I wrote a letter to the Cardinal, on the September 14th following, in acceptance of his Eminence's proposal. At the same time I asked among other questions, the very difficult one, how the expenses of the work were to be met.

To this question I did not receive any answer, owing to the great per-lexities attending it, till a few weeks ago, when Dr Clifford, Bishop of Clifton sent me the following official notice of 'resolutions passed at the Bishops meeting relating to the translation of the Bible March 10. 1858. "Dr N. [Newman] having proposed two alternatives respecting the expense of publish-ing a translation of the Holy Scripture, it was agreed to allow the copyright to be reserved to Dr Newman, etc"' Dr Clifford's letter is dated October 11 last[1]

And now, my Lord, I have told you every thing that has passed on the matter. Were I called on to relinquish the work at this moment, the only personal inconvenience I should sustain, would be the loss of a sum, considerable to me, though not great in itself which I have laid out in books etc etc for the prosecution of it.

As to considerations, which are not simply personal, but which have a just claim to decide my course of acting, on the one hand I feel the most extreme reluctance and pain in seeming to come into competition in such a matter with

---

[1] See note to letter of 18 July 1858 to Caswall. Meanwhile a copy of the Resolutions of the Council of Baltimore on 8 May was sent to Wiseman, with a covering letter signed by John McGill, Bishop of Richmond and P. N. Lynch, Bishop of Charleston, dated 8 Oct. Wiseman gave the Resolutions and letter to Ullathorne to show to Newman. The two Bishops, after explaining the position, said, 'Your Eminence and the Prelates of England cannot fail to see the many inconveniences, and evils which would arise should different versions be used in different countries where the English language is spoken. The Protestants would scoff and the simple Catholic laity would be cast into perplexity. National rivalries and wounded feelings would also scarcely fail to embitter, and prolong any controversies that might arise. The task of withdrawing a Version so widely spread among Catholics as is the Douay and substituting another recently prepared is one so delicate and difficult that it seems to us well, to give to the New Version, the highest and amplest authority possible, and carefully to avoid any unnecessary grounds of controversy. We hope therefore that your Eminence will receive favourably the proposition of the Resolutions and will exert your powerful influence with Dr Newman, and the others interested in his work so that instead of a Version prepared under the auspices of a single Province and of authority in one Nation only the English speaking Catholics of the world may receive a Version prepared under such circumstances as will ensure its ready acceptance by all. . . .' Newman returned this letter and the Resolutions, when writing to Ullathorne on 23 March 1859. Cf. also letter of 12 Aug. 1859 to Wiseman.

the Archbishop of Baltimore, a man so immeasurably superior to me, in station, in services to the Church, in theological knowledge, in reputation, in qualifications for the work, and in careful preparation for it, (who moreover has actually given to the world complete and ready for the use of the faithful, so great a portion of it); but on the other hand I am pledged to the Bishops of England by duty, by gratitude, and by my word.

May I then beg of your Lordship to present my humble respects to the Bishops of your Province, and, in answer to their condescending message, to assure them that I am quite ready to concur in any measure on which the bishops of England shall determine[1]

TO ROBERT ORNSBY

The Ory Bm Decr 7/58

Private

My dear Ornsby

I am sorry to give you more trouble.

This morning brings a letter from Z. [Zamoyski] and de L. [Ligne] dated the 5th at Morrison's Hotel.

If they are *still* there, for they *may* have written to me on their leaving for the continent, would you object to put the inclosed letter in the post? Read it and judge.

I suppose you will be easily able before doing so, to make out if they are there or not.[2]

Ever Yrs J H N

R Ornsby Esqr

[1] Wiseman, Grant and Ullathorne, who had been appointed, on 10 March by the English Bishops, 'to arrange with Dr Newman the conditions and duration of the copyright' never did so; nor did Wiseman and the English Bishops reply to the proposal made to them by the Council of Baltimore, with the concurrence of the rest of the American hierarchy. See letters of 2 April 1860 to John Gilmary Shea, and 8 July 1860 to Archbishop Kenrick, who eventually published his own version complete. It was no advantage for Newman to have the copyright of a translation, when there was a serious obstacle in the way of its publication.
Newman wrote to Miss Holmes on 20 Aug. 1864, 'I waited, in the matter of the translation of Scripture, *till* a great hitch should be taken out of the way. I found the Cardinal was washing his hands of the whole affair and throwing the responsibility upon me. First he threw all the money-transactions on me. I was to make all engagements with the publishers, and the Bishops were to have nothing to do with it. To this I had consented—but next he gave *me* to manage the *American* difficulty—not that he said so, but he sent me the American Bishops' letters, wished me to answer them, and did not answer them himself. If I am right, he did not send me a single line with the American letters, but simply the letters. I foresaw clearly that I should have endless trouble with publishers, American hierarchy, Propaganda etc etc if I took this upon me. So I waited *till* I heard something more about it, but I have never heard till this day any thing.' Cf. the rest of this letter to Miss Holmes, and *Ward* I, pp. 425–9; also letter of 7 June 1862 to Belaney.
[2] Zamoyksi and de Ligne left Dublin on 6 Dec., and Ornsby wrote on 8 Dec. returning Newman's letter to them. In their joint letter of apology on 5 Dec. they blamed Scratton's 'uncivil behaviour,' and thanked Newman 'for the kindness you have shown us during our stay in Dublin.'

TO JOHN HUNGERFORD POLLEN

The Oratory, Birmingham Decr 7. 1858

My dear Pollen

I suppose the inclosed should go to you. — the man you will see presses. I ought to have sent his letter on before.

We found the Baldacchino too large for the Chapel and have put it at the high altar — where it is seen to great advantage.

Is anything else to come?

Ever Yrs affly John H Newman of the Oratory

J. H. Pollen Esqr

FROM WILLIAM HENRY ANDERDON

6 Harcourt St. Dec 7. 1858

My dear Father,

In reference to your letter to Ornsby, which he came to read to me, I will say that a detailed statement has been sent to the Archbishop to Rome; and that upon any notification from his Grace of his wishes on the subject (which I have requested) I will proceed to act as he may direct, whether to the resignation of my Deanship, or any other measure.

Thro'out, I have kept strictly within the Statutes, as I have detailed to the Archbishop.

I may be wrong, but I do not at present see how, inasmuch as you have resigned the Rectorship, and declined repeatedly to exercise any Rectorial act, you can well call upon any department in the University to legislate or to assemble. I must go further, and express my surprise and concern that you should have permitted yourself to write at once so peremptorily and so indirectly; addressing yourself to a Professor who was unconnected with the matter, and not asking from me an explanation, or even a statement of facts.

I cannot wonder that Scratton feels so deeply moved at the tone of your communications with him, or so unwilling to continue responsible for a house about which he has met with such hindrances where he might have looked for help, and acknowledgments for service done. I share his feelings; for we have been together in an undertaking which certainly smiled on neither of us; and the wound has reached me also.

But I am still, with memories of 1835–6,[1] and of a thousand early kindnesses which later things have not yet effaced,

Affectionately yours W H Anderdon

The Very Revd Dr. Newman

[1] This was when Anderdon first went up to Oxford, aged nineteen. In 1885 Anderdon wrote, 'I met the dear Cardinal first at H. W.'s [Wilberforce] curacy in Hampshire, before I went up to Oxford, just when the Tracts for the Times were getting under weigh; and that meeting was the foundation for a series of kind acts and all-important helps to me, which it would be the height of ingratitude ever to forget.' *Letters and Notices of the English Jesuit Province*, 20, 1889–90, p. 394.

Copy.

The Oratory Birmingham. In fest. Imm. Con. [8 December] 1858.

My dear Anderdon,

I did not mean Ornsby to read my letter to you. When I found he had done so it took me by surprise.

Had I meant to send a message to you, I should not have written by another person. What I wished, though I seem not to have adequately expressed it to Ornsby, was to put him into such full possession of what I felt, that he might be in a position to act as if he were I, and as expressing my sentiments instead of me.

It was this that has made my letter seem peremptory to you, viz. that I was writing familiarly to a friend, not to an authority. In consequence I took no copy of it.

I wrote in no sense as Rector, or as having any authority whatever but as a friend of the two youths in their parents' absence.

I wrote to a private friend, and not to any authority, for the very reason that I wished to avoid seeming to write as if I were an authority myself. I think I said so in the first sentence of my letter to Ornsby.

I spoke of the Council, not as meaning in any sense to dictate, but in order to put Ornsby into possession of what I was aiming at, which was to prevent a stigma attaching to the youths through life.

I did not mean to summon any department of the University to 'legislate or assemble,' but in private I told Ornsby what seemed to me the way by which the just claims of the friends of the youths might be satisfied in the clearing of their characters. If my words fairly meant more, I disclaim that meaning.

Considering that the parents had committed their sons to me, and that I was the only person whom you could write to as regards Zamoiski (for I do not think you knew his mother's direction) I think I had a claim, that you should at once have informed me of their dismissal. On the other hand, it was not unnatural that on very first hearing the news, my interest in the two youths, and my sense of duty towards their parents, should have made me write at once and strongly to a friend who would interest himself in my place, in order to save the parents the distress of suddenly learning of a disgrace that had come on their children.

I am extremely surprised and concerned at your last words, which nothing I have done explain.[1]

I am, My dear Anderdon Yrs affly J. H N.

[1] Anderdon's reply is not to be found, but cf. Newman's letter of 24 Dec. In March 1859 Anderdon was writing to ask Newman's advice as to whether he should accept the headship of a Catholic College in the University of Sydney.

Copy   Dec 8. 1858

My dear Scratton

Neither of us entered into the negociation about Number 6, except for the sake of the University.[1]

For myself, I could sell my furniture tomorrow to good advantage — and out of it pay the rent to Mrs Segrave; but I had wished to preserve a house to the University, and I had intended to make a present of my furniture for the same purpose.

I will simply state what I thought I was doing, in our negociation, as regards your relation to the house, and there leave the matter. I thought you were holding the house as *Trustee* for the University, which does not imply possession or occupancy. I used the very word 'Trustee' to you, in speaking or writing, as you may recollect, when I spoke of putting the furniture into your hands.

Now, if you wish, I am quite ready to bring the bargain to an end at any time you name, so that it is not later than March 17, lest I should lose the opportunity of selling the furniture.

Pray pardon me, if I have, against my intention, said any thing harsh to you, particularly in a matter in which I know so well you meant to be kind to me[2]

I am &c J H N

Thos Scratton Esqr

TO JAMES STEWART

Confidential   The Oratory Birmingham Decr 9. 1858

My dear Stewart

I write to you, not as being Rector or as having any authority in the University, but simply as a friend of Zamoyski. And I write to *you* as Dean of your Faculty. And I write privately not wishing my name to appear.

[1] Scratton wrote on 6 Dec., complaining that Newman had judged him severely, and without a hearing. 'The whole truth of the matter is (what perhaps you are not prepared to hear) that Count Zamoyski grossly insulted me in (what I certainly consider to be) my own house. . . . With the full concurrence of Mr Anderdon I told him that I would not have him any longer in the house. . . .

If it be supposed that I am bound to submit to any insults that the students in Harcourt Street choose to put upon me . . . I say advisedly that you have made a great mistake in committing the care of the House to me, and the sooner you relieve me of the charge the better . . .'

[2] Scratton replied on 9 Dec. 'Many thanks for your kind letter—As far as I am myself concerned I should be very glad to shut up St Mary's but I feel it would be felt as a *blow* to the University.' Scratton added that he would consider for a few days about taking it on. See letter of 16 Dec. to him.

I inclose a letter I have received from him this morning. I have *told* him that I shall send it to *you*, as *Dean*.

As you know well, I have several times been on the point of recommending him to leave the University myself — I have no great idea of his diligence. I know he has been rude — but I take his part, first as his mother's representative, to whom I conceive I have a *duty* — secondly because I think he has been hardly treated; thirdly because I do not think it expedient to let a foreigner go away from a country, whose fame used to be *hospitality*, so abruptly, when he sincerely prizes the honor which the University can give him, I mean a degree, when so few persons are found to do so.

Will you consider this letter addressed to you as Dean — and let my name drop out of the matter. Whether the Statutes allow of his being a non-resident and taking a degree as he wishes, I cannot say — nor can I say whether the authorities of the University will grant his request, even if it be possible.[1]

Ever Yours affly John H Newman

J. Stewart Esqr

TO THE EARL OF DUNRAVEN

The Oratory Birmingham Decr 10. 1858

My dear Lord Dunraven,

I sent Father Flanagan to two physicians in London, that I might have a last chance of being able to send him to Adare, in case you allowed me still to do so. Both on account of your strong wish, the reason for which I so well understood and sympathised in, and for his own sake, that he might be under so careful an eye as yours, and in so large and well-protected an abode, I wished it very much.

Alas, the medical men confirmed my most anxious apprehensions, as I expressed them in my first letter to you. One of them was the friend who had seen him at Pau and was so anxious for his going abroad — the other a stranger to him.[2] They find the mischief just where it was, dormant but present. It is in what they called the most 'significant,' that is, dangerous place — at the top of the lungs, under the collar bone — in the front of the right and in the back of the left lung. It is either a tubercular deposit, or inflammation — they cannot tell which. Of course it may lay [sic] dormant for years, but it is death, if it rouses. The chances are, I fear, rather, that it will be a slow

[1] See letter of 13 Dec. to Stewart.
[2] De Castro was the doctor from Pau. The other doctor's name was Walsh. They had their consultation on 30 Nov., and Flanagan decided to leave for Brussels on 2 Dec., to join his cousin Stephen Woulfe Flanagan and his wife, at Paris, and go with them straight to Palermo. He sailed from Marseilles on 11 Dec.

wasting evil, bringing him down gradually to the grave. He does not know all this.

Then they said — 'He may be kept quite safe from illness at Adare — but it will be at the sacrifice of never going out. Now, his only chance is to be out in the air through the winter. A continual air bath may give him that increase of strength which will enable him to throw it off — and of course his increase of strength through the past summer is hopeful.'

I am sorry to say he writes from Brussels that he has symptoms of a returning cough, and cannot say Mass — but he is to cross from Marseilles to Palermo, as tomorrow.

My impression is that the physicians almost give him up. On the other hand, it is just a case for prayer — and prayer has done so much already, that I trust that we shall not slacken, and that we shall get more still

Believe me, My dear Lord Dunraven with great attachment, Yours most sincerely in Xt

John H Newman of the Oratory

The Earl of Dunraven

P.S. What dreadful trials are on Hope Scott. Now his boy is lying between life and death.

TO HENRY HENNESSY

The Oratory, Birmingham. Dec. 10th. 1858.

My dear Professor Hennessy,

I have not written sooner to acknowledge your letter, and your masterly Lecture, because I wished to do justice to it, and I have been so closely engaged in finishing my Article for the Atlantis, and in correspondence, that I have not till now found time to do so. I am sure it will be of service to the cause of the University, and hope you have dispersed it abroad widely. It contains a great deal of matter, and a great deal to think about. Your illustration by means of the rotatory and annual motions of the earth is very happy.[1]

Thank you for all you so kindly say about my own difficulties in continuing at my post in Dublin consistently with my duties to the Oratory. I wish it had been otherwise.

I am concerned to say that the time is passed when I could have done anything in the way of influence to gain you what sums were necessary towards an Observatory — but I don't think, on that account, that you will

---

[1] This was Hennessy's Inaugural Lecture in the Faculty of Science.

539

not succeed in the object. Recollect, that at Rome, as you have suggested in your Lecture, there is a great desire that Physical Science should be well represented in the University. I have signed a cheque making over my balance to others — and this some weeks ago, though I believe the transaction has not yet been completed.[1]

Yours most sincerely, John H. Newman of the Oratory.

H. Hennessy Esq.

P.S.   I made a suggestion to Mr. Stewart lately about the Address of the evening Students to me. Will you bear in mind 1. that I did it merely as a *friend*, and not in any sense as Rector or as an authority — 2. that *I did not like it* in itself, but considered it might be thought *more* practicable than for the Evening Students to Address the Government. But, if you ask me, *on the whole* I had *much rather* nothing was done with the address.[2]

TO ROBERT ORNSBY

The Oratory Bm Decr 11. 1858

My dear Ornsby

I am very much obliged to you for taking so kindly my letters to A [Anderdon] and S. [Scratton] for I had some fear lest you should think I had thrown you over. And on reading over my letter to A. which you return, I think I ought to have taken more blame from you than I have.[3]

I value most exceedingly the kind promptness of your communications on all subjects; and the punctuality with which you so generously follow out any suggestion of mine. Pardon me, if I have misled you on this occasion.

I hope (entre nous) good will come of it, in making certain persons more cautious in future. Scratton has written a kind letter, and we are friends again. As to A., his letter to me was a most improper one — bumptious and severe. I fear I cannot expect any explanation from him, though you have seen mine to him. I shall be greatly relieved, if I have one

Ever Yrs affly J H N

R. Ornsby Esqr

[1] See letter of 11 Dec. to Scratton.
[2] See postscript to letter of 3 Dec. to Ornsby. Hennessy replied on 12 Dec. agreeing that an address from the Evening Classes would be premature.
[3] When returning these letters on 10 Dec., Ornsby wrote that he thought them 'the best you could possibly have written to remedy the difficulty into which I so unfortunately brought you.'

TO THOMAS SCRATTON

(Copy)   Decr 11. 1858

My dear Scratton

I am much obliged to you for your letter of this morning; and willingly wait for your answer, as you propose.[1]

I was not prepared to find that Anderdon had used my cheque for the balance of account, £1500 odd, without my knowing.

You may recollect that I wanted to sign a cheque for £500 in his favour for current expenses.

When you sent me one to sign for the whole balance, not to be ungracious, I signed it; but I said (I think) that I wished for some authorization from Dr Leahy before it was used.

You answered that the cheque was safely locked up.

I expected to have heard before it was actually used; and, in my last letter, which you now answer, I said that, if used, I ought to have a receipt. You tell me now of it, but you don't send me one.

Now I wish you would be so good as to gain for me from Anderdon two things: —

    1 a statement that Dr Leahy authorized the transfer.

    2. a stamped receipt of the money.

Certainly one or two letters on the part of Anderdon to me would have been a condescension not out of place. These two documents, however, I must require, not as a matter of condescension, but of right[2]

                                                  I am &c J H N

TO ROBERT ORNSBY

                                                  ⌐Decr 12. 1858

An article, of a most favourable character, has appeared in the Irishman.[3] Send, or not, the inclosed to him, according to your judgment.[4] The only objection I see is, that the Editor might publish it; and this, besides other inconveniences, would seem uncivil to the Nation, and look like gratitude to

---

[1] See second note to letter of 8 Dec. to Scratton.

[2] On 13 Dec. Anderdon wrote explaining that he had been authorised by Archbishops Dixon and Leahy to take over the balance of the University 'Cullen and Newman' account, £1558, 8s. 11d., and Scratton sent Newman a receipt.

[3] The *Irishman* made an amende for the letter it published against the University. See end of letter of 1 Dec. and postscript to first letter of 6 Dec. to Ornsby.

[4] Ornsby sent the letter Newman enclosed, to the Editor of the *Irishman*, marking it 'private.'

enemies greater than to friends. Perhaps this might be obviated by a line to the Nation, thanking the Editor for *his* Article.

J H N.[1]

MONDAY 13 DECEMBER 1858   went to London to Lintott, Hope Scott, Burns and back

TO JAMES STEWART

The Oratory Birmingham December 13. 1858

My dear Stewart

I have just returned from London, and find your letter, which I cannot answer by return of post. Thank you for it, and for the promptness with which you have done the matter.

Yet I have some difficulty of leaving the matter to Anderdon's good-nature — he has shown himself so very un-tender in the affair hitherto. He might stick to his first resolve as an act of faith, and refuse to give Zamoyski permission to stand except at the price of an apology, to Scratton — which Z will never give.

Might I ask in confidence, have you not, can you not have, a second string to your bow? You have in your reply waived the question of non-residence — not liking, I suppose, to entertain it. But what *will you do*, if, after saying to him in the name of the Professors of Faculty, 'there is no reason *as far as they are concerned*, why you should not present yourself for examination,' it should turn out that there is every reason as far *as the Dean* is concerned? He will say, 'This has been an evasion. If you, the Faculty, had not the power to give leave, you should not have implied you had; you should not have answered my question. You should have said, The question does not belong to us, but the Council.'

I hope you will be able to remove this scruple from my mind. As it stands, I think I could hardly send him the letter, without drawing his attention to the fact, that a line is drawn under the words 'as far as they etc.'

Even, if you were inclined to grant non-residence, it struck me whether the statute allowed you to grant it except to those who *reside in colleges*. But, on second thoughts, I think it was Butler whose proposition this was, but the statute itself goes further.

Ever Yours affly, John H Newman.

James Stewart Esqr.

P.S.   One thing has struck me but of course do not mention my name any more than before, else, a suggestion is magnified into a command, — why should not Z ask leave to transfer himself to St Patricks? — it would be only a matter of form, and I suppose the new Dean of St P certainly would not refuse, when the time came, to let him proceed to his Examination.[1]

You must be so good as to send me Zamoyski's direction. I thought it was '6 Union Street, Berkeley Square,' but I can't find any such street in the Postal Guide.[2]

TO HENRY HENNESSY

The Oratory, Birmingham Dec. 14th. 1858

My dear Mr. Hennessy,

I think you may fairly ask to be reimbursed for any expenses you have actually incurred in the researches you speak of — and I do not at all doubt that you will succeed in that object, if Dr. Leahy is but made acquainted with it.

Very truly yours, John H. Newman

H. Hennessy Esq.

P.S. I have never properly congratulated you as I now do heartily, on your F.R.S.

TO THOMAS ARNOLD

Not sent[3]   The Oratory Bm [15] Decr 1858

My dear Arnold,

As I said I would give you the refusal, before I wrote to any one else on the subject of the Mastership, I send this to you, not expecting, I am sorry to say, to change your decision, but having been strongly urged to make the attempt by friends who are interested in our plan.

---

[1] After this letter of Newman's, Stewart approached Anderdon again, and secured a promise that he would give Zamoyski the certificate of residence necessary for him to sit for his degree, 'provided he had not to give a certificate that he approved of his conduct.' Zamoyski came to Dublin and took his degree in Jan. 1859.

[2] The address was correct.

[3] Realising that the proposed economies at the University and the wish to employ Irishmen rendered his position there insecure, Arnold was looking for another post. He wrote on 3 Dec. to Newman that 'the school at Birmingham would certainly have many attractions for me,' but asked for a week to consider it, as he had the opportunity of a post in Ireland under the National Board of Education, which, however, did not materialise. Bellasis returned this draft of a letter to Newman on 16 Dec. Arnold did not come as a master to the Oratory School, until 1862, after the departure of Darnell.

I have not a little compunction, at aiming to withdraw from the University so zealous and able a member of the Professorial body — but I can truly say that my fears for the stability of your position there are simply prior to, and independent of, my wish to gain you for the School — and, if they are not fulfilled in the event and you stay in Dublin, it will be a great rejoicing to me, both for the sake of the University and your own, that I have been instrumental in settling you there.

Also I can say, that I had given you up — till my friends in London urged me on again. I say all this, lest I should seem to any one to be shabby to the University; but I do not forget that you are *otherwise* looking about for a more lucrative situation, and I reflect that the University might lose you still, without our gaining you.

Now for my terms.

I offer you £50 down, for the expense of moving etc. And £300 a year With an increase of £5 per annum on each boy over the number of 20 lasting for a year, and I offer this arrangement for 3 years certain from next Lady Day — at the end of which time we are both free for a fresh arrangement.

Your work would be little more than Musa, musae — amo, amavi. And, say, six hours a day. You would have no duties whatever towards the boys out of school hours — except indeed looking over exercises etc.

Take a week to think over this.

Ever Yours affly (signed) J H N

THURSDAY 16 DECEMBER 1858   Exposition. [of the Blessed Sacrament] *Quarant'Ore*

FROM SIR JOHN ACTON

Aldenham Park Bridgnorth December 10 1858

My dear Father Newman,

I have been prevented from writing by a house full of company and a couple of days' illness into the bargain.

Your objections to the proposed alteration in the atlantis seem to refer chiefly to the injury it might do to the professors individually, and in general to the university. I do not think it would be any disadvantage to either if the atlantis, without changing its character, were to extend its scope. It cannot be extended beyond the limits of what is taught at a University. Indeed I should say that nothing can be more suitable than that the review which is to represent and lead Catholic opinion on every variety of subject should be conducted by the members of the Catholic University. It would be a great security against that levity and superficial popularity by which the English reviews have done so much harm to literature. It is quite right that a review should both popularise the results of research and contain the first announcement of them. I have in my eye the publications of some of the German universities and academies, as the Göttingen Gelehrte auseigen, the Heidelberger Jahrbücher, and the old

544

Wiener Jahrbücher. All the papers that appeared in them bore indeed the character of reviews, but that is a barrier which in England has never confined the range of writers. Holding, in a general way, to this analogy, I do not quite feel the importance of your second objection, that most subjects of the day, politics, ecclesiastical matters, theology, must be excluded. The Roman Jesuits are obliged to treat of all such questions in their official organ, and whilst they have more caution to observe than the University, they have manifestly less claim to be heard than those whose business it is to teach the various sciences at a university. If the body of professors is complete and if each science which belongs to a Universitas litterarum is represented in their number, they will be equally authorised to discuss each question. The professors of canon law, of political science, of speculative philosophy, are surely in every respect as much fitted to publish their opinions and their researches as the professors of mathematics or chemistry, and they are justified in instructing the public through the press by their appointment to teach the youth in the lecture room. Certainly their enquiries are the most important of all, and those upon which the public will be most curious. The objection that all these places may not be filled at the University does not obtain, if the contributors are not confined exclusively to members of the University. Indeed it seems that those are the very subjects on which, in the midst of warring opinions, people may expect to find enlightenment among the teachers of the highest school of Catholic learning. Some authority is required on such points, and in a review conducted by the professors of Dublin it is always certain that each subject will be treated by a competent person who has made it his study and not by an amateur. I do not believe that there is less certainty in these sciences than in others, and I am sure they are the most important. I should imagine too that the scientific treatment of these matters, without party vehemence, would be of great weight and value. I cannot conceive any other nucleus of Catholic thinkers who could form our opinions with some sort of harmony and agreement. This I confess strikes me as the thing most wanted, and I hope you will forgive me if I express my feeling clearly, not because it can help to induce you, but because it explains the motives which make many think as I do, who would be able to be of great assistance in carrying on the review. The great influence exercised by the British critic came from the fact that there were many able men, living more or less together, and all thinking and writing under the influence of the ideas which in sermons, books, essays and private conversation, you were putting forth. There was a stamp upon them all which I can yet often trace distinctly upon both Catholics and Protestants that I know, who belonged to the Tractarian party in those days. It would be much regretted if the Dublin University failed to do a similar service among ourselves. A quarterly review in your hands, written by your professors, and by all other competent Catholics who would be ready to join, would be of all things the one most likely to be of benefit to the Church in England. We have been long afflicted with a real calamity in the Dublin Review, and it has accustomed a large portion of our number to that intellectual lethargy which it displayed. On the other hand many are carried away by a superficial brilliancy to errors of thought and feeling which are still more dangerous. The Rambler would not be so outspoken and so ill humoured if these things were not felt as disasters by most of those who read it. But a monthly, especially with such traditions, can do no more than excite discontent and a wish for something better. If I had succeeded in obtaining the new Dublin Review it was my wish to conduct it for the ends I have alluded to with your assistance and under your guidance. The thing will be much better done if you will undertake it yourself, with the assured help of the University.

You say that the atlantis must be essentially Irish—if so it has a more exclusive character than the University itself. As to remuneration for scientific articles, I must mention Simpson's suggestion that there might be a scientific supplement, say half yearly. It will be a greater advertisement of the capacity of professors if the review has a wider scope, and therefore a greater number of readers.

I must mention one thing that occupied my thoughts very much when the transfer of the DR. [Dublin Review] to me was spoken of. A large portion of Anglicans are very attentive to Catholic writings and are always looking out for things to interest them. Almost every number of such a print as the 'Literary cabinet' is cited in the Union. Faber's books are read by thousands of copies by Protestants. There is a great deal to be done here, and few Catholics know the importance of it. None I am sure know how to deal with it except yourself. The influence of a review in your hands upon the higher schools of Protestant, and also upon such men as the writers in the 'Saturday' and even the 'Westminster' Reviews, would be quite as great as among Catholics.

I do not know whether anything I have said diminishes the force of the objections you named, but I hope it will induce to attach some weight to the advantages which the plan will offer.

Ever faithfully Yours   John D. Acton

TO SIR JOHN ACTON

The Oratory Birmingham Decr 16. 1858

My dear Sir John,

I inclose a prospectus of the Atlantis in order to show you how definite its object is.[1] I do not see how it can possibly depart from that object. It was set up, not as a strictly University organ, but as an organ of the Faculties of Arts and Science. We have had some difficulty (to speak to you in confidence) in keeping clear of medical articles — and only by keeping to the rule, that it is intended for Literature and Science. Again, if we let in Theology *as such*, we should have a great difficulty in keeping our course steady. And we should get into trouble with Theological Censors, an inconvenience, which, even as it is, we have not altogether escaped.[2]

And therefore, whatever is desirable, whatever not, the Atlantis will not be any thing but literary and scientific — not religious, not ecclesiastical, not political.

Nor could it be for another reason. Think of Irish politics! where should we be, if we once committed ourselves to such a whirl pool? There are among our members, Whigs, Conservatives, Young Irelanders, Tories. Contrast the prospect thus opened with our Prospectus.

On the other hand, if I may venture to give an opinion, I don't think the time has quite arrived for such a periodical as you propose. I think you ought to feel your way more. You would come too with far more weight to the management of a Review, if you first showed, which no one could do better than you, that you had given such time to patient study and thought, that you had a right to take part in current events. A year or two is nothing in your life, or Simpson's, whatever it may be in mine.

My difficulty about payment of articles is not quite removed — and then there is a difficulty in your *promising* to continue your contributions; else, I should propose your joining the Atlantis as literary contributors, making the work half literary, with distinct pagings, allowing the scientific parts to sell

[1] See second note to letter of 20 Oct. 1857 to Sullivan.
[2] See the letters of 25 May, and that of 2 Aug. 1858 to Morris.

separately, and publishing quarterly. Could you engage yourselves to this for three years? would the conductors of the Atlantis allow three years as sufficient?

The conductors might not be unwilling to be independent of the University, though conducted by University men. They would be very willing, if a plan was proposed to them which gave them money for their printing. At present printing and paper cost a good £100 a number; the University has paid hitherto — but I cannot predict it will do so longer.

Now, having thus brought out what I have to say — , I will answer any points in your letter in detail, which, on re-perusing it, seem to me to require notice.

Well, on reading your letter, I have nothing to say. One great point of difference is, whether a Review should be started *at once*.

Another is as to my capacity to take any great part in any periodical. Now first, I often feel that I am used up — at least for such purposes. A person should be younger in age, in mind, in thought, in experience, and in views, than I am, to write with freshness and energy. And then, things seem to have gone past me, and I don't know whom I am likely to influence. And moreover, I wanted now at length, the University being off my hands, to go back to my old studies, and to do something, if life is given me, more solid than I have done hitherto — And lastly, as to the moment, I intended to lie fallow this next year — for I am very tired.

> Ever Yours most sincerely John H Newman of the Oratory

Sir John Acton Bart

P.S.   I hope you have got well.

TO THOMAS SCRATTON

(Copy)   Decr 16. 1858

My dear Scratton,

I have taken some days to answer the proposal contained in your letter of December 4, because I did not wish to act without deliberation, and I waited for the letter you have now sent me, to see if any thing in it was likely to affect the question one way or the other.

Now I write to say that our arrangement as to Number 6 is accompanied with so many difficulties, that I think I had best avail myself of the offer contained in your letter of December 4, in which you say, 'I never wished to take the House, but I *did* undertake it for the sake of the University. I have taken upon myself a great anxiety and responsibility, but am ready and delighted to surrender it all to you tomorrow, if you will do me the kindness to relieve me of the burden.'

These are my reasons: —

You say in your letter of December 9 'It cannot, I suppose, pay its way, unless we can contrive to fill it; but I shall not grudge £100 or so, provided any real good is done.'

Now I have no wish at all on my own account for your keeping the house; your doing so is no good to me; and on your own account personally I wish you not to do so, for I don't wish you to risk pecuniary loss. You will say, that this is your own look-out; yes, but it is mine too. Two months ago I did not think you would lose; but, looking at things as they stand now, I think you *will*. But I shall lose also; I shall have the credit of causing you to lose, I shall be said (however unjustly, but it *has* been said already) to have secured my rest at your expense; to have driven a hard bargain with you, and the like. And then I shall be bound, not by you, but in honour, and according to the opinion of the world, to take part in the loss, and that after all for the sake of the University, which stands by and lets us both suffer.

Both for your sake then, who are so generous in the matter, and for my own, I think it will be right for me to accept your offer, as quoted above.

What strengthens me in this view is the circumstance that I cannot concede the two proposals in your letter now received. I cannot in honour depart from my arrangement with Penny, while the house continues; and, never having charged Mrs Segrave for any repairs, though I have even gone out of my way to paint, I cannot do so in the last year of my tenancy.[1] Here then are additional reasons for anticipating loss to you, and consequently odium on me.

When you resign the house to me is a matter of indifference, except that I should not like the date to be later than March 17 next.[2]

I am &c J H N

TO WILLIAM MONSELL

The Oratory Bm Decr 19. 1858

My dear Monsell

I am very much disappointed and mortified to think that you must have got to Town without calling here. It must have arisen from my stupidity in not writing to you. I hope there is a chance of your coming as you go back. There are so many things I want to talk to you about[3]

Ever Yours affly John H Newman

P.S. The account of Stanislas is not satisfactory.

[1] Scratton wrote on 13 Dec., ready to continue as lessee of St Mary's House, but wishing to charge repairs to the owner, and to ask from Penny if he remained on as tutor, a financial contribution.

[2] Scratton wrote on 20 Dec. agreeing to hand back the House on 16 March 1859.

[3] Monsell had written on 12 Dec., when returning Newman's extracts of his correspondence with the Irish Archbishops, concerning his resignation, 'but what is there to say about the whole question? I must admit that you could not have acted otherwise than you did, and that the responsibility of the, I fear, too probable failure of the University rests with others and in no degree with you. I never heard the name of Dr Gartlan . . . I do not think that either your resignation or his appointment is generally known.'

MEMORANDUM, DEFAMATORY TALK IN LONDON

Dec 20. 1858[1]

Some time ago, I suppose on his return here in June, Stanislas said that he had seen Wallis in London, who said that the differences between me and the London House etc were the talk of the Stafford Street Club — [2] that Father Faber said [had] a letter of mine (addressed to the Cardinal) and that the Cardinal said to him, 'The impudence of the fellow to write such a letter to me.'[3]

Also I think he said that Fr Faber had shown my letters or part of them to young Harry Bowden

When Ignatius [Ryder] came back here after his holiday at Brompton, he asked of Ambrose an explanation how it was that he heard there that I positively hated Fr Faber.

Stanislas persisted his stating his belief from what he heard that Fr Faber showed my letters to all comers.

Pollen brought down the news in November that Fr Faber showed my letters — and that it could not rest there, but that I should be driven to explain; — (that the Cardinal had said, 'the insolence of my letter to him' declining to have his dedication to myself and Fr Faber, I think Pollen said this)

Sir John Acton brought down word that Allies had been to Father Faber, and he said to him such things about me that he (Sir John) went down to him himself, and that he (Fr Faber) repeated to him (Sir John) what he (Fr Faber) had said to Allies. He took down my letter to the Cardinal from some repository and said that the Cardinal had given it to him (Fr Faber) as a record that he (the Cardinal) had done all he could to make up matters, that the Cardinal stood before the fire a long time, and then brought out 'the insolence' of Dr Newman, or the fellow, I don't know which. ⟨The Cardinal also said that I had 'shelved' myself.⟩ Fr Faber said that he (Fr Faber) had showed some letters of mine to the Duke of Norfolk — and that he, after hearing and reading said 'Shall we then never have a Saint.' — that he (Sir John) went to the Duke of Norfolk about the School — and the Duke who

[1] Newman collected evidence of 'what hard and wrong things are said of me, by those who ought not,'—talk which could jeopardize the success of the proposed school. See letter of 4 Dec.and second letter of 21 Dec. 1858 to Bellasis; also notes to letters of 9 Feb. and 1 April 1858 to him. Cf. Acton's letters to Simpson, preserved at Downside Abbey, which describe Faber as 'meddling against' Newman.
[2] This was the Catholic laymen's club, 3 Stafford Street, off Old Bond Street. It was registered in 1853. The leading Catholic laymen belonged to it, and held meetings there. By 1862 it had moved to 2 Savile Row. It appears to have come to an end in 1875, after which year it was no longer registered.
[3] This was Newman's letter of 7 June 1856 to Wiseman, which is preserved among Newman's letters to Faber at the London Oratory.

had given his name for the plan and promised £50 in the early spring, said to him 'that the Birmingham Oratory was not the place for a school.'

In September the Cardinal had asked of Bellasis whether Dr Newman was at the theological meeting at Sir John Acton's — i.e. the party to meet Döllinger. This under the circumstances was significant.[1]

⟨Also vid the notice of my Occasional Sermons in the Dublin[2]

Also J B Morris told Sir John Acton that Fr Faber said to him that every thing I had done since I was a Catholic had failed.⟩[3]

Stanislas had put down on paper the statements of Fr Guerratore of Naples, when he was in Birmingham in July 1857, as to what the London House had written about me in Christmas 1855–6.[4]

TUESDAY 21 DECEMBER 1858   Fr Frederic taken ill about this time

FROM SIR JOHN ACTON

Aldenham Park Bridgenorth Monday December 20 1858

My dear Father Newman,

If your difficulty about making the Atlantis a Quarterly proceeded simply from the narrow scope given it in the Prospectus, I should have only to quote the list of subjects: 'poetry, philosophy, history, philology, archaeology, fine arts, law, political economy, mathematics, and the sciences of experiment and observation' embracing 'every subject taught in a university.' There is very little theology fit to be treated in a review which does not allow of being included under some of these heads. But that which reduces me to a cheerful silence is what you say of your own plans. My wish and object was simply to obtain for the Catholic body the advantage of having its chief organ, and the chief director of its opinions, under your immediate influence.

[1] See letters of 18 Oct. 1858 to Allies and Hope-Scott.
[2] D R, XLIII, (Dec. 1857), pp. 511–14. This review hardly mentioned Sermons Preached on Various Occasions or Newman's labours as a Catholic, but, while praising him as the leader of the Tractarian Movement, was careful to mention 'the errors and defects,' the inaccuracies and faults of his teaching at that period. The review continued, 'any ordinary man would probably have yielded to the usual vanity of a party leader, and have attempted, after his conversion, to retain the influence which he certainly possessed before it. But Dr. Newman is no ordinary man. . . . In Dr. Newman the Catholic, we see no traces of the former leader of the once powerful tractarian party. Like some of those great men of olden times who fled from honours into the solitude of the desert . . . Dr. Newman hides himself in the comparative obscurity of a provincial town, rather than occupy positions where he would be certain to continue the pre-eminence of his former prestige.' The reviewer thought Newman 'ought not always to remain silent on the theological controversies of the day. There are certainly some subjects which seem as if they naturally fell to his province. Who can enter into controversy with latitudinarian writers more ably . . . Who can discuss better such questions as . . . miracles — the eternity of future punishments. . . . Nothing coming from his pen will ever be questioned as incorrect, rash, ill-advised, or ill-digested.'
Cf. also Newman's Q in the Corner letter of 16 Jan. 1858.
[3] Cf. Volume XVII, Appendix 3, p. 559.
[4] See letter of 16 July 1857 to Flanagan.

I saw, and still see, no other way of introducing some authority and order into the deplorable confusion prevailing, and I felt that from certain occupations which absorbed your time, from your retirement, if I may use the word, during the last few years, at least so far as England is concerned, we are delivered over to the influence of very questionable masters, and compelled to spend in controversy and disputes energies which might, under your auspices, be better employed. But something much better than to see you conducting our reviews is to know that you are at length again busy at works which will be a treasure not only to our own time and country. I will only beg you to foregive my importunity. I am sure you did not misunderstand its motives.

I have no difficulty in agreeing with that part of your letter which I can construe into advice for myself. I shall never obtain in the Rambler any sort of real influence, and the hurry and haste of writing monthly articles harasses and disgusts me. The things that I have accumulated in the course of my studies can find no place in it, and whatever I write in a review of such a popular character seems pedantic.

You think the time not yet come for such a review as I imagined. I did not so much think people prepared for it as that the decline of the Dublin gave an opportunity that ought not to be lost. It appears that the plan of Ward, Thompson and Oakeley failed of satisfying the Cardinal, partly for the very reasons which caused mine to be rejected.

The proposed 'Index of Reviews' is an excellent idea. Is there not rather too much classification? I suppose it is not finally corrected, for there are many misprints.[1] 'Job' is being retouched, with many growls. J B M. [Morris] talks (privately) of translating the book, on his own behalf.

Believe me Ever sincerely Yours J D Acton

TO SIR JOHN ACTON

The Oratory Birmingham Decr 21. 1858

My dear Sir John,

I somehow think I have not quite said all I meant to say in my letter to you. I contemplated in the plan I suggested, the Atlantis *being quarterly*. If I did not say so in words, it was an omission. But I will not say more — waiting till the next time I have the pleasure of seeing you. I seem to agree, and thought I did agree, with the main view of your letter, which I answered, i.e. with the propriety of treating *all* subjects in *substance*; the question being whether they should take the shape of a review, or again of politics of the day.

Very sincerely Yours John H Newman of the Oratory

Sir John Acton Bart

P.S. I *quite* understand it was your most kind thought of *me* which made you suggest your plan — but I will write no more — when it is so difficult to say every thing one should say.

We should thank you very much for corrections in the List of Reviews.

[1] Besides the Prospectus of the *Atlantis*, a 'Prospectus of an Index of Science and Literature,' which was to be an annual index of the periodical literature of the world, was also printed. This Prospectus was inserted in the first pages of the *Atlantis* for July 1858.

TO EDWARD BELLASIS, I

sent in substance   The Oratory Birmingham Decr 21 1858

Private

My dear Bellasis

As there is no London post for you to write by today,[1] I give you the further trouble to read this, in order to complete what I said on Thursday or Friday This is the practical conclusion in which that letter issues.[2]

I do not see how we can begin without a large sum, I will not say in hand, but to draw on and to risk.

E.g. the Duke could *guarantee* £2000 by a wave of his hand, or a flourish of his pen. Now unless we can do the like, I don't see how our scheme has any chance of bearing up against its difficulties.

I cannot hunt up about 10 to 12 or to 15 persons who would send boys, at least at first — now how many would give £100? I doubt whether half a dozen would. Would Mr Birks? would Lord Charles Thynne? — Then when there were two brothers! — would Mr Fitzgerald give two hundred for his two boys?

I declare I think we cannot ask above £80. I think we are more likely to get 15 boys at £80, than 12 at £100 — and the former raises a larger sum.

On the other hand, as to our expenses — In my last I said that 15 at £100 would only just cover the expenses — and that, if we had fewer than 15, we should have a deficit — for that deficit on three years, and for furniture etc etc. we have your collection, viz of £500 or £600. In what sense can that be called sufficient?

Well, we can lower our expenses thus: — instead of Arnold, get a young general grinder ⟨There is *this* plausibility in this plan, viz that Arnold might come a *year hence*, when we got on.⟩ (Manning seems to know of none) at £100 — sink the Head Master's £100 — try to bring down Prefects to £100, by cutting off one of them — then the expenses of House, Staff, etc, are £500 instead of £900. Then say 15 at £80, and let half of the £80 go for board, washing, coals, candles etc, then you would had [sic] the other £40 × 15 = £600 to meet the above £500. This seems to me the best scheme, but supposing even so small a coming short as 12 boys instead of 15, (and, considering we are supposing each boy to run out his *full* year, I fear 14 is as many as we could expect) then $12 \times £\dfrac{80}{2} = £480$, which you see is not enough to meet the

---

[1] Newman first dated this letter 19 Dec., a Sunday, and then altered it.
[2] The letter of Thursday or Friday was that of 17 Dec., described in the first note to the second letter of 21 Dec. to Bellasis.

expenses of even the very reduced calculation (£500) for House etc which I have been supposing.

Well then, can we move without a guarantee, in some shape or other, against losses, or without a larger sum to begin with?

Yours most sincerely John H Newman

TO EDWARD BELLASIS, II

The Oratory Birmingham Decr 21. 1858

sent these two letters in substance

Private

My dear Bellasis

Thank you for your letter.[1] On second thoughts I think you will feel with me, that I could not be a party to asking Fr Faber any such question as you propose; for the very supposition I made in my letter implied a want of confidence in him on my part, greater than any answer to that question, such as he might give, would remove.

Of course it is quite intelligible that those gentlemen who are hazarding a considerable sum on our scheme should ask any wealthy person, who would be likely to carry through a scheme of Fr Faber's, whether he would do so after they had actually hazarded their money and before the experiment was brought to an end, without my knowing any thing of what they did, and without their entering into communication with Fr Faber.

It will be observed, however, that this does not touch the main difficulty viz of Fr Faber doing his best to destroy our scheme, whether or not he had one of his own.[2]

I think then that what you have steadily to face is this, whether Fr Faber's active opposition against us reduces our probability of success so low that it is unwise in you to risk any sum.[3]

[1] Newman had written to Bellasis on 17 Dec. a letter, no longer to be found, about the danger threatening the proposed Oratory School from Fr Faber. See Memorandum of 20 Dec. Bellasis replied on 18 Dec., 'The possibilities mentioned in your letter must have careful consideration. If there really is a risk of active opposition from the quarter you name, either in the form of a rival school near London, or of private discouragement, it might run a Birmingham school hard no doubt. . . .

Would it be possible for some one, not supposed to be speaking from you, to obtain some kind of assurance from Faber that he would not oppose? . . . . Suppose for instance, (I do not know in the least whether this is practicable,) the Duke of Norfolk could obtain from Faber an assurance that he would not oppose, or start any rival school, for a certain number of years at all events.

The attraction to me of the proposed Birmingham school consists in the founders, and this would with me much outweigh position. Nonetheless there is no doubt that, with many a more Southern situation would be more attractive, considered by itself.'

Bellasis sent Newman's letter of 17 Dec. to Hope-Scott for his opinion. His reply is dated 20 Dec. 'Tell Father Newman from me to *go on*—What he apprehends *ought* not to take place and I think will not. If it does I do not fear it as much as he does. London and its neighbourhood are not the places for such a thing.'

[2] Newman cancelled here the words 'which might be to him of less consequence.'

[3] On 3 Feb. 1859 Acton wrote to Darnell, 'People anticipate opposition from Brompton, but, as I think erroneously. They object to the plan 1. as inconsistent with the [Oratorian]

And next it seems to me that it is worth while considering whether £500 or £600, which you have, is not a middle measure, too little to succeed with, and too much to throw away.[1]

TO WILLIAM HENRY ANDERDON

(Copy)

The Oratory Birmingham Decr 24. 1858

My dear Anderdon

I write a hasty line on a busy day to acknowledge your note for £100 just received, for which I inclose a receipt. I am very sorry you are obliged to anticipate the prospect of giving up the Church — [2] The choicest blessings of this joyful season from all of us.

I am, Yours affly John H Newman of the Oratory

The Revd W H Anderdon

TO EDWARD BELLASIS

The Oratory Bm Decr 28/58

My dear Bellasis

I return most cordially your Christmas greetings, to yourself, Mrs Bellasis, to all your children, and especially to Richard, begging your good prayers for

rule. This prevents them from setting up an opposition establishment. 2. Because of the Padre's [Newman] general incompetency. The confutation of this will be a practical one in your hands, but if they say anything too loud, I can quote Faber's express promise to me, that he would not only tolerate but assist the school. The promise of course is worthless, but the publication of it by a 'wellwisher who is happy to know etc' might in case of need, be of use. It was made indeed when Faber yet had a fair opinion of me, and had not yet denounced me as you wot.' On this last point see letter of 31 Dec. 1858 to Acton.

[1] The draft ends here. Bellasis replied on 25 Dec., 'I have talked over your last letter with Hope Scott, and we think—first—that no attempt at a rival school is likely to be made by Faber without the concurrence and aid of the Duke, and we do not think that, under the circumstances, and considering that the Duke knows of your plan and even promised to aid pecuniarily towards it, he would be likely to get encouragement from that quarter.

Secondly, it is possible that Faber may try to embarrass and defeat the scheme, and that if he did so he would influence a certain number of persons, but this would produce no permanent effect, unless he proposed a substitute, which, as said before, we think he would not do.

Thirdly, this consideration, that is, that you will have to contend with a certain amount of hostility from the convert side, should affect the amount at which you should put the pension, and we both agree that £80 would be better than £100. It would look better for the reason you give, that in case of a rival school proposing a less sum you would be obliged to come down yourself, which would be undignified, yet necessary.

Lastly, you may assume that you will be guaranteed to the extent of an additional £500 beyond the £500 already promised . . .'

[2] Anderdon wrote on 23 Dec. that, as he would presumably cease to be Dean of St Mary's House on 17 March, and would cease to be Pro-Vice-Rector on the appointment of a Rector, the situation was too uncertain for him to continue his lease of the University Church. He therefore gave six months' notice of his resignation, which would take effect on 25 June 1859.

us — and my own greetings include those of all our Fathers here. As years go on, one feels most piercingly what it is to have a good friend — and such you are to me and to us. I ought to have told you that we are holding another earnest novena, which finishes tomorrow, on the subject of the School — but I was not writing to you just when we began, and I did not like to write on purpose.[1]

Would not it be well for Fr Darnell to show himself in London now? for after your most satisfactory letter of the 25th, I consider it decided we shall begin. I should like him to make Mrs Bellasis's acquaintance, and Master Richard's. I *think* he has some reluctance, from the feeling that there are those in London, who might have taken him up and have not — as if it would hurt our prospects, if he came to London and did *not* go to certain houses. I have not hinted to him the important precedent of Mr Squeers, who, I think, showed himself in the Metropolis with a view to increasing his connexions.[2]

Decr 31. I have delayed this, hoping to tell you we had got a Master — but the negociation lingers — so I will add my happy wishes to you for the New Year and subscribe myself

Yours affectly in Xt   John H Newman of the Oratory

Mr Serjeant Bellasis

TO JOHN HUNGERFORD POLLEN

The Oratory, Bm Decr 28. 1858

My dear Pollen,

Our best and warmest congratulations to you and yours, of the coming of this Sacred and happy time.

As to the Altar, ladies have their views — Miss F's [Farrant] is to have nothing sham — I am told that she pronounces, I don't know why, the spars to be sham. And would rather have marble or inlaid work. Also, she will begin with the altar itself. Also, she does not like the truncated pillars — nor do I quite myself.

I enclose William's measurement for the curtains you speak of.

Yours affly John H Newman

J. H. Pollen Esq.

WEDNESDAY 29 DECEMBER 1858   Arnold came

[1] Newman's Chapter Address of 20 Dec. on the purpose of this novena, 'O St Philip, give us no new mortification—but either prevent the school or prosper it,' will be included in the volume of Newman's Oratorian Papers.
[2] *Nicholas Nickleby*, Chapter IV.

The Oratory Birmingham Decr 29. 1858

My dear Johnson,

I have just now received from Octavius an announcement of his marriage.[1] It is very kind of him to have thought of me; and, did not I know that during the honey moon people have no direction and are not to be found, I would write to him straight. In consequence I write to you, sending you and yours the best wishes of this sacred season, and begging your wife to be so kind, at a fitting time, to convey to him from me my truest congratulations, and my earnest prayers that the Good Providence of God may be with him and Mrs O.O. here and hereafter. And I congratulate you and your wife upon it — and Janet, and any other of your party, who are within reach of voice or pen.

I have little to tell you of myself — I have left Dublin for good, unless the Pope lugs me back, which he won't do, I know. We are in some excitement about the prospect of a Charter, which the Tory Minister is said to be intending for us. It will be a pleasant termination of my engagement — but, if the University does not get it now, it will get it from the Whigs, when they next come in; that is all.[2]

Young Arnold, who is one of our Professors, is coming here in an hour's time. How wonderful! what changes! As life gets on, one understands the wisdom of the Greek saw, that we should always behave towards enemies, as tho' they would one day be friends, and with friends as though they would one day be enemies. Not that I had ever the temptation to consider Arnold an enemy.[3]

When will you ever pass thro' Birmingham? When will you ever come and see how old I am? When shall I have an opportunity of telling you how pleased Hennessy is with his F.R.S. and how much he thinks of you?

With my love to your wife and to your large unknown circle

Ever Yrs affly John H Newman[4]

M. Johnson Esqr

P.S. On looking again, I see the announcement is from Octavius's *wife*, a still great[er] kindness.

[1] That of Octavius Ogle, Johnson's brother-in-law, to Maud Burland.
[2] Newman copied part of a letter of 20 Dec. from Arnold, 'I have lately heard from two Protestant sources, both likely to be well informed and both hostile to us, . . . that the present Government intend, not only to grant us a charter, but to recommend us a money grant.' Dunne also wrote at this time of an approach by the Catholic Members of Parliament to Disraeli, and if that failed, of plans for a stronger memorial to Lord Derby. See last note to letter of 19 July 1858 to Disraeli.
[3] Newman was thinking of Thomas Arnold the elder. Cf. *Trevor*, 1, pp. 263–5.
[4] Johnson replied on 30 Dec., 'Not many days pass without thinking of you and my old friends now dispersed in so many ways. But at this time you all rush upon one with unusual force. How many Christmas days did we pass together! . . . Caroline [Johnson's wife] continues strong and active—and, it is a great comfort to me, to believe that no one retains more

TO JAMES STEWART, I

Ory Bm Dec 29/58

My dear Stewart

Accept my best Christmas greetings for yourself, Mrs Stewart, and all your circle — especially for your poor little boy, who passes the sacred season so penitentially.[1]

I inclose my letter. I have said at the end, that, for my own personal convenience, I had rather the house Number 6 were closed on March 17. This is quite true — but you must not interpret this to mean that I *wish* it closed. It is not much to say, that the sorrow at the chance of an eye of the Faculty of Philosophy and Letters being extinguished would be far greater than my own convenience in the matter. But I have said it, because (between ourselves) Anderdon has said that Scratton did me a favor in taking Number 6 and the rent off my hands, and that I was ungrateful to him. Now if your Faculty thought this (the favor) to be the fact, they might come into the notion of taking Number 6 . . . . (whereas kindness to me would go the other way really,) and I wish them to act without reference to me, and consulting *solely* for the good of the University. If they determine to close, I shall think they see better what is good for the University than I at . . . .[2]

TO JAMES STEWART, II

The Oy Bm Decr 29. 1858

(Copy)

My dear Professor Stewart

I write to you in your capacity of Dean of your Faculty, but in no capacity myself except that of tenant of Number 6 Harcourt Street, which is at present occupied by St Mary's University House.

Since this is one of the Houses in the Faculty of Philosophy and Letters, it is right that I should acquaint you that my possession of it ends in November next, when it returns to the owner, Mrs Segrave. As the lady in question has always shown a special interest in the University, I do not think it will be

affectionate recollections of you than she and her sisters.' Johnson went on to describe his own ill health. He died on 28 Feb. 1859. In reply to the mention of Hennessy, Johnson wrote, 'The fellow coolly cribs a set of experiments of *mine* calls them *his own* and then still more coolly asserts that certain other experiments of mine seem to show the same thing. . . . The whole affair is an Irishcism [sic] from beginning to end.'

[1] He had the measles.
[2] The copy ends here.

difficult, should it then be considered desirable, to obtain of her a longer term of years.

The point, however, to which I have especially to draw the attention of your Faculty, requires an earlier consideration; for, as matters stand at present, though Number 6 is mine till the above-mentioned date, it will be necessarily closed as a University residence, after the 17th of March next, unless the University interferes to prevent it.

The state of the case is thus: —

The Secretary of the University (Mr Scratton) who has so much to do with its accounts, very kindly undertook the pecuniary affairs of the establishment at the beginning of this Session, receiving from that date the pension of the inmates and discharging the expenses which they incurred or occasioned.

In the course of the present month, however, he has seen reason to write to me offering to give back his charge into my hands, and expressing the relief which it would give him to be released from the responsibility which it involved. In a subsequent letter he stated his apprehension that he should lose a considerable sum, if the arrangement continued, though for the sake of the University he was willing to continue it, a result, which it is scarcely necessary to say, I did not at all anticipate, when I suffered him to make it.

It stands to reason that I could not let him be the victim of his generosity; and therefore I accepted after some deliberation the offer he made me; and it is settled between us that he resigns his charge by March 17 next, when the half session pensions end.

My object then in writing to you now is to know from your Faculty, whether they think it worth while to bring the matter before the University, with a view to the University renting Number 6 of me from March 17 to November 3 next; or whether they prefer any other mode of providing an abode for the Dean and students of St Mary's.

My terms would be the payment of the rent to Mrs Segrave during that interval, viz 2 quarters and a half, which, at £27. 10 a quarter amounts to £68. 15. I propose to lend my furniture to the University without charge up to July 22, when the Session ends.

I hope you will not think me importunate, if I request an answer by February 2 next. Perhaps I ought to add, that I have no pecuniary interest in your decision either way; but, that, as far as my own present convenience is concerned, I should prefer the closing of Number 6 on March 17.[1]

I am etc J H N

THURSDAY 30 DECEMBER 1858   Arnold left   Sir John Acton called

[1] Stewart replied officially on 11 Jan., asking if Anderdon might take over Number 6 Harcourt Street in March. Stewart added privately that it had been discovered that the House was not being run at a loss. Cf. letter of 20 Jan 1859 to Scratton.

TO SIR JOHN ACTON

The Oratory Bm ⌐Decr 31. 1858¬[1]

Private.

My dear Sir John[2]

I have thought over what we talked of yesterday, and, as I promised, I write to you.[3]

Deeply as it pained me to hear from you the indignity to which Dr D. [Döllinger] was to be subjected, I am on the whole disposed to make light of it. Perhaps the denunciation won't be made. If it is, he is able to hold his own. And they will be shy of meddling with him at Rome. And on what plea? for what kind of offence is it, to take a certain historical view of the person of

---

[1] In 1862 Newman copied out his draft of this letter, on which he had written 'in substance.' There are slight differences in the letter as sent, and small additions.

[2] Acton had stirred up opposition to the *Rambler*, of which he was the chief proprietor. In the *Rambler*, (Aug. 1858), p. 135, he had described St Augustine as 'the father of Jansenism.' This gave offence and an explanation, of which Acton disapproved, was published, (Sept. 1858), p. 216. He persuaded Döllinger to write a letter on the subject, which he, Acton, translated and published as the first article in the *Rambler*, (Dec. 1858), 'The Paternity of Jansenism.' Newman wrote on 2 Dec., 'I have been exceedingly interested by Döllinger's Article.' However, Wiseman wrote on 20 Dec. to Charles Russell that it was 'giving great pain and perhaps scandal' and two days later to Simpson, the editor of the *Rambler*, that it was 'exciting considerable uneasiness, likely to lead to the principles and opinions contained in it being deferred to authority superior to mine.' Dr Newsham saw no reason for a delation, but Wiseman also consulted Faber. He replied in a letter signed jointly by himself and Dalgairns, and now in the Westminster Diocesan Archives, 'We had already formed an independent judgment upon the letter which has appeared in the Rambler, before reading the opinion of the theologian sent us by your Eminence, and we had both been engaged in a correspondence of remonstrance with Sir John Acton on the subject. . . .' After giving various reasons against Döllinger's article, they concluded, 'For all these reasons we cannot help thinking that it belongs to the pastoral solicitude of your Eminence to denounce to the Holy See the letter published in the Rambler as containing propositions liable to lead the faithful into error, scandalous and offensive to pious ears, [signed] Frederick Wm Faber Congr Orat
John Bernard Dalgairns Congr Orat'
Cf. the end of the quotation from a letter of Acton's, in third note to second letter of 21 Dec. to Bellasis. See also *MacDougall*, pp. 36–9, (from whom the two quotations from letters of Wiseman are taken); *Gasquet*, pp. 34–8; *Atholz*, pp. 77–81; and A. Watkin and H. Butterfield, the *Cambridge Historical Journal*, x, (1950), pp. 88–91.

[3] Acton on 1 Jan. 1859 wrote to Simpson his account of this meeting, at which Döllinger's delation was discussed: 'I had a 3 hours' talk with the venerable Noggs who came out at last with his real sentiments to an extent which startled me, with respect both to things and persons, as H E [His Eminence], Ward, Dalgairns, etc., etc., natural inclination of men in power to tyrannise, ignorance and presumption of our would-be theologians, in short what you and I would comfortably say over a glass of whiskey. I did not think he could ever cast aside his diplomacy and buttonment so entirely, and was quite surprised at the intense interest he betrayed in the Rambler. He was quite miserable when I told him the news and moaned for a long time, rocking himself backwards and forward over the fire, like an old woman with the toothache. He thinks the move provoked both by the hope of breaking down the R. [Rambler] and by jealousy of Döllinger. He asked whether we suspected any one, and at last inclined to the notion that the source is in Brompton. He has no present advice, being ignorant of the course of such affairs in Rome, except that we should declare, if you can make up your mind to do so, that we do not treat theology in our pages.' *MacDougall*, pp. 38–9, *Gasquet*, p. 47.

heretics, while condemning their writings?[1] Mayn't I say that Luther was a loving and amiable papa, and yet abominate him? ⌐So I don't think, if this is all, much will come of it.

No one, however, can deny, that it is the bad repute of the Rambler which causes it, if it is done.

I certainly have long thought that the Rambler was in a false position. If I recollect rightly, it commences as a literary work. At one time it called itself Journal of the Fine Arts etc. It generally had a Tale in series. It was properly a Magazine. I think it was a mistake to treat of Theology proper at all; and a double mistake to treat it in Magazine fashion. And a third mistake, for laymen to do so.

Every one has his own line. I should be surprised to find myself writing on Contingent Remainders. It requires an explanation, when a layman writes on theology. From all I hear, I believe Ward has done good at St Edmund's, but even he surely was in a false position, though he had the direct sanction of his Diocesan, for what he did. Here then is mistake the fourth, that the Rambler on the contrary has attacked ecclesiastical authorities and their organs.

It is true that the Holy See, or its representatives, have sometimes taken up laymen, as Dr Brownson — nay, against local superiors, as M. Veuillot; but such persons have been thorough going partizans of its rights and claims.[1] The position of the Holy See must be considered, especially in a missionary country. It has to act, to act promptly and forcibly, and is forced to use such instruments as come to hand. It is common indeed with statesmen, of necessity to look to the present, and to live from hand to mouth. They adopt courses which are immediately effective, and measure services by what is showy, telling, and successful. If there be a power which need not look to the future, it is one which has a promise that it cannot fail, and is told not to be sollicitous about the morrow. We are in a world of imperfection — truth and its propagation is committed to 'earthen vessels — '[2] Hence even saints, as St Basil, St Jerome, St Thomas M. [Martyr],[3] St Joseph Calasanctius, St Alfonso, have been neglected at Rome during their lifetime. There is need constantly, in this or that locality, if the work is to go on, of rough and ready instruments, of thick and thin supporters, of vehemence, of severity. When a house is in flames, you may rightly expostulate with the fireman who curses and swears, but it may be his way, his only way, of waking you.

However, it is quite another matter, what is to be thought of this freedom of tongue, when exercised not in the cause of the great interests to which I

[1] During the fifties Orestes Brownson was a forthright defender of the papal claims, even those concerning the temporal sphere. The extreme ultramontane Louis Veuillot was supported by the Holy See against the Archbishop of Paris. See letter of 5 April 1853 to St John, Volume XV, p. 342.
[2] [[(N.B. Novr 27. 1862. Some of these sentences, to my surprise, were without any leave of mine, inserted in an article which appeared soon after in the Rambler.)]] This may refer to Acton's article in the Rambler, (Feb. 1859), 'The Catholic Press.'
[3] [[St Thomas of Canterbury]]

have referred; and still more, when, without benefitting them, it is directed against venerable authorities at home.

When Lucas, e.g. went to Rome, I was glad of it, because I thought that on the one hand kindness would have been shown him for his loyal service — and on the other that by means of that kindness he would have been persuaded to modify his political views. I forgot that, while the particular cause that took him to Rome was not Ultramontane, he had his Bishop[1] against him in it. In consequence, he could hardly find a person to introduce him to the Pope — and, zealous servant as he was of the Holy See, he wandered about the Churches of Rome, seeking consolation where consolation is ever to be found.[2]

How different from the case of La Mennais, whose future was not contemplated, since he was doing a present direct service to religion![3]

So again Wallis — he has found it simply impossible to hold his ground against Dr Cullen, considering he was not undertaking any direct championship of any special Roman interest.[4]

It is then to me quite clear, that, if the Rambler perseveres in its present course, it will find it cannot hold on — but must come to an end. A change of rulers in the diocese of Westminster will not mend matters.

Moreover, the question occurs whether, even for the sake of its other objects, it should not abstain from theology. While it teaches it, it provokes opposition — and this opposition is practically a siding with the parties whom the Rambler assails, nay, and will become so actually and avowedly. These parties have Catholic society with them at present, for society naturally sides with authority. But, if the Rambler retires from the field of controversy, they, united as they may be at present, will quarrel with each other. Restlessness must have an object to attack; pride of intellect will not bear a rival; men in rule will become suspicious of others who are *not* writers in Magazines. The general proposition, 'All converts are dangerous,' at present is applied to such as Simpson; let him be silent in theological matters, and that eternal truth, as it is felt to be, must find its fulfilment in other converts.[5]

---

[1] [[(N.B. Novr 27. 1862. At that time he lived, or at least the Tablet was published, in Dublin.)]] Thus Lucas's bishop was Archbishop Cullen.

[2] [[the Churches of Rome disconsolate]] Frederick Lucas went to Rome at the end of 1854 to appeal on behalf of the Tenant League. He arrived on 6 Dec., and was strongly opposed by Cullen, who was already there. Lucas had two audiences with Pius IX, on 9 Jan. and 26 Feb. 1855, but left Rome in May, having failed in his mission.

[3] When Lamennais, who was championing the papal claims in France against the Gallican bishops, appealed to Rome in 1824, he received a warm welcome from Leo XII, and it was thought that he might be made a Cardinal. In 1831 he again appealed to Rome, to approve of his teaching on liberty. He was admitted to one formal audience by Gregory XVI, and his doctrines were condemned.

[4] Wallis had just moved the *Tablet* from Dublin back to London.

[5] Döllinger wrote to Acton early in January, that it was 'very possible, yea not improbable, that the number of the Rambler may be put on the Index on account of, and with express mention of the letter. . . . The best thing will be to make as little noise as possible, and to hold your peace. The Rambler will very easily get over it, particularly if you follow Newman's wise advice to avoid theological matters, and must make its way through the thornbushes of ill will, of misrepresentation, and of its own faults.' Acton's translation, in A. Watkin and H. Butterfield, *art. cit.*, p. 91.

When I was a Protestant, I used to say, that no cause could progress without a view or theory: and, when I came to be unsettled in religious opinion, I thought that, even humanly speaking, my work was over in the Anglican Church, because I had no principles to put forth. But I was wrong. The Xtian Remembrancer and the Guardian have gone on with as much éclat without principles, as the British Critic with them. How have they gone on? simply by clever writing, by attacking their opponents, by hitting blots, though they made themselves responsible for little or nothing positive.

Here is a suggestion for the Rambler, supposing it feels the duty to give up theology, aims at escaping the displeasure of its ecclesiastical Superiors, yet wishes to promote the good ends to which it is devoted.

Let it adopt the policy of Wellington in the lines of Torres Vedras, who kept within shelter, while the enemy scoured the plain, but kept a sharp eye on him, and took him at disadvantage, whenever it was possible.

Let it go back to its own literary line. Let it be instructive, clever, and amusing. Let it cultivate a general temper of good humour and courtesy. Let it praise as many persons as it can, and gain friends in neutral quarters, and become the organ of others by the interest it has made them take in its proceedings. Then it will be able to plant a good blow at a fitting time with great effect — it may come down keen and sharp, and not only on Protestants — and without committing itself [1] to definite statements of its own, it may support authority by attacking views which authority will be the first to be jealous of, if the Rambler is not the first to attack them — Power, to be powerful, and strength, to be strong, must be exerted only now and then — It then would be strong and effective, and affect public opinion ⌈without offending piety or good sense.⌉

I don't think all this is a mere dream — but, to be realized, it requires the grace of patience.

The best wishes of the new year to you. The clock is now striking 12[1]

Very sincerely Yours in Xt   John H Newman of the Oratory

Sir John Acton Bart.

---

[1] Acton replied on 4 Jan. 1859, 'I am extremely grateful to you for your very important and instructive letter. Though he had not yet seen it Simpson writes that he entirely agrees with what you say of the necessity of disclaiming everything of a theological character in the Rambler, and the disclaimer shall be made in the next number. [The Rambler, (Feb. 1859), p. 89] I do not feel very confident however that it will diminish the animosity felt towards us. People of the kind we have to conciliate are quite as sensitive and intolerant in such subjects as history or politics as in theology. A sincere article on the government of the papal states, or on the state of the church in Sardinia, or on the character of Leo X or of Lewis XIV would I am sure give the greatest offence. It seems to me that these narrow and timid habits will last as long as the general ignorance on which they are founded. There is a dread not only of particular conclusions, but of the free and sincere inquiry which may lead to them, and I almost think people will become reasonable in one department as soon as in the others. With respect only to the imprudence of laymen in discussing theology in the Rambler I ought to observe that such papers have often been by priests—I do not say it as implying that the articles were good—and that the papers on original sin were in the shape of letters, not of what the Americans call editorials.'

Appendixes

Appendix 1

The six leading articles Newman wrote for the *Weekly Register*[1]

THE CATHOLIC UNIVERSITY

I

23rd JANUARY, 1858

When we opened our columns to the letters of a correspondent, who assumed an almost hostile tone towards the Catholic University of Ireland, we were perfectly aware that we exposed ourselves to the imputation of a disregard of great Catholic interests in the judgment of a large section of our readers, whose zeal in its behalf is more than enough to refute the charge of apathy urged against them generally by the writer in question. We published, however, his animadversions, for such they were in effect, because we really have greater confidence in the University than to imagine that it can be overset by a few rude words of an anonymous objector; because we are sure on the contrary, that it will only gain by discussion; because we have the strong feeling that to smooth things over, and to hush them up, to have a mortal dread of scandal — to be suspicious of light, and to speak by formulas, to give a hearing to one side only, and to garble or mutilate the evidence or arguments of the other — is not the way to recommend undertakings and to succeed in measures in this age and country, and in a matter such as the present. Above all, a newspaper is the very embodiment of the principle of free discussion in those things which are to be discussed at all. As to sacred things, these we accept as our fundamental principles, not as subjects for argument, and as little encumber them with our logic as we profane them with our scepticism; but when once a thing is acknowledged to be matter for discussion at all, it is matter for free discussion, and unless a given University be a point of faith or a trial of obedience, it affords a legitimate field for scrutiny and examination till the controversy is exhausted, or till public opinion is made up one way or the other. Authority and prescription are good in their place; and so private judgment, competition, and the voice of the community are good in their place too. The duty of a journalist is to be fair in admitting facts and arguments, and circumspect in coming to conclusions; and

---

[1] These articles, headed 'The Catholic University' appeared in the *Weekly Register* on 23 Jan., 30 Jan., 6 Feb., 13 Feb., 6 March, 13 March 1858. They were reprinted with a few omissions in *Campaign*, pp. 345–81.

as we wish to set Protestants an example of honesty in our controversial dealings with Protestants, so, in the case of Catholics, there is a call on us, and a still more urgent call, to be patient and tolerant of such sentiments and maxims as are open to Catholics to adopt, though different from our own.

If this view of our own position be correct as regards the varieties and conflicts of Catholic opinion in general, still more necessary is it in relation to matters which are still future, to experiments which are only in progress, and to results for which there is no parallel in the past. Now, together with an absolute confidence in the mission of the Catholic University, we candidly confess to great indistinctness ourselves as to the direction, the character and the range of that Mission; and if such ignorance is culpable, we must ascribe it to the teaching of the Rector himself, for he expressly tells us, in his University Papers, that 'each age has its own character and its own wants,' and he trusts 'that in each a loving Providence shapes the institutions of the Church as they may best subserve the objects for which she has been sent into the world.' Then he continues: '*We cannot tell what* the Catholic University ought to be at this era; doubtless neither the University of Scotus nor that of Gerson, in matters of detail; but, if we keep great *principles* before us, and *feel our way* carefully, and ask guidance from above for *every step* we take, we may trust to be able to serve the cause of truth in our day and according to our measure, *and in that way which is most expedient and most profitable*, as our betters did in ages past and gone.' [1]

Fortified by these avowals on the part of a writer who, if any one, must be accounted true to the University, we are not ashamed to confess that we cannot predict the full work which it will do, and the definite ground which it will cover, in the years which lie before it; though the very form of such a confession implies that a work and a territory it will have. And as to the particular question which has come into controversy in our columns, the connection of the new University with England, we frankly avow that we will not dogmatize upon it, nor reduce those to silence whose anticipations about it may be different from our own. We will not stop the mouths of Catholics who refuse to admit it. We will not pay the University the bad compliment of saying that England is necessary for its life. The University of Ireland is calculated, indeed, to do us English Catholics good service; but no one forces it upon us. It will have a great work, though, as our cross correspondent says so triumphantly, it is not seated on our soil, nor governed by our Bishops, nor supported by our money, nor filled by our youth. It is not at once an object whether of compassion, or contempt, because the high and mighty grumbler JOHN BULL, refuses to take part in its benefits. It may consider, indeed, that an alliance with the Catholics of England would be an advantage both to itself and to them; but if, with a few noble exceptions, they do little or nothing for it, it can witness their reserve with equanimity, and listen with

---

[1] *The Office and Work of Universities*, London 1856, p. 268; H.S., III, pp. 177–8.

candour to their explanations. Now our correspondent's peculiarities of manner are his own; but putting them aside, we certainly do think that there are many Englishmen who keep silence, indeed, from kindness and delicacy, or from a nervous dislike to their opinion being known, or from thinking it no business of theirs, or that it would be injudicious to make a noise, or from having their own views about the future, but still who have a clear opinion that the University of Ireland is in no sense, and never can be, an institution for this country.

Moreover, there are many influential and excellent persons who find themselves bound up with the University of London by the ties of old recollections and perhaps attachments, and who have no wish, and feel it no duty, to break them. There are others, perhaps, who look hopefully to the future of Oxford, to the chance of rallying round them converts who have imbibed its academical traditions, and of finding themselves in positions favourable to exerting an influence on the place; and who, in consequence, are indisposed to look across St. George's Channel for an Alma Mater who cannot be reached without the penalty of sea sickness. There are others, again, who think the very idea of a University premature, and the establishment of it unsound, until those peculiar methods and habits have been introduced into our primary and secondary education, which the Protestant public schools inherit, and of which a University should be the development.

These various opinions need not be inconsistent with the conviction that the University inaugurated in Stephen's Green is a great Catholic work; that, at least, it must powerfully react upon our education in this country and indirectly subserve our general interests. They need not hinder us from giving it our attention, our sympathy, our intercessions, for its own sake, and from joyfully recognizing in its success the social advancement of a generous and oppressed people — oppressed, moreover, to our shame be it spoken, by our own government and our own countrymen. And this being so, they surely may be tolerated by a Catholic Journal; and the more so, that, as we said when we began, their free expression is for the advantage of the University itself, on the one hand by impressing its presence and its importance on men's minds, and on the other hand, by gaining for its authorities and friends the benefit of those various lights which the agitation of any practical question by a number of independent intellects cannot fail to throw upon its bearing and prospects. We intend to return to this subject.

II

30th JANUARY, 1858

We confess to having a great jealousy of authority, prescription, prerogative, protection, so far as they are not based upon ecclesiastical principle and enjoined by a sacred sanction. Where religion speaks, social science is superseded; but in those matters which are left to ourselves, it is but an acquiescence in the custom of our country and the traditions of the day to adopt private judgment and free trade for our watchwords, and to denounce monopolies. We apply this broad statement to the case of the new University of Ireland. We do not wish to see it forced upon the Catholics of England. We should, in a particular case, obediently take what our spiritual governors, in their greater wisdom, felt it their duty to urge upon our acceptance; but, left to ourselves, we consider in this as in other matters, that a fair stage and no favour is the most congenial rule and the best policy for an Englishman to adopt. We have no wish to make the University a dogma of the WEEKLY REGISTER. We should be as sorry to hear that our Colleges were compelled to affiliate themselves to it, as to find that fathers of families were bound to send their sons to this or that College. The Colleges give a good preliminary education, and therefore fathers are only too glad to avail themselves of it for their children. Let the University in like manner gain a reputation for completing what the Colleges have begun, and the Colleges will find it in their interest to connect themselves with the University, in preference to other rival institutions.

This being the state of the case, its business obviously is to show what it can do. Till it has time to show what it can do, we shall not be surprised if the Catholics of England delay to make up their minds in its favour; but so far forth as it is in a condition to give evidence of its capabilities we shall be surprised indeed if they do not make up for lost time by availing themselves of it without hesitation. It is true, another line of conduct was open to them, at least, in idea, viz., to have been co-founders of the University; but if the work is to be carried out by the hierarchy and money of Ireland, English Catholics cannot be called upon to use it till they find it worth using. Here, then, their only duty meanwhile is to be fair to it, under circumstances in which there are abundant opportunities for unfairness. So large a work as a University cannot be carried out all at once; there will be necessarily much of incompleteness — many a desideratum, many an hiatus, in its provisions for a long time to come. For a long time to come, therefore, it will be easy enough to find fault with it, and to ask a multitude of questions which it will be very difficult to answer. It will be easy to say: 'Where is your recognition by the State? How do you mean to get it? Where are your degrees? Where are your theological students? Where are your lectures in law? Where are your collegiate buildings?' And this is what we mean by *unfairness;* for, on the other hand, it is just as easy, and far more amiable and more equitable, to inquire into what has actually been effected, or is in train to be effected, and to dwell upon the *positive* side of the subject. If bystanders will be content to put aside their own notions of what ought to be done first, what secondly, if they come to inquire about the University, willing to find what is in fact to be found, though they would rather have found something else, we think there would be much to tell them about it, and much to excite their Catholic sympathies; but it is too much the case with English Catholics to look with a sort of incredulity and despair at every undertaking of which the Sister Isle is the scene.

This arises from their want of confidence, as they say, that Irishmen can persevere in any matter whatever. They say that Repeal Agitations, anti-Establishment Leagues, and Defence Associations make an ephemeral noise and die away, and they anticipate the same fate for the Catholic University. We consider this to be a particularly unfair view of Ireland, as a few words will serve to explain. Because the phases of secular politics change with the moon, therefore among that people who have kept to this day the Faith which they possessed before the English were converted, great religious undertakings are to start and to come to nought; to begin with promises and end with disappointments! Now, are political measures and combinations much more variable and short-lived in Ireland than in England? It is the very nature of constitutional government and the rivalry of parties, to be ever in motion— now surging, now subsiding, now rolling in one direction, and now in the other. How few English statesmen have retained their consistency in the present day! What leader of Irish interests has changed as often as Lord PALMERSTON? Who has unsaid his first words, and renounced his old supporters so bravely as Lord JOHN RUSSELL? Was Sir ROBERT PEEL a martyr to political principle? Have there been no late English coalitions which have suddenly been dissolved? Has not Mr. GLADSTONE himself been accused of wavering between Lord DERBY, Sir JAMES GRAHAM, and the Whigs? Have there been no formations and reformations of party, no vicissitudes in societies, unions, protests, and periodicals, in the High Church portion of the Establishment, or among the Tractarians? How are similar political changes in Irish politicians in point, when we speak of the solemn foundation of a University with the direct sanction and blessing of the Holy See?

To hear some persons talk, one would think that the foundation of a University was an every-day occurrence. Modifications of moment are, of course, conceivable in the Institution now commenced in Dublin, but we wish to be put into possession of the precedents on which is grounded the anticipation of its failure. It has a set of Professors superior, perhaps, in zeal and *esprit de corps*, and equal in ability, to the professorial staff anywhere; it has students as many as are found in German Universities of the first rank and name; it has a sufficiency of means, at present from the annual collections, and in prospect from the falling in of legacies; it has a Medical School in full operation; it has a periodical publication, as the register of its researches and experiments in the various departments of literature and science; it has libraries accumulating on its hands faster than it can house them; it has a church of its own, handsome and large enough for all ecclesiastical and academical ceremonies. These are some of its positive achievements, to which it becomes English Catholics to have regard. What is to stop its course? What is to overset it? What does it lack? Well, it has one great want, certainly:

the internal consolidation, the strength of traditional thought and usage, the definitiveness of duties, the prestige and renown, which time alone can give. It wants other things too; but those who have the proof that it has realized so much, need not scruple to accept its promise that it will accomplish in good time what remains to be done.

III

6th FEBRUARY, 1858

Did the new Catholic University aim at nothing more than the establishment in the metropolis of Ireland of a School of Medicine, presided over by men who profess the Catholic religion and reverence its tenets, it would have proposed to itself an end sufficient to excite a powerful interest in its behalf among the Catholics of other lands; and were its only success, in consequence, that of stocking the country which has given it birth with Catholic practitioners, it would have received an adequate recompense for much greater labours and anxieties than those which have been involved in securing so valuable a result. We have no intention here of enlarging upon the importance of the Art of Medicine. Its services to mankind at large are as necessary as those of Religion itself, and far more widely and vividly recognized. It follows that while its professors occupy every part of a country and divide and subdivide its length and breadth among them, they everywhere come across the Parish Priest either as friends or as rivals, for neutrality is impossible where the territory is common to both. There cannot be a worse calamity to a Catholic people, than to have its medical attendants alien or hostile to Catholicity; there cannot be a greater blessing, than when they are intelligent Catholics, who acknowledge the claims of religious duty, and the subordination and limits of their own functions. No condition, no age of human life can dispense with the presence of the doctor and the surgeon; he is the companion, for good or for evil, of the daily ministrations of religion, its most valuable supporter or its most grievous embarrassment, according as he professes or ignores its creed. And especially at those critical eras in the history of the individual, at birth and at death, he is often engaged in the solution of practical questions which come under the jurisdiction of a higher teaching, and is forced, whether he will or no, into co-öperation or collision with Theology. Much, of course, might be said of Medicine regarded as a science, claiming to be one of the five departments of University knowledge, and connected with speculative philosophy generally. In this respect, too, it involves considerations of the highest moment; for it will be either the ally or the adversary of Revealed Truth, according to the hands which have the treatment of it; but we put aside this further view of it here. Looking at it merely as an art, and that one of the primary and most necessary arts of life, the difference which results to a Catholic population is incalculable between the presence of a body of practitioners who recognize the principles and laws of its religion, or of a body of men who are ignorant or make light of them.

Such being the need of Catholic training for the Medical Faculty of a Catholic country, what, on the other hand, has hitherto been in matter of fact the state of the Medical Schools of Ireland before the establishment of the new University? Those who are made acquainted with it for the first time, those who know nothing of the tyrannous contempt with which Ireland has been in all matters habitually treated by the British Government, will not be able to credit the fact that a nation of many millions of Catholics is subjected to those disadvantageous circumstances which are disclosed by the authoritative statements which are now lying before us. From them we gather too certainly that the medical establishments of Dublin are absolutely in the hands of the small Protestant minority of the country. At the date of the document which we use, and which is not much more than a year old, it appears that, out of all the Dublin hospitals, only three had any Catholic practitioner in them at all; and even in those three the Catholic officials did not exceed the number of Protestant. On the other hand, out of sixty-two medical officers altogether in the various hospitals, the Catholic portion did not exceed the number of ten. Again, out of five Medical Schools in Dublin (exclusive of the University) three had no Catholic lecturer at all, and the other two one apiece; so that out of forty-nine lecturers only two were Catholic. Putting the two lists together, we find that out of one hundred and eleven Medical Practitioners in situations of trust and authority, twelve were Catholic and ninety-nine Protestant; and this, we repeat, in the metropolis of a Catholic people. It is scarcely necessary to draw the conclusion, that the body of medical men to whom the care of the population is committed are either Protestant, or, at least, have in the whole course of their education imbibed a Protestant atmosphere, from the infection of which they could only be preserved by some happy prophylactic obtained from accidental and external sources. That there are those who have thus been preserved, and who are nothing else but an honour to Catholicity, we know well. How many we do not know; but for such alleviations of the evil we owe no thanks to the Dublin establishments themselves, and we have no sort of guarantee that those alleviations may not at any moment cease to exist or to operate.

Now, the Catholic University is reversing this unseemly state of things. Of course, it does not grudge Protestants their rightful stations and their merited rewards; nor has it any intention of denying them the consideration due to their virtues, their abilities, and their professional reputation; but it has set about, on the other hand, providing for Catholics also a position and an influence of their own. It has determined that monopoly shall cease, that free trade shall be the rule in medicine as well as in commercial transactions. It is providing for Catholic students an authoritative school and a safe home, where they may profess their religion without hesitation, practise it without shame, and carry its august decisions into the teaching of the lecture-room and the hospital. Already it has set up Professorships of Anatomy, Practice of Medicine, Surgery, Pathology, Chemistry, Materia Medica, and Medical Jurisprudence; and these departments of science are brought together in an establishment worthy of the distinguished persons who fill them. Its Medical House is one of the most complete in Ireland, or out of London, and contains under its roof two theatres, dissecting-rooms, rooms for anatomical preparations, and a chemical laboratory. This laboratory is especially deserving of notice. It is fitted up on the plan of those established in connection with certain German Universities, and, besides answering the purposes of the medical student, is designed to meet the wants both of those who pursue chemistry for purely scientific objects, and, again, of those who wish to apply it to manufactures. Moreover, it contains a very complete steam apparatus, to afford the student an opportunity of acquiring a knowledge of practical pharmacy. For his more enlarged literary inquiries, the University authorities have obtained from abroad a medical library well known to men of science in Germany. The library in question is the gradual aggregation of various collections, made ever since an early part of the eighteenth century by some eminent philosphers of that country. It has been recently enriched by the additions of Dr. VON RINGSEIS, Rector of the University of Munich, from whose hands it passed into the possession of the Irish University. It comprises above 5000 volumes, including some of the richest and rarest works in medical literature from the earliest times of printing. Indeed, it may be said to represent the select works of the chief European schools, and includes treatises in the Greek, Latin, French, German, Dutch, Italian, as well as English language. This library was going to America, and its purchase by the University is a specimen of the zeal and vigilance which its Professors have shown, as far as the brief period has allowed during which it has been established, in making its establishments worthy of the metropolis of a great Catholic nation.[1]

Hitherto the influx of students into its Medical School has been most promising, amounting already, as we understand, to sixty young men, whose examinations have shown, that, to say the least, they are not inferior to the attendants in any other lecture-rooms. For the purposes of discipline, a medical lodging-house has been opened, which is presided over by a University official, and contains accommodation for such students as are willing to avail themselves of it.

Here, then, is what we consider one of those great *positive results* of the new Catholic University, to which we referred last week. Its ultimate benefit to the Irish people at large, to poor even more than to rich, is both momentous and inevitable; and we recommend this consideration to one of our correspondents, who insinuated that the Irish people will have no return for their contributions, unless the Faculty of Arts be given up to the purposes of a grammar and commercial school.

[1] See letter of 10 Jan. 1857 to Pollen.

IV

13th FEBRUARY, 1858

It is not easy for a visitor at first glance to determine whether, on a particular beach, the tide is on the ebb or on the flow. In both cases there is a great deal of tumult on the face of the water; billows rising and falling, curling, foaming, dashing against cliffs and falling back again, exhausting themselves and each other in a quarrel which has no meaning and no end. Yet wait a while in patience, and you will have infallible signs that the ocean is coming in, and is soon to submerge in one triumphant sweep the outlying rocks and the broad sand. So it is at this time with the Sister Island. The Englishman looks at the party contests, which he has neither curiosity nor wit to investigate, and is impressed, at sight of them, with the one only thought that Irishmen have quarrelled and will quarrel. And yet all this while the commotion is not without a result; it is the return of the waters; it is the flowing in of Catholicity. Look back ten years, and you will see what has been gained, and will anticipate what will be gained in the ten years next to come.

We consider the Catholic University to be the event of the day in this gradual majestic resurrection of the nation and its religion. Careless spectators will confuse it with those ephemeral projects, which do but discourage patriotism by ensuring failure. They will pronounce it to be nothing else than one of those many political movements, not in Ireland only but (at least, in times past) in England, which rather express the sense of wrongs under which their promoters labour, than guarantee the redress of them. And we will not deny that they have had some excuse for the mistake, in the circumstance that there are those who, having taken up the cause of the University as politicians, have, as politicians, proceeded to lay it down again. The warfare of politics is governed by the expediency of the moment; what is advisable at one time is not advisable at another. Statesmen have very different views of the posture of affairs, and of the measures which it demands, according as they are in office or in opposition. The battlefield is shifted, and a fresh arm of the service is necessary for victory. If such were the formal use of the Catholic University, we should not wonder at finding that it had done its work in three or four years, and, starting in 1854, was closing its gates and disposing of its premises in 1858. But there is a higher view, surely, which may be taken of its office and its destiny. It is possible for men to have thrown themselves into its cause, from a conviction of the social advantages which necessarily follow on the cultivation of literature and science. It is possible for them to have at heart the removal of the great civil penalty, under which, both here and in Ireland, Catholics for centuries had lain, from the unjust denial to them of facilities for the culture of the intellect.

It is possible, without forgetting, nay, while deeply feeling, how much the last generation owes to political efforts, to hold at the same time that something besides efforts, even successful ones, is necessary for making the most of their results, viz., that high *status*, that commanding position in society, which an educated intellect and the reputation for mental attainments are the means of securing.

We have no intention here of dwelling on the grievances of Ireland. We do but take the fact as we find it, that, *quo jure quave injuria*, the dominant class has hitherto been Protestant; that the standard of literature refinement and fashion has lain among Protestants, and has had to be sought for among Protestants; that Protestantism has been identified with every secular advantage, of whatever moral complexion, which men are accustomed to covet. In Dublin especially, whatever there has been of high society, of high education, of erudition, of literary fame, of wealth, of power, or rank, of splendour, has been, to say the least, in most intimate alliance with Protestantism. The old religion and the old pedigrees have been for three centuries out of date; new gods have reigned in Olympus. As in the Greek drama, old Cadmus and old Tiresias, if they were to have a chance of preferment, have been bound to adopt the new mode, to practise the new shuffle, and to shout the Dithyrambic.[1] The Castle and Trinity College gave the tone to society and the law to thought.

We are intending no disrespect to the talent and learning of the celebrated foundation to which we have referred, nor to the persons of its authorities and officials. We doubt not, did we come into their neighbourhood, we should cheerfully take part in the good-will and echo the praises, which their social qualities elicit from those who have the hnoour of their acquaintance. Yet, looking at them from the point of view from which the impartial historian must regard them, we see in the magnificent institution of Elizabeth nothing more or less than an instrument of monopolizing literature and science for the uses of the State religion; of making the name of Protestant synonymous with mental illumination, and of Catholicity with bigotry and ignorance. And, as no Catholic can endure the very idea of the continuance of this tyrannical monopoly, so there is no Catholic but ought to hail with thankfulness whatever opens upon Ireland the prospect of its overthrow.

Such a prospect, indeed, existed before the Catholic University commenced, and is rather realized than created by its establishment. We do not, indeed, pretend to have any intimate knowledge of Dublin society or its history; but, if the testimony of those who have such knowledge is to be taken, a process has been going on for some years, tending towards the formation there, at length, of an upper class worthy of their country. The old names of the Irish race are mounting up into station and power; and the generation now entering upon the stage of life is in no slight measure free from depend-

---

[1] The reference is to the effect of the introduction of the Bacchic dithyramb upon Greek drama.

ence on Protestant patrons and the deterioration of Protestant influences. And, as year passes after year, doubtless the structure of society will be still further purified from ingredients which are foreign to the Irish faith and character, and will more faithfully represent the Catholic millions on which it is erected.

Short as has been the career of the University hitherto, it has already given evidence of the part which it is to play in this peaceful revolution. It is perhaps invidious to select individual cases, when many might be given in illustration in all the three faculties which it has already set up; but as last week we dwelt upon the benefits to be anticipated from its School of Medicine, so now we wish to draw attention to one out of various instances which occur of such benefits in the School of Arts, or, as it is called, more intelligibly than tersely, of Philosophy and Letters. Considering the standing, as well as the history and special character of his reputation, we shall not be considered disrespectful to others, who might be named, in singling out the Professor of Irish Archaeology as a specimen of the great social change on which we have been dwelling. Here is a branch of learning recondite, rarely pursued, and from its title especially Irish, and moreover especially Catholic; and here is a scholar, *facile princeps* in his own department of it, who has been, during his hitherto career, cramped in his attempts, dwarfed in his designs, to give to the world the unrivalled treasures still extant of the antiquities of his country, for want of Catholic patronage. At Rome, at Paris, at Brussels, in London, in Oxford, all over Europe, as we are told, lie buried the most precious memorials of the national history, both before and since the Christian era. Few even know where they are; few know what they contain; few can decipher their contents; but Mr Curry, the gentleman in question, in spite of his singular qualifications for doing justice to this branch of antiquarian literature, has hitherto been determined in the direction of his researches by the caprice of a Parliamentary vote, or the accident of local Protestant co-öperation; and, while in his investigations generally he has had to follow the paths of others rather than to strike out his own, he has been definitely debarred from such as were to terminate in illustrations of primitive Catholicism. He is said, before now, to have been instrumental in the conversion of a Protestant clergyman by showing to him MSS., ritual or devotional in their subject, which he could not get the means of giving to the Press; and had it not been for the Catholic University, the probability is that this eminent scholar would have carried to the grave with him, unvalued, unused, the keys which might unlock a world of curious and momentous knowledge. He would have shed lustre on Government commissions and on Trinity College publications; and there would have been the end of his biography. But a happier and more appropriate destiny is in store, we may hope, both for him and for his favourite pursuit. Negotiations, we understand, have been opened for the possession, or, at least, for the use of the foreign MSS. to which we have referred; and an advertisement has already appeared of an instalment of what is to be

575

expected from him, in the shape of twenty-one lectures, delivered in the University Schools, in which he discusses the existing unpublished materials of ancient Irish history from its Pagan period down to the seventh century of Christianity.[1]

V

6 *MARCH*, 1858

There is a class of undertakings, not uncommon in the world, which are ushered in with noise; and wise men feel that where noise is there is seldom anything besides noise. The University lately set up in Dublin is, at least, safe from this criticism. Whatever be its faults, no one can accuse it of puffing itself too loudly, or of becoming a rallying point for party zeal. It is engaged in working, not for the present merely, but for the future; and accordingly it is not exposed to the temptation, which otherwise might beset it, of essaying brilliant displays, or of courting an ephemeral popularity. One cannot be surprised that it has not attained what it has never sought. Its sobriety and modesty certainly were not likely to commend it to those who think that work is got through by talk and profession, and have not shielded it from the importunate question, What has the University done? What is the University doing?

It is possible to be extreme in disregarding public opinion. A *quantum* of reputation is necessary for making progress in any great undertaking; it is the ready money, or rather the credit, which furnishes the exigencies of the day. It imparts to the parties engaged therein the strength of self-reliance and of sympathy. There is an impropriety in trying the strength of well-wishers too rudely, and in appealing simply to a future which they may never live to see. And there is an inconvenience in allowing the growth of a popular disrespect, which may be a provocation to acts of insult or of injury. The authorities of the University seem to be aware of this danger, and of the duty under which they lie of meeting it. And this is the view we take — we shall presently say why — of their new scientific and literary periodical, the *Atlantis*: it is one of their ways of fulfilling a serious obligation.

This publication, though not many weeks old, has already made a considerable sensation; and we venture to affirm that, if its first number is to be a sample of what is to come, it cannot fail to continue to do so. It is an ambitious attempt, certainly; it aims at installing the University among our recognized oracles of intellectual activity, and it claims for it a European position. It will either be a great success, or a great failure. It implies that the University is already prepared for a trial of strength in the open field of

---

[1] Eugene O'Curry's *Lectures on the Manuscript Materials of Ancient History* were published in Dublin in 1861. For the foreign MSS. see letter of 5 June 1854 to Talbot.

literature and science. Its conductors, in their recent prospectus, inform us, that 'In undertakings such as theirs, success, from the nature of the case, is another name for merit; and failure can only arise from causes traceable to themselves. If they are sanguine that they shall be able to answer to the profession which they make in the very fact of their commencing, it is because they trust they have the elementary qualifications of zeal, industry, and determination.' [1]

To any one who has followed the course of official and semi-official documents, with which the proceedings of the University have been accompanied, the motives for so bold a step will be easily understood. What the Professors are at present doing on the very scene of their labours, the schools they are bringing into shape, the students they are collecting, the minds they are forming, the plans of education they are systematizing, and the traditions they are establishing, cannot be seen or valued except on the spot. Their friends are those who know them; beyond this personal range is the cold and dim region of uncertainty, ignorance, scepticism and ill-will, as regards their proceedings, of rumour, fiction, slander, and gossip. On this side of the water their cause is sometimes pronounced to be failing — a staff of Professors without academical heads, without students, without lectures, quarrelling among themselves, and quaking at the falling off of the funds. Such as this being the absurd representations which are made concerning them, they are reduced to the necessity of adopting the ancient disputant's method of refuting his sophisticated opponent, *Solvitur ambulando*, or the modern philosopher's dictum, *Cogito, ergo sum*. Their learned labours, recorded in the *Atlantis*, will be the summary sovereign demonstration that their University both is alive and is thriving, in spite of all that is conjectured to the contrary.

In taking this view of their proceedings, we are availing ourselves of statements made four years ago, before the University had commenced its operations. The present Rector, to whom the task of conducting them was committed, laid it down as the historical idea and almost the essence of a University, that 'demand and supply were all in all'; and (which is the particular principle in point here) that '*the supply must be before the demand*, though not before the need.' [2] He clearly anticipated then, what indeed it was not hard to anticipate, that at first Professors would have to create the public interest, instead of merely satisfying it, and to draw students to their lecture-rooms, instead of finding them there ready to their hand. Nay, he thought it prudent to go beyond what was probable in his anticipation; for, in fact, their lecture-rooms have been fairly attended from the first. Starting, however, on this cautious assumption, he made it his great object, as far as possible, to set up the Professors in such advantageous circumstances, and in such an independent position, as would give full scope to their talents, even though they had no pupils at all, and would furnish the best opportunities, for their

[1] See letter of 20 Oct. 1857 to Sullivan.
[2] *The Office and Work of Universities*, p. 76; *H. S.*, III, p. 51.

at least acting upon public opinion. In a word, since he could not at his will create lecture classes, he determined to create institutions.

This policy is laid down in a printed document of April, 1854, from which we proceed to quote a few sentences: 'Considering,' it said, 'that we have the whole weight of government, not only against us, but in favour of a rival system, it is imperative that the Professors appointed should be men of celebrity. Such celebrity is the only secular inducement to bring students to us in preference to the government colleges. Even able men, if they have not yet made a name, will be unequal to the special necessity of the moment.' An important conclusion follows: 'Since students, as has been said, are to be gained specially and pre-eminently by means of the celebrity of the Professors, it is plain that the Professors must be appointed independent of, and prior to, the presence of students. This has been the case in the history of Universities generally. This brings us to another practical conclusion: *we must commence by bringing into position and shape various large departments of knowledge* — by founding *institutions* which will have their value intrinsically, whether students are present or not. This, if we can manage to do it, will have a double advantage; such institutions, first, will attract students; next, they will have a sufficient object before students come.' After giving instances of the institutions which might be founded, it proceeds: 'Not that such institutions are all of them possible all at once, but some of them are; and these, and such as these, might set to work, and would be producing results *before and during and until* the actual formation of classes of students in each department, for whose sake they are really set up. Astronomical observers, Professors of medical science, the decipherers and editors of ancient writings, chemists and geologists, would in various ways subserve the social interests of Ireland, even though their lecture-rooms at first were but partially filled.[1]

Some of these institutions, as the writer calls them, have already been called into existence; such are the Medical House, the Chemical Laboratory, the Irish Archaeological Department; the Libraries and Museums, which are in course of formation; and the University Church and its accompaniments. Now, the *Atlantis* is one of these, and, in some respects, the most important of all, because it is, in a certain sense, the organ and the record of their proceedings; and, again, because it is not of a local nature, but world-wide in the most emphatic way, increasing the 'celebrity' of the Professors of the University, and making them useful to the literary and scientific world, even though they had no classes of students to instruct at home.

Our readers may now be interested to compare what we have been saying with the views professed in the original advertisement of the *Atlantis*, as it was published in the newspapers in the spring of last year: 'The University,' said the *pro tempore* Editor, 'has already had a greater measure of success than even its most zealous friends, looking calmly at the difficulties under

[1] Memorandum of 29 April 1854, Volume XVI, Appendix I, pp. 558–9; *Campaign*, pp. 95–7.

which it started, ventured to anticipate for it. It has at present in its lecture-rooms from a hundred and ten to a hundred and twenty students. It has, moreover, done much to vanquish the most formidable of difficulties which can beset a public institution, struggling into existence and position; and that is, the apathy, the incredulity, the scorn, with which the very idea of its establishment was variously received, and that, even among those very classes for whose advantage it was specially designed. The fact of its being actually commenced, the number of able men whom it has enlisted in its service, the recognition and the prospects of its "Medical School," the popularity which has attended upon its New Church, the homage paid to it by the foreign youth who have sought it out from abroad in preference to their own schools, have all combined to mitigate the prejudice and to overcome the disinclination of the public mind towards it. But its success supplies a lesson as well as an encouragement. It teaches its members that they must, and may safely, *depend on themselves*. Up to this time, they have made their way, not by favour of external parties, patrons, influences, or contingencies, but *by means of their own reputation, courage, confidence, resources and energy*, under the blessing and protection of Heaven. If they are true to themselves, others will come over to them. They have but to proceed in the course which they have begun, and they are sure to make progress. It is in order, then, that the University may be taking another step in advance that a periodical is contemplated, as the repository and record of its intellectual proficiency. Such an undertaking naturally follows on the entrance of the Professors upon their respective provinces of labour. Nor will it only serve to tell the public what they are doing and what they can do; it will be their contribution to the science and literature of the day; it will be their advertisement, recommendation, and bond of connection, with the learned bodies of Great Britain and the Continent, and it will gain for them, in exchange for what they send, the various journals of a similar kind, many of them important and valuable, which issue periodically from those great centres of thought.'

Some excellent and true friends of the University have criticised the business-like tone and austere technicality of the number which has appeared, and have, in their kind interest for the fame of the University, wished somewhat of more indulgence to ordinary readers, by the introduction of matter less inexorably high and abstruse. But the very object of the publication is to record the successful diligence of the Professors in their respective studies—not to write eloquent reviews or essays, *currente calamo*, on curious or entertaining subjects. Ornamental writing is about as much out of place in the *Atlantis*, as *ormolu* clocks, Dresden china, and Axminster carpets in Pump Court or Copthall Buildings.[1] Scientific schools and circles abroad, where English is not vernacular, would not be impressed by fine periods, or edified by miscellaneous information.

[1] i.e. law or business offices.

VI

13th MARCH, 1858

One of the main secrets of success is self-reliance. This seems a strange sentiment for a Christian journalist to utter; but we speak of self in contrast, not with a higher power, but with our fellow-men. He who leans on others, instead of confiding in his own right arm, will do nothing great. Here, again, we must explain; for is not this the sentiment of every wild religionist who makes himself his own prophet and guide, and despises Holy Fathers and ecclesiastical rulers? Well, then, we are censuring dependence on others, when others are not representatives, in so far as they are relied on, of a higher and more sacred authority. We hope we have expressed ourselves without any paradox at last.

Now, there is a strong existing temptation, to which some men are more exposed than others, but all men under circumstances, of *not* relying on themselves. And this has been a special temptation of literary men and intellectual bodies, from the time of Pericles or Maecenas down to that of Leo or Louis le Grand. And in the case of Universities in particular, as the schoolboy gets his themes done for him, as the undergraduate buys a *cram*, so the venerable Mother to whom he belongs may chance to have it firmly imprinted in her academical intellect, that she cannot possibly prosper without the sanction of the State and the favour of great personages. This has never been the weakness, *exceptis excipiendis*, of the English Universities. They have been dragooned, indeed, by tyrannical despotism; they have had theories, or have felt the passion of loyalty; they all but worship the law as the first of all authorities in heaven or upon earth; but when the question is that of submitting to the Government of the day, or to persons in power, it requires but little knowledge of the history, for instance, of Oxford, to be aware that it has been its rule to rely upon itself—upon its prejudices, if we will, but still on what was its own. Rather than consent to stultify its received principles and recorded professions by a sudden change in favour of Catholic emancipation, it rejected from its representation its favourite son, the Leader of the Commons, when he had deserted his own opinions and invited Alma Mater to follow him. Nor could it honourably have taken another course; and, while we have no relish for political traditions which would have stood in the way of our having at this day any Catholic University at all, we hope that no Catholic University that is or that shall be, with its vantage-ground of higher principles, will ever show less self-respect, consistency, and manliness, than Protestant Oxford, in standing on its own sense of right and falling back upon its own resources.

However, old Universities are but partially exposed to the temptation of courting the secular power and of shifting with the times. It is when an academical body is struggling into position that the offers of the State are at once apposite and effectual; it is when it needs a principle of permanence, which the State can impart, whether in the form of legal recognition or of pecuniary aid. Under such circumstances, imagination is busy with those parties who are interested in its welfare, spreading out before them attractive pictures of the liberality and security of Government grants, and of the satisfactory *status* which is the result of a Charter and of the privilege of conferring degrees. And, on the other hand, memory is busy, too, holding out an over-true record of the anxious or the teasing warfare with a host of difficulties, great and little — the tedious and uncertain progress; the ups and downs, neither dignified nor pleasant; the wear and tear of mind, the discouragements from public opinion or popular rumour, amid which the private individual or body fights its way into station and prosperity. The temptation is strong to attempt a short cut to greatness; though, to tell the truth, a body which has been welded into one mass by the various strokes of fortune is likely to be less brittle, and to have more work in it, than if it had been cast in some external mould, and were subjected to conditions of size and shape which had been determined before its existence.

This, however, is a speculation, interesting indeed to pursue, but beside the purpose of these remarks; for we are contemplating, as is obvious, in what we have been saying, the new Catholic University; and, as regards this particular Institution, we are not called to the delicate task of adjusting the balance of advantages between State patronage and private enterprise in such great scientific and educational undertakings, for a very simple reason. It is true, indeed, that the new University has not the legal *status* and the Government favour, which have abstractedly so many recommendations; but it is certain also, as we consider, that, in matter of fact, in Ireland and at this time, its Professors, whatever else they might gain, would not gain much or anything towards the special objects for which it is instituted, by having those coveted distinctions. And though such an assertion may at first sight look like hazarding a second paradox, we are prepared to defend it.

What will be called, by enemies and timid supporters, the special hitch in the proceedings of the University at present, is, we suppose, not that its Professors are second-rate, nor that they idle away their time, nor that their salaries are insecure, nor that they are without a fair number of students; but that the students, though increasing, are not increasing in the exact ratio of the age of the University. If, then, State recognition can do anything at all for the University at this moment, here, and here only, is the one definite service which it is to render. The one *desideratum*, as hostile critics urge it, concerns, not the Professorial, but the Undergraduate body. Let there be no mistake on this point. Government need not be invoked to do for the Professors what the Professors can do for themselves, but what they cannot do without the Government. If Government does not do as much as this one thing, it does nothing at all. When these objectors cry out to them: 'You will not get on without the Government your talents, your attainments, your honest diligence, your reputation, are worth nothing without Parliament and Law to back you;' what they really say, when brought to book, is this: 'Your students, indeed, at present do not exceed those of one Oxford College; but with Government patronage, they will infallibly be as many as two, three, or four.' If they do not mean this, it is hard to say what they mean which is to the purpose. Taking this, then, for granted, that the advocates for seeking Government aid put it forward as their strong point, that it will fill brim-ful the lecture-rooms of the Professors, we beg attention to the case of the Queen's University and Colleges in Ireland — institutions, of which the very name is suggestive of those high privileges which the Crown and Parliament can alone bestow; and let us ask whether the present condition of those Government bodies, composed, as they are, of Professors of first-rate ability and attainments, is such as to inspire us with any very sanguine hope that the Catholic University would gain much in that one respect in which it is supposed to need to gain by the circumstance of a legal recognition.

We shall not attempt any elaborate investigation into the state of the institutions in question, which we leave to the Blue-book, promised the world as long ago as August last, whenever it shall make its appearance. In a matter so notorious, it will be enough to refresh the memory of any persons who have interested themselves in the subject by one or two documents which we happen to have at hand. It seems, then, that, as late as last year, the sum of £1625 was voted in Parliament for the Queen's University of Ireland, and £3200 for the Queen's Colleges. It appears, too, that the Cork College, in particular, has in its gift as many as fifty-five scholarships, for proficiency in literature, science, medicine, law, civil engineering, and agriculture; in all which departments of study it grants, by the medium of its University, diplomas and degrees. Of these scholarships, ten are of the value of £40 a year each, and forty-five of sums ranging between £24 and £15; making a total of £1400, as the educational encouragement given in one city and neighbourhood in the course of the year. Further, out of the whole number of students of the three Colleges, who presented themselves in Dublin in 1856 at the degree examination, as many as one-fourth were presented with a gold medal, and another fourth with a £12 prize. And yet, in spite of these inducements, the matter of fact is such that the College books do not fill, and even the students who come cannot be persuaded to present themselves for examination, but leave without taking a degree. Moreover, it appears that in 1856 there were only forty-eight examinees from all the three Colleges in the course of the year, or an average of sixteen per College, while the examiners amounted to as many as twenty-one. It appears also that, at the same date, there had only been one engineer's diploma gained in the course of six years, while the expense of the Professorship during that time had been £560. When the subject came before Parliament last session, statesmen of the most various shades of opinion — Whigs, Tories, Peelites, and Orangemen — seemed to acquiesce in these facts, and the only arguments by which Government carried the vote in behalf of the Colleges were such as these: — that the scheme had certainly issued in disappointment but that it was originally Sir ROBERT PEEL'S; that it was now established by Act of Parliament; that it was the expression of a principle of national policy; that it involved a theological question; that measures were in progress for its revision; that a Commission was to publish a report upon it in the course of a few weeks; and that it was unbusiness-like to decide against it before having had the opportunity of reading what the Commissioners had to say.

Such is the result of a paper University, imposed *omnibus numeris* on Ireland. Why should Government be thought able to secure a great accession of students for the Catholic University, when it is unable to collect them for its own favourite institution? Why should not our friends be content to work quietly? and to confide in themselves and in the future?

Appendix 2

November 11, 1858[1]

University Annual Expenses

IN June 1856 I asked the Bishops, and in October 1857 the Archbishops, for the following yearly sums — £5000 from annual collections — £1260 Interest of the Trustees Fund. £600 from University Fees, viz (say) 60 students at £10 — the deficit of the £600 to be made up by the Trustees — Total — £6800

Allocation of the annual £6800.

1. Allocation of the £5000

Faculty of Theology

			£		
Fr O'Reilly	— Dogmatics	—	300		Fr O'Reilly does not draw his whole Salary
Dr Forde	— Canon Law	—	250		
The church—for accommodation, mass, choir, Preachers at £1 a quarter, for 50 sittings for *three* quarters		—	150		
Margin—for other Professorships		—	300		
				1000	

Faculty of Law

Mr O'Hagan	— Jurisprudence	—	100—	100	The arrangement with Mr O'Hagan for £200 a year half from Law, half from Phil and Letters has not yet come into effect, though it ought to be settled at once. I heartily and earnestly wish it carried out. I have not rightly the title of Mr O'Hagan's Professorship Law.

Faculty of Medicine

Dr Lyons	— Practice of Med.		150		
Ellis	— Surgery	—	150		
Hayden. 1.	Anatomy	—	125		
Cryan 2.	Anatomy	—	125		
Sullivan	Chemistry	—	150		Mr Sullivan should have an assistant in the Laboratory vid. below.
Macdermott	— Mat. Med.	—	100		
Macswiney	— Jurisprudence	—	100		
Three Demonstrators		—	100	1000	The Salaries of the Demonstrators was till lately £85. I think I have lately increased it to £100.

[1] This was the paper Newman sent to Anderdon on 16 Nov. 1858. It is preserved at University College, Dublin.

Faculty of Phil. and Letters   £

		£	
Mr Ornsby	— Classical Literat.	300	
Stewart	— Classical Languag.	300	
Renouf.	Ancient Hist and Chron.	200	
Robertson	Modern do	200	
Arnold	— English Literature	200	
Dunne	Logic	250	To Mr Dunne's Salary £50 has been added, to come into effect Feby 12/59, in consequence of his having to lecture to the Medical Students.
Curry	Celtic Archaeol.	200	
Schurr	French. German ⎱	150	
Marani	Italian. Span. ⎰		
Penny.	Catechism	100	
O'Hagan.	Political Econ.	100	vid above under Law
MacCarthy.	Architecture —	0	Mr McCarthy ought to have
		—— 2000	some annual pecuniary ack-knowledgement of his trouble and zeal

Faculty of Science

Mr Butler.	Mathematics	—	300	
Hennessy.	Nat. Phil.	—	300	
Sullivan.	Chemistry	—	150	
Dr Lyons	— Physiology	—	150	
Mr Flanagan	Engineering	—	0	Mr Flanagan has been prom-
		—	900	ised £300 a year, but has not yet put himself into a position
		£5000		to claim it.

2. Allocation of £1260 (Payments more or less provisional)

Officers.

Mr Anderdon	— Pro-Vice-Rector.	160	If this office, lasts, or become Vice Rector, unless a Pro-fessorship is attached to it, the salary ought to be made up to £200
Scratton	Secretary	200	The Secretary ought in addition to his £200, to have a percentage of the Fees.
Servants	— say	100	The Servants have never cost near £100. £50 of it might go to an assistant in the Labora-tory, who is much wanted.
Debt upon Fees Account as below	—	445	
Margin for Examiners in Phil and Letters and in Science. for occasional lectures for affiliated schools for Stationary for Printing etc. ⎱		355	The Examiner System has never been formed—I ought to write a separate paper upon it.
		1260	

The Margins at *present* are

Theology — 300

Officers — 355

3. Allocation of £600 Fees.

		£	
Advance to Houses, say	—	500	
10 Burses at £45	—	450	
2 Exhibitions	—	70	
5 Prizes	—	25	
	—		1045
Debt on Fees Account to be supplied as above		445	
		600	

655 — of this surplus £300 should go to a good staff of Examiners—£50 to Mr Renouf—£50 to Mr Arnold. (Indeed I wish all the Professors in that Faculty, who have £250 or £200, had £300.) Percentage on Fees to Mr Scratton.

J H N

List of Letters by Correspondents

List of Letters by Correspondents

Abbreviations used in addition to those listed at the beginning of the volume:

A.	Original Autograph.
Bayswater	Oblates of St Charles, Bayswater, London.
C.	Copy, other than those made by Newman.
D.	Draft by Newman.
Georgetown	Georgetown University, Washington, D.C.
H.	Holograph copy by Newman.
Harrow	Dominican Convent, Harrow, Middlesex.
Lond.	London Oratory.
Magd.	Magdalen College, Oxford.
Pr.	Printed.
Pusey	Pusey House, Oxford.
Rankeillour	The Lord Rankeillour
S.J. Dublin	The Jesuit Fathers, 35 Lower Leeson Street, Dublin.
S.J. Lond.	The Jesuit Fathers, 114 Mount Street, London.
Stoke	The Dominican Convent, Stoke-on-Trent.
Todhunter	Mrs Todhunter, Gillingham Hall, Suffolk.
Ushaw	Ushaw College, Durham.

The abbreviation which describes the source is always the first one after the date of each letter. This is followed immediately by the indication of its present location or owner. When there is no such indication, it means that the source letter is preserved at the Birmingham Oratory. It has not been thought necessary to reproduce the catalogue indications of the Archives at the Oratory, because each of Newman's letters there is separately indexed, and can be traced at once.

After the source and its location have been indicated, any additional holograph copies (with their dates) or drafts are listed, and then enclosed within brackets, any references to previous publication in standard works.

Lastly, when it is available, comes the address to which the letter was sent.

Correspondent	Year	Date	Source	Location, Owner, Address
Acton, Sir John	1857	25 Nov	A	
	1858	8 Mar	A	
		26 Mar	A	
		5 April	A	
		8 July	A	Mr Douglas Woodruff
		10 July	A	Mr Douglas Woodruff
		14 July	A	Mr Douglas Woodruff
		27 July	A	Mr Douglas Woodruff
		2 Aug	A	Mr Douglas Woodruff
		2 Dec	A	Mr Douglas Woodruff
		16 Dec	A	Mr Douglas Woodruff
		21 Dec	A	Mr Douglas Woodruff
		31 Dec	A	Mr Douglas Woodruff (*Ward*, 1, pp. 482–5; Acton, *Essays on Church and State*, ed. D. Woodruff, p. 18)
			D	(Two)
			H of D	
Allies, T. W.	1957	6 Nov	C	
		12 Nov	C	
	1858	8 Jan	C	
		11 Jan	C	
		19 Jan	C	
		26 Jan	C	
		28 Jan	C	
		31 Jan	C	
		21 Mar	C	
		7 Oct	C	
		18 Oct	C	
Allies, Mrs T. W.	1858	12 Mar	C	
Anderdon, William Henry	1857	12 April	D	
	1858	28 Sept	D	
		5 Oct	D	
		16 Nov	D	
			H	1872
		8 Dec	C	
		24 Dec	D	
Archbishops of Ireland	1857	6 Aug	A	Diocesan Archives, Dublin
			D	
			H	
	1858	12 Nov	D	(Two)
Arnold, Thomas	1857	30 Nov	D	
	1858	15 Dec	D	
Badeley, Edward	1857	22 April	A	
	1858	16 Mar	A	
		26 Mar	A	

Correspondent	Year	Date	Source	Location, Owner, Address
Bathurst, Catherine Anne	1857	27 June	A	Harrow
		5 Nov	A	Harrow
	1858	22 Mar	A	Harrow
Beardwood, William Houghton	1858	16 July	D	
Bellamy, Theodora	1858	3 Sept	D	
Bellasis, Edward	1857	21 Oct	A	
		28 Oct	A	
		6 Nov	A	
	1858	2 Feb	A	
		9 Feb	A	
			D	
		12 Feb	A	
			D	
		7 Mar	A	
		12 Mar	A	
			D	
		1 April	A	
		6 April	A	(*Ward*, I, pp. 453–4)
			D	
		13 April	A	
		23 April	A	
			D	
		25 Nov	A	
		4 Dec	A	(*Ward*, I, pp. 454–5)
		21 Dec (I)	D	
		21 Dec (II)	D	
		28 Dec	A	(*Ward*, I, p. 456)
Bianconi, Charles	1857	8 July	H of A	1876
			D	
			H of D	1872
Bittleston, Henry	1857	29 June	A	*Ad.* The Revd Fr Bittleston/The Oratory/Hagley Road/ Birmingham /England
	1858	22 April	A	
		30 April	A	(*Trevor*, II, p. 180)
		21 May	A	
		8 Aug	A	(*Trevor*, II, pp. 184–5)
Blake, Michael	1857	2 April	D	(*Ward*, I, p. 632)
			H	1872
Blount, Gilbert	1857	8 July	D	
Blount, Michael	1857	13 June	D	
		29 June	D	
Bloxam, J. R.	1857	3 July	A	Magd. MS. 307
	1858	22 Mar	A	Pusey, 'Cardinal Newman' volume
		18 Sept.	A	Pusey, 'Cardinal Newman' volume

Correspondent	Year	Date	Source	Location, Owner, Address
Bowles, F. S.	1857	8 June	A	
		26 June	A	
		6 Nov	A	
			D	
		7 Nov	A	
Bretherton, Peter	1858	5 Mar	C	
Browne, George	1857	2 April		See Blake, Michael
Browne, James	1857	2 April		See Blake, Michael
Buckle, Mrs William Henry	1858	14 Feb	C	
Butler, Edward	1857	15 Nov	D	
		19 Nov	D	
			H	1872
		24 Nov	D	
			H	1872
		17 Dec	A	
	1858	11 Jan	D	(Telegram)
			H	1872
		19 Jan	D	
		23 Mar	A	
			H	1872
		20 July	A	S.J. Dublin
		18 Nov	D	
			H	1872
Campden, Viscountess	1857	13 May	C	
Cantwell, John	1857	2 April	D	(*Ward*, I, p. 631)
			H	1872
Capes, J. M.	1857	6 April	A	
	1858	17 May	A	(*Ward* I, p. 439; *Gasquet*, pp. xxiv–xxv)
		10 Aug	A	(*Ward*, I, 440–1)
			D	
		22 Sept	A	(*Ward*, I, p. 441)
		27 Sept	A	(*Ward*, I, p. 441)
Capes, J. M.	1858	1 Oct	A	(*Ward*, I, pp. 442–3)
			D	
Caswall, Edward	1857	10 July	A	
	1858	29 June	A	
		18 July	A	
Circular Letter	1858	24 Feb	Pr	
Clifford, William	1858	4 Mar	A	Diocesan Archives, Clifton
Collins, Edward Francis	1857	1 June	A	F. I. Connolly, 33 Parkside, Wimbledon
Copeland, George	1858	4 Feb	A	*Ad.* George Copeland Esqr/ MD/ &c &c/Cheltenham
Coppinger, Mrs	1858	14 June	A	
Cullen, Archbishop	1857	2 April	A	(*Ward*, I, p. 632)
			H	1872

Correspondent	Year	Date	Source	Location, Owner, Address
Cullen, Archbishop	1857	29 April	A	Diocesan Archives, Dublin
			D	
		8–10 July	A	Diocesan Archives, Dublin
		18 July	A	Diocesan Archives, Dublin
			D	
		17 Aug	D	
	1858	17 June	Pr	*Campaign*, pp. xxxvii–viii
			D	
		21 July	A	Diocesan Archives, Dublin
			D	
			H	1872
		31 Aug	A	Diocesan Archives, Dublin
		28 Sept	A	Diocesan Archives, Dublin
			D	
			H	Cashel Diocesan Archives
Dalgairns, J. D.	1858	4 April	A	Lond. Vol. 12
Daunt, W. J. O'Neill	1857	30 Oct	A	St John's Seminary, Camarillo, California
	1858	6 April	A	National Library of Ireland
Delany, William	1857	2 April	D	(*Ward*, 1, p. 631)
			H	1872
Denison, George Anthony	1858	2 Nov	D	
Denvir, Cornelius	1857	2 April		See Delany, William
Derry, John	1857	2 April		See Delany, William
Disraeli, Benjamin	1858	19 July	C	
			D	(Two)
Dixon, Joseph	1857	2 April	D	(*Ward*, 1, p. 630)
			H	1872
		15 April	D	
		2 July	D	
			H	1872
		18 July	D	
			H	1872
		17 Aug	D	
		8 Dec	A	St Patrick's College, Maynooth
	1858	27 Oct	D	
			H	1872
		12 Nov	D	
			H	1872
Dodsworth, William	1857	26 July	C	
		29 Sept	C	
		7 Oct	C	
Dunne, D. B.	1857	20 April	A	Miss Doreen Powell, County Cork *Ad.* D. Dunne Esqr D.D. &c &c/ Catholic University House/ 86 Stephen's Green/Dublin
		1 May	A	Miss Doreen Powell *Ad.* D. Dunne Esqr &c &c/ University House

Correspondent	Year	Date	Source	Location, Owner, Address
Dunne, D. B.	1857	11 May	A	Miss Doreen Powell *Ad.* the same
		6 July	A	Miss Doreen Powell *Ad.* D. Dunn Esqr D.D./28 Lower Mount Street
		16 Sept	A	Miss Doreen Powell
		17 Dec	A	Miss Doreen Powell *Ad.* D. B. Dunne Esqr/Catholic University House/86 Stephens' Green/Dublin
	1858	27 Mar	D	
			H	1872
		26 July	D	
		30 July	D	
Dunraven, Earl of	1858	20 June	A	
		14 July	A	
		20 Oct	A	
		8 Nov	A	
		10 Dec	A	
Durcan, Patrick	1857	2 April	D	(*Ward*, I, p. 632)
			H	1872
Editor of the Weekly Register	1857	12 Dec	Pr	The *Weekly Register*, (12 Dec. 1857), p. 5
	1858	2 Jan	Pr	The *Weekly Register*, (2 Jan. 1858), p. 7
		16 Jan	Pr	The *Weekly Register*, (16 Jan. 1858), p. 4.
Ellis, Andrew	1857	26 April	A	*Ad.* A. Ellis Esqr M D/110 Stephen's Green/Dublin
		1 Aug	A	*Ad.* the same
		7 Dec	A	*Ad.* the same
	1858	11 Jan	A	*Ad.* the same
		16 Aug	A	*Ad.* the same
		22 Aug	D	
		13 Sept	A	Castleknock College, Dublin *Ad.* the same
		24 Sept	D	
Faber, F. W.	1857	17 Dec.	A	Lond. Vol. 9
Fallon, Patrick	1857	2 April		See Blake, Michael
Feeny, Thomas	1857	2 April		See Blake, Michael
Flanagan, John Stanislas	1857	4 April	A	
		29 April	A	
		15 May	A	
		17 May	A	(*Trevor*, II, p. 159)
		19 May	A	
		29 June	A	
		4 July	A	
		9 July	A	
		16 July	A	
		31 Oct	A	

Correspondent	Year	Date	Source	Location, Owner, Address
Flanagan, John Stanislas	1858	21 Feb	A	
		22 Feb	A	(*Trevor*, II, p. 175)
		23 Feb	A	
		24 Feb (I)	A	(*Trevor*, II, p. 180)
		24 Feb (II)	A	
		25 Feb	A	
		26 Feb	A	
		28 Feb	A	(*Trevor*, II, p. 175)
		5 Mar	A	(*Trevor*, II, p. 175)
		12 Mar	A	
		15 Mar	A	(*Trevor*, II, p. 176)
		5 April	A	(*Trevor*, II, pp. 179–80)
		30 April	A	
		13 May	A	
		19 May	A	(*Trevor*, II, p. 180)
		31 May	A	(*Trevor*, II, p. 184)
		23 June	A	
		17 July	A	
		18 July	A	
		7 Oct	A	
		21 Oct	A	
		25 Oct	A	
Flanagan, Terence	1858	3 Mar	D	
Flanagan, Thomas	1857	28 July	Pr	*Apo.* pp. 396–8
			D	
Flannery, Michael	1857	23 May	D	
		18 Nov (I)	D	
			H	1872
		18 Nov (II)	D	
			H	1872
		19 Nov	D	(Two)
			H	1872
		28 Nov	D	
		30 Nov	D	
			H	1872
		18 Dec	D	
	1858	11 Jan	D	
		13 May	D	
Forde, Laurence	1857	20 June	D	
		1 Nov	D	
		26 Nov	A	Diocesan Archives, Dublin
			D	(Two)
			H	1872
Froude, Isy	1858	29 Oct	C	(*Harper*, p. 114)
Froude, Mrs William	1857	22 April	A	*Ad.* Mrs Wm Froude/Dartington Rectory/Totnes/Devon

Correspondent	Year	Date	Source	Location, Owner, Address
Froude, Mrs William	1857	28 Oct	A	(*Harper*, p. 111) *Ad*. Mrs Wm Froude/Dartington Parsonage/ Totnes/Devon
		11 Dec.	A	(*Harper*, pp. 111–12) *Ad*. the same
	1858	5 April	C	
Fullerton, Lady Georgiana	1857	28 Oct	Pr.	The *Month*, CXXIX, (April 1917) p. 336
Furlong, Thomas	1857	2 April		See Durcan, Patrick
		14 April	D	
Gartlan, James	1858	30 Nov	D	(*Campaign*, p. lix)
			H	1872
Giberne, Miss M. R.	1857	13 July	A	
		14 Aug	A	
	1858	9 April	A	
		24 June	A	
Gillooly, Lawrence	1857	2 April		See Durcan, Patrick
Godwin, Thomas	1858	30 July	A	
Gordon, Mrs	1858	13 Feb	A	Lond. Vol. 11
Hallahan, Mother Margaret Mary	1857	18 May	C	
Hayden, Thomas	1857	15 June	A	National Library of Ireland
			D	
		27 June	D	
			H	1872
		31 July	Pr	*Castleknock College Chronicle*, 1954, p. 16
			D	
		8 Sept	Pr	*Castleknock College Chronicle*, 1854, p. 17
	1858	24 April	D	
		13 June	D	
		1 July	Pr	*Castleknock College Chronicle*, p. 17
Haydon, Frank Scott	1858	24 April	D	
Hennessy, Henry	1858	20 Mar	C	
		26 Mar	C	
		15 July	C	
		10 Dec	C	
		14 Dec	C	
			D	
Holmes, Miss	1857	16 May	A	
		9 July	A	
		10 Oct	A	
		4 Nov	A	
	1858	29 July	A	
		10 Aug	A	
		7 Nov	A	

Correspondent	Year	Date	Source	Location, Owner, Address
Hope-Scott, James	1857	1 April	H	1873
		5 June	A	Rankeillour
			H	1873
		29 July	A	Rankeillour
			H	1873
		5 Aug	A	Rankeillour
			H	1872
			H	1873
		24 Dec	A	Rankeillour
				(R. Ornsby, *Memoirs of James Robert Hope-Scott*, II, pp. 143 and 151; *McGrath*, p. 454)
			H	1873
	1858	1 Jan	H	1873
		27 Sept	A	Rankeillour
			H	1873
		18 Oct	A	
			H	1873
		28 Oct.	A	Mrs Maxwell Scott, Abbotsford
		31 Oct	A	Mrs Maxwell Scott, Abbotsford
Hope-Scott, Mrs	1857	8 July	A	Mrs Maxwell Scott, Abbotsford
Johnson, Manuel	1857	23 June	A	*Ad.* M. Johnson Esqr/Observatory/Oxford/England
		28 Sept	A	*Ad.* Manuel Johnson Esqr/Observatory/Oxford
		4 Nov	A	*Ad.* the same as 23 June
	1858	29 Dec	A	*Ad.* the same as 28 Sept
Jones, Daniel	1857	30 Oct	A	
Keane, Augustus Henry	1858	31 Aug	D	
Keane, William	1857	2 April		See Blake, Michael
		14 April	D	
Keefe, M.	1858	13 Feb	D	
Kelly, Francis	1857	2 April		See Blake, Michael
Kelly, John J.	1857	17 Nov	D	
			H	1872
Kelly, Matthew	1858	5 Oct	D	
Kerr, Lord Henry	1858	22 Mar	C	Todhunter
Kerr, Lady Henry	1857	8 Dec	C	Todhunter
	1858	14 Feb	C	Todhunter
		31 Oct	C	Todhunter
Kilduff, John	1857	2 April		See Durcan, Patrick
Leahy, John	1857	2 April	A	S J. Dublin (*Ward*, I, p. 631)
			D	
			H	1872
		15 April	Pr	The *Irish Monthly*, (Dec. 1890), p. 651
			D	

Correspondent	Year	Date	Source	Location, Owner, Address
Leahy, Patrick	1857	23 May	D	
			H	1872
		17 June	A	Cashel Diocesan Archives
			D	
		20 June	A	Cashel Diocesan Archives
			D	
		28 June	D	
		17 July	D	
		31 July	A	Cashel Diocesan Archives
		8 Aug	D	(*McGrath*, p. 446)
			H	(Three)
		11 Aug	A	Diocesan Archives, Dublin
		17 Aug	D	
			H	(Two)
		26 Aug	D	
			H	
		12 Sept	D	
		16 Oct (I)	A	Cashel Diocesan Archives
		16 Oct (II)	A	Cashel Diocesan Archives
			D	
			H	(Four)
		30 Oct	D	
			H	(Two)
		1 Nov	A	Diocesan Archives, Dublin
			H	(Two)
	1858	3 Feb (I)	A	Diocesan Archives, Dublin
			D	
			H	
		3 Feb (II)	A	Cashel Diocesan Archives
		27 Feb	A	Cashel Diocesan Archives
			D	
			H	
		17 Aug	D	
			H	1872
		27 Aug	D	
		2 Oct	A	Cashel Diocesan Archives
			D	
			H	1872
		5 Oct (I)	A	Cashel Diocesan Archives
			D	
			H	1872
		5 Oct (II)	D	(Two)
		27 Oct	D	
		12 Nov	D	
			H	1872

598

Correspondent	Year	Date	Source	Location, Owner, Address
Leigh, William	1857	7 Oct	A	Dominican Priory, Woodchester *Ad*. William Leigh Esqr/Woodchester Park/Stroud/Gloucestershire
		10 Oct	A	Dominican Priory, Woodchester *Ad*. William Leigh Esq/Woodchester Park/Stroud/Gloucestershire
Lissoni, D. D.	1857	27 July	A	College of the Holy Cross, Worcester, Massachussetts
Lynch, Henry J.	1857	10 July	C	
		13 July	C	
Lynch, P. N.	1858	7 Dec	D	
Lyons, Robert D.	1857	4 July	D	
			H	1872
		5 July	A	
		23 Nov	D	
		26 April	A	
	1858	15 June	A	(*Campaign*, p. xxvi)
		14 July	A	
		28 Sept	D	
			H	1872
MacDermott, Robert	1857	5 Dec	D	
	1858	14 Feb	D	
			H	1872
		26 July	D	
		31 July	D	
		18 Aug	D	
		21 Aug	D	
			H	1872
		13 Sept	D	
		24 Sept	H	
McEvily, John	1857	2 April		See Durcan, Patrick
McGettigan, Daniel	1857	2 April		See Durcan, Patrick
McGettigan, Patrick	1857	2 April		See Blake, Michael
MacHale, John	1857	2 April	Pr	B. O'Reilly, *John MacHale, Archbishop of Tuam*, New York, 1890, II, p. 520. (*Ward*, I, p. 633)
			D	
			H	1872
McNally, Charles	1857	2 April		See Blake, Michael
Manning, H. E.	1857	25 June	A	Bayswater
		30 Sept	A	Bayswater
		6 Oct	A	Bayswater
		21 Dec	A	Bayswater
Marshall, T. W.	1858	14 Mar	D	
Maxwell, Patrick	1857	28 May	D	
Mills, Austin	1857	5 July	A	

Correspondent	Year	Date	Source	Location, Owner, Address
Molloy, James Lynam	1857	26 Dec	D	
	1858	9 Jan	A	Miss Doreen Powell, County Cork *Ad.* James Molloy Esqr/St Patrick's House/86 Stephen's Green/ Dublin
Monsell, William	1857	29 April	A	
		8 Aug	A	
		9 Oct	A	
		22 Dec	A	
	1858	12 Mar	A	
		9 May	A	
		28 May	A	
		11 June	A	
		5 July	A	
		19 July	A	
		30 July	A	
		18 Oct	A	
		19 Dec	A	
Morris, J. B.	1857	2 Dec	A	St Edmund's College, Ware
		11 Dec	A	St Edmund's College, Ware
	1858	2 Aug	A	St Edmund's College, Ware
		7 Sept	A	St Edmund's College, Ware
Mozley, Mrs John	1857	15 May	A	J. H. Mozley, Haslemere, Surrey
		31 Aug	A	J. H. Mozley
	1858	28 Feb	A	J. H. Mozley
Mulholland, John	1857	26 Dec	D	
Neville, William	1857	8 July	A	In note to letter to Gilbert Blount
		10 Nov	A	
Newsham, Charles	1858	13 April	A	Ushaw
Norfolk, Duke of	1857	30 June	D	
	1858	8 Feb	A	The Duke of Norfolk
		7 April	A	The Duke of Norfolk
Norfolk, Duchess of	1857	29 Nov	A	The Duke of Norfolk
	1858	26 Nov	A	The Duke of Norfolk
O'Brien, Dominic	1857	2 April		See Leahy, John Pius
		14 April	D	
Ogle, Octavius	1857	20 Oct	D	
O'Hagan, John	1858	15 June	A	S.J. Dublin
		14 July	A	S.J. Dublin
		28 Sept	D	
			H	1872
		11 Oct	A	S.J. Dublin (*McGrath*, p. 471)
		14 Nov	A	S.J. Dublin
O'Reilly, Edmund	1857	18 July	D	
		18 Dec	D	(Two)
	1858	18 Jan	D	
		27 Feb	D	(*McGrath*, p. 458)

Correspondent	Year	Date	Source	Location, Owner, Address
O'Reilly, Edmund	1858	27 Feb	H	1872
		22 April	A	(*Campaign*, pp. xl–xli)
		25 May	A	
		31 May	C	
		8 June	C	
		9 July	C	
		25 July	A	S.J. Dublin
		23 Aug	C	
Ornsby, Robert	1857	9 Aug	A	
			H	1872
		6 Sept	A	
			H	1872
		30 Sept	A	
		12 Dec	A	
			H	1872
		21 Dec (I)	A	
			H	1872
		21 Dec (II)	A	(*Ward*, I, pp. 379–80; *McGrath*, p. 453)
			H	1872
		31 Dec	A	
	1858	5 Jan	A	
			H	1872
		9 Jan	A	
			H	
		12 Jan	A	
			H	1872
		14 Jan	A	
			H	1872
		19 Jan	A	
			H	1872
		23 Jan	A	
			H	1872 (Two)
		4 Feb	A	
			H	1872
		13 Feb	A	
			H	1872
		20 Feb	A	
			H	1872
		12 Mar	A	
			H	1872
		30 Mar	A	
			H	1872
		12 April	A	
			H	1872
		22 April	A	
			H	1872

Correspondent	Year	Date	Source	Location, Owner, Address
Ornsby, Robert	1858	29 April	A	
			H	1872
		8 June	A	
			H	1872
		22 June	A	
			H	1872
		29 June	A	
			H	1872
		11 July	A	
			H	1872
		20 July	H	1872
		26 July	H	1872
		17 Aug	A	
			H	1872
		7 Sept	A	(*McGrath*, p. 466)
			H	1872
		9 Sept	A	
		15 Sept	A	(and 19 Sept)
			H	1872
		7 Oct	A	(*Ward*, I, pp. 446–7)
			H	1872
		11 Oct	A	(*Ward*, I, p. 447)
			H	1872
		17 Oct	A	(*Ward*, I, p. 448)
			H	1872
		18 Oct	H	1872
		31 Oct	A	
			D	(Two)
			H	1872
		8 Nov	A	
			H	1872
		12 Nov	A	
			H	1872
		16 Nov	A	(*Campaign*, p. lix)
		1 Dec	A	
			H	1872
		3 Dec	A	
		6 Dec (I)	A	
		6 Dec (II)	A	
		7 Dec	A	
		11 Dec	A	
		12 Dec	H	1872
Patterson, James Laird	1858	26 June	A	
			D	
Phillipps, A. Lisle	1857	1 July	C	(*de Lisle*, I, pp. 367–9; C. Butler, *The Life and Times of Bishop Ullathorne*, I, pp. 343–4)

Correspondent	Year	Date	Source	Location, Owner, Address
Phillipps, A. Lisle	1857	4 July	C	(*de Lisle*, I, p. 369)
		9 July	C	(*de Lisle*, I, pp. 369–70)
		13 July	C	(*de Lisle*, I, p. 370)
		30 July	C	(*de Lisle*, I, pp. 371–2)
		24 Nov	C	
Platt, Ralph	1857	17 Oct	A	Ushaw
Plumer, Julius	1858	12 Aug	D	
			H of D	
Pollen, John Hungerford	1857	5 Aug	C	
		28 Aug	C	
		8 Nov	C	
		17 Nov	C	
		26 Nov	C	(*McGrath*, p. 450)
	1858	24 Jan	C	(Anne Pollen, *John Hungerford Pollen*, p. 267)
		16 May	C	
		21 May	C	
		28 May	C	
		2 June	C	
		10 June	C	
		19 June	C	
		16 July	C	
		21 July	C	
		2 Aug	C	
		10 Aug	C	
		20 Aug	C	
		31 Aug	C	
		27 Sept	C	
		8 Oct	C	
		7 Dec	C	
		28 Dec	C	
Poole, Mary Imelda	1858	21 April	C	
		29 April	C	
Pope, Thomas Alder	1857	17 Nov	A	
Professors, etc of the University	1858	6 Nov.	D	(Two)
			H	1872
Pusey, E. B.	1858	13 April	A	Pusey (*Liddon*, IV, p. 78)
		21 April	C	(*Liddon*, IV, p. 78)
		17 May	A	Pusey
		7 June	A	Pusey
Quinn, James	1858	12 April	A	
			D	
Ratcliff, Sir John	1858	19 June	A	Oscott College
Renouf, Peter le Page	1858	10 Feb	A	Pembroke College, Oxford
		11 Oct	A	Pembroke College, Oxford
Robertson, J. B.	1858	28 Sept	D	
			H	1872

Correspondent	Year	Date	Source	Location, Owner, Address
Rossi, Carlo	1857	1 July	D	
Russell, C	1858	23 June	A	S.J. Dublin
		11 Oct	A	S.J. Dublin
			D	
		27 Oct	C	
		4 Dec	A	S.J. Dublin
			H	1872
Ryan, John	1857	2 April		See Leahy, John Pius
St John, Ambrose	1857	4 May	A	
			H	1875
		6 May (I)	A	(*Ward*, I, p. 374)
			H	(Two)
		6 May (II)	A	
		7 May	A	(*Ward*, I, pp. 437–8; *Trevor*, II, p. 169)
		12 May (I)	A	(*Ward*, I, pp. 377–8; *McGrath*, pp. 441–2)
			H	1875
		12 May (II)	A	(*Ward*, I, pp. 376–7; *Trevor*, II, p. 159; *McGrath*, pp. 442–3)
			H	1875
		19 May	A	
			H	1875
		25 June	A	
			H	1875
		29 June	A	
			H	1875
		2 July	A	
			H	1875
		8 July	A	
			H	1875
		14 July	A	(*Trevor*, II, pp. 161–3)
			H	1875
		5 Nov	A	
			H	1875
		12 Nov	A	
			H	1875
		17 Nov	A	
			H	1875
	1858	21 Jan	A	
		8 June	A	
			H	1875
		9 June	A	
		10 June	A	
			H	1875
		13 June	A	(*Ward*, II, pp. 345–6; *Trevor*, II, pp. 181, 183)

Correspondent	Year	Date	Source	Location, Owner, Address
St John, Ambrose	1858	13 June	H	1875
		15 June	A	
			H	1875
		16 June	A	
		20 June	A	
			H	1875
		23 June	A	
			H	1875
		25 June	A	
			H	1875
		31 Oct	A	
			D	
			H	1875
Scott, W. M.	1857	28 Nov	A	
		18 Dec	A	
	1858	25 May	A	
		7 June	A	
		9 June	A	
		5 Sept	A	
Scott-Murray, C. R.	1858	7 July	D	
Scratton, Thomas	1857	11 May	A	S.J. Dublin
		12 May	A	S.J. Dublin
		28 May	A	S.J. Dublin
		13 June	A	S.J. Dublin
		21 Oct	A	S.J. Dublin
		28 Oct	A	S.J. Dublin
		24 Nov	A	S.J. Dublin
		1 Dec	D	
		3 Dec	A	S.J. Dublin
		7 Dec	A	S.J. Dublin
	1858	5 Jan	A	S.J. Dublin
		19 Jan	A	S.J. Dublin
		8 Feb	A	S.J. Dublin
		22 Mar	A	S.J. Dublin
		27 Mar	A	S.J. Dublin
		31 Mar	A	S.J. Dublin
		21 April	A	S.J. Dublin
		22 April	A	S.J. Dublin
		23 April	A	S.J. Dublin
		29 April	A	S.J. Dublin
		11 May	A	S.J. Dublin
		23 May	A	S.J. Dublin
		24 May	A	S.J. Dublin
		26 May	A	S.J. Dublin
		28 May	A	S.J. Dublin
		1 June	A	S.J. Dublin

Correspondent	Year	Date	Source	Location, Owner, Address
Scratton, Thomas	1858	14 June	A	S.J. Dublin
		16 June	A	S.J. Dublin
		24 June	A	S.J. Dublin
		28 June	A	S.J. Dublin
		1 July	A	S.J. Dublin
		2 July	A	S.J. Dublin
		19 July	A	S.J. Dublin
		22 July	A	S.J. Dublin
		25 July	A	S.J. Dublin
		26 July	A	S.J. Dublin
		22 Sept	A	S.J. Dublin
		End of Sept	A	S.J. Dublin
		18 Oct	A	S.J. Dublin
		22 Oct	A	S.J. Dublin
		15 Nov	A	S.J. Dublin
		8 Dec	A	S.J. Dublin
		11 Dec	D	
		16 Dec	D	
Simeon, Sir John	1857	17 April	C	
			D	
	1858	4 Feb	A	Sir John Simeon, Bart.
Simpson, Richard	1857	14 May	A	
		27 May	A	
Stanton, Richard	1857	18 June	A	
		22 June	A	
		30 July	A	
		25 Nov	D	
Stewart, James	1857	1 June	A	*Ad.* James Stewart Esqr/10 Great Charles Street/Dublin
		17 June	C	
		30 Sept	C	
	1858	17 Feb	C	
		15 May	C	
		2 June	C	
		7 June	C	
		2 July	C	
		12 July	C	
		7 Oct	C	
		15 Nov	C	*Ad.* [A] James Stewart Esqr/10 Great Charles Street/Dublin
		22 Nov	A	Convent of the Sacred Heart, Hove, Sussex
		26 Nov	C	
		9 Dec	C	
		13 Dec	C	
		29 Dec (I)	C	
		29 Dec (II)	D	

Correspondent	Year	Date	Source	Location, Owner, Address
Sullivan, William Kirby	1857	13 June	D	
		9 Aug	A	
		28 Aug	A	
		9 Sept	A	
		9 Oct	A	
		10 Oct	A	
		20 Oct	A	
		28 Dec	A	
	1858	6 Jan	A	
		8 Jan	A	
		4 Feb	A	
		5 Feb	A	
		20 Mar	A	
		5 April	A	
		20 April	A	
		15 May	A	
		25 May	A	
		30 May	A	
		31 May	A	
		16 June	A	
		28 June	A	
		9 July	A	
		21 July	A	
		12 Aug	A	
		18 Aug	A	
		23 Aug	A	(*Ward*, 1, p. 430)
		31 Aug	A	(*Ward*, 1, pp. 430–1)
		27 Sept	A	
		28 Sept	A	
			D	
			H	1872
		29 Sept	A	
		7 Oct	A	
		11 Oct	A	
		23 Nov	A	
		30 Nov	A	(*Ward*, 1, p. 432)
Tate, Robert	1857	17 Oct	A	Ushaw
Taylor, J. I.	1857	End of April?	D	(*Ward*, 1, pp. 375–6; *McGrath* pp. 440–1)
Thompson, Edward Healy	1857	6 April	C	
		12 April	C	
Throckmorton, Sir Robert	1857	12 Nov	A	Coughton Court, Throckmorton MSS. Folder 39
		1 Dec	A	Coughton Court, Throckmorton MSS. Folder 39
Thynne, Lord Charles	1858	25 Nov	C	
Thynne, Lady Charles	1857	28 Oct	C	

Correspondent	Year	Date	Source	Location, Owner, Address
Tillotson, Robert Beverley	1858	10 Mar	A	
		20 Mar	A	(*Trevor*, II, pp. 176–7)
Todd, William Gowan	1857	7 Oct	A	
Tyrrell, Henry	1858	24 Sept	D	
Ullathorne, Bishop	1857	7 May	A	
		10 May	A	
	1858	2 Mar	A	
			D	
		3 Mar	A	
		30 Mar	A	
Unknown Correspondent	1858	2 Oct	C	
Vaughan, Daniel	1857	2 April		See Blake, Michael
		23 June	D	
Vere, Aubrey de	1858	25 July	A	National Library of Ireland
Walford, Edward	1858	16 June	A	St John's Seminary, Camarillo, California
		14 July	A	St John's Seminary, Camarillo, California
Walker, J., of Scarborough	1857	17 Oct	A	
Wallis, John	1858	21 April	A	
		5 Sept	A	
Walsh, Edward	1857	2 April		See Leahy, John Pius
Walsh, James	1857	2 April		See Blake, Michael
Ward, Mrs F. R.	1858	4 Feb	A	
Ward, W. G.	1857	17 April	A	Mrs Sheed (*Ward*, I, at p. 420; W. Ward, *William George Ward and the Catholic Revival*, London 1893, pp. 216 and 459–60)
			D	
			H of D	
		6 July	C	Mrs Sheed
	1858	13 Feb	C	(W. Ward, *op. cit.*, p. 460)
Weedall, Henry	1858	29 April	A	Stoke
Welply, David	1858	8 Mar	D	
Whitty, Robert	1857	19 May	A	S.J. Lond.
Wilberforce, Henry	1857	18 April	A	Georgetown
			H	1876
		20 May	A	Georgetown (*McGrath*, p. 443)
			D	1876
		27 May	A	Georgetown
			H	1876
		4 June	A	Georgetown
		9 June	A	Georgetown
		13 June	A	Georgetown
		15 July	A	Georgetown
			H	1876
		30 July	A	Georgetown
			H	1876

LIST OF LETTERS BY CORRESPONDENTS

Correspondent	Year	Date	Source	Location, Owner, Address
Wilberforce, Henry	1857	10 Sept	A	Georgetown
			H	1876
		2 Nov	A	Georgetown
			H	1876
		18 Nov	A	Georgetown
			H	1876
		8 Dec	A	Georgetown
			H	1876
		12 Dec	A	Georgetown
			H	1876
	1858	12 Jan	A	Georgetown
			H	1876
		15 Jan	A	Georgetown
			H	1876
		17 Jan	A	Georgetown
		19 Jan	A	Georgetown
			H	1876
		24 Jan	A	Georgeotwn
		22 Feb	A	Georgetown
			H	1876
		7 Mar	A	Georgetown
			H	1876
		8 Mar	A	Georgetown
			H	1876
	1858	12 July	A	Georgetown
			H	1876
Wiseman, Cardinal	1857	27 Aug	A	
			D	
		14 Sept	D	(*Ward*, I, p. 419; *Trevor*, II, p. 170)
		7 Nov	D	
	1858	14 Feb	D	
		19 Feb	D	
		7 Mar	D	(with letter to Bellasis)
Wood, Thomas W. B.	1857	11 Nov	D	
		24 Nov	D	
	1858	15 Jan	D	
Woodlock, Bartholomew	1857	24 May	D	
Wootten, Mrs	1858	6 Aug	A	
Wyse, John	1857	14 May	D	

*   *   *   *

MEMORANDA, Etc.

Subject		Date	Source	
Concerning Henry Ignatius Ryder	1857	6 April	A	(In note to letter of 4 April to Flanagan)
Plan for a theological dictionary	1857	27 April	A	(In note to letter of 29 June to Bittleston)

Subject	Date		Source	
Suggested requests to the Irish Archbishops	1857	16 May	A	(In note to letter of 17 May to Flanagan)
Prospectus of the *Atlantis*	1857	3 Nov	Pr	(In note to letter of 20 Oct. to Sullivan)
On the request to translate Scripture	1857	End of Nov	A	(*Trevor*, II, pp. 171–2)
Leading Articles in the *Weekly Register* on the Catholic University	1858	23, 30 Jan 6, 13 Feb 6, 13 Mar	Pr	(Appendix I, p. 565) (*Campaign*, pp. 345–81)
The project for the Oratory School	1858	9 Feb	A	(In note to letter of 9 Feb to Bellasis)
Rules for the translation of Scripture	1858	19 Feb	A	(In note to letter of 19 Feb to Wiseman)
University Annual Expenses	1858	11 Nov	A	University College, Dublin (Appendix II, p. 584)
Prospectus for the Oratory School	1858	End of Nov	D	(In note to letter of 4 Dec. to Bellasis)
Defamatory Talk in London	1858	20 Dec	A	
Conditions Newman ought to have made before accepting the Rectorship of the Catholic University	1872	23 Nov	A	(In note to letter of 12 Nov. 1858 to the Irish Archbishops)

*   *   *   *

LETTERS TO NEWMAN

		from	Inserted before Newman's of
1857	20 July	The Archbishops of Ireland	6 Aug
	25 Aug	Archbishop Leahy	26 Aug
	26 Aug	Cardinal Wiseman	27 Aug
	27 Sept	William Dodsworth	29 Sept
	6 Oct	Cardinal Wiseman	16 Sept to Dunne
1858	13 Feb	Cardinal Wiseman	14 Feb
	15 Feb	Cardinal Wiseman	17 Feb to Stewart
	5 Mar	Cardinal Wiseman	7 Mar to Wilberforce (Questions about the proposed school)
	20 July	Archbishop Cullen	21 July
	29 July	Sir John Acton	2 Aug
	3 Oct	Archbishop Leahy	5 Oct to Anderdon
	8 Oct	Archbishop Leahy	7 Oct to Allies
	31 Oct	The Professors of the Catholic University	6 Nov
	7 Dec	William Henry Anderdon	8 Dec
	10 Dec	Sir John Acton	16 Dec
	20 Dec	Sir John Acton	21 Dec

Index of Persons and Places

The index to Volume XI contains notices of almost all the persons who occur in that volume, and the indexes to subsequent volumes notices of those who occur in them for the first time. These are not repeated, and so, for persons and places already mentioned in those volumes, reference back is here made by an (XI) or (XII) etc. inserted after such names.

References are given, in the case of persons mentioned for the first time in this volume, to *The Dictionary of National Biography* or *The Dictionary of American Biography*, and failing them, to Frederick Boase, *Modern English Biography*, or Joseph Gillow, *Bibliographical Dictionary of the English Catholics*; also occasionally to other printed works. Much of the information is derived from the correspondence and other material in the archives of the Birmingham Oratory, and from various private sources.

volumes, Naples 1959, and *La Vita di San Filippo Neri*, Naples 1879 (English translation 1882, new edition 1926). He became Archbishop of Capua in 1889, Vatican Librarian in 1893, and Cardinal in 1895, 185.

Capes (XI), Frederick (1816–88), 242, 349.

Capes (XI), John Moore (1812–89), 10–11, 30, 120, 349, 437–40, 461, 463–4, 471–2, 488.

Caprioli, Commendatore, 54.

Cardwell, Edward (1813–86), at Winchester and Balliol College, Oxford, double first in 1835 and a Fellow, entered politics as a follower of Sir Robert Peel. He was Secretary for Ireland in Palmerston's cabinet, in 1859–64, then Secretary for the Colonies, and Secretary for War from 1868 until 1874, when, on Gladstone's resignation, he was made a Viscount. (*DNB*, III, 952), 358–9.

Carlisle (XVII), George William Frederick Howard, seventh Earl of (1802–64), 42, 61–2.

Castlerosse (XVI), Viscount (1825–1905), Earl of Kennare 1871, 519.

Castro, Dr de, of a Portuguese family, was brought up in England as a Protestant. After studying medicine in London, he practised in Manchester. He became a Catholic, and in 1858 was at Pau in France, suffering from consumption, 340, 371–2, 507, 538.

Caswall (XII), Edward (1814–78), 62, 88, 125, 131–2, 167, 175, 248, 252, 266, 298, 362, 368, 372, 376–8, 388, 391, 413–14, 441, 470, 512.

Caswall, Thomas (1816–62), brother of Edward, went to Clare College, Cambridge, 1835, B.A., 25th Wrangler, 1839. He was a Fellow of his College from 1840 until 1846, when he became a Catholic. In 1858 he went to America, and died in New York, as a result of an accident, 248.

Charles, laybrother, Charles Goodrich, 23, 371, 376, 390, 395, 436.

Charlton, Barbara Tasburgh, Mrs William Henry (1815–98), daughter of Michael Anne, who changed his name when he married the heiress of the Tasburghs. Both were ancient Yorkshire Catholic families. Barbara was educated by the Dames Anglaises in Paris, and then at the Sacred Heart Convent in the rue de Varennes. In 1839 she married the heir of another old Catholic family, William Henry Charlton of Hesleyside, Northumberland, but they mixed in circles wider than those of the old Catholics. Their three sons were sent to the Oratory School. Mrs Charlton was a staunch Catholic, not afraid to criticise what she held to be Catholic deficiencies. Hearing a rumour in the autumn of 1858 that the School was not to be started she wrote

that 'the eyes of the most bigoted, must be open to the cruelty and disadvantage of sending sons to our underbred Colleges.' Her husband, one of the promoters of the Border Counties Railway, died in 1880. (L. E. O. Charlton, *The Recollections of a Northumbrian Lady 1851–1866*, London 1949), 444.

Charlton (XI), Edward (1814–74), 266.

Cheyne, Patrick, 368.

Clarendon (XIV), fourth Earl of (1800–70), 62, 370.

Clifford (XI), Hugh Charles, seventh Baron (1790–1858), 281, 283.

Clifford (XI), William Joseph Hugh (1823–1893), 281, 413, 533.

Coffin (XVII), Edmund, 173, 296.

Coffin (XI), Robert Aston (1819–85), 112.

Coleridge (XV), Henry James (1822–93), 74.

Collins, Edward Francis. (*Boase*, I, 679), 50.

Colthurst, probably Robert, youngest son of Sir Nicholas Conway Colthurst, fourth Baronet, of Cork. Robert became a Catholic, and died in 1864, aged about 33, 462.

Copeland (XI), George Ford (1804–85), 245–6.

Coppinger, Mrs, 378.

Cotton, Henry (1789–1879). (*DNB*, IV, 1229), 246.

Crawley (XIV), George John Lloyd (1820–74), 68, 86, 213, 242, 266, 272–3, 276, 298–300, 353.

Crofton (XIV), Morgan William, 75.

Crowther (XV), Thomas (1820–98), 132, 136, 198.

Cruice (XVI), Patrice, 217.

Cryan (XVI), Robert (1826–81), 425.

Cullen (XII), Paul (1803–78), 5, 9, 20, 23, 25, 28, 33–5, 41, 44, 48, 56–7, 67, 83–4, 95–7, 110–23, 135–6, 140, 143–4, 159, 170, 174, 179, 182, 186, 196, 200, 217–18, 221, 233–235, 303, 307, 317–18, 343, 359, 369–70, 374, 379, 385, 397, 401, 407, 419–23, 426, 440–5, 448–51, 457, 467–70, 473–80, 483, 486–91, 505, 509–12, 515–17, 535, 561.

Curry, see O'Curry, Eugene.

Dalgairns (XI), John Dobrée (1818–76), 74, 111, 176, 311, 393, 559.

Dalton, John (1814–74), of Irish origin, spent his early years at Coventry, and was educated at Sedgley Park School and Oscott. He worked as a priest in East Anglia, and was one of the first Canons of Northampton. The years 1858 and 1859 he spent at the English College in Valladolid, and on his return settled at Norwich. He was the translator of a number of Spanish and Italian books, including works of St Teresa. (*DNB*, V, 435), 147, 233.

Darnell (XII), Nicholas (1817–92), 17, 62, 68, 72–4, 83–5, 95, 110–11, 139, 143, 149, 153,

623